T0350299

Auditing Corporate Surveillance Systems

News headlines about privacy invasions, discrimination, and biases discovered in the platforms of big technology companies are commonplace today, and big tech's reluctance to disclose how they operate counteracts ideals of transparency, openness, and accountability. This book is for computer science students and researchers who want to study big tech's corporate surveillance from an experimental, empirical, or quantitative point of view and thereby contribute to holding big tech accountable. As a comprehensive technical resource, it guides readers through the corporate surveillance landscape and describes in detail how corporate surveillance works, how it can be studied experimentally, and what existing studies have found. It provides a thorough foundation in the necessary research methods and tools, and introduces the current research landscape along with a wide range of open issues and challenges. The book also explains how to consider ethical issues and how to turn research results into real-world change.

ISABEL WAGNER is an associate professor in the Cyber Technology Institute at De Montfort University. She is a senior member of IEEE and ACM. Her research in privacy, computer networks, and experimental research methods is the foundation for this book on transparency and web measurement. She has given tutorials on this topic, for example at the 2020 International World Wide Web Conference, and taught undergraduate and postgraduate courses on experimental methods to study corporate surveillance.

Auditing Corporate Surveillance Systems

Research Methods for Greater Transparency

ISABEL WAGNER
De Montfort University

CAMBRIDGE
UNIVERSITY PRESS

University Printing House, Cambridge CB2 8BS, United Kingdom

One Liberty Plaza, 20th Floor, New York, NY 10006, USA

477 Williamstown Road, Port Melbourne, VIC 3207, Australia

314–321, 3rd Floor, Plot 3, Splendor Forum, Jasola District Centre,
New Delhi – 110025, India

103 Penang Road, #05–06/07, Visioncrest Commercial, Singapore 238467

Cambridge University Press is part of the University of Cambridge.

It furthers the University's mission by disseminating knowledge in the pursuit of
education, learning, and research at the highest international levels of excellence.

www.cambridge.org
Information on this title: www.cambridge.org/9781108837668
DOI: 10.1017/9781108946940

First published 2022

A catalogue record for this publication is available from the British Library.

Library of Congress Cataloging-in-Publication Data
Names: Wagner, Isabel, (Computer Scientist), author.
Title: Auditing corporate surveillance systems : research methods for
greater transparency / Isabel Wagner.
Description: New York : Cambridge University Press, 2022. |
Includes bibliographical references and index.
Identifiers: LCCN 2021029681 (print) | LCCN 2021029682 (ebook) |
ISBN 9781108837668 (hardback) | ISBN 9781108946940 (epub)
Subjects: LCSH: Data protection. | Electronic surveillance. |
Privacy, Right of. | BISAC: COMPUTERS / Security / General
Classification: LCC HF5548.37 .W34 2021 (print) |
LCC HF5548.37 (ebook) | DDC 658.4/78–dc23
LC record available at https://lccn.loc.gov/2021029681
LC ebook record available at https://lccn.loc.gov/2021029682

ISBN 978-1-108-83766-8 Hardback

Contents

Figures

Tables

Listings

Preface

News headlines about privacy invasions, discrimination, and biases discovered in the platforms of big technology companies are commonplace today. The headlines – ranging from comprehensive profiling of users, to microtargeting of political messages, to discrimination based on gender, race, and age – show that big tech's operations cause real-world harm.

However, big tech companies are reluctant to disclose how they operate and typically do not give out specific information, such as what data they collect or how their algorithms make decisions. This secretive operation counteracts ideals of transparency, openness, and accountability. Investigative journalists have used traditional journalistic means to study big tech's operations: interviews, leaked documents, and freedom-of-information requests. However, these techniques are often limited in that they investigate only one particular aspect of one particular company. They cannot make claims about the big tech landscape as a whole.

In recent years, a new strand of research has appeared to fill this gap. This research uses large-scale experiments that systematically interact with the publicly accessible elements of big tech's platforms to infer details about their hidden operations – in essence, conducting *meta*-surveillance against big tech. These experiments have investigated, for example, how user tracking works, what the extent of tracking is on the web today, and how the collected information is used for algorithmic decision-making and ad targeting.

Beyond raising awareness, transparency established through experimental means has already resulted in real-world change, for example, in the creation of browser plug-ins that help users defend against corporate surveillance, and in the provision of technical evidence for lawsuits and regulatory action.

However, resources to learn about the relevant research methods and their application are still scarce and scattered across a large number of research papers. When I wanted to teach experimental methods to study digital corporate surveillance (in a postgraduate course in the 2018/19 academic year), I therefore had to create the syllabus and materials from scratch. This book extends and updates these materials and provides a comprehensive introduction to the field and its research methods.

How This Book Is Organized

This book focuses on how transparency can be created through technical experimentation with online black-box ecosystems. In four parts, the book explains what these black-box ecosystems are and what is known about how they work; how experiments with these systems can be designed, conducted, and analyzed; what previous research has found; and what the gaps and challenges are.

Part I: Corporate Surveillance Landscape

Part I describes the landscape of corporate surveillance, explains what black-box online ecosystems are, and discusses how they work by explaining the underlying technical mechanisms and protocols.

Chapter 1, Corporate Surveillance and the Need for Transparency, explains what corporate surveillance is, describes the corporate surveillance ecosystem and its evolution, and analyzes the human rights risks associated with corporate surveillance. The chapter also motivates the need for transparency and accountability in the modern ecosystem of big technology companies.

Chapter 2, Technologies for Corporate Surveillance, focuses on the inner workings of networked services – what technologies they use and how they work – which will enable a deeper understanding of the methods used for corporate surveillance. The chapter first introduces the internet protocol suite and its most important protocols, and then explains the systems and languages used to deliver web-based and mobile content.

Chapter 3, Methods of Corporate Surveillance, explains how corporate surveillance works on a technical level: how individual users can be tracked across their use of web and mobile services, for example through stateful tracking with cookies or stateless tracking with fingerprinting; how information collected through tracking is consolidated in comprehensive user profiles;

how analytics services contribute to tracking and profiling; and how advertising technology works, including ad targeting and ad sales.

Part II: Methods

Part II discusses how experiments can be designed, conducted, and analyzed. It provides in-depth explanations of methods for experiment design, data collection, and data analysis for transparency research.

Chapter 4, Experiment Design, explains how to design experiments to study black-box corporate surveillance systems. The chapter first examines the kinds of research questions that can be asked about corporate surveillance systems. Then, it describes different high-level study designs for transparency research, followed by a look at longitudinal studies. After examining the challenges that transparency researchers face in designing these experiments, the chapter focuses on input variables that are influenced and varied during an experiment, variables that are outside the experimenter's influence, and response or output variables that are measured during an experiment.

Chapter 5, Data Collection, describes methods for executing the designed experiment and recording the response variables. The ethical implications of experiments have to be considered before starting data collection, with the aim to minimize harmful impacts. Various data sources and data collection methods are available: archival data sources, passive data collection, active data collection with methods to influence input variables, data collection from mobile apps, and data collection via crowdsourcing. The chapter also describes methods to store the collected data.

Chapter 6, Data Analysis, explains how the collected data can be processed with the aim of extracting meaningful measures, and how statistical analysis can be used to support significant conclusions. This chapter first introduces common quantitative measures for transparency research, including measures for tracking, privacy, fairness, and similarity. To compute most of these measures, data need to be preprocessed to extract the response variables of interest from the raw collected data, for example using simple transformations or heuristics, machine learning classifiers or natural language processing, or static and dynamic analysis methods for mobile apps. Finally, the chapter explains statistical methods that allow to make meaningful and statistically significant statements about the behavior of the response variables in the experiment.

Part III: Results

Part III gives details on experimental results published in the last decade, including results on corporate surveillance methods, results on user-facing services, and results on countermeasures.

Chapter 7, Transparency for Corporate Surveillance Methods, examines findings from transparency research that shed light on the methods used for corporate surveillance, including tracking, profiling, analytics, and advertising. The chapter focuses on key results obtained for the research questions described in Chapter 4 and explains the experimental designs used to achieve them.

Chapter 8, Transparency for Corporate Services, discusses results for user-facing services that show whether the services are biased toward specific groups of users; whether they comply with policies, laws, and regulations; and how they use user data in providing their services. The chapter first focuses on network-level services, such as server-side blocking and the provision of wireless internet access. Then, the chapter discusses web-based services, including privacy policies, search, social networks, and e-commerce. The chapter closes by discussing results for mobile services, such as the characteristics of app stores, third-party libraries, and apps.

Chapter 9, Effectiveness of Countermeasures, examines the arms race between corporate surveillance and the countermeasures that allow users to defend themselves against advertising, tracking, and profiling. The chapter first explains ad blockers as the most common countermeasure, and shows how the industry is using anti-ad blockers to block ad blocker users. The chapter then discusses specialized blockers for tracking and fingerprinting, as well as countermeasures based on obfuscation and tools that aim to increase user awareness, before closing with a discussion of countermeasures for mobile devices and applications.

Part IV: Gaps and Challenges

Part IV focuses on the gaps and challenges in transparency research by describing methods for effecting real-world change and open research questions.

Chapter 10, Making It Count: Towards Real-World Impact, explains how transparency research can lead to real-world change. After introducing impacts that are commonly realized by transparency research, the chapter systematizes types of impact and explains a process for planning impact throughout a research project. Finally, the chapter explains, using real-world examples, how various groups of stakeholders can be engaged, including the public, policy-makers, courts, regulatory bodies, standardization bodies, nongovernmental organizations, publishers, and developers.

Chapter 11, Future Directions in Transparency Research, examines the formidable challenges that remain in transparency research, not least due to the rapid evolution of technology. This chapter highlights four areas of challenges: methodological challenges that call for new methods for transparency research; open research questions related to existing systems; research questions related to new and emerging systems such as the Internet of Things; and challenges related to systems that are pervasively embedded into real-world systems and infrastructure, such as smart cites.

Acknowledgments

I am indebted to friends, family, and colleagues whose inspiration and guidance made this book possible. In particular, I am thankful to Falko Dressler for inspiring me to stick with science and for being a great mentor throughout my career; to my husband Andrey Revyakin for being an inspiring scientist and for reminding me that good writing is concise; and to Eerke Boiten for long and fruitful discussions about privacy, privacy risk, and corporate surveillance. I am also grateful to the group of privacy and data protection activists, consultants, and officers who participated in our focus groups on privacy impact assessments in 2018. Their suggestion to use virtual personas to measure privacy risk sparked the initial idea for this book. Last but not least, I would like to thank my editor at Cambridge University Press, Kaitlin Leach, and all the staff at the Press for their support during the writing and production of this book.

PART I

Corporate Surveillance Landscape

1

Corporate Surveillance and the Need for Transparency

The term *corporate surveillance* describes the ubiquitous monitoring of the behavior of individuals by corporations. Corporate surveillance has become commonplace today, and most internet users are subject to it every day. Corporate surveillance powers the dominant business models on today's Internet, but it also has the power to curb individuals' rights and create a fundamentally unequal surveillance society. This power, coupled with corporate secrecy surrounding their methods of corporate surveillance, motivates the need for more transparency.

This book is a guide to performing systematic experiments to create more transparency for corporate surveillance and its algorithms. This chapter begins with a high-level overview of corporate surveillance and how it has evolved over time, including the players in the corporate surveillance ecosystem, the reasons why corporations conduct surveillance, and the negative effects caused by it. Finally, the chapter will argue why these characteristics of corporate surveillance mean that there is an urgent need to subject it to greater transparency and audit the algorithms it relies on.

1.1 Evolution of Online Corporate Surveillance

To illustrate how online corporate surveillance evolved, we can follow the history of Google, which, according to Zuboff (2019), was the first to use data not just to improve their service but for monetization. In 1998, Google launched their first service, Google Search. In their drive to improve search results for users, Google used the *collateral data* that accumulated as a by-product of people using the search engine, including the "number and pattern of search terms, how a query is phrased, spelling, punctuation, dwell times, click patterns, and location" (Zuboff, 2019). Initially, this data was used solely to improve the search engine, for example, to improve the relevance of search results shown to users. During this time, users and search engine relied on each other: the search engine needed users to improve its functionality, and users needed the search engine to find resources on the web.

With the burst of the dot-com bubble in 2000, however, Google began to focus on advertising as a source of revenue. Initially, keyword-based ads were shown to users who searched for specific keywords. Later, Google's strategy shifted to targeting *individuals* instead of keywords. The collateral data that Google already collected for optimizing the search engine was used to create and analyze user profiles, which allowed Google to display ads related to the user's interests, not just their current search term. Google's 2003 patent for "Generating User Information for Use in Targeted Advertising" describes how data points that form a user profile, such as gender, age, and interests, can be inferred from collateral data. This approach allowed Google to optimize ad placement: instead of prioritizing the placement of ads with a high price per click, Google could prioritize ads that had a higher likelihood of a user actually clicking on them. This approach was then refined and expanded, for example, by tracking users on websites other than Google Search, which allowed Google to collect more profiling information, offer more precise targeting, and further optimize ad placement.

This increase of Google's trackers on non-Google websites was confirmed by longitudinal studies of tracking on the Internet. In 2005, trackers from `doubleclick.net` and `google-analytics.com` were embedded on 18% and 0% of first-party websites, respectively. In 2008, these numbers had already grown to more than 30%. Taking into account all companies acquired by Google, such as its acquisition of DoubleClick in 2007, Google's *reach*, i.e., the number of websites that embed Google's trackers, grew from under 10% in 2005 to almost 60% in 2008 (Krishnamurthy and Wills, 2009).

As a result of its advertising innovations and its increasing market dominance, Google's advertising revenue increased from $1.4 billion in 2003 to $134.8 billion in 2019 (Clement, 2020).

Even though Google is the most prevalent tracker on the Internet, it is not the only corporation to track users, and the reach of other trackers has also increased. For example, the ten third parties most commonly embedded in websites reached approximately 10% of websites in 1996–2000, 20% of websites in 2005, and over 60% in 2016 (Lerner et al., 2016). Figure 1.1 shows how the reach of confirmed trackers, the reach of embedded third parties, and Google's advertising revenue have evolved between 1996 and 2016.

To illustrate the extent of what these trackers know about users, three examples from a 2020 data leak from the tracking company BlueKai are illuminating (Whittaker, 2020):

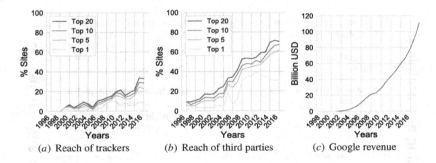

Figure 1.1 Three time series illustrating the evolution of corporate surveillance between 1997 and 2016. (*a*) The percentage of websites that are reached by the top trackers, (*b*) the percentage of websites reached by the top third parties, and (*c*) Google's advertising revenue. (*a,b*) adapted from Lerner et al. (2016), (*c*) adapted from Clement (2020).

- "One record detailed how a German man, whose name we're withholding, used a prepaid debit card to place a €10 bet on an esports betting site on April 19. The record also contained the man's address, phone number and email address."
- "The record detailed how one person, who lives in Istanbul, ordered $899 worth of furniture online from a homeware store. We know because the record contained all of these details, including the buyer's name, email address and the direct web address for the buyer's order."
- "A record detailing how one person unsubscribed from an email newsletter run by an electronics consumer, sent to his iCloud address. The record showed that the person may have been interested in a specific model of car dash-cam. We can even tell based on his user agent that his iPhone was out of date and needed a software update."

Even though these records are highly detailed and specific, it is important to keep in mind that BlueKai is not the largest tracker: it tracks only about 1% of all web traffic. Google and Facebook have greater reach, and the content of their databases can be expected to be at least as fine-grained and most likely encompass more individuals.

1.2 Ecosystem of Corporate Surveillance

The ecosystem of companies participating in corporate surveillance has steadily expanded during the last decade. In 2012, there were six main

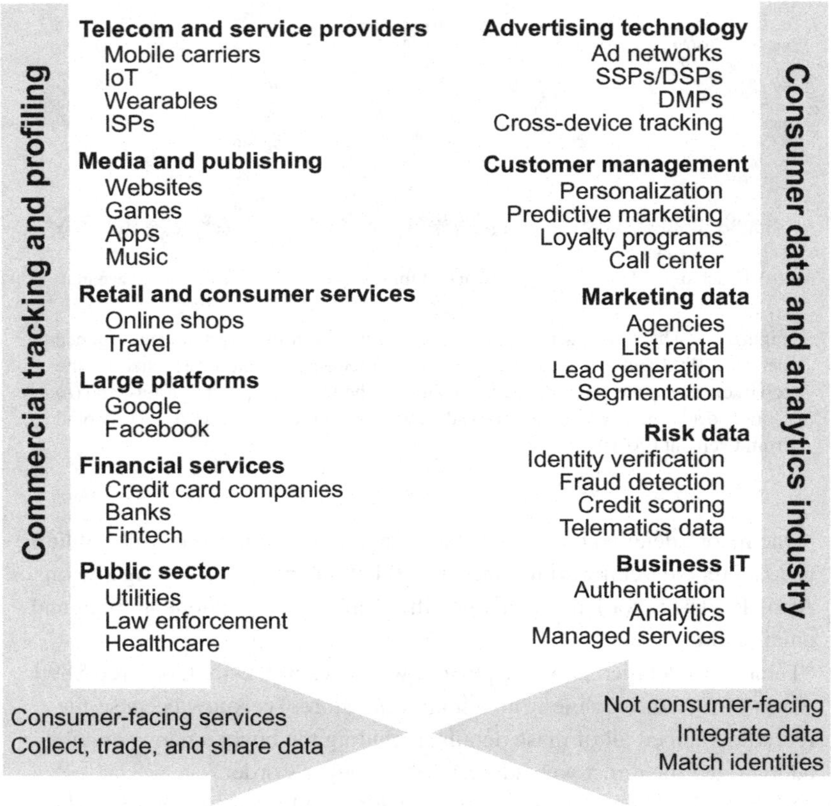

Commercial tracking and profiling

Telecom and service providers
Mobile carriers
IoT
Wearables
ISPs

Media and publishing
Websites
Games
Apps
Music

Retail and consumer services
Online shops
Travel

Large platforms
Google
Facebook

Financial services
Credit card companies
Banks
Fintech

Public sector
Utilities
Law enforcement
Healthcare

Advertising technology
Ad networks
SSPs/DSPs
DMPs
Cross-device tracking

Customer management
Personalization
Predictive marketing
Loyalty programs
Call center

Marketing data
Agencies
List rental
Lead generation
Segmentation

Risk data
Identity verification
Fraud detection
Credit scoring
Telematics data

Business IT
Authentication
Analytics
Managed services

Consumer data and analytics industry

Consumer-facing services
Collect, trade, and share data

Not consumer-facing
Integrate data
Match identities

Figure 1.2 Tracking and profiling landscape. Adapted from Christl (2017).

business models for third parties on websites: advertising, analytics, social networks, content providers, front-end services, and hosting platforms (Mayer and Mitchell, 2012). Through their being embedded on websites, these third parties were generally in a position to track and profile users, although not all of them actually would do so.

In 2017, however, a large number of additional participants in the ecosystem were identified (Christl, 2017). These additional participants include both first-party sectors – sectors that offer consumer-facing services, shown on the left-hand side of Figure 1.2 – and third-party sectors – sectors that collect and analyze consumer data without offering consumer-facing services, shown on the right-hand side of Figure 1.2.

First parties that were traditionally associated with tracking and profiling were large platforms as well as media and publishing companies. However, the range of first parties has expanded so that now nearly every sector that has some online presence engages in tracking and profiling, including retail, internet and telecommunications providers, device manufacturers, financial services, and even the public sector. First-party participants in the corporate surveillance ecosystem typically collect data about individuals or allow third parties to do so; process and analyze the collected data for their own use; and share or sell the collected data, or access to it.

Third parties, in addition to advertising and analytics companies, now include companies that offer customer management, such as providers of call centers and loyalty programs; companies that provide marketing data; companies that offer risk management, such as background checks, screenings, or credit scores; and companies that offer business services such as authentication, identity verification, or fraud detection. Third-party participants in the corporate surveillance ecosystem focus on integrating data and matching user identities from multiple first parties. The collected data is also increasingly accessed for the purpose of government surveillance (Christl, 2017).

1.3 Motives for Corporate Surveillance

Various reasons have been brought forward for why companies engage in corporate surveillance, including economic motives, arguments from a business intelligence and optimization perspective, convenience, and the drive to achieve and maintain monopolies.

The economic motives for corporate surveillance rest on advertising-funded business models. These business models differ between the participants in the corporate surveillance ecosystem. Publishers can offer free web services if they have enough advertising revenue to support their operation (Couldry, 2016). Advertising revenues are higher if individuals with specific characteristics can be targeted. Advertisers can save money by targeting those individuals who will then go on to buy their product (Couldry, 2016). In addition, tracking allows advertisers to evaluate the effectiveness of their targeting (Yu et al., 2016).

The business model of large advertising platforms such as Google and Facebook consists of enabling – and profiting from – the publishers' and advertisers' business models. They collect comprehensive digital dossiers about individuals, including personally identifiable information, behaviors, and interests. Instead of selling these dossiers directly, which would give the buyer the ability to make unlimited use of it after the sale, corporations sell the ability to make limited use of the data without transferring the data itself. For example, corporations may sell the ability to target an individual without revealing who the individual is. This gives corporations with large databases the ability to control how everyone else can use their data, giving rise to the claim that data is "the new oil" (Amnesty International, 2019).

Google and Facebook employ this business model by first offering useful digital services to consumers. The data collected from people who use these services can be mined to create detailed profiles about individuals that can be used to predict behaviors. The platforms then sell access to these profiles to other entities, such as advertisers, who want to target groups of people with specific attributes (Amnesty International, 2019). The valuation of Google and Facebook shows that this can be a very profitable business model, so much so that surveillance – not advertising – may be the true "business model of the internet" (Rashid, 2014).

To maintain and expand the viability of this business model, the corporations strive to collect ever more data to make ever more precise predictions about individuals. To do so, they intensify surveillance on products they already offer and branch out to new products and markets. For example, Facebook's Free Basics service attempts to dominate markets in the Global South, and Google's Nest and Assistant products attempt to dominate the smart home and smart city markets (Amnesty International, 2019). In addition, these corporations use their surveillance capabilities to identify potential competitors with the goal of either acquiring them as an additional source for data or forcing them out of the market by introducing a product with similar features. For example, Android, Maps, and YouTube were competitors acquired by Google; and Instagram was a competitor acquired by Facebook with the aim of crushing another competitor, Snapchat. In this way, big tech corporations are continually striving toward becoming monopolies and maintaining their monopoly status (Doctorow, 2020).

Business intelligence is another argument for corporate surveillance. Information about how users use an online service can be used to improve it, as Google did with its search engine (Couldry, 2016). This may also justify the use of analytics services by websites, because analytics services allow website owners to acquire this information without having to implement the data collection themselves (Yu et al., 2016).

Finally, some have argued that corporate surveillance can be convenient and even desirable for users. For example, social buttons and social logins are often seen as convenient because they can save time (Yu et al., 2016). In addition, many users are keen to optimize aspects of their own lives, for example through health monitoring, the convenience of smart home applications, or the *quantified self* movement (Couldry, 2016).

1.4 Undesirable Effects of Corporate Surveillance

However, many authors have argued that corporate surveillance exhibits a range of undesirable effects, both for individuals and for society as a whole. For example, Zuboff (2019) wrote that "surveillance capitalism is a rogue force driven by novel economic imperatives that disregard social norms and nullify the elemental rights associated with individual autonomy that are essential to the very possibility of a democratic society."

Amnesty International (2019) frames these undesirable effects as *human rights risks* that can negatively affect the right to privacy, the right to freedom of expression, and the right to equality and nondiscrimination. In addition, the scale of platforms such as Google and Facebook can amplify these human rights risks because they allow manipulation of users at scale and feature addictive platform designs that aim to maximize the time users spend on the platform.

1.4.1 Right to Privacy

The right to privacy is often dismissed with the argument of having "nothing to hide." However, as Snowden (2019) memorably wrote, "saying you don't care about privacy because you have nothing to hide is like saying you don't care about free speech because you have nothing to say."

In fact, privacy is often argued to be a prerequisite to the enjoyment of other human rights, such as freedom of speech, freedom of thought, and freedom of assembly (Wachter, 2017; Rachovitsa, 2016; Buttarelli, 2017). This is because privacy is essential to develop a sense of our own identity and is therefore essential to human autonomy and self-determination (Amnesty International, 2019). Surveillance, however, curtails this right by creating a pressure to conform. In addition, corporate surveillance can define individuals' identities for them by creating profiles of individuals and using these profiles for targeting.

Big tech corporations have repeatedly made public promises to protect user privacy. However, they have also repeatedly failed to uphold their promises. Examples include Google's location tracking on Android, undisclosed microphones in Google's Nest devices, and Facebook's knowledge of the Cambridge Analytica data misuse (Amnesty International, 2019).

In addition, storage of large amounts of potentially sensitive data about individuals presents not just a privacy risk in the context of the company storing the data. For example, there are many known cases where privacy was breached by hackers or disgruntled employees, where data was sold after bankruptcy, and where data was subpoenaed by government agencies (Yu et al., 2016).

1.4.2 Right to Freedom of Expression

Freedom of expression includes not just freedom of speech but also the "freedom to seek, receive and impart information and ideas of all kinds" (United Nations, 1948). Corporate surveillance can threaten freedom of expression, for example by biasing search result rankings and by limiting the right to read anonymously.

Search result rankings are important because humans predominantly focus on the top of a search result list, and only a very small portion of search results beyond the first page are ever accessed (Hannak et al., 2013). Biases in these rankings, if they exist, would affect the ability of individuals to find information. For example, search results could be ordered in such a way that the top results always reinforce a user's existing worldview, thereby trapping users in filter bubbles. Even though existing studies suggest a limited extent of personalization (Hannak et al., 2013; Cozza et al., 2016), platforms are not transparent about their search result–ranking algorithms.

The right to read anonymously was affirmed by the US Supreme Court in 1962 because surveillance of reading habits is likely to create a chilling effect that makes individuals self-censor what they read. However, e-readers show how this right may be under threat from corporate surveillance. For example, Amazon reserves the right and claims the technical capability to record information regarding a user's interaction with Kindle content, including which books a user reads, which sections of a book have been read, what annotations were made, which geographical locations the e-reader was used at, how quickly a user is reading, and what the user's preferred complexity of reading material is (Wicker and Ghosh, 2020). However, Amazon does not confirm that it is indeed collecting these comprehensive records of Kindle users' reading habits, nor does it give users access to data collected about them.

1.4.3 Right to Equality and Nondiscrimination

The right to nondiscrimination can be violated by online advertising platforms when they allow the targeting of individuals based on protected characteristics.

In addition, discriminatory targeting can also be enabled by other targeting mechanisms and the ad delivery process.

Facebook's advertiser interface allowed advertisers to place ads that were targeted at protected characteristics such as age (Angwin et al., 2018), gender (Scheiber, 2019), and race (Angwin and Parris, 2016). This was possible even when the ads were for housing, finance, or jobs, where this discrimination is illegal according to US law. For example, Facebook allowed advertisers to target housing ads exclusively at white users, and ads for high-paying tech jobs exclusively at male users. Following lawsuits brought by the American Civil Liberties Union (ACLU), Facebook was forced to stop allowing discriminatory targeting on its platform (Scheiber and Isaac, 2019). As part of the settlement, Facebook agreed to create a separate advertising portal for housing, finance, and job ads, which would not offer the possibility to directly target protected characteristics. Advertisers would be mandated by Facebook's policy to use the new portal.

However, Facebook's other targeting mechanisms allow for discriminatory targeting even without direct use of protected characteristics (Speicher et al., 2018). For example, discrimination can be based on custom audiences, if the custom audience is constructed from audiences such as voter records for which the protected characteristics are known. Discrimination can also be based on attribute-based targeting, if attributes can be found that correlate well with a protected characteristic. Finally, discrimination can be based on look-alike targeting, if the advertiser knows identifiable information such as email addresses for a small group of people with the desired protected characteristic.

Discrimination can also result from the ad delivery process, where budget allocation and the use of stereotypical imagery can both lead to skewed ad delivery (Ali et al., 2019a). For example, the audience for ad campaigns with low budgets may consist of more than 55% men because women are more expensive to target. In addition, ads with stereotypically female images can reach audiences with more than 90% women. This skewed delivery affects all ads on Facebook, including ads for real-world employment and housing opportunities.

1.5 Need for Transparency

These undesirable effects emphasize the need for greater transparency of corporate surveillance systems and the algorithms they use. Big tech platforms themselves have recognized this need and provide a small set of transparency tools to their users.

Facebook, for example, gives users access to ad explanations that inform users why they are seeing a specific ad. However, these ad explanations are incomplete and misleading because they omit the most salient targeting attributes (Andreou et al., 2018).

In addition, Facebook provides a library of political ads to make it easier to analyze political advertising including how political ads are targeted. However, this library of political ads is incomplete, does not show microtargeting attributes, and requires advertisers to self-report their political ads (Silva et al., 2020). These shortcomings make Facebook's ad library unsuitable as a transparency tool.

Transparency tools provided by other platforms have similar shortcomings, which indicates that big tech is at best an unreliable source of meaningful insight into the characteristics and extent of its surveillance operations. However, transparency is essential for four reasons: to hold big tech accountable, to ensure a functional democracy, to ensure human autonomy and individuality, and to collect evidence for the need and effectiveness of laws and regulations.

Transparency to hold big tech accountable is needed to bring to light when big tech uses corporate practices that are unlawful, whether intentionally or not (Scheiber, 2019). For example, the case of Facebook allowing advertisers to place discriminatory ads would not have been uncovered without transparency research conducted by investigative journalists. However, the concentration of power in big tech platforms is an obstacle to accountability (Amnesty International, 2019), which further emphasizes the need for transparency.

Transparency to ensure a functional democracy is needed, for example, to uncover biases in big tech that can influence elections. For example, Hargreaves et al. (2018) found bias at the top of Facebook's news feed that favored some parties over others in an Italian election. In addition, Facebook has repeatedly experimented with displaying social messages to motivate users to vote on election days (Bond et al., 2012; Jones et al., 2017). Even though Facebook showed that their interventions on the Facebook news feed led to an increase in voters, they did not provide evidence that they used this power to influence voters in an equitable way. Transparency is needed to assure the public that Facebook did not selectively display their intervention to people they estimated to vote in a certain way.

Transparency to ensure human autonomy and individuality is needed not just because of the negative impacts of pervasive surveillance described above but also because big tech platforms, in particular Facebook, have admitted to performing experiments on their users (Kramer et al., 2014). For example, Facebook experimented with *emotional contagion* by manipulating the news feeds of Facebook users to display more posts with positive or negative emotions. Facebook then measured the extent to which users were influenced by this manipulation by observing the positive or negative emotions expressed in the user's subsequent posts. Importantly, the users in this experiment were not informed and did not give consent, even though Facebook argues that their experiments were covered by their terms of use. This example shows that big tech platforms are in a position of great power but do not necessarily demonstrate responsibility and respect toward users. Transparency is needed so that the public can discover these cases and debate the desirability and acceptability of big tech's behavior.

Transparency to show the effects and effectiveness of laws and regulations is needed to verify claims of compliance made by big tech. For example, transparency research has evaluated whether the EU's General Data Protection Regulation (GDPR) affected tracking practices on the web (Libert et al., 2018; Sørensen and Kosta, 2019), and whether the regulation led to a geographical differentiation in website delivery that would result in users seeing different content depending on their location (van Eijk et al., 2019). Other studies have evaluated to what extent tracking data flows across data protection boundaries (Iordanou et al., 2018), whether apps targeted at families and children meet the requirements of the Children's Online Privacy Protection Act (COPPA) (Reyes et al., 2018), and whether cookie notices meet the requirements of the GDPR (Matte et al., 2020). In each of these cases, researchers have found problematic behaviors, which shows the need for transparency even when regulations are in place.

2

Technologies for Corporate Surveillance

Corporate surveillance is based on networked services used by consumers, such as browsing websites and interacting with mobile applications. The Internet and its protocols form the basis for most of these services.

This chapter therefore focuses on the inner workings of these networked services – what technologies they use and how they work – which will enable a deeper understanding of the methods of corporate surveillance introduced in Chapter 3. This chapter first introduces the internet protocol suite and its most important protocols, and then explains the systems and languages used to deliver web-based content and mobile content.

2.1 Networking Services

The Internet operates on a stack of protocols called the *internet protocol suite*. Each layer of the protocol suite has distinctive tasks and is designed so that it relies on the services provided by the layer directly below and provides services to the layer above.

2.1.1 Internet Protocol Suite

Figure 2.1 shows the four layers of the internet protocol suite and gives some examples for the protocols on each layer (Kurose and Ross, 2016).

The link and physical layer handle communication over a specific one-hop network link, such as Ethernet or Wi-Fi, for example the hop from a computer to a Wi-Fi router. The link layer is responsible for moving data packets called *frames*, while the physical layer moves individual bits. These layers do not include routing functionality to send packets along a path through a network. Their implementation is specific to the characteristics of the physical link. Each

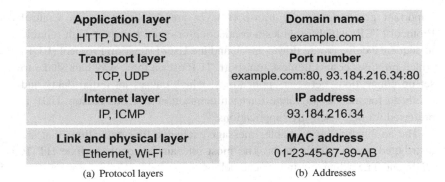

Application layer	Domain name
HTTP, DNS, TLS	example.com
Transport layer	**Port number**
TCP, UDP	example.com:80, 93.184.216.34:80
Internet layer	**IP address**
IP, ICMP	93.184.216.34
Link and physical layer	**MAC address**
Ethernet, Wi-Fi	01-23-45-67-89-AB

(a) Protocol layers   (b) Addresses

Figure 2.1 Internet protocol suite. (a) four layers of the internet protocol suite and example protocols, (b) addresses used on each layer.

network interface has a link-layer address called Media Access Control address (MAC). MAC addresses are designed to be globally unique and are assigned to each network interface card by its manufacturer.

The network or internet layer is responsible for moving data packets called *datagrams* from one host to another, and for finding a route between the two hosts. On the Internet, all hosts must be able to communicate using the Internet Protocol (IP). IP provides best-effort transmission, i.e., it does not guarantee reliable or in-sequence delivery. IP uses IP addresses to identify hosts. IPv4 addresses consist of four bytes that are hierarchically structured, so that they identify not only individual hosts, but also the network the host resides in. Although IP addresses are not technically bound to a specific geolocation, they are often stable and reassigned infrequently. As a result, there are databases that map IP addresses to geolocations, such as the RIPE Atlas (Iordanou et al., 2018) and Maxmind (Papadopoulos et al., 2017; Invernizzi et al., 2016; Callejo et al., 2017). Traffic on the network layer can be summarized in NetFlow records which summarize the data transmissions that have taken place between a single application on specific hosts. NetFlows indicate the time when the flow started, its duration, the source and destination IP addresses, source and destination ports, and the number of transmitted packets and bytes. Internet Service Providers (ISPs) collect NetFlow data for performance and security monitoring, and sometimes provide data to researchers for analysis (Iordanou et al., 2018).

The transport layer is responsible for moving application-layer packets called *segments* between applications. These applications may reside on different hosts and are differentiated by their port numbers. The two most important protocols on the transport layer are the Transmission Control Protocol (TCP) which provides a connection-oriented transport with reliable in-sequence delivery and flow control, and the User Datagram Protocol (UDP) which provides connectionless transport. TCP uses a three-way handshake to set up connections between applications, which causes an initial delay and overhead for maintaining state for each connection. For this reason, UDP is preferred for delay-sensitive applications.

The application layer enables message exchange for applications that are distributed over multiple hosts. The most relevant protocols include HTTP, DNS, and TLS which are introduced below.

2.1.2 Application Layer: TLS

The Transport Layer Security (TLS) protocols sit on top of the transport-layer protocol TCP and provide confidentiality, integrity, and server authentication (Kurose and Ross, 2016). From the perspective of an application-layer protocol, TLS is used in the same way as TCP, through sockets. This design makes it easy to run application-layer protocols over secured TLS instead of unsecured TCP. For example, HTTPS designates the HTTP protocol run over TLS instead of TCP.

TLS uses a combination of protocols to provide its services. The two most important protocols are the TLS handshake protocol which sets up the cryptographic keys between communicating parties, and the TLS record protocol which is used for secure data exchange after the handshake has been completed. Because the TLS handshake is expensive in terms of messages exchanged and computations needed, the TLS session resumption feature allows to resume a previous TLS session. To realize this feature, TLS uses key material from a previous session to accelerate the handshake. The TLS cache in browsers is used to store key material for this purpose (Sy et al., 2018). To allow running of several HTTPS servers at a single IP address, TLS provides the server name indication (SNI) extension. When the SNI extension is used, the first message of the TLS handshake includes the domain name requested by the user. The disadvantage of this approach is some loss of confidentiality due to the leak of the requested domain name (Gonzalez et al., 2016).

2.1.3 Application Layer: HTTP

The hypertext transfer protocol, or HTTP, is a stateless application-layer protocol that enables communication between clients and servers. It is used on the web as well as for mobile applications. HTTP is a request-response protocol where a client, or user agent, sends a request message to a server, and the server answers with a response message.

HTTP Requests

An HTTP request consist of three parts: a request line that indicates the request method and the resource that is requested; request header fields; and an optional message body. The most commonly used request methods are GET and POST, where GET is typically used to retrieve data from the server, and POST allows to transmit data, such as the values of form fields. The resource that is requested from the server is specified as a uniform resource locator (URL) (Reschke and Fielding, 2014). URLs can not only include the server (host) name and the path to the requested document, but also authentication information (username and password), the port the request is sent to, a query string with parameters and their values, and a fragment identifier. In contrast to the other parts of the URL, the fragment identifier is not sent to the server but instead processed on the client-side. Most HTTP request header fields are specified in RFCs 7230 to 7235 (Reschke and Fielding, 2014; Fielding and Reschke, 2014), and the Internet Assigned Numbers Authority (IANA) maintains a registry of header fields.[1]

For the purpose of transparency research, the most commonly studied header fields are *Cookie*, *Referer*, *User-Agent*, and Do Not Track (*DNT*). The *Cookie* header contains data, in the form of a name-value pair, that was previously sent by the server in a *Set-Cookie* response header. Cookies enable identification of clients, which is needed for logins and shopping carts, but also used for tracking (see Chapter 3). The *Referer* header contains the URL for the resource that led to the current request. For example, the referer for an embedded image is the website that embeds the image. The referer can also point to external resources, for example when a user clicks on a link to another website (Nikiforakis et al., 2012). The *User-Agent* header contains information about the user's browser. The user-agent string identifies the browser name, version, operating system, and operating system architecture (e.g., x86_64). The *DNT* header, although supported by some browsers, is not an official header in the HTTP standard and has not found widespread adoption.

---

[1] www.iana.org/assignments/message-headers/

HTTP Responses

An HTTP response similarly consists of three parts: a status line, response header fields, and an optional message body (Fielding and Reschke, 2014). The status line indicates the server's status with regard to the user's request. The standard defines five groups of status codes: codes in the 100 group are informational, the 200 group indicates success (e.g., 200—OK), the 300 group indicates redirections (e.g., 301—Moved Permanently), the 400 group indicates errors originating on the user side (e.g., 400—Bad Request or 404—Not Found), and the 500 group indicates server-side errors (e.g., 504—Gateway Timeout). Like HTTP requests, response messages can contain a number of response header fields. The *Content-Type* header indicates the MIME type of the data sent in the message body, for example image/png for images in PNG format, or text/html for HTML documents. The *Last-Modified* header indicates when the document was last modified on the server-side. To assist with caching of resources, the entity tag (*ETag*) header can contain a fingerprint (e.g., a hash) or revision number of the resource. The format of the ETag header is not defined and can be freely chosen by the server. The *Location* header is used with 300 status codes to indicate the redirection target. The *Set-Cookie* header contains cookies to be stored by the client. Each cookie contains a name and value, and can contain additional attributes, for example an expiration date, whether the cookie should only be sent back through a secure channel, and whether the cookie should be accessible through means other than HTTP (e.g., through JavaScript). The client is responsible for storing cookies and handling them according to the set attributes. The tracking status (*Tk*) header is intended to hold the response to the *DNT* header, for example, indicating that the server is tracking (T), not tracking (N), or disregarding the header (D).

HTTPS

The HTTP protocol provides several headers that relate to the use of TLS. HTTP Strict Transport Security (HSTS) allows websites to declare that browsers connecting to it have to use an encrypted connection. This can protect users against TLS stripping attacks. Websites can transmit their HSTS requirement using the *Strict-Transport-Security* header in their HTTP response when a browser first visits, and browsers can also use a public preload HSTS list to find out in advance which websites require encrypted connections. Browsers use an HSTS cache to keep a record of which domains require HTTPS (Dabrowski et al., 2016). The Content Security Policy (CSP) is a mechanism that allows web developers to specify which content should be trusted by the browser. This can protect users against cross-site scripting and clickjacking. A website's CSP can be transmitted in the HTTP *Content-Security-Policy* header or in an HTML meta tag (Roth et al., 2020).

2.1.4 Application Layer: Domain Names

Domain names, or host names, are the human-readable way to identify hosts on the Internet. The Domain Name System (DNS) is responsible for translating host names to IP addresses (Kurose and Ross, 2016).

The DNS realizes a distributed database of mappings from host names to IP addresses through a hierarchy of DNS servers. DNS defines a hierarchy of *zones*, where each zone provides at least one authoritative name server that can map domain names to IP addresses for all names in its zone. The root zone is the top of the hierarchy, followed by zones representing top-level domains such as *.com* on the next level, and zones for domain names that can be registered by individuals and organizations, such as *google.com*, on the level below that. The sub-domains on the next level can be freely chosen by the individual or organization who owns the domain.

The DNS protocol, running over UDP port 53, allows hosts to query this database. The client-side software that initiates queries is a DNS resolver. To answer queries, DNS servers use the tree hierarchy to recursively query other DNS servers until the authoritative server is found who can send the correct reply. To speed up this operation, DNS servers and clients can cache responses to queries (Klein and Pinkas, 2019). Reverse DNS (rDNS) provides the reverse lookup service, from IP address to host name (Invernizzi et al., 2016).

DNS can be used for load balancing, for example when a single website is served from multiple web servers. In this case, the authoritative DNS server can return one of several IP addresses for queries to the same host name.

By default, DNS queries and responses are not encrypted, which means that the DNS queries reveal information about the websites a user visits. Different options have been introduced to encrypt DNS lookups including DNS-over-TLS (DoT) and DNS-over-HTTPS (DoH). The disadvantage of both is that the DoT or DoH provider still learns which websites a user wants to visit (Siby et al., 2020).

In small networks that do not have a local DNS server, multicast name resolution can be used to resolve host names (Cheng et al., 2013). This is often used to resolve *.local* names in networks provided by Wi-Fi hotspots.

In addition to the technical infrastructure that supports a mapping from human readable domain names to IP addresses, there is also an infrastructure that allows individuals and organizations to register domain names for their own use (Arshad et al., 2017; Binns et al., 2018b). The *whois* system is part of this infrastructure and allows individuals to look up the contact details of domain owners (Ali et al., 2019b; Clayton and Mansfield, 2014). The whois system is a distributed database where top-level domain registries operate whois servers, and clients can use the whois protocol to request a lookup. While originally all information about domain owners was public, the use of whois privacy solutions allows domain owners to either hide their contact details (so-called *privacy service*) or both their name and contact details (*proxy service*). The use of whois privacy solutions has increased over the years (Clayton and Mansfield, 2014). This can make transparency research more difficult (see Chapter 4).

2.1.5 Wi-Fi Hotspots

Wi-Fi hotspots provide access to the Internet in public locations such as airports or coffee houses. Historically, many hotspots were open, with no restrictions on access. Although connection without authentication was convenient, it came at the cost of no encryption on the wireless link. Alternatively, hotspots used one of the standard Wi-Fi encryption methods (WEP, WPA, or WPA2) which required users to acquire the password from staff or noticeboards at the location (Cheng et al., 2013). The inconvenience of distributing these passwords made this method less popular, even though it offered improved privacy and security.

Today, many hotspots are open, but restrict internet access through captive portals (Dabrowski et al., 2016). Captive portals display a login page or acceptable use policy that the user has to agree to before they can connect to the Internet. Technically, captive portals redirect the user's first HTTP request to a portal site, often by spoofing an HTTP 302 *moved temporarily* response code. Only after logging in and/or paying and/or accepting the policy, the user is connected to the Internet by allowlisting the user's MAC or IP address in the Wi-Fi router. This allowlisting entry can be valid for a limited period of time. Captive portals are often operated by third parties. A captive portal in a coffee shop, for example, might be run by a large telecommunications provider or a specialized third party company instead of the coffee shop owner. Although registration on captive portals is often free, it requires users to provide personal information or to log in via their social media account. Compared to the traditional methods explained above, this method offers no encryption on the wireless link, but instead allows the provider of the hotspot, including the third party that operates the captive portal, to collect data about their users. In addition to captive portals, many hotspots redirect users to a landing page after passing the captive portal (Ali et al., 2019b).

2.2 Web-Based Services

On the Internet, the protocol stack described above is used to transport web content that will be displayed in the user's browser. Web content can consist of different content types that the browser has to render in a way intended by the web developer. Web developers use different languages to specify how content should be rendered: the Hypertext Markup Language (HTML) describes the semantic structure of the website, Cascading Style Sheets (CSS) specify elements of the visual style, and JavaScript (JS) is used to implement interactive elements such as mouse-over menus.

HTML is the standard way to describe how documents transmitted via the Hypertext Transfer Protocol should be displayed in a web browser. The standard is maintained and developed by the Web Hypertext Application Technology Working Group (WHATWG), whose steering group consists of Apple, Google, Microsoft, and Mozilla.[2] The current version is HTML5.

Each HTML document consists of a hierarchy of nested *tags* which can be customized through attributes. To display an HTML document, the browser has to parse the HTML markup to create an internal representation of it. This internal representation is called the Document Object Model or DOM tree.

Listing 2.1 shows an example HTML document, and Figure 2.2 shows the resulting DOM tree. As shown in the listing, HTML documents typically start with a document type declaration (DOCTYPE) which is used by browsers to decide how each element should be rendered. The doctype in the listing indicates an HTML5 document. The doctype is followed by the `<head>` tag which contains metadata such as the document title and style definitions. The style definition is specified using Cascading Style Sheets and can be inline as in the example, or included from a separate file. The `<body>` of the document contains tags that describe content elements and their semantic relationships, such as headings `<h1>`, paragraphs `<p>`, links `<a>`, or forms `<form>`. In Listing 2.1, the form contains embedded JavaScript code in the `<script>` tag that changes the value of the `<output>` tag as well as the `href` target of the earlier link. The DOM in Figure 2.2 shows the representation of the HTML document after the JavaScript has been processed, and as such displays the updated link target.

The HTML specification contains many additional features, for example, embedding of external resources, such as CSS, JS, or images, and various other tags. In HTML5, several new features were introduced, such as the `<canvas>` tag (Mowery and Shacham, 2012) or WebAPI calls (Diamantaris et al., 2020).

---

[2] https://html.spec.whatwg.org/

Listing 2.1. *Example HTML document*

```html
<!DOCTYPE html>
<html lang="en">
  <head>
    <title>Sample page</title>
    <style>
      body { background: beige; color: navy; }
    </style>
  </head>
  <body>
    <h1>Sample page</h1>
    <p>This is a <a href="demo.html">simple</a> sample.</p>
    <!-- this is a comment -->
    <form name="main">
      Result: <output name="result"></output>
      <script>
        document.forms.main.elements.result.value = 'Hello World';
        var a = document.links[0];
        a.href = 'sample.html';
      </script>
    </form>
  </body>
</html>
```

```
├DOCTYPE: html
└HTML lang="en"
   ├HEAD
   │  ├TITLE
   │  │  └#text: Sample page
   │  └STYLE
   │     └#text: body { background: beige; color: navy; }
   └BODY
      ├H1
      │  └#text: Sample page
      ├P
      │  ├#text: This is a
      │  ├A href="sample.html"
      │  │  └#text: simple
      │  └#text: sample.
      ├#comment: this is a comment
      └FORM name="main"
         ├#text: Result:
         ├OUTPUT name="result"
         │  └#text: Hello World
         └SCRIPT
            └#text: document.forms.main.elements.result.value = 'Hello World';
               var a = document.links[0]; a.href = 'sample.html';
```

Figure 2.2 DOM tree for the example HTML document.

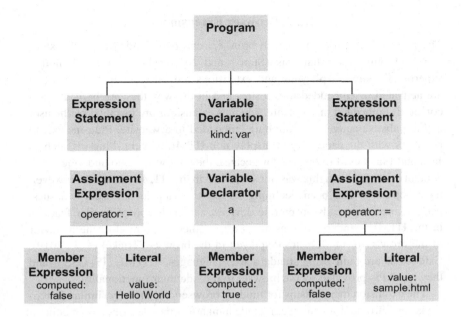

Figure 2.3 The abstract syntax tree for the JavaScript snippet in Listing 2.1.

2.2.1 JavaScript

JavaScript is a programming language that is supported by all modern browsers (Acar et al., 2013). It is mainly used to manipulate the DOM and thereby support interactivity on websites, such as pop-up menus, asynchronous requests/responses, data display, and data filtering.

To execute JavaScript code, web browsers rely on JavaScript engines. The JS engine runs alongside the browser's rendering engine. JS engines in use today include V8 (Chrome/Google), SpiderMonkey (Firefox/Mozilla), and Chakra (Edge/Microsoft). JavaScript engines can be realized as interpreters or, to improve performance, as just-in-time compilers (Mulazzani et al., 2013). They can also be a combination of interpreter and compiler, as, for example, in V8 (Chen and Kapravelos, 2018).

JavaScript, like other programming languages, can be parsed and represented as an abstract syntax tree (AST). For example, the AST in Figure 2.3 corresponds to the JavaScript code embedded in Listing 2.1.

2.2.2 Browser Extensions

The functionality offered by web browsers can be extended through extension and plug-in mechanisms (Starov and Nikiforakis, 2017a). Although superficially similar, plug-ins and extensions are different in the way they are activated or embedded in websites and in the way they are built. Plug-in content is embedded in a website, whereas extensions are installed by the user and are always active without being embedded in a website. Plug-ins extend browsers with the capability to display non-HTML content. Plug-ins such as Java and Flash used to be popular because they allowed audio and video web content at a time when this was not supported in the HTML standard. However, their popularity has been declining in recent years due to security issues, performance overheads on mobile devices, and inclusion of similar features in the HTML standard. Extensions, on the other hand, modify the behavior of the browser or of websites displayed in the browser (Trickel et al., 2019). Extensions are built using standard web languages – HTML, JS, CSS – and they use APIs provided by the browser to provide their functionality.

The extension mechanisms for modern browsers are broadly similar. Extensions for Chrome, for example, include a manifest that describes what content scripts, web accessible resources, and background pages are included in the extension.The manifest also declares which permissions from the extension API the extension is asking for (Chen and Kapravelos, 2018). Background pages contain the main logic of the extension, consisting of standard HTML, and run in their own JS execution environment. Content scripts are JS code that can communicate with the background page as well as modify the current website using the DOM API. Content scripts can be static or dynamically injected into websites, and they run in their own JS execution environment. As a result, content scripts are sandboxed from main website's JavaScript code. Web accessible resources are the only resources directly accessible from websites (Trickel et al., 2019). Background pages can use the entire Chrome extension API, but content scripts are limited to a subset of API calls, and API calls cannot be used in websites. To allow communication between content scripts and background pages, the extension API offers a message passing API.

The security features of extension mechanisms, such as sandboxing and permissions for API use, have been designed to avoid security issues that were common with earlier plug-in mechanisms.

2.3 Mobile Services

Similarly to web-based services, services for mobile devices also use internet networking technologies and are therefore also subject to corporate surveillance. Mobile browsers can be used to access regular web-based services, and mobile apps offer services tailored to mobile devices.

The two most widely used operating systems for mobile devices are Google's Android and Apple's iOS. Apps for both operating systems are normally obtained through their corresponding app stores. All app stores offer millions of apps, including free apps, paid apps, apps with in-app purchases, and apps supported by advertising.

2.3.1 Android

At its core, Android is an open source operating system that is based on the Linux kernel. However, the proprietary Google Play Services are necessary to use Google's Play Store and are required by many apps. In addition, many devices already come with preinstalled proprietary software (Gamba et al., 2020).

The Play store is the official source for Android apps, and it is bundled with the stock version of Android (Carbunar and Potharaju, 2015; Viennot et al., 2014). To use the Play store, users need to sign into a Google account. There are numerous independent app stores that can either be installed as regular apps or come preinstalled by the phone manufacturer. Because Google Play is not accessible in some countries including China, many independent app stores exist in the Chinese market, for example, provided by phone vendors and large tech companies (Wang et al., 2018). F-Droid is another independent app store that distributes open-source apps.

Android apps are distributed as files in the Android Package (APK) format. APK files are signed archives that contain compiled code, resources such as images, and a configuration file called *manifest* which lists the name of the app package, the app's components, and the required permissions (Pham et al., 2019). The signature on the APK files is generated by the app developer, not by Google as the operator of the app store. Apps for Android can be developed in Java or Kotlin, possibly combined with C/C++. They can use the Android SDK to access Android features. APKs can be downloaded and unpacked for analysis using apktool.[3]

Access to some Android features is protected by *permissions*, for example, permissions to access the camera, internal storage, or network communication. Permissions have to be granted by the user on a per-app basis, either when installing the app or when the permission is first needed by the app. Permissions are grouped into normal, signature, and dangerous permissions

---

[3] https://ibotpeaches.github.io/Apktool/

(Pham et al., 2019). Normal permissions need to be declared by the app, but are then automatically granted when the app is installed. Users cannot revoke these permissions. For example, network access via the INTERNET permission is a normal permission. Signature permissions are a type of custom permission that apps can use to control access to their components by other apps from the same developer. Signature permissions are granted when the app is installed, provided that the app's signature matches the signature on the app that defines the permission. Dangerous permissions are intended to protect the user's private information, including stored data and other apps. Before Android 6, dangerous permissions were requested at install time, but with later Android versions they are requested when they are first used. Dangerous permissions include access to a user's location, contact list, or device storage. Unique device identifiers, such as the mobile advertising identifier (MAID) or the International Mobile Equipment Identity (IMEI), can be accessed if the corresponding dangerous permissions are granted (Pham et al., 2019). The Android platform code or the underlying Linux kernel act as a reference monitor that grants or denies access to permissioned resources (Reardon et al., 2019). However, some APIs are not protected with permissions. For example, the list of installed applications, which can be used for fingerprinting, can be retrieved using an unprotected API (Grace et al., 2012).

2.3.2 iOS

Apple's iOS is a proprietary operating system that is often seen as more secure and more privacy-friendly than Android. The iOS app store is the only official source for iOS apps (Egele et al., 2011). Installing apps from other sources like Cydia requires the device to be jailbroken. The iOS app store uses a vetting procedure for apps to make sure that they conform to the licensing agreement.

Apps for iOS are developed in Objective-C and Swift, and use the iOS SDK to access iOS features (Egele et al., 2011). iOS apps are delivered as a signed zip archive which contains the application binary in Mach-O format, data and resource files, and metadata information. The signature on the archive is generated by Apple, which is in contrast to Android where the developer signs their own apps. This has implications for the trust model: users of iOS only have to trust Apple, whereas Android users have to trust multiple independent developers.

iOS also differs in its app permission model (Agarwal and Hall, 2013) where iOS relies on an app review process (vetting) to ensure that all apps meet the app store guidelines, that is, they request permissions for user data only when the permissions are actually required for the app's functionality

(Egele et al., 2011). Starting with iOS 5, user notification and control over permissions has gradually increased (Agarwal and Hall, 2013).

Whereas access to unique device identifiers is easy on Android, it is restricted on iOS. Apps do not have access to unique device identifiers such as IMEI or MAC address, and Safari, the default browser on iOS, uses intelligent tracking prevention (Zhang et al., 2019a). The only identifier accessible to apps is the advertising identifier, provided that the app actually displays ads. Users can change the advertising identifier at any time, and it can be made unavailable if the user activates the *limit ad tracking* option (Corner et al., 2017).

3

Methods of Corporate Surveillance

Corporations conduct surveillance based on internet technologies and web and mobile services. The chapter explains how different aspects of corporate surveillance work on a technical level: how individual users can be tracked across their use of web and mobile services based on stateful tracking with cookies and stateless tracking with fingerprinting; how information collected through tracking is consolidated in comprehensive user profiles; how analytics services contribute to tracking and profiling; and how advertising technology works, including ad targeting and ad sales.

3.1 Tracking

Since the introduction of HTTP cookies in 1994, a variety of different tracking mechanisms has been created and existing tracking mechanisms have been continuously refined to improve their tracking capabilities. This section reviews stateful and stateless tracking methods as well as methods to track users across devices, on mobile devices, and via email.

3.1.1 Stateful Tracking

Stateful tracking denotes all mechanisms that allow to reidentify users by storing information on the user's machine. Different storage mechanisms have been used for stateful tracking. This section first explains the most common mechanism, HTTP cookies, then Flash, Java, and HTML5 cookies, and, finally, cache-based tracking.

HTTP Cookies

Cookies are a mechanism in the HTTP protocol that allows web servers to store small amounts of data on the user's machine (Bujlow et al., 2017). Defined in

RFC6265 (Barth, 2011), cookies are the most common mechanism for state management in the otherwise stateless HTTP protocol. State management is a useful mechanism because it enables, for example, shopping carts with persistent contents or website logins without frequent reauthentication.

Servers can set cookies in the user's browser by sending the *Set-Cookie* header in their HTTP response. On subsequent requests to the server's domain, the browser will then automatically include the *Cookie* header containing the value of the previously set cookie. Cookies can also be set and read via JavaScript.

Figure 3.1 shows what information is stored in cookies by showing two example cookies set by a visit to two different websites. The first line shows the cookie name which is chosen by the server and allows to disambiguate between different cookies set by the server, followed by the cookie value which is a string limited to a size of 4 KiB. The subsequent lines show properties of the cookie. The *Domain* property identifies the website that set the cookie. The *Expires* property indicates when the cookie will expire and then be deleted by the browser. Session cookies are deleted when the session ends (e.g., when the user closes browser window), whereas persistent cookies specify the date when they will expire. A long expiration time, such as two years in Figure 3.1, is an indicator that the cookie may be used for tracking (Li et al., 2015). The *Secure* flag indicates that this cookie should be transmitted securely, i.e., via HTTPS, and the *HttpOnly* flag indicates whether the cookie can be accessed via HTTP only (when the flag is set to true), or whether it can also be accessed programmatically via JavaScript (when set to false).

i18n-prefs: "GBP"
Created: "Wed, 14 Oct 2020"
Domain: **".amazon.co.uk"**
Expires: "Thu, 14 Oct **2021**"
HostOnly: false
HttpOnly: false
Last Accessed: "Wed, 14 Oct 2020"
Path: "/"
SameSite: "None"
Secure: true
Size: **13**

mid: "X4dh0gAEAAHu4V6AnrOajXbuJgeK"
Created: "Wed, 14 Oct 2020"
Domain: **".instagram.com"**
Expires: "Fri, 14 Oct **2022**"
HostOnly: false
HttpOnly: false
Last Accessed: "Wed, 14 Oct 2020"
Path: "/"
SameSite: "None"
Secure: true
Size: **31**

Figure 3.1 Attributes of two example cookies set by visits to Amazon (*left*) and Instagram (*right*). Differences are highlighted in bold. Note that Amazon's cookie contains a preference for a currency (GBP) that is not unique for each user, whereas Instagram's cookie contains a string that can uniquely identify a user.

First-party cookies are set by the website that the user is visiting. Third-party cookies, on the other hand, are set by third parties, i.e., by web content that is included in the first-party website, such as advertisements or JavaScript libraries. Using third-party cookies, the third party learns the browsing history of users for all websites that its content is included on. This is particularly critical when the third party provides content for many first party websites, such as popular JavaScript libraries. For this reason, all major browsers allow users to block third-party cookies.

The same-origin policy is the main security mechanism for cookies. It specifies, first, that cookies can only be set for the domain that the loaded content is from, and second, that cookies will only be sent to the domain that is specified in the cookie. This policy effectively restricts cross-domain tracking of users. However, the same-origin policy can be circumvented through redirect tracking and cookie synchronization.

In redirect tracking (Koop et al., 2020), when a user clicks on a link or visits a URL, the desired content is served only at the end of a chain of redirects, often implemented using HTTP redirects with a 3xx status code. Each redirect host in this chain can set first-party cookies, which avoids the limitations of the same-origin policy and allows the redirect hosts to track users.

Cookie synchronization (Papadopoulos et al., 2019) is used when two different third parties, who each have their own cookies that uniquely identify users, want to match their unique identifiers so they can learn more about the user, for example, to improve their ad targeting. Once two third parties have an agreement that they wish to match their cookie identifiers, they can execute a cookie synchronization protocol (Acar et al., 2014; Olejnik et al., 2014). Figure 3.2 shows an example message exchange that allows two servers, A and B, to synchronize their cookies. It begins when the user requests a resource from website A, which includes the existing cookie for A. A then replies with a HTTP 302 redirect, which redirects the browser to a resource on website B. The URL indicated in this redirect includes, for example as a query string, the value of A's existing cookie. The browser then requests this resource from B, including the existing cookie for B in the HTTP request. At this point, B can match their user identifier to A's identifier. To allow A to match user identifiers as well, B can then reply with a similar redirect, redirecting the browser back to A, and including the value of B's existing cookie. This concludes the cookie synchronization between A and B, and they can now merge their back-end databases using their cookie matching tables. This back-end merge can be executed infrequently (e.g., daily).

To avoid having to set up multiple cookie synchronization agreements, A and B can also match their cookies with a central third party and thereby gain

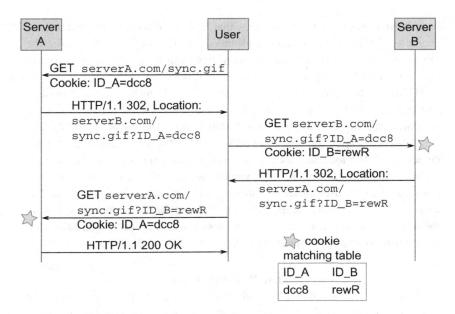

Figure 3.2 Sequence diagram showing how the cookie synchronization protocol can play out between two servers A and B, triggered when a user loads a resource from A. The point during the message exchange when each server completes their cookie matching table for this user is marked with a star.

cookie matches with all servers that match with the central third party. This model is favored by Google's DoubleClick which hosts the match database for their customers.[1]

Flash, Java, and HTML5 Cookies

Besides HTTP cookies, Flash, Java, and HTML5 each offer their own mechanisms for storing information on the user's machine. Flash cookies, or local shared objects (LSO) (Soltani et al., 2009; Acar et al., 2014; Ayenson et al., 2011) are files stored on disk by the Flash plug-in. These files, up to 100 KiB each, can be set and read when websites embed Flash content. Unlike cookies, they do not expire. In addition, Flash cookies are stored per Flash installation, which means that they can be accessed from different browsers on a single machine, i.e., they allow cross-browser tracking of users and circumvention of private browsing mode (Bujlow et al., 2017). Because browsers initially didn't offer an in-browser mechanism to delete Flash cookies, they have

---

[1] https://developers.google.com/ad-exchange/rtb/cookie-guide

been used to respawn HTTP cookies that had been deleted by the user, for example, as part of the evercookie (Kamkar, 2010). For the Java plug-in, the *PersistenceService* offers similar storage mechanisms as Flash, with similar capabilities for tracking users (Bujlow et al., 2017).

HTML5 offers three storage mechanisms: local storage, session storage, and IndexedDB. Local storage is a key-value store, shared between browser windows, that supports objects up to 5 MiB in size (Bujlow et al., 2017). The entries do not expire, but are emptied when HTTP cookies are deleted. Like cookies, HTML5 local storage follows the same-origin policy. Session storage is similar to local storage, but only available within a browser window, and it is emptied when the user closes the browser window. IndexedDB is intended as a storage mechanism for larger objects and files. Like local storage, it follows the same-origin policy, and its entries do not expire. It has been used as another mechanism to respawn deleted HTTP cookies (Acar et al., 2014).

Cache-Based Tracking

Cache-based tracking methods exploit various caches that the browser or operating system use for performance reasons. An early example of cache-based tracking was to use JavaScript to read the display color of links – assuming that visited links are displayed in a different color from unvisited links – to probe a user's browsing history (Bujlow et al., 2017; Weinberg et al., 2011). The defense mechanism implemented in modern browsers always returns the color for unvisited links when the link status is queried via JavaScript.

A cache-based tracking method that has been observed as a method to respawn deleted HTTP cookies (Ayenson et al., 2011) relies on the fact that some HTTP headers, notably the *Last-Modified* and *ETag* headers, can contain arbitrary values (Bujlow et al., 2017). When a user first requests a website or object, the web server can set these values to a new user identifier. At each subsequent user request, the browser will transmit these values in the *If-Modified-Since* and *If-None-Match* headers, respectively, which allows the server to reidentify the user. Originally, the purpose of these HTTP headers was to reduce traffic by allowing the server to check whether the document had been modified since it was last sent to the user. If it was not modified, the server could send a short HTTP 304 not modified response instead of the full response.

Several other cache-based tracking methods have been proposed, but it is not known whether they are used for corporate surveillance. These methods include timing attacks on caches for web objects and the DNS cache (Felten and Schneider, 2000), exploiting the DNS cache to build statistically unique identifiers (Klein and Pinkas, 2019), and using the HTTP 301 redirect cache and the HTTP strict transport security cache (HSTS cache) (Bujlow et al., 2017).

3.1.2 Stateless Tracking

Stateless tracking denotes all methods that attempt to reidentify users without keeping state on the user's side. This overcomes a key weakness of stateful tracking, namely that users may delete their local state. Stateless tracking methods, known as *fingerprinting* methods, are used for long-term reidentification of users. Fingerprinting uses different features to reidentify users, including the user's device and its hardware components such as network interfaces and sensors, the user's operating system, and the user's browser. Fingerprinting assumes that these features, called *fingerprinting attributes*, change infrequently enough that a combination of attributes can yield a unique fingerprint.

Network Fingerprinting

The user's IP address is a fingerprinting attribute that is readily available because a unique network address is required for network communication to take place (Bujlow et al., 2017). IP addresses can reveal the name of the user's internet service provider, whether the user is using a proxy server, and can approximate the user's geolocation. The geolocation estimate is most accurate for residential users, but can be inaccurate for many mobile devices, Virtual Private Network (VPN) users, and Tor users. IP addresses are suitable for fingerprinting because public IP addresses are quite stable: 87% of users have an IP address that is stable for more than a month (Mishra et al., 2020).

However, several users may share a public IP address, for example, users in a local network who connect to the Internet via a shared router. To overcome this limitation to fingerprinting, WebRTC can be used to collect the combination of a user's local and public IP addresses. This combination is suitable for fingerprinting because it is very likely to be unique (Englehardt and Narayanan, 2016). WebRTC is a protocol for real-time peer-to-peer communication within the browser. To discover the best path between peers, WebRTC collects all IP addresses from the local client, including its addresses in the local network and its public-facing address, and makes them available to peers. Websites can exploit this behavior for tracking by creating an *RTCDataChannel*, triggering collection of IP addresses with *RTCPeerConnection.setLocalDescription()*, and reading the collected IP addresses with *RTCPeerConnection.onicecandidate*. This is possible despite the permission model: WebRTC only needs user permission for audio/video transmission, but not for transmission of IP addresses.

Other network protocols such as Bluetooth can also be used for fingerprinting (Zuo et al., 2019). For example, Bluetooth Low Energy (BLE) broadcasts unencrypted advertisement packets, that allows pairing with mobile apps. These packets contain universally unique identifiers (UUIDs) that describe the services offered by the BLE device (e.g., heart rate, battery status). The set of UUIDs broadcast by a device can be used as a fingerprint for its device type.

Device Fingerprinting

Device fingerprinting relies on measuring imperfections in hardware components that were introduced during the manufacturing process. These imperfections make devices discernible from each other even if they are otherwise identical.

An early example is fingerprinting based on clock skew (Kohno et al., 2005). Clock skew is the first derivative of a clock's offset and describes differences in clock frequency. No two hardware clocks are fully identical, which results in small differences in the skew of each clock. The skew of each clock is assumed to be constant over time and can be estimated from the timestamps sent in the TCP *Timestamps* option. Clock skew can thus be used as a fingerprinting attribute which is accessible remotely without modification or cooperation of the fingerprinted device.

Wireless network interface cards (NICs) are another hardware component whose imperfections can be used for fingerprinting (Brik et al., 2008). The imperfections in NICs are caused by variations in the physical properties of the NIC components that help transmit the wireless signal and include quadrature errors, self-interference, amplitude clipping, and frequency offset. To measure the fingerprint, the fingerprinter must be within wireless range.

Clock skew and NIC imperfections can be used together to fingerprint wireless devices remotely (Uluagac et al., 2013). This method relies on the observation that clock skew and NIC imperfections cause variations in the timing of packet transmissions which can be measured as variations in packet inter-arrival times on the receiver side.

Microphones and speakers are also affected by manufacturing imperfections which introduce anomalies in how sound is generated and received (Das et al., 2014). If the fingerprinter is able to play and record audio samples, acoustic features such as mel-frequency cepstral coefficients can be used as fingerprinting attributes. This is particularly relevant for smart devices that have microphones and speakers.

Modern mobile devices have a large range of sensors that can be used for fingerprinting. For example, fingerprinting attributes have been derived from the time and frequency domain of accelerometer signals (Dey et al., 2014) and a combination of accelerometer and gyroscope sensor values (Das et al., 2016, 2018a). These fingerprints can be improved if the sensors can be stimulated by playing inaudible audio files. In addition, the factory calibration data of accelerometer, gyroscope, and magnetometer can be inferred and used to construct a fingerprint (Zhang et al., 2019a).

The batteries of mobile devices can also be used as fingerprinting attributes. The HTML5 BatteryStatus API offers access to charge level, chargingTime, and dischargingTime, which can be used to infer the battery capacity (Olejnik et al., 2016).

Browser Fingerprinting

Browser fingerprinting is the most common type of fingerprinting deployed on the Internet today. The central idea is that a combination of fingerprinting attributes, derived from characteristics of the user's browser, can serve as a global identifier for users if the combination is unique enough. Panopticlick introduced a set of fingerprinting attributes, including the HTTP *User-Agent*, the HTTP *Accept* headers, whether cookies are enabled, the screen resolution (accessible via JavaScript's *window.screen* object), the user's timezone, the list of installed browser plugins, plugin versions and MIME types, the list of system fonts (accessible via Flash or a Java applet), and the presence of supercookies (Eckersley, 2010). All these attributes – and more – have been confirmed in fingerprinting scripts in the wild (Nikiforakis et al., 2013).

Additional attributes can enhance a fingerprint's uniqueness and provide more accessible ways of querying the values of known attributes: a list of basic fonts installed on the system can be queried from JavaScript using the *offsetWidth* and *offsetHeight* DOM variables (Boda et al., 2012); the font rendering can be fingerprinted by checking the sizes of bounding boxes for unicode glyphs in different CSS font families (Fifield and Egelman, 2015); the JavaScript *navigator* object can be used to reveal details about browser vendor and version, supported plugins and MIME types, and operating system and architecture (Acar et al., 2013); the presence and configuration of browser extensions can be fingerprinted by testing for their Web Accessible Resources (Sjösten et al., 2017) or by testing for their effects (e.g., NoScript allowlists can be deduced by attempting to load scripts and then testing whether they were executed) (Mowery et al., 2011); the list of websites a user is logged into can be fingerprinted via redirection URL hijacking and CSP violation reports (Gulyas et al., 2018); and the presence of the *DNT* header, the WebGL vendor

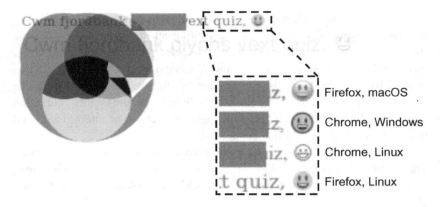

Figure 3.3 Grayscale rendering of the canvas fingerprint drawn by the *fingerprint2.js* library. Part of the rendering has been magnified to show the differences between four different platforms.

and renderer, and the use of an ad blocker can be queried from JavaScript (Laperdrix et al., 2016).

The browser's JavaScript engine can be fingerprinted as well by using JavaScript test suites that are designed to fail for different browsers (Mulazzani et al., 2013). Reasonably small test suites are sufficient to distinguish browser and operating system combinations, including major and minor versions. In addition, performance tests on the JavaScript engine also allow to infer browser, operating system, and microarchitecture (Mowery et al., 2011).

Features introduced with HTML5 provide additional ways to improve fingerprinting. Most importantly, canvas fingerprinting and canvas font fingerprinting have contributed to increasing the uniqueness of fingerprints. Canvas fingerprinting works by rendering text or WebGL scenes onto a HTML5 `<canvas>` element and then inspecting the rendered pixels (Mowery and Shacham, 2012). A popular string for canvas fingerprinting is "Cwm fjordbank glyphs vext quiz" because it is a perfect pangram – a phrase that contains every letter of the English alphabet exactly once. For example, Figure 3.3 shows the canvas rendered by the *fingerprint2.js* library[2] on four different platforms. Due to differences in the systems' graphics drivers and graphics processing units (GPUs), the rendered outputs vary and are unique enough to serve as fingerprinting attributes. For example, Figure 3.3 shows differences in the smiley and the width of the rendered text.

---

[2] https://github.com/fingerprintjs/fingerprintjs

Table 3.1. *List of fingerprinting attributes available in fingerprint2.js.*

userAgent	webdriver	language
colorDepth	deviceMemory	pixelRatio
hardwareConcurrency	screenResolution	availableScreenResolution
timezoneOffset	timezone	sessionStorage
localStorage	indexedDb	addBehavior
openDatabase	cpuClass	platform
doNotTrack	plugins	canvas
webgl	webglVendorAndRenderer	adBlock
hasLiedLanguages	hasLiedResolution	hasLiedOs
hasLiedBrowser	touchSupport	fonts
fontsFlash	audio	enumerateDevices

Canvas font fingerprinting also relies on the HTML5 `<canvas>` (Englehardt and Narayanan, 2016), but instead of taking a measurement based on all rendered pixels, canvas font fingerprinting measures only the width and height of the rendered text. To make this measurement more unique, canvas font fingerprinting enumerates fonts that may be present on a system and takes width/height measurements for each font.

The HTML5 *AudioContext* interface, part of the web audio API, can be used for fingerprinting a system's audio hardware. AudioContext fingerprinting works by generating audio signals and then checking their properties from JavaScript (Englehardt and Narayanan, 2016).

The ability of the HTML5 `<canvas>` element and *AudioContext* interface to fingerprint not only the user's browser, but characteristics of the underlying hardware can also allow for cross-browser fingerprinting (Cao et al., 2017) to track users across different browsers on one machine. Cross-browser fingerprinting combines various rendering tasks and uses features including WebGL lines, curves, anti-aliasing, vertex shaders, fragment shaders, transparency via the alpha channel, image encoding and decoding, and various installed writing scripts (e.g., Chinese, Korean, or Arabic).

To summarize the current state of the art in browser fingerprinting, Table 3.1 shows a list of all attributes that are currently available in the *fingerprint2.js* library.

3.1.3 Cross-Device Tracking

In addition to tracking users on a single device or browser, the tracking industry also aims to track users across all the devices they might use. Cross-device tracking consists of two main steps: first, to identify and track unique devices, and second, to correlate those devices belonging to the same person (Zimmeck et al., 2017). For the first step, any combination of stateful and stateless tracking methods can be used. For the second step, devices are represented in device graphs where edges between devices are included if the devices belong to the same user. Sometimes deterministic matching is possible, for example when a user logs into a service from two different devices. At other times, probabilistic matching methods can be used (Brookman et al., 2017). For example, when two devices have the same public IP address, they may share the same NAT behind the same router. Especially for residential IP addresses, this indicates some relationship between the users of the devices. The colocation of two devices at the same IP address can also indicate that both devices belong to the same user, such as a mobile device that is colocated with a user's work PC during the day and with their home PC during the night. Probabilistic matching can also be based on the similarity of browsing patterns across devices.

3.1.4 Tracking on Mobile Devices

On mobile devices, most of the stateful and stateless tracking methods discussed above are applicable as well. However, there are some differences.

Stateful tracking using cookies is more difficult on mobile devices because each app has its own cookie store (Vines et al., 2017). While mobile web browsing can be tracked through cookies in the mobile browser app, cookies are not useful to track users across other apps they use. However, mobile devices have additional unique device identifiers that are available to apps, provided they have been granted the corresponding permission, and that can serve the same purpose as cookies on desktop systems. For example, the mobile advertising ID (MAID) uniquely identifies Android devices, and similar advertising identifiers are available on Apple and Microsoft devices (Christl and Spiekermann, 2016).

Stateless tracking on mobile browsers yields a similar uniqueness for fingerprints, even though the uniqueness is due to different combinations of attributes (Laperdrix et al., 2016). For example, the lack of plugins and fonts on mobile browsers reduces the number of fingerprintable attributes, but, in turn, the user-agent and canvas attributes are more fingerprintable: the user-agent string is more fingerprintable due to the number of different mobile vendors and firmware versions, and the canvas is more fingerprintable due to differences in mobile hardware and differences in emojis that depend on the manufacturer and on the version of the operating system.

3.1.5 Email Tracking

Similar to the web, tracking can also be performed on the basis of emails, in particular when emails have HTML bodies or when webmailers are used to read email. Although JavaScript execution is typically blocked in email readers (Englehardt et al., 2018), embedded images and CSS are still requested from third-party servers and cookies can be set. As a result, email offers similar tracking opportunities as the web.

3.2 Profiling

Profiling is the process of analyzing data about users with the aim to make inferences and predictions. Profiling therefore produces knowledge, in particular nonrepresentational knowledge – knowledge that does not represent a current state of affairs (Gutwirth and Hildebrandt, 2010). In this sense, profiles represent patterns in past data. Profiles are based on correlations, but not causes or reasons, and they are developed into probabilistic knowledge about individuals, i.e., predictions about how individuals are expected to behave or react in the future. Profiles can influence the future, for example, by shaping what options are available to individuals. Profiling can thus help to create the reality that it infers from data about the past. Compared to traditional statistical approaches which validate hypotheses about proposed correlations, profiling aims to detect new correlations.

Issues with profiling have been known for more than a decade (Gutwirth and Hildebrandt, 2010). Profiling can threaten personal autonomy by influencing the behavior of individuals (Zuboff, 2019). The constant algorithmic classification of individuals can lead to social sorting, where groups of individuals are treated differently, which can have profound effects on choices and life chances of individuals (Lyon, 2003). In addition, power inequalities between those who possess profiles and the individuals who are being profiled threaten privacy, fairness, and due process. Profiles may lead to wrong decisions, including discrimination, because of false positives and false negatives. These decisions about individuals cannot be audited or contested easily. Finally, consent given by an individual is not meaningful if the individual is not aware of the profiles that are created as a result.

This section reviews what these user profiles may contain, how anonymity and profiling relate to each other, and how data brokers have created a marketplace for user profiles.

3.2.1 Contents of User Profiles

Three main information sources are useful to learn about contents of user profiles: profile attributes made available to users by corporations; profile attributes offered to other corporations, for example, as ad targeting attributes; and inferences researchers have shown to be possible.

Table 3.2 shows profile attributes from four major profilers – Google, Facebook, BlueKai, and eXelate – that appear in each profiler's *ad preference manager*, which is the interface they offer to users to inspect their profiles. Note that most profile attributes are broad interest categories, however, some attributes can serve as proxies for sensitive attributes, such as "Consumers of Christian Television Network" (proxy for religion) or "Spanish Language Spoken" (proxy for Hispanic ethnicity).

In contrast, Figure 3.4 shows profile attributes that are present in profiles maintained by Acxiom (Christl, 2017). These attributes include much more personal and sensitive data, such as specific information about health, personal finances, and political views.

Because profilers are unlikely to reveal how they arrived at each attribute in a user's profile, researchers have demonstrated for a range of attributes how they might be inferred.

For example, the demographics of website visitors, such as age, gender, education, and occupation, can be derived from an individual's clickstream,

Table 3.2. *Selection of attributes in profiles collected by four profilers that allow users to view their profile (Bashir et al., 2019b; Andreou et al., 2018; Degeling and Nierhoff, 2018).*

Google	Computers and Electronics, Fruit and Vegetables, Mobile and Wireless, Lawn Mowers, Movies, Games, Fantasy Sports, Finance, Celebrities and Entertainment News, Shopping
Facebook	Instant messaging, Steam, Social network, Steak sauce, Instagram, Cricket For India, Entre Rios Province, Food, International Federation of Accountants, Education, New Parents, Allergy relief, Recent homebuyer, Likely to Engage in Politics (Liberal)
BlueKai	Computer, Outdoor Activities, Windows, Truck Rental, The Academy Awards, Travel, Grocery Locations, Halloween Buyers, Pakistan, Summer Olympics Enthusiast, Consumers of Christian Television Network (Broadcast), Spanish Language Spoken
eXelate	Pets, Diet and Weight Loss, Jewelry and Watches, Shopping, Auto Buyers—Sedan, Home and Garden, Lighting, Bed and Bath, Finance and Insurance

Age
Gender
Education
Employment

Purchases

Political views

Religion

Loans
Income
Net worth
Vehicles owned
Properties owned

Search history

Type of home
Size of home
Number of bedrooms

Relationship status
Number of children
Likelihood of:
  - planning to have a baby
  - planning to adopt

Alcohol and tobacco interests

Gaming and lottery interests

Residential history
History of name changes

Health interests:
  - Arthritis
  - Cardiac health
  - Diabetes
  - Disabilities

Likelihood of:
  - being a social influencer
  - being socially influenced

Figure 3.4 Example attributes contained in data broker user profiles, adapted from the Acxiom profile in Christl (2017). According to Christl (2017), Acxiom maintains 3,000 attributes and scores for over 700 million people.

i.e., the sequence of websites visited by the individual, with 67% accuracy (De Bock and Van den Poel, 2010). Google's inferences of age and gender have been confirmed to be mostly correct (Tschantz et al., 2018a).

Another method for predicting personal attributes in addition to demographics is based on Facebook likes (Kosinski et al., 2013), which allows to predict the user's sexual orientation, ethnicity, religious and political views, personality traits, intelligence, happiness, use of addictive substances, parental separation, age, and gender with accuracy between 85%–95%.

The big-5 personality traits – extraversion, agreeableness, conscientiousness, neuroticism, and openness to experience – can be predicted from mobile phone usage data (Chittaranjan et al., 2013; de Montjoye et al., 2013a) and data available at the mobile phone carrier (de Montjoye et al., 2013a), with a classification performance 10%–20% better than chance.

The emotional state of users, such as confidence, hesitance, nervousness, relaxation, sadness, tiredness, anger, or excitement, can be predicted based on keystroke patterns, i.e., the timing of key press and release events, with accuracy between 77%–88% (Epp et al., 2011).

Finally, the future behavior of users can also be predicted. For example, a user's future relationships can be predicted based on the structure of the user's social network graph, such as connections and interactions between mutual friends, with 70% accuracy (Backstrom and Kleinberg, 2014). In addition, a user's future locations can be predicted up to three hours into the future based on their location history and the location histories of their friends (De Domenico et al., 2013).

Contrary to research studies, commercial profilers do not specify the accuracies of their inferences. It is therefore possible that profile attributes are assigned to users – and treated as users' true attributes – based on low-accuracy inferences.

3.2.2 Anonymity versus Profiling

Many profilers and proponents of targeted advertising claim that profiles are harmless if they retain a user's anonymity, that is, they do not contain any personally identifiable data. At its core, this claim relies on the distinction between singling-out and identifying, assuming that singling users out is harmless while identifying users is not.

However, harm can be done even if an individual is not identified by name, for example, by unfair or discriminatory targeting (Borgesius, 2016). In this sense, the data used to single out a person *is* a form of personal data as defined in data protection law.

From a technical perspective, many studies have shown the reidentification risk of purportedly anonymous profiles. For example, when AOL published 20 million search queries from 650,000 of their users, each user was given a persistent pseudonym and could be reidentified from the contents of their search queries (Ohm, 2009). The Netflix prize dataset, which contained movie ratings from 500,000 Netflix subscribers, was de-anonymized using data from the internet movie database IMDb as background knowledge (Narayanan and Shmatikov, 2008).

The reidentification risk of datasets can be quantified by computing their *unicity* as the percentage of individuals that can be reidentified if the adversary knows a specific number of pieces of information. For example, knowing four location points is enough to uniquely identify 95% of individuals (de Montjoye et al., 2013b), assuming hourly location points and spatial resolution at the mobile carrier level. Similarly, knowledge of three credit card transactions uniquely identifies 90% of individuals (de Montjoye et al., 2015), knowledge of four installed mobile apps uniquely identifies 95% of individuals (Achara et al., 2015), and knowledge of the complete list of installed apps identifies 99% of users.[3]

3.2.3 Data Brokers

Data brokers are companies that specialize in trade with user profiles, particularly in acquiring and reselling personal data about individuals (Christl and Spiekermann, 2016; Christl, 2017). Most of these companies, including Acxiom, Core Logic, Datalogix, eBureau, ID Analytics, Intelius, PeekYou, and Rapleaf, do not offer user-facing services and thus are largely unknown to users. The business of data brokers includes collecting information, classifying this information and linking it to individuals, and selling the information to their clients. To collect information, data brokers rely on various sources: data purchase or exchange with other data brokers; clients who upload their customers' data in exchange for enriching it with additional information; web trackers including social media; the payment card industry; telecommunications and mobile carriers; and public records, such as bankruptcies, driver's licenses, voter records, property records, and telephone directories (Christl, 2017; Christl and Spiekermann, 2016).

Data brokers then use globally unique identifiers to link data from these sources to individuals and classify or infer further information, including personally identifiable information, demographics, political views, financial information, and health information (see Figure 3.4) (Christl, 2017).

Instead of selling (access to) their entire databases, data brokers offer different services to their clients. For example, clients can buy: lists of consumers with specific attributes; additional attributes for their own consumer data; scores and ranks on their own consumer data; identity verification; risk scores associated with specific transactions; verification of consumer-submitted information; fraud detection; and dossiers on individuals compiled from all available sources (Christl and Spiekermann, 2016).

The data collected by data brokers covers an enormous number of individuals. For example, Acxiom claims to have 3,000 attributes or scores for over 700 million people, Oracle claims more than 30,000 attributes on 2 billion people, and Experian claims more than 500 attributes on 2.3 billion people (Christl, 2017), which is more than one-quarter of the world population.

---

[3] Note that this reidentification risk is in addition to the privacy risk associated with revealing *which* apps are installed.

This data is collected largely without the knowledge or explicit consent of individuals, and data brokers make it hard to opt out of their data collection. For example, when one journalist attempted to opt out of data collection by 212 different data brokers (Angwin, 2014), only 92 of them accepted opt-outs. Of these, 70% required submission of government-issued identification such as driver's licenses to complete the opt-out, and 26% required submission of this identification by postal mail or fax.

3.3 Analytics

Web analytics is a service offered to website owners to better understand who their users are and how they interact with the website, for example, by presenting user statistics, device statistics, events, and errors (Starov et al., 2018). Free analytics services often combine data from their clients and aim to monetize the data, for example, by creating and selling user profiles. From a technical perspective, website owners who want to use a free analytics service such as Google Analytics embed JavaScript code into their website. When executed in a visitor's browser, this code sends information to the analytics back-end, including user identifiers and information about the visited website (Starov et al., 2018). Analytics services can also be included in browser extensions and mobile apps.

To use analytics on mobile platforms such as Android, app developers have to include analytics libraries into their app (Liu et al., 2017). The app developer can configure how much information is sent to the analytics platform by customizing how the analytics API is called from the app. Because the analytics library shares the host app's permissions, a wide range of information about the user is potentially accessible to the analytics library, including unique device identifiers such as the IMEI and MAC address. This can make profiles collected through mobile analytics libraries even more comprehensive than web analytics and increases the privacy risk to users.

Web analytics is also performed by audit bureaus of circulation (ABCs) which aim to verify the popularity of websites (Deußer et al., 2020). Advertisers rely on these estimates of popularity to judge the relevance of different publishers. Technically, ABCs collect click traces, i.e., timestamped sequences of websites visited by users, through JavaScript *tags* inserted into websites. Whenever a user visits a website with such a tag, the tag sends identifiers for the visited website and the visited subsite to the ABC. The ABC can enrich this data with further information such as the IP address geolocation, the user's device type (from the *User-Agent* header), the user's identifier (from the *Cookie* header), the category of content, and the timestamp.

3.4 Advertising

The business model of many big tech corporations relies on advertising. This section first gives a brief history of internet advertising and introduce the modern advertising ecosystem, before discussing in detail how ad targeting, real-time bidding, and ad audience estimation work. Then, the section examines the user-facing side of advertising: ad preference managers and ad explanations, and closes with a look at mobile advertising.

3.4.1 History of Internet Advertising and Modern Ecosystem

The basic premise of internet advertising is that users access web content for free, while publishers of websites sell space on their website to advertisers (Gill et al., 2013). Figure 3.5 shows some of the milestones and key developments during the first 20 years of internet advertising. During these years, pricing models and interactions between publishers and advertisers have changed significantly (Mayer and Mitchell, 2012). Initially, publishers dealt directly with advertisers in the *direct buy* model. In this model, it was not necessary for websites to include content from third parties, and as such it caused few

Web		Mobile
HotWired sells banner ads to AT&T and Coors	1993	
First central ad servers	1995	
DoubleClick sells ads priced per impression, first rich media ad	1996	
Search engines use keyword auctions	1998	
Google AdWords	2000	SMS advertising
	2003	MMS advertising
First ad exchange: RightMedia	2005	
Facebook Ads	2006	AdMob
YouTube rolls out in-video ads, Google acquires DoubleClick	2007	First mobile ad exchange, AdSense for Mobile
Real-time bidding adopted by many ad exchanges	2009	In-app ads and mobile video ads, Google acquires AdMob
Promoted tweets on Twitter	2010	Apple iAd
	2012	Facebook Ads on Mobile

Figure 3.5 Timeline of web and mobile advertising. Based on data from Chen et al. (2016a) and Pujol et al. (2015).

privacy or tracking related concerns. However, this model is least common today because of the effort involved in setting up direct agreements between publishers and advertisers.

Advertising networks were the next model that introduced middlemen between advertisers and publishers. This allowed publishers to display ads from many advertisers, and advertisers to place ads on many publisher websites. In addition, ad networks introduced the capability of targeting ads to users based on audience, location, website content, or the user's browsing history.

The most common model today is based on advertising exchanges and includes a number of new intermediary businesses, like demand-side platforms, supply-side platforms, and data providers (Bashir et al., 2016). In this model, illustrated in Figure 3.6, supply-side platforms (SSPs) work with publishers to offer the available inventory of ad space to multiple ad networks and exchanges. Demand-side platforms (DSPs) work with advertisers to bid for ad space in multiple ad exchanges. The ad exchanges take bids from advertisers or DSPs to fill the ad slots offered by publishers or SSPs. The ad pricing in this model is no longer based on fixed rates, but instead on the highest price a bidder (advertiser) is willing to pay to display their advertisement to a specific user. When advertisers are able to bid in real-time on individual ad impressions, they can adjust their bid prices based on the targeting data sold to them by data providers. This model necessarily relies on cookie synchronization to help SSPs and DSPs match their cookies. Without cookie synchronization, information about the user which is available at the SSP would not be available at the DSP, and the DSP would not be able to adjust the bid price based on the specific user who will view the ad.

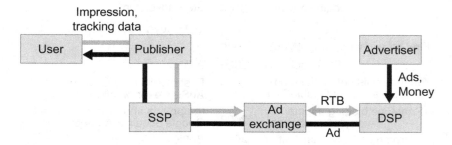

Figure 3.6 Entities in the modern advertising ecosystem (Bashir et al., 2016). Gray arrows indicate the flow of impressions and tracking data from the user through the ad ecosystem, and black arrows indicate the flow of ads and revenue from the advertisers.

This modern advertising ecosystem crucially relies on tracking and profiling techniques which enable the placement of ads targeted at narrowly defined audiences (Parra-Arnau et al., 2017). However, a consequence of the decoupling between publishers and advertisers is that it is now easier for malicious advertising – malvertising – to be displayed on well-known publisher sites (Zarras et al., 2014). Malvertising encompasses scams, drive-by downloads that infect users with malware, click fraud, deceptive downloads that trick users into installing malicious browser extensions, or link hijacking attempts that redirect users to the attacker's website. Due to the opacity of the ad ecosystem, the multitude of involved players, and the increasing placement of ads by unknown third parties, even reputable websites have displayed malvertising, such as the *New York Times* in 2009 (Chen et al., 2016a).

3.4.2 Ad Targeting

Publishers increasingly want to target their advertising at very specific audiences. For example, a sports shoe company may want to target "users who live in Madison, WI, from 6AM to 9AM on business days, and the ad must not be shown to the same user more than 7 times on any given day" or "male users aged [25–30] who are interested in 'sports', 'healthy lifestyle' and 'jogging'" (Barford et al., 2014).

Different types of ad targeting can be distinguished, including profile targeting, contextual targeting, and behavioral targeting (Lécuyer et al., 2014). The examples above illustrate *profile targeting*, that is, targeting based on a static view of the user's profile including demographics such as age and gender, location, and interests. *Contextual targeting*, on the other hand, targets ads based on the web content that is currently being displayed, such as the currently opened email or the currently watched video. The final type of targeting, *behavioral targeting*, is based on a user's past actions, such as emails sent, videos watched, or websites visited (Lécuyer et al., 2014).

Retargeted ads – ads for a specific product that a user has previously visited on an e-commerce site – are an example for behavioral targeting (Bashir et al., 2016). To enable retargeting, information about the user's browsing history needs to be present at the demand-side platform (DSP), which can be realized through cookie synchronization between SSP and DSP.

Facebook's ad platform offers additional targeting options. To improve profile and behavioral targeting, advertisers can use free-text attributes that Facebook will match against the pages a user has liked (Andreou et al., 2019) and data broker targeting, where the targeting attributes are supplied by from data brokers instead of relying solely on a user's behavior on

Facebook (Andreou et al., 2018). In addition, Facebook offers targeting at custom audiences, or *PII targeting*. In this case, the advertiser uploads a list of personally identifiable information (PII) of individuals they want to target, for example email addresses or phone numbers. Facebook links these identifiers with Facebook accounts and displays ads only to users in this group. Advertisers only learn the estimated audience size, but not which specific Facebook accounts are targeted (Andreou et al., 2018). Finally, Facebook offers *lookalike targeting*. On the advertiser side, this is similar to PII targeting in that the advertiser uploads a list of PII of individuals they would like to target. However, different from PII targeting, Facebook will then determine *similar* Facebook accounts, and will display ads to users in this group of similar accounts. However, Facebook does not reveal how they define similarity and how similar users are selected (Andreou et al., 2019). Advertisers can also use combinations of these targeting options, for example, to narrow down a custom audience by demographic or behavioral attributes.

Platforms keep developing new ad targeting strategies. For example, in 2020, Twitter offered 30 different targeting types (Wei et al., 2020).

To help advertisers tailor their targeting options, Facebook displays an estimate of the *audience size*, i.e., the number of users who can be reached with a set of targeting options (Chen et al., 2013), and of the *potential reach*, i.e., the number of daily active Facebook users who match the targeting criteria (Venkatadri et al., 2018).

3.4.3 Real-Time Bidding and Header Bidding

Since its introduction in 2009, real-time bidding (RTB) has become the most common mechanism to determine the price paid by an advertiser for one particular ad impression (Cook et al., 2020). Real-time bidding, as its name suggests, means that an auction takes place, in real-time, for every single ad placed in this way. The specific auction mechanism differs depending on the RTB platform: Google, Bing, and Yahoo use generalized second price auctions where the winning bidder pays the price bid by the first unsuccessful bidder, whereas Facebook uses Vickrey-Clarke-Groves auctions, where the winning bidder pays according to the potential loss of all other bidders (Chen et al., 2016a).

The most common payment model for RTB auctions is cost-per-mille (CPM), or the cost per 1,000 ad impressions (Olejnik et al., 2014). Advertisers who prefer instead to pay per click (cost-per-click, or CPC), can rely on middlemen. For example, the demand-side platforms Criteo has specialized in buying ad impressions via RTB and selling them as ad clicks to advertisers.

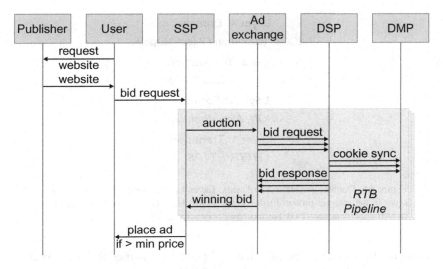

Figure 3.7 Message exchange during real-time bidding ad auctions (Bashir and Wilson, 2018; Cook et al., 2020). The sequence in the gray *RTB Pipeline* box can be repeated with other ad exchanges if the winning bid price is too low.

Figure 3.7 shows the messages exchanged during an RTB auction (Cook et al., 2020; Parra-Arnau et al., 2017; Bashir and Wilson, 2018), which is typically completed in under 100 ms. The auction is triggered by a user's visit to a websites whose ad space is served through RTB. The website served by the publisher contains an embedded resource that triggers a bid request to the supply-side platform. The supply-side platform manages the publisher's ad space and is responsible for selling the ad space at RTB auctions. The SSP therefore contacts the ad exchange to initiate the auction. The ad exchange then sends bid requests to auction participants, such as different demand-side platforms. Different ad exchanges may work with a different set of demand-side platforms.

The bid requests sent to DSPs contain information about the ad space and the user the ad will be displayed to, such as the URL of the visited website, the topic category of the website, the user's IP address, information about the user's browser, and a DSP-specific user identifier. This user identifier allows the DSP to identify the user in its own database or in the database of a data management platform (DMP). This step relies on previously executed cookie synchronization for this user. Each DSP then decides how much to bid for displaying an ad to this user based on the user's profile and the bidder's targeting goals, and submits a bid response to the ad exchange. The ad

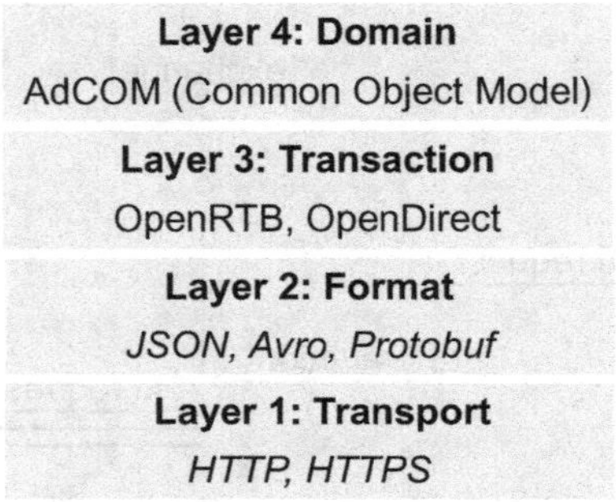

Layer 4: Domain

AdCOM (Common Object Model)

Layer 3: Transaction

OpenRTB, OpenDirect

Layer 2: Format

JSON, Avro, Protobuf

Layer 1: Transport

HTTP, HTTPS

Figure 3.8 OpenRTB v3.0 protocol stack. Layer 1 corresponds to the *application layer* in the internet protocol suite. Only protocols on layers 3 and 4 are defined in IAB specifications (IAB Technology Laboratory, 2018).

exchange then determines the winning bidder and notifies the SSP. At this point, if the bid price does not meet the SSP's minimum price, the SSP can initiate another auction with another ad exchange, proceeding in a "waterfall" of ad exchanges. If the bid price is acceptable, the ad exchange sends the ad to the SSP, which places it on the visited website.

It is also possible that the winning bidder is not a DSP, but another ad exchange. In this case, the winning ad exchange will initiate another auction among its own set of participants to determine who will display the ad (Bashir and Wilson, 2018).

Participating in RTB offers additional tracking opportunities for the DSP even if it does not win the auction: because all participants are sent a bid request with information about the user, the DSP can track this user's activity (Parra-Arnau et al., 2017). However, besides being able to display its ad, the winning bidder also gains the right to initiate cookie synchronization with the ad exchange, which can improve targeting and inform bidding strategies for future auctions (Olejnik et al., 2014).

The industry body IAB (Interactive Advertising Bureau) has published specifications to standardize the RTB protocol and message formats. The openRTB standard, shown in Figure 3.8, describes different protocols and their layering on top of standard internet protocols (IAB Technology Laboratory, 2018), as well as the message formats for BidRequest and BidResponse.[4]

---

[4] Appendix C of the AdCOM specification shows an example BidRequest, with all the components described above: https://github.com/InteractiveAdvertisingBureau/AdCOM/blob/master/AdCOMv1.0FINAL.md

Facebook's ad platform also uses RTB, but with modifications due to Facebook acting as publisher, SSP, ad exchange, and DSP. Facebook avoids showing ads from the same advertiser repeatedly, and aims to spread an advertiser's budget over a period of time instead of spending it all at once. Most importantly, ads on Facebook win auctions not just according to their bid price, but according to their total value, which is a combination of bid price, estimated click rates, ad quality, and ad relevance (Ali et al., 2019a). To estimate relevance, Facebook computes a relevance score based on expected feedback from the target audience. This score can have a large influence on which users get to see specific ads (see Section 7.4).

Header bidding is a new protocol for ad auctions (Pachilakis et al., 2019; Cook et al., 2020) which aims to avoid the disadvantages of the waterfall model of running RTB auctions. In the waterfall model, the SSP uses a prioritized list of ad exchanges to run successive ad auctions, starting with the highest priority ad exchanges. Each level of the waterfall can start only after the previous auction has failed, which introduces additional delays. In addition, the waterfall model can result in lower revenues for publishers due to lower competition on each level of the waterfall, compared to a model where all possible participants bid simultaneously.

This is exactly what header bidding, or parallel bidding on mobile platforms, does (Pachilakis et al., 2019). Figure 3.9 illustrates the message exchange during a header bidding auction. When a user loads a website, the

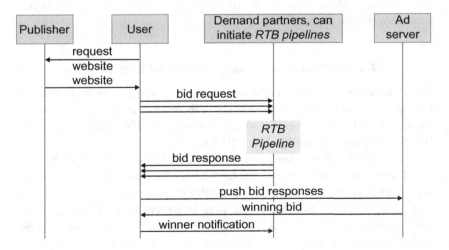

Figure 3.9 Message exchange during header bidding (Pachilakis et al., 2019; Cook et al., 2020).

publisher responds by sending the website header. Embedded in the header are bid requests to all advertising partners, including DSPs, ad exchanges, direct orders, auctions, and fallback channels. As with RTB, each bid request contains information about the user and the visited website, and bid responses contain bid prices. Differently from RTB, it is not the ad exchange that decides who wins the auction. Instead, bids are collected at the publisher's ad server which decides whether the highest bid wins, or whether an ad from another channel is selected. The ad server then provides the ad image to the user's browser, and the winning bidder is notified from the user's browser when the ad is rendered. The header bidding process gives more control to the publisher and allows them to maximize revenue more effectively.

The complexity introduced with RTB and header bidding auctions means that advertisers cannot easily tell whether the auctioneer is actually authorized to sell ad slots for specific publishers (Bashir et al., 2019a). This has led to a type of domain spoofing fraud where fraudsters create bid requests for high-value publishers to draw high bids from advertisers. However, instead of displaying the ad on the high-value publisher's site, the fraudster displays the ad on a low-value website, if at all. The industry standard *ads.txt* was designed to counter this type of fraud (IAB Tech Lab, 2019). Ads.txt is a plain-text file, publicly available at the domain root of the publisher's website, which allows publishers to specify which third party SSPs and ad exchanges they are working with. Even though ads.txt was introduced as an anti-fraud measure, it can be used to increase transparency because it makes public information about business relationships in the advertising space that were previously not accessible (Bashir et al., 2019a).

3.4.4 Ad Preference Managers and Ad Explanations

Some platforms provide ad preference managers (APMs) which allow users to inspect the ad targeting data held about them and, in some cases, correct the data. In 2017, researchers found four functional APMs: Google, Facebook, BlueKai, and eXelate (Bashir et al., 2019b).

These APMs differ in the functionality offered to users: Google shows a list of topics that it believes the user likes or dislikes, and allows users to add and remove topics. However, Google's APM does not show sensitive topics such as health, even though they are used in ad targeting (Wills and Tatar, 2012; Datta et al., 2015). Facebook's APM shows a list of user interests based both on the user's likes and on inferences from browsing behavior, and a list of advertisers that users have interacted with. Users can remove interests and block advertisers. BlueKai's APM shows inferred interests based on the

"One reason you're seeing this ad is that **[advertiser]** wants to reach people interested in Facebook, based on activity such as liking pages or clicking on ads.
There may be other reasons you're seeing this ad, including that **[advertiser]** wants to reach people ages **[age]** and older who live in **[location]**.
This is information based on your Facebook profile and where you've connected to the internet."

Figure 3.10 Pattern of ad explanations on Facebook (Andreou et al., 2018).

BlueKai cookie in the user's browser. The interests are not editable, but users can opt out. Finally, eXelate's APM shows interests based on the eXelate cookie and allows users to remove interests.

Ad explanations are another user-facing tool, which are intended to explain why a user is seeing a particular ad. Facebook's ad explanations follow a generic pattern, shown in Figure 3.10. This pattern mentions specific advertisers, several potential targeting attributes, such as age and location, and gives a vague explanation of the data used for targeting, such as "your Facebook profile" or "what you do on Facebook."

3.4.5 Mobile Ads

Compared to ads served in the context of a web browser, ads embedded in mobile apps differ in the available ad types, the integration of ads into the mobile app, the targeting options, and the messages exchanged to request an ad.

Due to the limited display space on mobile devices, most mobile ads are either banners or interstitials (Chen et al., 2016a). Ads in system notifications and icons are possible as well, but violate the Google developer content policy.

To display ads, mobile apps have to include one or more advertising libraries (Demetriou et al., 2016). Different types of ad libraries are available, including mobile web libraries, rich media libraries, and ad mediators which can manage multiple ad libraries within one app. Because ad libraries share host app's permissions, the ad library can read files generated by the host app, can observe user input to the host app, and can use all APIs covered by the app's permissions. In addition, no same-origin policy can be enforced for mobile ads. Because ad library and host app run in the same process, users of the app cannot distinguish between actions taken by the ad library and actions taken by the host app.

On Android, when an app with an integrated ad library runs, the ad library instantiates a WebView that fetches the *advertising creative*, i.e., a small snippet of HTML or JavaScript which in turn is responsible for fetching and

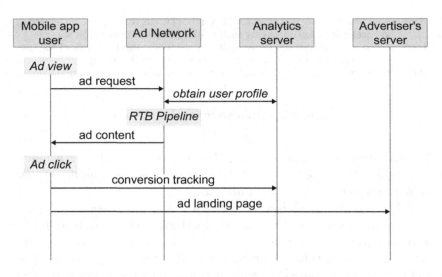

Figure 3.11 Mobile ad serving message exchange (Ullah et al., 2014; Nath, 2015). The ad request contains targeting information, such as the app name, device properties, or user location. The ad network can synchronize its user profile with the analytics server and/or use real-time bidding to collect the ad. The analytics server can use cookies, tracking pixels, and/or redirects to track the user.

displaying the ad content (Son et al., 2016). The network request to fetch the ad creative can include various targeting options. These targeting options can be taken from the full range of data available to the host app, including the user's location and unique device identifiers. Unique identifiers enable ad servers that are embedded in many different apps to build comprehensive user profiles. Targeting can then be based on this user profile in addition to the attributes in the ad request (Nath, 2015; Ullah et al., 2014).

Figure 3.11 shows an example of the entities and exchanged messages when an ad is served to a mobile app. However, it is important to keep in mind that different ad libraries may use different patterns and different technologies to serve ads. For example, AdMob uses plain-text HTTP GET requests, InMobi uses one HTTP POST request per ad, and Millenial Media uses two HTTP connections to retrieve the ad and associated content from separate servers (Chen et al., 2016a).

The top part of Figure 3.11 shows how the mobile app, via an ad control or ad view that is provided by its embedded ad library, requests an ad from the ad network. To select which ad is served, the ad network may run an RTB auction and serve the winning bidder's ad to the app. The bottom of the figure shows what happens when a user clicks on an ad. In this case, the click is first registered at an analytics server that tracks conversions, and a separate connection to the advertiser's content server retrieves the landing page associated with the ad. Alternatively, some ad libraries use standard HTTP redirects with a single connection to the analytics and advertiser's servers (Nath, 2015).

PART II

Methods

4

Experiment Design

Experiments are a way to find out how systems work, in particular to understand how changes to a system's inputs change its outputs (Montgomery, 2019). Designing an experiment means to make a detailed experimental plan before actually doing the experiment.

This chapter explains how to design experiments to study black-box corporate surveillance systems. The chapter will begin by examining the kinds of research questions that can be asked about corporate surveillance systems. Then, it describes different high-level study designs for transparency research, followed by a look at longitudinal studies and how they can be conducted. After examining the challenges that transparency researchers face during their studies, the chapter then focuses on the variables that researchers may encounter, including variables that are outside the experimenter's influence, variables that can be influenced (input variables), and variables that the experimenter aims to measure (response or output variables).

4.1 Research Questions

A well-formulated research question, or set of research questions, is the first step towards a successfully executed transparency experiment. Creating the research questions may take time, require several iterations, and even initial exploratory experiments, before the final formulation is arrived at. Research questions consist of different components that each address a different aspect of the planned experiments. Not all research questions need to include every aspect, but these are good starting points when thinking about research questions. Research questions can delineate:

- The *scope* of the study, for example, by mentioning what the system under study is.

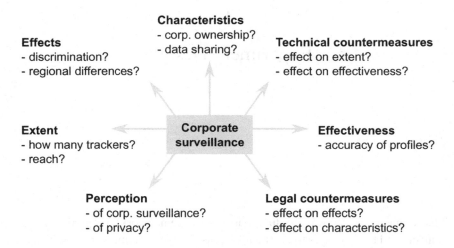

Figure 4.1 Categories of research questions to study corporate surveillance.

- What *questions* are asked of the system under study, for example, whether the study aims to quantify some phenomenon, or to find out what its causes are.
- The *scale* of the study, for example, whether one system will be studied in detail, or whether the study investigates widespread patterns on a large scale.
- What the most important *input and response variables* are.

In the context of studying corporate surveillance systems, research questions can be classified into seven categories, as shown in Figure 4.1. The following sections examine each category in detail, beginning with research questions aimed at the characteristics of corporate surveillance, followed by research questions about the extent of corporate surveillance, its effectiveness, its purpose and effects, the effectiveness of countermeasures, the effectiveness of laws and regulations, and the users' perception of corporate surveillance. In practice, research questions for a particular study need not be restricted to one category. In fact, it is often beneficial to combine research questions from different categories.

4.1.1 Characteristics of Corporate Surveillance

Research questions about the characteristics of corporate surveillance aim to understand *how* corporate surveillance works, for example, asking what data is

Table 4.1. *Research questions about characteristics of corporate surveillance.*

Research questions	Reference
Who has what data? How long is data used after its owner deletes it? Who shares data with whom?	Lécuyer et al. (2014)
What is the general size and nature of the hidden Web, and what are the corporate ownership patterns that affect user privacy?	Libert (2015)
Does behavioral targeting affects search ads? Do past searches affect ads on websites? what profile data affects social network ads?	Guha et al. (2010)
How frequently is Online Behavioral Advertising (OBA) used in online advertising? Does OBA target users differently based on their profiles? Is OBA applied to sensitive topics? Is OBA more pronounced in certain geographic regions compared to others? Do privacy configurations, such as Do-Not-Track, have any impact on OBA?	Carrascosa et al. (2015)
How much do advertisers pay to reach a user?	Papadopoulos et al. (2017)
What are all the different ways in which a Facebook advertiser, out of malice or ignorance, can target users in a discriminatory manner (i.e., include or exclude users based on their sensitive attributes like race)?	Speicher et al. (2018)
In the retargeting ecosystem, who is sharing user data, and how does the sharing take place?	Bashir et al. (2016)
A content distributor may make more money displaying some content versus others. Are content recommendations influenced by this revenue (payola)?	Sandvig et al. (2014)

collected, which technologies are used to share data, which entities participate, and what the relationships between these entities are (e.g., corporate ownership patterns).

Table 4.1 shows a selection of research questions from the literature that are aimed at understanding the characteristics of corporate surveillance.

4.1.2 Extent of Corporate Surveillance

Research questions about the extent of corporate surveillance aim to *quantify* aspects of the corporate surveillance ecosystem, for example, how many trackers there are, how widespread different tracking methods are, how many websites trackers can reach, and to what extent different services are

Table 4.2. *Research questions about the extent of corporate surveillance.*

Research questions	Reference
How many European Facebook users have been assigned potentially sensitive ad preferences?	Cabañas et al. (2018)
How often do search engines surface Wikipedia links and links to other types of user-generated content?	Vincent et al. (2019)
To what degree is state surveillance facilitated by commercial tracking mechanisms?	Libert (2015)
How often do real users receive personalized search results?	Hannak et al. (2013)
How widespread is personalization on today's e-commerce websites? How are e-commerce retailers choosing to implement personalization?	Hannak et al. (2014)
Does price discrimination, facilitated by personal information, exist on the Internet?	Mikians et al. (2012)
How many popular extensions introduce on-page changes and are thus fingerprintable?	Starov and Nikiforakis (2017a)

Table 4.3. *Research questions about the effectiveness of corporate surveillance.*

Research questions	Reference
What information is actually contained in advertising interest profiles, and are these profiles accurate?	Bashir et al. (2019b)
How accurate are Google's gender and age inferences?	Tschantz et al. (2018a)
How fingerprintable are the extension profiles of real users?	Starov and Nikiforakis (2017a)

personalized. Table 4.2 shows a selection of research questions aimed at the extent of corporate surveillance.

4.1.3 Effectiveness of Corporate Surveillance

Research questions about the effectiveness of corporate surveillance ask *how well* corporate surveillance works, for example, how accurate the profiling inferences are or how well fingerprinting can identify users. Table 4.3 shows some of these research questions from the literature.

4.1.4 Purpose and Effects of Corporate Surveillance

Research questions about the purpose and effects of corporate surveillance ask *why* corporate surveillance is conducted, who benefits from it, and what the

Table 4.4. *Research questions about the purpose and effects of corporate surveillance.*

Research questions	Reference
To what degree and by what means may advertising platforms themselves play a role in creating discriminatory outcomes?	Ali et al. (2019a)
How biased are the search results for political topics on social media sites like Twitter? Where does this bias in the search results come from?	Kulshrestha et al. (2017)
Does a user's vantage point influence whether they are shown cookie notices?	van Eijk et al. (2019)
For what purposes is the data used? Are the uses in the data owners' best interests?	Lécuyer et al. (2014)
If a person's digital life demonstrates a political bias, does that person receive personalized search results and do those search results reflect that person's bias?	Le et al. (2019)
Are racial minorities less likely to find housing via algorithmic matching systems? Does algorithmically controlled personalization systematically restrict the information available to the economically disadvantaged?	Sandvig et al. (2014)
Do gig economy workers' perceived demographics correlate with their position in search results?	Hannák et al. (2017)

effects are on individual users. For example, research questions can be aimed at understanding economic gains, regional differences, discrimination, or the characteristics of personalized content. Table 4.4 provides examples of real research questions from the literature.

4.1.5 Effectiveness of Countermeasures

Countermeasures are tools or methods that individual users can deploy to protect themselves against corporate surveillance (see Chapter 9). Research questions in this category aim to understand *how effective* these countermeasures are, for example, by measuring their effects on the extent and effectiveness of corporate surveillance. Some examples for these research questions are shown in Table 4.5.

4.1.6 Effectiveness of Regulations and Feedback Mechanisms

Besides countermeasures deployed by individuals, other mechanisms to restrict corporate surveillance include laws, regulations, and public

Table 4.5. *Research questions about the effectiveness of countermeasures against corporate surveillance.*

Research questions	Reference
How well do different ad blockers filter ads?	Gervais et al. (2017)
To what extent can tracker-blocking tools protect users against trackers?	Merzdovnik et al. (2017)
How have the filter rules in anti-ad block filter lists evolved over time? How has the coverage of anti-ad block filter lists evolved over time?	Iqbal et al. (2017)

Table 4.6. *Research questions about the effectiveness of regulations and feedback mechanisms.*

Research questions	Reference
Did the GDPR have an effect on the presence of third parties on European websites?	Sørensen and Kosta (2019)
What effect did the GDPR have on privacy policies on the web?	Linden et al. (2020)
Does the service adhere to its own privacy policy?	Lécuyer et al. (2014)
To what extent do security and privacy relevant reviews trigger security- and privacy-related app updates in apps? What kind of security- and privacy-related app updates do app developers implement in consequence of security and privacy relevant reviews?	Nguyen et al. (2019)

user feedback. Research questions in this category aim to understand to what extent new laws and regulations affect the operation of corporate surveillance, and to what extent corporate surveillance reacts to user feedback. Table 4.6 shows examples of this type of research question from the literature.

4.1.7 Perception of Corporate Surveillance

The final group of research questions aims at understanding how corporate surveillance is perceived by users. These research questions are important to explain user behavior and can inform the design of countermeasures, regulations, and feedback mechanisms. Table 4.7 gives some examples of research questions studying user perceptions.

Table 4.7. *Research questions about the perception of corporate surveillance.*

Research questions	Reference
What are the ideal privacy settings desired by users? Is there potential to aid users in selecting the correct privacy settings for their content?	Liu et al. (2011)
How do perceived gender, race, and other demographics influence the social feedback gig economy workers receive?	Hannák et al. (2017)
How do users perceive and evaluate existing ad explanations? When exposed to typically hidden inner attributes of an algorithmic advertising platform (such as users' algorithmically derived attributes and how advertisers use them), how do users think about and evaluate these attributes?	Eslami et al. (2018)

4.2 Study Designs

After creating a set of research questions, the next step is to select an appropriate study design that allows to answer the research questions. Historically, the term *audit study* has designated a field experiment aimed at detecting discrimination (Sandvig et al., 2014). These audit studies followed the method of randomized controlled trials, which is the standard experimental method followed in medical research (see Section 4.2.6). Due to their careful design and execution, the results of audit studies were often used as evidence in discrimination lawsuits.

In transparency research, the goal is to design and execute audit studies in a similarly methodical way so that the results can serve as evidence in courts and for policymakers. This section introduces several study designs that have been used in the literature and discusses their use cases, advantages, and disadvantages.

Figure 4.2 shows the blueprints for five different study designs: code audits, noninvasive user audits, scraping audits, sockpuppet audits, and crowdsourced audits (Sandvig et al., 2014). In all but the first design, the system under study is represented as a black box where the experimenter is only able to influence some of the system inputs and observe some of the system outputs, which are together represented as a gray circle (Wills and Tatar, 2012). Typically, the goal is to detect whether information can flow from specific, possibly sensitive, inputs to specific outputs. Detection of these information flows can then allow to uncover some of the internal operations of the black-box or reveal whether the black-box system adheres to its own policies.

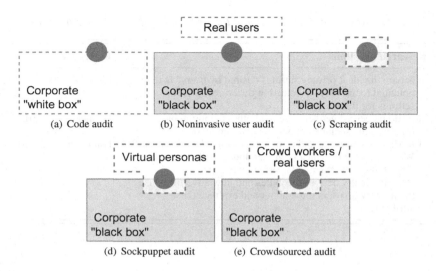

Figure 4.2 Five types of study designs for transparency research. Dashed lines indicate the subject of study in each design. The dark circle represents possible interactions with the corporate black-box system.

4.2.1 Code Audits

Code audits can be used when researchers have access to the internals of the systems, such as the code used by the system. Code audits are often used to study the behavior of specific algorithms and can allow definitive answers to research questions. However, when studying large corporate surveillance systems, code audits have two significant drawbacks. First, corporations are usually reluctant to share their code, especially code that their platforms are running on. This reluctance comes, in part, from a fear that people will try to *game* their algorithms (Sandvig et al., 2014) and in part from the conception of algorithms as valuable intellectual property that needs to be protected as a trade secret (Pasquale, 2015). Second, modern codebases can be so large as to make it infeasible to detect where exactly the code creates undesired effects such as discrimination. In addition, systems based on machine learning models rely not only on their code, but also on the data used to train the model. As a result, it is not sufficient to audit the code, rather, an audit has to encompass both code and data.

However, there are some cases where code audits are feasible in the study of corporate surveillance, namely, those cases where code is executed on a user device as opposed to on corporate servers. Most notably, these cases include JavaScript code executed in browsers and mobile apps executed on mobile devices. In these cases, decompiling and analyzing code can be a useful method to answer research questions.

4.2.2 Noninvasive User Audits

Noninvasive user audits do not interact with the system under study directly, but rather ask users about their experiences with the system. This type of audit is typically conducted using social science research methods such as surveys and interviews. User audits are most useful for research questions that study user perceptions of corporate surveillance. However, they are less suitable for the other categories of research question, in particular due to the unreliability of human memory, participants' cognitive biases, and the need for careful question design to avoid leading questions (Sandvig et al., 2014).

4.2.3 Scraping Audits

Scraping audits interact with the system under study directly and repeatedly, for example, by issuing requests and observing the corresponding responses. By carefully designing which requests are issued, in which order, and with what properties, scraping audits can allow to make inferences about behaviors and properties of the system under study. However, platforms may be able to discern scraping audits from real user behavior, for example, if the researcher uses an API to send HTTP requests instead of a fully-fledged web browser, and as a result the platform may alter its behavior. This can invalidate the research and lead to wrong conclusions. Another disadvantage of scraping audits is that they may be illegal in some jurisdictions because they may violate the terms of service of the system under study. For example, the Computer Fraud and Abuse Act (CFAA) in the US may prohibit scraping audits (Sandvig et al., 2014). However, a federal court has ruled that terms of service violations do not violate the CFAA if they are part of research into online discrimination (American Civil Liberties Union, 2020). In addition, many researchers have argued that research in the public interest should not be prevented by terms of service clauses, but this argument and its ethical implications have to be considered carefully on a case-by-case basis (see Section 5.1).

4.2.4 Sockpuppet Audits

Sockpuppet audits interact with the system under study using artificial users, called *virtual personas*, that are created specifically for the audit study. By attempting to recreate realistic user interactions as closely as possible, sockpuppet designs avoid the disadvantage of scraping designs. In addition, sockpuppet designs offer the best control over experiment variables because virtual personas can be created to closely match the experiment's requirements. Sockpuppet designs also allow the experimenter to randomize experiments and scale the number of samples collected from the system under study, thereby allowing causal inferences to be drawn (Tschantz et al., 2015). Similar to scraping audits, however, sockpuppet audits may be illegal in some jurisdictions and may violate terms of service.

4.2.5 Crowdsourced Audits

Crowdsourced audits rely on real human users to interact with the system under study. Crowdsourcing platforms such as Amazon Mechanical Turk have made it easy to distribute short, repetitive tasks to real users in exchange for a small fee. The advantage of this approach is that the collected data is based on the system's responses to real user profiles and, as such, most closely resembles the true system behavior. However, the number of human users needed for a reasonably sized study can be quite high, leading to a much higher cost for this study design compared to the other designs. In addition, data collection may be affected by details in each user's profile and past interactions with the system, so that the data analysis has to account for more noise factors in the collected data than with a sockpuppet design.

4.2.6 Randomized Controlled Trials

The last three study designs, scraping, sockpuppet, and crowdsourced audits, can all be framed as randomized controlled experiments or randomized controlled trials (RCT). RCTs are a method used in experimental science that allows checks as to whether input variables have an effect on response variables and thus allows *causal* inferences to be made about the effects observed in a system.

Generally, the goal of an RCT is to check whether experimental factors, or input variables, have an effect on the behavior, or response variables, of a black-box system. To do this, each experimental unit is randomly assigned to receive either control treatment (e.g., no treatment) or experimental treatment. In the experimental treatment condition, the experimental factor(s) are varied while all other factors are kept constant as much as possible. Starting from the null hypothesis that the treatment has no effect, the experimenter then measures the response of each experimental unit to determine the size of the effect and possibly reject the null hypothesis.

Table 4.8. *Terminology from randomized controlled trials, applied to an example from transparency research (Tschantz et al., 2015).*

RCT terms	Mapping to behavioral advertising
Effect	Use of data for behavioral advertising?
Experimental unit	Web browser instance
Experimental factor	User behavior
Treatment	Behavioral profiles
Constant factors	IP address, time of day, etc.
Response variable	Sequences of ads
Noise factors	Other users, advertisers

In transparency research, an example application of RCTs is the study of behavioral advertising, for example, to understand what user data is used to target behavioral advertising. The experimental factor in this example is user behavior, which can be specified as a set of websites the user likes to browse. Browser instances are randomly assigned a treatment, consisting of a specific user behavior, and the observed response variable is the sequence of ads shown in this browser instance. Table 4.8 shows how the general terms of RCTs map to this example (Tschantz et al., 2015).

In experiments with more than one input variable, the variation pattern for input variables needs to be carefully designed. Simplistic designs, for example, designs that vary one variable at a time while keeping the others at a constant baseline level, limit the conclusions that can be drawn from the experiment and should be avoided. Better designs include: factorial designs that explore all possible combinations of values for each input variable; randomized block or Latin square designs that reduce the effect of noise variables; and fractional factorial designs that reduce the number of combinations needed compared to factorial designs (Montgomery, 2019).

After the experiment, the collected data needs to be analyzed (see Chapter 6) to determine the effect size. Importantly, researchers have observed variability in the data collected by some experiments, which means that experiments need to be repeated, or *replicated*, multiple times and the data analysis needs to use statistical tools to draw correct conclusions from the experiments (Zeber et al., 2020; Urban et al., 2020a; Mazel et al., 2019).

Study designs can also be enhanced by interacting with the system under study from more than one perspective. For example, some studies combine interactions with two different user-facing services to learn about the data flows between the services (Bashir and Wilson, 2018), or interactions with a user-facing service as well as services for corporate clients such as advertisers (Vines et al., 2017; Kondracki et al., 2020).

4.3 Longitudinal Studies

Longitudinal studies aim to understand long-term effects in the system under study, including how the system evolves over time or how the system behavior differs before and after a specific event. To do this, longitudinal studies rely on the same types of research questions and the same study designs as previously discussed. In addition, longitudinal studies have to consider the temporal scope of the study, specifying what time period will be studied, and the data collection method, for example, specifying whether the study will be set up in advance and then collect data repeatedly, or whether it will rely on existing data sources with historical data.

Table 4.9 shows examples of longitudinal studies from the literature. While their methods and results will be described in more detail in the following chapters, the table highlights the diversity of longitudinal research questions and shows what temporal scopes existing studies have selected and how they have addressed the need for repeated data collection.

4.4 Challenges of Studying Black-Box Systems

Studying black-box systems is difficult due to a variety of factors. Some of the difficulty stems from the fact that the internals of black-box systems are not accessible to researchers, with some systems actively trying to thwart research efforts, which can make it necessary to design creative solutions and workarounds. Additional challenges arise from the scoping of studies, commonly made assumptions, the need to control for noise factors, the influence played by constant factors, and the measurement of response variables.

4.4.1 Scoping

Scoping of an experimental study of black-box systems often requires a high degree of background knowledge about the system under study. To acquire this background knowledge, researchers can ask a series of questions (Tschantz et al., 2015):

- Which black-box should be studied? Which aspects of this black-box should be studied? What is known about entities and components in the

Table 4.9. *Research questions and temporal scope for longitudinal studies.*

Research question	Category	Historical data?	Repeated collection?	Time period	Reference
How have app permissions evolved in subsequent app releases?	Characteristics	✓	–	9 years	Calciati and Gorla (2017)
How do top app lists on app stores evolve? Are apps updated frequently and priced appropriately?	Characteristics	–	daily	6 months	Carbunar and Potharaju (2015)
How have the permissions used by ad libraries evolved?	Characteristics, Extent	–	✓	3 years	Book et al. (2013)
How did the prevalence and complexity of trackers evolve?	Characteristics, Extent	✓	–	20 years	Lerner et al. (2016)
How did the prevalence and depth of third-party presence on websites evolve?	Extent	–	5x	4 years	Krishnamurthy and Wills (2009)
How did the reach and penetration of trackers evolve?	Extent	–	9x	3 years	Metwalley et al. (2015)
How has the fingerprintability of browser extensions evolved?	Effectiveness	–	2x	4 months	Starov and Nikiforakis (2017a)
How have PII leaks from apps evolved?	Effects	✓	–	8 years	Ren et al. (2018)
How has the coverage of anti-ad block filter lists evolved over time?	Countermeasures	✓	–	5 years	Iqbal et al. (2017)
How have ad block filter lists evolved?	Countermeasures	–	✓	9 years	Alrizah et al. (2019)
Did the number of third party requests decrease after GDPR?	Regulations	–	21x	8 months	Sørensen and Kosta (2019)

black-box? Which mechanisms are available to interact with the black-box? What data flows into and out of the black-box? Which factors influence the behavior of the black-box?

The answer to the first two of these questions need to be chosen carefully while considering the study design. For example, in an RCT study to understand whether the ads shown by Google are influenced by a user's behavior, Google could be selected as the system under study. However, keeping all system inputs constant (except for experimental factors) would mean keeping Google's interactions with advertisers constant, which is outside of the experimenter's influence. As a result, a better choice for the system under study is *Google and its ecosystem of advertisers*.

In addition, Google could also be selected as the experimental unit. However, randomized controlled experiments require multiple experimental units that can be treated differently. This is not possible because there is only one Google. Instead, *interactions with Google* is a better choice for the experimental units. For example, all interactions of one person, or one virtual persona, can be grouped into one experimental unit (Tschantz et al., 2015).

4.4.2 Assumptions

The second challenge relates to common statistical assumptions that are often made in the analysis of randomized controlled experiments. In particular, three common assumptions for significance testing do not hold when studying big tech systems (Tschantz et al., 2015). First, parametric statistical tests assume that the system behavior follows a known distribution where only the distribution's parameters are unknown. Second, many statistical tests assume that the experimental units are independent and identically distributed. Third, some tests assume the absence of cross-unit effects, i.e., that giving or withholding treatment from one unit will not affect the other units. Each of these assumptions were violated when studying Google's ad serving behavior (Tschantz et al., 2015). This result likely applies to many other black-box studies.

As a result, it is important to consider already during the study design how the data analysis will be conducted and which statistical tests will be used. Otherwise, the configuration of the experiment or the number of experimental trials may turn out to be insufficient to support meaningful data analysis.

4.4.3 Controlling for Noise Factors

Noise factors are influences outside the experimental treatment that cause a variation in the behavior of an experimental unit. Due to the complexity of the corporate surveillance systems under study, a variety of noise factors are possible, and indeed to be expected, in every study.

Controlling for noise factors involves two steps: first, the identification of the noise factor and its cause; and second, the application of a method to control the noise factor.

A common source of noise is the distributed and layered nature of internet infrastructure. Measurement results may be influenced by the behavior of lower-layer protocols, protocols used on the server-side, such as DNS load balancing, or effects arising from distribution of the measurement itself onto multiple machines which can cause differences in HTTP headers (Guha et al., 2010).

Another source of noise is the dynamic nature of many black-box systems. For example, e-commerce sites may frequently update their prices and available products (Hannak et al., 2014); websites may use A/B testing to determine how to increase visitor engagement (Mikians et al., 2013); and the ads displayed on a website may change with every refresh (Barford et al., 2014).

Finally, the act of measurement itself is also a source of noise because it can influence the future behavior of the black-box. This is often referred to as *profile contamination*. For example, consider a study that sets up virtual personas with interests in specific categories of e-commerce products, such as sports shoes. If the study then measures the ads displayed on a news website to determine whether the interest category influences which ads are shown, then the act of visiting the news website may change the virtual persona's profile, perhaps by adding an interest in news. Each subsequent measurement is then based on the updated profile instead of the original one, and the measurement may become more and more diluted (Barford et al., 2014).

Controlling these noise factors can be difficult, and researchers have employed a variety of strategies to do so. For example, noise due to distributed and layered infrastructure has been addressed by using static DNS entries so that all measurements will be served by the same data center, and by sending all measurement-related requests from the same /24 subnet (Hannak et al., 2013; Kliman-Silver et al., 2015).

Noise due to the dynamic nature of the system under study has been addressed by executing measurements in lock-step, i.e., by sending related requests in parallel (Kliman-Silver et al., 2015), and by synchronizing the measurement time if measurements are taken from multiple vantage points (Mikians et al., 2013). In addition, researchers have employed different strategies for replicating measurements, for example, following the randomized controlled trial method (Tschantz et al., 2015) and including a control account to quantify the baseline level of noise (Hannak et al., 2014; Barford et al., 2014).

Finally, system-specific strategies are also useful when attempting to limit noise factors. For example, when studying search engine personalization, researchers have used the normal search page instead of the search API and have introduced a wait time between subsequent queries to avoid carry-over effects (i.e., the effect that an initial search influences the results shown for subsequent searches) (Hannak et al., 2013; Kliman-Silver et al., 2015).

4.4.4 Influence of Constant Factors

Factors that are held constant during an experiment, such as the vantage point from which measurements are taken or the measurement time, can also influence the results.

For example, results may differ depending on the type of vantage point: vantage points at residential IP addresses can be subject to more censorship than vantage points located in data centers (Ramesh et al., 2020). In addition, the geographic location of the vantage point can influence, for example, how many cookies will be placed and whether cookie banners are shown to users (van Eijk et al., 2019; Dabrowski et al., 2019) and how many websites are subject to server-side blocking (McDonald et al., 2018).

4.4.5 Measurement of Response Variables

The final challenge in studying black-box systems is that it is difficult to accurately measure response variables. This difficulty is partly technical and partly conceptual.

Technical difficulties stem, for example, from difficulties to identify which text ads are semantically equal (Guha et al., 2010), what part of a website's content is advertising (Barford et al., 2014), or which third parties are trackers.

Conceptual difficulties, on the other hand, relate to response variables that are inherently difficult to measure. For example, studies attempting to measure *bias*, such as political bias in search results, may struggle to obtain a ground truth of what the relevant bias is because even the opinions of human raters may diverge (Pitoura et al., 2018).

Possible solutions for both technical and conceptual challenges will be described in detail in Chapter 6.

4.5 Input Variables

Input variables are the experimental factors that are systematically varied in experiments to study the behavior of black-box systems. Depending on the research question and the system under study, there are many possible input variables. This section introduces a wide range of input variables and discusses how values for each input variable can be selected. First, the section focuses on variables that are directly under the experimenter's control and often relate to scraping or sockpuppet study designs. Then, the section describes variables in crowdsourcing studies that the experimenter cannot control directly but wants to treat as input variables in the analysis. Finally, the section describes how virtual personas for sockpuppet studies can be designed.

4.5.1 Variables under Experimenter's Control

Variables that are directly under the experimenter's control can be grouped into a number of categories, including: variables relating to websites; browsers; specific web services like search, e-commerce, or travel; vantage points; names; advertising; geolocations; and mobile apps.

Websites
One of the most common input variables is the list of websites that will be studied. Considerations for selecting these websites include their popularity, their interest category, and their geographical origin.

At least three organizations publish toplists that include one million websites, ranked by their popularity: Amazon (Alexa); Cisco (Umbrella); and Majestic. A fourth toplist by Quantcast was discontinued in 2020. The Alexa ranking is based on visitors and page views, Umbrella on DNS traffic to Cisco resolvers, and Majestic on backlinks to websites. However, these rankings have a number of weaknesses: their composition changes frequently and substantially; they do not provide historical versions; their ranking algorithms are proprietary; they may be open to adversarial manipulation; and ranks below 100,000 are not statistically meaningful (Pochat et al., 2019). To mitigate these weaknesses, the hardened Tranco[1] list combines the three toplists. Updates to the Tranco list are published daily and historical versions are accessible by date. This allows researchers to specify exactly which version of the list was used in their study, which is necessary to allow others to reproduce results.

Traditionally, the Alexa list was most commonly used in transparency research due to its historical availability going back to the early 2000s. The number of sites included in studies has ranged from a few hundred (Mayer and Mitchell, 2012) up to one million (Englehardt and Narayanan, 2016). How many sites should be included in a study depends not only on the available computational resources, but also on how the study is designed – a study that fetches each website only once can include more websites than a study that fetches each website with multiple different browser configurations or virtual personas.

---

[1] https://tranco-list.eu/

Stratified sampling is often used to increase the range of website ranks in a study by including a sample of lower-ranked sites in addition to the top sites. This sampling method is intended to more closely reflect the time spent by users on top, middle, and bottom websites (Habib et al., 2019). For example, studies have used the top 500 sites plus 500 sites sampled uniformly at random from the top 1 million (Gervais et al., 2017), 50 random websites each from ranks 1–200, 201–5,000, and >5,000 (Habib et al., 2019), or the top 100,000 sites plus 2,000 sites from each subsequent 100,000 bracket (Yang and Yue, 2020).

The use of categories in addition to rank can improve the diversity of the website sample, ensuring a "wide sample of [...] websites across various categories" (Bashir et al., 2018). For example, studies have used the top sites from each of Alexa's top-level categories (Bashir et al., 2018), a random selection of sites from each category (Lecuyer et al., 2015), top sites in a selection of interesting categories (Brookman et al., 2017), or top sites from one specific category such as news sites (Datta et al., 2015). In addition to the categories included in the Alexa list and SimilarWeb (Trevisan et al., 2019), domain classification or tagging services can match websites to interest categories. These services can also be used in combination, for example, combining categories from Google AdWords, Cyren, and McAfee (Carrascosa et al., 2015).

The use of country-specific rankings can also improve diversity, in particular increasing the representation of websites from smaller or less-developed countries (Urban et al., 2020b; Englehardt et al., 2015). Country-specific rankings are also helpful to limit studies to one particular geographical region such as the EU, for example, to study differences between the EU countries (Degeling et al., 2019; Linden et al., 2020).

Websites can also be selected to make them resemble real browsing behavior, for example, by including subsites, sampling from the AOL query log, and sampling links from Reddit. Subsites – websites that are not a domain's main landing page – include more cookies and more tracking behaviors than landing pages (Urban et al., 2020a) as well as more advertising (Aqeel et al., 2020). This means that it is essential to include subsites in most studies to avoid incomplete measurements. To retrieve a list of subsites, researchers can crawl landing pages and extract links shown there, focusing on local links pointing to the same website (Zeber et al., 2020) or on outgoing links to other websites (Koop et al., 2020). In addition, subsites can be found by sampling URLs based on social media shares (Hils et al., 2020) or from the Hispar toplist[2] which includes 100,000 sites from 2,100 domains.

---

[2] https://hispar.cs.duke.edu/

The AOL search query log can be used to construct website lists by submitting each search term to a search engine and adding the first few links to the website list (Liu et al., 2013; Englehardt et al., 2015). Other studies have used the Reddit API to request random posts and constructed website lists by extracting links from the corresponding user's posts (Degeling et al., 2019).

To study particular types of websites, websites can also be identified manually, selected using specialized services, or selected based on custom search methods. For example, researchers have manually selected websites that display ads from specific ad networks (Wills and Tatar, 2012; Tschantz et al., 2015), news websites in specific countries (Libert et al., 2018), or websites from public organizations (Sørensen and Kosta, 2019). Studies have also used lists of malicious websites from VirusTotal (Starov et al., 2018; Ikram et al., 2017a), search engines for onion services (Overdorf et al., 2017), and custom searches for pornographic websites (Vallina et al., 2019). In these cases, to make the study reproducible, researchers need to publish the complete list of websites that was studied.

Browsers and Browser Extensions
When research questions are concerned with differences between browsers or with the behaviors of different browser extensions, such as in studies of fingerprinting, it is important to use different browsers and different operating systems. For example, one study considered 48 browsers across desktop and mobile platforms (Sy et al., 2018), selected so that browsers with large market shares were included as well as browsers that offered advanced privacy features. The main platforms to consider are Windows, Linux, and MacOS on the desktop (Mikians et al., 2012) and Android, iOS, and Windows phone on mobile devices (Ren et al., 2016).

Browser extensions are usually downloaded from each browser's extension store, with studies using between 1,000 (Starov and Nikiforakis, 2017a) and more than 100,000 different extensions (Chen and Kapravelos, 2018).

Without access to many different systems with different hardware and software configurations, browsers and operating systems can be emulated by configuring virtual machines (Datta et al., 2019) or by configuring the browser used for data collection (Hupperich et al., 2018).

E-Commerce and Travel
Studies focusing on corporate surveillance in the e-commerce realm need to select specific vendors and specific products to focus on because the multitude of available product options makes it impossible to conduct comprehensive studies.

To make the selection of e-commerce sites representative both in terms of the diversity of products and in terms of the number of users exposed to them, most studies first select a variety of categories, for example, from Alexa's list of e-commerce categories (Bashir et al., 2016) or from Google's product taxonomy list (Solomos et al., 2019), and then select the most popular e-commerce sites from each category, aiming for tens (Hannak et al., 2014) to hundreds (Mikians et al., 2012) of sites. Other studies focus in depth on the largest sites, such as Amazon Marketplace (Chen et al., 2016b).

After selecting e-commerce sites, studies need to select specific products to study. The selection should aim for diversity in the products, for example, including products with low, medium, and high price (Mikians et al., 2012), but products can also be selected randomly (Iordanou et al., 2017) or by choosing best-selling products first (Chen et al., 2016b). The number of products selected is typically lower for studies with many e-commerce sites, for example, up to 10 products (Bashir et al., 2016; Mikians et al., 2012), and higher in studies focusing on one or few e-commerce sites, for example, close to 1,000 (Chen et al., 2016b). Because the e-commerce landscape changes rapidly – only 20% of best-selling products are still best-selling after nine months (Chen et al., 2016b) – longitudinal studies are both interesting and complicated by these rapid changes.

Studies investigating travel-related e-commerce face similar issues when selecting e-commerce sites and products (travel destinations) as described above. Most studies use the three to five most popular travel sites, and select destinations either randomly (Eslami et al., 2017) or based on their popularity as destinations for tourist or business travel (Hunold et al., 2018).

In addition, studies of travel sites need to consider a temporal dimension: when the trip will take place, and for how long. This could be either one fixed date for the entire study (Vissers et al., 2014) or a flexible date that is always one or two weeks ahead of the time when data collection takes place (Hunold et al., 2018).

Search

The input variables for studies of search engines most commonly consist of the search terms, or queries, used in the study. It is difficult to select a representative sample of search terms because of the unlimited possibilities and variations. The most common strategy for selecting search terms is to first decide on specific categories or events, such as major political events (Robertson et al., 2018b), categories such as *tech* or *lifestyle* (Hannak et al., 2013), products (Guha et al., 2010), or geolocations (Kliman-Silver et al., 2015; Ballatore et al., 2017).

Then, concrete search terms for each of the selected categories are chosen. The method for choosing concrete search terms could be a manual selection (Robertson et al., 2018b), a selection from the most frequent hashtags on Twitter (Kulshrestha et al., 2017), a selection from Google Trends' *Year in Search* (Hannak et al., 2013), or a selection from relevant datasets, such as entities from a set of news articles (Cozza et al., 2016). Studies often include hundreds of different search terms.

Search result rankings can also serve as input variables, for example, in studies with human participants who use researcher-controlled search results. This has been used, for example, to study ranking biases and countermeasures against ranking biases (Epstein et al., 2017).

Vantage Points

A *vantage point* is the geographic location from which data collection is performed. The choice of vantage point is important because it can influence what content is served to the user and which corporate surveillance behaviors can be observed.

Most commonly, researchers use the vantage point of their own university's network. However, this can be problematic: some ad networks do not serve ads for nonresidential IP addresses (Vadrevu and Perdisci, 2019); results may differ depending on whether the vantage point indicates a residential or data center IP address (Ramesh et al., 2020); and the accessibility of HTTP hosts can depend on the geographical region of the vantage point (Wan et al., 2020).

As a result, studies increasingly consider their vantage points carefully, for example, by combining different types of vantage points, including IP addresses from universities, VPN services, data centers, residential addresses, and Tor exit nodes. For example, a study from a European university could use a VPN service with US IP addresses to replicate, or at least validate, its results (Urban et al., 2020b). Another strategy is to combine university, data center, and residential IP addresses (McDonald et al., 2018).

Residential IP addresses in different countries can be obtained through the service *Luminati*.[3] However, use of Luminati can be expensive: Samarasinghe and Mannan (2019) paid more than \$800 to crawl 1,000 URLs from vantage points in 56 countries. It may also be possible to recruit participants for use of their residential internet connection (Ramesh et al., 2020). Data center IP addresses can be obtained through renting Virtual Private Servers in target countries (McDonald et al., 2018). Another type of vantage point that can be

---

[3] https://luminati.io

considered is users who browse the Internet through Tor. The Tor exitmap can be used to crawl websites through all available Tor exit nodes (Khattak et al., 2016).

To ensure that the selection of vantage points is a representative sample, a simple strategy is to select at least one vantage point per continent (Ramesh et al., 2020). Alternatively, vantage points can be selected by country, based on the gross domestic product of each country. For example, McDonald et al. (2018) have selected every tenth country in a list of countries ordered by GDP.

To geolocate vantage points on mobile devices, it may be possible to override the JavaScript Geolocation API to specify arbitrary coordinates (Kliman-Silver et al., 2015). However, experimental validation is needed to ensure that the system under study relies on the Geolocation API as the location source, instead of deriving it from the device's IP address.

Names

The names of individuals can cause biased or discriminatory behavior of web services, for example, when the name is stereotypically black-identifying or white-identifying (Sweeney, 2013).

A sample of first names can be chosen from public lists of names given to black and white children, for example, from Massachusetts between 1974 and 1979 (Bertrand and Mullainathan, 2004) and California between 1961 and 2000 (Sweeney, 2013).

Fake full names are easy to generate, but real full names, if required, may have to be harvested manually, for example, by searching for a first name, and noting all full names that appear on the first few result pages (Sweeney, 2013).

Advertising

Studies of the advertising ecosystem often make use of ad campaigns run by the researchers. The input variables for these campaigns include ad targeting attributes, including the characteristics of custom audiences, and sometimes the ad creative used in the campaign.

Targeting options are often used to restrict a study to a limited set of countries (Ikram et al., 2017a; Marciel et al., 2016), to allow data analysis by country (Lambrecht and Tucker, 2019), or to ensure that ads are only shown to a previously known set of participants (Andreou et al., 2018). Targeting options can also include topics or interests, based on lists provided by the ad platform, for example, to study audience sizes or ad prices (Marciel et al., 2016).

Custom audiences can be selected to improve data analysis. For example, custom audiences based on public voter records that include information about the ethnicity of individuals (e.g., from North Carolina) allow to create all-black and all-white custom audiences (Ali et al., 2019a).

While the ad creative is often held constant, some studies have focused on effects caused by characteristics of the ad creative. For example, the text, headline, and image of an ad could be chosen as stereotypically male (bodybuilding) or female (cosmetics) to study whether the ad will be shown to different audiences (Ali et al., 2019a).

Geolocations

Geolocations or origin-destination pairs are important in a wide variety of studies. Two uses of geolocations – for studies of travel sites and for vantage points – have already been discussed above. In addition, geolocations have been used for studies of ride-sharing services, route planning services, personalization, and price discrimination.

The specification of geolocations as input variables varies in the needed granularity. For some studies, granularity at the continent or country level is sufficient (Mikians et al., 2012), while others need to select specific cities (Chen et al., 2015; Johnson et al., 2017), census tracts (Riederer et al., 2016; Thebault-Spieker et al., 2017), or even locations within cities (Schirck-Matthews et al., 2019; Tannert and Schöning, 2018). Locations within cities can be specified as explicit origin-destination pairs (Tannert and Schöning, 2018) or as a grid overlay. The properties of this grid can be adjusted based on the practically feasible number measurement points (Chen et al., 2015), or based on the density of activity in each part of the grid (Jiang et al., 2018).

Studies can also combine different granularities, such as Kliman-Silver et al. (2015) who combined the national, state, and county levels. This combination reduces the number of geolocations needed to observe effects across small, medium, and large distances.

While it would be most desirable to study representative samples of geolocations, for example, in terms of the characteristics of the populations inhabiting each location (Ge et al., 2016), some studies have additional practical constraints such as the availability of locations in existing datasets. Some studies also use locations the researchers are familiar with as a convenience sample (Vissers et al., 2014; Schirck-Matthews et al., 2019).

Mobile Apps

Studies of corporate surveillance on mobile devices are commonly based on a selection of mobile apps. Google Play is the most commonly used app store to retrieve mobile apps. Other app stores include AppChina, Mi.com, and Anzhi (all for Android) (Pan et al., 2018) or iTunes and BigBoss (for iOS) (Egele et al., 2011). Rankings created by third parties are also available, for example, from App Annie (Ren et al., 2016).

Criteria for selecting apps include popularity, app categories, and specific features or permissions. As with websites on desktop systems, mobile apps are often chosen based on their popularity, i.e., how often they were downloaded from the app store. Some studies focus only on very popular apps, such as apps with more than 50 million downloads (Nguyen et al., 2019), while others select a fixed number of apps from a list of apps sorted by popularity (Reyes et al., 2018). Some studies also include a sample of less popular apps (Continella et al., 2017).

In addition to popularity, many studies consider the category of apps to increase the diversity of apps in the study (Wang et al., 2019) or to focus on a specific type of app such as apps for families (Reyes et al., 2018) or ride-sharing apps (Zhao et al., 2019).

Some studies also focus on the features of apps and only include apps that display ads (Ullah et al., 2014) or that request specific permissions, such as camera permissions (Srivastava et al., 2017), network permissions (Crussell et al., 2014), Bluetooth permissions (Zuo et al., 2019), or microphone permissions (Pan et al., 2018). To study malicious apps, researchers have relied on app samples from VirusTotal (Urban et al., 2020b) or used third-party app stores that do not perform strict app reviews (Li et al., 2017a).

In addition to striving for a representative sample of apps in a study, practical considerations often lead to the exclusion of apps, for example, apps that require credit cards (Ren et al., 2018), apps that block TLS interception (Leung et al., 2016), apps that crash in the testbed (Ren et al., 2018), or apps that obfuscate the tracking API (Liu et al., 2019).

Depending on the scope, depth, and available resources of a study, studies include between a few hundred (Ren et al., 2018) up to more than one million apps (Binns et al., 2018b; Li et al., 2017a). Although most studies focus on free apps, some also include a sample of paid apps (Reardon et al., 2019).

Others

Besides the input variables introduced above, it is easy to imagine a multitude of other input variables. Due to the evolving nature of the web and the continuous introduction of new technologies, new and different input variables will be needed over time. For example, to study newly introduced voice assistants, input variables are needed for voice assistant apps and voice commands (Natatsuka et al., 2019); to study TV streaming devices, input variables are needed for streaming TV channels (Moghaddam et al., 2019);

and to study cookie notices after introduction of the GDPR, input variables are needed for the visual properties of cookie notices (Utz et al., 2019).

Two properties are important when using new types of input variables and selecting specific values for them. First, the variable values should be as *comprehensive* as possible, for example, by selecting all TV channels, or all possible placements of cookie notices. Second, they should be *representative* in all dimensions that are relevant to them, for example, by sampling from all relevant user demographics, by sampling from the most and least popular items, or by sampling from the full range of realistic values.

4.5.2 Variables Outside of Experimenter's Control

In study designs that involve human participants, the researcher often cannot directly choose the values of variables that should be treated as input variables in the data analysis. For example, the researcher cannot control the age of each participant, or the specific websites a user visits. However, studies with real users are often necessary because realistic behaviors, such as news reading patterns (Munson et al., 2013) or social media profiles (Chen et al., 2013), may be hard to synthesize and because the results for virtual personas may differ from those for real users, such as ad prices (Papadopoulos et al., 2017).

In these cases, researchers have to select a *representative sample* of participants to ensure that the study yields meaningful results. In a representative sample, the characteristics of the sample are similar to the characteristics of the underlying population, and the sample size is large enough to allow estimation of the sample characteristics. The consequence of not selecting a representative sample is that the results of the study cannot be generalized to all users of the system (the underlying population).

A common pitfall is the selection of a convenience sample. Convenience samples may draw from the population of undergraduate students at the local university (Bashir et al., 2019b; Zimmeck et al., 2017), from the social circle of authors or fellow conference attendees (Andreou et al., 2019), from users of a crowdsourcing service (Iordanou et al., 2018; Liu et al., 2011), or from users who are willing to install a specific app or browser extension (Mikians et al., 2013; Munson et al., 2013).

Sometimes, it is possible to obtain a true unbiased sample, for example, from the users of a specific platform. For example, Chen et al. (2013) obtained an unbiased sample of Facebook profiles by first scraping all unique user names, and then randomly sampling from this list of user names. This is based on the notion that an unbiased sample from a population can be obtained by sampling uniformly from the entire population. In Facebook's case, the population can be enumerated using the 32-bit space of Facebook user identifiers. Because this is typically not feasible, sampling algorithms based on random walks can be used to approximate an unbiased sample (Gjoka et al., 2010).

Another method to improve the representativeness of a sample is to combine different data sources. For example, Iordanou et al. (2018) used a limited number of human participants from a crowdsourcing service to precisely identify trackers, and then used a large NetFlow dataset to analyze tracking at scale. Each data source on its own would be insufficient for the study's conclusions: the human participants because of their small number, and the NetFlow dataset because of its lack of payload that does not permit to identify trackers. Only in combination, the two data sources provided the desired precision and scale.

It is often not possible, especially given real-world resource constraints, to create truly representative samples. In these cases, however, it is necessary to discuss and acknowledge limitations caused by limited representativeness. Ideally, this also includes a discussion of how any representation biases may have influenced the study outcome.

For example, studies can report on the demographics (e.g., in terms of location, gender, age, or income) of their sample (Bashir et al., 2019b) and analyze whether the sample population consists of a close social circle (Liu et al., 2011). In addition, the composition of the sample can be compared to the composition of the underlying population. For example, studies sampling from Facebook users can compare the characteristics of their sample to the characteristics of the global Facebook population. These estimates for the global Facebook population are accessible via Facebook's advertiser interface, by examining audience size estimates for the relevant targeting attributes (Andreou et al., 2019). The sample characteristics can include not only demographic attributes, but also interests or behavioral attributes that a platform assigns to users.

In some cases, studies can result in useful insights even if nonrepresentative data was used. In particular, studies introducing new methods to study corporate surveillance and studies examining new methods used for corporate surveillance may only need a proof-of-concept evaluation instead of a full large-scale evaluation (Papadopoulos et al., 2017; Hu et al., 2019b).

4.5.3 Virtual Personas

Virtual personas are synthetic user profiles used for data collection. They are designed so that the resulting profile resembles specific aspects of real user profiles, for example, specific interests in website categories, e-commerce, or political views. When designing and creating virtual personas, the researcher needs to choose what specific interests each persona should have and how these interests can be *induced*, that is, communicated to the black-box system under study. This process depends on the specific black-box system that will be studied and can involve, for example, creation and configuration of user accounts, browsing websites, or installing and using apps on mobile devices. Finally, the researcher needs to address the challenge of profile contamination.

Inducing Interests

Most commonly, the interest profile for a virtual persona is induced by browsing a specially designed set of *training* websites. The websites in this set are chosen depending on what the virtual persona should represent, for example, affluent or budget conscious customers (Mikians et al., 2012), individuals with a narrow set of interests (Lecuyer et al., 2015), individuals with specific demographics (Hannak et al., 2013), or individuals with specific system configurations (Urban et al., 2020b).

The training websites for e-commerce customers can include price aggregators and discount sites (budget conscious) or vendors of high-end luxury products chosen from Alexa categories such as Retail/Jewelry or Luxury goods (affluent) (Mikians et al., 2012). They can also be defined based on keywords from Google's product taxonomy. In this case, the training websites can be extracted from sponsored links on the search result pages when searching for each keyword plus a shopping term like "sell," "buy," and "offer" (Solomos et al., 2019).

The training websites for specific interests are often chosen from websites assigned to interest categories such as the Alexa categories or Google AdWords categories. To this end, Google AdWords provides a list of related websites for each of their 2,000 categories (Carrascosa et al., 2015), similar to the Alexa API. To avoid overly broad interests, researchers often choose categories from lower levels of the category tree, for example, second-level categories from Google or third-level categories from Alexa (Barford et al., 2014). Alternatively, interests can also be defined as free-text topics, and training websites are chosen from the search result pages for these topics (Balebako et al., 2012), or they can be defined by liking Facebook posts and pages from selected publishers (Hargreaves et al., 2019).

Interests can also be induced by clicking on ads that are relevant to a persona's theme (Nath, 2015). In this case, it is important to determine whether the ad is truly relevant without contaminating the persona's profile. This can be achieved by using a dummy persona to verify relevance, for example, by visiting the ad's landing page.

It is also possible to create virtual personas on mobile devices. In this case, the persona is not defined by the websites it visits, but rather by the apps it installs and uses. For example, a persona corresponding to a Google Play category can be trained by executing the top ten apps in that category (Ullah et al., 2014).

The number of training websites to use for each category has to be large enough to induce the interest, but small enough to keep the profile focused, i.e., to avoid inducing additional interests. Studies have used as few as 10 training pages per persona (Carrascosa et al., 2015) ranging up to 100 (Mikians et al., 2012; Urban et al., 2020b). The number of personas in a study depends on the specific research question, but has ranged from under ten (Mikians et al., 2012) to several hundred (Barford et al., 2014; Urban et al., 2020b).

To make the behavior of virtual personas resemble real user behavior, training and data collection can be limited to daytime hours in the persona's timezone, and delays between requests can be used according to an exponential distribution with a mean of two minutes (Mikians et al., 2012).

It is often useful to verify the contents of a virtual persona's profile, for example, by visiting the ad preference manager provided by the system under study. In particular, this can be used to tweak the list of training websites by retaining only those that add the category of interest to the Google ad preferences profile of a clean browser (Carrascosa et al., 2015).

After configuring the virtual persona, *control* websites are used for data collection. These control websites should be chosen according to two criteria. First, they should represent a neutral interest or be orthogonal to the interests of the virtual personas, for example, by choosing weather sites (Carrascosa et al., 2015; Solomos et al., 2019) or general interest sites such as news (Barford et al., 2014). Second, they need to allow collection of the response variables relevant to the study. For example, studies investigating the advertising ecosystem need control pages that display ads (Barford et al., 2014; Solomos et al., 2019).

Email and Social Media Accounts

Some systems require accounts to set up virtual personas, while others benefit from an account but do not require it. For example, an ad profile on Google can be induced by browsing websites, but with a Google account for each persona, the researcher gains more control over the profile contents. For example, Hannak et al. (2013) used a number of Google accounts that each varied in a specific feature, such as the browser's user-agent string, the IP address or geolocation, age, gender, search history, browsing history, and search click history.

Systems that require accounts for the creation of virtual personas include Facebook (Hargreaves et al., 2019) and Gmail (Lecuyer et al., 2015). While creating accounts on these platforms used to be easy to automate, the platforms have made the process more difficult by including captchas, requiring valid phone numbers, and implementing other anti-abuse measures (Farooqi et al., 2020a). As a result, account creation can now require a significant investment of time and possibly money, which makes studies with many virtual personas difficult. To overcome this difficulty, studies can be designed to use a small number of accounts with rotating email addresses (Farooqi et al., 2020a).

Profile Contamination

Profile contamination refers to the situation where data collection on control websites adds additional interest categories to a virtual persona's profile that are not related to that persona's desired theme. For example, browsing 50 random websites can double the number of interests assigned to a virtual persona (Barford et al., 2014). These additional interests may influence the collected data and make the study results unreliable.

Therefore, studies need to carefully consider profile contamination and, if possible, take measures to prevent it. For example, the effect of profile contamination can be limited by synchronizing measurements, using identical virtual machines, ensuring all measurement machines use the same external IP address, and ensuring a clean browser history (Balebako et al., 2012). Another method is to use private browsing mode (Leung et al., 2016) and to use a separate browser to collect information about the observed response variables. For example, if ads are collected as response variable, the associated landing pages should be visited from a separate browser (Carrascosa et al., 2015).

4.6 Response Variables

Response variables are the quantities of interest that are measured and subsequently analyzed in a study. In many cases, it is necessary to post-process the measured data to extract the response variables of interest from the raw collected data. As with input variables, a wide range of response variables has been used in transparency research, depending on the system under study and the research question.

Most commonly, response variables are extracted from network communication observed either directly on a device or on a router in the network. However, many response variables are also extracted from artifacts such as mobile apps or the rendering process of websites.

The definition and extraction of response variables often requires in-depth knowledge of the system under study and is a highly creative process. As such, this section can only provide an overview of common examples of response variables. It is likely that new studies will define entirely new response variables, or invent new and improved methods to extract response variables from raw data. This section focuses on raw response variables and outlines briefly how they can be post-processed for further analysis (see Chapter 6).

4.6.1 Response Variables for Network Communication

The most commonly collected raw data, which is the basis for many different response variables, is network communication. Network communication can be collected at different layers of the internet protocol stack, for example, the application and transport layers, and the properties of different protocols can be used as response variables, for example, HTTP, DNS, or TCP.

Response variables on the lower layers include the TCP connection state and the output of the *traceroute* command, which can indicate censorship or server-side blocking (Niaki et al., 2020).

HTTP response codes can be recorded to study server-side blocking (focusing on 4xx and 5xx codes) (Afroz et al., 2018) and some forms of tracking (focusing on 3xx codes) (Koop et al., 2020).

The HTTP *Referer* and *Location* headers can be used to construct *request trees*. Request trees, visualized in Figure 4.3(c), are a logical grouping of all HTTP requests that belong to the loading of a single website (Crussell et al., 2014). This grouping enables further analysis, such as detection of ad impressions and clicks. To construct a request tree, all HTTP requests are treated as nodes. Edges between two nodes are added in three cases. First, when the two requests are linked via the *Referer* header, the URL indicated in the *Referer* header is considered the parent of the request containing the *Referer* header. Second, when two requests are linked via the *Location* header, the URL indicated in the *Location* header is considered the child of the request containing the *Location* header. Third, when a request does not contain a *Referer* header, all future requests to URLs which are in the body of its HTTP response message are considered children of the current request.

The HTTP *Cookie* headers can be recorded to analyze stateful tracking. Some studies collect the browser's cookie store from disk instead of from HTTP requests. This can save processing time if no other response variables need to be extracted from HTTP requests (Englehardt and Narayanan, 2016). The *Cookie* and *Referer* headers can also be used to construct a *cookie linking graph* (Englehardt et al., 2015). This graph allows to analyze which part of a user's traffic can be linked by a passive adversary as belonging to a single user. To construct a cookie linking graph, all observed URLs and cookies are treated as nodes. Edges between URLs are added if they are linked via the *Referer* header, and edges between a URL and a cookie are added when specific cookie values (typically values of *identifying* cookies that are unique for each user) are observed in the request or response headers for the URL.

The URLs in HTTP requests can be used to analyze domain names and domain ownership. The most common method to identify the domain name from a full URL is to use the URL's public suffix *plus one* (Mayer and Mitchell, 2012). The public suffix list,[4] maintained by Mozilla, lists all suffixes under which users can register domain names, such as .com or .co.uk. "Plus one" indicates that one additional label from the hierarchical name should be included, for example, google.com or google.co.uk. These two examples show that relying on the public suffix list is cleaner than simply using the two right-most labels because suffixes can consist of more than one label. Based on domain names, a third-party graph can be constructed and domains can be labelled as third-party domains if they are requested by multiple websites or apps (Vallina-Rodriguez et al., 2016). To construct the graph, two types of nodes are created: one node for each website or app; and one node for each domain. Edges are added if a flow from a website or app to a domain is observed. Then, domain nodes with a degree ≥ 2 are potential third party domains.

If TLS is used, some properties of TLS can also be used as response variables. For example, the session resumption identifier can be used to estimate session resumption lifetimes (Sy et al., 2018) and TLS certificates can be used to detect the identity of app developers or website owners by inspecting the *Issuer* or *Organization* fields (Gamba et al., 2020).

4.6.2 Response Variables for Web-Based Services

Response variables for websites include properties of the underlying web technologies, such as embedded JavaScript, HTML and DOM trees, and the browser itself. In addition, response variables have been defined for services relying on these web technologies, such as advertising, cookie notices and privacy policies, search results, social networks, pricing, ratings, route planning, and ride-sharing.

---

[4] https://publicsuffix.org

JavaScript

JavaScript code itself is used as a response variable because it is executed on the client and thus allows to analyze *programs* used for corporate surveillance, not only the network communication with corporate surveillance programs. JavaScript code can be detected via its content-type or file extension and then downloaded for further analysis (Englehardt and Narayanan, 2016). Features of JavaScript code have also been used as response variables, such as lines in JS programs (Ikram et al., 2017b), nodes in the abstract syntax tree (Iqbal et al., 2017; Chen and Kapravelos, 2018), or usage of relevant API calls (Das et al., 2018b). Finally, because JS code is executed locally, it is also possible to instrument the JS engine to monitor the execution trace, for example, to detect which branches are taken and which functions are called (Zhu et al., 2018).

HTML

Properties of the HTML code for a website can also serve as response variables. For example, changes in DOM elements and DOM attributes can be used to analyze the effectiveness of countermeasures such as ad blockers (Mughees et al., 2017). In addition, the use of HTML5 elements such as *HTMLCanvasElement* or *AudioContext* can be recorded to analyze fingerprinting (Englehardt and Narayanan, 2016).

However, in some cases, analysis of HTTP requests and DOM trees on their own is not enough because they do not reveal where resources were included from, especially if third-party dynamic code is present (Bashir et al., 2016; Arshad et al., 2017): DOM trees can be dynamically modified to include new resources, which means that the parent/child relationship in a DOM tree does not allow the conclusion that the parent must have included the child. In addition, the referer in HTTP requests for embedded resources is always the first party, even if the resource was embedded by a third-party JavaScript. To overcome this limitation, *inclusion trees* (see Figure 4.3(a)) record which HTML or JavaScript initiated a resource request, and an inclusion chain indicates the chain of inclusions that resulted in inclusion of a particular resource. Inclusion trees can be constructed through two methods: first, by modifying the browser's HTML parsing engine and extension engine (Bashir et al., 2016; Arshad et al., 2017); and second, by using the Chrome Debugging Protocol (Bashir et al., 2018). Both methods construct inclusion trees by tracking static and dynamic resource inclusions.

While inclusion trees can be constructed for each individual page load, inclusion graphs represent the union of all inclusion trees in a dataset (Bashir and Wilson, 2018). In inclusion graphs, each domain name is represented as a node, and edges are inserted if the dataset contains any information flow

Listing 4.1. *Contents of the <body> tag of a first-party HTML document*

```
<script src="tp1.com/script1.js"></script>
<!-- pixel is dynamically inserted by script1.js -->
<img src="tp2.com/pixel.gif"/>
<iframe src="tp3.com/frame.html">
 <script src="tp4.com/script4.js"></script>
</iframe>
```

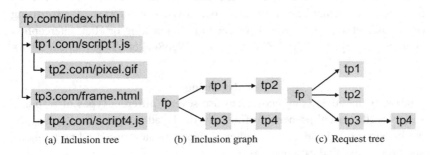

(a) Inclusion tree   (b) Inclusion graph   (c) Request tree

Figure 4.3 Example inclusion tree, inclusion graph, and request tree (or referer graph) for the first-party HTML document from Listing 4.1.

between two nodes, such as resource inclusion. Inclusion graphs are somewhat similar to request trees, but edge insertion in request trees is more constrained because edges are only inserted for HTTP requests to one node that include another node in the referer header. Therefore, request trees capture less detail than inclusion graphs. Inclusion graphs can also be weighted, where edge weights are computed based on the number of times resource inclusion was observed on each edge. Figure 4.3 shows the differences between request trees, inclusion trees, and inclusion graphs.

Browser

Properties that are influenced by the user's browser and system configuration are useful for studies of fingerprinting. These properties can include standard fingerprinting attributes, for example, extracted from HTTP headers such as *User-Agent, Accept,* or *Content-Encoding*; from JavaScript, such as the list of plugins, timezone, or screen resolution; or from Flash, such as the list of fonts (Laperdrix et al., 2016). In addition, they can include the list of installed browser extensions, list of web logins (Gulyas et al., 2018), WebGL rendering tasks (Wu et al., 2019), or sensor readings from a mobile device's gyroscope, accelerometer, or magnetometer (Zhang et al., 2019a). These properties may be further analyzed by determining the frequency of values in the whole dataset and the number of distinct values (Gómez-Boix et al., 2018).

Some fingerprinting studies have also collected the fingerprinting counter-measure employed by a user (Vastel et al., 2018b), including countermeasures in browsers (Firefox, Brave) and browser extensions (FPGuard, FPRan-dom, User Agent Spoofer), or the generic type of fingerprinting protection employed, such as attribute standardization or variation (Datta et al., 2019).

Further response variables collected from web browsers include the latency of page loads which can be useful to analyze some forms of advertising (Pachilakis et al., 2019), the occurrence of clickjacking or click interception attempts (Zhang et al., 2019b), or the use of WebSockets (Bashir et al., 2018).

Advertising

Studies of the advertising ecosystem use several different types of response variables: the visual properties of displayed ads, ad categories, ad prices, the performance of ad campaigns, audience size estimates, users' ad preferences, and properties of ad explanations.

Properties of ads. The visual properties of displayed ads include: the title, URL, and text (Datta et al., 2015; Lecuyer et al., 2015); media content such as images; the identity of the advertiser (Andreou et al., 2019); and the timestamp of the ad impression. Some studies have also analyzed the ad's topic (Solomos et al., 2019) and landing page (Guha et al., 2010), for example, identifying the domain name, corporate domain owner, and category of the advertiser (Galán et al., 2019).

Ad targeting types include behavioral targeting, contextual targeting, retar-geting, geographic targeting, demographic targeting, and static targeting (Car-rascosa et al., 2015). In addition, some studies have investigated the specific selection of targeting attributes available to advertisers on different platforms (Angwin et al., 2018).

The cost of ads is often difficult to measure, but two mechanisms in modern advertising allow to observe bid prices from the client-side: header bidding (Pachilakis et al., 2019) and unencrypted real-time bidding (Papadopoulos et al., 2017). In both cases, the ad's CPM can be extracted from the observed messages. In addition, observing the number of displayed and clicked ads on Facebook can allow to estimate the revenue generated for Facebook by a specific user (González Cabañas et al., 2017). Suggested bid prices can also be collected from the advertiser interface, for example, for YouTube and Facebook (Marciel et al., 2016).

Performance of Ad Campaigns. The performance of researcher-run ad campaigns can be extracted from the ad platform's advertiser-facing website. The reporting on these websites is often not real-time but subject to delays which can range from under five minutes (Vines et al., 2017) to half an hour or more (Conti et al., 2015).

Performance indicators include statistics for ad impressions and ad clicks (Conti et al., 2015), the click-through rate (Galán et al., 2019), the reach in terms of unique users, and the demographics of the ad audience (e.g., age, gender, location) (Ali et al., 2019a; Korolova, 2010). Some studies have collected these performance indicators repeatedly, for example, every two minutes (Ali et al., 2019a), to study how they evolve over time.

Ad Preferences. Ad preferences are those attributes of a user's profile that are shown to the user on an ad platform's ad preference manager. They can be used to compare attributes shown to users with those available to advertisers (Angwin et al., 2016b), to evaluate the accuracy of assigned attributes (Bashir et al., 2019b), to study the algorithms used by profilers (Degeling and Nierhoff, 2018), and to study how profiles evolve over time (Wills and Tatar, 2012).

Audience Size Estimates. Estimates of the audience size for a particular ad campaign or a particular combination of targeting attributes is available on Facebook's advertiser interface. The audience size estimate has been used, for example, to study the uniqueness of user profiles (Chen et al., 2013) and the frequency of the most common profile attributes (Cabañas et al., 2018). The audience size estimate has also been used to study the characteristics of Facebook's rounding algorithm for the audience size estimate, to find out whether advertisers can use the estimate to infer hidden information about Facebook users (Venkatadri et al., 2018, 2019).

Properties of Ad Explanations. Ad explanations are intended to explain to users why they are seeing a particular ad. The properties of ad explanations include explanations of the used targeting type and the targeting attributes. This information can be augmented by measuring the audience size estimate for each targeting attribute (Andreou et al., 2019). However, Facebook aims to prevent automated retrieval of ad explanations: Facebook initially allowed automated clicks on the "Why am I seeing this" button, then introduced rate limits (Andreou et al., 2018), and then disallowed automated clicks entirely (Merrill and Tobin, 2019).

Cookie Notices and Privacy Policies

Response variables related to website policies and regulations include properties of cookie notices and properties of privacy policies.

Visual properties of cookie notices include their dimensions, location offset, inner HTML, height, number of words, and number of links/buttons (van Eijk et al., 2019). In addition, information about the behavior of cookie notices can be recorded, including whether they block or allow user interaction before consent is given and whether they employ nudging or dark patterns (Utz et al., 2019). The choices offered by cookie notices can also be recorded, including information only, confirmation only, and choices to accept or decline individual cookies or groups of cookies (Degeling et al., 2019). The text of cookie notices can also be recorded to extract information about data collection, the data processor, the collection purpose, and whether the notice offers a link to more information (Utz et al., 2019).

The use of third-party cookie consent libraries and their properties have also been studied, including their mechanism, user interface type, technical details, and legal details (Degeling et al., 2019).

To study how users interact with different types of cookie notices, researchers have recorded: the user's consent decision depending on the properties of the consent notice (Utz et al., 2019); the time spent to make the consent decision; and the user's attention, either via eye tracking, for example, by measuring the fixation count and the average fixation duration, or via questionnaires that ask to recall information from cookie notices (Karegar et al., 2020).

Privacy policies are the legal text that websites use to explain their data collection, processing, and sharing practices to users. When a user consents to the use of cookies in a cookie notice, websites interpret this as the user agreeing to the website's privacy policy. Privacy policies can be analyzed with respect to their linguistic properties, such as their length and readability. Length is often measured as the number of sentences, words, or syllables (Linden et al., 2020). Readability can be measured with readability measures such as the Flesch Reading Ease (Libert, 2018), and by counting the number of sentences in passive voice (Degeling et al., 2019) or the frequency of obfuscating words (Shipp and Blasco, 2020). They can also be analyzed with regard to their visual attractiveness, the frequency of updates, and the time it takes to read them (Libert, 2018).

The semantics of privacy policies, i.e., the privacy choices offered in the policy, can also be analyzed, for example, in terms of privacy categories and attributes (Linden et al., 2020). In addition, the privacy choices may include opt-outs, data deletion, and do not track, and the number of actions required for the user to make a choice can also be recorded (Habib et al., 2019).

Search

Response variables for studies of search engines mainly focus on properties of the search engine result pages (SERPs). Search engines include not only general-purpose search engines such as Google or Bing (Robertson et al., 2018b), but also search functions included in social media platforms such as Twitter (Kulshrestha et al., 2017), on e-commerce and travel sites (Hunold et al., 2018), and on job and gig economy sites (Chen et al., 2018).

Most commonly, studies record the specific items displayed on a SERP and how they are ranked (Hannak et al., 2013; Hunold et al., 2018). The properties of search results can also be recorded, such as prices on e-commerce sites (Hannak et al., 2014), sellers on e-commerce sites (Chen et al., 2016b), or biases in searches for political terms (Kulshrestha et al., 2017).

The ranking on SERPs can be analyzed both in terms of search result items (Cozza et al., 2016) and in terms of the order of components on the SERP (see Figure 4.4), such as Google's general, map-card, general-video, Twitter, knowledge, news-card components (Robertson et al., 2018b).

The properties of autocomplete suggestions can also be recorded, including their linguistic features and churn (Robertson et al., 2018a).

Finally, the user interaction with SERPs has been studied, for example, in terms of the query reformulation rate, page click count, and successful click count (Mehrotra et al., 2017).

Social Network Activity

Response variables for social networks include user profiles and activity on social networks as well as properties of the social network itself, such as characteristics of its news feed or online status indicator.

The properties of friend lists, such as the number of friends, relationships between friends, and whether the friend list is public, can be analyzed, for example, to find out whether a Facebook account belongs to a regular user or to a like farm (De Cristofaro et al., 2014; Ikram et al., 2017a). A user's interaction with their social news feed, including reading and sharing, can be recorded to study how users interact with different content types (Bakshy et al., 2015).

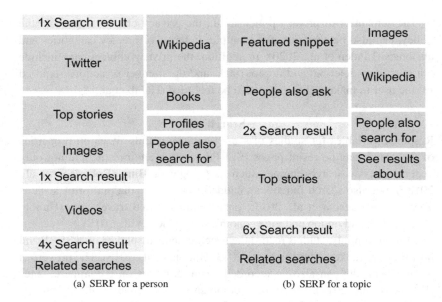

(a) SERP for a person   (b) SERP for a topic

Figure 4.4 Components shown on search engine result pages (SERPs), for two example searches on Google. The size of each component is proportional to the real SERP, except for multiple search results, which have been compressed into the space of a single search result.

The social network news feed is the primary interaction point of users with the social network. Its properties include the number of posts on the news feed, the number of displayed ads and the average user exposure to ads (Galán et al., 2019). In addition, biases in the composition of the news feed can be measured by comparing the rates of posts coming from specific publishers (Hargreaves et al., 2019, 2018).

Some social networks offer online status indicators that show whether other users are online or not. Their properties include: the delay until a user appears online/offline; whether the user's last online time is displayed; whether the user can see their own status; and whether the status is visible globally, within the service, or to friends only (Cobb et al., 2020).

Pricing, Rating, Route Planning

Prices are most often used as response variables in studies of price discrimination and differentiation, for example, on e-commerce sites (Chen et al., 2016b) and travel sites (Hupperich et al., 2018). They are also used to study sharing economy sites such as ride sharing (Kooti et al., 2017) and housing (Mashhadi and Chapman, 2018).

Ratings, for example, of hotels, drivers, or workers, can be collected as response variables to audit rating algorithms (Eslami et al., 2017) or to study biases on gig economy platforms (Ge et al., 2016; Hannák et al., 2017).

Response variables for route planning applications include route complexity, externalities, and other characteristics of the route. Route complexity can be measured as the length (Tannert and Schöning, 2018), number of turns, and number of intersections in a route (Johnson et al., 2017). Externalities measure effects of the routing system on the surrounding world and include socioeconomic characteristics of the neighborhoods traffic is routed through or the percentage spent on highways (Johnson et al., 2017). Finally, routes can also be analyzed with respect to their beauty and convenience (Schirck-Matthews et al., 2019), such as the number of Flickr images per kilometer, or the percentage of tree cover.

Ride-Sharing Services

Response variables for ride-sharing services include variables relating to the user, characteristics of the service, and variables that quantify externalities caused by use of the ride-sharing service.

On the user side, response variables include the user's geolocation which is regularly sent to the service while the app is running (Chen et al., 2015), as well as the geolocations of cars and their drivers which the service sends to the user (Zhao et al., 2019).

Service characteristics that are often used as response variables include the estimated wait time (Thebault-Spieker et al., 2017), prices and the surge multiplier (Cooper et al., 2018), the length of trips, the portion of canceled or declined trips (Ge et al., 2016), and the identifiers and positions of nearby cars (Zhao et al., 2019). These variables allow to study the supply and demand in the ride-sharing system.

To study externalities caused by ride-sharing services, such as congestion and public transport ridership, response variables include predicted travel times, the travel delay based on actual travel times, and the daily metro ridership (Agarwal et al., 2019).

4.6.3 Response Variables for Mobile Services

In contrast to web-based services that are almost exclusively observable through network communication, mobile services can also be studied by examining static properties and dynamic behaviors of the mobile applications themselves. Static properties relate to characteristics of mobile applications that can be analyzed by inspecting the binary application without executing it, while dynamic properties focus on the run-time behavior of apps. The most commonly recorded static response variables are app permissions, the use of third-party libraries in apps, and the API calls used in apps.

App permissions are contained in the app's manifest (Grace et al., 2012). They can be recorded as an intermediate response variable to filter apps for the main study, so that only apps that use certain features of interest are retained (Demetriou et al., 2016; Pan et al., 2018), or they can be recorded as final response variables. For example, they have been used to study the evolution of permission usage over time or the permission use by a certain category of apps (Nguyen et al., 2019; Book et al., 2013; Calciati and Gorla, 2017). The use of permissions can also serve as a proxy for the privacy level of an app.

Third-party libraries are included in apps for a variety of purposes. For example, some libraries provide additional functionality such as image processing (Srivastava et al., 2017), while others are used for tracking, analytics, and advertising (Wang et al., 2018). Due to the use of code obfuscation, it is difficult to reliably identify the libraries included in an app, for example, known package names cannot be used when apps use code obfuscation (Ma et al., 2016). Instead, researcher have used call frequencies of different APIs (Ma et al., 2016) or reference and inheritance relationship patterns (Li et al., 2018) to infer the identities of third-party libraries. The release dates of third-party libraries can also serve as response variables to study to what extent old library versions are used in apps (Book et al., 2013).

The APIs called by an app allow some inferences about the app's expected behavior without executing it. For example, an app's control flow graph, created from its binary, can be combined with a list of privacy-relevant API calls (He et al., 2019). Analysis of the control flow graph then allows to infer whether the app has the potential for leaking private information over the network (Grace et al., 2012; Egele et al., 2011). The parameters given to API calls, for example, APIs offered by analytics or tracking libraries, can be recorded to study to what extent user behavior and information can be revealed by these libraries (Liu et al., 2019). Based on API calls relating to particular features or libraries, researchers can analyze how often a feature or library is used in a corpus of apps. For example, this has been used for APIs relating to media access (Pan et al., 2018) and for ad libraries (Book and Wallach, 2013).

Response variables for dynamic behaviors of apps include the characteristics of local files generated by apps, which allows to study whether they may leak information to third-party libraries (Demetriou et al., 2016), and whether apps use cloud services, which can be detected from network traffic (Henze et al., 2017).

4.6.4 Response Variables for User Characteristics

Response variables for user characteristics include demographics, user identifiers, and user attributes or preferences.

Demographics

User demographics include gender, age, ethnicity, income level, educational attainment, marital status, number of children, employment, and residence location. Demographics can be recorded in user surveys as ground truth to compare with the inferences made by profilers (Bashir et al., 2019b), they can be used to assess the representativeness of a population sample (Ikram et al., 2017a), and they can be collected as ground truth to compare with predictions made by machine learning models (Mehrotra et al., 2017; Riederer et al., 2016).

If they are not available for direct collection, demographic attributes can also be inferred. For example, ethnicity can be inferred from users' profile photos (Mashhadi and Chapman, 2018), and gender can be inferred based on first names (Chen et al., 2018; May et al., 2019).

User Identifiers

Unique user identifiers are most often used as response variables for detecting identifiers in outgoing network traffic. Depending on the user's device, different identifiers are available.   On Android devices, they include the international mobile subscriber identity (IMSI), IMEI, SIM number, Android serial number, Android advertising ID, phone number, and MAC address (Razaghpanah et al., 2018). On desktop systems, they include the IP address, MAC address, and fingerprinting attributes like the operating system, user agent, and desktop resolution (Urban et al., 2018). On IoT devices, they can include device serial numbers, device names, software versions, account names, and Wi-Fi SSIDs (Moghaddam et al., 2019).

User Attributes and Preferences

Response variables for other user attributes have been used in a variety of studies. The timestamps of user actions can be recorded to infer behavioral patterns (Conti et al., 2015; Kooti et al., 2017). A user's expected privacy settings on social media can be collected to compare with their actual settings (Liu et al., 2011). The profiles of job applicants, including the relevance of their skills, education level, experience, and willingness to relocate, can be used to study biases on résumé search engines (Chen et al., 2018). Users' voting preferences can be recorded to study ranking biases in search engines (Epstein et al., 2017).

Finally, the properties of a user's emails – or of emails received by virtual personas – can be recorded to study email-based tracking. Response variables include the type of received emails (account registration emails, password reset emails, authentication emails, or spam), the category of the sender's domain, the presence of trackers (Hu et al., 2019b), and whether links in emails leak referers or email addresses to third parties (Englehardt et al., 2018).

5

Data Collection

Data collection entails executing the designed experiment and recording the response variables. The ethical implications of the experiment have to be considered before starting data collection, with the aim to minimize its harmful impacts. Some experiments need approval from an Institutional Review Board or Ethics Committee. Various data sources and data collection methods are available: archival data sources, passive data collection, active data collection including methods to influence input variables, data collection from mobile apps, and data collection via crowdsourcing. Data collection also needs to consider how the collected data will be stored.

5.1 Ethical Considerations

The ethical implications of transparency research need to be considered to determine whether the research has the potential to negatively affect real-world humans or organizations, and if so, to justify and minimize the harmful effects. This section discusses ethical issues that can arise in transparency research as well as methods to mitigate or prevent harmful effects.

5.1.1 Guidelines for Ethical Considerations

Universities normally have a process in place that allows researchers to gain approval for any research activity involving humans. To apply for approval, researchers have to: explain their intended research, including their research objectives and methods; identify possible ethical issues; and explain how these issues will be addressed. A research ethics committee or institutional review board (IRB) – consisting of ethics specialists but not necessarily subject specialists – will then consider the application and either approve, request changes, deny the application, or conclude that the study is outside of the IRB's purview (McDonald et al., 2018; Chen et al., 2015).

The need for researchers to gain IRB approval is triggered by the characteristics of the proposed research. For example, these characteristics can include the following, all of which may be met by transparency research:

• Gathering information from or about individuals and organizations.
• Using archived data in which individuals are identifiable.
• Research into criminal activities.

Ethical considerations can be informed by codes of ethics, such as the ACM Code of Ethics[1] or the IEEE Code of Ethics.[2] These codes of ethics explain what professional conduct is expected of members of these professional organizations. In addition, the principle of privacy by design (Cavoukian, 2013) and ethical research guidelines (Kenneally and Dittrich, 2012) can help guide ethical considerations.

However, in some cases, transparency research may violate the requirements of a code of ethics. The most common case relates to research violating a company's terms of service, whereas codes of ethics may mandate that researchers comply with terms of service. Terms of service violations may occur when the terms of service forbid research methods like automated queries, reverse engineering, or scraping. However, some research problems cannot be solved while complying with terms of service, and it is possible that the research's benefit for society outweighs any harm to the companies (Vaccaro et al., 2015).

The revised 2018 version of the ACM code of ethics recognizes this situation. Specifically, the code states that researchers must follow the rules (i.e., laws, regulations, policies) "unless there is a compelling ethical justification to do otherwise," and it recognizes "that some exceptions to a creator's control of a work are necessary for the public good."

An example of a compelling ethical justification was given by AdNauseam, one of the most controversial works in the transparency research space (Howe and Nissenbaum, 2017). At its core, AdNauseam is a browser extension that hides advertisements and, in the background, clicks on a certain portion of the hidden ads.

The ethical and moral justification for AdNauseam's approach rests on three main arguments: whether the aim is laudable, whether alternatives exist, and whether it is different from click fraud.

---

[1] www.acm.org/code-of-ethics
[2] www.ieee.org/about/corporate/governance/p7-8.html

Howe and Nissenbaum (2017) argue that their aim is laudable because ubiquitous and surreptitious corporate surveillance violates the tenets of liberal democracy and often goes against the user's wishes. The design goal for AdNauseam is, therefore, that privacy as a societal value should be infused in systems, and systems should be able to protest against tracking by disrupting the corporate surveillance business model. In this case, the disruption is caused by polluting the aggregate data held by profilers through random ad clicks which reduces the value of the data, and by inserting mistrust into the advertising ecosystem by making publishers pay for decoy ad clicks. As a result, they argue, their obfuscation-based approach is morally defensible.

Regarding the existence of alternative approaches at lower cost, they argue that the best alternative would be regulations, which seemed unlikely to be realized. Regarding costs, they argue that the bandwidth and server resources spent for processing fake ad clicks is negligible compared to the resources spent on serving ads in the first place.

Regarding click fraud, they agree that both click fraud and AdNauseam are forms of lying. However, they argue that fraud normally involves financial benefit for the perpetrator, which is not the case with AdNauseam.

This example shows that compelling ethical justifications can be multi-faceted arguments that consider implications of and benefits from research projects on different levels, including the individual level and the organizational, systemic level. The following sections give more examples of ethical considerations on these levels.

5.1.2 Harmful Effects on Individuals

Let us start by considering specific types of harm that transparency research may cause to individuals and how these harms can be addressed. Harmful effects may be caused by several research methods that involve humans: data collection from researcher-controlled apps or browser extensions; data collection using surveys or interviews; data collection from websites that display information about individuals; data collection through residential internet connections; and use of synthetic data that may be visible to users.

Data Collection from App or Browser Extension Created by Researchers Studies that involve collecting data from an app or browser extension that was created for this purpose by the researchers are quite common, for example, to study price discrimination (Iordanou et al., 2017), cloud usage by mobile apps (Henze et al., 2017), Facebook ad explanations (Andreou et al., 2018), Facebook ad prices (González Cabañas et al., 2017), or tracking on mobile devices (Razaghpanah et al., 2018).

These studies closely resemble classic human research and normally need IRB approval, although some IRBs have argued that approval is not necessary if the goal is not to study human behavior, but the behavior of software (Razaghpanah et al., 2018). Researchers may also have to ensure compliance with data protection regulations such as the GDPR, and possibly seek approval from the data protection authority (Iordanou et al., 2017).

Most studies use a combination of methods to minimize harm to individuals, including informed consent and data minimization. Informed consent means that users are informed about the extent and purpose of data collection so that they can freely decide whether to participate or not (Henze et al., 2017; González Cabañas et al., 2017; Iordanou et al., 2017). To make participants more comfortable with giving consent, researchers sometimes restrict the publication of datasets derived from the collected data (Henze et al., 2017).

Data minimization means restricting data collection to only what is necessary to achieve the study objectives (Andreou et al., 2018). Researcher-controlled apps or extensions are commonly designed so that they do not collect or store personally identifiable information (PII) (González Cabañas et al., 2017). This may include very detailed considerations: account management pages on e-commerce sites may have to be excluded because they can include PII; full URLs may include PII and therefore may have to be shortened to the domain level (Iordanou et al., 2017); user identifiers, statistics of users, and statistics of user behavior may allow reidentification and may have to be omitted from collection (Henze et al., 2017). In addition, it can be good practice to delete accidentally collected PII and use blocklists to avoid collecting this type of PII again (Iordanou et al., 2017).

The operation of the app or extension can also be limited so that only data from a specific set of target sites or apps is collected, for example, a list of known e-commerce sites (Iordanou et al., 2017), a specific social media platform (González Cabañas et al., 2017), or apps that are not mobile browsers (Razaghpanah et al., 2018). Another way to limit data collection is to give users the option to turn off data collection (Razaghpanah et al., 2018; Henze et al., 2017) or to preprocess data on the user's device so that only summary data is transmitted to the researchers (Henze et al., 2017; Razaghpanah et al., 2018). Any data transmitted back to the researchers should use modern methods for transport encryption such as TLS (González Cabañas et al., 2017).

Studies with Human Participants

Studies with human participants include all studies that use surveys or crowdsourcing services and need IRB approval. These studies normally have to ensure that participants give their informed consent before participating.

However, in some cases, there are additional considerations. For example, a study that aims to find out whether manipulated search result rankings could have any effect on the outcome of an election (Epstein and Robertson, 2015) needs to make sure that the study does not accidentally influence a real-world election. This can be achieved by using past elections for the study, by ensuring that the sample of participants is too small to influence election outcomes, or by studying elections of another country, such as using candidates from an Australian election in a study with US participants.

In some cases, studies can only be conducted if participants are not aware that they are participating in a study, for example, to ensure the ecological validity of the study and to be able to collect unbiased results (Utz et al., 2019). In this case, participants cannot give their informed consent and as a result researchers have an additional duty to ensure that participants are not harmed. For example, in a study of user reactions to different kinds of cookie notices on a real website, the interventions (kinds of cookie notices) were designed so that they work as expected by users and respect users' choices. In addition, data collection was limited to pseudonymized data, data sharing was restricted, and participants were informed as soon as possible after their participation – as short as 30 s in this case (Utz et al., 2019).

Data Collection from Websites or Apps That Display User Data
When collecting data from websites that display user data, such as freelance marketplaces or résumé search engines, it is unlikely that informed consent can be obtained from every user because contact information may not be available or because removing users who do not consent may invalidate the study design.

Besides data minimization and refraining from collecting PII (Hannák et al., 2017) two additional methods are used in this case.

First, following the notion of contextual integrity (Nissenbaum, 2004), the sharing of datasets should be limited because it may violate the participants' expectations about their data (Chen et al., 2018). Second, the study needs to ensure that it does not cause negative effects on users. For example, job candidates from résumé search engines should not be contacted (Chen et al., 2018), no tasks should be booked with freelance workers (Hannák et al., 2017), no rides should be requested from ride-sharing drivers (Chen et al., 2015), and, in general, no operations should be performed that would change the normal user behavior (Zhao et al., 2019).

Data Collection through Residential Internet Connections
Some studies rely on human participants to benefit from the properties of their internet connection. Because study results can differ depending on the

vantage point of the crawler, some researchers use services like Luminati that allow crawling from residential IP addresses (McDonald et al., 2018). In this case, the researchers' activities may be traced back to the residential user who has no connection to the researchers. Therefore, researchers need to take steps to reduce the possible negative effects on these users. This can include data minimization, for example, by collecting the geolocation of the user, but not their IP address, and it can include refraining from crawling certain content, including pornography, malicious sites, and sites that are often censored (McDonald et al., 2018).

Synthetic Data That May Be Visible to Users

In cases where researchers create synthetic data that may be displayed to users – for example, when researchers run their own ad campaigns – researchers should ensure that users are not negatively affected. For example, when running ad campaigns, the ads should not pollute users with meaningless ad impressions. To make ad impressions meaningful, researchers can, for example, show ads for a real non-profit organization in the area of data transparency (Papadopoulos et al., 2017). This also ensures that the resources needed to run the campaign are aligned with the values of the research.

Another study that created synthetic measurement clients to investigate Uber (Chen et al., 2015) ensured that drivers would not see their measurement clients as potential clients, and that their measurement would not affect Uber's surge pricing.[3]

5.1.3 Harmful Effects on Organizations

The two main considerations to address harmful effects on organizations are whether and how to comply with all applicable rules, and how to minimize the impact of running experimental studies on real organizations.

Compliance with Laws, Regulations, and Policies

Different countries have different laws that may be applicable to transparency research. While this section gives some examples, it is not possible to exhaustively cover all applicable laws.

As an example for the legal situation in the United States, Reyes et al. (2018) have considered how US laws may apply to their study, which included the installation and execution of mobile apps. They argue that they do not observe

---

[3] Surge prices are determined as a multiplier of the regular price for a ride. They are typically used in times of high demand.

human communication, which means that the Electronic Communications Privacy Act does not apply; that they do not attempt to access restricted content, which means that the Computer Fraud and Abuse Act (CFAA) does not apply; and that their research is both in the public interest and uses only lawfully acquired devices and software, which means that the Digital Millennium Copyright Act does not apply. In addition, they argue that terms of service noncompliance is common practice in research, and that some US courts have confirmed that this noncompliance is not a violation of the CFAA (American Civil Liberties Union, 2019, 2020).

In another study, Andreou et al. (2018) found that they are in compliance with Facebook's terms of service. The study included the collection of user data from Facebook via a browser extension and, in these cases, Facebook requires that the extension obtains user consent, explains to users that data is not collected by Facebook but by third-party researchers, and explains what information will be collected and how it will be used.

Several studies have found that they do violate terms of service, but have concluded that "algorithm audits are necessary to ensure civil rights in the digital age" (Hannák et al., 2017) or that prior studies had already argued convincingly why terms of service noncompliance is acceptable (Chen et al., 2018; Sandvig et al., 2014). For example, Soeller et al. (2016) argued that "non-commercial research for the public good that deals with issues of societal importance must be able to access public Web resources for research purposes as long as automated processes do not produce an unreasonable load."

These examples show that legal compliance requires careful and nuanced consideration that depends on the specific details of the planned study.

Limiting Impact on Organizations

Many studies have considered how they can study corporate surveillance while limiting negative impacts on the organization under study, for example, in terms of server resources, bandwidth, and cost.

The creation of virtual personas, including accounts, is necessary for some studies, but it may interfere with the operation of the system under study. For this reason, researchers have chosen to limit their use of accounts. For example, Chen et al. (2018) uploaded only two researcher-controlled résumés to a résumé search engine so that the search result rank of real candidates was decreased by, at most, two. Hannak et al. (2014) limited the use of accounts on e-commerce systems by reserving, at most, one hotel room per hotel, making reservations far in the future, and canceling reservations as soon as the experiments were complete. This ensured that the e-commerce sites had enough time to attract real users after the cancellation, and that availability of hotel rooms was not subject to artificial scarcity.

Even when accounts are not used, studies may need to limit their use of server resources and bandwidth of the system under study. To do so, researchers have limited the rate of their requests to the service, for example, to one query every 30 s (Chen et al., 2018), have decided to respect `robots.txt` files (Hannák et al., 2017), or have compared the number of their measurement clients to the system's active number of users (Chen et al., 2015).

Researchers may also have to consider their responsible disclosure strategy when the research discovers vulnerabilities in the system under study (Zhao et al., 2019). Responsible disclosure means that the service is notified of a vulnerability before the finding is made public. This reduces the chance that the vulnerability is exploited by malicious actors (Stock et al., 2016).

Finally, studies have also attempted to limit the cost induced by their experiments, particularly studies of the advertising ecosystem where ad impressions and ad clicks incur a cost to advertisers (Barford et al., 2014). It can be possible to estimate this incurred cost based on knowledge about ad pricing. For example, Vadrevu and Perdisci (2019) have estimated that the worst-case cost incurred to individual advertisers was under $5, and on average was only $0.04.

5.2 Archival Data Sources

Archival data sources are public datasets that can support studies as primary or supplementary data sources. They can also help with longitudinal and historical studies where live data collection is not possible.

5.2.1 Traffic

The most commonly used archival data source is the Internet Archive and its Wayback Machine.[4] The Internet Archive has been archiving full websites since 1996, including embedded resources like images, JavaScript, and CSS. The archive is accessible through web browsers, which means that mechanisms for browser automation (see below) also work for retrieving historical data from the Wayback Machine. In addition, the Internet Archive enables APIs to locate the times for individual snapshots for specific URLs. The Wayback

---

[4] https://web.archive.org/

Machine has been used for many studies, including to analyze the historical coverage of ad block filter lists and the presence of anti-ad block scripts (Iqbal et al., 2017), to analyze websites that triggered false positives or false negatives in EasyList ad filtering (Alrizah et al., 2019), to analyze historical privacy policies (Linden et al., 2020), and to analyze the evolution of online tracking (Lerner et al., 2016). However, when using the Wayback Machine, it is important to keep in mind its limitations. The Wayback Machine does not archive all websites on the Internet, nor does it archive every single changed version of the sites in its archive. The vantage point from which a website is archived may change between snapshots so that a website's localization may change between snapshots. In addition, some embedded resources may not be archived, and the embedded resources may have been archived at different times. This can lead to inconsistent views of some websites (Lerner et al., 2016).

The Open Observatory of Network Interference (OONI)[5] provides an open dataset of internet measurements from vantage points in hundreds of countries, mostly relating to various forms of blocking and censorship. Contributions to the dataset are made by volunteers through the *ooniprobe* software. For example, the *http_requests* test downloads each URL in a list twice – once through the regular internet connection and once through Tor. The request pairs recorded for this test can be used to detect instances where Tor and non-Tor users are treated differently, either because of censorship (non-Tor user sees errors) or because Tor is blocked (Tor user sees errors) (Khattak et al., 2016). Other tests are designed to find out which websites or messaging apps are blocked, whether VPNs are blocked, and whether middleboxes are present in a network (McDonald et al., 2018). The OONI dataset is available from an AWS bucket and via an API.

The Common Crawl dataset[6] is a large dataset of crawls of about three billion websites with regular snapshots since 2013. The dataset is available on AWS buckets. Even though the dataset includes mainly HTML pages and does not fetch embedded resources like images or scripts, it has been used to extract tracking graphs and analyze the extent of tracking on the web (Schelter and Kunegis, 2018).

The OpenWPM project has released measurement data for up to one million websites between 2015 and 2019[7] (Englehardt and Narayanan, 2016). This dataset includes HTTP requests and responses, JavaScript, and cookies.

[5] https://ooni.org/
[6] https://commoncrawl.org/
[7] https://webtransparency.cs.princeton.edu/webcensus/data-release/

5.2.2 Lists

Some data sources provide information in list form that can be used to define input variables or help with data analysis.

Whotracks.me, run by the company that develops the Cliqz browser and Ghostery browser extension, provides a dataset of trackers and the companies who own them, including all domains they operate under.[8] The dataset includes: additional information, such as the reach of each tracker; the percentage of requests that set cookies; the percentage of requests that contained a unique identifier in a query parameters which can be used as an indicator for cookie synchronization; and the types of resources used by the tracker (e.g., JS, iFrames, images, or CSS). This dataset has been used to compare tracking on a specific type of website with tracking on the general web (Agarwal et al., 2020) and to analyze parent-subsidiary relationships (Bashir et al., 2019a).

Ad block filter lists and anti-ad block filter lists are used in many studies, for example, to identify traffic that belongs to the advertising ecosystem (Razaghpanah et al., 2018) or to evaluate the performance of ad blockers (Gervais et al., 2017) and anti-ad blockers (Iqbal et al., 2017). The most common ad block filter lists are EasyList and EasyPrivacy, and anti-ad block filter lists include the Anti-Adblock Killer list[9] and the ad block warning removal list.[10] Chapter 9 discusses these lists in more detail.

Studies of the Tor ecosystem and the experience of Tor users often rely on Tor blocklists that contain a list of all Tor nodes, such as dan.me.uk and TorDNSEL. For example, they have been used to analyze how the quality of Wikipedia edits from Tor compares to those made by non-Tor editors (Tran et al., 2020).

5.2.3 Data Sources for Specific Purposes

There are many other data sources available that can support specific studies.

The Usable Privacy project maintains a set of corpuses of privacy policies.[11] Some of these corpuses are annotated by legal experts with the ground truth of the privacy practices described in the policies. This makes these corpuses especially useful for work on automatic classification of privacy policies (Linden et al., 2020; Harkous et al., 2018).

---

[8] https://whotracks.me/trackers.html
[9] https://github.com/reek/anti-adblock-killer
[10] https://easylist-downloads.adblockplus.org/antiadblockfilters.txt
[11] https://usableprivacy.org/data

Specialized search engines for source code[12] index the HTML, JS, and CSS of websites. This allows researchers to find common code fragments or instances of common libraries across domains (Papadopoulos et al., 2020).

For studies of the mobile app ecosystem, several repositories allow easier access to Android apps than the Google Play Store. For example, apkpure.com provides a repository of historical Android app versions, and the AndroZoo dataset[13] contains more than 12 million apps that can be filtered according to various criteria (Allix et al., 2016).

5.3 Passive Data Collection

Passive data collection refers to the recording of live network traffic that has not been influenced by the experimenter. This live traffic is usually captured at points where the traffic from many users converges, for example, at internet service providers, Wi-Fi hotspots, or VPNs.

The advantage of passive traffic capture is that it offers a large-scale view of real user behavior. This allows the experimenter to make statements about the behavior of black-box systems and the interaction of users with black-box systems *in the wild*.

However, the disadvantage is that the experimenter cannot set up different experimental conditions, but instead has to work with the behaviors that are are present and distinguishable in the captured traffic. Typically, there is no information about user characteristics such as demographics. Depending on how the traffic was anonymized, traffic originating from one user may be linkable to a user pseudonym, or may not be linkable at all.

Whether passive traffic capture is a feasible option may depend on the experimenter's employer or connections to other organizations. For example, to capture traffic at an internet service provider or internet exchange point, experimenters may need an existing working relationship with the ISP or IXP.

5.3.1 Network Traffic Capture

To capture traffic from the network stack, researchers typically record full HTTP packets at the application layer, i.e., HTTP headers and the full payload of HTTP requests and responses. Existing studies have used traffic captured at large European ISPs (Pujol et al., 2015; Metwalley et al., 2015; Iordanou et al., 2018), at neighborhood networks and residential gateways (Varmarken et al.,

---

[12] https://publicwww.com/
[13] https://androzoo.uni.lu

2020), at university networks and countrywide mobile networks (Gill et al., 2013), and at VPN proxies for mobile users operated by ISPs (Papaodyssefs et al., 2015).

However, a disadvantage of passively collected network traffic is that it is not easily possible to decrypt HTTPS traffic. Man-in-the-middle techniques would require that the experimenter can route traffic through their own infrastructure, which is not feasible with the typical setup and traffic volume of passive capture. As a result, passive traffic capture is limited to plain-text HTTP traffic. With the increasing adoption of HTTPS, both on the web and on mobile platforms (Felt et al., 2017) the study designs for experiments that use passive traffic capture may become more difficult.

5.3.2 Application Data Collection

Another form of passive data collection is when researchers use application data that is available within a black-box system. Researchers have used this data either to derive insights on the performance of their own service, or to analyze the characteristics of an unrelated third-party service.

For example, researchers at Microsoft have used data from the Bing search engine to characterize how satisfied users are with their search results (Mehrotra et al., 2017). Even though these researchers used data that is only available internally, such as user demographics, click counts on the search result page, and the reformulation rate of queries, they argue that their technique can also be used for external audits of search engines by observing search queries, search engine result pages, and user clicks in network traffic.

Researchers at Yahoo have used emails that Uber sent to users of Yahoo's email service to analyze characteristics of Uber's service (Kooti et al., 2017). These emails included ride receipts and weekly reports and, combined with demographic data available at Yahoo, allowed a detailed comparison of riders and drivers, for example, in terms of their ages and incomes.

Researchers at Cliqz have used data from the browser usage of 200,000 Cliqz users to study tracking (Yu et al., 2016).

Research at Facebook and Google has also taken advantage of the data available there, for example, to study the interactions of 10 million Facebook users with shared news articles (Bakshy et al., 2015), or to analyze statistics of right-to-be-forgotten requests received by Google (Bertram et al., 2019).

5.4 Active Data Collection

Active data collection refers to the recording of data that results from actions taken by the experimenter. For example, an experimenter could browse a particular website and record the sequence of requests and replies until the website has loaded.

Active data collection has several advantages: it can be easily influenced by the experimenter; it allows traffic to be decrypted at the application layer; it allows the definition of control and experimental groups; and it allows noise factors to be eliminated more easily than in passive data collection.

However, the traffic generated may not resemble traffic generated by real users. For example, human users see fewer third-party requests than web crawlers (4.5 for humans versus 11.6 for crawlers), fewer requests to tracking domains, and a different composition of fingerprinting scripts (crawlers see more anti-fraud scripts than humans) (Zeber et al., 2020). Determining how more human-like traffic can be generated can be difficult (Bashir and Wilson, 2018). In addition, large-scale crawls may need additional hardware or infrastructure to enable the data collection.

While passive data collection needs to identify suitable data sources and find methods to analyze the data that is available, active data collection needs to design methods for creating traffic with the desired properties, recording the desired response variables, and automating the data collection.

5.4.1 Network Communication

Network communication other than HTTP is often used in studies of server-side blocking and censorship (Afroz et al., 2018). Because these studies focus on the availability of internet resources and the reasons for their unavailability, they need to focus less on engineering human-like traffic. Instead, they can rely on tools like ZMap which scans the IPv4 address space on the transport layer (TCP protocol) (Khattak et al., 2016). In addition, these studies often issue DNS requests directly, using different resolvers, instead of relying on the browser and operating system to perform this function behind the scenes (Afroz et al., 2018).

5.4.2 Web Traffic

Creating web traffic often consists of assembling a list of websites to be crawled and executing the crawl as quickly as possible, focusing on crawl efficiency. Methods to simulate human-like browsing sequences exist. For example, one method makes a fresh browsing decision at every timestep, where the simulated user either remains on the current publisher's site and follows an internal link, or visits a new publisher (Burklen et al., 2005). However, because these methods aim to mimic realistic browsing behavior, they cannot be targeted as closely to the aims of transparency studies, such as triggering the creation of profiles by advertisers and trackers (Bashir and Wilson, 2018).

While Chapter 4 introduced a range of possible response variables, researchers need to find concrete ways to record each variable. For web traffic, this can include intercepting network traffic on the measurement machine, recording data stored on disk, and recording data from within the browser (Englehardt and Narayanan, 2016).

Intercepting network traffic, for example, with *mitmproxy*, allows researchers to record all HTTP requests and responses. If the browser is configured with a self-signed certificate, mitmproxy can also decrypt TLS connections (Englehardt and Narayanan, 2016). Mitmproxy also allows the extraction of JavaScript files and Flash objects from the network traffic.

Data that can be recorded from the measurement machine's disk include the browser's cookie database and Flash LSO.

To record data from within the browser, browser extensions can be used to record dynamic behavior and extract the final HTML or DOM tree of the rendered page. Browser extensions can be used, for example: to record usage of JS APIs by instrumenting the getter and setter methods of various objects (Englehardt and Narayanan, 2016); to extract specific properties of the rendered website, such as the ads shown to the user or the values in the ad preference manager (Datta et al., 2015); to export the rendered page can as a screenshot (Zhang et al., 2019b; Vissers et al., 2015); and to support semiautomated experiments with human interaction (Matte et al., 2020).

Even though some researchers have used instrumented versions of the browser itself (Zhang et al., 2019b), this is usually not practical because the instrumentation has to be updated frequently to keep up with the browser's development (Acar et al., 2013). However, such instrumentation can be necessary, for example, to construct inclusion trees to analyze which first or third party was responsible for including a specific resource in a website (Bashir et al., 2016).

Although traffic can be recorded manually for individual websites and apps, automated data collection is needed especially for large-scale experiments that allow conclusions about the web landscape as a whole. Table 5.1 summarizes the features of browser automation tools that have been used in transparency research. These tools combine different feature classes: features for config-uring the crawler, such as JavaScript execution or setting of HTTP headers; features for automating crawls, such as parallelization and rate limitation;

Table 5.1. *Features of browser automation tools. The year of the latest update is indicated in brackets.*

Tool	Features	Reference
Selenium (2021)	Mature tool to automate browsers, many language bindings available	Tschantz et al. (2015)
PhantomJS (2018)	JavaScript-enabled headless browser, discontinued 2018	Libert (2015)
BrowserMob Proxy (2017)	Scriptable proxy, can be integrated in Selenium, can rewrite HTTP requests, decrypt TLS, simulate bandwidth/latency, export traffic	Starov et al. (2016)
openWPM (2021)	Experimentation environment based on Selenium, extensible through Python, supports parallelization, records HTTP requests and responses via mitmproxy, cookies and JS API usage via browser extension	Englehardt and Narayanan (2016)
AdFisher (2018)	Based on Selenium, can detect personalization in ads with automated experiments, supports permutation tests, records values in Google ad settings and ads shown to user	Datta et al. (2015)
FPDetective (2015)	Based on PhantomJS/CasperJS and Selenium/Chrome, response variables related to fingerprinting, records JS API usage and Flash function calls	Acar et al. (2013)
FourthParty (2015)	Firefox extension, can be automated via Python, records HTTP traffic, DOM, cookies, resource loads, JS API calls on window, navigator, screen objects	Mayer and Mitchell (2012)
Tracking Observer (2015)	Firefox extension, driven by list of websites, collects HTTP requests and responses, cookies (inc. local storage and Flash LSO)	Roesner et al. (2012)
Tracking Excavator (2017)	Chrome extension, records historical versions of websites, driven by list of websites and timestamps, collects third-party requests, cookies, JS API usage	Lerner et al. (2016)
CookieCheck (2017)	Instrumented version of chrome, records cookies, isolation between instances through Docker	Trevisan et al. (2019)
Cookinspect (2021)	Semi-automated: browsing and interaction driven by human, browser extension records response variables	Matte et al. (2020)

features for recording results at different layers; and features for automating entire experimental designs, including synchronized crawls and error recovery (Ahmad et al., 2020).

Tool selection is an important step because it can influence the research result and how research hypotheses are answered (Ahmad et al., 2020).

For example, the observed number of third-party trackers depends on whether the tool executes JavaScript or not. To make research results reproducible, it is therefore important to declare the tools and their versions that were used to obtain the results.

In addition, it is important to note that tools that are not actively maintained can quickly cease to work as intended due to the rapid changes in browsers, extension APIs provided by browsers, and the internet ecosystem.

5.4.3 Mobile Traffic

In addition to the considerations for web traffic, active data collection for mobile devices needs different methods for interacting with apps and needs to overcome obstacles related to instrumenting apps and recording traffic on-device or off-device. Table 5.2 summarizes the features of tools for app automation and mobile device instrumentation.

Because human interaction with apps is not scalable for large-scale studies, so-called *monkey* tools create synthetic input events that can exercise app functionally automatically. Input events can be generated purely randomly, which is simple but may take a very long time to exercise all possible app behaviors (Pan et al., 2018). Guided generation of input events analyzes the UI elements offered by apps and creates input events that are targeted at exercising the available behaviors more quickly (Jin et al., 2018).

Instrumenting apps on mobile platforms is harder than instrumenting desktop browsers because there is no generic extension mechanism for apps. In addition, mobile platforms are less open than desktop platforms because they employ more stringent security mechanisms. This is especially the case for iOS.

One solution that circumvents having to instrument mobile apps, in particular mobile browsers, is to imitate mobile browsers on a desktop platform (Das et al., 2018b). Another solution is to use software for dynamic instrumentation, such as Frida, Xposed, or Cydia Substrate. Although this software typically requires rooted or jailbroken devices, it offers similar functionality as instrumentation through a browser extension on the desktop.

To record mobile traffic on-device, the most commonly used method is a local VPN (Henze et al., 2017). This mechanism allows a researcher-controlled app to act as a VPN provider for the apps under study, and thus allows access to their network traffic.

To record mobile traffic off-device, researchers commonly use *mitmproxy* on the wireless router. Without configuration of TLS certificates, mitmproxy can only usefully collect plain HTTP traffic (Papadopoulos et al., 2019). Using

Table 5.2. *Features of tools for app automation and mobile device instrumentation. The year of the latest update is indicated in brackets.*

Tool	Features	Reference
UI/Application Exerciser Monkey (2020)	Generates completely random input events, portion of event types is configurable, app-agnostic	Pan et al. (2018)
DroidBot UI automation (2021)	Creates state transition models for apps, then generates inputs that traverse UI elements, no instrumentation needed, can trigger behaviors faster than Exerciser Monkey	Li et al. (2017b); Jin et al. (2018)
Monkeyrunner (2020)	API to load apps and execute events from Python, can script app execution	Binns et al. (2018a)
AndroidView Client (2020)	Python tool to automate test input generation and drive Android apps, scriptable based on views present in an app	Liu et al. (2017)
PUMA monkey tool (2014)	PUMAScript (a Java extension) can script monkey and react to events	Hao et al. (2014); Nath (2015)
openWPM-Mobile (2018)	Extends openWPM, emulates plausible sensor values for mobile browsers	Das et al. (2018b)
Cydia Substrate (2020)	Hook into running Android and iOS apps, e.g., hook APIs used for tracking, needs rooted/jailbroken device	Liu et al. (2017)
Xposed (2018)	Allows development of third-party plug-ins to customize Android apps, e.g., allows hooking into privacy-related APIs, needs rooted device	He et al. (2019)
Pluto (2015)	Uses UI/Application Exerciser Monkey, collects files created by the app	Demetriou et al. (2016)
Appium (2021)	API to control iPhone simulator on macOS	Bandy and Diakopoulos (2019)
Frida (2021)	Dynamic instrumentation framework, can inject own code into native apps on most platforms	Shuba and Markopoulou (2020)
JustTrustMe (2020)	Module for Xposed framework, modifies Android to disable TLS certificate checking, thus helps to bypass certificate pinning	Moghaddam et al. (2019)
AntMonitor (2021)	VPN-based packet collection for Android	Varmarken et al. (2020)

a self-signed root certificate on the mobile device, mitmproxy can decrypt mobile HTTPS traffic (Ren et al., 2018; Jin et al., 2018) and JustTrustMe can be used to circumvent certificate pinning (Rao et al., 2015).

When collecting data from apps, it is important to reduce background traffic that is not relevant to the study, for example, by using a factory-reset phone, turning off background synchronization, closing all background apps, and filtering traffic to known service domains (e.g., Apple iCloud, Google Play) (Leung et al., 2016).

5.5 Data Collection from Mobile Apps

In addition to traffic from mobile apps, data collection from mobile apps encompasses static data like app permissions and dynamic data like stack and function call traces.

The first step in collecting static data from mobile apps is to acquire the app package and unpack it, for example, using APKTool on Android. This will yield its bytecode (in DEX format on Android) and metadata (Binns et al., 2018b) as well as the app's class hierarchy via the extracted directory structure (Li et al., 2017a). The metadata lists the permissions requested by the app and can be extracted using tools like the Android Asset Packaging Tool *aapt*.

Further data can be extracted by decompiling the app's binary Dalvik byte-code from the DEX format into Smali format, for example, using baksmali[14] or Androguard.[15] Smali code allows the extraction of function call graphs (He et al., 2019) and calls to specific APIs (Pan et al., 2018) as well as inclusion and inheritance relationships (Li et al., 2017a).

Dynamic data can be collected by instrumenting the Dalvik VM directly or by using software like the Xposed framework that simplifies this instrumentation. Most commonly, interesting API calls are hooked so that their execution during the app's runtime can trigger dynamic analysis, such as recording the API call and its parameters (Liu et al., 2017).

5.6 Crowdsourcing

Data collection via crowdsourcing encompasses methods where data is collected from human participants, including traffic, settings, opinions, ratings, or a combination thereof. Crowdsourcing can rely on paid participants via crowdsourcing platforms such as Amazon Mechanical Turk or on participants recruited via a researcher-controlled website, browser extension, or app.

When using crowdsourcing methods, it is important to make sure that participants are fairly compensated for their efforts, in addition to the ethical

---

[14] https://github.com/JesusFreke/smali
[15] https://github.com/androguard/androguard

issues discussed above. Fair compensation could be monetary, such as a fair payment above the minimum wage, or intangible, such as benefits derived from using a researcher-provided browser extension or app.

The following sections examine studies that have used crowdsourcing and highlight how many participants were recruited, what the benefits for participants were, and what the benefit for the researchers was.

5.6.1 Paid Participants

Traditionally, participants for experimental research were recruited locally and paid after performing their tasks in the researchers' lab. This method is still used to some extent, and it can have advantages especially for long-term data collection. For example, Zimmeck et al. (2017) paid participants between $15 and $50, depending on how much data was returned by the browser extension and Android app that participants were asked to use.

However, Internet-based crowd working platforms are far more common today. Platforms to recruit paid participants include Amazon Mechanical Turk (AMT), Prolific Academic, and CrowdFlower. However, workers on all platforms struggle to be fairly compensated for their work. On Amazon Mechanical Turk, 96% of workers earn less than the US federal minimum wage of $7.25 (Hara et al., 2018), and almost no workers earn more than the US effective nationwide minimum wage of $11.80. This is partly because the median payment set by task requesters is only $4.57/h, and partly because compensation for tasks does not take into account unpaid work, for example, the time workers spend searching for tasks, completing qualification tasks, and completing tasks that are then rejected.

The characteristics and population sizes of workers on crowdsourcing platforms vary, but in general crowd workers are a reliable and inexpensive source of experimental data (Peer et al., 2017). However, there are differences between the platforms. Peer et al. (2017) found that participants on Prolific Academic and CrowdFlower are more naive, more diverse, less dishonest and return higher quality results. In general, researchers have to validate that participant samples from crowdworking platforms are representative of the whole population of interest. For example, a study of political ideology verified that the distribution of liberal and conservative values among AMT participants is close to the distribution in representative off-line samples of the population and concluded that AMT is a suitable tool (Clifford et al., 2015). Similar validations may be needed for transparency-related study designs.

General guidelines to make crowdsourced experiments successful include paying participants above the minimum wage, making tasks fun and engaging, including questions to check participants' comprehension of the task, and avoiding to exclude participants except for obvious abuse. Publications resulting from crowdsourced experiments need to report any restrictions on inclusion, such as based on suspicious or odd behaviors, as well as participant dropout rates because these may interact with the study results (Crump et al., 2013).

Crowd Worker Tasks

Studies of corporate surveillance have relied on crowd workers in different ways, from traditional surveys, to labeling images, executing searches, and creating accounts for the researchers' virtual personas.

Surveys are often used as stand-alone instruments or combined with other tasks to collect information about the demographics of participants (Robertson et al., 2018b). Surveys have also been used to compare the expected and actual privacy settings of Facebook users (Liu et al., 2011).

Image labeling tasks, and labeling tasks in general, are useful to collect labels for machine learning training data. This is a repetitive, time-consuming task that often does not require expert knowledge and can thus be easily outsourced. For example, Bashir et al. (2016) asked AMT workers to identify which ad creatives were retargeted ads, Soeller et al. (2016) asked crowd workers to identify whether the borders on two map tiles differed (e.g., from Google Maps), and Srivastava et al. (2017) asked crowd workers to label the image processing task performed by a mobile app.

Search tasks often require users to perform searches while logged into their own social media accounts. This allows researchers to measure search personalization based on real user profiles. To make the tasks easier for workers, they can be set up so that they do not require manual execution of searches but rather configuration of a proxy (Hannak et al., 2013) or installation of a browser extension (Robertson et al., 2018b), which then performs the searches automatically.

Quality Control

Quality control for tasks submitted by crowd workers is important to ensure the reliability of research results. Quality control is performed partly in the screening of workers and partly in the distribution of tasks and analysis of results. Screening criteria or questions for workers include their approval rating (Soeller et al., 2016), their location (Liu et al., 2011), and whether they use the corporate surveillance platform under study (Hannak et al., 2013).

Once participants have been screened, the two most common quality control measures are to replicate tasks and to include controls in each task. The idea behind replicating tasks is to have each task or subtask performed by more than one crowd worker. A simple majority vote can then be used to filter out bad results (Soeller et al., 2016), and researchers can manually analyze results to break ties (Bashir et al., 2016). If tasks are replicated 10 or more times, a consensus threshold can be used instead of a majority vote (Srivastava et al., 2017).

Controls are tasks with a known result which can be included as sub-tasks within a larger task. For example, when having crowd workers label ad images as retargeted, Bashir et al. (2016) designed each task to consist of 30 images, where 27 were previously unlabeled and 3 were known retargeted ads. Results from workers who incorrectly labeled the controls could then be excluded.

Crowd Worker Compensation

The compensation for crowd workers is set as the price for each completed task. To estimate the hourly wage that could be achieved by workers, researchers need to estimate how long it takes to complete each of their tasks, and how much unpaid work workers have to complete in addition to that. Even though many studies report the price per task, very few provide the estimated completion times. Prices per task vary widely, from $0.10 for creating a Google account (Viennot et al., 2014), to $0.18 to label 30 images (Bashir et al., 2016), to $0.85 to label 10 map tiles (Soeller et al., 2016), to $2 to configure a proxy and visit a website that automatically collects search result pages (Hannak et al., 2013). Liu et al. (2011) reported average hourly wages of $9.23 for their study by combining their price per task ($1) with the participants' average completion times (6.5 min).

5.6.2 Browser Extensions

Researchers have used browser extensions in many different studies, for example, to investigate ad prices and ad preferences on Facebook (González Cabañas et al., 2017), ad preferences on Facebook (Angwin et al., 2016b), ad explanations on Facebook (Andreou et al., 2019), the composition of Facebook's news feed (Hargreaves et al., 2019), third parties and trackers embedded in websites (Falahrastegar et al., 2016; Iordanou et al., 2018), price differentiation on e-commerce sites (Mikians et al., 2013), real-time bidding prices (Olejnik et al., 2014), browser fingerprints (Vastel et al., 2018a), and characteristics of users' browsing histories (Kawase et al., 2011).

These studies differ in how they recruit users, the number of users they report on, and the benefits that users derive from installing the browser extension.

The most common method to recruit users is to ask colleagues, students, or friends to install the extension (Olejnik et al., 2014; González Cabañas et al.,

2017; Falahrastegar et al., 2016). This typically results in small user bases (tens of users) that are unlikely to be representative of any wider population because participants have been sampled from a small social circle. Extensions that recruit users via crowdsourcing platforms (Iordanou et al., 2018) sample from a much larger population and thus can benefit from more a representative user base. Some extensions provide a significant benefit to users and thereby attract users through social media promotion, posts on tech websites, and press coverage (Angwin et al., 2016b; Galán et al., 2019; Iordanou et al., 2017; Vastel et al., 2018b). In this way, researchers can benefit from thousands of users for their extensions. Although users are sampled from a large population in this case, they are unlikely to be representative because they self-select due to an interest in, and perhaps prior knowledge of, the extension's topic.

The benefits for users can include satisfying the user's curiosity, providing access to new features, and tangible monetary benefits.

A user benefit that is common to many crowdsourcing methods is that many people are keen to contribute to science even though they are not scientists, and crowdsourced science offers the opportunity to do that. For example, the Facebook Data Valuation Tool (FDVT) is an extension for Chrome and Firefox that records Facebook ads and ad preferences (González Cabañas et al., 2017; Cabañas et al., 2018; Galán et al., 2019). The extension shows the user a real-time estimate of the value they generate for Facebook by viewing and clicking ads. This can satisfy the curiosity of users who are interested in finding out how Facebook makes money.

The nonprofit news organization ProPublica published a Chrome extension to record Facebook ad preferences (Angwin et al., 2016a,b). The extension showed users what their assigned ad preferences were. Although this information is accessible on Facebook, it can be hard to locate, so the users benefited from having this information easily accessible. Users were given the opportunity to rate the preferences for accuracy and send them back to ProPublica. Without user action, the extension did not collect any data.

\$heriff is a browser extension that can compare prices for any product from vantage points around the world, with different browser configurations (Iordanou et al., 2017; Mikians et al., 2013). This price comparison can allow users to save money on purchases. The extension collects information relating to the price comparison while performing its task, and users can additionally opt in to donating even more data, including cookies and browsing history.

5.6.3 Apps

Mobile apps are in many regards similar to browser extensions provided by researchers, for example, in their recruitment of users and provision of user benefits. However, apps like Lumen (Razaghpanah et al., 2018) or Meddle (Pan et al., 2018; Rao et al., 2015) are built to allow the analysis of the entirety of a user's mobile traffic. Technically, they use the mobile device's VPN permission, possibly combined with a self-signed CA certificate, to analyze plain-text as well as encrypted traffic. Users gain information on how other apps use their sensitive information such as unique identifiers and PII (Razaghpanah et al., 2018), improved privacy, transparency, and control (Rao et al., 2015), or information about the cloud use of installed apps (Henze et al., 2017).

Some apps also provide user benefits over and above just information. For example, ProtectMyPrivacy detects accesses to private data and gives users a choice to block, allow, or replace the accessed data with obfuscated versions. Users can also contribute their decisions to drive the researchers' recommendation engine and receive recommendations as a reward (Agarwal and Hall, 2013).

5.7 Data Storage

The data collected as part of experimental transparency research is often very large, especially for large-scale studies that collect the entire network traffic and screenshots. As a result, researchers have to carefully consider how to store the data so that it is both stored as a permanent record and fast to access for data analysis.

Data preservation guidelines published by the US Library of Congress (Library of Congress, 2020) recommend platform-independent, character-based formats that are based on well-known schemas. In particular, their recommendations include comma-separated values (CSV) and SQLite.

Depending on the planned data analyses, researchers have often used combinations of data storage systems to achieve performance and permanence aims. For example, OpenWPM relies on a combination of SQLite for relational data and LevelDB for deduplicated compressed web content (Englehardt and Narayanan, 2016). By keying all data to identifiers for the top-level website and browser, they ensure that the two databases can be linked for analysis.

It is also possible to use one database system for data collection and convert to another database system for analysis. For example, Brookman et al. (2017) have used OpenWPM's schema for data collection, but switched to the MS SQL server for analysis.

Table 5.3 summarizes the advantages and disadvantages of several common data storage systems that have been used in transparency research.

Table 5.3. *Characteristics of different data storage systems.*

Database type	Advantages	Disadvantages	References
LevelDB NoSQL key-value store	• fast writes • fast sequential reads • compression with Google Snappy • no server (linked library)	• corruption possible after crash or power failure • no indexes • no SQL	Englehardt and Narayanan (2016)
SQLite SQL	• no server (linked library) • ACID transactions • Library of Congress approved • parallel reads despite table-level locking • most SQL features	• slower than LevelDB in some cases	Acar et al. (2014); Ali et al. (2019b); Englehardt and Narayanan (2016)
MongoDB NoSQL document-oriented with JSON-like documents	• ACID transactions • server can load-balance and replicate • indexes • queries can include JavaScript and aggregation (e.g., MapReduce)	• server needed • default security configuration too permissive	Degeling and Nierhoff (2018); Degeling et al. (2019)
Redis NoSQL in-memory key-value store	• values can be abstract data types • persistence through binary dumps or journaling	• size limited by RAM	Duan et al. (2017); Moghaddam et al. (2019)
MySQL SQL	• ACID transactions • most SQL features • indexes • row-level locking	• server needed	Marciel et al. (2016); Acar et al. (2013)
MS-SQL SQL	• ACID transactions • most SQL features • indexes • row-level locking • faster than SQLite	• server needed • proprietary	Brookman et al. (2017)
PostgreSQL SQL	• ACID transactions • complete support of SQL • indexes • row-level locking • faster than SQLite	• server needed	Corner et al. (2017); Schirck-Matthews et al. (2019)
IndexedDB NoSQL database of JSON objects	• available in-browser through JavaScript API • can be used by browser extensions		Weinshel et al. (2019)

6

Data Analysis

During data analysis, the collected data are processed with the aim of extracting meaningful measures and subjecting them to rigorous statistical analysis that supports significant conclusions. First, this chapter will introduce common quantitative measures for transparency research, including measures for tracking, privacy, fairness, and similarity. To compute most of these measures, data needs to be preprocessed to extract or compute the response variables of interest from the raw collected data. In some cases, response variables are already contained in the collected data and do not need to be processed further. In other cases, however, the collected data needs to be processed to extract response variables. This can be done either with simple transformations or heuristics, with machine learning classifiers or natural language processing, or with static and dynamic analysis methods for mobile apps. Finally, the chapter explains the necessary statistical methods that allow making meaningful and statistically significant statements about the behavior of the response variables in the experiment.

6.1 Quantitative Measures for Transparency Research

Quantitative measures have been defined to quantify characteristics of the corporate surveillance ecosystem. This section introduces measures that are commonly used. To make new studies comparable with prior work, it is important to reuse existing measures whenever they are appropriate.

6.1.1 Measures for Tracking

The *prevalence* of tracking can be measured as the number of trackers that a website or app is using (Razaghpanah et al., 2018). Because it can be difficult to identify exactly which third parties are trackers, some studies use the number of third-party requests or third-party domains and the number of identifying cookies to avoid having to determine which third parties are trackers (Mazel et al., 2019; Gervais et al., 2017) (see Section 6.2.1 for heuristics that can be used to determine which network requests are trackers). Prevalence can also be expressed in relation to other quantities, for example, the percentage of tracking requests among all requests a website makes, or the reduction of tracking requests when ad blockers are used (Merzdovnik et al., 2017).

The *reach* of a tracker (also called *coverage* or *tracking range*) is expressed as the portion of all websites or apps in a given sample that are tracked by a given tracker (Libert, 2018). Reach can be computed on a domain level (Gervais et al., 2017) or on a corporation level (Merzdovnik et al., 2017). On the corporation level, for example, the corporation Alphabet owns domains like google-analytics.com and doubleclick.net. The domain-level reach is easier to compute, but the corporation-level reach more closely expresses the real-world reach of a tracker.

To take into account that trackers on low-ranked websites observe less traffic than those on higher-ranked websites and can thus be seen as less important for the reach of a tracker, the *prominence* measure de-emphasizes trackers on low-ranked websites (Englehardt and Narayanan, 2016; Schelter and Kunegis, 2018). As a side effect, this also makes prominence robust to the number of websites in a study, which makes it suitable for comparisons and longitudinal studies. Using the indicator function present(s,t) to indicate whether tracker t is present on a website s, prominence is computed as

$$\text{Prominence}(t) = \sum_{\text{present}(s,t)} \frac{1}{rank(s)}.$$

The *concentration of power* in the tracking ecosystem as a whole can be measured using the Herfindahl–Hirschman Index (HHI) from economics (Binns et al., 2018a). The HHI is based on a measure of reach and thus can be computed differently depending on the chosen measure. For example, the PROWISH-HHI uses a measure of reach that takes into account prominence as well as parent-subsidiary relationships. The index is computed as

$$\text{HHI} = \sum_{i=1}^{N} s_i^2,$$

where s_i is the market share of a company i, and N designates the number of companies in the market. The market share s_{t_i} of a tracker can be estimated based on prominence as

$$s_{t_i} = \frac{\text{prominence}(t_i)}{\sum_{j=1}^{N} \text{prominence}(t_j)}.$$

The *penetration* of trackers has been defined differently in different studies. Metwalley et al. (2015) define the penetration of a tracker as a user-focused metric that indicates the percentage of users that send at least one request to a tracker over duration of 1, 2, 5, or 10 days. On the other hand, Razaghpanah et al. (2018) define penetration based on the percentage of apps that use a specific advertising or tracking domain or as the percentage of apps that is covered by a specific corporation (which may own multiple domains).

Graph-based measures can be used to analyze the tracking ecosystem as a whole. In a *tracking graph*, nodes represent companies, and edges represent relationships between them, for example, cookie synchronization relationships or relationships defined by resource embedding. The graph can then be analyzed using common measures from graph theory, such as the node degree, diameter of the graph, clustering coefficient, average path length, and algebraic connectivity (Urban et al., 2020b). This is particularly useful when analyzing longitudinal changes, for example, when comparing two graphs at different points in time.

Stateless tracking via fingerprinting is often studied by analyzing the fingerprintability of browsers, which is measured using the uniqueness of users and the information content, or entropy, of fingerprints. The *anonymity set size* is the most common measure for the uniqueness of browsers or users (Gómez-Boix et al., 2018). The anonymity set size indicates the number of users that a fingerprinter cannot distinguish. For example, an anonymity set size of n means that n browsers are indistinguishable, and an anonymity set size of one means that the browser is uniquely identifiable in the given dataset, based on the fingerprinting attributes in the study. The distribution of anonymity set sizes and the percentage of unique users can be used to compare different datasets and fingerprinting methods (Gulyas et al., 2018).

The amount of identifying information in a fingerprint is measured using *entropy* (Laperdrix et al., 2016). Given a fingerprinting attribute X and its possible attribute values x_i, $P(x_i)$ is the frequency of the attribute value x_i in the dataset. The entropy of a fingerprinting attribute, $H(X)$, is then computed as

$$H(X) = -\sum_{i=0}^{n} P(x_i) \log_b P(x_i),$$

where, usually, $b = 2$, which means that entropy is measured in bits. Entropy can also be computed over an entire fingerprint instead of individual attributes.

One additional bit of entropy doubles the probability of the fingerprinter for uniquely identifying a browser. Higher entropy thus indicates a more unique and identifiable fingerprint. Entropy depends on the number of fingerprints in a dataset and is therefore not suitable for comparisons between datasets. For this purpose, entropy can be normalized using *max-entropy* H_M. Max-entropy indicates the highest entropy value that would result if all attribute values were unique, and it is computed as $H_M = \log_2(N)$, where N is the number of fingerprints in the dataset. Normalized entropy is then defined as

$$H_N(X) = \frac{H(X)}{H_M}.$$

6.1.2 Measures for User Privacy

Measures for user privacy are often concerned with *identifiability*, also called unicity or uniqueness, which indicates how many pieces of information an adversary would need to know to uniquely identify a user in a dataset of anonymized user records (de Montjoye et al., 2013b; Achara et al., 2015; Deußer et al., 2020). The less an adversary needs to know, the higher the privacy risk for users.

For example, given an anonymized dataset D of the combinations of mobile apps installed by real users and a set U of some of the apps installed by a specific user, uniqueness is the size of the subset $S \subset D$ that contains the user's apps. If uniqueness is 1, the user can be uniquely identified based on their combination of installed apps (Achara et al., 2015). Uniqueness has also been used to evaluate identifiability based on spatio-temporal points (de Montjoye et al., 2013b), purchases (de Montjoye et al., 2013a), click traces (Deußer et al., 2020), and browsing histories (Bird et al., 2020). In practice, it is computationally expensive to compute the full expressions of these sets, which means that sampling techniques are used to estimate uniqueness.

Another way to measure privacy risk is to combine measures for the scale and sensitivity of information leaks (Wagner and Boiten, 2018; Ferra et al., 2020). This can be based, for example, on the number of attribute-value pairs in ad requests sent to ad networks, the number of attributes that allow targeting in each ad request (Nath, 2015), or the type and frequency of PII leaks (Ren et al., 2018). For example, Ren et al. (2018) have constructed equations for privacy risk based on the type of leaked PII, the destination domain, and the fraction of unencrypted flows. To do so, they classified the severity of PII items available to Android apps into severity levels and then recorded the percentage of apps leaking a particular PII item or type, grouped by the app category, whether the leak is via HTTP or HTTPS, and whether the leak goes to the first-party or a third-party.

6.1.3 Measures for Fairness and Discrimination

Discrimination is often grouped into direct discrimination and indirect discrimination (Žliobaitė, 2017). Direct discrimination, analogous to the notion of *disparate treatment* in US labor law, occurs when an algorithm takes a protected characteristic as input. In the context of advertising, for example, direct discrimination may occur when an advertiser selects protected characteristics like ethnicity or gender as targeting attributes. Indirect discrimination, analogous to *disparate impact*, occurs when an the output of an algorithm is correlated with a protected characteristic even though the algorithm did not take the feature as an input.

Two notions of fairness have been proposed to address indirect discrimination (Dwork et al., 2012): individual fairness states that similar individuals should be treated similarly; and group fairness states that subsets of the population, according to a protected characteristic or sensitive attribute, should be treated similar to the entire population.

To evaluate these notions of fairness in the context of a search engine that ranks job candidates' résumés, Chen et al. (2018) use statistical tests to determine whether the ranking algorithm exhibits individual and/or group fairness. In particular, they define a regression model to estimate an individual's rank based on their sensitive and nonsensitive attributes, and then observe whether the influence of the protected characteristic on this model is significant.

To capture the notion of disparate impact in the context of discrimination in ad targeting, the *representation ratio* indicates how much more likely a user with the sensitive attribute is to be targeted compared to a user without the sensitive attribute (Speicher et al., 2018). The representation ratio rr is expressed as the frequency of users from the relevant audience R being in the target audience T when they have or do not have, respectively, a sensitive attribute s:

$$rr_s(T, R) = \frac{|T \cap R_s|/|R_s|}{|T \cap R_{\neg s}|/|R_{\neg s}|}.$$

Based on the representation ratio, *disparity* in ad targeting can be defined as

$$disp_s(T, R) = max(rr_s(T, R), \frac{1}{rr_s(T, R)}).$$

Targeting is discriminatory if the disparity exceeds a threshold. For example, a threshold of 1.25 would correspond to the 80% rule for disparate impact (Speicher et al., 2018).

6.1.4 Measures for Similarity and Distance

Similarity and distance measures are often used to express the difference between two experimental groups, or between an experimental group and the control. The two most commonly applied measures for similarity are the cosine similarity and the Jaccard index. The cosine similarity measures similarity between two vectors, whereas the Jaccard index measures similarity between two sets. For both measures, 0 indicates no similarity and 1 indicates equality.

For two vectors A and B, the *cosine similarity* $\cos(\theta)$ is computed by dividing the dot product of the two vectors by their magnitudes:

$$\cos(\theta) = \frac{\mathbf{A} \cdot \mathbf{B}}{\|\mathbf{A}\| \, \|\mathbf{B}\|} = \frac{\sum\limits_{i=1}^{n} A_i B_i}{\sqrt{\sum\limits_{i=1}^{n} A_i^2} \sqrt{\sum\limits_{i=1}^{n} B_i^2}}.$$

Cosine similarity has been used, for example, to compare topic categories, sets of ads, and browsing histories. A common method to define the vectors for cosine similarity is term frequency–inverse document frequency (tf-idf). For example, to compare the browsing histories of different users, Papaodyssefs et al. (2015) represent each user as a vector where each element represent an individual website. Each element is weighted based on tf-idf, where the term frequency *tf* is the number of times a user has visited a specific website, and the document frequency *df* is the number of users who have this website in their history. This weighting reduces the impact of very popular websites on the similarity computation. To match the topic categories in Google's Play store with those defined by Alexa, Ullah et al. (2014) represent all categories as text and create their tf-idf vectors. Cosine similarity can then be computed on pairs of tf-idf vectors, and categories are assumed to match if the similarity is 1. To compare sets of ads, Balebako et al. (2012) use two cosine similarities, one based on the URLs of ad landing pages, and the other based on the words in the titles and texts of ads. In both cases, a vector is constructed that represents the frequency of a given URL or word in the set of ads. In this case, the elements of the vectors are URL or word frequencies. Another option is to construct vectors so that the elements represent individual ads, and weight each element based on the logarithm of the number of page reloads that contained the ad (Guha et al., 2010).

For two sets A and B, the *Jaccard index* is computed by dividing the intersection of the two sets by their union:

$$J(A, B) = \frac{|A \cap B|}{|A \cup B|} = \frac{|A \cap B|}{|A| + |B| - |A \cap B|}.$$

The Jaccard index has been used, for example, to compare different versions of privacy policies and to measure personalization of search results. To compute the similarity between different versions of privacy policies, Degeling et al. (2019) first split each policy into sentences and compute the hash for each sentence. The similarity is then based on the set of sentence hashes, which means that policies are taken to be similar if they contain many equal sentences, regardless of their order. To measure search result personalization, Hannak et al. (2013) define sets containing the search results received by different virtual personas. A Jaccard index of 1 indicates no personalization (the search results in both sets are equal), and lower values indicate increasing personalization. Importantly, this does not take into account differences in the ranking of search results.

A variant of the Jaccard index is the *overlap coefficient* which indicates the overlap between two sets A and B, computed as

$$\text{overlap}(A, B) = \frac{|A \cap B|}{\min(|A|, |B|)}.$$

The overlap coefficient is particularly suitable if the sizes of the two sets are very different. In this case, the Jaccard index would indicate low similarity, but the overlap may be high if the smaller set is a subset of the larger set. This has been used, for example, to find the overlap between two communities of users (Ribeiro et al., 2020).

Distance measures can also be used to compute the similarity between ranked lists, such as search results. In this case, it is not just the identity of elements that is important, but the order of elements as well.

A measure for the amount of reordering between two search result lists is the edit distance, such as the *Damerau-Levenshtein distance*. This distance indicates the smallest number of list operations, i.e., insertion, deletion, substitution, or transposition, that are needed to transform one list into the other (Hannak et al., 2013; Le et al., 2019).

The *Kendall Tau distance* indicates how many pairwise disagreements there are between two search result lists. This can be used to define the Kendall rank correlation coefficient which is 1 if the two lists have the same order and -1 if the order is reversed (Cozza et al., 2016).

Finally, the *rank-biased overlap* is a measure suitable for lists with indefinite length where the top items are assumed to be more important than the lower-ranked items (Webber et al., 2010). Because the rank-biased overlap (RBO) applies to lists of infinite length, it iteratively evaluates the agreement A_d between two lists S and T at increasing depths d, so that A_d is the proportion of overlapping elements at depth d. The parameter p determines the top-weightedness. For example, $p = 0.9$ means that the top ten ranks account for 86% of the evaluation. Then, rank-biased overlap is defined as

$$RBO(S, T, p) = (1 - p) \sum_{d=1}^{\infty} p^{d-1} A_d.$$

In the context of search result rankings, Robertson et al. (2018b) found that the top 13 ranks account for 80% of all user clicks and, therefore, they set $p = 0.938$.

6.2 Heuristics for Extracting Response Variables

Heuristics, as practical but not optimal approaches to problem-solving, are often used to extract response variables from collected data, including for tracking, advertising, network traffic, web services, and mobile services. Heuristics are often the only feasible way to extract response variables because many response variables are embedded in a fast-changing, dynamic web environment in custom and nonstandard ways. Although many response variables can be extracted manually with better precision than with heuristics, heuristics allows researchers to automate the process and perform experiments at larger scales.

6.2.1 Heuristics for Detecting Tracking

Heuristics for detecting response variables related to tracking include methods to detect which entities own domains or apps, which cookies can identify users, which third parties can track users, and whether cookie synchronization or fingerprinting are taking place.

Detecting Who Owns a Domain
After identifying domain names, the whois service can be used to find out who the domain owner is. This can be difficult when domain owners use

whois privacy solutions (Clayton and Mansfield, 2014). The use of whois privacy solutions is very common. For example, one study failed to look up information for about 40% of domain names (Gervais et al., 2017). Some studies have discarded domains that use whois privacy solutions (Ren et al., 2018), however, this can severely bias the sample of domains in a study.

Instead, researchers have worked around this limitation with combinations of imperfect methods, for example: by loading the website and, if it redirects to another domain, querying whois for the other domain; by inspecting the whois registration email address; by inspecting the `Organization` field in the website's TLS certificate (Ali et al., 2019b); or by manually investigating the corresponding website (Libert, 2018).

To find out whether the domain owner is a subsidiary of a parent company, researchers have relied on hand-curated lists of parent-subsidiary relationships (Binns et al., 2018b; Libert, 2018), the email addresses in the domain's SOA (Start of Authority) record (Falahrastegar et al., 2016), and databases such as Crunchbase, Hoovers, and opencorporates (Ali et al., 2019b; Binns et al., 2018a).

Analytics services can be used to identify websites that have a common owner (Starov et al., 2018). In particular, when a website owner manages different websites under a common analytics account, the analytics identifier can be used to link groups of websites together. Once the analytics identifier for one website is known, search engines that index website source code can be used to discover other websites using the same identifier.

Detecting Who Owns an App

To detect which organization owns a mobile app, the app store listing and the app binary provide information. Regular expressions can be used to identify host names from the contents of Android APKs (Binns et al., 2018b), and at least one of the identified host names is likely to belong to the app's owner. In addition, the Play store on Android lists the name and contact information of the app's developer. This information can be combined with whois records and with the package names from the APK, for example, to find out whether the domain of the contact email address is contained in a package name (Ren et al., 2018).

Detecting Which Cookies Contain Identifiers

Not all cookies are suitable for tracking users, for example, cookies with generic values that are the same for many users. To track individual users, cookies must contain some form of user identifier either in the cookie name or value.

The heuristic most commonly used for detecting identifying cookies consists of four steps (Englehardt and Narayanan, 2016; Acar et al., 2014; Englehardt et al., 2015).

First, session cookies and cookies with an expiration date of less than 90 days in the future are unlikely to be used for tracking. However, some researchers disregard the cookie lifetime criterion because lifetimes can be updated every time the cookie is accessed (Fouad et al., 2020).

Second, the cookie value is parsed, taking into account common delimiters that separate multiple values stored in a single cookie, such as —, &, and ∴. In addition, the cookie name, or key, also needs to be parsed because some sites store identifiers in the key instead of the value (Fouad et al., 2020).

Third, parsed values that are shorter than eight characters cannot hold enough information to distinguish many users.

Finally, the parsed values are compared across the entire set of experiment results. The values of identifying cookies should remain the same throughout the experiment, and they should differ between measurement machines and between virtual personas. The level of difference between parsed values is often determined via the Ratcliff-Obershelp algorithm which computes a similarity score for two strings. Cookies whose similarity is lower than a threshold similarity are assumed to differ. Different studies have chosen different threshold values, for example: 66% (Englehardt and Narayanan, 2016); 33% (Acar et al., 2014); and 55% (Englehardt et al., 2015), respectively. In addition to computing similarity, some studies have simply labeled cookies as nonidentifying if their value also exists in a different user's browser (Papadopoulos et al., 2019) or if their value occurs in an independent crawl (Fouad et al., 2020).

Detecting Which Third Parties Are Trackers

Third parties are easily identified as hosts whose names differ from the host name of the first-party website. This heuristic can lead to false positives, for example, when websites use a different domain name for their content servers. On mobile devices, third-party domains can be distinguished from first-party domains by checking information on the app store, in TLS certificates, and by checking whether a domains is contacted by apps from more than one developer (Razaghpanah et al., 2018).

However, it is not as straightforward to identify which of these third parties are trackers. A common heuristic is to use public blocklists to identify trackers. For example, advertising-related trackers are likely to be present in EasyList, while nonadvertising trackers are present in EasyPrivacy (Englehardt and Narayanan, 2016). EasyList and EasyPrivacy are often used but not the only options: the Ghostery, Disconnect, Fanboy, and Pi-hole lists are also suitable blocklists (Ali et al., 2019b; Moghaddam et al., 2019). These lists either contain domain names that are always assumed to be trackers, or regular expressions that each HTTP request URL is matched against to check if a specific request in the context of a specific website is a tracker.

Another list-based method to identify trackers is to look up third-party domain names in manually curated lists of known tracking domains (Libert, 2018) or to check whether domains are listed as advertising or tracking in domain classification services (Razaghpanah et al., 2018).

However, the disadvantage of relying on manually curated lists to identify trackers is that they may miss new trackers and may falsely report third parties as trackers. In addition, blocklists can be web-focused and may miss mobile trackers (Binns et al., 2018a).

When used to classify third parties as trackers, these lists should be used only to classify, but not to block. This is because blocking tracking requests can result in missing trackers that would subsequently be loaded by blocked trackers (Iordanou et al., 2018).

Trackers can also be identified from their behaviors, for example, based on the components of their URLs. Domains that include cookie values in URL parameters, and thus leak their cookie values to others, are likely to be trackers (Lerner et al., 2016). HTTP requests with GET arguments that include tracking-related keywords, such as *usermatch*, *rtb*, or *cookiesync*, are also likely to be trackers (Iordanou et al., 2018). In addition, URL parameters can be combined with list-based tracker identification. For example, if the referer in an HTTP request is contained in a list of trackers, and the URL has GET arguments, the requested domain is likely to be a tracker (Iordanou et al., 2018).

Trackers can also be identified by their use of invisible pixels (Fouad et al., 2020). The rationale is that invisible images do not contribute any meaningful content, but are instead a method to send data to third parties. Therefore, domains that provide invisible pixels are likely to be trackers.

On mobile devices, another option to identify trackers is to check whether a domain receives unique identifiers from the user's device (Razaghpanah et al., 2018).

Detecting Cookie Synchronization

Cookie synchronization can be detected by searching for identifying cookie values in HTTP requests, responses, and referers (Englehardt and Narayanan, 2016). For example, the requested domain learns the identifier if the URL of an HTTP request contains an identifier from a cookie, or if an identifier is included in the referer. Additionally, if the domain redirects to a third domain, then the third domain also learns the identifier. Finally, if an identifier is included in the location of an HTTP redirect, then the location domain learns the identifier (Acar et al., 2014). In this case, a cookie synchronization relationship exists if one party has a cookie value that matches a parameter sent to another party (Olejnik et al., 2014).

However, this method relies on the value of the user's cookie being the same as the value used for cookie synchronization. The heuristic fails if the cookie synchronization API uses hashing or encryption, or if its identifiers depend on the website initiating the synchronization. Both are increasingly common. In these cases, it may be possible to detect cookie synchronization by matching against the URL parameters found in the public documentation of cookie synchronization APIs, such as DoubleClick's (Olejnik et al., 2014).

Detecting Fingerprinting

Attempts to fingerprint a user's browser can be detected by analyzing the API calls made by embedded JavaScript. Each fingerprinting attribute needs to be detected separately, and the more attributes are detected, the higher the confidence that the detection relates to an actual fingerprinting attempt.

Possible canvas fingerprinting scripts include all scripts that access *HTML-CanvasElement* or *CanvasRenderingContext2D*. Additional criteria can filter nonfingerprinters from these candidates (Englehardt and Narayanan, 2016; Acar et al., 2014): canvas fingerprinting scripts need a canvas size greater than 16x16px to reliably identify differences between browsers; they typically include text in at least two colors, with more than 10 different characters, and configure the text properties with the *fillText* and *strokeText* methods; they call *toDataURL* or *getImageData*, but do not call *save*, *restore*, or *addEventListener*; and finally, the canvas image must not be requested in a lossy compression format such as JPG.

Scripts perform canvas font fingerprinting if they set the font properties to at least 50 different values and call *measureText* at least 50 times (Englehardt and Narayanan, 2016). WebRTC based fingerprinting relies on the *RTCPeerConnection* interface, uses the *createDataChannel* and *createOffer* methods, and accesses the *onicecandidate* property. AudioContext fingerprinting uses *AudioContext* and *OscillatorNode*. Access to other fingerprinting attributes can be detected by analyzing JavaScript calls to *navigator*, *screen*, *window*, and *HTMLElement* (Lerner et al., 2016).

The Don't FingerPrint Me browser extension[1] includes most of these detection methods (Ali et al., 2019b).

---

[1] https://github.com/freethenation/DFPM

When evaluating fingerprinting countermeasures, it can be important to detect what type of fingerprinting protection is used, or whether the observed fingerprinting attributes are inconsistent. To detect the type of fingerprinting protection, such as attribute standardization or variation, attribute values are compared between a control and treatment configuration. The protection type relies on attribute variation if the attribute value is stable in the control configuration but varies in the treatment configuration. The protection type is attribute standardization if it is stable in the treatment configuration but different from the control. However, if the attribute varies in the control configuration, or if the experiment does not include enough platforms to rule out partial standardization, this method cannot distinguish between protection types (Datta et al., 2019).

To detect inconsistent fingerprinting attributes, each attribute can be checked against values that are typically observed for the reported browser and operating system, which may have been altered by a fingerprinting protection (Vastel et al., 2018b). For example, the client-side *navigator.userAgent* should equal the server-side *User-Agent* header. The client-side *navigator.platform* should be consistent with the operating system from the *User-Agent* string. The WebGL *renderer* and *vendor*, the file names for *navigator.plugins*, and media queries for themes should all be consistent with values that are expected for the user's the operating system. In addition, error messages, internal function representations, the navigator object, and browser features should be consistent with the user's browser, while browser events and sensors should be consistent with the user's platform.

Detecting Other Tracking Methods

As new tracking methods are uncovered, researchers continue to devise new methods for detecting these new trackers. In recent years, this has included redirect tracking, pixel tracking in emails, and cross-device tracking.

Redirect tracking can be detected by monitoring the domains loaded as the top window document. All domains except the first and last in a redirect chain are potential redirect trackers. Among these, redirects that set a first-party identifying cookie during the redirect are likely trackers (Koop et al., 2020).

Pixel tracking in emails relies on embedded images and can therefore be detected by analyzing the URLs of these images. The URL is a likely tracker if the URL contains the recipient's email address or obfuscated email address, and if the image is invisible (HTML tags *hidden* or *invisible*) or its size is below a threshold (Hu et al., 2019b).

Probabilistic cross-device tracking relies on various heuristics and can therefore be difficult to detect directly. Instead, researchers have focused on detecting features that would allow cross-device tracking, such as the sharing of potentially hashed identifiers with third parties (Brookman et al., 2017), and on detecting the effects of cross-device tracking, for example, by observing desktop ads after mobile browsing (Zimmeck et al., 2017; Solomos et al., 2019).

6.2.2 Heuristics for Advertising

Several types of response variables for advertising can be extracted from raw collected data: ads and their properties, ad traffic, types of ad targeting, the identities of advertisers, and properties of the advertising technologies.

Detecting Ads

Detecting ads in HTTP responses or DOM trees is challenging because advertising relies on a complex DOM structure, deep nesting of elements, and dynamic JavaScript execution (Liu et al., 2013). As a result, the crawler either needs to be based on a full browser, or needs to be able to execute JavaScript (Barford et al., 2014). In addition, some ad platforms attempt to defeat automatic detection of ads by frequently updating the names of advertising-related DOM elements (Merrill and Tobin, 2019).

One of the simplest methods to identify ads is to use filter lists provided by ad blockers. This can be achieved either by modifying an ad blocker so that any match with the filter list is labeled as an ad instead of blocked (Lecuyer et al., 2015), or by separately matching the URL, iFrame URL, div class, and landing page URL of candidate elements against the filter list (Barford et al., 2014; Liu et al., 2013). Candidate elements are all `iFrame`, `img`, and `embed` tags in the DOM. In addition to matching the filter list, the elements can also be checked for their dimension to ensure that they match a standard ad dimension, and their links can be checked to verify that they point to an external resource (Barford et al., 2014).

On some platforms, it can be easier to detect ads by looking for specific DOM elements. For example, researchers have extracted ads from Facebook by finding the *Sponsored* tag in the DOM (Andreou et al., 2019; Silva et al., 2020), which works for both ads that appear as posts in the main news feed and ads that appear on the right-hand side.

Besides the properties of the ad creative – the ad's image and text – the ad's URL and the associated landing page are often recorded because they allow researchers to associate a topic category with the ad and to identify who the advertiser is by detecting the owner of the corresponding domain (Galán et al., 2019). Landing pages can be identified by analyzing the ad URL. The ad URL may directly point to the advertiser's landing page, however, in many cases, the

URL points to an advertising or analytics server first, which then redirects to the landing page. In these cases, the landing page URL can be extracted from URL parameters. For example, 80% of ad landing pages can be extracted by matching patterns like *adurl=* or *redirecturl=* (Liu et al., 2013).

To classify the topic of landing pages, researchers have used online tagging services such as McAfee (Galán et al., 2019; Solomos et al., 2019), Alexa (Ullah et al., 2014), Google AdWords, or Cyren (Carrascosa et al., 2015). Different tagging services can be combined to obtain more robust results, for example, by using keywords only if they are assigned by more than one service. The coverage of tagging services tends to be high: 95% of URLs in the dataset collected by Carrascosa et al. (2015) were found in a tagging service.

To detect specific types of ads, such as political ads or malvertising, additional work is needed to detect whether an ad matches the desired type. For political ads, ads can be manually labeled as political or nonpolitical (Silva et al., 2020). In addition, Facebook offers a library of known political ads.[2] For malvertising, researchers have relied on VirusTotal (Liu et al., 2020) as well as different malware and phishing blocklists (Zarras et al., 2014) to classify ads as malicious or benign.

Detecting Ad Traffic

Ad traffic consists of all traffic that is used by the advertising ecosystem to serve ads. It consists of signaling traffic for accounting and control, content delivery traffic, and analytics traffic (Ullah et al., 2014). The most commonly used heuristic to identify ad traffic is to rely on ad block filter lists (Pujol et al., 2015). This method works for both active and passive data collection.

On mobile devices, another way to identify ad traffic is based on lists of known ad libraries and known ad domains. Both lists are expanded as more traffic is analyzed: when an HTTP request to a known ad domain is observed, the originating library is added to list of ad libraries; and when a known ad library makes a request to a new domain, this domain is added to the list of ad domains (Liu et al., 2020).

Once ad traffic has been identified, the ad responses contained in the traffic can be used to detect the content of ad impressions by analyzing embedded images, scripts, and URLs (Liu et al., 2020). However, not every ad response corresponds to an ad impression because ad impressions can be resold. In this case, the ad response can initiate a new ad request (Nath, 2015; Crussell et al., 2014).

---

[2] www.facebook.com/politicalcontentads

Ad clicks on mobile devices can be detected by analyzing the *request tree* of the corresponding ad request. When an ad has been clicked, the subtree of the ad request often contains an HTTP redirection because ads often communicate with the ad server first before receiving the ad content from the advertiser (Nath, 2015; Crussell et al., 2014).

Ad traffic can also be used to identify users of ad blockers (Pujol et al., 2015). Two heuristics are useful to detect ad blocker users: first, they are expected to make fewer ad requests than users who do not use an ad blocker, and second, they are expected to make requests to the servers hosting updated versions of the ad block filter list.

Detecting Targeting Types

To detect how observed ads have been targeted, i.e., why the user has been served this ad and not another, heuristics can be used to distinguish between static ads, contextual ads, demographic or geographic ads, profile-based ads, and retargeted ads. Researchers are often interested in only one type of targeting, and in this case the heuristics follow a process of exclusion where a series of criteria defines how ads with a different targeting type can be filtered out.

To detect behavioral or profile-based targeting, Carrascosa et al. (2015) filter out contextual ads, retargeted ads, static ads, demographic ads, and geographic ads. For retargeted ads, they compare the ad's landing page with the sites previously visited by the virtual persona. If the persona has visited the ad's landing page, the ad is a potential retargeted ad. Ads that are collected with a clean browser profile can be static, contextual, or geographic, but they cannot be targeted at a user's profile and thus can be filtered. To filter demographic and geographic ads, they analyze virtual personas that have received the same ad. If these personas have dissimilar behavior, the ad cannot be targeted at the persona's profile.

An alternative approach to distinguish profile-based and contextual ads is to compute the similarity of the ad's landing page with the interest categories from the user's profile, and with the category of the website or app where the ad is displayed. After filtering static ads, i.e, ads that are delivered to all virtual personas, ads are labeled as contextual if their similarity with the website or app category is high. On the other hand, if the similarity with the user's interest categories is high, the ad is profile-based (Ullah et al., 2014).

To detect retargeted ads, Bashir et al. (2016) combine four criteria. First, the ad image has to be larger than 50x50 pixels. Second, ads that are shown to a control persona that did not visit any e-commerce sites cannot be retargeted. Third, ads shown to more than one persona cannot be retargeted if all personas were configured to visit different e-commerce sites. Finally, the remaining ad images are manually labeled to decide whether the ad image matches the categories and e-commerce sites visited by the virtual persona. This manual step is needed if ads are not clicked and thus the true landing page is unknown.

Detecting Bidding Technologies

Real-time bidding messages are only partially observable from the client-side. In particular, the bid requests and bid responses exchanged between the ad exchange and the bidders cannot be observed. However, messages exchanged with the user's browser can be observed, and this includes messages from the ad exchange that contain the ad and the winning bid price as well as a message sent to the winning bidder that contains the winning price notification (Olejnik et al., 2014). These messages can be detected by comparing recorded HTTP requests and responses with public documentation of RTB message formats, for example, from DoubleClick or the IAB. The winning price notifications sometimes contain clear-text prices, but increasingly the price is encrypted, for example, following a format specified by Google (Olejnik et al., 2014; Papadopoulos et al., 2017).

In header bidding, a larger portion of the message exchange can be observed by the client. Pachilakis et al. (2019) propose three methods to detect the presence of header bidding. First, websites can be analyzed statically, for example, with regular expressions, to determine if they include well-known header bidding libraries, such as `prebid.js`, `gpt.js`, or `pubfood.js`. However, this method leads to both false positives and false negatives when unrelated JavaScript libraries use the same names or when header bidding libraries are renamed, respectively. Second, DOM events caused by header bidding can be detected from within the browser. This can be achieved by adding event listeners for relevant events, for example, for the end of the bidding phase (*auctionEnd*), after the winning bidder has been determined (*bidWon*), or after an ad has been successfully rendered (*slotRenderEnded*). When a DOM event is triggered, the subsequent HTTP requests should be recorded because they contain potential response variables such as the bids received, the bidder who won, the CPM, the ad size, or the currency. Third, header bidding can be detected on the network level by analyzing HTTP requests sent to header bidding entities. Based on a list of well-known header bidding Demand Partners, HTTP requests and responses to those partners can be monitored. In addition, HTTP requests and responses can also be monitored for the presence of header bidding parameters such as *bidder*, *hb_partner*, or *hb_price*.

6.2.3 Heuristics for Analyzing Network Traffic

Response variables that are often extracted from network traffic include media files and personally identifiable information (PII).

A common method to extract media from network traffic is to rely on the tool MediaExtract[3] which recognizes a wide range of file formats by analyzing the file headers (Pan et al., 2018).

To recognize PII in network traffic, researchers commonly use experimental designs that allow control over the exact values of PII such as names and email addresses. This allows choosing unique PII values that can be distinguished from other information in the traffic (Leung et al., 2016; Ren et al., 2016; Starov et al., 2016). In the simplest case, the PII is transmitted as-is and can be recognized easily.

However, a challenge with detecting both media and PII in network traffic is that the information is often encoded (e.g., base64, Unicode, gzip), encrypted, or otherwise obfuscated.

Deterministic obfuscation can be detected by repeating the experiment three times: twice with identical PII and once with control PII. A potential PII leak is then detected if the same parameters are detected in HTTP requests for the first two experiments, but different ones for the third (Starov et al., 2016).

Another method to detect obfuscated information leakage is to attempt de-obfuscation. For example, Pan et al. (2018) decode base64 encodings before using MediaExtract to detect encoded media files. However, base64 is not the only encoding method that can be used: Starov and Nikiforakis (2017b) have observed URL encoding, repeated base64 encoding, compression with gzip, and JSON packing, as well as combinations of these methods. Since the corresponding decoding methods are not computationally expensive, it can be feasible to try several decoding methods to check for PII leaks.

Differential analysis is a similar but more refined method designed to detect PII leaks even when the app performs encryption and obfuscation, and even with multiple nested instances of encryption and obfuscation (Continella et al., 2017). For example, they observed an app which hashed the Android ID with SHA-1, then XOR'ed with a random key, then encoded with base64, then appended to a JSON string, then encrypted with RSA, then encoded again with base64, and finally sent over the network. They first instrument Android to replace API calls that are sources of nondeterminism, like random values, timing, or data received from the network, with deterministic versions, and record nondeterministic API calls where replacement was not possible. Then, they execute apps multiple times to establish a baseline for the app's network

---

[3] https://github.com/panzi/mediaextract

traffic. Finally, they vary PII on the device and observe nondeterminism in the subsequent network traffic. They use the Needleman-Wunsch algorithm to align strings between network requests and quantify how much the new traffic differs from the baseline with the Hamming and Levenshtein distances.

6.2.4 Heuristics for Web Services

Heuristics for web services have been designed to detect similar JavaScript on different websites, the policies and cookie banners used on websites, the demographics of users, the political leaning of websites, and instances of server-side blocking.

Detecting Similar or Obfuscated JavaScript

Methods to detect similar JavaScript used by multiple websites are used to detect similar functionality, such as similar methods to detect use of ad blockers (Nithyanand et al., 2016; Mughees et al., 2017).

Two heuristics have been used to compute similarity between JS. The first method starts by removing reserved words from the JS code and then represents each JS file with a vector of keyword weights computed with tf-idf. Similarity can then be computed using the cosine similarity between tf-idf vectors (Nithyanand et al., 2016). Although this method is insensitive to white space, rearranging of code, and small changes to the code, it fails for obfuscated JS. The second method parses each JS file to create its abstract syntax tree (AST) and then transforms each AST into a node sequence by traversing the AST in fixed order. Finally, a vector is created that contains the frequency of each node in the sequence, and similarity can be computed based on this vector (Mughees et al., 2017). ASTs represent the logical structure of code and as such are not sensitive to changes in variable names. This makes AST-based similarity suitable for obfuscated code.

Based on one of these similarity measures, JS from the same source can be detected through maximal clique finding (Nithyanand et al., 2016) or clustering (Mughees et al., 2017). For maximal clique finding, each JS is regarded as a node. Edges between nodes are added if their similarity is above a threshold. The maximal cliques in the resulting graph indicate JavaScript that comes from the same source. The threshold can be calibrated to achieve a desired true positive rate. For example, Nithyanand et al. (2016) used a threshold of 0.8 to achieve a true positive rate of 0.85. For clustering, Principal Component Analysis (PCA) can be used to reduce the dimensionality of vectors, and clusters can be identified visually in two- or three-dimensional plots (Mughees et al., 2017).

Methods for detecting obfuscated JavaScript are important because they allow treating obfuscated JavaScript differently, for example, by attempting de-obfuscation. A combination of static and dynamic analysis can be used to detect whether JavaScript code is obfuscated: browser API calls are monitored during execution of the JavaScript code (i.e., dynamic analysis), and code is obfuscated when these calls are inconsistent with static analysis of the source code (Sarker et al., 2020).

Detecting Policies and Cookie Banners

The presence of cookie banners on websites can be detected by matching the website's DOM against a manually curated list of CSS elements used in cookie banners, for example, from the "I don't care about cookies" browser extension (van Eijk et al., 2019). This method can result in false negatives if new CSS elements have not yet been included in the manually curated list, and in false positives if websites use CSS elements with the same names for different purposes.

The privacy policies used by websites can be detected by analyzing the links on a website. Links that contain keywords that are often used for privacy policies, either in their URL or title, can then be followed to find the privacy policy. The list of keywords often includes *privacy*, *statement*, *notice*, and *policy* (Linden et al., 2020). However, for non-English websites privacy policies are usually written, and linked to, in the local language. It can therefore be necessary to compile a dictionary of phrases that indicate privacy policies in different languages. For example, Degeling et al. (2019) have created such a dictionary for 24 languages spoken in Europe.

To extract the text of a privacy policy, researchers have used tools that remove a website's headers and footers and only retain its main text, such as Boilerpipe (Degeling et al., 2019) or Mozilla's Readability.js library (Libert, 2018).

Heuristics can also be used to process the content of privacy policies (Libert, 2018). For example, whether a policy mentions trackers found on the website can be determined by searching the policy text for the name of the domain owner and its parent organizations. Similarly, compliance with the *DNT* header can be detected by searching for the corresponding text in the policy and manually labeling whether the policy states that *DNT* is respected or not. It is also possible to judge how easy policies are to read by computing readability measures such as the Flesch Reading Ease (Shipp and Blasco, 2020).

Detecting User Demographics

Facebook's ad audience size estimation tool can be used to detect the demographics of a website's audience (Ribeiro et al., 2018). By targeting ads at the website's Facebook page, the estimated ad audience size includes only users who have liked that page. The demographics of these users can then be used as a proxy to measure the true demographics of the website's audience. To retrieve estimated demographics, the audience size estimate has to be recorded once for each demographic attribute by setting targeting attributes to the website's Facebook page plus the demographic attribute.

To detect the gender of website users, different tools are available that try to guess gender based on lists of first names (e.g., baby name datasets) or lists of first names, last names, and countries. These tools include genderComputer,[4] Gender Guesser,[5] and Genni[6] (Chen et al., 2018; May et al., 2019). However, these tools can be imprecise. For example, May et al. (2019) found that their manual labels only agreed with 44% of labels for female names classified by genderComputer. They were able to increase accuracy (to 84% agreement for female names) by combining two tools and labeling names only when both tools agree.

Detecting Political Leaning

The political leaning of websites, news outlets, or tweets is often used to analyze biases in search ranking algorithms. There are three main approaches to detect political leaning: audience-based, content-based, and rater-based.

Content-based approaches are based on linguistic features that measure differential use of phrases. Content-based approaches rely on accurately labeled training data and can be computationally expensive. In addition, they may be inaccurate when text samples are very small, such as tweets (Robertson et al., 2018a).

Rater-based approaches rely on human raters to evaluate political leaning. However, rater-based approaches can be expensive and suffer from rater bias (Robertson et al., 2018a). A well-known source of rater-based estimates that follows a defined methodology to minimize rater bias is Media Bias/Fact Check,[7] which provides estimates for 1,500 media domains (Le et al., 2019).

Audience-based approaches are based on the principle of homophily, which assumes that the political leaning of a news outlet is similar to the political leaning of its audience. However, audience-based approaches can be limited if they rely on self-reported political affiliations or on black-box classifications by ad platforms such as Facebook (Robertson et al., 2018a).

---

[4] https://github.com/tue-mdse/genderComputer
[5] https://pypi.org/project/gender-guesser/
[6] http://abel.lis.illinois.edu/cgi-bin/genni/search.cgi
[7] https://mediabiasfactcheck.com

Because information about audiences is increasingly more available through social media and advertiser interfaces, several audience-based approaches have been proposed in recent years. For example, Kulshrestha et al. (2017) detect the political leaning of Twitter users by comparing their interest vectors with the interest vectors of prototypical left- and right-leaning users. Interest vectors are tf-idf vectors defined by the topics that each user's followers have been tagged with. Ribeiro et al. (2018) detect the political leaning of news outlets by analyzing how many Facebook users with each political leaning are reported by Facebook's ad audience estimation tool when targeting the news outlet and a particular political leaning. Finally, Robertson et al. (2018a) have linked Twitter accounts to US voter records – which indicate whether the voter is a registered Democrat (left-leaning) or Republican (right-leaning) – based on names and locations indicated in Twitter profiles. To determine the political leaning of URLs included in tweets from these users, a bias score can be computed based on the frequency with which Democratic and Republican users shared each URL.

Detecting Server-Side Blocking

Websites use server-side blocking to restrict access for some users, for example, based on the user's geographic region or use of anonymizing services like Tor.

To distinguish websites that are unavailable due to server-side blocking from those that are unavailable due to censorship or ISP blocking, Afroz et al. (2018) have designed heuristics to exclude the latter two. A combination of the path lengths reported by *traceroute* and whether TCP responses are spoofed can determine if HTTP requests are blocked before they arrive at the server, which indicates censorship or ISP blocking, or if the server receives the request but does not serve a website, which indicates server-side blocking.

Some websites implement server-side blocking by serving block pages instead of ignoring HTTP requests. To detect whether a website is a block page instead of the requested website, heuristics based on page length, clustering, and comparisons with known block pages can be used. The page length heuristic relies on the idea that block pages are typically shorter than the requested pages (McDonald et al., 2018). However, the accuracy of this heuristic depends on the type of block page which means that the heuristic should not be used on its own. Instead, it can be combined with clustering to identify groups of block pages from a set of candidates. The number of clusters is small enough to inspect each cluster manually and identify the type of block page. Comparisons with known block pages rely either on the frequency of

HTML tags, represented as a vector, for both potential and known block pages, or on clustering based on the block page text (Niaki et al., 2020).

6.2.5 Heuristics for Mobile Services

The most commonly used heuristics for mobile services are to detect the use of third-party libraries, and to detect the release dates of libraries to allow for versioning.

The simplest approach to detect third-party libraries is to match the library name against a list of known package names (He et al., 2019). The main disadvantage of this approach is that it can only work if the library does not use obfuscation which changes the package names (Ma et al., 2016). However, because the approach is much faster than alternative approaches, it can be used as a first step to identify nonobfuscated libraries.

To identify obfuscated libraries, signatures for each library can be compared with signatures of known libraries and clustered to detect when the same library is used in different apps. Signatures can be based on different features, including the call frequency of Android APIs (Ma et al., 2016), the reference and inheritance relationships between classes and methods (Li et al., 2018, 2017a), and the function call graph (He et al., 2019). To detect obfuscated libraries in new apps, these approaches rely on a database of signatures that is generated in a precomputation step. This step can be time-consuming depending on the number of apps and the complexity of the signature. Over time, the precomputed signature databases become obsolete when new libraries and new library versions are released, and thus have to be updated incrementally (Ma et al., 2016) or recomputed from scratch (Wang et al., 2018).

The release dates and versions of third-party libraries are not listed explicitly in the app binary. Signature-based approaches are suitable to detect library versions (Ma et al., 2016) but a hash over the entire library can also be used as a version string (Book et al., 2013). Based on the detected versions, the release date of an app that contains a third-party library can serve as an upper bound for the release dates of the library because the library must have been released prior to the release of the app. This upper bound can become reasonably tight if a large corpus of apps is analyzed (Book et al., 2013).

6.3 Machine Learning and Natural Language Processing

Machine learning and natural language processing are useful in transparency research when manual analysis is too time-consuming in large-scale experiments and when manually defined heuristics are not good enough to correctly

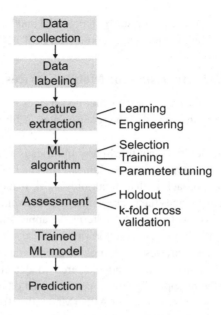

Figure 6.1 Overview of the process for developing a machine learning model.

classify all cases. This section discusses machine learning approaches that can help answer research questions in transparency research, for example, by labeling response variables in collected data.

Machine learning can be grouped into supervised and unsupervised approaches (Murphy, 2012). Supervised machine learning is used to predict categories (*classification*) or numeric values (*regression*), and unsupervised learning is used to group data (*clustering*). To create a machine learning model (see Figure 6.1), the first step is to collect relevant data that will be used to train and test the model. When using a supervised model, the next step is then to label the data instances, for example, with the true categories that the model will be trained to predict. The next step involves extracting features from the data. Machine learning algorithms learn to associate vectors of features with the corresponding labels (classification) or to group vectors (clustering). Feature extraction is therefore a critically important step that can influence the performance of the trained model. Feature engineering is a manual process for extracting features, possibly with the help of data mining algorithms. Feature engineering can also be aided by unsupervised learning methods such as dimensionality reduction. After features have been extracted, the machine learning algorithm can be selected, configured, and trained.

Training is usually performed on a subset of the collected data (often 70%), and the remainder of the data is used to evaluate the performance of the trained model. There are different methods for splitting the collected data into training and testing sets. The Holdout method simply splits the data into fixed training and testing sets according to the specified percentage. The problem with this approach is that a *lucky* split can have a large impact on the performance of the model, so that repeating the training with a different split can lead to different results. To counter this disadvantage, the k-fold cross validation method splits the data into k random subsets. Then, k experiments are performed where each experiment uses one of the k subsets for testing and the remaining $k - 1$ subsets for training. The results from the k experiments can then be averaged to estimate the true model performance. Most of the classifiers discussed in this section use k-fold cross validation with $k = 5$ or $k = 10$.

Model performance is commonly evaluated using four metrics: accuracy, precision, recall, and F1 score. They are computed based on the numbers of true positive samples (TP), true negatives (TN), false positives (FP), and false negatives (FN) observed during the testing phase. The precision p indicates the portion of positive results that are truly positive:

$$p = \frac{TP}{TP + FP}.$$

Recall r, or true positive rate, indicates how many of the truly positive results were classified correctly by the model:

$$r = \frac{TP}{TP + FN}.$$

Accuracy a indicates the portion of all data points that were classified correctly:

$$a = \frac{TP + TN}{TP + TN + FP + FN}.$$

Finally, the F1 score is the harmonic mean between precision and recall:

$$F = 2 \times \frac{p \times r}{p + r}.$$

These metrics can also be generalized for use with multi-class classifiers.

Natural language processing applies machine learning techniques to text (Clark et al., 2013). In a first step, text is preprocessed, for example, by separating sentences, converting to lowercase letters, and stemming. Stemming algorithms such as Porter-Stemmer detect and normalize word endings so that, for example, *walk*, *walks*, *walked*, and *walking* can be recognized as the same word.

In a second step, text is represented as a numerical feature vector so it can be used as input for machine learning. For example, a bag-of-words consists of the number of times a word occurs in a text. For a set of texts, bag-of-word models can be constructed based on the combined vocabulary of the texts, and feature vectors are chosen as the vector of frequencies without the vocabulary. More advanced word embeddings, based on neural networks, are available in software packages like Word2vec, GloVe, BERT, fastText, or Gensim.

The remainder of this section introduces machine learning models that have been used in transparency research, explaining what each model does, for example, classification or clustering, what data was used to train the model, which features were extracted from the data, and which machine learning algorithms were chosen.

6.3.1 Classifiers for Tracking

To overcome the shortcomings of identifying trackers based on manually curated filter lists, researchers have used machine learning classifiers to identify trackers, for example, based on HTTP requests or JavaScript programs.

To detect trackers based on HTTP traffic, Li et al. (2015) focus on cookie-based third-party tracking. Their input data consists of HTTP requests and responses to/from third-party websites that were recorded while crawling a set of first-party websites. The data was manually labeled based on an inspection of the third-party website, look-up in blocklists, and inspection of the cookie properties. From this HTTP traffic, they extract all cookies and compute three features: the minimum cookie lifetime, the number of third-party cookies, and the augmented lifetime, i.e., the sum over cookie lifetimes multiplied by the length of the cookie value. These features were identified from a larger set of candidate features using recursive feature elimination. The chosen machine learning algorithm is a binary support vector machine (SVM). It is important to note that the features used in this classifier closely resemble the heuristics that have been designed to detect cookies carrying user identifiers.

In contrast, two classifiers that have been designed to detect whether a given JavaScript program performs tracking use much larger features sets that do not resemble any of the heuristics introduced above (Ikram et al., 2017b; Wu et al., 2016). Both classifiers use 2,000 JavaScript programs collected by visiting a sample of websites, but differ in their approaches for labeling and feature extraction. JavaScript programs can be labeled manually based on a set of twelve rules (Ikram et al., 2017b), or by matching against Ghostery, EasyList, and EasyPrivacy (Wu et al., 2016). Features can be based on the

JavaScript APIs used in a JavaScript program, or on a tf-idf representation of the JavaScript programs. To create the tf-idf representation, Ikram et al. (2017b) use a beautifier to format each JS program and use the lines as terms for tf-idf, selecting the top 200 terms and the 7-grams, i.e., sets of 7 lines, as features. For both classifiers, SVM, C4.5 decision trees, and random forests performed best, with accuracies above 96%. Importantly, both classifiers were able to identify more trackers than were included in manually curated filter lists.

Another approach to identifying trackers is based on text extracted from the candidate tracker's landing page and from search results for "about <tracker domain>" (Razaghpanah et al., 2018). All words, bi-grams and tri-grams found in the tokenized text were used as features, and the final feature vector was constructed as the normalized count of feature occurrences. A linear-kernel SVM classifier, trained on text for 4,000 domains – half tracking samples from EasyList, and half benign samples from the Alexa list – achieved an F1 score of 0.95.

On mobile devices, the process of labeling HTTP requests as tracking or nontracking can be improved by first labeling third-party libraries (Shuba and Markopoulou, 2020). This approach greatly reduces the effort to create a labeled training dataset because there are much fewer candidate libraries than HTTP requests. Based on a list of known tracking libraries, the stack traces for outgoing requests can be inspected to determine whether the request originated from a tracking library or not. The labeled dataset can then be used to train classifiers, such as decision trees, that label HTTP requests based on a bag-of-words representation of the request.

To detect cookie synchronization even when the synchronized identifiers are hashed or encrypted, Papadopoulos et al. (2019) built a classifier that uses HTTP requests as input data. To label true cookie sync events, they used a heuristic (see above) to identify cleartext cookie sync events. The features extracted from the HTTP requests included the domain of the recipient, the type of recipient company (content distribution, social, advertising, analytics, or other), the URL, referrer, names of URL parameters, HTTP status code, browser, and number of parameters. Based on these features, a decision tree classifier was found to perform better than SVM or random forest, with an average F1 score of 0.98.

To detect whether two browser fingerprints, collected at different times, belong to the same browser instance, Vastel et al. (2018a) built a classifier based on a dataset of fingerprints collected over two years. The dataset included ground truth labels that identified the browser instance for each fingerprint. The features extracted from this dataset, computed for pairs of fingerprints, included binary indicators for each attribute indicating whether the attribute value is equal, the similarity between the attribute values, the number of changed attributes, and the time difference between the fingerprints.

Features were selected based on an evaluation of feature importance and a random forest classifier was trained. A random forest is an ensemble of decision tree classifiers. It is often used because decision trees are robust against outliers and the nodes in a decision tree can be used to explain the outcome of the classifier. Their classifier was able to correctly link fingerprints for 54 days, compared to 42 days for a rule-based algorithm.

6.3.2 Classifiers for Advertising

To detect ad impressions and ad clicks in HTTP traffic, particularly from mobile devices, features can be extracted from request trees, URL parameters, and HTTP headers (Crussell et al., 2014). Because their input dataset was imbalanced – it contained many more benign HTTP requests than ad-related requests – they used the SMOTE algorithm to oversample the minority class. This can improve the classifier's sensitivity to the minority class. Their random forest classifier achieved an accuracy of 85%.

To estimate the prices for real-time bidding auctions that use encrypted bid price notifications, Papadopoulos et al. (2017) attempt to predict the winning price of an ad auction based on the HTTP requests that contain the encrypted price. The ground truth for ad prices is drawn from two sources: prices from cleartext RTB auctions, and prices from their own ad campaigns. They identify more than 200 features that may explain the variability in ad prices, including the time of the auction, the HTTP headers, the ad content, the DSP, the publisher, and the user's interests and location. They use dimensionality reduction and feature importance estimation to reduce the number of features. They find that regression models, which would be able to give a numerical estimate of ad price, perform badly due to highly variable prices. Instead, a random forest classifier that only estimates which of four price ranges a price is in, performs better with a precision of 83%.

To detect the topic category of an ad, Nath (2015) constructs a classifier based on the content of the ad's landing page. To train the classifier, they use the top 1,000 websites from each Alexa category and use the category as the ground truth label. Notably, their training data does not explicitly include landing pages of real ads. They extract features from the title and keywords in the HTML header by removing stop words, applying a stemming algorithm, and constructing a bag-of-words consisting of stemmed words and 2-grams. Based on this bag-of-words feature representation, Nath (2015) uses multi-class logistic regression to classify the topics of ad landing pages, which achieves 76% accuracy across all categories.

Instead of identifying the topic of ads directly, classifiers can also be used to detect whether an ad belongs to a certain category. For example, Silva et al. (2020) use a Convolutional Neural Network to identify which ads on Facebook are political. Neural network classifiers are more complex to design than other machine learning models because they consist of several interconnected layers. The composition, connection, and configuration of these layers opens a large design space and it can be difficult to determine how a neural network needs to be changed to improve its performance. For example, Silva et al. (2020) use a continuous bag-of-words model to encode the text of Facebook ads, and then use a sequence of layers (see Figure 6.2): a dropout regularization layer, a convolutional layer, a ReLU activation layer, a max-pooling layer, another ReLU activation layer, and another dropout layer. The output layer is a sigmoid activation function that generates the political/nonpolitical label. This classifier achieved an accuracy of 94%.

Natural language processing can also be used to detect which of Facebook's ad preferences are likely to be sensitive in the sense of data protection regulation, i.e., related to ethnicity, political opinions, religious beliefs, health, and sex life or sexual orientation (Cabañas et al., 2018). Facebook assigns ad preferences to users from a pool of over 120,000 different preferences. Since this is too large for manual analysis, NLP can be used as a prefiltering step by computing the semantic similarity between Facebook ad preferences and words from sensitive categories. Ad preferences with a similarity score above a threshold (e.g., 0.6) can then be classified by experts. To construct a word list for sensitive categories, Cabañas et al. (2018) use a list of controversial issues on Wikipedia. This process identified 4,400 potentially sensitive ad preferences, 2,000 of which were verified as sensitive by experts.

Two machine learning models have been proposed to detect anti-ad blockers. The first aims to classify whether a website is using an anti-ad blocker or not (Mughees et al., 2017), while the second classifies whether JavaScript code is an anti-ad blocker (Iqbal et al., 2017). For the first approach, the input data consisted of the HTML content of websites. Benign websites were chosen from the Alexa toplist, and known anti-ad block websites were added from anti-ad block filter lists. Both were visited with and without an ad blocker, and features were constructed based on these pairs of visits. Features included changes in the number of HTML tags, tag attributes, lines, words, and characters, the cosine similarity of the entire HTML document, and changes in the URL. A random forest classifier was found to perform better than decision trees or Naive Bayes, with a precision of 94% (Mughees et al., 2017).

For the second approach, input data consisted of 1 million JS snippets that were not identified as anti-ad block by filter lists and 372 anti-ad block scripts from crowdsourced filter lists. The anti-ad block label was manually verified for 10% of scripts. Features were constructed based on the abstract syntax trees of the JS snippets and included all text elements, text elements from literals, and text elements from keywords of JS and the JS Web API. This approach generated a very large number of features (1.7 million for the text elements alone). The feature set was narrowed down by removing duplicate features and features that did not vary much. Then, features were ranked according to their chi-square correlation, and the top 1,000 features were selected. Because the input dataset was imbalanced – it contained few anti-ad block samples compared to benign samples – AdaBoost was selected as an ensemble classifier that builds a meta-classifier from multiple weak classifiers during several rounds. The classifier achieved a recall of 99% (Iqbal et al., 2017).

6.3.3 Classifiers for Analyzing Network Traffic

Machine learning can also identify data in network traffic, for example, PII (Ren et al., 2016) and other data types including geolocations (Jin et al., 2018).

To classify whether an outgoing HTTP request contains PII or not, Ren et al. (2016) combine natural language processing for feature extraction and decision trees for classification. Their input data consisted of traffic from 950 apps, some of which contained unique PII values that could labeled based on heuristics. Features were then defined by identifying delimiters in HTTP requests (e.g., ,;/(){}[/]), defining text between delimiters as words, and constructing a bag-of-words model based on these words. To reduce the number of features, words with low frequency were removed, and rare PII leaks were oversampled to ensure that they were not removed. The general-purpose classifier achieved an accuracy of 80%. Classifiers for individual domains were not only faster to train but also performed better.

To detect and label arbitrary data types in network traffic, Jin et al. (2018) combine generative NLP and Bayesian classification. Generative NLP reduces the need for manually labeled training data because it requires only a small initial set of manually identified patterns, for example, common key names for data types such as locations, email addresses, unique identifiers, and network addresses. For each pattern, matching keys and values in key-value pairs observed in traffic are identified and the most frequent text patterns are added to the pattern set. This step is repeated until the size of the pattern set stabilizes. The probabilistic Bayesian classifier then uses key-value pairs extracted from traffic as input and determines what the pair's data type is, achieving a precision of 93% or higher, depending on the data type.

6.3.4 Classifiers for Web Services

Machine learning classifiers for web services can be used to detect the topic of a website, classify malicious behaviors, and analyze the contents of privacy policies.

Detecting Topics of Websites

Similar to the landing pages for ads, the topics of websites in general can be detected through heuristics such as online tagging services (Carrascosa et al., 2015). However, this can be inaccurate if a single domain offers a variety of content categories, or if the category of interest is not present in an online tagging service, such as parked domains. In addition, the labeling methods and taxonomies differ significantly between domain classification services, and many services have low coverage especially for less popular domains. As a result, the selection of domain classification service should be considered carefully to ensure that it matches the needs of the study (Vallina et al., 2020).

To detect the topic of a website in general, topic modeling based on tf-idf can be used. To prepare for topic modeling, a list of topics and a corpus with documents for the categories of interest is needed. For example, Weinshel et al. (2019) used the 1,932 Google AdWords categories as topic list and the top 10 Wikipedia articles for each topic as document corpus. The corpus was preprocessed by extracting the 1,000 most relevant words for each topic with tf-idf. To prepare websites for classification, they were preprocessed by extracting visible text and HTML metadata, removing stop words and non-English words, and applying a stemming algorithm. For each topic T, a weighted matching score can then be computed between the words on the website W and the relevant words for the topic as

$$\text{score}_T = \sum_{i=0}^{1,000} \sum_{K_i^T \in W} \frac{1}{i},$$

where K_i^T is the i-th most relevant word for topic T. The highest-scoring topic is then taken as the inferred topic for the website. The accuracy of this approach, evaluated through a user study, reached 61% and was similar to the performance of a long short-term memory network (LSTM), but much quicker (Weinshel et al., 2019).

To detect whether a given domain is a parked domain, Vissers et al. (2015) developed a random forest classifier based on the web content of 3,000 verified parked domains and 3,000 verified nonparked domains from the Alexa list. Their classifier used 21 features, including the average and maximum link length, the average HTML length, the external link ratio, and the presence of redirection mechanisms. Based on these features, they train a random forest classifier, which achieves a true positive rate above 97%. The random forest classification threshold can be adjusted to achieve different trade-offs between true positive and true negative rates.

Similarly, random forests can be used to detect whether a domain is a free live streaming (FLIS) domain (Rafique et al., 2016). To collect input data, FLIS domains have to be located manually through search engines. The non-FLIS pages in the input dataset can be selected either randomly from the Alexa list or from Alexa's *sports* category which matches the topic of many FLIS sites. The second option is useful because training with sites that have a similar topic will make the classifier better able to distinguish FLIS pages from non-FLIS sports pages. The features selected for this classifier included the number of sports-related words in URLs, sports-related n-grams and widgets, the presence of *reporting* links, the presence of media traffic, and the use of nonstandard ports for streaming. The classifier achieves a true positive rate above 99%.

Sensitive websites, in the sense of data protection regulation, are websites on health, ethnicity, religion, sexual orientation, and political beliefs. A multinomial Naive Bayes classifier can be used to detect whether a website is sensitive, and if so, its category (Matic et al., 2020). This classifier is based on labeled URLs from Curlie,[8] a public crowdsourced taxonomy of websites. The features consist of the content and metadata of each website, processed with tf-idf, but limited to the top 5,000 features. The classifier achieves an F1 score of 0.9 for nonsensitive websites, and F1 scores between 0.55 and 0.91 for the topics of sensitive websites. Importantly, classifying URLs based on the content of their top-level domain is inaccurate, which means that Alexa and SimilarWeb are inadequate for identifying sensitive URLs (Matic et al., 2020).

Classifiers for Malicious Behaviors

Similar to website topics, classifiers can also detect a range of malicious behaviors by websites and browser extensions, including the use of cloaking techniques, malicious third-party content inclusions, and data leaks from browser extensions.

---

[8] https://curlie.org/

Cloaking techniques, or black-hat search engine optimization techniques, are used by websites to return different content depending on whether the visitor is a search engine spider or a regular user. This can trick users into clicking on search results that look benign but are actually malicious. The training data for a classifier to detect cloaking techniques needs to include web content crawled with different browser configurations, so that some configurations mimic search engine spiders and some mimic real users. A set of known cloaking domains can be obtained, for example, from lists of domains representing counterfeit luxury storefronts (Wang et al., 2014a). Features include the similarity of visible text between browser configurations, HTML, screenshots, embedded links, and request trees. A decision tree classifier to detect cloaking techniques achieved an accuracy of 95% (Invernizzi et al., 2016).

Third-party content inclusions can be malicious even on reputable websites, for example, through malicious advertising (Chen et al., 2016a). To build a classifier that can detect malicious inclusions, Arshad et al. (2017) used the Alexa top 200,000 sites as input data and used VirusTotal's URL scanning service to label resource loads as benign or malicious. The features include the type of top-level domain, the number of subdomains, the Alexa rank, the number of nonalphabetic characters and unique characters in domain names, the randomness in domain names, and whether a domain is an ad network, CDN, or URL shortening service. Because the input dataset is imbalanced – 3.7 million benign inclusion sequences and only 25,000 malicious ones – a separate Hidden Markov Model (HMM) can be trained for each class. The advantage of HMMs is that they can model interdependencies between resources in inclusion sequences. The HMM parameters can be estimated using the Baum-Welch algorithm. To combine the two HMM classifiers when predicting labels of unknown sequences, each HMM computes its own likelihood and the HMM with the higher likelihood determines the label. This approach achieved a recall of 93% (Arshad et al., 2017).

To detect whether a browser extension leaks a user's browsing history, a classifier can be built based on the API call trace of extensions. To reduce the effort for building a labeled input dataset, Weissbacher et al. (2017) combine unsupervised learning, which identifies candidates for manual labeling, and manual labeling. The unsupervised step consists of a regression model based on the amount of data sent by the extension, depending on the size of the browsing history. The features for the extra randomized tree classifier consist of all 2-grams from the API call trace, i.e., all combinations of two subsequent API calls, and it achieves an F1 score of 0.96.

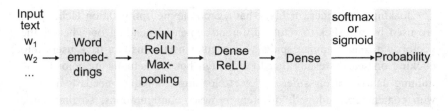

Figure 6.2 Architecture of a CNN-based classifier, for example, used to detect whether text is a privacy policy, or to label the contents of privacy policies.

Classifiers for Privacy Policies

To analyze privacy policies, machine learning has been used to detect whether a given website is a privacy policy, and to label the privacy practices described in the policy.

To detect whether a given text is a privacy policy, Linden et al. (2020) built a classifier based on an existing dataset of 1,000 privacy policies and a non-policy sample of English pages extracted from links on the landing pages of the Alexa top 500 sites. To transform this data into feature vectors suitable as input for a one-layer convolutional neural network (CNN), they tokenize the text and use a word embeddings layer to map words into vectors. Then, they use a convolutional layer, followed by a rectified linear unit (ReLU), a max-pooling layer, a fully connected layer, and another ReLU. A softmax layer finally outputs the probability that the given document is a privacy policy. Figure 6.2 illustrates this common CNN architecture. The classifier in Linden et al. (2020) achieves 99% accuracy, however, the performance of the classifier can depend on the sites chosen as nonpolicy samples. For example, to ensure that the classifier can separate privacy policies from legal documents and terms of service, the nonpolicy sample should include these types of documents.

CNNs can also be used to detect the privacy categories described in a policy as well as their attributes. For example, *data retention* is a category and its attributes refer to the retention period, purpose, and information types. A hierarchy of classifiers can be used to perform this complex labeling task, so that one classifier is trained to label the different categories, and then a separate classifier for each category labels the attributes within the category (Harkous et al., 2018). To define this hierarchy, a taxonomy of the possible privacy categories and attributes is needed, along with input data where the categories and attributes are correctly labeled on a set of privacy policies. Because this labeling process relies on a detailed understanding of the nuances of privacy policies, Harkous et al. (2018) have relied on law students to annotate their corpus of 115 privacy policies. The architecture of their CNN follows Figure 6.2, with a domain-specific word embeddings layer built from unlabeled privacy policies and a sigmoid function at the output layer which determines the probabilities for each class.

Other approaches for labeling privacy practices are to use separate binary classifiers for specific issues, for example, whether a policy allows collection of personal information (Zimmeck and Bellovin, 2014), or to use a separate classifiers for each combination of data types and parties that the privacy policy affirms or denies, such as affirming use of location data by third parties (Zimmeck et al., 2019). For the latter approach, Zimmeck et al. (2019) split the policy text into paragraphs and created a vector representation of each paragraph based on its tf-idf vector and manually crafted features like the presence or absence of indicative strings like *not collect* which indicates a negative modality. Their input data consisted of 350 privacy policies, annotated by legal experts, and their support vector classifiers achieved F1 scores between 0.78 and 1.

Natural language processing can also be used to detect internal contradictions in privacy policies. For example, Andow et al. (2019) extract named entities and data objects from privacy policies and use part-of-speech tagging to process each policy sentence into four-tuples consisting of actor, action, data object and entity (e.g., we, share, personal information, advertisers). A formal logic can then identify contradictory sentences, for example, when a statement claiming that a broad data type will not be collected is followed by a statement affirming the collection of a more specific data subtype.

To detect opt-out choices in privacy policies, Kumar et al. (2020) used active learning to reduce the manual labeling effort. Active learning uses a classifier trained on a small initial set of labeled policies. Based on the classifier's confidence about its classification of policies that are not in the training set, additional instances for manual labeling are identified and the classifier is retrained. The selection of additional instances can be guided by entropy: if the classifier is very uncertain (high entropy) about a particular classification, manually labeling this instance is more helpful than labeling a low entropy instance. This approach reduces the number of samples needed to achieve high classifier performance. Their logistic regression classifier, with a feature set consisting of words and bigrams, achieved an F1 score of 0.87.

6.3.5 Classifiers for Mobile Services

Classifiers for mobile services have been developed to identify the purpose of network accesses in Android apps, the type of image processing an app performs, whether an app is malicious, and which app reviews are about privacy or security issues.

To predict the purpose of network accesses from Android apps, Jin et al. (2018) define a taxonomy of four data types – phone identifier, phone status, personal data, and sensor – and associated purposes. For example, the possible purposes for the phone identifier are tracking for advertising, tracking for analytics, signed-out personalization, anti-fraud, and authentication. Based on outgoing HTTP requests and the observed key-value pairs, their feature set includes a bag-of-words constructed from the URL and data values, whether the app package name occurs in the URL, the app's category on Google Play, the business' category from Crunchbase, and whether the domain occurs in the source code of other apps. The maximum entropy algorithm is then used to identify the purpose, based on the candidate purposes in the taxonomy, with a precision of 95%.

To predict what kind of image processing is performed by an app, such as barcode detection, computer vision, or optical character recognition, Srivastava et al. (2017) interpret the app's log of function calls as a string, compute its word embeddings vector, and use one CNN per image processing type to label which type is performed by the app. To create appropriate training data for these classifiers, they identify libraries that perform a known type of image processing and create execution traces from apps that use these libraries while the app performs image processing and while it does not. Their classifiers achieve a precision of 96%.

One way to identify malicious apps is by analyzing their requested permissions as a proxy for their potential to perform malicious operations. The feature set includes a binary indicator for the presence or absence of each permission, and features can be ranked by importance using mutual information or the Pearson correlation coefficient. The most risky sets of permissions can then be identified using principal component analysis, and a random forest classifier can label apps as malicious or benign, with a true positive rate of 94% (Wang et al., 2014b).

Finally, machine learning can be used to identify which of an app's user reviews describe privacy or security issues. Based on a manually compiled list of keywords that indicate privacy or security issues, such as names of Android permissions or resources that are protected by default, Nguyen et al. (2019) label 4,000 reviews as security/privacy relevant or not. After removing stop words and applying a stemming algorithm, their features consist of a bag-of-words vector based on character n-grams, which limit the influence of typos. They use SMOTE to oversample the smaller class and train an SVM classifier with a linear kernel, achieving an accuracy of 93%.

6.4 Analysis of Mobile Apps

Analysis methods for mobile apps are often based on *taint tracking*: information acquired from specific sources, such as API calls that access protected information, is marked as tainted, and the use of this information is then tracked throughout the app's execution, for example, to detect whether it arrives at a problematic information sink such as the network. Static analysis focuses on the possibility that tainted information flows to a specific sink, whereas dynamic analysis can detect – and react to – actual occurrences of these information flows while the app is running.

6.4.1 Static Analysis of Mobile Apps

Static analysis has been used for two main purposes: to conduct reachability analyses to find possible leaks of sensitive data, for example, to identify the use of specific APIs by third-party libraries, and to detect the presence of specific software components in apps.

Reachability analyses begin with a list of *interesting* information sources, such as API calls for dangerous permissions (Grace et al., 2012) or other privacy-relevant APIs (Book and Wallach, 2013). For each API call, the reachability analysis creates a control flow graph by tracing backwards to find the sources of the API call and forward to find its sinks. This type of reachability analysis is implemented, for example, in the tool FlowDroid (Arzt et al., 2014).

Based on a list of third-party libraries included in an app, the reachability analysis can be used to identify all API calls from an app to an embedded library (Book and Wallach, 2013) or to identify access to PII (Gamba et al., 2020).

The string literals in an Android app, its exported functions, and its class signatures can be used to compute a *birthmark*, i.e., a feature that identifies the app (Duan et al., 2017). These birthmarks can be compared, using a similarity score, with birthmarks from other sources, such as open source software, and thereby detect whether software from other sources is present in an app. For example, this has been used to detect possible violations of open source policies in Android apps (Duan et al., 2017).

6.4.2 Dynamic Analysis of Mobile Apps

The principle of dynamic analysis is to place hooks into API calls or underlying system calls so that researcher-controlled dynamic analysis code is triggered every time a function of interest is called.

One of the simplest analyses that can be performed with this method is to record the parameter values of API calls, which can be used to identify what values are given to advertising or tracking libraries (Liu et al., 2017, 2019).

More in-depth analyses use taint tracking, i.e., they mark sensitive information as a taint source, then track the taint through app execution and record if it arrives at a taint sink. The taint tracking step can be based on variables within applications, messages passed between applications, method calls to native libraries, and access to files to ensure that taint can be tracked over persistent information and the network. TaintDroid was one of the first frameworks to propose real-time taint tracking for Android apps (Enck et al., 2014; Wang et al., 2019). Their evaluation was based on manual interaction with apps, including account creation, instead of automated interaction with monkey applications.

Newer approaches to taint tracking ensure that taint tracking continues to work with changes introduced in Android such as the new Android RunTime environment. For example, TaintMan (You et al., 2018) instruments both the target application and system libraries with taint enforcement code, and taint tracking is then performed based on low-level instructions instead of the higher-level concepts used in TaintDroid.

To support the evaluation of new taint tracking tools, DroidBench provides a test suite consisting of hand-crafted apps with test cases for interesting static and dynamic analysis problems (Arzt et al., 2014; Chen et al., 2017).

6.4.3 Combined Static and Dynamic Analysis

In many cases, a combination of techniques – static and dynamic analysis, or static analysis and traffic analysis – can result in better insights compared to the individual methods on their own.

One method to combine static analysis with traffic analysis is to use static analysis to identify apps that use specific API calls, and then observe the results generated by these API calls in network traffic. For example, to identify apps that exfiltrate audio or video data, Pan et al. (2018) focused on apps that use API calls related to camera, audio, and screen capture, and then executed the apps to detect media files in traffic.

Another method is to use traffic analysis to detect PII in network flows, followed by static analysis to find out what caused the PII to be sent. For example, Reardon et al. (2019) used this method to reverse engineer apps that circumvented the Android permissions that were supposed to protect the PII.

A common method of combining static and dynamic analysis begins by identifying sources and sinks for information leakage, for example, privacy-sensitive API calls as sources, and calls to the network or into analytics or tracking libraries as sinks (He et al., 2019; Liu et al., 2017). Then, static analysis is used to construct function call graphs (He et al., 2019) or perform reachability analysis (Yang et al., 2013). Dynamic analysis then relies on the knowledge gained from the static analysis. For example, He et al. (2019) analyze flows from sources to sinks to identify whether the call chain includes third-party libraries, and Yang et al. (2013) emulate user actions found in event sequences from the static analysis to determine whether data transmissions were intended by the user or not.

Combinations of static and dynamic analysis do not have to be limited to a combination of one static analysis technique and one dynamic analysis technique. For example, HybriDroid (Chen et al., 2017) combines two static analysis techniques with a dynamic analysis technique. They first analyze the app metadata to extract permissions, components, and intent filters. Then they use the static analysis tool FlowDroid to extract intents and sensitive data flows. Finally, they use TaintDroid to refine the model created by static analysis.

6.4.4 Dynamic Analysis for JavaScript and Browser Extensions

Dynamic analysis techniques are not restricted to mobile apps. They can, in principle, be applied to any software that can be executed in a researcher-controlled environment. Besides mobile apps, this is most commonly the case for JavaScript code and browser extensions.

To detect information leakage from Chrome browser extensions, Chen and Kapravelos (2018) combine static and dynamic analysis. Starting from a list of sensitive data sources and taint sinks, they use static analysis to construct data flow and control flow graphs and then link these graphs to dynamic JavaScript runtime objects. In this way, taint can be propagated among dynamic objects based on information from static analysis. This approach is possible because the JavaScript source code of browser extensions is available during runtime.

JavaScript code embedded in websites can also be subjected to dynamic analysis. For example, Zhu et al. (2018) instrumented Chrome's V8 JavaScript engine to record execution traces of JavaScript code, that is, which statements were executed in what order. In particular, these execution traces record which branches were taken during execution. Differences between execution traces, for example, resulting from two browsing sessions, can then be analyzed to detect whether the JavaScript code differentiates between the two sessions. This approach can be used to detect JavaScript that blocks users who use ad blockers.

6.5 Statistics

Statistical methods are used to analyze and interpret the meaning of the collected and post-processed response variables. This section focuses on statistical methods that have already been applied to transparency research, beginning with an overview of descriptive statistics. Then, three groups of methods from inferential statistics are explained in detail: hypothesis tests, regression, and estimation of causal effects. The section closes with a brief discussion of statistical methods for special use cases, such as spatial analyses.

6.5.1 Descriptive Statistics

Descriptive statistics are included in almost all analyses of experimental data in transparency research. They describe the characteristics of a data sample and therefore give a quick, high-level overview of individual response variables, including their central tendency, dispersion, and value ranges. However, descriptive statistics do not allow conclusions about the causes or the significance of effects or differences.

Descriptive statistics include the mean and median which indicate the central tendency and standard deviation, variance, percentiles, and extreme values which indicate dispersion. The five-number summary indicates the five most important percentiles of a data sample: the smallest observation, 25% percentile or lower quartile, median, 75% percentile or upper quartile, and the largest observation.

Descriptive statistics are often visualized in plots, including bar charts, box plots, scatter plots, or histograms. These visualizations can also include a breakdown of the response variable by different values for the input variables, or show how the response variable evolved over time. While these visualizations can give an intuitive understanding of the result of an experiment, they need to be backed up by further statistical analysis to support statements about causes or statistical significance.

6.5.2 Hypothesis Tests

Statistical hypothesis testing commonly follows three steps. First, the value of a *test statistic* is computed based on the observed data. Second, the *p-value* is calculated. The p-value indicates the probability that a test statistic at least as extreme as the observed one is sampled under the null hypothesis (i.e., assuming that the experimental treatment has no effect). Finally, the null hypothesis is rejected if the p-value is below a predefined significance level α. The significance level represents the risk of rejecting a true null hypothesis and is typically chosen as a small value, often $\alpha = 0.05$. If the p-value is above the significance level, the null hypothesis cannot be rejected and the evidence does not support further conclusions. In particular, this means that it would be wrong to "accept" the null hypothesis.

When multiple hypotheses are tested on a single observed dataset, the significance level has to be corrected to ensure that the risk of rejecting a true null hypothesis remains at the chosen significance level. The most common method to do this is the Holm-Bonferroni method. If m hypotheses are tested, Holm-Bonferroni adjusts the significance level by dividing it by the number of hypotheses, i.e., $\alpha = \frac{\alpha}{m}$ (Lecuyer et al., 2015).

Which test statistic can be used depends on the intended comparison, the assumptions required by the test statistic, and the characteristics of the observed data.

Three types of comparisons are common. One-sample tests compare the observed sample to a known population. Two-sample tests compare samples from two experimental conditions, for example, an experimental treatment with a control treatment. Paired tests are used to compare samples measured from the same subjects, for example, before and after treatment, or when treatment and control subjects are matched, for example, in observational as opposed to experimental studies.

Many common test statistics make assumptions about the distribution of the population that the observed data is sampled from, about the independence of observations and experimental units, and about the absence of cross-unit effects. These assumptions are typically not satisfied in transparency research (Tschantz et al., 2015). As a result, nonparametric test statistics should be chosen which do not rely on assumptions about the distribution of the underlying data.

Pearson's Chi-Squared Test

Pearson's chi-squared test statistic can be used to evaluate goodness of fit and homogeneity. Goodness of fit compares the distribution of observed data with a theoretical distribution, whereas homogeneity compares the distribution of observed data for two or more groups. Both versions have been applied in transparency research.

The goodness of fit test was used to test whether ads shown on mobile devices are targeted (Nath, 2015). They used a set of virtual personas, each trained with a single interest so that each persona matches a single targeting attribute. Then, they observed how frequently ads are shown to each persona. The null hypothesis is that the distribution of ads over interest categories is uniform, i.e., that ads are shown with the same frequency to all personas.

If the null hypothesis was true, it would mean that no behavioral targeting was taking place. The chi-squared test then compares the uniform distribution with the observed distribution of ads over targeting attributes represented by personas.

The homogeneity test was used to test whether the ads shown alongside searches for black-identifying names have different characteristics compared to ads shown when searching for white-identifying names, with the null hypothesis stating that there are no differences (Sweeney, 2013). They observed the frequency with which ads using the word *arrest* appeared alongside search results for black-identifying versus white-identifying names. The chi-squared test was then used to compare the differences between the two observed frequencies. The p-value for this test indicates the likelihood that the observed frequency is due to chance, and the null hypothesis can be rejected if the p-value is smaller than the significance level.

The homogeneity test can also be used to evaluate what factors the accuracy of Google's inference of demographic attributes depends on (Tschantz et al., 2018a). In particular, they observed whether the age and gender inferred by Google was correct, and tested whether this correctness depends on a range of other factors, including whether a user is logged into Google, whether the user uses an ad blocker, whether and how frequently the user clears cookies, whether first and third-party cookies are allowed in the user's browser, and whether the user is using private browsing mode. A separate chi-squared test was used for each factor to compare the frequency of Google's inference being accurate with the frequency of observing the factor. Because this is a case of multiple hypothesis testing – each chi-squared test tests one hypothesis – the Holm-Bonferroni correction needs to be applied. However, to limit the number of hypotheses they needed to test with the correction applied, they split their dataset into an exploratory portion and a confirmatory portion. The exploratory portion of the dataset was used to compute chi-squared tests *without* the correction, and the results were only used to identify candidate factors that might be statistically significant. The confirmation portion was then used *with* the correction, but only on the reduced set of hypotheses identified with the exploratory analysis.

Kolmogorov-Smirnov Test

The Kolmogorov-Smirnov test statistic is a nonparametric test that can be used to compare the distribution of observed data with a known distribution (one-sample test), or between two sets of observed data (two-sample test). The two-sample test is particularly useful in transparency research because it allows comparing the outcomes of two experimental treatments.

The two-sample Kolmogorov-Smirnov test has been used to test whether the observed number of third-party requests differs between two browser configurations (Mazel et al., 2019). In particular, they observed the number of third-party requests per website, averaged over 10 replications of the experiment, while browsing the top 1,000 websites. Their experimental treatment used a browser with an ad blocker, whereas the control treatment did not use an ad blocker. The null hypothesis is that the two distributions of observed third-party requests are equal, and the Kolmogorov-Smirnov test determines the likelihood that differences in the observed distributions are due to chance.

Kruskal-Wallis, Mann-Whitney, and Wilcoxon Signed-Rank Tests

The Kruskal-Wallis H test, Mann-Whitney U test, and Wilcoxon signed-rank test are nonparametric tests to determine whether groups of observed samples have the same distribution. The Mann-Whitney test, also called Wilcoxon rank-sum test, relies on *independent samples* and can only compare two groups. The Wilcoxon signed-rank test relaxes the assumption of independent samples and can therefore compare dependent and paired samples. The Kruskal-Wallis test, like Mann-Whitney, relies on independent samples, but can compare more than two groups. Because these tests rely on the *ranks* of individual observations instead of numerical values, they can be used with ordinal data such as the scores from Likert scales that are often used in surveys. The null hypothesis is usually that the distributions of populations are the same.

The Kruskal-Wallis test has been used to compare the number of third-party cookies and requests received at vantage points in different countries (Fruchter et al., 2015). The p-value indicates the likelihood that the observed differences between countries are due to chance, and a p-value below the significance level allows the conclusion that the differences between countries are statistically significant.

The Kruskal-Wallis and Mann-Whitney tests can also be combined within a single study, for example, to compare the likelihood of voting for one of two candidates between three groups of participants: a control group that received neutral search result rankings, and two bias groups that received manipulated search result rankings (Epstein and Robertson, 2015). They used the Kruskal-Wallis test to compare voting behaviors of the three groups before treatment, and pairwise Mann-Whitney tests between the control group and each bias group to compare voting behavior after treatment.

Other Nonparametric Tests

Other nonparametric statistical tests can be used for specific purposes. For example, McNemar's test can be used to test for differences between paired percentages, for example, the difference before and after treatment (Epstein and Robertson, 2015), and the Friedman test can be used to evaluate differences in treatments across multiple repetitions of the experiment (Hupperich et al., 2018).

Confidence Intervals

Confidence intervals are related to hypothesis testing and can be used to test specific null hypotheses. A confidence interval is an estimate for the value range of an unknown parameter, commonly the mean. Confidence intervals are computed for a specific confidence level, such as 0.95 or 0.99. The confidence level indicates the probability that a given confidence interval contains the true value. For a null hypothesis that states that a specific mean equals zero, confidence intervals can be used instead of test statistics to reject the hypothesis: if the confidence interval does not contain the value zero, then the null hypothesis can be rejected, and the likelihood of rejecting a true null hypothesis, i.e., the significance level, corresponds to the confidence level. Similarly, for a null hypothesis that states that the means for two groups are equal, the null hypothesis can be rejected if the confidence intervals for the two groups do not overlap.

Ali et al. (2019a) have used confidence intervals for this purpose. In particular, they test whether the audience demographics for ads differ depending on characteristics of the ads. They use confidence intervals with a 99% confidence level for the probability of *success*, where success is interpreted as one possible outcome, such as the probability that an ad audience member is male. Because they test multiple hypotheses, they also apply the Holm-Bonferroni correction.

6.5.3 Regression

Regression is used to model the relationship between a response, or dependent, variable and one or more explanatory, or independent, variables. Although regression models can be used to predict values of the response variable, they are most commonly used in transparency research to explain to what extent variation in the explanatory variables contributes to variation in the response variable.

A generic linear regression model can be written as $y = X\beta + \epsilon$, where y is the vector of observations of the response variable, X is the matrix of values of explanatory variables, β is the vector of model parameters (or regression coefficients) that is estimated, and ϵ is a vector of noise or error terms that summarizes all influences on the response variable that are not contained in the explanatory variables.

In addition to estimating the values of the regression coefficients, the statistical estimation process also performs hypothesis tests to determine whether the true value of each regression coefficient is different from zero. If a coefficient is not statistically significantly different from zero, it does not have explanatory power in predicting the response variable. The results of these hypothesis tests are often given by indicating which of three significance levels each hypothesis test achieved, either $p < 0.1$, $p < 0.05$, or $p < 0.01$, all of which indicate that the coefficient is different from zero for the given significance level.

Regression has been used to analyze what factors influence the rank of hotels on travel booking sites (Hunold et al., 2018). Their explanatory variables included, for example, the hotel's price on different booking sites, its star rating, user ratings, and cancellation policy. They combined several different regression models, including rank-ordered logit regression models and linear regression models, to analyze how hotel prices influence hotel rankings on different booking sites.

Hannák et al. (2017) used regression to analyze what factors influence the ratings and reviews received by workers on freelance marketplaces. They combined negative binomial regression models and ordinal regression models to analyze the two response variables. Negative binomial regression was used because the number of reviews received follows a binomial distribution (it indicates a number of "successes"), and ordinal regression was used to analyze rating scores because ratings are given on an ordinal scale, for example, low to high or 1 to 5, instead of arbitrary numerical values. Their explanatory variables included the workers' age, gender, experience, join date, last online time, response time, and profile image.

In addition to identifying which explanatory variables contribute to explaining variation in the response variable, regression-based methods can also estimate what portion of the difference in outcomes is explained by different explanatory variables. For example, the Oaxaca-Blinder decomposition (May et al., 2019) is a method from econometrics used to estimate how much variation of the response variable is due to individual explanatory variables or combinations of explanatory variables.

6.5.4 Estimation of Causal Effects

Methods that can determine what *causes* an observed effect are more powerful and allow researchers to draw stronger conclusions than methods that only analyze *correlations*. To determine causation, correct statistical analysis is not enough: it needs to be accompanied by an experimental design that allows reasoning about causation. Experimental designs differ depending on whether the experiment is an active, experimental study, or a passive, observational study.

Causal Effects for Active, Experimental Studies

A method that has been shown to be suitable for determining causation for experimental studies is a permutation test with randomization and blocking (Tschantz et al., 2015; Datta et al., 2015). To apply this method, a suitable test statistic has to be defined and the permutation test has to be performed. Additional strategies like blocking, applied during data collection, can help manage performance and noise levels. As with traditional hypothesis tests, corrections like the Holm-Bonferroni correction need to be applied when testing multiple hypotheses.

The test statistic is a measure of distance between the control and experimental groups. It should take on a high value if the response variable differs between the two groups. For example, it can be chosen as the difference in the number of interest-related ads that are shown to the treatment and control groups (Tschantz et al., 2015). The test statistic can be challenging to choose because it is not necessarily clear from the outset which test statistic will show the differences between treatment and control groups most clearly. A pilot study can help decide which test statistic to use. Test statistics can also be selected automatically based on the collected data. For example, Datta et al. (2015) train machine learning classifiers on a subset of the collected data, so that the classifier predicts which treatment an experimental unit received based on the observed response variables. This classifier's accuracy – the number of correctly classified units – can be used as a test statistic.

To perform a permutation test, the labels of control and experimental groups are randomly permuted. The hypothetical value of the test statistic is then computed for each permutation and compared with the actually observed test statistic for the true assignment of labels. If the null hypothesis is true, i.e., there is no difference between the control and experimental groups, then the values of the test statistic should be similar regardless of the permutation. On the other hand, if the null hypothesis is not true and there is a difference between the groups, then the value of the actually observed test statistic should be higher than most hypothetical test statistics. This intuition can be formalized to compute the p-value of the permutation test: the p-value is given by the proportion of hypothetical test statistics that were greater or equal to the actually observed test statistic. If the p-value is smaller than the significance level, the result is statistically significant and the treatment applied to the experimental group is the likely cause for the observed difference in the response variable.

Permutation tests require the random assignment of experimental units to either the control or the experimental group. To reduce noise in the measurement, all experimental units should perform data collection in parallel. However, this can be difficult in practice, for example, due to limitations on available hardware or bandwidth for data collection. Blocking is a strategy that groups experimental units into blocks. Within each block, data collection is performed in parallel, and multiple blocks can be executed in sequence to ensure that the overall number of experimental units is large enough. The permutations are then performed *within* blocks. To improve performance of the test when the number of possible permutations is large, Datta et al. (2015) have used random sampling to select a random subset of permutations, and used confidence intervals to estimate the true p-value based on the random sample.

Causal Effects for Passive, Observational Studies

Observational studies, such as studies that rely on passive data collection, cannot randomly assign treatment and control groups to their experimental units. Instead, the treatment label is predetermined by the observed data. Therefore, different methods are needed to determine causal effects.

These methods rely on finding "quasi-experiments" in the data, i.e., cases where experimental units, also called subjects, have different values for the treatment variable, but otherwise same or similar values for the control variables (Jiang et al., 2019). Control variables are confounding factors that may be alternative explanations for observing the treatment effect (Li et al., 2020). Methods to systematically identify these quasi-experiments are called matching methods, and their aim is to pair each subject in the treatment group with a similar subject in the control group. Matching can be performed based on exact values for each control variable, however, this normally results in a low number of matches in a dataset (Stuart, 2010). Another option is to match based on a distance metric, such as the Mahalanobis distance. However, similar to exact matching, this method matches separately on every control variable and thus the number of matches can be too small (Jiang et al., 2019).

The propensity score is a matching method that mitigates this disadvantage. A propensity score represents the probability of an experimental unit having the *treatment* label, based on the values of all control variables. Propensity scores can be estimated, for example, with logistic regression that includes all possible confounding factors as independent variables (Miroglio et al., 2018). Subjects are then matched based on their estimated propensity scores so that each treatment subject is matched with the control subject with the closest propensity score, provided the propensity score is within a threshold. Subjects that cannot be matched are excluded from the rest of the analysis. As a result of the matching process, the distributions of treatment and control subjects, based on their control variables, are as as similar as possible. The quality of the matches can be evaluated for both categorical and continuous control variables with appropriate hypothesis tests, for example, a chi-squared test for independence or a Kolmogorov-Smirnov test.

After the matching is complete, the data can be analyzed using the hypothesis tests and regression models discussed above, or using methods specifically adapted to observational studies. For example, propensity-score-stratified regression can group subjects into groups with similar propensity scores, which allows simulating a randomized blocked trial (Foong et al., 2018).

Another common method is the difference-in-differences method (Li et al., 2020; Zhao et al., 2020). This method can be used with observational data where data is available before and after the treatment was applied. For example, the treatment variable in a study could be whether a subject uses an ad blocker or not, and subjects could make the decision to install an ad blocker at some point during the observation period. The data therefore includes observed response variables for all subjects without treatment (before treatment was applied for the treatment group, and before and after treatment was applied for the control group), and for some subjects with with treatment (after treatment was applied for the treatment group). The difference-in-differences method then compares the change over time in the response variable for both the treatment group and the control group, and the treatment effect corresponds to the difference between these changes. This can be formally represented as a regression model and analyzed accordingly.

6.5.5 Statistics for Spatial Analyses

Statistical analyses that include geographical locations have to consider possible spatial autocorrelation, i.e., the fact that locations are not independent (Thebault-Spieker et al., 2017). In this case, regression models are not suitable because they would overestimate the real effects (Jiang et al., 2018). Instead, the analysis has to account for three types of spatial effects: correlated, endogenous, and exogenous spatial relationships. Correlated spatial relationships occur when neighboring locations have similar response variables. In this case, a spatial error model can account for the spatial relationship (Thebault-Spieker et al., 2017). Endogenous spatial relationships occur when the response for one location depends on the responses of neighboring locations. This can be estimated using a spatial lag model that introduces a weight for the dependent variable (Jiang et al., 2018). Finally, exogenous spatial relationships occur when the response for one location depends on predictors of neighboring locations. In this case, a spatial Durbin model can be used that includes versions of each variable for endogenous and exogenous spatial relationships (Thebault-Spieker et al., 2017).

PART III

Results

7

Transparency for Corporate
Surveillance Methods

This chapter examines findings from transparency research that shed light on the methods used for corporate surveillance, including tracking, profiling, analytics, and advertising. It focuses on key results obtained for the research questions described in Chapter 4 and explains the experimental designs used to achieve them.

7.1 Tracking

Figure 7.1 shows the prototypical experiment design followed by many studies that evaluate the prevalence of tracking on the Internet. The data collection is configured based on input variables including websites, browsers, timeouts, and vantage points. The raw collected data – HTTP requests and responses as well as JavaScript calls – are then postprocessed to detect domain owners, identifying cookies, trackers, and the use of fingerprinting. These response variables allow the computation of quantitative measures such as prevalence, reach, and prominence.

7.1.1 Stateful Tracking

Prevalence and Reach

Many studies have found that embedding of third parties and third-party trackers is very common on the web. In 2015, for example, 88% of websites made third-party requests (Libert, 2015) and 46% of websites had at least one third-party tracker (Li et al., 2015). Table 7.1 summarizes studies that have evaluated the prevalence and reach of stateful tracking. The differences in findings stem from a number of factors: the true use of stateful tracking at the time of the study, the selection of websites, the use of trackers or third parties as response variable, and the method to identify trackers.

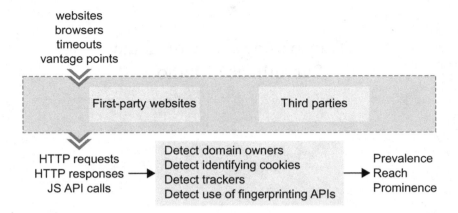

Figure 7.1 Experimental design of studies that measure web tracking. Inputs variables are shown on top of the black-box system under study and observed output variables are shown on the bottom. Next to the output variables, the figure indicates possible methods for processing the observed data and response variables.

Organization-based reach is generally larger than domain-based reach. For example, the top tracking organization (Google) identified by Schelter and Kunegis (2018) has more than twice the reach of the top tracking domain. Online tracking has been found to have a long, thin tail, meaning that there are many trackers with a very small reach, and only a few trackers with a very large reach (Englehardt and Narayanan, 2016).

Reach has also been evaluated in terms of how many users can be reached within a certain amount of time. Metwalley et al. (2015) found that the top trackers reach more than 90% of users within just 10 days. The time a user spends browsing before contacting the first tracker is smaller than 1 s for 77% of users, and less than 100 s for 100% of users in their sample.

Influence of Vantage Point, Website, and Browsers

The choice of vantage point can have a large influence on the results of tracking studies. For example, studies consistently find that Google is the tracker with the largest reach, except if the vantage point is in China (Hu et al., 2020a), Russia (Schelter and Kunegis, 2018), or Iran (Samarasinghe and Mannan, 2019). In addition, studies have shown differences in the tracking ecosystem depending on the country. Vantage points in the UK observe more trackers than other countries (Samarasinghe and Mannan, 2019; Hu et al., 2020a), and the ecosystem of trackers observed when visiting the top ten most popular sites

Table 7.1. *Overview of results for prevalence of tracking and the reach of the top tracker for stateful tracking. Results for organization-based reach are marked with *.*

Year	Websites	Third parties or trackers?	Prevalence	Reach	Reference
2008	Alexa 1,000	Third parties	n/a	~35%	Krishnamurthy and Wills (2009)
2012	Alexa 500	Trackers	91%	39%	Roesner et al. (2012)
2012	Common Crawl	Trackers	89%	25%, 51%*	Schelter and Kunegis (2018)
2015	Alexa 10,000	Trackers	46%	n/a	Li et al. (2015)
2015	Alexa 1 million	Third parties	87%	46%	Libert (2015)
2015	350,000	Trackers	n/a	42%*	Yu et al. (2016)
2016	Alexa 500	Trackers	n/a	~40%	Lerner et al. (2016)
2016	Alexa 1 million	Third parties	n/a	~65%	Englehardt and Narayanan (2016)
2017	Alexa 200,000	Third parties	n/a	~70%	Merzdovnik et al. (2017)
2018	Alexa 1 million	Third parties	n/a	82%*	Libert (2018)
2019	68,000	Trackers	n/a	44%	Samarasinghe and Mannan (2019)

in the UK from a UK vantage point is disjoint from the ecosystem seen when visiting the ten most popular sites in China, from China (Hu et al., 2020a).

Tracking also differs between categories of websites. For example, Englehardt and Narayanan (2016) found that news websites contain the most trackers among all categories. In a study of pornographic websites, Vallina et al. (2019) found that the trackers embedded in porn sites only partially overlap with trackers in the rest of the web, with common web trackers like Facebook being almost completely absent on porn sites, and specialized porn advertisers being almost absent from the rest of the web. Website tracking behaviors may even differ depending on the political leaning of websites, where hyper-partisan websites embed more trackers than the general web, and right-leaning more than left-leaning websites (Agarwal et al., 2020). Tracking is also common on captive portals and landing pages of public Wi-Fi hotspots, with captive portals hosting 7.4 trackers on average, and tracking often beginning before the user accepts the hotspot's terms of use (Ali et al., 2019b).

Most studies on web tracking visit the landing pages of a set of websites. However, this may lead to an underestimation of tracking experienced by real users. For example, one study found that subsites set 36% more cookies, tracking increased by 6%, device fingerprinting by 25%, and cookie synchronization by 15% (Urban et al., 2020a). Visiting only landing pages therefore misses a large chunk of interesting behavior that should be the subject of measurement studies.

Compared to the vantage point and the selection of websites in a study, the browser used for the study has a smaller influence on the observed tracking behaviors. However, Samarasinghe and Mannan (2019) found that some trackers are only observed from specific browsers, but not others.

Cookie Synchronization

Cookie synchronization is very common in the modern web. Even considering only cookie synchronization that can be observed from the client-side, 91% of users are affected by cookie synchronization (Olejnik et al., 2014), and 96% of user-identifying cookie values are shared between at least two parties (Falahrastegar et al., 2016).

From the user's viewpoint, 20% of users experience their first cookie synchronization within the first day of browsing, and 38% within the first week (Papadopoulos et al., 2019). Cookie synchronization happens even when the website has a sensitive topic such as health (Falahrastegar et al., 2016), and it increases the number of third parties that can learn about a user's browsing history by a factor of 6.75 (Papadopoulos et al., 2019).

From an organizational viewpoint, trackers with higher reach participate in more cookie synchronization relationships than less popular trackers (Falahrastegar et al., 2016; Olejnik et al., 2014), with 85% of the top third parties engaging in cookie synchronization (Englehardt and Narayanan, 2016). The party engaged in the most cookie synchronizations is DoubleClick (Olejnik et al., 2014; Englehardt and Narayanan, 2016), which has positioned itself as a middleman that other entities have to synchronize with. DoubleClick achieves this by not sharing their cookie identifiers directly, but instead sharing party-specific identifiers (Papadopoulos et al., 2019). Taking parent-subsidiary relationships into account, most cookie synchronizations cross organizational boundaries (Falahrastegar et al., 2016).

Data sharing between third parties can also be performed between servers directly, making it not observable in traditional measurement studies. However, advertisers' header bidding behavior can be used as a proxy to infer the existence of server-side data sharing (Cook et al., 2020). This assumes that advertisers will bid differently (most likely higher) if they know a user's browsing history, which can be used to infer that data sharing relationships exist even if no observable cookie synchronization takes place. Cook et al. (2020) find several instances of inferred server-side data sharing, some of which could be verified, for example, through news articles announcing collaborations.

7.1.2 Stateless Tracking (Fingerprinting)

Extent of Stateless Tracking

Compared to cookie-based tracking, fingerprinting is much less prevalent. For example, only 0.4% of the top 10,000 websites use one of three commercial fingerprinting providers (Nikiforakis et al., 2013). All features introduced in Panopticlick (Eckersley, 2010) are used in the wild, but commercial fingerprinters use additional attributes to extract browser-specific features and attempt to circumvent proxies to determine the user's real IP address (Nikiforakis et al., 2013).

Canvas fingerprinting is less common on top websites: 5.5% of the top 100,000 websites use canvas fingerprinting, but only 1.8% of the top 1,000 (Acar et al., 2014). Canvas font fingerprinting, even though used by less than 1% of the top 1 million sites, is much more prevalent among the top 1,000 sites (2.5%) (Englehardt and Narayanan, 2016). Other fingerprinting methods, for example, based on WebRTC, AudioContext, or the BatteryAPI, are used even less frequently (Englehardt and Narayanan, 2016).

Characteristics of Stateless Tracking

Despite its relatively low prevalence, the characteristics of stateless tracking have been well studied, in particular relating to the fingerprintability of web browsers and the effectiveness of new fingerprinting attributes. Figure 7.2 shows a common experimental design for fingerprinting studies. The input variables include browser configurations and fingerprinting attributes. The recorded attribute vectors allow analyzing quantitative measures including the anonymity set size and entropy.

Many studies have evaluated the fingerprintability of new attributes, for example, the list of installed browser extensions (Starov and Nikiforakis, 2017a), which websites a user is logged into (Gulyas et al., 2018), unnecessary modifications browser extensions make to websites (Starov et al., 2019), and intra-browser messages sent by extensions (Karami et al., 2020). Combined with previous fingerprinting attributes, these new attributes contribute to making fingerprints more unique.

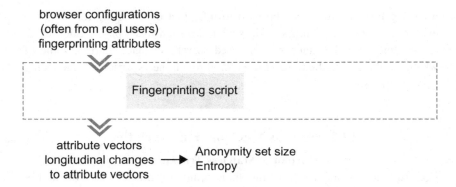

Figure 7.2 Experimental design of studies that measure fingerprintability. The fingerprinting scripts under study are white boxes because the JavaScript code for fingerprinting scripts is available, and because researchers often run their own servers to collect fingerprints.

For example, installed browser extensions can be fingerprinted by querying the web accessible resources they provide (Sjösten et al., 2017), or by observing changes they make to a website's DOM (Starov and Nikiforakis, 2017a). 9% of extensions in Google's Chrome store make detectable changes on arbitrary websites, and 5.7% are fingerprintable due to changes that are not functionally relevant. The likelihood that a user's combination of extensions is unique increases with the number of installed extensions (Gulyas et al., 2018), but as few as four extensions may be enough to re-identify most users (Achara et al., 2015).

Fingerprinting based on WebGL rendering is possible because of its inclusion in the HTML5 *canvas* element. In contrast to other fingerprinting methods, WebGL based fingerprinting allows the linking of different browsers running on the same machine (Cao et al., 2017) because the underlying hardware and graphics driver produce the same rendering output regardless of the browser.

A shortcoming of fingerprinting is that the link to a unique user may be lost when the fingerprint evolves over time, for example, due to browser or operating system updates, updates of other software in the environment, or user actions like changes in screen resolution or timezone, cookie deletion, or change of the *DNT* option (Li and Cao, 2020). In these chases, subsequent versions of fingerprints can be linked using heuristics or machine learning algorithms, so that users remain trackable for longer periods of time. For example, Vastel et al. (2018a) were able to accurately link fingerprints over 20 evolved versions. However, this method may not scale to datasets with millions of fingerprints (Li and Cao, 2020).

Fingerprinting may also become less effective when a very large number of users needs to be distinguished. For example, in a comparison of the fingerprintability of browsers based on three datasets of fingerprints – the Panopticlick dataset with 470,000 fingerprints (Eckersley, 2010), the AmI-Unique dataset with 120,000 fingerprints (Laperdrix et al., 2016), and a dataset with 2 million fingerprints (Gómez-Boix et al., 2018) – the uniqueness of fingerprints depended on the size of the dataset, with 83% unique fingerprints in the Panopticlick dataset, 89% in the AmIUnique dataset, and only 35% in the third dataset (Gómez-Boix et al., 2018).

7.1.3 Tracking on Mobile Devices

Almost all studies of tracking on mobile devices have focused on the Android platform. On Android, tracking is more prevalent than on the web, and the reach of the top trackers is higher as well. The top tracker on Android is Alphabet with near 100% coverage, followed by Facebook (Razaghpanah et al., 2018). 90% of apps include at least one tracker (Binns et al., 2018b; Seneviratne et al., 2015), and even 60% of paid apps include trackers (Seneviratne et al., 2015). Most trackers collect persistent unique identifiers that enable them to track users across apps, and many trackers have a presence both in mobile apps and on desktop websites, which can enable them to track users across devices (Razaghpanah et al., 2018).

When comparing trackers found on websites optimized for mobile versus desktop users, about 30% of trackers appeared only on the desktop versions of websites, whereas 13% of trackers were specific to the mobile versions of websites (Yang and Yue, 2020).

7.1.4 Cross-Device Tracking

The prevalence of cross-device tracking can be estimated by analyzing how many third party domains collect information that is suitable for probabilistic cross-device tracking. By visiting 100 websites from different devices, Brookman et al. (2017) observe connections to 1,130 third-party domains, of which 861 collect enough information to allow for some form of cross-device tracking. Heuristics can also be used to identify cross-device trackers. For example, Zimmeck et al. (2017) were able to identify 124 distinct cross-device trackers in a dataset of 3,200 trackers.

Tracking companies report accuracies well above 90% for their cross-device trackers. Even though this number is not easily verifiable, this level of accuracy appears feasible based on experiments with different cross-device tracking techniques (Solomos et al., 2019).

7.1.5 Email Tracking

To study the prevalence of email tracking, Englehardt et al. (2018) collected 12,000 emails from commercial mailing lists and found that 85% of emails contained embedded third-party content and 70% contained resources that were included in tracker-blocking filter lists. 11% of links embedded in these emails leak the recipient's email address to a third party when clicked.

Similar findings hold for emails from disposable email services, where 31% of embedded images contained tracking links, and 6.5% of emails contained third-party tracking links (Hu et al., 2019b). In addition, emails from popular domains contained more trackers than from less popular domains.

7.1.6 Influence of Regulations on Tracking

Web and mobile tracking is subject to regulations, including competition regulations and data protection regulations. The influence of competition regulation on the tracking ecosystem has not been widely studied, but the effect of data protection regulation has been subject of intense study, especially after the new European data protection regulation (GDPR) came into force in 2018.

One study on competition regulation estimated the market concentrations of web and mobile tracking companies (Binns et al., 2018a). Based on the prominence-weighted Herfindahl-Hirschman Index (HHI), which is a measure for market concentration, the market concentration among web tracking companies is 0.12, which meets the standard for regulatory intervention in the EU where the threshold is 0.1, but not in the US which uses a threshold of 0.25. However, even if the market overall is unconcentrated, mergers that raise the HHI by more than a threshold may be subject to regulatory scrutiny. This threshold is 0.025 in the EU. The acquisition of DoubleClick by Google in 2007 raised the HHI by 0.039 (Binns et al., 2018a), which would meet the EU regulation threshold. This indicates that competition regulation, in addition to data protection regulation, could be applied to constrain the web tracking ecosystem.

When studying the impact of data protection regulations, geographical aspects are relevant, for example, when data is sent across data protection boundaries or when regulations lead to geographical differences in the prevalence of tracking. IP address geolocation can be used to determine where tracking flows start and end. Almost 85% of tracking flows from users in the EU end at tracking servers in the EU (Iordanou et al., 2018). Even though this is a positive result in terms of the likely GDPR compliance of trackers, 12% of tracking requests end in North America which has less stringent data protection rules. To study whether the prevalence of trackers differs by country, Fruchter et al. (2015) focused on four countries with different privacy regulatory models: Germany with a comprehensive privacy model where privacy is regarded as a human right; the US and Japan with a sectoral privacy model where privacy rules differ depending on the sector; and Australia with a coregulatory model where industries develop their own privacy policies. Even though they observed significant differences between countries, the differences could not be fully explained by the privacy regulatory model. For example, the highest number of third-party cookies was observed in the US and the lowest number in Japan, although both countries follow the same (sectoral) privacy regulatory model. This indicates that the regulatory model is not the only factor that determines the prevalence of tracking.

Several studies have observed changes in the tracking landscape around the time when the GDPR came into force in May 2018, for example, a 22% drop of third-party cookies and a 7% drop of social media content on European news sites (Libert et al., 2018); a decrease in the number of third parties on European websites in general, but particularly on privately owned news, entertainment, and shopping sites (Sørensen and Kosta, 2019); and an increase of 16% in the websites that display cookie notices (Degeling et al., 2019). However, the reach of the most prevalent third parties decreased only slightly: Alphabet's reach decreased by 1% to 96%, and Facebook's reach decreased by 5% to 70% (Libert et al., 2018). In addition, only about 1% of websites stopped using tracking libraries and even fewer websites asked users for consent before setting cookies (Degeling et al., 2019).

Websites that operate globally must comply with the GDPR for their European users. Correspondingly, the top 100,000 websites on average reduced their use of cookies by 46% across the GDPR introduction (Dabrowski et al., 2019). However, the GDPR also led to a diversification of website behavior: among the top 100,000 websites that set at least one cookie, 26% set cookies only for the US vantage point, but not for the EU vantage point (49% of the top 1,000 websites) (Dabrowski et al., 2019). This diversification can make measurement studies of tracking behaviors more difficult due to the increased need for taking multiple vantage points into account.

The EU ePrivacy Directive states that websites must ask for consent before placing identifying cookies. However, almost half of the websites analyzed by Trevisan et al. (2019) placed cookies before consent, with large variations depending on the website category: 86% of news/media websites placed cookies before consent, compared with only 14% of law/government websites. The trackers with the largest reach were most responsible for placing cookies that may violate the ePrivacy Directive.

The GDPR also had effects on information-sharing links between companies: cookie synchronization links between companies reduced by 40% when comparing measurements before and after May 2018 (Urban et al., 2020b).

7.2 Profiling

Resesarch on profiling mainly focuses on questions about the effectiveness and effects of profiling, for example, asking whether the contents of user profiles are accurate, and how identifiable users are based on their profiles. Figure 7.3 shows an experimental design for profiling studies. The input variables include the interests of real users or virtual personas, including their browsing history. The main response variables are the profile attributes shown in ad preference managers of different profilers that can be processed to detect categories of interests and websites and to compute the overlap between – and accuracy, consistency, and size of – profiles.

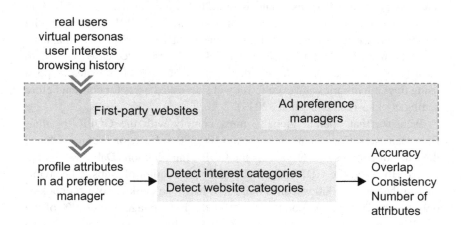

Figure 7.3 Experimental design of studies that analyze profiling.

7.2.1 Contents of User Profiles

On Facebook, the median user is assigned 310 profiling attributes. In a dataset with 114 users, Andreou et al. (2019) found 17,000 unique attributes, which indicates a relatively small overlap between profiles of different users.

To find out whether these assigned attributes correspond to real user interests or characteristics, Bashir et al. (2019b) asked users to rate the accuracy of attributes in their profiles. Profile attributes were quite inaccurate, with participants rating only 27% of attributes as strongly relevant. In addition, the participants' recent browsing history explained less than 10% of profile attributes on Facebook, BlueKai, and eXelate (45% on Google), indicating that many profile attributes may be outdated. Only about one-quarter of attributes overlapped between the profiles assembled by the four profilers.

The consistency of profiles can be evaluated by comparing the profiles of virtual personas that visit the same set of websites. Based on simulated web sessions that started with clean browser instances, Degeling and Nierhoff (2018) found that BlueKai profiles created by visiting the same series of websites overlap only around 50% on average. Even when more than 1,000 URLs are visited, the overlap is less than 75%. This indicates that BlueKai's profile creation process is not self-consistent.

7.2.2 Anonymity versus Identifiability

The uniqueness of the attribute combinations shown on public Facebook profiles is an indication for how easy it can be to reidentify users based on some of their attributes. Facebook's ad audience estimation can measure the frequency with which profile attributes occur on public Facebook profiles and thereby evaluate uniqueness. Chen et al. (2013) estimated that a Facebook profile is unique if its entropy reaches 29 bit, which can be achieved by combining just four profile attributes: a user's current city (13 bits), their age (10.5 bits), their gender (1.4 bits), and their relationship status (4.4 bits). This result means that a profiler that can accurately infer these four attributes might be able to look up the user's Facebook profile.

Click traces – a timestamped sequence of website visits – can also reidentify users. Deußer et al. (2020) evaluated the unicity of click traces and found that individuals in click trace databases can be reidentified based on very few pieces of information, such as a partial browsing history which can be obtained by shoulder surfing or by observing the timestamps when links were shared on Twitter. The high unicity of click trace databases means that click traces can be interpreted as pseudonyms of individuals, which may have legal implications, for example, the GDPR requires explicit informed consent to collect and store pseudonyms.

7.3 Analytics

Analytics services are commonly included in studies of third-party tracking, so that the results above also apply to analytics services. In addition, on mobile devices, analytics libraries receive user information linked to unique device identifiers. For example, if an app developer uses analytics to analyze their app's performance based on gender, the analytics company receives all users' genders together with their device identifiers, and can thus build comprehensive profiles (Liu et al., 2017, 2019).

7.4 Advertising

Many studies have focused on the advertising ecosystem. For example, studies have attempted to characterize different aspects of the ad ecosystem, analyzed the characteristics of ad targeting mechanisms and the effects of ad display algorithms, studied the functionality of bidding mechanisms, evaluated the properties of ad transparency mechanisms like ad explanations and ad preference managers, compared web and mobile advertising, and explored adversarial advertising as well as the use of advertising *as a service*, i.e., the use of online advertising as part of a research method.

7.4.1 Advertising Ecosystem

To characterize the advertising ecosystem as a whole, researchers have studied server-side infrastructure and behaviors as well as user-side exposure to ads.

In 2015, 17% of all HTTP requests and 1.1% of all transferred bytes on the Internet corresponded to advertising-related traffic (Pujol et al., 2015). Dedicated ad servers served almost one-third of all ads, and the top ten autonomous systems delivered more than half of all ads. The fact that the top ten autonomous systems include several cloud providers indicates that the ad industry relies heavily on cloud resources and CDNs, which means that many websites use the same back-end infrastructure to deliver both content and ads. HTTP traffic related to advertising was also found to have a longer delay between request and response than traffic related to other content, indicating the presence of the time-consuming real-time bidding process.

The ad ecosystem consists of many different entities which form a web of interdependent entities where types of companies cannot be clearly delineated. The graph between advertising-related domains is dense, with short paths and a high clustering coefficient (Bashir and Wilson, 2018). This means that user data can spread quickly within the ecosystem. The top advertising domains – Google, Facebook AppNexus, and Integral Ad Science when ranked by betweenness centrality – are able to see the vast majority of a user's browsing history. For example, DoubleClick observes 90% of all page impressions. Even with ad blocking, the top ad domains can still observe 40%–80% of page impressions, depending on the ad blocker (Bashir and Wilson, 2018).

Malicious ads, or malvertising, has been the focus of studies after even reputable publishers were found to sometimes serve malicious ads. All publishers that do not have exclusive agreements with their advertisers are potential publishers of malvertising because most publishers trust their advertisers and do not apply additional filters before displaying ads. Around 1% of ads observed by Zarras et al. (2014) showed malicious behavior. 82% of these malicious ads were served by the top 10,000 websites, compared to 76% of ads overall. This indicates that cybercriminals do not preferentially target top websites to serve malvertising, but rather distribute malvertising similarly to regular ads.

Some entities in the ad ecosystem have been observed in attempts to block transparency research. For example, a browser extension developed by journalists at ProPublica was recognizing ads on Facebook by searching the DOM for the word "sponsored," but was found to stop working after Facebook changed the text to "Sp*SonSso*SredS," interweaving invisible letters *S* and placing groups of one or two letters into separate *span* elements (Merrill and Tobin, 2019). The text kept changing, and at one point read "SpSpSononSsosoSredredSSS." In addition, Facebook disabled automated clicks on the button that shows ad explanations to users, preventing browser extensions from automatically collecting ad explanations (Merrill and Tobin, 2019).

From the user perspective, the average Facebook user sees 70 ads per week from 33 different advertisers. On average, this translates to six ads per session and 0.8 ads per minute (Galán et al., 2019). In relation to the other content users see on Facebook, ads represent 10%–15% of the information in a user's news feed. Increasing the portion of ads in the news feed by only 1% can increase Facebook's weekly revenue by an estimated $8 million. However, users are likely to be over-profiled because only 23% of user interests are related to the ads they receive (Galán et al., 2019).

7.4.2 Ad Targeting and Ad Delivery

Two main factors determine which ads are shown to specific users: the targeting attributes selected by the advertiser, and the ad delivery algorithm used by the ad platform. Researchers have studied both the characteristics and effects of these two factors.

Ad Targeting

A recurring theme in ad targeting studies is that ad platforms allow ads to be targeted at users' sensitive attributes. Although Google's policy states that ads would not be shown based on sensitive information, Wills and Tatar (2012) showed that ads targeted at sensitive information were indeed being shown to users, even though sensitive interests did not show up in Google's ad preference manager. Gmail ads were targeted at the contents of emails received by users, including emails with sensitive contents concerning the user's health, race, religion, sexual orientation, and financial situation (Lecuyer et al., 2015). Behavioral advertising was shown to virtual personas that were trained with only sensitive keywords (Carrascosa et al., 2015). Facebook assigns, on average, 16 potentially sensitive attributes to each user, and 60% of European Facebook users were tagged with at least one of the ten most common sensitive attributes (Cabañas et al., 2018). On a population level, 40% of EU citizens, corresponding to 73% of European Facebook users, were assigned at least one of the 500 most common sensitive attributes. Women and young people were assigned sensitive attributes at higher rates, and advertisers were indeed able to use these attributes for targeting (Cabañas et al., 2018).

Facebook allows advertisers to target users based on PII, but does not specify which PII sources are targetable. Venkatadri et al. (2019) found that most potential PII sources are targetable: PII mentioned in user profiles is targetable if the user has completed the verification for the PII. For example, a phone number is only targetable if the user has verified that they can access messages sent to the phone number; PII provided by users for the purpose of two-factor authentication or for the purpose of sending alerts about unrecognized logins is targetable; PII provided to Facebook Messenger and PII from address book synchronizations, i.e., a user's PII found in another user's address book, are also targetable. The only two sources of PII that were not targetable were PII provided to WhatsApp and PII uploaded by other advertisers. This indicates that Facebook does not consider purpose limitations for data provided to them.

Targeted ads are increasingly common. For example, half of the websites in 2014 placed targeted ads in 80% of their ad slots (Barford et al., 2014), and 5% of web ads were targeted at a user's profile, compared to 14% of ads on

Gmail (Google has since disabled ads on Gmail) (Lecuyer et al., 2015). More recently, researchers have studied to what extent different targeting strategies are used, finding that 20% of targeting strategies are potentially invasive (e.g., PII-based) or opaque (e.g., look-alike audiences). 12% of ads are retargeted ads and 24% of advertisers use multiple attributes for targeting. In addition, many advertisers change the content of their ads depending on the user, targeting attributes, or over time (Andreou et al., 2019).

Newer ad targeting methods, such as look-alike targeting or custom audiences based on PII lists, are less well understood by users compared to traditional targeting methods based on demographics or keywords (Wei et al., 2020).

Ad Delivery

The ad delivery process may result in biased ad delivery and discriminatory outcomes even when ads are not explicitly targeted at sensitive attributes. An experimental design to study discriminatory ad delivery is shown in Figure 7.4. Input variables include ads, the ad budget, and targeting attributes. The main response variable is the number of ad impressions by age, gender, race, and location, based on which gender and racial biases can be analyzed.

For example, a gender-neutral STEM career ad, even if targeted at any gender, was shown to over 20% more men than women. This was the case even though women had higher click rates, and could be replicated on several different ad platforms (Lambrecht and Tucker, 2019). This bias occurred because young women are a more expensive demographic to show ads to: low-budget ad campaigns on Facebook reach more than 55% men and campaigns

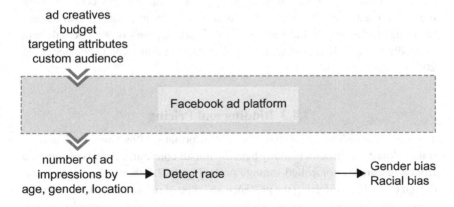

Figure 7.4 Experimental design of studies that analyze ad delivery mechanisms.

with high budgets more than 55% women (Ali et al., 2019a). Therefore, if the ad delivery algorithm optimizes for cost-effectiveness, it can distribute ads in a discriminatory way. This indicates that economic incentives may exacerbate existing discrimination (Lambrecht and Tucker, 2019).

The content of an ad – its headline, text, and image – can also influence ad delivery on Facebook. For example, ads for stereotypically male interests, such as bodybuilding, reach more than 80% men, even if the ad is targeted at all genders. Similarly, ads for stereotypically female interests such as cosmetics reach more than 90% women, ads for stereotypically black interests such as hip-hop reach more than 85% black users, and ads for stereotypically white interests such as country music reach more than 80% white users (Ali et al., 2019a). Ad delivery is skewed even when the ad has a neutral headline and text, and the ad image, representing a stereotypical interest, is invisible to human users (by using a 98% alpha channel). This indicates that Facebook automatically classifies ad images to estimate the relevance of the ad, which results in skewed ad delivery. This effect persists for ads for job search and housing where discrimination based on protected characteristics is illegal (Ali et al., 2019a).

Even when ad platforms disallow targeting specific sensitive attributes, advertisers can still create ad audiences that are discriminatory, for example, based on custom audiences or proxy attributes. To construct discriminatory custom audiences, advertisers need PII from a group of individuals that have the desired value of the sensitive attribute, for example, groups with a specific gender or ethnicity. This information can be found in public records such as voter records in the United States. Based on Facebook's lookalike audience construction, ads can then be targeted at a wider audience while still exhibiting the discriminatory feature. In addition, attributes that strongly correlate with the desired sensitive attribute can be used as a proxy to create discriminatory targeting, for example, the audience for "Marie Claire" is 90% female and the audience for "BlackNews.com" is 89% African American (Speicher et al., 2018).

7.4.3 Bidding and Pricing

The real-time bidding ecosystem and the information flows involved in real-time bidding are difficult to study because not all communication is observable from a researcher-controlled vantage point. Figure 7.5 shows an experimental design that allows inferring the presence and type of information flows in the ad ecosystem. The input variables include virtual personas and control personas that visit a set of products on e-commerce sites, followed by a visit to publisher

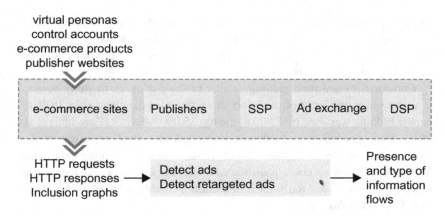

Figure 7.5 Experimental design of studies that analyze information flows in the ad ecosystem.

sites. Inferences about information flows can be made based on the ads and retargeted ads detected in the observed HTTP requests and responses.

To show a retargeted ad – an ad for a product that the user has previously viewed on an e-commerce site – the demand-side platform has to know that the user who is served an ad on a publisher's website has previously viewed the product on an e-commerce website. However, this information is spread between different entities, which means that cookie synchronization is an essential prerequisite for serving retargeted ads. Observing retargeted ads allowed Bashir et al. (2016) to identify 31% more cases of cookie synchronization than indicated by heuristics for detecting cookie synchronization.

A user's browsing history can also leak through real-time bidding even when no cookie synchronization is taking place (Olejnik et al., 2014). Because bid requests include both the URL that the user is visiting and the ad exchange's cookie for this user, bidders can record the URLs and identifying cookies they observe in bid requests and thereby build up a partial view of the user's browsing history. This allows bidders to observe up to 11% of a user's browsing history (Olejnik et al., 2014).

The ads.txt standard was introduced by the IAB to combat fraud in real-time bidding auctions. Its adoption has increased since its introduction in May 2017, with 20% of the top 100,000 websites adopting ads.txt in 2019. This corresponds to 62% of websites that are using RTB to display ads (Bashir et al., 2019a). Compliance with the standard also increased, with more than 70% of buyer-seller pairs in a dataset of 135 million RTB ads complying with ads.txt. However, a challenge for more systematic investigation of ads.txt is that it is difficult for researchers to act as participants in the system – which is necessary for randomized controlled experiments – because ad exchanges are not interested in working with a publisher whose website does not have millions of unique visitors per month.

Compared to real-time bidding, header bidding is easier to study because it allows observing most of the information flows on the client-side. In 2019, header bidding was used by 5,000 of the top 35,000 websites (Pachilakis et al., 2019). Half of websites used only one demand partner, and Google was used as a demand partner by more than 80% of websites, thus dominating the market. The latency before a website is displayed to the user increases with the number of demand partners and the number of ad slots available, with a median latency of 600 ms (Pachilakis et al., 2019).

The prices advertisers pay to place ads, and how these prices depend on the used targeting options, can be studied by observing the winning prices of RTB auctions where the prices are sent in clear-text. The average price for 1,000 ad impressions (its CPM) is $0.36, with the highest price around $3, depending on the category of website that displayed the ad, the time of day, and the location of the user (Olejnik et al., 2014). Shopping, restaurant, and reference sites attracted the highest ad prices, while humor and sports sites were less expensive by a factor of at least two. Ad impressions during nighttime were more expensive than during daytime, and ads shown to users in the US were more expensive than ads shown to French users, which in turn were more expensive than Japanese users. In contrast to users valuing their presence on a website at €7 (Carrascal et al., 2013), during RTB auctions this information is sold for less than $0.0005 or $0.5 CPM.

However, RTB auctions are moving towards encrypted prices, making ad prices more difficult to observe. In 2017, 68% of desktop ad prices were encrypted, and 26% of prices for mobile ads. In addition, encrypted prices were around 1.7x higher than clear-text prices (Papadopoulos et al., 2017).

In 2019, prices for ads observed during header bidding were lower than those observed for RTB in 2014, with only 20% of header bidding bid prices higher than $0.5 CPM, and the median cost between $0.00084 CPM and $0.096 CPM, depending on the ad size (Pachilakis et al., 2019).

The amount of behavioral advertising received by a user depends on whether that user's interests are seen as valuable: virtual personas with more valuable interests received more ads targeted at the corresponding interests (Carrascosa et al., 2015). To observe the value of ad targeting categories, the suggested bid prices for ad targeting combinations on YouTube and Facebook can be used. Users in the US are the most expensive to target, and 17 of the 20 most expensive countries are countries with "very high human development."

The prices for interest categories varied widely and were not consistent between YouTube and Facebook (Marciel et al., 2016).

7.4.4 Ad Transparency Mechanisms

Ad preference managers and ad explanations are presented as transparency mechanisms by ad platforms such as Google and Facebook. It is important to study how well these mechanisms fulfill their transparency function, for example, with respect to user awareness and completeness.

An important requirement for transparency mechanisms is that users are aware of them. However, in 2019, 90% of users were unaware of BlueKai and eXelate, and 48%–68% were unaware of Google's and Facebook's ad preference managers (Bashir et al., 2019b).

Another requirement is that APMs are complete, that is, they show all inferred interests that are available to advertisers for targeting. However, interest categories for some targeted ads were never shown in the APM (Wills and Tatar, 2012) and Google's APM never shows sensitive interests, even though it allows ads to be targeted at these interests (Datta et al., 2015). For example, a virtual persona interested in substance abuse was shown statistically significantly more ads on the topic of substance abuse, but the interest was not displayed in the APM. This is particularly problematic because it prevents effectful choice: when a user removes an interest from the APM, they should be shown fewer ads relating to that interest. While Google's APM enables effectful choice for those interests shown in the APM, it is not available for interests that are omitted from the APM (Datta et al., 2015).

Ad explanations are intended to explain to users why a particular ad was shown to them. To be satisfactory, explanations should be personalized, complete, consistent, correct, and deterministic. Facebook's ad explanations, while personalized and consistent, are often incomplete, misleading, and lack specificity: 97% of ad explanations that mentioned page likes or ad clicks did not state the specific page liked or ad clicked (Andreou et al., 2018). In addition, Facebook's ad explanations show, at most, one targeting attribute in the first part of the ad explanation (see Figure 3.10), even if the advertiser used multiple attributes. When selecting which targeting attribute to show to users, Facebook chooses the attribute that is most common among its users and prefers demographic attributes over PII-based attributes and behavioral attributes. This selection strategy results in incomplete ad explanations that lack explanatory power (Andreou et al., 2018). In addition, targeting attributes from data brokers are never used in ad explanations (Angwin et al., 2016b) and, even when PII targeting is used, Facebook does not explain which piece of PII was used, such as email address or phone number. Finally, even though Facebook's ad explanations correctly included the user's attributes, they also included attributes that were not used for targeting at all, such as the user's age and location. This results in misleading ad explanations (Andreou et al., 2018).

A user study confirmed that users prefer more detailed ad explanations to those deployed on Twitter or Facebook. However, more detailed ad explanations also decreased user trust in the advertiser, which can explain why the currently deployed ad explanations are incomplete, misleading, and nonspecific (Wei et al., 2020).

7.4.5 Mobile Ads

The market for in-app mobile ads is more concentrated than the market for browser-based ads. For example, 73% of ad flows on both Android and iPhone are served by Google (Vallina-Rodriguez et al., 2012). Figure 7.6 shows two experimental designs for the study of mobile ads, based on static and dynamic analysis. The design for static analysis (Figure 7.6a) uses apps and ad libraries as inputs, and quantifies prevalence, use of permissions, and possible information leaks based on a reachability analysis on control flow graphs. The design for dynamic analysis (Figure 7.6b), on the other hand, uses interactions with apps as inputs and records network traffic. The targeting attributes and methods are then analyzed based on the detected ads, ad requests, and ad categories.

In-app ads are realized by ad libraries included in apps. As a result, ad libraries share the permissions of the host app, and this means that ad libraries can have access to a wide range of sensitive data. Free apps, which are more popular than paid apps, request more permissions and are more likely to include ad libraries (Chen et al., 2016a). In 2012, one-third of apps contained one ad library, 10% contained two, and 3% of apps contained five or more ad libraries (Grace et al., 2012). The number of permissions available to ad libraries has also increased over time. Dangerous permissions were available to more than 20% of ad libraries in 2013, compared to under 10% in 2011. In addition, most of the permissions newly available to ad libraries were related to uniquely identifying users and extracting user data (Book et al., 2013).

Ad libraries can use these permissions in two ways: they can collect information to improve their ad targeting, and they can expose information to the advertiser.

80% of ad requests from mobile devices contained more than ten attribute-value pairs. These attribute-value pairs can contain, for example, unique device identifiers (66% of ad requests), the user's location (28% of ad requests),

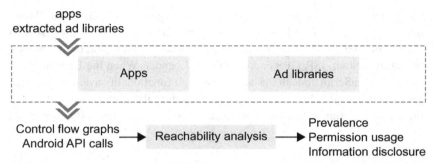

(a) Static analysis (e.g., Grace et al., 2012) allows analyzing what ad libraries are capable of, but not what they actually do during run-time.

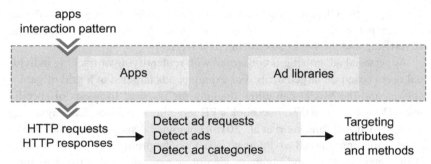

(b) Dynamic analysis (e.g., Nath, 2015) allows analyzing the actual behavior of ad libraries during run-time.

Figure 7.6 Experimental design of studies that analyze mobile advertising.

and static targeting attributes such as the app category (3% of ad requests). The most common targeting attribute is the app name, whereas location is only used by 4 of the top 10 mobile ad networks. Behavior-based targeting where the ad network identifies the user based on their device identifier and targets based on its internal records, for example, about app usage patterns, was only used by one ad network, Google's DoubleClick, for 80% of their ads (Nath, 2015).

Regarding data exposed to advertisers, ads can read file names in a user's local storage (but not their contents). This allows ads to test for the existence of files created by other apps, and thereby infer that a user has installed specific apps. This can allow inferences, for example, about medication, gender preference, browsing history, and the user's social graph (Son et al., 2016). In addition, some DSPs allow advertisers to insert macros into the URL parameters of tracking pixels that are delivered together with ad content. These macros are replaced with user values by the DSP and allow advertisers to learn about the app the user is using, the user's device identifier, device model, operating system, ISP, GPS coordinates, and gender. When the DSP supports ad tags – JavaScript code in the ad creative – all functionality available through JavaScript is available to the advertiser, including the BatteryStatus API and the amount of time taken for downloads or computation tasks (Corner et al., 2017) .

7.4.6 Adversarial Advertising and Advertising as a Service

This exposure of data to advertisers has enabled two distinct uses of advertising that are not related to the original goals of the ad ecosystem: adversarial advertising and the use of advertising *as a service.*

Adversarial advertising is concerned with reidentifying or tracking individual users based on targeted ads. For example, ads targeted at a grid of geolocations and the MAID can allow tracking the physical locations of specific users (Vines et al., 2017); Facebook's PII targeting can allow deanonymizing website visitors (Venkatadri et al., 2018); combined demographic and interest-based targeting can allow inferring the Google profile of website visitors (Conti et al., 2015); and common identifiers can allow advertisers to infer social connections between users (Wang et al., 2019). These individual attacks show that the advertising ecosystem does not only enable corporate surveillance of users, but also adversarial surveillance by potentially malicious third parties.

The specificity of ad targeting and ad audience size estimation can enable scientific studies. For example, ads can be used to perform measurement tasks, such as measuring the bandwidth observed for US-based mobile carriers, grouped by device model, battery level, charge status, and hour of the day (Corner et al., 2017). By targeting the same devices repeatedly, which is enabled by unique device identifiers, the same approach can be used for longitudinal studies. Compared to the cost of performing similar measurement studies through other means, ad-based measurement can be very cost-effective: a measurement consisting of one million ads can be performed for under $1,000 (Corner et al., 2017).

Facebook's ad audience size estimate allows researchers to conduct demographic studies. For example, the urban/rural divide can be studied by comparing inequalities between urban and rural municipalities, including the likelihood of college education, the likelihood of being married, the likelihood of being interested in the Catholic church, or the likelihood of using specific mobile platforms. In addition, linear regression based on this data allows the prediction of income levels (Rama et al., 2020).

Similarly, the ad audience size estimate allows researchers to study the cultural similarity of countries by obtaining ad audience size estimates when targeting different countries and cultural indicators. For example, targeting the names of 20 Brazilian dishes allowed Vieira et al. (2020) to obtain a measure of how culturally similar different countries are to Brazil.

8

Transparency for Corporate Services

The user-facing services offered by corporations have been studied to find out whether the services show biases towards specific groups of users, whether they comply with policies, laws, and regulations, and how they use user data in providing their services. This chapter first focuses on network-level services, such as server-side decisions on the accessibility of services and the provision of wireless internet access. Then, the chapter discusses web-based services, including privacy policies, search, social networks, and e-commerce. The chapter closes by discussing results for mobile services, such as the characteristics of app stores, third-party libraries, and apps.

8.1 Networking Services

Networking services are concerned with enabling access to web and mobile services. This section focuses on two networking issues in particular, server-side blocking and wireless internet access.

8.1.1 Server-Side Blocking

Server-side blocking refers to the decision, made by individual website owners, to make their website entirely or partly unavailable to specific groups of users. Reasons for server-side blocking include blocking of EU users for GDPR compliance, blocking of regions due to economic sanctions, blocking of regions due to third-party liability in that region, blocking due to hosting costs (Tschantz et al., 2018b), blocking due to security concerns, or blocking to prevent fraudulent traffic from particular regions (Afroz et al., 2018).

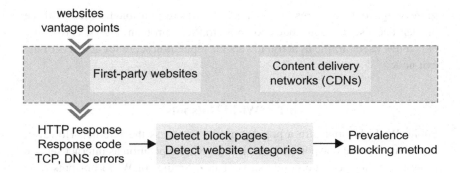

Figure 8.1 Experimental design of studies that measure server-side blocking.

Studies of server-side blocking have investigated the extent of blocking – how many regions or users are blocked, and how many websites engage in it – as well as the mechanisms used to perform blocking. Figure 8.1 shows how experiments to study server-side blocking can be designed. Based on sets of websites and vantage points as input variables, data is collected on different layers of the internet protocol suite, including HTTP responses, TCP errors, and DNS errors. The prevalence of blocking and blocking methods is analyzed based on detected block pages and website categories.

The extent of server-side blocking on the web depends on the selection of vantage points. For example, with vantage points in Africa and Pakistan, Afroz et al. (2018) found that less than 1% of websites engaged in geoblocking, with some websites blocking access entirely from large regions. Similarly, 0.6% of websites that use Cloudflare performed country-based blocking (Tschantz et al., 2018b). Blocking for security reasons, however, was about 10 times more common and included blocked IP ranges, blocked browsers, and soft blocking with captchas. With vantage points in 177 countries, McDonald et al. (2018) found that 4.4% of websites blocked access from at least one country, with shopping websites engaging in most geoblocking, and Iran, Syria, Sudan, and Cuba being the most frequently blocked countries. However, most countries are subject to at least some geoblocking, indicated by a median of four blocked websites per country.

Besides geoblocking, some websites also block users who browse the web anonymously via Tor. 367 of the Alexa top 1,000 websites block at least some of Tor users' traffic, but no website succeeds in blocking traffic from *all* Tor exit nodes. In addition, blocking behavior differed for different subsites. For example, Google's main website was never blocked, but the search function was blocked for 23%–40% of exit nodes (Khattak et al., 2016). The reputation score assigned to IP addresses by Cloudflare was responsible for most of these blocks: because Tor exit nodes combine traffic from many users, classifying only a few users' traffic as abuse lowers the reputation score for all users of the exit node.

8.1.2 Wi-Fi Hotspots

Public Wi-Fi hotspots are a popular means to access the Internet. However, providers of these hotspots can use their privileged position as internet service provider to engage in corporate surveillance. Studies of Wi-Fi hotspots have focused on the types of information hotspots can learn about their users, and on the prevalence of data collection behaviors at hotspots.

More than two-thirds of users of open hotspots at airports leak some private information while using the hotspot, for example, through multicast name resolution, broadcasting their list of known wireless access points, contents of plain-text HTTP browsing, and device identifiers (Cheng et al., 2013). In addition, the operators of captive portals can access the browsing history of users, for example, by embedding invisible references to a large number of websites. By observing cookies in the HTTP requests from users, the captive portal can infer which websites the user has already visited (Dabrowski et al., 2016).

Large-scale studies of hotspot data collection behavior have so far not been conducted, owing to the requirement of being physically close to a hotspot to observe its behaviors. However, a small-scale study of hotspots in Montreal revealed widespread data collection (Ali et al., 2019b). For example, 40% of hotspots used a social login or registration page to collect PII, 95% of hotspots used tracking methods on their captive portals and landing pages, with 7.4 third-party tracking domains on average, and 59% of hotspots created long-term cookies with up to 20 years validity. 38% of these hotspots set cookies even before getting user consent. In addition, user data was widely shared with third parties, including device identifiers like the MAC address (59%) and PII including name, email address, gender, and age (8%).

8.2 Web-Based Services

Web-based services can exhibit a range of behaviors that surveil users or take advantage of the collected user data Although user data can help improve web services, it can also be shared with third parties or used to discriminate. Figure 8.2 shows typical elements in the experimental design of studies that analyze specific web services. Input variables include websites of specific cate-

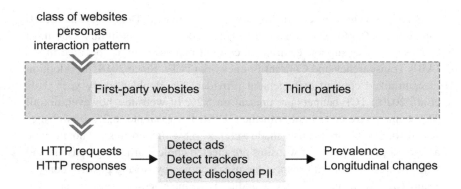

Figure 8.2 Generic experimental design for study of specific web services.

gories, virtual personas, and interaction patterns. HTTP requests and responses
are the most commonly collected data, and prevalence or longitudinal changes
are analyzed depending on, for example, the ads, trackers, or PII detected in
the HTTP traffic.

8.2.1 Privacy Policies and Cookie Notices

Privacy policies and cookie (or consent) notices are the key mechanisms for
communicating privacy practices to users and for collecting consent for the
intended data collection, processing, and sharing activities. Privacy policies
also explain to users how they may complain or opt out.

The European General Data Protection Regulation (GDPR) introduced
new requirements for websites to ensure a lawful basis for their privacy
practices. Many websites implemented these requirements by collecting user
consent via cookie notices. As a result, cookie notices have become more
prevalent after the GDPR came into force in 2018. For example, 40% of global
websites display cookie notices post-GDPR (van Eijk et al., 2019), whereas
the prevalence of cookie notices in Europe increased from 46% (pre-GDPR)
to 63% (post-GDPR) (Degeling et al., 2019).

Even though the GDPR is a European regulation, a user's location has
almost no influence on whether a cookie notice is displayed. Instead, the
display of a cookie notice correlated with the top-level domain of a website.
This means that cookie notices were displayed for the expected audience in
the website's own country instead of the real user location. However, .com
domains were an exception: they displayed cookie notices to EU users with
32% increased odds compared to other users (van Eijk et al., 2019).

Focusing on how the cookie notices are implemented, Degeling et al. (2019) found that 15% of websites use a third-party cookie consent library. One-third of these libraries support centralized consent management as specified in the IAB's Transparency and Consent Framework (TCF). Since 2018, the adoption of centralized consent management providers has doubled every year (Hils et al., 2020). TCF banners are present on 6.2% of websites, however, not all TCF banners are compliant with the GDPR. For example, 6.2% of websites stored consent before the user made a choice, 6.8% of websites did not provide a way to opt out, 46.5% of websites preselected choices affirming consent, and 5.3% of websites did not respect the user's choice by storing positive consent in any case (Matte et al., 2020). In addition, the interfaces of consent dialogues are often designed so that denying consent takes longer than giving consent. For example, users take a median of 3.2 s to give consent in one version of Quantcast's consent dialog, but a median of 6.7 s to deny, which indicates a significant time cost for privacy-conscious users (Hils et al., 2020).

Privacy policies have been studied with regard to their length, readability, and content. The readability of privacy policies can be measured using the Flesch Reading Ease (FRE) score, which is based on the counts of words, sentences, and syllables in a text. Higher FRE scores indicate easier readability, and scores above 45 are required for insurance policies in some jurisdictions. The average FRE for privacy policies has been measured as 39.83, and the average score for the policies of the most prominent trackers at 35.48. This indicates that privacy policies are very hard to read for the average website user (Libert, 2018).

After the GDPR was introduced, 15% of websites newly introduced a privacy policy, and 72% of websites updated their existing privacy policies. At the same time, privacy policies became between 25% and 40% longer (Degeling et al., 2019; Linden et al., 2020).

Besides length and readability, the content of privacy policies has been harder to study at scale due to the difficulty of automatically analyzing the semantics of legal text. As a result, studies have focused on specific aspects: the disclosure of third-party trackers, contradictory statements, opt-out statements, and the disclosure of data use in Android apps.

Data flows to third-party trackers, which are observable by visiting a website, should be disclosed in the website's privacy policy. However, only 38% of websites disclose that they embed Google trackers, even though Google trackers are present on 82% of websites. Overall, only 14.8% of third-party trackers are disclosed in privacy policies (Libert, 2018). Similarly, 42% of apps disclose privacy-relevant data flows in their privacy policies either incorrectly or not at all (Andow et al., 2020).

Contradictory statements in privacy policies include logical contradictions, narrowing definitions, and redefinitions of common terms, for example, policies stating that email addresses or device identifiers are not personally identifiable information. In a study of 11,000 privacy policies, 14% contained logical contradictions and 17% contained logical contradictions or narrowing definitions (Andow et al., 2019). In addition, the majority of policies – 60% – contain at least one negation. This feature makes policies harder to read for humans as well as harder to analyze for automated tools.

Opt-out statements are links that allow users to opt out of specific practices. In a set of 6,800 privacy policies, less than 3% of policies offered any kind of opt-out, with higher ranked sites offering opt-outs at a slightly higher rate. Most opt-out links were to allow users to opt out from receiving targeted advertising (Kumar et al., 2020).

The privacy policies of Android apps can be compared with the apps' actual behavior in terms of permission requests, API usage, and inclusion of third-party libraries. In a study of 1 million apps, 88% performed at least one privacy practice that would have to be disclosed in a privacy policy, but only half had a privacy policy. In addition, 12% of apps have at least one compliance issue related to location, with a median of three compliance issues per app (Zimmeck et al., 2019).

Subject access requests (SAR) are a mechanism introduced in the GDPR that gives users the right to request from any company the data that is being held about them. Companies are required to respond to requests within one month (or three months for complex requests). To evaluate to what extent companies comply with SARs, Urban et al. (2019) selected 38 companies that engaged in cookie synchronization, and sent SARs asking for all information related to their cookie identifiers. However, only 39% of companies granted access to the data in the required timeframe. 3% denied the request, 31% did not finish granting access on time, 11% of companies did not respond at all, and the remaining companies claimed that they do not store any data (Urban et al., 2019).

8.2.2 Search

Search engines are what makes information on the web accessible to users. This puts search engines in the powerful position of being able to decide what information users can find and how easy it is to find certain information. As a result, many studies have evaluated what information is presented on a search result page (SERP) and whether and to what extent the information is personalized or biased. Figure 8.3 shows a prototypical experimental design for studying search engines.

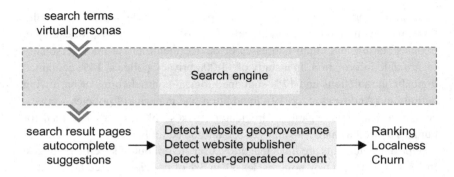

Figure 8.3 Experimental design for studies that measure search result personalization and bias.

Search results are typically presented with a title and a text snippet. These text snippets influence which links the user clicks, but biased text snippets can also influence users who only scan them while deciding which links to visit (Hu et al., 2019a). The partisanship of text snippets indicates whether snippets for political queries disproportionately use words associated with a political leaning, such as the use of "gun rights" (right) versus "gun violence" (left) in search results relating to the gun control debate in the US. Around half of text snippets amplify partisanship, which means that the text snippet has higher partisanship than its corresponding website, and 20% of snippets have inverse partisanship (Hu et al., 2019a). However, this is likely not due to a bias in Google's snippet algorithm, but rather due to the practices of including partisan quotes at the beginning of news articles and starting articles with strong language to attract clicks.

Google's top stories algorithm is the algorithm that selects three news articles that are highlighted in searches for trending stories. A relatively small set of publishers is selected to provide the majority of stories for the top-stories spots. Specifically, less than 20 publishers provide approximately 50% of all top stories, and the top 20% of publishers provide almost 90% of all stories (Lurie and Mustafaraj, 2019; Trielli and Diakopoulos, 2019). In addition, only one-third of publishers appears at least once in the first spot, whereas two-thirds of publishers appear at least once in the third spot (Lurie and Mustafaraj, 2019). This indicates that Google chooses less well-known publishers for the third spot in an attempt to expose users to more diverse search results.

User-generated content, for example, from Wikipedia and Twitter, is often included in Google search result pages. Specifically, Wikipedia is present on 58% of search result pages. For high-volume queries for trending and popular topics, Wikipedia appears on more than 75% of search result pages (Vincent et al., 2019). This illustrates the importance of open, user-generated content for Google's ability to satisfy user information needs and raises the question of whether Wikipedia editors should receive a share of the economic benefit Google derives from their work (Vincent et al., 2019).

The autocomplete suggestions shown while users are typing a search query have the potential of influencing the specific terms that users search for. This can have a significant effect on determining what kinds of information sources come up in the search results. Bing's suggestions included negative emotions at a higher rate than Google's, and Google included social media references twice as often as Bing (10% compared to 4.6%, respectively). Google's social media references most often pointed to YouTube, indicating that Google's autocomplete algorithm tends to favor Google's own products (Robertson et al., 2019). In addition, the majority of suggestions appeared for less than 10 days in a 10-week dataset. Higher-ranked suggestions were more stable over time which may indicate attempts to reduce the effects of inaccurate or misleading autocomplete suggestions.

Search result pages may show different results for different users. Overall, less than 12% of search results are personalized, with most personalized results towards the bottom of search result pages (Hannak et al., 2013). The highest amount of personalization was observed for news, local queries, and political queries, all of which are discussed in the following sections.

News Curation

News curation algorithms that personalize news and news search results have been audited due to their potential of creating filter bubbles in which users only see the type of news that matches their preexisting world view.

On Google News, statistically significant personalization of search results reinforced the partisanship of virtual personas. Specifically, for virtual personas trained to be either pro- or anti-immigration, searches for current policy issues resulted in an average difference of the search result list of 3.2%, with larger differences towards the bottom of the list, and an edit distance of 8.4 in 100 search results (Le et al., 2019).

On Apple News, the top stories are curated by humans, while trending stories are algorithmically curated. Bandy and Diakopoulos (2019) did not observe personalization based on location or user accounts, but did find differences between the human- and algorithmically curated news feeds. The human-curated top stories had a lower concentration of publishers: three publishers accounted for 23% of stories, compared to 45% of algorithmically curated stories. In addition, the selection of topics differed: the algorithmically curated trending stories featured more celebrities and sensational news, whereas the human-curated top stories included more substantive policy issues and international news (Bandy and Diakopoulos, 2019).

Location Biases

Location can influence search results in two ways: first, through the location of the user who is performing the search, and second, through the locations that search results originate in.

The impact of the user's location can serve as a proxy for other traits, such as race, income, education, or political affiliation. To study this impact, Kliman-Silver et al. (2015) designed a series of vantage points that represent locations on national, regional, and local scale. There was almost no location-based personalization for political or controversial queries, but queries for local terms were personalized: 18–34% of results were different and 6–10 URLs were reordered. Even though results were very noisy – two users from the same location could receive different results – the personalization level for local queries increased with the distance between two searchers.

The localness of search results indicates where search results originate from. When applied to searches for geographical information, localness expresses "which countries are producing their own representations and which are represented by others" (Ballatore et al., 2017). Localness is highest in the US, and other wealthy countries also have more locally produced content. However, most content is produced in countries in the Global North, even when searching for information on a country in the Global South in the local language. For example, content produced in the US supplied more than half of the search results on the first page for 61 countries. This means that content producers in relatively few countries can determine what information is available about other countries, which Ballatore et al. (2017) call a *digital hegemony*.

Political Biases

Political biases in search results and search result rankings can influence the formation of political opinions and ultimately the voting behavior of individuals.

On Twitter, although the input bias of all tweets relating to a search term is slightly left-leaning, the output bias of the top 20 tweets is on average more left-leaning for candidates from the left and more right-leaning for candidates from the right (Kulshrestha et al., 2017). This indicates that Twitter's ranking algorithm amplifies the input bias of tweets.

Search engine result pages for political queries on Google show no significant difference in weighted bias (where the top results are weighted higher than the bottom results) between searches where users are logged into Google and searches from incognito windows. This indicates the absence of filter bubble effects (Robertson et al., 2018a). However, results shown in Google's *twitter-card* are more right-leaning than search results in other components of the SERP, and results towards the bottom of the SERP are more left-leaning. On average, Google's ranking algorithm shifts the lean of SERPs to the right, although the magnitude of the effect varies widely depending on the search term (Robertson et al., 2018a).

In a study of queries suggested by Google's autocomplete, Robertson et al. (2018b) found that search result pages resulting from autocomplete suggestions are significantly personalized. Personalization increased with the amount of Alphabet services that participants used regularly and was 19% higher for logged-in users. Participants that showed weak preferences for or against a candidate received significantly more personalization than other participants. This is an important result because these individuals are most susceptible to being influenced by biased rankings.

To study the extent to which individuals can be influenced by biased rankings, the so-called *search engine manipulation effect*, Epstein and Robertson (2015) used a lab-based experiment to analyze voter behavior. They found that the voting preferences of undecided voters could be shifted by 20% or more. They presented participants with a choice to vote in a foreign election, but gave three groups of participants different search results for gathering information before casting their vote: one group received search results with an unbiased ranking, while the rankings for the other two groups were biased towards either of the two candidates. Most participants were not aware that their search result rankings were manipulated, and even participants who were aware were influenced by the manipulation. In real elections, a shift in voting preferences of the observed magnitude, if only 10% of voters are undecided, could shift the election outcome by 2.5%, which is larger than the winning margin of many real-word elections (Epstein and Robertson, 2015).

8.2.3 Social Networks

The importance of social networks for today's internet users can hardly be understated. However, the importance of *auditing* social networks is best illustrated by three experiments that Facebook performed on their users. These experiments demonstrate the power that Facebook's algorithms have over user behavior and even emotions.

In the first experiment, Facebook experimented with *emotional contagion* (Kramer et al., 2014). The 689,000 participants in the experiment were not aware that they were participants, and had not given informed consent. However, Facebook argued that their data use policy covers experiments and thereby constitutes informed consent. In the experiment, Facebook classified emotions in users' posts as positive or negative, and then reduced posts with either positive or negative emotions in users' news feeds, aiming to determine whether this reduction in emotional posts would affect the emotions in the user's subsequent posts. They found that they could indeed affect users' emotions: users who received fewer positive posts then posted 0.1% fewer positive words and 0.04% more negative words, whereas users who received fewer negative posts subsequently posted 0.07% fewer negative words and 0.06% more positive words.

In the second experiment, Facebook experimented with political mobilization and voting behavior during the 2010 US congressional election. Facebook displayed different types of mobilization messages – intended to remind users to vote – and aimed to analyze which messages were most effective. Users were divided into three groups: the first group received an *informational* message, reminding them of the election day, providing a link to find the closest polling place, showing how many Facebook users already voted, and providing a button for the user to indicate that they voted; the second group received a *social* message which, in addition to the contents of the informational message, contained pictures of friends who had already voted; and the third group was used as a control group and was not shown a message (Bond et al., 2012). Actual voting behavior was assessed by matching Facebook account data to voter records. Based on this matching, Facebook found that users in the social group were 2% more likely to click the "I voted" button, and 0.39% more likely to actually vote than users in the other two groups. In addition, for each close friend who received the social message, a user was 0.22% more likely to vote than if their friend had not received the message. As a result, Facebook estimated that their political mobilization messages resulted in 60,000 additional votes, and the effects of friends resulted in another 280,000 additional votes.

The third experiment was similar, but performed during the 2012 US presidential election. In this experiment, users in the social group were 0.24% more likely to vote, with each additional close friend in the social group increasing the likelihood by 0.1%, resulting in a total of 270,000 additional votes (Jones et al., 2017). This amount of additional votes may be enough to influence the real-world outcome of an election. Even though Facebook *has the power* to use this political mobilization in a discriminatory way, for example, by displaying more mobilization messages to users with a particular political leaning, independent research is needed to find out whether this power is used.

Biases and Personalization in News Feeds and Recommendations
According to Facebook, "the order in which users see stories in the News Feed depends on many factors, including how often the viewer visits Facebook, how much they interact with certain friends, and how often users have clicked on links to certain websites in News Feed in the past" (Bakshy et al., 2015). Although this statement describes some of the inputs to Facebook's news feed curation algorithm, it does not describe the resulting properties of the news feed. Audit studies have investigated personalization and biases on social media platforms, for example, biases in Facebook's news feed or the effects of YouTube's video recommendation algorithm.

To evaluate political biases in Facebook's news feed, Hargreaves et al. (2018, 2019) configured virtual Facebook personas with different political preferences in the 2018 Italian election. Personas only followed a set of Facebook pages representative of all parties in the election, and political preferences induced by liking and commenting on corresponding posts. The top-most position in the news feed was strongly biased towards the persona's political leaning. In addition, only a small number of publishers appeared in the top positions of the news feed, and some publishers consistently appeared with a lower frequency than would be expected in an unfiltered news feed. The news feed for an "undecided" persona with no obvious political leaning was similar to that of a right-leaning user.

The topical composition of the *information diets* of social media users is skewed more towards entertainment, compared to the topical composition of broadcast mass media which is skewed more towards politics (Kulshrestha et al., 2015). For individual users, the contribution of the top topic, i.e., the topic that users consume most information about, was 30% higher on social media compared to mass media. For 80% of users, their top two topics determined half of their information diet, and the bottom twelve topics contributed only between 10% and 20% (Kulshrestha et al., 2015). This indicates that social media personalization leads to narrow information diets that consist of only few topics, which can create and enhance filter bubble effects.

YouTube's video recommendation algorithm allows viewers to discover new content, but it may also steer viewers towards more radical content. Ribeiro et al. (2020) found some evidence for a pipeline of users migrating to more extreme communities: 23.3% of users who wrote one or two comments on alt-right videos in 2018 commented only on alt-lite videos in 2006–2012; 7% commented only on videos from the intellectual dark web; and 5.5% commented only on control channels. They found similar indications of a radicalization pathway in YouTube's recommendations. However, their analysis did not encompass enough videos and recommendations to draw conclusions founded on statistically significant causal evidence.

In a study of YouTube's strategy for moderating comments on videos, Jiang et al. (2019) found no difference in moderation rates between left- and right-leaning content. Comments on extreme videos were 50% more likely to be taken down, and comments on factually true videos were 60% less likely. Comments made after a video was fact-checked were 20% more likely to be moderated. Even though there is a *correlation* indicating that comments on right-leaning videos are moderated more frequently, Jiang et al. (2019) find no *causation*. Instead, differences in moderation rates are likely caused by higher rates of misinformation, extreme partisanship, and linguistic cues indicating hate speech.

Misuses of Social Media Platforms
Social media platforms are also used by actors outside of the platform, for example, by using deceptive link previews to lure users to potentially malicious external content.

When users share links on social media, many social media platforms generate a visual link preview that is displayed instead of the URL shared by the user. However, these link previews can be manipulated, for example, so that the resulting link preview hides the malicious target. Most social media sites generate previews only infrequently, about every two weeks, which gives attackers time to run malicious campaigns based on previously generated link previews. In addition, 90% of social media sites do not employ any countermeasures against sharing of malicious links. Social media sites, as mediators between their portals and external web links, are responsible for at least not misrepresenting the contents of external links to their users (Stivala and Pellegrino, 2020).

8.2.4 Pricing

The pricing of products or services on the Internet can easily be personalized algorithmically. This means that e-commerce sites could attempt to ask the maximum price each individual is willing to pay for a product, thereby maximizing their profits. Many audit studies have evaluated whether price discrimination on the Internet exists, and if so, what its effects are. In addition, the effects of algorithmic pricing strategies and the presence of dark patterns on e-commerce sites have been audited.

Three possible triggers for price discrimination include the user's underlying system, their location, and personal information, such as whether a user is affluent or budget-conscious. Mikians et al. (2012) did not find evidence for discrimination based on the operating system or browser, but found that prices for digital products varied up to 166% based on the user's location, and prices for physical products at Staples varied up to 11% depending on location. In addition, biased search result rankings were used instead of price discrimination, for example, to show more expensive products to affluent users and cheaper products to budget-conscious users. Another study found that 3.8% of retailers vary prices based on the country of users, with variations of up to a factor of seven. Only 0.4% of retailers varied prices within countries, for which the most likely explanation was A/B price testing (Iordanou et al., 2017).

However, not all studies found evidence for systematic price discrimination or steering. For example, Hannak et al. (2014) only observed personalization strategies, including reduced prices for members, reduced prices for users of certain mobile platforms, and re-ordered search results lists to show more expensive products first. A study of airline pricing did not find evidence for price discrimination either: the observed price fluctuations could be fully explained by other factors, such as real changes in price and increased tax (Vissers et al., 2014). Similarly, a study of hotel and rental car bookings found no evidence for price discrimination. The price differences in 1.1% of data points were small and could be explained by currency conversion issues (Hupperich et al., 2018). These results indicate that outright price discrimination may be much less frequent on the Internet than commonly speculated.

Algorithmic pricing means that prices are determined by an algorithm instead of a human merchant. A heuristic to detect algorithmic pricing, for example, on the Amazon Marketplace, is based on the assumption that algorithmic prices are likely to be set, at least in part, in response to other sellers' prices. Based on frequent observations of prices for specific products, four time series can be constructed: the seller's price, the lowest price, Amazon's price, and the second-lowest price. The similarity between these time series, computed using Spearman's Rank Correlation ρ, indicates whether prices change at the same time (large ρ). Instances of algorithmic pricing can therefore be assumed when $\rho \geq 0.7$ and $p \leq 0.05$, i.e., ρ is statistically significant (Chen et al., 2016b).

Based on this heuristic, 2.4% of sellers on Amazon Marketplace use algorithmic pricing. In most cases, the target price for algorithmic pricing is set to the current lowest price: 70% of sellers are within $1 of the lowest price, and 40% are within $1 of Amazon's price. Some sellers set prices to 15%–30% above Amazon's price to account for Amazon's commission fees. Comparing algorithmic sellers to nonalgorithmic sellers, algorithmic sellers are active for longer but sell fewer products, possibly because they focus on products they can obtain in bulk at low price. In addition, algorithmic sellers have slightly better feedback scores and significantly more feedback ratings than nonalgorithmic sellers (Chen et al., 2016b).

Dark patterns are another method to maximize profits from e-commerce sites. Dark patterns are patterns in user interface design which are intended to steer users towards making decisions favorable not to themselves, but to the site employing the dark pattern. Privacy dark patterns have been identified on many websites (Bösch et al., 2016). On e-commerce websites, 11% of shopping sites employed dark patterns, and specialized third-party entities exist that provide dark patterns as turnkey solutions. Among the most common dark patterns are low-stock messages that create an impression of scarcity, countdown timers that claim that a special deal or discount will expire, and social activity messages that create social pressure by informing users how many others have already purchased the product (Mathur et al., 2019).

8.2.5 Ratings and Rankings

Algorithms for ratings and rankings are used not only in general-purpose search engines (see Section 8.2.2), but also for specialized products or services, such as hotels, hotel bookings, and résumé search.

Different hotel booking websites use different rating algorithms, but it is not clear whether the resulting ratings for the same hotels are consistent across different booking websites. Eslami et al. (2017) found that the rating interface of booking.com suggests that the lowest possible rating is 1 out of 10. However, because the final score is computed from a set of component scores, the rating algorithm outputs a lowest score of 2.5, even if all component scores are at their lowest level. As a result, the ratings for hotels in their sample did not differ significantly between Expedia and hotels.com, but both ratings differed significantly from the booking.com rating. Differences were largest when ratings are below 7 out of 10, with a mean difference of up to 37%. This indicates that rating algorithms can be designed to create scores that may be misleading for users.

In addition to biased rating algorithms, the ranking algorithms on hotel booking websites may also be biased. The extent to which the rank of a hotel on a booking website depends on the price offered for the same hotel on other booking sites, including the hotel's own website, can be used to study these biases. Booking websites have often used price parity clauses – and still do so in North America – requiring hotels to match the price on the booking site to the lowest price offered elsewhere. However, between 2013 and

2018 European competition regulators have prohibited price parity clauses. Hotels have suspected that booking websites adapted their ranking algorithms in response, to find alternative ways of punishing hotels that offer lower prices elsewhere. In a sample of 18,000 hotels, Hunold et al. (2018) observe many cases where either the hotel's own website (25%) or a competitor booking website (15–20%) offered lower prices. Taking into account a wide range of factors that could influence a hotel's ranking, a 10% lower price elsewhere had the same effect on ranking as if the user rating was decreased by 0.3 points out of 10. This indicates that this ranking strategy reduces the search quality for consumers because the ranking does not reflect the user's search criteria, but rather the booking website's profit maximization.

Résumé search websites are websites that allow recruiters to search for job candidates. A concern on résumé search sites is gender bias, which would result in candidates of one gender being ranked lower than the other. Chen et al. (2018) found no evidence for direct discrimination, where gender is used as an input to the ranking algorithm. However, the ranking algorithms did not meet individual and group fairness criteria. Individual fairness requires that candidates with similar features should be placed at similar ranks, regardless of gender. However, at position 30, female candidates appeared 1.4 ranks below similar male candidates. Although this was statistically significant, it is a small effect. Group fairness requires that the distribution of ranks should be similar among men and women. Around 10% of job title/city combinations showed group unfairness, with the job title determining whether males or females were the disadvantaged group.

8.2.6 Browser Extensions

Browser extensions can leak user data to third parties. This phenomenon has almost exclusively been studied for Chrome extensions. 6.3% of the top 10,000 extensions for Chrome leaked some data, although the majority were accidental leaks through the HTTP Referer header. However, some extensions also shared browsing history with third parties and leaked search queries, form data, and information about other extensions (Starov and Nikiforakis, 2017b). In addition, 2.1% of the top 178,000 extensions leaked sensitive information (Chen and Kapravelos, 2018), and 1.9% of extensions tracked their users including their browser history (Weissbacher et al., 2017). Some of these extensions used encryption or exfiltrated data using WebSockets to evade detection.

Importantly, this issue does not exclusively concern low-ranking extensions with small users bases: the top ten leaking extensions had over 60 million users

(Chen and Kapravelos, 2018), and more popular extensions leaked data more frequently (Starov and Nikiforakis, 2017b).

8.2.7 Malicious Web Services or Practices

Audit studies have also been conducted to find out about the prevalence and characteristics of potentially illegal web services or practices, such as click interception, cloaking, and free live-streaming sites.

Click interception or clickjacking is an attempt to make users perform clicks that they did not intend, for example, by overlaying invisible iFrames over benign-looking buttons. These unintended clicks can be used, for example, for generating clicks on ads or for distributing malicious content. To detect clickjacking, a browser extension can monitor accesses to HTML anchor elements, creation and modification of hyperlinks, and use of JavaScript event listeners. Using this method, Zhang et al. (2019b) found 437 unique third-party scripts that performed click interception on 613 websites, or about 25% of websites in their sample. This indicates that techniques are needed to ensure link integrity and limit the privileges of third-party JavaScript.

Cloaking techniques are used to make websites appear benign to search engines, but then serve malicious content to human users. The prevalence of cloaking on the Internet can be evaluated by comparing the titles and text snippets of search results with the real contents of the website. Cloaking techniques are more common when searching for high-risk terms, such as luxury products or weight loss products. In these cases, 11.7% of the top 100 search results and 4.9% of ads cloaked against the Google crawler (Invernizzi et al., 2016). This indicates that detection of cloaked search results is needed on the client-side in order to protect users from malicious content.

Free live-streaming sites (FLIS) are websites that offer video streams without the consent of the content owner. Besides the issue of copyright infringement, these websites are also likely to exploit users for monetary gain. The most highly ranked FLIS domain had an Alexa rank of 1,553, and 64% of FLIS domains had been reported at least once for copyright violation (Rafique et al., 2016). Visitors of these domains were exposed to a large amount of ads, often deceptive and/or malicious. For example, video players had, on average, five or six overlay ads which hid more than 80% of the area of the player. On average, about 50% of the displayed ads were malicious, and 16% of domains used anti-ad blockers to ensure ad revenue.

8.2.8 Other Web Services

Other web services include contact forms, user registration, domain parking, and paywalls, and mapping.

Contact forms allow users to contact the website, however, they frequently leak personal information to third parties. In particular, 29% of websites had more third-party JavaScript embedded on their contact form compared to their main page, which represents a large potential for PII leaks. In addition, 6.1% of websites intentionally leaked PII to third parties, for example, through third-party form builders and marketing tools, and a further 2.5% of contact forms leaked PII accidentally, for example, through poor coding practices (Starov et al., 2016).

More than 50% of websites that allow users to sign up, but are not social networks, leak private information, such as profile data and search strings, from registered users to at least one third party. Half of these leaking websites leak the user identifier, such as the user's email address, which can allow third parties to link records belonging to the same user (Krishnamurthy et al., 2011).

Domain parking refers to domains that the domain owner is not using to display user-facing content or services, but instead is holding in their domain portfolio for future development or resale. Domain parking services are used to monetize the domain by displaying advertising. Parked domains are often typosquatting domains that users visit when they mistype common URLs, or domains that have been repurposed after command and control servers used for malware distribution have been taken down. 60% of parked domains are parked with three popular services, Sedo Parking, Internet Traffic, and Cash Parking. Half of parked domains were owned by only 15% of domain owners, indicating that some parked domain owners have very large portfolios. Google is the most common ad syndicator for parked domains, present on almost 90% of parked domains (Vissers et al., 2015).

Paywalls

Paywalls are becoming more prevalent for financing web services, such as news sites, in cases where advertising revenue is not sufficient. There are two main paywall policies: *soft* paywalls allow access to some free articles but require a subscription after the free article quota has been exceeded. They enforce reading limits on the client and thus can be circumvented; *hard* paywalls require a subscription to access any content. They enforce reading limits on the server-side and cannot be easily circumvented (Papadopoulos et al., 2020).

Heuristics and machine learning can be used to detect the presence of paywalls on websites. Heuristics based on crowd-sourced datasets can use paywall recognition rules from browser extensions such as "bypass paywalls" and "anti-paywall," and from Fanboy's enhanced tracking list (Papadopoulos et al., 2020). A machine learning classifier can be trained based on a dataset labeled with this heuristic. The classifier uses three types of features: text features for key phrases like *subscribe* or *sign up* in different languages; structural features like the presence of an RSS or ATOM feed, changes in the number of text nodes between crawls, and the difference in the amount of text visible in the browser's reader mode; and visual features like the number of obscured text nodes or the number of text nodes in overlay elements. A random forest classifier achieved a precision of 77% (Papadopoulos et al., 2020).

The prevalence of paywalls doubles approximately every six months, with the adoption rate differing by country and industry: 80% of paywalled sites are news sites, and the US and Australia have the highest rate of paywall use. However, paywalls exhibit two undesirable effects. First, paywalls lead to fewer page views, a shorter average time spent on a site, and fewer incoming links. Second, even paywalled sites use trackers and advertising, which indicates that even paying users are subject to corporate surveillance (Papadopoulos et al., 2020).

Mapping

Maps allow people to navigate and learn about the world. However, there is no world-wide consensus about country borders: in cases of border disputes, countries may have differing opinions about border lines. This means that big tech map providers have to decide which version of the border to display on their service. Google Maps and Bing Maps have opted to use personalization to display a divergent view of international borders to users in different countries. Both services roll out hundreds of tile updates every week, and tiles with borders are personalized based on the country of the user. In most cases, there are three versions of tiles with disputed borders: one version for each of the two countries having the border dispute, and one version for the rest of the world indicating that this border is subject to a dispute. For seven world regions with known border disputes, Soeller et al. (2016) found that Google Maps shows personalized border tiles in five cases, and Bing Maps in four cases. In addition, updates to these personalized borders are much more dynamic than updates to print maps. For example, Google updated their borders for Crimea one to two months after its annexation by Russia. This indicates that audits of border personalization are important because it prevents archiving and preservation of historical map material and promotes a diverging world view.

8.3 Mobile Services

Transparency studies of mobile services have focused on the characteristics and extent of corporate surveillance in three key parts of the mobile ecosystem: app stores, third-party libraries, and individual apps.

8.3.1 App Stores

App stores are the main mechanism for users to obtain apps for their mobile devices. The characteristics of these app stores have been studied, including the characteristics of apps available in them, however, mainly for Android and the Google Play store.

The top 1% of free apps account for 81% of all downloads from the Play store, based on an index of 1.1 million apps (Viennot et al., 2014). Two-thirds of popular apps with more than 50,000 downloads use ad libraries, and half of less-popular apps, compared to 55% of iOS apps (Egele et al., 2011). In addition, 15% of free apps embedded social libraries such as the Facebook SDK or Twitter4J. Paid apps caused only 0.05% of all downloads, and there were 3.5 times more free apps than paid ones. On average, more than 3,000 new apps are published every day, and their average rating is above 4 out of 5 (Viennot et al., 2014).

Less than 50% of the sampled apps on Google Play were updated within the last year, and less than one-quarter of apps within a six-month observation period (Carbunar and Potharaju, 2015). App updates correlated with a decrease in the prices of paid apps and with an increase in permissions. The distribution of apps, downloads, and reviews per developer followed a power-law distribution, i.e., few developers had a large number of apps, but developers with the highest number of apps did not have the highest numbers of downloads or reviews.

Wang et al. (2018) compared the characteristics of Google Play with 16 Chinese app stores with respect to app update rates, use of ad libraries, use of permissions, and prevalence of malicious, fake, or cloned apps. Popular apps were likely to be published in multiple app markets simultaneously, but more than half of Google Play developers did not publish on Chinese app markets, and vice versa. The app update rates differed significantly: only 5% of apps on Chinese app markets were updated within a 6-month period compared to 23% of apps on Google Play. Only 53% of apps on Chinese markets included ad libraries compared to 70% of apps on Google Play. However, apps on Chinese markets requested more dangerous permissions and were more over-privileged than apps on Google Play. On the average Chinese app store, more than 2% of apps were fake compared to 0.03% on Google Play. The percentage of cloned apps was higher, with 10% of apps sharing package names but not developer signatures (4% on Google Play) and up to 24% of apps sharing code (18% on Google Play). However, this is likely caused by the cloning of apps from Google Play into Chinese markets. Twelve percent of apps were malicious on Chinese app markets compared to 2% on Google Play, and malicious apps were removed at a much lower rate in Chinese app markets: between 0.01% and 34% on Chinese markets compared to 84% on Google Play.

8.3.2 Third-Party Libraries

Ad and analytics libraries are common third-party libraries included in apps. However, there is a large variety of libraries available for many other purposes. For example, Li et al. (2017a) found more than 60,000 different third-party libraries in Android apps. Some of these libraries may leak private data over the network, including device identifiers (IMEI and IMSI), user locations, and other sensor data (He et al., 2019).

The lack of an updating mechanism for third-party libraries puts burden on app developers to monitor whether new library versions are available and manually update the library versions in their apps. As a result, the use of outdated libraries, possibly with security vulnerabilities, is common. In a study of 90 libraries included in 1.2 million apps, 85% of library inclusions were not the most recent versions, but could be upgraded by at least one version without additional effort for the developer. 48% of libraries could even be upgraded to the latest version without additional effort. Security vulnerabilities in these libraries can affect many thousands of users. For example, eight libraries had known vulnerabilities in specific versions, and these were used by 18,000 apps. In 98% of cases, these libraries could have been updated to a secure version without modifying the app's code (Derr et al., 2017).

8.3.3 Apps

Privacy leaks from mobile apps have been widely studied. Table 8.1 summarizes the findings of seven studies for iOS, Windows Phone, and Android. The table shows that leaks of device identifiers are common, allowing apps and possibly third parties to track users. Leaks of user identifiers, location data, contact information, and media data are less common, but more sensitive than device identifiers.

The increasing use of permissions is one reason why this data leaks from mobile apps. Across the subsequent app releases, 95% of new releases do not change the permission requests, but releases that do add 0.64 new permissions on average. The most frequently added permissions are permissions to access the user's location, phone state, camera, and contacts (Calciati and Gorla, 2017). Correspondingly, the privacy risk to users and the risk of data leaks increases over time with subsequent app releases (Ren et al., 2018).

Comparing the privacy practices of paid and free apps based on apps that have both a free and paid version, of those apps where the free version uses at least one third-party library or at least one dangerous permission, 45% retain those libraries and permissions in the paid version. In addition, only 55% of

Table 8.1. *Prevalence of different types of privacy leaks from mobile apps.* *"–" indicates that leaks of this type were not reported.*

Platform	Number of apps	Device identifiers	User identifiers	Locations	Contacts	Media	Reference
iOS	1400	50%	—	3%	0.4%	—	Egele et al. (2011)
iOS	225,000	48%	—	13%	6%	—	Agarwal and Hall (2013)
iOS	100	47%	14%	26%	2%	—	Ren et al. (2016)
Windows	100	55%	3%	8%	—	—	Ren et al. (2016)
Android	100	52%	14%	14%	1%	—	Ren et al. (2016)
Android	100	42%	—	1%	—	—	Continella et al. (2017)
Android	9,100	—	—	—	—	0.2%	Pan et al. (2018)
Android	524	62%	8.5%	53%	—	—	Ren et al. (2018)
Android	46	33%	4%	2%	—	—	Feal et al. (2020)

apps provide a privacy policy, and only 3.7% of apps differentiate in their policy between the two app versions (Han et al., 2020).

Incentivized app installs are a method for app developers to acquire new users for their apps. Even though this practice is banned in Apple's app store, and discouraged on Google Play, third-party platforms offer paid app installs to developers. This increase in apparent popularity and user numbers can help app developers acquire funding from investors: apps using incentivized installs had more than twice the rate of funding raised compared to baseline apps (Farooqi et al., 2020b).

Many services provided by mobile apps can also be accessed via the corresponding mobile website. For 50 services with both a web frontend and a mobile app, Leung et al. (2016) analyzed the difference between the types and amounts of information leaked. Overall, PII leaked from 90% of apps and 76% of websites. The mobile app tended to leak more information types than the website, but both apps and websites leaked locations, names, genders, phone numbers, and email addresses. Web frontends leaked locations and names more frequently and contacted more trackers and advertisers, whereas mobile apps leaked unique identifiers and device information more frequently.

Like websites, mobile apps make use of cloud services. Ninety percent of apps and 92% of mobile websites use cloud services. On average each app connects to 3.2 cloud services, and each website to 4.8. About 50% of the apps send 95% of their traffic to cloud services, and one-third of apps send all of their traffic to cloud services. The most popular cloud services are Google (54% of apps and 84% of websites) and Amazon (65% of apps and 76% of websites). This *cloud entanglement* of mobile websites and apps potentially exposes sensitive user data to cloud services, which most users are not aware of (Henze et al., 2017).

User reviews that mention privacy and security issues can lead to privacy and security improvements in apps. Sixty percent of apps with a security- or privacy-relevant review made subsequent security or privacy updates, and reviews were a significant predictor of app updates that make apps more privacy-friendly (Nguyen et al., 2019). Seventeen percent of these privacy-relevant app updates could be attributed to updates of the app's code, and 48% to updates of libraries. This indicates that user reviews have a positive influence on privacy protection in apps, especially where developers were not aware of the privacy practices of third-party libraries.

App store owners can nudge developers to remove permission requests. Google, for example, identified groups of functionally similar apps by analyzing textual app descriptions and user click data on Google Play. If an app requested a permission that almost no similar apps request, they displayed a nudge to the developer. Even when nudges were only displayed when confidence was very high, they displayed warnings to 19,000 apps between 2017 and 2019, and 59% of apps removed at least one permission as a result (Peddinti et al., 2019). However, this approach is unlikely to affect libraries and apps provided by the app store owner itself.

Ride-Sharing Apps

Ride-sharing apps like Uber and Lyft have become extremely popular. However, the companies providing these services are reluctant to give insight into how their services work and to what extent they are used. For example, Uber and Lyft were not willing to share data regarding the number of trips and vehicle miles with a local transport agency for planning and policy decision making (Cooper et al., 2018). As a result, a number of studies have audited the characteristics and effects of ride-sharing services.

Supply, demand, and pricing of Uber can be analyzed by emulating the Uber app in a grid of geolocations to collect the price estimates for all car types, the expected wait times, and the nearest cars. Supply is then given as the number of unique car identifiers across measurement points, demand is the number of cars disappearing between measurement times, and price is the average surge price over five-minute windows. Chen et al. (2015) found that Manhattan has an order of magnitude more taxis than all Ubers combined, and that San Francisco has 58% more Ubers than Manhattan. Surge pricing is more frequent in San Francisco compared to Manhattan, and uses higher multipliers: the average multiplier is 1.36 in San Francisco compared to 1.07 in Manhattan. Surge prices are in effect 57% of the time in San Francisco, compared to 14% of the time in Manhattan.

To study the demographics of riders and drivers, Kooti et al. (2017) used their position within Yahoo to correlate information about rides from emailed ride receipts with information about demographics from the associated Yahoo accounts. They found that the average Uber rider is white (81%), in their mid-20s, with above-average income, and equally likely to be male or female. Younger riders tended to take more rides whereas older riders took longer rides. The median number of rides was 0.2 per week, and only 1.1% of riders were highly active with more than 20 rides per month. The demographics among Uber drivers were different, with 60% of drivers being white, and 76% of US drivers male. 19% of drivers worked 40 hours per week or more whereas 73% worked fewer than five hours per month. Generally drivers had lower income than riders, and only 17% of drivers were also riders.

Comparing the temporal availability of ride-sharing services with taxis, the supply of Uber and Lyft has strong peaks during rush hour times, whereas the supply of taxis is more constant through the day (Jiang et al., 2018). This is likely caused by the difference in employment model between ride-sharing services (drivers are paid per ride) and taxis (drivers are regular employees paid by hour).

Regarding spatial availability, most cars are available downtown, and numbers decrease with increasing distance to the city center, regardless of the service. In addition, a higher ratio of families in an area correlates with lower supply and demand. City infrastructure – parking lots, parking meters, and public transit stops – has a positive effect on supply and demand for ride-sharing services. A 1% increase in off-street parking increased the availability of Ubers by 0.12%, Lyfts by 0.1%, and taxis by 0.28% (San Francisco) (Jiang et al., 2018). Similarly, higher population density leads to significantly reduced wait times. For example, a doubling of density reduces the wait time by 70 s. In addition, a higher median income in a geographical region reduces the wait time, with a doubling of median income reducing wait times by 190 s (Thebault-Spieker et al., 2017). This indicates that the sharing economy is more effective in dense areas with high socioeconomic status.

Ride-sharing services may also cause negative externalities including an increase in congestion. Comparing congestion levels and public transit ridership on days when ride-sharing drivers were on strike with days when they were not, Agarwal et al. (2019) found that ridership of public transport increased during strike days, and congestion levels decreased. The decrease in congestion was large, roughly half of the decrease observed during public holidays, and the largest decrease was observed on the most congested routes. This indicates that ride-hailing services contribute to congestion and draw commuters who otherwise would use public transit.

Finally, ride-sharing services can also have an impact on the privacy of drivers because of the use of unique and fixed vehicle identifiers. Based on regular measurements from ride-sharing apps in a grid of geolocations, drivers' daily routines, working patterns, home location, and employment status can be tracked (Zhao et al., 2019).

Route Planning Apps

Similarly to ride-sharing apps, route planning apps can cause externalities, such as a redistribution of traffic and increased route complexity. These externalities can be caused by the optimization criteria used for route planning, including travel time, simplicity, safety, or beauty. For example, Waze routes around high-violence neighborhoods in Rio de Janeiro. In a sample of 5,000 origin-destination pairs in four cities (San Francisco, New York City, London, and Manila), safe and scenic routes were significantly more complex (i.e., they had more turns) than fast and simple routes. Scenic routes increased traffic around parks and tourist destinations, thereby subtracting traffic from nearby highways, and safe routes increased traffic in wealthier areas (Johnson et al., 2017).

Route planning apps are also important for wheelchair users who have additional requirements for routes, including a preference for paved routes, a lack of steps, and a maximum height for curbs. Google Maps does not offer wheelchair routing, but the routes computed by OpenRouteService and Routino are generally longer than pedestrian routes by about 15%, but not significantly more complex (Tannert and Schöning, 2018).

When comparing bicycle routes suggested by Google Maps and MapQuest with real routes used by cyclists from Endomondo, Schirck-Matthews et al. (2019) found that real trips were significantly longer than what route planners suggested, especially for sport cycling. Real routes also had higher turn frequency, a higher share of residential roads, and fewer traffic lights.

These studies can inform improvements to routing algorithms and help make sure that negative externalities from mass use of route planning apps are minimized.

9

Effectiveness of Countermeasures

This chapter examines the arms race between corporate surveillance and countermeasures that allow users to defend against advertising, tracking, and profiling. The most common countermeasures are ad blockers, which the corporate surveillance industry is countering with anti-ad blockers. Specialized blockers for tracking and fingerprinting have also been proposed, as well as countermeasures based on obfuscation and tools that aim to increase user awareness. The chapter closes with a discussion of countermeasures for mobile devices and apps.

9.1 Ad Blockers

Online advertising is associated with tracking and profiling of users. A popular countermeasure for privacy-conscious users is therefore to use an ad blocking tool that blocks advertisements before they are displayed to the user.

9.1.1 How Do Ad Blockers Work?

The two main differences between ad blockers are: how they decide what an *ad* is, and how they block ads (see Table 9.1).

How to Block

Some blocking methods rely on blocking network requests outside of and independent from the browser or application that is making the requests (Merzdovnik et al., 2017).

DNS blocking, or *sinkholing*, uses blocklists of domain names or IP addresses. Any network request to an entry in the blocklist is blocked or redirected (e.g., to *localhost*) by the operating system. A common approach is to use a *hosts* file to specify the blocklisted domains and the redirection target.

Table 9.1. *Ad blockers differ in how they decide what to block, and how to block it.*

Ad blocker	What?	How?
MVPS list	public blocklist	DNS blocking
Peter Lowe's list	public blocklist	DNS blocking
Privoxy	public default ruleset	interception proxy
Adblock Plus	public filter lists	browser extension
Disconnect	centralized filter list	browser extension
Ghostery	centralized filter list	browser extension
Privacy Badger	heuristics	browser extension
uBlock Origin	public filter lists	browser extension

Listing 9.1. *First entries in Peter Lowe's DNS blocklist showing the redirection target 127.0.0.1 (localhost) on the left and the blocked domain on the right.*

```
127.0.0.1 101com.com
127.0.0.1 101order.com
127.0.0.1 123found.com
127.0.0.1 123freeavatars.com
127.0.0.1 180hits.de
```

Publicly available DNS blocklists include the MVPS list[1] and Peter Lowe's list.[2] Listing 9.1 shows the first few entries in Peter Lowe's list. A disadvantage of DNS blocking is that it does not allow fine-grained blocking: it can only block entire domains or subdomains, not individual resources.

Another network-based blocking method relies on an external interception proxy such as Privoxy[3] to filter network requests. These proxies provide fine-grained blocking of network resources based on their URI. However, they are limited when handling encrypted traffic. In theory, interception proxies could be configured as man-in-the-middle proxies that decrypt and re-encrypt TLS traffic, but this is generally seen as an unacceptable security risk for users. In addition, this technique would only work if the website did not use certificate pinning (Kranch and Bonneau, 2015).

Other blocking methods rely on extensions running in the user's web browser. These extensions modify the browser so that it blocks network requests from inside the browser, before the resources are requested from

---

[1] http://winhelp2002.mvps.org/hosts.htm
[2] http://pgl.yoyo.org/as/
[3] www.privoxy.org/

the server. Some of the most common browser extensions are uBlock Origin, Adblock Plus, Ghostery, Disconnect, and the EFF Privacy Badger. The advantage of browser extensions is that they allow fine-grained blocking of network requests regardless of whether the website uses HTTPS. However, they rely on the API that browsers offer to extensions. This is a disadvantage for mobile browsers and especially mobile apps that often do not have extension APIs. It can also be a disadvantage if the browser's vendor decides to change the API in such a way that blocking incurs a performance overhead or even becomes impossible. For example, Google has announced in 2019 that it intends to change Chrome's extension API in this way (Wagner, 2018; Shankland and Mihalcik, 2019).

Some browser extensions, most notably Adblock Plus, also allow specifying CSS filters that hide advertising elements within the displayed content. A similar approach is perceptual ad blocking (Storey et al., 2017), which uses computer vision techniques to identify and hide ads marked with the AdChoices icon. However, these approaches do not offer effective privacy protection because tracking and profiling is performed when the resource is requested from the server. Simply hiding ads from view is, therefore, only a visual relief for users.

What to Block

Most ad blockers decide what constitutes an advertisement based on a list of rules: blocklists specify which domains or resources should be blocked, and allowlists specify which resources should not be blocked. Ad blockers usually allow the user to subscribe to several different filter lists. For example, uBlock Origin lists more than 60 filter lists with emphasis, for example, on ads (e.g., EasyList), tracking (e.g., EasyPrivacy), Malware (e.g., Disconnect's Malvertising list), annoyances (e.g., Fanboy's Annoyance list), and regional lists (e.g., EasyList Germany as a supplement to EasyList). These lists are updated regularly, sometimes as often as daily, to keep up with changes in the web. Listing 9.2 shows a selection of entries from EasyList. Each line is a regular expression that specifies a pattern that the URLs of all network requests are matched against, and matching requests are blocked.

Allowlisted entries in filter lists are mainly used to fix cases when a benign network request matches a pattern, or when blocking the request would break a website's functionality. Adblock Plus is the only ad blocker that additionally uses allowlists to allow so-called acceptable ads.[4] It is important to note that the criteria for acceptable ads focus on visual features: size, placement, and

---

[4] https://acceptableads.com/

Listing 9.2. *Entries from EasyList. (The last two lines show allowlisted entries.)*

```
&act=ads_
&ad.vid=$~xmlhttprequest
,160x600;
,468x60-
&link_type=offer$popup,third-party
&popunder=$popup
###A9AdsMiddleBoxTop
||007-gateway.com^$third-party
||0755.pics^$popup,third-party
||07zq44y2tmru.xyz^$popup
-api.adyoulike.com
-smartad.s3.amazonaws.com^
@@|blob:resource://$image
@@||ad.linksynergy.com^$image,domain=extrarebates.com
```

clear labeling of ads. There is no requirement for acceptable ads to refrain from tracking or profiling. In late 2020, this allowlist of acceptable ads had over 16,000 entries.

Some ad blockers do not use rules, but instead rely on heuristics to identify unwanted network requests. The EFF Privacy Badger, for example, analyzes third-party requests to identify common tracking techniques, such as identifying cookies, cookie synchronization, or canvas fingerprinting. As soon as a third-party host has been observed to use these techniques on at least three first-party sites, Privacy Badger blocks all subsequent requests to the third-party host.

New Approaches to Ad Blocking

Because the creation of filter lists and heuristics requires time-consuming manual effort, newer approaches to ad blocking use machine learning to identify which HTML elements and network requests are advertising-related and therefore should be blocked.

To define the features for a machine learning model, websites can be represented as graphs with four types of nodes: *HTML* nodes for each HTML element, *network* nodes for each HTTP request, *script* nodes for each JavaScript code segment, and a *parser* node for the browser's inbuilt HTML parser. Based on this graph, features include *structural features* such as the numbers of nodes and edges, node degrees, numbers of siblings, or node attributes, and *content features* such as request types, ad-related keywords in network requests, ad dimensions in network requests, query string parameters, or the presence of semi-colons in query strings (Iqbal et al., 2020).

A labeled training dataset can be obtained by crawling the Alexa top 10,000 websites and labeling each fetched URL as *ad* if it matches a rule in a public filter list (including EasyList, EasyPrivacy, and Peter Lowe's list), and as *non-ad* otherwise. A random forest classifier consisting of 100 decision trees achieved 95% accuracy and 86% recall (Iqbal et al., 2020).

Importantly, the assumption is that this machine learning model generalizes to advertising and tracking related resources that are not captured by manually curated filter lists. If this assumption holds, the machine learning model could improve ad blocking performance in areas where filter lists have low coverage (such as less popular websites), while at the same time reducing the effort to curate filter lists.

9.1.2 Effectiveness of Ad Blockers

Given the different approaches to ad blocking introduced above, it is important to evaluate how well each approach works. These evaluations can then inform further development of ad blockers and guide recommendations given to users.

To measure the effectiveness of ad blockers, most studies do not analyze the visual effectiveness in terms of blocked advertisements. From a privacy perspective, it is more meaningful to instead measure the amount of tracking that users are exposed to. On a technical level, this can be achieved by measuring the prevalence and reach of third parties, either on the level of the domain name or on the level of legal entities.

Experimental designs need to consider not just which ad blockers to evaluate, but also how each ad blocker should be configured. Importantly, experiments need to include conditions for each ad blocker's default settings because users may never change the default settings. Each combination of ad blocker and configuration represents one experimental condition. The experiments should also include a baseline condition without an ad blocker to allow for comparisons between ad blockers, as well as a combined condition that evaluates the case of users who install multiple ad blockers. Table 9.2 summarizes the experimental designs of five studies that evaluated ad blockers.

Taken together, these studies indicate that the best ad blockers can succeed in blocking slightly above 80% of third-party requests. However, they are much less effective in reducing the reach of third-party tracking companies. For example, even when a user uses a combination of five ad blockers that succeed in blocking around 85% of third-party requests, Google can still reach 60% of websites visited by the user.

The efficiency of ad blockers indicates the performance of the browser and the underlying operating system when privacy extensions are/are not in use. Contrary to claims by browser vendors, Borgolte and Feamster (2020)

Table 9.2. *Summary of the experimental designs of five studies that evaluated the effectiveness of ad blockers.*

Ad blockers	Websites	Performance measures	Reference
baseline, Adblock Plus, Disconnect, Ghostery, Privacy Badger, uBlock Origin, all combined	top 200,000 sites, two random subsites for each site	third-party requests, reach	Merzdovnik et al. (2017)
baseline, Adblock Plus, Ghostery, Do Not Track (each with default and maximum protection settings)	top 500 sites, 500 sites from the top 1 million	third-party requests, reach	Gervais et al. (2017)
baseline, Adblock Plus, Ghostery (each with maximum protection, ad block only, privacy only)	top 1,000 sites	HTTP and HTTPS requests	Pujol et al. (2015)
Abine, Adversity, EasyList, EasyPrivacy, Ghostery, Fanboy list	top 500 sites	third-party requests, cookies	Mayer and Mitchell (2012)
baseline, Ghostery, Abine TACO, Do Not Track	hand-selected pages on different topics	domains that set cookies	Balebako et al. (2012)

found that the use of privacy extensions can improve browser and system performance as well as user experience, for example, by reducing the page load times and page load sizes.

9.1.3 Effectiveness of Filter Lists

Creating and maintaining effective ad block filter lists relies on crowdsourced reports of false positives (possibly legitimate content that is blocked, but breaks some features of websites) and false negatives (advertisements that are not blocked) followed by manual list updates. The effectiveness of this mechanism can be evaluated based on historical versions of EasyList and crowdsourced reports from the EasyList forum. Alrizah et al. (2019) found that about 30% of community effort is spent correcting false positives. However, the reporting of false positives was slow, with half of errors persisting for more than one month. After their reporting, updates to the list were available quickly, on average within two days. False negative reports were more than twice as frequent as false positive reports. However, many false negative reports were insufficiently detailed or did not report real errors. List updates as a result of false negative reports took three times longer (six days on average) than updates based on false positive reports.

The effectiveness of filter lists can also be evaluated based on the overlap of tracking or advertising detected by heuristics or machine learning with tracking or advertising detected by filter lists. For example, invisible pixels are present on 94% of domains and represent more than one-third of third-party images. Comparing a heuristic based on invisible pixels with the filter lists from Disconnect and EasyList/EasyPrivacy, Fouad et al. (2020) found that the Disconnect list misses 30% of the trackers detected with their heuristic, and EasyList/EasyPrivacy misses 25%. This shows the need for finding more effective ways for blocking and for maintaining filter lists.

9.1.4 Prevalence of Ad Blockers

Much of the Internet's business model depends on advertising revenue. When a large portion of users decides to block ads from being displayed, ad impressions and ad clicks will decrease, potentially affecting the economic viability of Internet companies. Therefore, it is important to study to what extent ad blockers are actually deployed, and to what extent this may cause a loss of revenues.

Active measurements are not suitable to evaluate how many users have ad blockers enabled. Instead, it is necessary to analyze passively collected traces of a large number of users, which are hard to obtain in practice.

Based on anonymized traces from a large residential broadband provider covering traffic from several thousand households, 22.2% of browsers are likely to use Adblock Plus because they request list updates from Adblock Plus servers. Another 15.3% of users have a low percentage of ad requests[5] and thus may be using another ad blocker that does not contact Adblock Plus servers (Pujol et al., 2015). Adblock Plus is the most popular ad blocker used by 10%–18% of users (Metwalley et al., 2015). A large-scale analysis in 2016 found ad block prevalence to vary between 17% in the US and UK and 37% in Germany (Malloy et al., 2016).

The economic impact of between 10% and 37% of ad blocker users can be analyzed by its influence on the generated advertising revenue. Gill et al. (2013) proposed a model to compute advertising revenue based on the base

---

[5] To determine an appropriate threshold for the percentage of ad requests, Pujol et al. (2015) used an active measurement study comparing a baseline browser without ad blocking to two ad blockers (Adblock Plus and Ghostery) with different configurations. Based on this active measurement, they found that a user is very likely to use an ad blocker if less than 5% of HTTP requests are ad requests.

price for ad impressions, the quality of the publisher displaying the ads, and the user's purchasing intent approximated by the interests the ad network has inferred about the user. To estimate real-world ad revenues, they used published figures for base prices, estimated the quality of publishers based on their rank in the Alexa toplist, and used a set of passively collected HTTP traces to first estimate users' purchasing intent and then compute revenues. They found that, while the top 5%–10% of ad networks earn 90% of the total ad revenue, the user base generating this revenue is more widely spread, with 35%–55% of users generating 90% of the total ad revenue. According to this analysis, if the top 5% of users were to block ads entirely, advertising revenue could drop by 35%–60%.

Ad blocking also has an economic impact on the users of ad blockers: advertisers claim that ads help users find cheaper deals faster, and that ads therefore save time and money for users. However, this claim was refuted in a lab study that analyzed user's shopping behavior depending on whether ad blockers were used or not. The study found no significant differences between the two groups in terms of the time needed to complete shopping tasks and the prices paid (Frik et al., 2020).

Reduced advertising revenue is a serious threat to the internet business model. Unsurprisingly, therefore, there are proposals that would allow *some* ads to be displayed under certain conditions. For example, Adblock Plus has a designated allowlist for so-called acceptable ads. Another approach is to allow users to control which ads may be displayed to them (Parra-Arnau et al., 2017). Their approach detects the interest categories for ads, ads that are targeted to a user's browsing profile, and the uniqueness of a user's browsing profile as seen by the ad network. Based on these three criteria, users can then specify policies to block or allow ads. For example, a policy could state that profile-based ads in a particular interest category should be blocked, but only when the browsing profile is above a specific uniqueness threshold.

9.1.5 Anti-Ad Blockers

Ad blockers threaten the business models of many companies in the advertising industry. The industry has, therefore, developed methods to circumvent ad blockers, and to detect and counter-block users of ad blockers.

Circumvention of Ad Blockers

The most common technique to circumvent ad blockers, i.e., to display ads even to users who use ad blockers, is to keep changing how ads are delivered and/or embedded in websites. For example, publishers can change the domain names that serve ads or change the HTML element identifiers that display ads (Zhu et al., 2018). Both techniques allow publishers to display ads as long as the ad blocker's filter lists have not been updated, effectively forcing frequent update cycles on filter list maintainers.

The advertising industry is also actively exploiting known bugs in browsers to display ads. For example, a bug in the Chrome browser between 2012 and 2017 had the effect of treating WebSocket connections differently from HTTP connections, such that WebSocket connections did not trigger callbacks in Chrome's extension API (Bashir et al., 2018). WebSockets, as specified in RFC 6455, are socket-like connections that can be opened by JavaScript running on a client. In Chrome, these WebSocket connections did not trigger *chrome.webRequest.onBeforeRequest*, which is the part of the extension API that ad blockers use to block outgoing network requests. As a result, advertisers could display ads even to users with ad blockers. More than two-thirds of WebSocket connections were related to advertising and tracking, with some companies using WebSockets to extract sensitive information such as browser fingerprints or even the entire DOM (Bashir et al., 2018).

Finally, web push notifications (WPN) are also used to deliver advertising. To receive ads via WPN, users have to allow notifications for the website they are visiting. The website can then push notifications to the user which can contain ads. Half of ads delivered via WPN are malicious, and most are not included in current ad block filter lists (Subramani et al., 2020).

Counter-Blocking of Ad Blockers
The second strategy how publishers address the threat of ad blockers is to detect the use of ad blockers and then block the user from accessing their website, often in conjunction with a request to turn off the ad blocker, allowlist the publisher's website, or donate to the publisher. However, the use of anti-ad blockers has a negative effect on user engagement, resulting in fewer page views and fewer revisits, especially for low-engaged users with no loyalty to the site (Zhao et al., 2020).

Technically, anti-ad blockers are implemented in JavaScript and work in one of two ways: using bait advertising elements or using bait scripts. Bait advertising elements are HTML elements such as *div* containers that are named specifically so that ad blockers will block them. The anti-ad block script can then attempt to access CSS properties of the bait element, for example, the width, height, or display properties (Nithyanand et al., 2016; Rafique et al., 2016). If this access fails, the script assumes that the user has blocked ads and can react, for example, by blocking the user from the website. Bait scripts are JavaScript code snippets that set a variable value or create an object.

The anti-ad block script can then check whether the variable value is correct or whether the object exists, and assume presence of an ad blocker if this check fails (Nithyanand et al., 2016).

Anti-ad blockers are more prevalent on some website categories than others. For example, anti-ad blockers are used on almost 20% of *general news* sites, even though these sites only represent 9.4% of the top 5,000 websites. In contrast, there are almost no anti-ad blockers on shopping sites (Nithyanand et al., 2016).

To evaluate the prevalence of anti-ad block scripts on the web, researchers have measured both the number of websites that use anti-ad block scripts, and the number of websites that make visible changes to their websites as a result. There is a large gap between these two numbers, which means that there are many websites that use anti-ad block scripts but do not take any visually apparent action. For example, 6.7% of the Alexa top 5,000 (335 websites) use anti-ad blockers, but only 6 of these websites make visible changes (Nithyanand et al., 2016). In 2017, 0.7% (686 websites) of the Alexa top 100,000 made visible changes in response to ad block (Mughees et al., 2017), and 5% of the Alexa top 100,000 triggered filter rules in the Anti-Adblock Killer List (Iqbal et al., 2017). One year later, anti-ad blockers were present on 30% of the Alexa top 10,000, with only 6.6% of these making visible changes to their website (Zhu et al., 2018).

The differences in the number of websites found to be using anti-ad blockers can partly be explained by the different methods used to detect anti-ad blockers. For example, methods that detect anti-ad blockers by identifying visual changes in websites cannot identify sites that use anti-ad block scripts only to record ad block usage (Mughees et al., 2017). Manually derived static JavaScript code signatures are unlikely to find anti-ad blockers in obfuscated JavaScript and involve a lot of manual effort to keep up with the changing anti-ad block landscape (Nithyanand et al., 2016; Storey et al., 2017). Automated JavaScript code analysis, whether static (Iqbal et al., 2017) or dynamic (Zhu et al., 2018), can improve on these drawbacks and thus is likely to detect more anti-ad blockers.

To protect ad block users from anti-ad blockers, ad blockers are adding anti-ad block filter rules to their lists. These filter rules can be implemented in different ways: they can block the anti-ad block script from being loaded; they can use exception rules to allow bait elements to load, thereby tricking the anti-ad blocker into believing that no ad blocker is in use; or they can block the visual elements that websites use to retaliate against ad block users. As with ad block filter rules, anti-ad block filter rules are created manually based on community feedback or suggestions. As a result, different filter lists may work for different anti-ad blockers. For example, filter lists have only a small overlap in the domains mentioned in filter rules: EasyList and Anti-Adblock Killer List only have 20% of domains in common (Iqbal et al., 2017). In addition, anti-ad block filter lists may have a long lag time between the addition of anti-ad block to a website, and the eventual creation of a matching filter rule: 90 days after the addition of anti-ad block, matching filter rules were available for only 32% (Anti-Adblock Killer List) and 82% (EasyList) of cases.

9.2 Tracker Blockers

Tracker blockers are broader in scope than ad blockers: they aim to block tracking in general, which includes advertising but also includes tracking that is independent of ad display. A wide range of tools and strategies are available to block tracking in some way, including ad blockers, replacing social media buttons with nontracking versions (ShareMeNot), hiding the user's IP address (Tor, VPNs), modifying HTTP requests to strip tracking information (Privoxy), enabling the Do Not Track header, disabling third-party cookies, and blocking the execution of Java, Flash, and JavaScript (NoScript) (Bujlow et al., 2017; Roesner et al., 2012). For email-based tracking, additional defense techniques include content proxying, HTML filtering, and blocking of cookies, referers, and requests (Englehardt et al., 2018).

However, some of these strategies are less effective than others. For example, blocking popups and enabling the Do Not Track header does not help reduce the number of trackers, but blocking of cookies and JavaScript is effective, reducing tracking by roughly two-thirds (Roesner et al., 2012). In addition, the average number of third parties per website dropped from 17.7 to 12.6 just by blocking third-party cookies, and Ghostery was further able to reduce this number to 3.3 (Englehardt and Narayanan, 2016). However, Ghostery was less effective when the prominence of the third party was low. This is likely a consequence of a manually curated filter list which focuses more on popular third parties.

The effectiveness of tracker blockers can be evaluated by comparing the reduction in third-party requests and reach. As Table 9.3 shows, tracker blockers can reduce the number of third-party requests quite effectively, but the reach of the top tracker is much less affected. The combination of five tracker blockers on desktop systems can reduce the number of third-party requests by 82%, but the top tracker (Google) still reaches 60% of websites, i.e., the reach of the top tracker was only reduced by 37%. On mobile devices, tracker blockers are even less effective because in-app tracking is harder to block.

Table 9.3. *Percentage of third party requests and reach of the top tracker for desktop (top) and mobile (bottom) tracker blockers (Merzdovnik et al., 2017).*

Tool	% requests to 3rd party	Reach of top tracker
No blocking	100	97
Adblock Plus	58	93
Disconnect	49	80
Ghostery	23	66
Privacy Badger	42	93
uBlock Origin	33	59
All tools combined	18	60
No blocking (mobile)	100	74
EasyList (mobile, proxy-based)	97	74
AdAway (mobile, DNS-based)	100	57
MOAB (mobile, DNS-based)	77	54

The best mobile tracker blocker only reduces the number of third-party requests by 23%, and reduces the reach of the top tracker by 20% (Merzdovnik et al., 2017).

A promising approach to improve tracker blocking on mobile devices is NoMoATS (Shuba and Markopoulou, 2020). This approach uses decision trees trained based on requests that originate from known tracking libraries. Pretrained decision trees can be evaluated on the mobile device and can label requests in about one millisecond, which makes it suitable for real-time use. The classifier is most effective if full URLs and HTTP headers are available to label requests (i.e., for plain-text traffic), but even on TLS traffic that cannot be decrypted, the classifier has an F-score of 90%, meaning that 90% of outgoing tracking requests can be blocked even for encrypted traffic.

Another approach to tracker blocking was pursued by the Cliqz browser, taking advantage of information about potential trackers extracted from the browsing data of Cliqz users (Yu et al., 2016). They defined *unsafe* data elements transmitted to third parties as those whose values are unique and unchanging among a large user population, i.e., values that could be used to uniquely identify users. A data element is considered *safe* if its value has been seen by at least k users over a time period t, for example, for $k = 10$ and $t = 7$ days, and the initial state of each data element is unsafe. The browser transmits information about safeness to Cliqz servers in a privacy-preserving way. The server then aggregates the information, compiles a list of potential trackers, and distributes it back to the browsers via an update mechanism. The browser then blocks requests that contain unsafe data elements if the domain matches a list of potential trackers. This method blocks fewer requests overall than the Disconnect extension (51.7% versus 66.1% of requests), but it blocks more requests that contain unsafe values (51.7% versus 40.4%). In addition, the number of requests with unsafe values that are not blocked is lower (4% versus 15.3%).

However, the blocking of trackers sometimes comes at the price of breaking the functionality of the website. Website functionality is difficult to test at scale in an automated way, but some studies have performed manual analyses of site breakage, usually for a small sample of websites (Mazel et al., 2019; Iqbal et al., 2020). Browser vendors can measure website functionality by measuring the increase of the page reload rate over the baseline. For example, in the Cliqz browser, the page reload rate increased by 10% for users of Adblock Plus, 25% if all requests to potential trackers are blocked, and 5% for their tracker blocker (Yu et al., 2016).

9.3 Fingerprinting Blockers

Blocking fingerprinting is harder than blocking stateful tracking because there is no client-side state that can be observed and blocked from being transmitted (Figure 9.1). Instead, fingerprinting blockers focus either on blocking JavaScript that accesses APIs known to be used for fingerprinting, or on modifying the attributes that may be used for fingerprinting and ensuring that only sanitized attribute values are included in outgoing requests.

Fingerprinting blockers are important because there is no effective way for users to opt out of fingerprinting. For example, although the Network Advertising Initiative (NAI) and European Interactive Digital Advertising Alliance (EDAA) offer opt-outs, opting out does not stop fingerprinting (Acar et al., 2014).

9.3.1 Fingerprinting Countermeasures

Several fingerprinting countermeasures have been introduced in recent years, both as countermeasures for individual fingerprinting attributes and as countermeasure strategies that can be applied to multiple attributes.

The two most common countermeasure strategies are to randomize fingerprinting attributes so that servers cannot link successive fingerprints to the same user, and to standardize fingerprinting attributes so that servers cannot distinguish between users.

An example for the randomization strategy is PriVaricator (Nikiforakis et al., 2015). PriVaricator relies on randomization policies that aim to generate

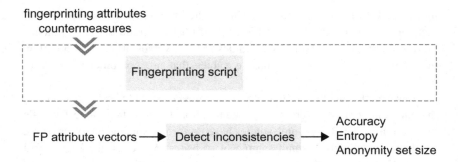

Figure 9.1 Experimental design for studies that measure the effectiveness of fingerprinting blockers.

randomized fingerprints that are consistent with realistic fingerprints and do not cause a negative impact on user experience, but are unique for each website visit. PriVaricator proposes policies for two fingerprinting attributes: plugin enumeration and access to screen properties (*offsetWidth*, *offsetHeight*, and *getBoundingClientRect*). The policies for screen properties can be configured to always return 0, to return a random number between 0 and 100, or to return the original number ±5% noise. Policies for plugin enumeration consist of the probability for hiding each entry. In addition, a threshold configures after how many property accesses and with what probability randomization/hiding should take place. Evaluated against three real-world fingerprinting scripts, the best policies make all tested fingerprinters ineffective, while only changing the visual appearance of 0.7% of the top 1,000 sites (Nikiforakis et al., 2015).

An example for the standardization strategy is the defenses implemented in the Tor Browser Bundle[6] (Acar et al., 2013). As of 2020, Tor implements more than 30 distinct fingerprinting countermeasures, for example, using a fixed window size, disabling HTML5 APIs that are used for fingerprinting, fixing the keyboard event resolution to 100 ms, and standardizing the user-agent string and HTTP headers.

Researchers have also proposed specific countermeasures for novel fingerprinting attributes, including sensor fingerprinting, extension fingerprinting, and WebGL fingerprinting.

Countermeasures for motion sensor fingerprinting include calibration, obfuscation, and quantization. Calibration improves sensor readings by configuring the sensor so that manufacturing imperfections are removed, and it can reduce the F-score for fingerprinting the accelerometer by 16%–25%, while at the same time improving the utility of the sensor. Obfuscation

---

[6] www.torproject.org/projects/torbrowser/design/#fingerprinting-linkability

adds noise to sensor readings to hide miscalibrations and thereby make them unavailable for fingerprinting. If noise is generated as Laplacian noise following the differential privacy definition, the F-score can be reduced by 30%–50%, but at a cost to utility. Quantization converts real-valued sensor readings into a step function. Quantization can reduce the accuracy of fingerprinting at a very small cost to utility, but is less effective than obfuscation (Das et al., 2016, 2018a).

A countermeasure for extension fingerprinting is client-side diversification that consists of altering, randomizing, or adding fingerprintable attributes of browser extensions while retaining their functionality. The structural changes introduced by extensions can be diversified by adding random tags and attributes into each website. In addition, the extension-related items that can be accessed from a website are diversified by renaming web-accessible resources, identifiers, and class names. This method makes more than 98% of fingerprintable extensions undetectable (Trickel et al., 2019).

As a countermeasure for WebGL fingerprinting, the results of floating point operations can be standardized to mitigate fingerprintability. This assumes that WebGL fingerprintability is caused by differences in the evaluation of floating point operations and integer conversions. An integer representation of numerator and denominator can make these operations consistent across platforms. This approach effectively standardizes the results of WebGL rendering tasks, thus making them unsuitable for fingerprinting (Wu et al., 2019).

9.3.2 Anti-Fingerprinting Blockers

Implementations of fingerprinting countermeasures can introduce inconsistencies into fingerprints that fingerprinters can use to deduce the presence of fingerprinting blockers, and in some cases even reconstruct the original values of fingerprinting attributes. For example, modifications to the user-agent string, randomization of canvas and audio attributes, and blocking of fingerprinting APIs can all be exploited by anti-fingerprinting blockers. FP-Scanner (Vastel et al., 2018b) was able to correctly identify all altered fingerprints and could infer the type of fingerprinting blocker by analyzing the pattern of inconsistencies observed in a fingerprint. In addition, FP-Scanner was able to recover the correct browser and operating system family in all cases, but not the correct version of the operating system or browser.

9.3.3 Effectiveness of Fingerprinting Blockers

The effectiveness of fingerprinting blockers can be evaluated by analyzing how much the uniqueness of browsers reduces if individual fingerprinting attributes are either unavailable or standardized. The unavailability of Flash reduces the percentage of uniquely identified browsers from 95% to 88%, and standardization of HTTP headers results in a reduction from 90% to 82% on the desktop and 81% to 60% on mobile browsers. A combination of unavailability of Flash and Java and standardization of HTTP headers could reduce uniqueness to 54%. In addition, unavailability of JavaScript would reduce uniqueness from 89% to 29%, albeit at the cost of breaking almost all websites (Laperdrix et al., 2016).

Fingerprinting blockers can also be evaluated by focusing on individual fingerprinting attributes instead of uniqueness, for example, by analyzing to what extent known fingerprinting attributes are masked by the fingerprinting blocker. Tracker blockers that are not designed to block fingerprinting can have the undesirable effect of making users more identifiable. For example, Adblock Plus and uBlock Origin both modify the *adblock installed* attribute. Most fingerprinting blockers mask less than half of fingerprinting attributes, with the exception of the Tor Browser Bundle which masked 19 out of 20. Correspondingly, the percentage of unique browsers was above 50% for most fingerprinting blockers, with the exception of Brave browser (7.2%) and Tor Browser Bundle (1%) (Datta et al., 2019).

The effectiveness of existing tracker blockers for blocking fingerprinting can be evaluated by analyzing to what extent known fingerprinting scripts are blocked. Disconnect and EasyList/EasyPrivacy block only 17.6% respectively 25.1% of canvas fingerprinting scripts. Scripts for other fingerprinting types, such as canvas font fingerprinting, WebRTC fingerprinting and AudioContext fingerprinting, are blocked at even lower rates. In addition, fingerprinting scripts with low prominence are blocked at lower rate than more prominent fingerprinters (Englehardt and Narayanan, 2016) . A combination of different tracker blockers can be effective at blocking most fingerprinters, but in a 2017 study some fingerprinters were still missing from filter lists, even though the fingerprinters had been known for over three years (Merzdovnik et al., 2017). This emphasizes the disadvantage of manually curated lists.

9.4 Obfuscation

Obfuscation-based countermeasures generally have three goals (Howe, 2015): first, to protect users against unwanted behaviors such as methods used for corporate surveillance; second, to provide users with a means to express their frustration with unwanted behaviors; and third, to insert noise and uncertainty into the system to subvert the effectiveness of unwanted behaviors.

Obfuscation strategies have been proposed as a protection against profiling and advertising (Clark et al., 2015). To confuse profilers, obfuscation traffic can be created in addition to a user's normal browsing. This obfuscation traffic makes individual users less distinguishable and thus allows users to participate in the online ecosystem without standing out. To create obfuscation traffic, Degeling and Nierhoff (2018) identified 170 domains where a single visit results in a change to the user's BlueKai profile. The user's regular browsing is then interspersed with 5% visits to dummy URLs, chosen so that the dummy URLs' interests are not present in the current user's BlueKai profile. This approach reduces the similarity of user profiles between subsequent observations, spaced 100 URL visits apart, by about 20% and thus introduces a considerable amount of uncertainty into the profile held by BlueKai.

To obfuscate a user's search terms, TrackMeNot (Toubiana et al., 2011) introduces obfuscated queries at an average rate of about three queries per minute with the goal that search engines should not be able to distinguish between genuine and obfuscated queries. To make obfuscated queries plausible, TrackMeNot uses a topic universe to select query topics, selects realistic frequency profiles across topics, and adjusts the timing to resemble the user's real weekly and daily patterns. In addition, TrackMeNot simulates user activity by visiting some search results. However, it is possible that machine learning can be used to distinguish these obfuscated queries from genuine queries (Peddinti and Saxena, 2010).

AdNauseam is an obfuscation tool for advertising that inserts uncertainty into the advertising ecosystem by automatically clicking on ads (Howe and Nissenbaum, 2017). The design goals for AdNauseam are to infuse privacy as a societal value into systems and to resist tracking through protest by disrupting the corporate surveillance business model. Because clicking on ads alters the information held by profilers about specific users, polluting this information makes aggregate statistics less accurate and thereby reduces the value of the data. Technically, AdNauseam is realized as a browser extension, which identifies ads based on uBlock Origin, downloads the identified ads, and probabilistically clicks on some of them. At the same time, AdNauseam protects users from tracking by blocking cookies that result from ad clicks and by blocking network accesses from trackers.

However, the effectiveness of obfuscation strategies is generally hard to measure, in particular of the third goal to subvert the operation of corporate surveillance.

9.5 Tools to Raise User Awareness

Although some users are comfortable with tracking in some situations, users are very uncomfortable with trackers that know personal information about them (Melicher et al., 2016). However, users also suffer from an awareness gap in that they do not realize how much trackers know about them. Researchers have proposed a range of user-facing tools that attempt to reduce this awareness gap by visualizing aspects of corporate surveillance. However, a common disadvantage of these tools is that they are not widely known or publicized. As a result, users need some initial awareness to find out about the tools, and therefore it is likely that the tools are mainly used by users who are already well-aware of the issues.

Lumen serves as an Android privacy monitor that alerts users when apps leak unique identifiers and PII (Razaghpanah et al., 2018). To provide this service, Lumen intercepts all network traffic via the VPN permission and inspects packets to detect instances of unique identifiers, such as IMEI, IMSI, advertising identifier, phone number, or MAC address. Lumen additionally sends summary data back to the researchers to enable studies based on real user traffic.

The Facebook Data Valuation Tool (FDVT) is a browser extension that displays to users how much money they make for Facebook (González Cabañas et al., 2017). FDVT queries the Facebook ad campaign API to retrieve ad prices per click and per impression, and then computes the value generated for Facebook by a user based on the user's Facebook usage, including the number of ads displayed during sessions, the number of ads clicked, and some personal information such as the user's country. The total value estimated by FDVT deviates only 12% from public figures reported by Facebook. FDVT additionally sends summary data back to researchers to allow studies of Facebook's ad ecosystem.

The Price $heriff is a browser extension that allows users to check for price discrimination (Iordanou et al., 2017; Mikians et al., 2013). The extension allows users to initiate a price check for supported e-commerce sites. The backend then checks prices for the requested product from various locations around the world with a clean browser state, and from the vantage points of other user installations with user-specific browser and cookie state. The price data collected by $heriff is also used for research studies.

Formlock is a browser extension that warns users when contact forms leak PII (Starov et al., 2016). Whenever a user visits a website with a contact form, the extension highlights form fields that are sent via GET requests or that are sent to third parties. A context menu provides an explanation why the fields are highlighted. The extension also provides some protection mechanisms against PII leaks, for example, by blocking requests that send form content to third parties and by stripping URL parameters.

Tracking Transparency is a browser extension that visualizes long-term information that trackers can infer from a user's browsing history (Weinshel et al., 2019). The extension stores a log of visited websites and encountered trackers, and uses client-side tf-idf topic modeling to categorize the visited websites. The user can then inspect the number of trackers on the current page, the total number of trackers seen, the number of pages visited, and the number of interests inferred. In addition, the extension shows which interests were inferred, how common these interests are (based on the audience size estimate from Google AdWords), how sensitive the interests are (based on a user study), and which trackers could have inferred each interest. Finally, the extension also shows the frequency with which each tracker was encountered, a word cloud with interests inferred by each tracker, and the first-party websites most associated with each tracker.

9.6 Tools for Mobile Applications

Some defense mechanisms are specific to mobile devices, for example, mechanisms that block permission requests, access to personal information, or access to the list of installed apps.

DroidNet is a modification of the Android framework that can quarantine permission requests from new apps and provide expert recommendations to users as to whether each permission requests can be safely granted (Rashidi et al., 2018). The framework collects user decisions for each permission request, identifies expert users, and then uses the experts' decisions to generate crowdsourced recommendations. However, even though this approach has been shown to work well, its practical applicability is limited because it requires a modification of the Android framework.

ProtectMyPrivacy follows a similar concept as DroidNet, but for jailbroken iOS devices (Agarwal and Hall, 2013). ProtectMyPrivacy quarantines access to sensitive information, such as unique device identifiers, MAC addresses, the address book, and the location. Users can then decide to substitute their real information with an anonymized version, and can receive crowdsourced recommendations from the ProtectMyPrivacy server.

Instead of sensitive data or permissions, HideMyApp aims to hide the presence of sensitive apps from other apps (Pham et al., 2019). This functionality is important because more than half of the most popular apps on Android query for the list of installed apps, and knowledge of only four apps is sufficient to reidentify 95% of individual users (Achara et al., 2015). If the installed apps include sensitive apps such as health apps, this is a privacy risk in addition to the fingerprintability of the app list. To hide the presence of apps, HideMyApp creates a container app with a generic package name for each sensitive app. During runtime, user-level virtualization is used to launch the sensitive app, which ensures that the app's correct identity is not registered in the operating system. Even though HideMyApp does not require rooting or modifications to Android, it does require that sensitive apps are installed from an alternative app store, which could be provided by developers of sensitive apps, such as a hospital that developed an mHealth app.

PART IV

Gaps and Challenges

10

Making It Count: Towards Real-World Impact

As the previous chapters have shown, corporate surveillance has been studied intensely over the last decade, and a variety of methods for its study have been developed. However, this has not led to a reduction in real-world corporate surveillance. Even though some individual corporate surveillance practices have been stopped or changed – for example, some discriminatory ads on Facebook have been prohibited (Scheiber and Isaac, 2019), while some apps have improved their privacy (Privacy International, 2019b; Peddinti et al., 2019) – these practices may have been replaced and new ones developed.

The academic community now knows more about corporate surveillance – a decade of research has created more transparency – but this has not solved two fundamental issues: (1) there are many other corporate surveillance practices that are still in the dark; and (2) the protection of privacy and other human rights in the online world has not improved as a result.

This chapter examines the question how transparency research might lead to real-world change. To do so, we will discuss how research studies can plan for real-world impact from the outset, and explain how different groups of stakeholders and communities can be engaged to maximize the chance of real-world changes. But first, let us examine the current state of impact from transparency research, and compare it to desirable impacts that have been repeatedly called for.

Most commonly, transparency research results in academic publications. This outcome is highly incentivized by academia and academic promotions processes. Unfortunately, academic publication remains the only outcome for many studies. Other outcomes include media engagement, responsible disclosure, publication of code, and provision of evidence to regulators.

Media coverage is most often achieved when research groups already have experience with media engagement, and when the research findings are directly relevant to the media outlet's target audience, such as stories about discrimination in digital advertising.[1] Media coverage can increase public awareness of corporate surveillance and thereby, indirectly, increase pressure on regulators and policymakers to take action. Companies that are directly implicated in the research results may also change their practices as a result, out of a desire to stay out of the public spotlight (Narayanan and Reisman, 2017).

Responsible disclosure is another impact that is realized especially by research groups that are already experienced in responsibly disclosing security vulnerabilities. Responsible disclosure of specific issues to specific companies can lead to companies changing their practices. For example, research by Privacy International resulted in several popular apps removing the Facebook SDK from their apps to protect users from tracking by Facebook.[2] However, the changes resulting from responsible disclosure are often localized and restricted to a small scale, such as individual web publishers or individual app developers, and typically do not result in big tech changing their fundamental business operations.

Publication of code and tools is a common practice. In most cases, this code is targeted at researchers who can expand or replicate research results. In some cases, however, code and tools are published for envisioned use by end users or regulators. For example, Matte et al. (2020) published a tool that regulators can use to check compliance of cookie notices with the GDPR which, with the support of the nonprofit organization *noyb*, has led to the filing of regulatory complaints against three web publishers.[3] However, research code is often not maintained after publication of the associated paper, due to time constraints or graduation of PhD students. Unfortunately, the rapid evolution of the web, web browsers, and mobile platforms means that research code becomes obsolete rather quickly which limits its potential impact.

In contrast to these commonly realized impacts, the impacts that have been repeatedly called for in published research are much more far-ranging and aimed at large-scale changes: calling for regulations to allow for auditability and external oversight, regulatory enforcement of existing rules, and effective countermeasures that are available to all users by default.

Auditability is the notion that it should be possible to subject platforms and algorithms to external oversight to ensure that they respect societal norms (Narayanan and Reisman, 2017). This includes designing platforms so that

---

[1] www.newscientist.com/article/2161442-facebook-may-guess-millions-of-peoples-sexuality-to-sell-ads/;www.economist.com/business/2019/04/04/facebooks-ad-system-seems-to-discriminate-by-race-and-gender

[2] https://privacyinternational.org/blog/2758/appdata-update;www.privacyinternational.org/long-read/3196/no-bodys-business-mine-how-menstruations-apps-are-sharing-your-data

[3] https://noyb.eu/en/say-no-cookies-yet-see-your-privacy-crumble

they allow external audit including of their network traffic (Moghaddam et al., 2019), allowing access to platform internals for audit purposes (Pitoura et al., 2018), and exceptions for auditing in laws like the CFAA and professional codes like the ACM Code of Ethics (Sandvig et al., 2014). In addition, Sandvig et al. (2014) call for financial and institutional resources to establish independent third-party auditors who hold platforms and algorithms accountable through regular audits. Audit rights have also been demanded by the European Data Protection Supervisor (EDPS) in their investigation into the use of Microsoft products by European institutions (EDPS, 2020).

Most countries have existing rules that cover many aspects of business, such as competition law or antitrust law, consumer protection law, and data protection law. For example, these include the Federal Trade Commission (FTC) rules, the Children's Online Privacy Protection Act (COPPA), and the CCPA in the US, and the Unfair Commercial Practices Directive and the GDPR in the EU. However, these laws are often not strictly enforced, especially for businesses that operate in the digital realm. A partial reason may be that new technologies can make it more difficult for regulators to investigate whether these laws have been violated. However, another reason is that enforcement especially of antitrust law in general has decreased in the last decades (Doctorow, 2020). For this reason, strict and rapid enforcement of existing rules is often called for in research (Mathur et al., 2019; Gamba et al., 2020).

Finally, users can be protected even in the absence of auditability and enforcement of existing rules by providing effective countermeasures to all users by default. This could be achieved, for example, by ensuring that platforms offer effective privacy controls (Moghaddam et al., 2019), by integrating countermeasures into all browsers by default (Mathur et al., 2019), by finding new mechanisms that can ensure truly informed consent especially on mobile and embedded devices (Gamba et al., 2020), and by ensuring that platforms provide visual explanations for algorithms they employ (Eslami et al., 2015).

All three of these areas of large-scale impact face formidable opposition by business interests and political opinion influenced by decades of lobbying. However, for the reasons set out in Chapter 1, it is essential that we make progress towards these goals. The remainder of this chapter outlines initial steps that can be taken.

10.1 Planning for Real-World Impact

To increase the chances of realizing impact from research, it is often helpful to plan for impact right from the start of a research project. This process can be

Table 10.1. *Types of impacts, following Reed (2018).*

Type of impact	Definition	Examples
Understanding and awareness	Research causes people to have better understanding or more awareness	Awareness of corporate surveillance practices
Attitudinal	Research causes people to change their attitudes or views	Views about the importance of privacy
Economic	Research causes monetary benefits or reduced costs	Positive impact through new business models, or negative impact caused by improvements in ad blockers
Health and well-being	Research causes better health outcomes and improved quality of life	Reduced stress caused by attention economy
Policy	Research causes contributions to new laws or regulations	Informing data protection regulation or contributing to its enforcement
Decision-making and behavior change	Research causes groups or organizations to change their behaviors or decisions	Website publishers removing trackers, browser makers enabling countermeasures by default
Social	Research causes benefits to society such as improvements to human rights	Freedom from discrimination when accessing online services
Capacity or preparedness	Research causes improved ability to cope with changes or improved capacity to derive benefits in the future	Automated evidence collection for regulatory action

divided into three steps: envisioning the impact, planning for the impact, and achieving the impact. The envisioning step asks about *who* and *what* – what impacts may result from the research, and who will benefit? The planning step identifies *how* – concrete pathways that can lead from the research idea and findings to real-world change. Finally, the achieving step follows the planned pathway and monitors progress along the way.

Generally, impact is understood as some form of change in the world. Impact can take many forms, including social and economic benefits for specific groups of people. Table 10.1 describes eight types of impacts (Reed, 2018) and gives examples for these impacts in the context of corporate surveillance and transparency research. Impacts can be evaluated according to their significance – how important the change is to the affected groups – and by their reach – how many people are affected by the change.

To envision which specific impacts may result from a particular research project and plan how these impacts may be realized, Reed (2018) proposes a series of questions that can serve as a guide to systematically identifying stakeholders and potential impacts:

- Identify the specific research that you want to plan impact for. This could be a new research project, an aspect of a research project, or a research idea. Importantly, the research must have potential to be interesting or useful to someone.
- What problems, needs, or barriers are there in policy, economy, practices or behaviors that this research could help address? Are there trends or current issues linked to the research?
- Who are the stakeholders that might be interested in the research (other than researchers)? This could be individuals, groups, or organizations.
- What would change for these individuals, groups, and organizations if they took an interest in or used the research? How would they benefit? Would some of them be disadvantaged as result of the research?
- How would you know that they have benefited? What specific things would you be able to measure?
- How can you engage each stakeholder group? What specific activities can you undertake, and how would you know that these activities were successful?

Tables 10.2 and 10.3 show examples of how the answers to these questions might look like for a generic research project investigating corporate surveillance. The tables show groups of stakeholders and outline why each might be interested in the research, what influence they can exert to facilitate or block impacts, and what types of impact they may derive. The following sections discuss concrete examples showing how these stakeholders can be engaged in practice.

10.2 Engaging Stakeholders and Communicating Results

Most stakeholders are not scientists. This means that they do not necessarily have a regular practice of deciphering academic publications, may not know how to find new publications, and may not be able to judge the quality of new publications. As a result, researchers need to understand what each stakeholder needs and what their constraints and concerns are (Baron, 2010). For example: policymakers are often concerned about what their constituents think about a particular policy issue; NGOs need to consider whether an issue fits their

Table 10.2. *Stakeholder analysis for research into corporate surveillance (1).*

Organization or group	Examples of stakeholders	Why are they interested?	What is their level of influence?	What type of impact?
Media and journalists	Newspapers, ProPublica, The Conversation, tech magazines	Tell truth to power Hold corporations accountable Tell a good story Sell papers/drive traffic	+ Can raise public awareness + Can increase pressure on other stakeholders to act − May not be able to report on nuanced findings or may need help with it + Can bridge gap between researchers and users	Understanding, awareness
Parliaments (legislative branch)	European Parliament, Council of Ministers, US Congress, UK House of Commons	Interest in transparency induced by public pressure Influenced by powerful tech and advertising lobby groups	+ Can propose and pass new legislation + Can amend legislation proposed by government	Policy
Governments (executive branch)	European Commission		+ Can propose new legislation	Policy
Courts (judicial branch)		Responsible for interpreting and applying laws and resolving disputes	+ Can force big tech to implement changes − Costly and time-consuming process	Policy
Oversight, regulatory bodies	FTC, EU data protection authorities e.g., ICO, CNIL, competition regulators	Responsible for regulating industries	− Investigations and processes can take a long time, uncertain outcome + Can impose fines and other sanctions	Policy

Table 10.3. *Stakeholder analysis for research into corporate surveillance (2).*

Organization or group	Examples of stakeholders	Why are they interested?	What is their level of influence?	What type of impact?
Advocacy groups, NGOs	ACLU, Privacy International, Amnesty International, noyb, La Quadrature du Net	Their core missions are to protect civil liberties, privacy, human rights	+ Can lobby legislators + Can support lawsuits with expertise and access to (pro bono) lawyers + Can raise public awareness with campaigns and reports + Can bridge gap between researchers and users	Understanding and awareness, attitudinal, policy
Big Tech corporations and other companies in the ecosystem	Google, Facebook, ad exchanges, analytics companies, SSPs, DSPs	May want to be seen doing *the right thing*, but this also means they are interested in blocking research (e.g., by changing their websites often)	− Can block research by making external audit difficult − Unlikely to change their behavior unless under extreme pressure, e.g., when forced by courts	Negative economic impacts
Browser developers	Mozilla, Google, Microsoft, Brave, Opera, Apple, mobile browser makers		+ Can implement protective technology and nudges, thus rolling out ad/tracker blocking to massive-scale userbase − Some have conflicting business interests	Decision-making and behavior change
Website publishers, app developers		Interested in commercial success (ad revenue). May not want to sell out their users. May not be informed about practices of third party services.	− May counter-block user defense mechanisms + May remove or consolidate the third-party tracking tools they embed	Decision-making and behavior change
Users		Some have interest in privacy, but many are not informed enough/cannot be bothered/don't see the harms	− Protective technologies favor tech-savvy users, resulting in inequality	Social (human rights), understanding and awareness, attitudinal, health

agenda; media organizations and journalists have to judge whether something is newsworthy, whether it is a good story, and whether it will sell; and citizens are interested in issues that directly affect their lives (Baron, 2010).

Based on an understanding of these needs and constraints, researchers can adapt their message to each stakeholder by selecting, interpreting, and presenting the research findings in the most appropriate way. The following sections present specific examples of successful stakeholder engagement as well as some background information on the constraints and concerns of stakeholders.

10.2.1 The Public: Media, Journalists, and Users

One way of directly engaging the public and benefiting users is to publish browser extensions and apps developed by researchers (see Sections 5.6 and 9.5). However, most of these extensions and apps are used by a small number of users, most of who were already tech-savvy and interested in privacy. In addition, not every research finding can be neatly packaged in an app or browser extension.

Media coverage, facilitated by journalists, is a more general way to spread awareness more broadly and reach wider audiences. Besides well-known mass media organizations, there is a wide range of smaller, more specialized media outlets who may be interested in publishing articles about research. However, journalists need to be made aware of interesting research findings that they can write about: simply publishing a paper is not enough. Making journalists aware of interesting stories can happen in at least three ways: through already existing contacts with journalists; through press releases, for example, facilitated by a university's press office; or through pitching articles directly to news organizations like The Conversation[4] that specialize in working with academics.

Press releases are a traditional way to notify journalists of potentially interesting stories. In an academic context, the process can work as follows (Schubert, 2018): after publishing a paper, the researchers contact the university's press officer who estimates whether the story will attract interest. If it does, the researchers draft a press release and work with the press officer to refine and 'polish' the final press release. Journalists can then contact the researchers to find out more information or to arrange an interview.

Pitching articles directly, for example, to The Conversation, is a more proactive way to publicize research findings. Articles in The Conversation are often republished by other news organizations which can increase exposure

---

[4] https://theconversation.com

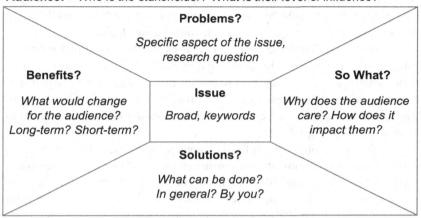

Figure 10.1 Message Box. Adapted from Baron (2010); COMPASS (2017).

to larger audiences. When writing for The Conversation, researchers draft the news article themselves with the assistance of an editor who helps to ensure that the writing is accessible and the article presents an engaging story.

In both cases, it is helpful for researchers to be clear about the message they want to convey. A structured way of turning an academic paper into a set of messages aimed at a particular audience is the *message box* (Baron, 2010; COMPASS, 2017). As shown in Figure 10.1, a message box consists of five fields that highlight different aspects of the research and its relevance to the audience.

The *issue* describes the context of the research in broad terms. For example, the context could be "discrimination in online advertising" or "preventing online tracking and surveillance." The *issue* often includes keywords that someone might use to search for information about the issue.

The *problem* describes the specific focus of the research. For example, the problem may be a subset of the research questions answered in a paper, selected to match the interests and needs of the audience.

The *so what?* explains why the audience should care about the results of the research. Because different stakeholders have different needs and interests, they will be interested in different aspects of the research and the consequences it may have for them. The *so what?*, therefore, depends heavily on the specific audience, their values, and what they care about.

The *solution* describes potential solutions to the problem. The solution does not necessarily correspond to research findings but rather to actions that could be taken to address the problem, based on what the research has found. For example, a solution could be a technical countermeasure that is available but needs to be rolled out more broadly, or it could be new legislation.

The *benefits* describe the positive outcomes that would be realized if the solution was implemented to address the problem. These can also be larger-scale benefits that may need a combination of solutions to be realized. For example, larger-scale benefits could be protection of specific human rights, while smaller-scale benefits could be that the solution gives users a sense of control over their digital life.

The clarity that often results from completing a message box can also help when sharing information about the research on social media. For example, a social media strategy identifies which audiences might be interested, and how social media content can be made actionable, shareable, and rewarding for these audiences (Reed, 2018). This might include sharing resources that make the research easier to understand such as short videos or infographics.

10.2.2 Policymakers: Parliaments and Governments

The processes for making new laws can differ substantially between countries, and as a result the ways to influence the policymaking process also differ. The University of Kansas' *Community Toolbox* proposes a general strategy for policy change focusing on "eight Ps" (Rabinowitz, 2020): preparation, planning, personal contact, pulse of the community, positivism, participation, publicity, and persistence.

Preparation emphasizes that background knowledge is needed about the current policy, about who makes and influences policy, and about potential allies and opponents. Planning involves creating a strategy for the desired policy change. Personal contact emphasizes that personal relationships with policymakers are important. Pulse of the community describes the need to understand what policies citizens support or resist. Positivism means that positive rather than negative aspects should be emphasized, for example, by giving positive rather than punitive reasons for policy change. Participation encourages to involve many people in the policy change, including established opinion leaders. Publicity should be used to keep people informed and ensure that the policy issue retains a high profile. Finally, persistence is important because it can take a long time to realize policy change.

Policymaking in the European Union

In the EU, the most common legislative process is the Ordinary Legislative Procedure (OLP) which has been used for 90% of all laws since 2009

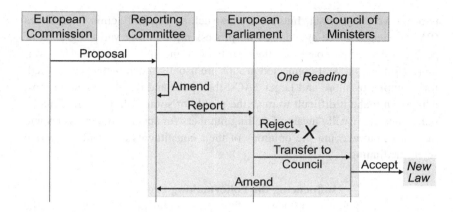

Figure 10.2 EU lawmaking process. Adapted from Kristof et al. (2020).

(Kristof et al., 2020). As shown in Figure 10.2, the process starts by the European Commission drafting a legislative proposal and submitting it to the appropriate committee of the European Parliament, which consists of members of the European Parliament (MEPs). The committee's rapporteur then seeks external expertise, and members of the committee can propose amendments and vote on them. The resulting *report*, i.e., the legislative proposal plus approved amendments, is then voted on by the full parliament. If Parliament rejects the proposal, the law is abandoned. On the other hand, if both Parliament and the Council of Ministers accept the proposal, a new law is created. The Council of Ministers can also propose amendments, in which case the proposal goes back to the original committee. At this point, one of up to three *readings* is complete. Other committees can also propose amendments which are sent to the main committee.

Policymaking in the United States

Compared to the EU, policymaking and political ideology in the US is much more partisan. As a result, there are additional considerations before engaging with the policymaking process (DiNitto and Johnson, 2015). A general risk in the policymaking process are nondecisions, i.e., cases where policy issues are not pursued because of pressure by lobby groups. To address this risk, various entities, such as individuals, interest groups, think tanks, and political candidates, engage in agenda setting. This often involves getting mass media to publicize a policy issue, which may create pressure that counters the pressure from lobby groups. Mass media often relies on policy images that create emotional reactions, which means that the wording and framing of policy issues is very important. Interest groups such as political action committees (PACs) engage in the agenda-setting process representing various groups of people, for example, based on their profession, income, or gender. However, more affluent and well-connected groups are usually much better represented, for example, by more and larger PACs, than poor and disadvantaged groups, which can make it difficult to raise the profile of some policy issues. Finally, politicians are usually aware of polling numbers for specific policy issues and may take into account the opinions of their constituents alongside objective scientific findings.

Influencing the Policymaking Process

The two main points of influence in the European lawmaking process are the external expertise given to the rapporteur, and the MEPs in the reporting committee who can propose amendments. In the US lawmaking process, the main influence points are connections to local congressmen, i.e., representatives for the local district, state senators, and their staffers, as well as congressional testimony on specific issues (Baron, 2010).

However, given the time frame and complexity of the policymaking process, influence on the policymaking process is most likely when researchers work with nongovernment organizations or advocacy groups that are able to pursue policy change over longer periods of time and with the needed legal expertise.

10.2.3 Lawyers and Courts: The Judicial Branch

Some findings from transparency research have direct legal implications because they point to a violation of laws or regulations. However, these legal implications are often difficult to judge for technically minded researchers, not least because laws vary widely around the world and require legal expertise to apply correctly.

For example, the employment and data protection laws that apply to discrimination in hiring processes are different in the UK compared to the US. For example, the Equal Employment Opportunity Commission (EEOC) in the US requires that the ratio of candidate selection rates for different demographic categories is not smaller than 0.8 (the 4/5ths rule), whereas UK law does not stipulate specific ratios and includes provisions where biases may be justifiable (Sanchez-Monedero et al., 2019). In addition, there are different definitions for "discrimination" in different regions (Žliobaitė, 2017), and the perspective on privacy and data protection varies widely, for example, between the comprehensive regulatory model in the EU and the sectoral model in the US (Fruchter et al., 2015).

For this reason, achieving legal impacts from research is often only possible through collaboration with legal scholars, lawyers, or advocacy groups.

For example, a collaboration between computer scientists and a researcher from a law school allowed to evaluate not just the technical functionality of cookie banners, but also their legal compliance with the GDPR (Matte et al., 2020). This collaboration ensured that the research findings could specifically show where stipulations of the law were not met, and this enabled follow-up work by the nonprofit organization noyb that filed complaints with the data protection regulator.

In another example, research by investigative journalists found that Facebook allowed advertisers to place ads for housing, jobs, and finance in a discriminatory manner (Angwin et al., 2018; Scheiber, 2019). In collaboration with nonprofit organizations, including the American Civil Liberties Union, the National Fair Housing Alliance, and the Communications Workers of America, they brought several court cases between 2016 and 2018 against Facebook and the specific companies that had placed discriminatory ads. These cases were finally settled in 2019 and Facebook had to promise changes to its advertising portal, including new rules where "advertisers in the areas of housing, employment and credit [are required] to use a separate portal that will not include gender or age as targeting options" (Scheiber and Isaac, 2019).

Finally, work on supercookies resulted in a class action lawsuit that was finally settled for $500,000 (Soltani et al., 2009).[5]

10.2.4 Oversight and Regulatory Bodies

The two most important regulators for research findings from transparency research are the Federal Trade Commission (FTC) in the US and the data protection authorities in the EU (e.g., CNIL in France and ICO in the UK).

The FTC's mandates include preventing *unfair* and *deceptive* business practices (Mayer and Mitchell, 2012). The FTC has a history of levying fines and imposing consent orders which order companies to stop unfair or deceptive practices, for example, against apps with deceptive privacy policies,[6] violations of COPPA,[7] apps that track users without permission,[8] and smart

---

[5] www.mediapost.com/publications/article/191409/kissmetrics-finalizes-supercookies-settlement.html
[6] www.ftc.gov/news-events/press-releases/2014/04/ftc-approves-final-order-settling-charges-against-flashlight-app
[7] www.ftc.gov/news-events/press-releases/2015/12/two-app-developers-settle-ftc-charges-they-violated-childrens
[8] www.ftc.gov/news-events/press-releases/2016/06/mobile-advertising-network-inmobi-settles-ftc-charges-it-tracked

TVs that record viewing histories without consent.[9] The FTC has also fined Google ($22.5 million[10]) and Facebook ($5 billion[11]).

Much of the FTC's enforcement is focused on entities that do not keep the promises in their privacy policies (Zimmeck and Bellovin, 2014). This has led to work on automatically labeling the privacy practices in policies so that they can be compared with experimentally observed behaviors (Zimmeck et al., 2019). The FTC is also actively investigating new areas such as cross-device tracking (Brookman et al., 2017) and algorithmic transparency (Lambrecht and Tucker, 2019).

With the introduction of the GDPR, the European data protection authorities can impose fines for GDPR violations of up to 4% of annual worldwide turnover. Google received the largest fine to date of 50 million, for not collecting valid consent for its processing of data about Android users (CNIL, 2019). The complaint was brought by two non-profit organizations, La Quadrature du Net[12] and noyb, the European Center for Digital Rights.[13] Even though Google filed a complaint against the decision, the fine was upheld in July 2020.[14] A number of further regulatory complaints is pending, including against Facebook, YouTube, Amazon, and Netflix.

Under the GDPR, data subjects may file data protection complaints in court or with their local data protection authority. For example, the ICO has a website that allows individuals to file a complaint.[15] However, the complexity of the complaint process (IAPP, 2016) means that it is beneficial to collaborate with legal experts throughout.

There are several examples of researchers filing regulatory complaints, either on their own or with the support of nonprofit organizations. For example, Zimmeck et al. (2019) designed a web interface for use by regulatory agencies that can highlight possible issues with COPPA compliance of apps. Even though the findings of their automated tool need to be verified by legal experts, it has the potential of simplifying evidence collection for regulators. Similarly, Trevisan et al. (2019) developed a tool that regulators can use to verify compliance with the EU ePrivacy directive, and Matte et al. (2020) developed a browser extension that collects evidence for GDPR violations by

[9] www.ftc.gov/news-events/press-releases/2017/02/vizio-pay-22-million-ftc-state-new-jersey-settle-charges-it
[10] http://money.cnn.com/2012/08/09/technology/google-safari-settle/index.html
[11] www.ftc.gov/news-events/press-releases/2019/07/ftc-imposes-5-billion-penalty-sweeping-new-privacy-restrictions
[12] www.laquadrature.net
[13] https://noyb.eu/
[14] www.conseil-etat.fr/actualites/actualites/rgpd-le-conseil-d-etat-rejette-le-recours-dirige-contre-la-sanction-de-50-millions-d-euros-infligee-a-google-par-la-cnil
[15] https://ico.org.uk/make-a-complaint

cookie consent libraries. This browser extension and screenshots obtained from it have been used in the official complaint against three websites filed with the French data protection authority CNIL.[16]

10.2.5 Standardization Bodies

Standardization bodies such as the World Wide Web Consortium (W3C) are in a position to consider privacy implications at design stage (Acar et al., 2014).

One example for a successful interaction between researchers, standardization bodies, and developers is the case of the Ambient Light Sensor API (Olejnik, 2020). The Ambient Light Sensor API was introduced into the W3C standardization process and implemented in Chrome and Firefox in 2017. However, researchers discovered attacks, based on reflection of light from human skin, that would allow websites to use readings from the light sensor to steal the user's browser history and cross-origin resources. In-depth discussions of this information leakage risk led to responses from browser developers: in 2020, the API has been dropped from Firefox, and Chrome offers only sanitized light sensor readouts by capping the resolution of the light value and the frequency at which new readouts are provided.

This example shows that practical demonstrations of attacks can help contextualize discussions and ultimately lead to real-world improvements. However, the interaction between researchers, standardization bodies, and developers can be time-consuming.

10.2.6 Nongovernment Organizations and Advocacy Groups

Besides engaging in the policymaking process, filing lawsuits, and filing regulatory complaints, nongovernment organizations and advocacy groups also engage in research, develop countermeasures, and communicate with the public.

For example, the Electronic Frontier Foundation (EFF) develops the Privacy Badger, a browser extension that uses heuristics to detect and block trackers[17] (Bau et al., 2013). The EFF has also contributed to research on fingerprinting through the Panopticlick project[18] (Eckersley, 2010), and Mozilla maintains the web privacy measurement framework openWPM[19] (Englehardt and Narayanan, 2016).

---

[16] https://noyb.eu/en/say-no-cookies-yet-see-your-privacy-crumble
[17] https://privacybadger.org/
[18] https://panopticlick.eff.org/
[19] https://github.com/mozilla/OpenWPM

Research by Privacy International investigated Android apps that enable tracking by Facebook through embedding of Facebook's SDK (Privacy International, 2019a,b). This work resulted in several apps removing Facebook's SDK and thereby improving their users' privacy. A study by ProPrivacy found widespread use of programmatic advertising in the charity sector and led to an open letter, addressed to UK charities, calling for the removal of tracking technologies from sensitive websites[20] (McGrath and Theodorou, 2020).

Other nongovernment organizations collaborate with academics in research projects. For example, Upturn[21] contributed to a study of discriminatory ad delivery on Facebook (Ali et al., 2019a), and authors from Mozilla regularly author research papers (Mishra et al., 2020; Zeber et al., 2020; Bird et al., 2020).

These varied fields of expertise and activities pursued by nongovernment organizations make them valuable partners for researchers.

10.2.7 Publishers and Developers

Like with security vulnerabilities, responsible disclosure of findings from transparency research can result in positive changes that protect users from at least some corporate surveillance. Responsible disclosure means that researchers who discover a vulnerability inform the corresponding vendor first, before publicizing their finding. This gives the vendor time to fix the issue before it becomes publicly known, which minimizes the risk that the vulnerability is exploited while a fix is not yet available. After a certain time period, and regardless of whether the vendor fixed the issue, the finding is made public. This increases pressure on the vendor to deploy fixes quickly. The deadline given to vendors varies depending on the organization that identified the vulnerability. For example, Google's Project Zero uses 90 days[22] whereas the CERT uses 45 days.[23]

The same responsible disclosure process has been used for findings from transparency research, for example: achieving the removal of Facebook's SDK from several apps (Privacy International, 2019b); the patching of security issues related to data-saving mobile browsers (Kondracki et al., 2020); the fixing of password leaks to third parties (Leung et al., 2016; Ren et al., 2016); and the fixing of an encrypted DNS vulnerability to traffic analysis (Siby et al., 2020). Besides patching, responses to responsible disclosure can also include

---

[20] https://proprivacy.com/reports/open-letter-to-uk-charities
[21] www.upturn.org
[22] https://googleprojectzero.blogspot.com/2015/02/feedback-and-data-driven-updates-to.html
[23] https://vuls.cert.org/confluence/display/Wiki/Vulnerability+Disclosure+Policy

additional entries for ad block filter lists and first parties limiting their use of third-party scripts (Acar et al., 2020b).

However, challenges in the practical use of the responsible disclosure process occur when many parties are affected. In this case, the selection of a suitable communication channel for each party, tracking of responses and fixes, and sending of follow-up reminders can take a considerable amount of time. To ease this process, disclosing findings to trusted third parties such as CERTs can have a higher success rate than using a direct communication channel (Stock et al., 2016). Reminder intervals, the effect of media coverage, and the effect of sender reputation are future directions to improve the responsible disclosure process and study its effectiveness (Stock et al., 2016).

11

Future Directions in Transparency Research

The rapid evolution of internet-connected devices, coupled with corporations that strive for opacity, leads to an increasing need for more transparency. This need can be satisfied by carefully designed experimental audit studies, following the methods introduced in this book.

However, formidable challenges to transparency research remain, giving rise to exciting opportunities for more research. This chapter highlights four areas of challenges: (1) methodological challenges that call for new methods for transparency research; (2) open research questions related to existing systems; (3) research questions related to new and emerging systems such as the Internet of Things (IoT); and (4) challenges related to studying systems that are ever more pervasively embedded into real-world systems and infrastructure, such as smart cites.

11.1 Methodological Challenges

Methodological challenges relate to all methods discussed in Part III: experiment design, data collection, and data analysis. The references in this section indicate publications that have identified the corresponding challenge and provide further context.

11.1.1 Experiment Design

Experiment design is challenging because it asks to systematically consider all aspects of an experiment before it is run, to anticipate possible issues with data analysis, and to improve the design of data collection accordingly. For example, these issues may relate to the ability of linking records, or to the need for collecting large enough numbers for each experimental group (Boda et al., 2012).

Selection of Values for Input Variables

The selection of values for input variables concerns both the initial selection of values for individual input variables and the selection of combinations for different input variables.

Many studies call for a broader selection of values for individual input variables, such as more browsers (Mazel et al., 2019), more demographic attributes (Riederer et al., 2016; Hu et al., 2020a), more search categories (Hannak et al., 2013), more search terms (Kulshrestha et al., 2017), more components of search result pages (Trielli and Diakopoulos, 2019), and more virtual personas (Hargreaves et al., 2018). The selection of values can be informed by actual frequencies of user types or traffic composition (Barford et al., 2014), by a thorough consideration of all possible values (Mikians et al., 2012), or from user input through surveys (Trielli and Diakopoulos, 2019).

The combinations of input variable values that are studied are often limited by varying one variable at a time while keeping other values at a baseline level. Better experimental designs result in more systematic combinations of values (Mikians et al., 2012; Nath, 2015) and include fractional factorial or Latin hypercube designs. However, they have so far not been widely applied in transparency research.

More systematic methods are also needed to build and verify the profiles of virtual personas (Agarwal et al., 2020).

Selection of Vantage Points

With increasing fragmentation of the web, for example, because of local legislation, the selection of vantage points becomes more important. For example, the prevalence of consent management providers (Hils et al., 2020) and the characteristics of cookie notices (van Eijk et al., 2019) depend on the vantage point. As a result, multiple vantage points should be used (Das et al., 2018b; Fruchter et al., 2015; Iordanou et al., 2018), ensuring the selection of at least two to three diverse vantage points (Wan et al., 2020). The selection of vantage points can take into account differences between regulatory environments (Binns et al., 2018a), between urban and rural areas (Thebault-Spieker et al., 2017), or between countries (Hu et al., 2020a; Fruchter et al., 2015).

A diverse selection of vantage points enables new studies, including regional differences in IoT device behavior (Ren et al., 2019), the effect of geolocation on tracking (Samarasinghe and Mannan, 2019), and the influence of location on the composition of search results (Vincent et al., 2019).

Selection of Websites

Recent work has emphasized that the effects observable on subsites, or internal pages, differ from the effects observable on top-level domains, or landing pages

(Aqeel et al., 2020; Urban et al., 2020a). As a result, many papers call for subsites to be used (Papaodyssefs et al., 2015; Cahn et al., 2016; Zhang et al., 2019b; Urban et al., 2020b), but it is not clear how subsites should be selected to ensure a representative sample. For example, subsites for the Hispar toplist are extracted from Google search results (Aqeel et al., 2020), whereas Urban et al. (2020a) extract subsites from links on landing pages.

In addition, with the consideration of sensitive categories in data protection legislation, both sensitive and nonsensitive websites should be selected for studies of tracking, profiling, and advertising (Matic et al., 2020).

Scope

The scope of many studies is limited to English-language websites, apps, or systems, located in the US. Although many studies point this out as a limitation (Hannak et al., 2013, 2014; Riederer et al., 2016; Hannák et al., 2017; Ribeiro et al., 2018; Thebault-Spieker et al., 2017; Degeling et al., 2019; Kumar et al., 2020; Hu et al., 2020a), only few studies have considered other languages and other locations. Opportunities include analyses of privacy policies for other languages (Zimmeck et al., 2019; Oltramari et al., 2018) and more diverse studies of search and e-commerce systems (Hannak et al., 2013, 2014).

Scope can also be limited by a focus on a single platform. For example, ad delivery (Ali et al., 2019a), PII targeting (Venkatadri et al., 2019), ad explanations (Andreou et al., 2019), and user exposure to ads (Galán et al., 2019) have all been studied for Facebook, but not for other ad platforms including Google, Instagram, Twitter, Pinterest, or LinkedIn (Venkatadri et al., 2018). Similarly, studies of mobile app ecosystems have largely focused on Google Play (Zimmeck et al., 2019), but not on other app markets for Android or app markets for other platforms.

Scale

The largest-scale studies to date have investigated tracking behaviors on up to one million websites (Englehardt and Narayanan, 2016; Libert, 2018). This scale captures the majority of web interactions for most users. Large-scale experiments have also been called for to evaluate cross-border tracking (Iordanou et al., 2018), data leaks from mobile apps (Jin et al., 2018) and websites (Starov et al., 2016), subject access requests (Urban et al., 2019), and anti-ad blockers (Nithyanand et al., 2016).

However, many research questions can only be answered with complex study designs that are not easy to scale and automate (Narayanan and Reisman, 2017). For example, studies that involve physical devices such as mobile phones or IoT devices can become prohibitively expensive if many devices have to be purchased, and prohibitively time-consuming if manual interactions have to be performed. In addition, studies that investigate how big tech's algorithms use personal data, such as studies of bias and discrimination, often need to set up virtual personas (Hargreaves et al., 2018) and maintain browser state for a longer period of time (Hannak et al., 2013; De Cristofaro et al., 2014), which limits their scalability.

To successfully address these challenges, new approaches are needed that can reduce cost in terms of time and resources (Lecuyer et al., 2015; Nath, 2015), including improved automation, reliable methods to reduce noise factors, and improved methods for experiments that require account creation (Farooqi et al., 2020a).

User Studies

User studies need to ensure that they select a large (Starov and Nikiforakis, 2017a) and representative sample of users (Eslami et al., 2015). User studies should be realistic enough to ensure that the study measures real effects, for example, by replicating the information from app store pages when evaluating apps (Srivastava et al., 2017).

User studies can help understand how users perceive many aspects of the corporate surveillance ecosystem such as: how users react to dark patterns (Mathur et al., 2019); why users choose privacy settings that do not correspond with their expectations (Liu et al., 2011); how users react to discrimination in different settings, such as search results or job ads (Plane et al., 2017); how the presence and ranking of components on search result pages influences users (Robertson et al., 2018b); when ads are seen as sensitive (Agarwal et al., 2013); which topics are perceived as sensitive (Dolin et al., 2018); and how users use countermeasures (Mazmudar and Goldberg, 2020).

In addition, user studies can help evaluate usability, for example, the usability of subject access requests (Urban et al., 2019) or the usability of animated privacy notices under repeated exposure (Karegar et al., 2020).

Another open challenge is how to attract users to awareness-raising tools (Riederer et al., 2016) and privacy-enhancing tools such as tracker blockers and ad blockers (Agarwal et al., 2013). In addition, the effectiveness of awareness tools should be evaluated, for example, by measuring user behavior change that results from the use of awareness tools (Henze et al., 2017).

Finally, studies that combine experiments, user studies, and longitudinal data collection are promising because they evaluate the system under study from different viewpoints (May et al., 2019).

Longitudinal Studies

Longitudinal studies are more often called for than reported on. They are important because they allow researchers to keep track of the continuously evolving techniques in the corporate surveillance ecosystem (Krishnamurthy and Wills, 2009; Wills and Tatar, 2012). For example, the consent interface design of Quantcast changed 38 times over two years, so studies that use one snapshot only see one state (Hils et al., 2020).

Longitudinal studies can contribute new insights in a variety of areas: the components of search engine result pages (Trielli and Diakopoulos, 2019), user exposure to ads (Galán et al., 2019), the app ecosystem (Zimmeck et al., 2019; Book et al., 2013), in-app ad targeting (Nath, 2015), redirect tracking (Koop et al., 2020), personalization (Le et al., 2019), price differentiation (Hupperich et al., 2018), online freelancing websites (Hannák et al., 2017), and online status indicators (Cobb et al., 2020).

Causality

Experiment designs that allow causal inferences are important because they allow researchers to attribute observed effects to their cause, which supports much stronger conclusions than correlational statements. For example, causal experiments have been called for to attribute the cause of price differences to user information (Mikians et al., 2013), to attribute discriminatory ad targeting to either the advertiser or the ad platform (Datta et al., 2015), to study compliance to ads.txt (Bashir et al., 2019a), and to confirm the effect of a user's browsing history on their search results (Hannak et al., 2013).

Transience and Nondeterminism

The web is a highly dynamic environment, which can have a large influence on web measurement. For example, two studies that measured the use of HTML5 WebAPIs based on domains from the Alexa list during 2018 only had an overlap of 8% of domains (Diamantaris et al., 2020; Das et al., 2018b). In addition, with increasing introduction of internet regulations by various countries, a user's vantage point increasingly determines which corporate surveillance methods users are exposed to (Dabrowski et al., 2019). This observed transience and fragmentation raise questions about how reliable, robust, and meaningful findings from individual studies are.

As a result, methods are needed to ensure and assess external validity of data collection, which could be caused by nondeterministic website behaviors or fragmentation depending on the vantage point (Fruchter et al., 2015). In addition, methods are needed to systematically deal with nondeterministic websites, for example, websites that employ anti-ad blockers only for some visits (Mughees et al., 2017).

Replication

The transience of corporate surveillance systems also results in difficulties repeating, replicating, or reproducing prior studies, with the purpose of confirming or reproducing the research findings, because the system under study changes too quickly.

However, reproducibility of experiments is a fundamental principle of the scientific method, and studies should ideally be repeatable (i.e., the original research group can produce the same results), replicable (i.e., a different research group can produce the same results), and reproducible (i.e., a different research group can produce the same results with a different experimental setup) (Cockburn et al., 2020). New approaches are therefore needed that can maintain reproducibility even if the system under study changes, or that can correctly attribute whether a failure to reproduce research findings is due to changes in the system under study, due to variables that were not appropriately controlled, or due to errors and mistakes in the experiment.

One method to help with reproducibility is to make all necessary resources and data publicly available (Iordanou et al., 2018; Jin et al., 2018), including a documentation of the full experiment design and all needed software (Engle-hardt and Narayanan, 2016). This can be achieved by publishing containers or virtual machines that contain the entire execution environment (Subramani et al., 2020).

Replication can also be used as a mechanism to bolster study results (Zeber et al., 2020), deal with nondeterminism (Mughees et al., 2017; Urban et al., 2020a), handle ad churn (Wills and Tatar, 2012), or observe changes after relevant events, such as new policy, increased enforcement, or widespread adoption of new technologies (Fruchter et al., 2015; Cabañas et al., 2018).

11.1.2 Data Collection

Challenges in data collection relate to the accessibility of data and data sources that are needed to answer research questions. Although many well-established data collection methods exist, open challenges include: stable methods to deal with encrypted (HTTPS) traffic for mobile and embedded devices (Dabrowski et al., 2016; Continella et al., 2017); data collection from closed systems, such as collecting routes from Waze (Johnson et al., 2017); methods to handle Android native code; methods to detect transformed or obfuscated media in traffic (Pan et al., 2018); and methods to deal with obfuscated tracking APIs in Android apps (Liu et al., 2017).

New data sources can also open up new opportunities for research. For example, user reviews can be used as a data source to evaluate changes in Android or effects of regulations (Nguyen et al., 2019).

Interaction

Realistic and automated interaction with websites and apps is an area with many open challenges. Interaction with websites during crawls includes mouse movements, scrolling, and keystrokes (Gervais et al., 2017). Making these interactions realistic, and evaluating whether realistic interaction patterns lead to different observed effects, is a challenge (Zhang et al., 2019b).

Interaction with apps needs to be designed so that interesting behaviors are triggered reliably and quickly (Reyes et al., 2018). In addition, automated interaction should be able to deal with app logins (Demetriou et al., 2016). One approach to improve interaction patterns for apps is to collect manual inputs to apps from crowd workers (Continella et al., 2017; Shuba and Markopoulou, 2020; Almeida et al., 2018).

Crowdsourcing

Crowdsourcing can help support large-scale data collection and labeling of data (Nithyanand et al., 2016; Starov et al., 2016). However, time synchronization and correct timestamping have been identified as challenges for some applications of crowdsourcing (Bandy and Diakopoulos, 2019).

11.1.3 Data Analysis

Most data analysis challenges relate to finding new quantitative measures and methods for extracting response variables from raw data. Additional opportunities for future work are in combining different analysis methods, for example, combining traffic analysis with dynamic analysis of apps (Vallina-Rodriguez et al., 2016), and in applying and developing statistical techniques, for example, differential testing in studies that attempt to find PII leaks (Englehardt et al., 2018).

Measurement

Measures for the effects of countermeasures are often restricted to client-side measures, such as a reduction in the number of third-party requests. However, additional measures are needed to quantify the effects on the server-side, such as effects on the resulting user profiles (Tschantz et al., 2018a) and the information advertisers learn about users (Wang et al., 2019). This is particularly important for obfuscation-based countermeasures (Howe and Nissenbaum, 2017; Degeling and Nierhoff, 2018).

In addition, measures are needed to quantify semantic differences, for example, between search result lists (Hannak et al., 2013) or between privacy policies (Andow et al., 2020), to quantify the effectiveness of solutions for discriminatory targeting (Speicher et al., 2018), and to quantify the effectiveness of dark patterns and their effects on users (Mathur et al., 2019).

Bias and discrimination. Better measures for discrimination should include measures that support continuous data types without binning (Galhotra et al., 2017). In addition, client-side measures that can indicate bias in search results (Kulshrestha et al., 2017) and better methods to measure media bias (Ribeiro et al., 2018) are needed.

Functionality. Measures of website functionality and functionality loss are important to evaluate side effects of client-side countermeasures (Starov and Nikiforakis, 2017a; Storey et al., 2017; Mazel et al., 2019), effects of geoblocking (McDonald et al., 2018), and effects of fine-grained discrimination against anonymous users, for example, by offering restricted services (Khattak et al., 2016). Similarly, measures of app functionality are also needed (Shuba and Markopoulou, 2020).

Methods for Extracting Response Variables

Improved methods for extracting response variables include better heuristics or machine learning classifiers. They are needed for many situations, including: to label political bias and ideology (Trielli and Diakopoulos, 2019); to detect paywalls (Papadopoulos et al., 2020); to detect anti-ad blockers (Mughees et al., 2017; Zhu et al., 2018); to detect cookie notices (van Eijk et al., 2019); to detect web push notification ads (Subramani et al., 2020); to detect side-channel privacy leaks (Chen and Kapravelos, 2018); to label the semantics of privacy policies (Andow et al., 2019); and to detect dark patterns that use color or style instead of textual features (Mathur et al., 2019).

In addition, the characteristics and biases of existing methods need to be well understood. For example, even though many domain classification services are available, their coverage and taxonomies vary. As a result, there is scope for research to evaluate the correctness of labels assigned by domain classification services, and to create custom taxonomies or custom classifiers (Vallina et al., 2020).

Resolving domains and IP addresses to entities. The entities responsible for traffic, websites, or apps are a very important response variable in many studies. However, existing methods for resolving domain names and IP addresses to entities are imperfect (Andow et al., 2020), especially when entities are using whois privacy services (Binns et al., 2018a). As a result, there is an urgent need to improve methods for the resolution of domains to entities

(Bird et al., 2020), including corporate ownership patterns (Zhang et al., 2019b; Farooqi et al., 2020a).

JavaScript. Methods to extract response variables from JavaScript need to take into account new techniques for obfuscating JavaScript (Sarker et al., 2020), and should be able to deal with JavaScript that is obfuscated, embedded, or composed of multiple sources (Nithyanand et al., 2016; Ikram et al., 2017b).

Machine Learning

Machine learning can help improve measurement studies in many ways. For example, better classifiers can be created to detect trackers (Englehardt and Narayanan, 2016), to automate image labeling (Soeller et al., 2016), to detect cookie synchronization (Papadopoulos et al., 2019), and to label the purpose of data collection in privacy policies (Andow et al., 2020).

Because machine learning can be used to defeat privacy protections, it is important to find methods for hardening privacy protections against machine learning (Peddinti and Saxena, 2010). Methods for retraining classifiers are important to cope with changes in the web or mobile environment while avoiding the cost of repeating the entire training phase (Srivastava et al., 2017).

Machine learning relies on large-scale input datasets (Epp et al., 2011). However, better methods are needed for collecting, cleaning, and labeling datasets, and for evaluating their bias (Wu et al., 2016). Crowdsourcing has been proposed to enable the labeling of large datasets (Nithyanand et al., 2016; Starov et al., 2016).

11.2 Open Research Questions

Open research questions exist in all areas of the corporate surveillance ecosystem, both in the methods used for surveillance and in the services provided to users.

Interdependent privacy, also called multiparty privacy, describes the situation where actions of one user leak information about another (Humbert et al., 2019). This has been studied conceptually in areas like location privacy and genomic privacy, but has not received much attention in transparency research and measurement studies (Krishnamurthy and Wills, 2009).

11.2.1 Corporate Surveillance Methods

Tracking, fingerprinting, and advertising are large areas with many open research questions. In addition, there are open questions regarding the economic effects of corporate surveillance methods.

Tracking

Besides the characteristics, prevalence, and longitudinal evolution of emerging tracking technologies like redirect tracking (Koop et al., 2020), tracking studies can also evaluate the effect of geolocation on tracking (Samarasinghe and Mannan, 2019), the impact of regulations such as GDPR not just on cookies but other methods of tracking (Dabrowski et al., 2019), and the diffusion of information in the tracking ecosystem (Krishnamurthy and Wills, 2006).

Cross-device and cross-platform tracking also need further research, including methods to study cross-platform tracking (Vallina-Rodriguez et al., 2016) and evaluations of the importance and usefulness of features for probabilistic cross-device tracking (Zimmeck et al., 2017).

Open issues also remain in email tracking, for example, evaluations of user-level tracking (Hu et al., 2019b) and evaluations that compare tracking by mailing list managers to tracking by senders (Englehardt et al., 2018).

New fingerprinting methods are discovered frequently and deserve to be studied. In general, fingerprinting studies should distinguish between mobile and desktop fingerprinting (Gómez-Boix et al., 2018) and make sure to use large fingerprinting datasets which can be difficult to collect (Gulyas et al., 2018). In addition, the stability of fingerprints over time (Gulyas et al., 2018; Li and Cao, 2020) and the large-scale uniqueness of fingerprinting attributes can be evaluated (Bird et al., 2020).

Advertising

One of the key open questions in the advertising ecosystem is to characterize the algorithms that match ads between advertisers and users (Andreou et al., 2018). This includes studies that can determine whether advertisers or ad platforms are responsible for discriminatory targeting (Datta et al., 2015), and studies that find out what exactly advertisers can learn about users (Wang et al., 2019). These are difficult questions because the internal information flows in the ad ecosystem are difficult to observe from the outside. A possible approach for addressing this issue is for researchers to act as participants in the ecosystem (Bashir et al., 2019a).

Industry bodies like the IAB regularly release new standards for advertising. In the past, these have included openRTB, ads.txt, and centralized consent management. Evaluating the characteristics and effects of new standards, such as seller.json, are open issues (Bashir et al., 2019a). In addition, the adoption of and compliance to existing standards are interesting topics for longitudinal studies (Bashir et al., 2019a) and studies that evaluate the effect of geolocation (Hils et al., 2020).

Another large area for further research are the information flows in the constantly changing ad ecosystem, new types of ads, new targeting mechanisms, and new ad platforms (Datta et al., 2015). This includes: studying the characteristics of more ad platforms, including Instagram, Twitter, Pinterest, and LinkedIn (Venkatadri et al., 2018); studying discriminatory ad delivery on platforms other than Facebook (Ali et al., 2019a); studying the sources of PII for targeting on Google's Customer Match and Twitter's Tailored Audiences (Venkatadri et al., 2019); studying less-common or novel ad targeting types (Wei et al., 2020); and studying new ad pricing mechanisms like header bidding, including their effect on PII leaks (Pachilakis et al., 2019).

From the users' point of view, the exposure to ads should be studied for platforms other than Facebook, and longitudinally (Galán et al., 2019). In addition, users appreciate better ad explanations (Wei et al., 2020), but their design and adoption are open issues.

Economic Effects

Economic effects are important because, seen from big tech's perspective, they drive the adoption of surveillance technologies. However, economic effects from the user's perspective are not well studied. Topics for further research include: the wealth transfer enabled by privacy-invasive techniques, for example, in terms of data exposure, computational cost, and user attention (Borgolte and Feamster, 2020); the economic impact of ad blockers and reasons why users use ad blockers (Pujol et al., 2015); the tension between commercial interests and privacy, and its limits and possibilities for resolution (Ermakova et al., 2018); and field experiments that compare economic welfare between ad blocker users and users without ad blockers (Frik et al., 2020).

11.2.2 Web Services

New types of web services, such as online freelancing marketplaces (Hannák et al., 2017), and new widely adopted features such as online status indicators (Cobb et al., 2020), are important areas for further research. In addition, the characteristics of existing features often deserve further study, such as PII leakage from registration forms and other web forms (Englehardt et al., 2018), as do the characteristics of specific types of websites, such as the use of third-party services in publicly owned websites (Sørensen and Kosta, 2019).

Further research is also needed to study the differences between platforms, for example, between the desktop, browser, and mobile versions of the same application (Cobb et al., 2020), to study different e-commerce pricing mechanisms such as bundle discounts, coupons, and sponsored listings (Hannak et al., 2014), and to study dark patterns on different types of websites, including email and travel booking (Mathur et al., 2019).

Privacy Policies

Many open issues in the study of privacy policies have already been mentioned, including labeling policy semantics (Andow et al., 2020), and extending research to policies in other languages (Zimmeck et al., 2019) and regions with different regulatory models (Oltramari et al., 2018).

In addition, an important topic is to automate the evaluation of flow-to-policy consistency, that is, whether observed data flows are consistent with the stated privacy policy (Degeling et al., 2019). This can help generate evidence for violations of regulations. However, besides semantic labeling of policies a major challenge in this area is to detect whether users have given consent. This includes comparing observed cookies with the cookie consent given by users (Dabrowski et al., 2019), linking consent to privacy policy statements (Razaghpanah et al., 2018; Reyes et al., 2018), and detecting when or whether apps have asked for consent, and what privacy practices are covered by consent (Andow et al., 2020).

Search

Besides more comprehensive and systematic selections of search terms (Hannak et al., 2013), and the study of search engines other than Google (Hannak et al., 2014), open research questions include: longitudinal studies of the composition of search engine result pages (Trielli and Diakopoulos, 2019) and their personalization (Le et al., 2019); the influence of geographic locations on the composition of SERPs (Vincent et al., 2019); and the influence that presence and ranking of SERP components have on users (Robertson et al., 2018b).

11.2.3 Mobile Devices

In the mobile device ecosystem, the characteristics of app stores other than Google Play are not very well studied (Zimmeck et al., 2019; Book and Wallach, 2013). Research opportunities for all app stores include: studying the development of app ecosystems by periodic sampling of app stores (Book et al., 2013); studying malware spreading strategies on app stores (Wang et al., 2018); studying economic aspects of app stores, such as network effects, bidding wars, and price elasticity (Carbunar and Potharaju, 2015); and studying the supply chain ecosystem, for example, apps preinstalled by phone vendors (Gamba et al., 2020).

Many aspects of mobile apps deserve further research, including: dark patterns in mobile apps (Mathur et al., 2019); in-app targeting strategies and their evolution (Nath, 2015); the information exchange between apps, embedded libraries, and ad servers (Book et al., 2013); app monetization models besides advertising, including crowdfunding and virtual currencies (Mhaidli et al., 2019); and platforms for incentivized app installs other than affiliate apps (Farooqi et al., 2020b). In addition, the characteristics of apps on mobile platforms other than Android are also understudied (Pan et al., 2018; Kondracki et al., 2020). Less-popular apps should be included to ensure a representative sample of apps (Hu et al., 2020b).

Further research questions relate to searches from mobile devices (Hannak et al., 2013), for example, studying the composition and personalization of search engine result pages on mobile devices (Vincent et al., 2019).

11.2.4 Countermeasures

Ad blockers are the most popular countermeasure. However, the prevalence of ad blockers is difficult to measure without access to proprietary data or NetFlow data from ISPs (Malloy et al., 2016). In addition, the characteristics of ad block filter lists offer opportunities for further research, including understanding the causes of false positives (i.e., rules that block of legitimate content) in ad block filter lists, and studying filter lists other than EasyList (Alrizah et al., 2019).

In general, more widely-adopted mechanisms are needed that provide users with transparency and control (Weinshel et al., 2019). These mechanisms should be suitable for end users, not just specialists (Agarwal et al., 2013), and should minimize loss of functionality (Mazel et al., 2019). Specific countermeasures that merit further research are countermeasures for redirect tracking (Koop et al., 2020); improved methods for blocking web push notification ads (Subramani et al., 2020); solutions for discriminatory targeting (Speicher et al., 2018); and countermeasures against fingerprinting, including evaluations of how fingerprinting is influenced by existing countermeasures (Li and Cao, 2020; Gulyas et al., 2018).

Finally, countermeasures for mobile device users are an important area of study, for example, developing countermeasures against data leaks through analytics libraries (Liu et al., 2019), evaluating the effectiveness of protection mechanisms for app users (Book and Wallach, 2013), and evaluating possible loss of functionality under countermeasures (Shuba and Markopoulou, 2020).

11.3 Internet of Things

Internet of Things (IoT) devices are increasingly common. Many IoT devices offer convenience and desirable features, such as home security, home automation, smart appliances, and smart features in home entertainment. However, there are two issues: these devices – including smart doorbells, thermostats, fridges, TVs, and voice assistants – are typically connected to the Internet, and they have access to sensitive information due to their privileged position in individuals' homes. For example, IoT devices have already leaked PII in network traffic, including leaks to third parties, exposed recordings of users and their activity to third parties, and sent traffic to third parties that allowed to infer the presence of devices, times of device activity, and usage patterns (Ren et al., 2019). In addition, security vulnerabilities frequently found in IoT devices can enable surveillance by third-party adversaries in addition to entities in the corporate surveillance ecosystem (Perdisci et al., 2020).

As a result, some aspects of IoT devices have already been the studied. For example, researchers have studied the destination of network traffic, the portion of traffic that is encrypted, the content types that are encrypted, the content types that are sent in plain-text, the exposure of sensitive information, and whether the exposure of information depends on the device location (Ren et al., 2019). For over-the-top streaming channels, which are often monetized using behavioral advertising, researchers have studied how widespread tracking is on these channels, and what tracking technologies are used (Moghaddam et al., 2019). For voice assistants, researchers have studied how voice apps identify users and what kind of personal information they access (Natatsuka et al., 2019), whether on/off buttons truly disable the microphone, whether any conversations that do not mention the wake word are recorded, and whether all user-issued commands are logged and available for user review (Ford and Palmer, 2019).

This section reviews some of the underlying technologies for IoT devices, existing results, and open challenges.

11.3.1 Communication Protocols for IoT Devices

In addition to internet-facing communication using the technologies as described in Chapter 2, IoT devices use additional protocols for local communication, including Wi-Fi, Zigbee, and Bluetooth Low Energy. The differences between these protocols have implications for research studies, for example, regarding what information can be recorded by sniffing network communication (Acar et al., 2020a).

Wi-Fi is often used to provide internet connection through a smart hub or access point. Wi-Fi devices can be identified by their IP and MAC addresses, but Wi-Fi encryption protects the protocol headers at the internet layer and above. In contrast, Zigbee devices can be identified using their MAC address and network address (NwkAddr) which are both not encrypted. The network coordinator in a Zigbee network, such as a smart hub, has a fixed address, and each network has a unique *personal area network* identifier.

In Bluetooth Low Energy, the IoT device acts as a "slave" node that starts by broadcasting advertising packets in randomized time intervals on channels 37–39. When a "master" node, such as a smartphone, receives these advertising packets, it can initiate a connection with the IoT device. Bluetooth Low Energy offers different pairing protocols that determine how nodes exchange pairing features (Zuo et al., 2019). The simplest but least secure option is *just works* which means that devices will pair with any master node without requiring credentials. Other options include *passkey entry*, *numeric comparison*, or *out of band*. After deciding the pairing protocol, the nodes negotiate encryption keys for the BLE connection, possibly based on passkey information. Based on this communication connection, the device provides services, such as reading or writing device properties. The data structures used are typically hierarchical and defined by the device's Generic Attribute Profile. In addition, each service, service characteristic, and service characteristic descriptor is identified by a UUID.

11.3.2 Detecting Presence/Properties of IoT Devices

The UUIDs broadcast by BLE devices allow the fingerprinting of IoT devices (Zuo et al., 2019). For this purpose, UUIDs can be extracted from the binaries of the corresponding mobile apps by searching for uses of the relevant Bluetooth APIs. Based on knowledge of the UUIDs used by IoT devices, the presence of specific devices can then be detected by anyone within communication range. Another method to identify IoT devices is through analysis of the DNS traffic they cause (Perdisci et al., 2020).

DNS traffic, in combination with DHCP and SSDP traffic, can also be used to detect the presence of smart TVs (Varmarken et al., 2020).

To detect when smart speakers are activated, Dubois et al. (2020) combined three different methods. First, they used a static lab setup with fixed positions for all smart speakers. A camera could then record the activation lights, and automated detection was achieved by comparing images against the known *off* state. This comparison was easy because the devices were never moved. Second, they used the provider's web interface to retrieve the list of activations. Third, they recorded the outgoing network traffic and empirically determined a threshold to distinguish between background traffic and activation traffic. Activation was then assumed to take place whenever the threshold was crossed.

11.3.3 Results for IoT Transparency

Voice assistants and smart TV platforms are the most commonly studied IoT devices to date. The smart TV platforms Roku and Amazon Fire are both subject to widespread tracking and advertising. Trackers are present on 69% of Roku channels and 90% of Amazon Fire channels. The most common tracker, Google Analytics, is present on almost half of all channels, and some channels contact more than 40 trackers. In addition, more than 30% of channels leak device identifiers like MAC addresses and serial numbers to trackers, and on-device options to limit tracking and advertising had little to no effect (Moghaddam et al., 2019).

However, countermeasures for smart TV platforms are still limited. Even the best combination of DNS-based filter lists like Pi-hole is only able to block 27% of trackers on Fire TV and 22% on Roku. In addition to simple leaks of device identifiers, many channels leak both the advertising identifier and a static identifier like the device serial number. This enables channels to relink user profiles if the user decides to change the advertising identifier, effectively preventing users from opting out (Varmarken et al., 2020).

Voice assistants, or smart speakers, react to user commands by detecting their *wake word* being spoken. However, smart speakers can misactivate – activate even when the wake word has not been said. For example, when audio was provided by playing TV shows, smart speakers misactivated 0.95 times per hour. These misactivations were nondeterministic, i.e., a repetition of the same TV show would not necessarily result in a repeated misactivation, and they differed between vantage points in the UK and the US. Misactivations can be long enough to capture sensitive content in conversations: depending on the device, half of the observed misactivations were longer than 1–4 s, and one-quarter were longer than 2–7 s (Dubois et al., 2020).

To find out whether adversarial activations of voice assistants have the potential of performing sensitive actions or retrieving sensitive information, the *skills* provided by voice assistants can be analyzed. 5.5% of skills have sensitive commands, such as locking or unlocking doors, starting camera feeds, or retrieving camera images (Shezan et al., 2020). Certification of skills, for example, offered for Google Assistant and Amazon Alexa, is intended to assure users that skills meet the voice assistant's policies. However, this does not mean that policy compliance is verified consistently by skill stores: one study succeeded in getting certifications for hundreds of policy-violating skills (Cheng et al., 2020). Approximately 3.5% of skills on Google's and Amazon's skill marketplaces request private information without following the market's developer specifications, and 68 skills continued eavesdropping after users sent the command to stop them (Guo et al., 2020).

11.3.4 Challenges

A major challenge in conducting measurement studies of IoT devices is that they are physical devices that often use closed platforms. As a result, existing methods to automate user interactions are not applicable, and use of TLS with certificate pinning means that existing methods to intercept outgoing traffic may not be able to provide cleartext for all traffic (Moghaddam et al., 2019). In addition, the cost of purchasing physical devices for study introduces a barrier that may prevent some research studies from taking place: a study of "One million IoT devices" is much more expensive, and therefore much less feasible, than a comparable study of one million websites.

A further methodological challenge in the IoT ecosystem is the interaction with IoT devices. For example, open research questions include: automating interactions with voice assistants like Google Assistant (Natatsuka et al., 2019); using voice synthesizers and machine learning to mimic user voices (Celosia and Cunche, 2020); developing data-driven dialogue systems to automate interaction with skills (Cheng et al., 2020); and creating crawlers that are able to log into channels (Moghaddam et al., 2019).

Studies of IoT devices have so far focused on relatively few devices, including two TV streaming services and two voice assistants. Studying TV streaming besides Roku and Amazon Fire (Moghaddam et al., 2019), and studying voice assistants besides Google Assistant and Amazon Alexa (Natatsuka et al., 2019) are opportunities for further research.

In addition, regional differences in IoT device behavior have not been well studied (Ren et al., 2019), and data use in the smart speaker ecosystem is another open question (Dubois et al., 2020).

Finally, improved countermeasures and protection mechanisms are needed for smart home and IoT devices (Acar et al., 2020a; Varmarken et al., 2020).

11.4 Smart Cities

Smart cities are cities that employ new technologies to become *smarter*, for example, aiming to improve the quality and efficiency of services provided by the city, to improve the quality of citizens' lives, or to stimulate sustainable economic growth (Eckhoff and Wagner, 2018). Smart cities can encompass many different applications, and individual cities may only implement a small subset. For example, smart city applications include smart mobility, smart utilities, smart buildings, smart environment, smart public services, smart governance, smart economy, smart health, and smart citizens.

To realize these diverse applications, cities rely on a combination of new technologies, including ubiquitous internet connectivity, smart cards, open data, sensing including participatory sensing, wearable and IoT devices, autonomous systems, intelligent vehicles, and cloud computing. The more pervasive the use of these technologies in a city, the higher the potential for ubiquitous surveillance of its citizens, either by the city itself or by third parties that provide services as part of public-private partnerships. Because it is hard for citizens to *opt out* of a smart city – it may have to involve moving out of the city and stopping any visits to the city for employment or entertainment – it is crucial that smart cities respect the rights of their citizens, including the rights to privacy, freedom of expression, equality, and nondiscrimination. However, with increasing use of algorithms and outsourcing of city operations to private corporations, this is by no means guaranteed. As a result, smart cities are an important target for transparency research.

This section outlines some examples of real-world smart cities, discusses key concerns for privacy and transparency, and describes some of the challenges for transparency research in smart cities.

11.4.1 Example Smart Cities

Three examples of real-world and envisioned smart cities include Hong Kong, Eindhoven, and Toronto. Citizens in Hong Kong have been relying on some smart city services for many years already. The *Octopus Card* is a smart card that is not only used to pay for public transport and parking, but also for payments in shops as well as for access to buildings, schools, and hospitals. Importantly, the privacy policy permits the collection of data about users and their usage of the card, as well as use of the collected data for marketing (Eckhoff and Wagner, 2018).

The city of Eindhoven employs smart city technology in its most popular nightlife street, the Stratumseind. In particular, the street is subject to surveillance, for example, through monitoring of noise levels and Wi-Fi tracking, with the goal of de-escalating social situations such as street fights. Depending on the situation, the "smart street" can deploy nudges such as changing the lighting and smells on the street (cold light and pleasant smells are thought to have a calming effect), or it can dispatch police officers. To protect privacy, data collected by the sensors on this street is processed directly on the sensors wherever possible, and raw data are not stored.

Finally, Toronto is an example of a smart city that has not yet been realized. Toronto was planning a large project to redesign its Quayside neighborhood, and a company called Sidewalk Labs was the commercial partner to realize the project. What makes this partnership noteworthy is that Sidewalk Labs is owned by Alphabet, Google's parent company. Unsurprisingly therefore, almost every aspect of the city redesign involved data collection.[1] For example, the vision for the redevelopment referred to *ubiquitous sensing*, including Google Nest thermostats in every home and office as well as pervasive use of cameras in public spaces to monitor and direct traffic and more generally "respond to data."

Ann Cavoukian, the former privacy commissioner of Ontario, Canada, who is known for her work on privacy by design, was hired as a privacy consultant to ensure that the data collection did not infringe on the privacy rights of citizens. In particular, Sidewalk Labs assured that all collected data would be de-identified at the source. However, in October 2018 Cavoukian resigned, citing concerns that "third parties might have access to identifiable data."[2] It is not clear how her resignation influenced the course of the project, but in May 2020, Sidewalk Labs withdrew from project, citing the global pandemic Covid-19.[3] Even though this withdrawal may mean that Toronto's Waterfront may not become a corporate surveillance hotspot just yet, it is easy to imagine that corporations will continue their attempts to extract data about individuals from smart city infrastructures.

11.4.2 Privacy and Transparency Concerns in Smart Cities

As the example of Sidewalk Labs and Toronto Waterfront shows, public-private partnerships can be a cause for concern in smart cities. In particular, it is often not clear how risks and rewards are split between the public and private partners,[4] and companies may claim to own the data collected by smart city infrastructure. The latter has happened in The Netherlands where a company that manages traffic lights and lamp posts claims to own the data collected from sensors on this infrastructure and declines to share them with the municipalities.[5] Most large tech companies are already offering products in the smart city space, including Google, Microsoft, IBM, and Cisco, which

---

[1] www.theatlantic.com/technology/archive/2018/11/google-sidewalk-labs/575551/

[2] https://globalnews.ca/news/4579265/ann-cavoukian-resigns-sidewalk-labs/

[3] https://medium.com/sidewalk-talk/why-were-no-longer-pursuing-the-quayside-project-and-what-s-next-for-sidewalk-labs-9a61de3fee3a

[4] www.thestar.com/news/gta/2019/07/01/who-should-share-in-the-risks-and-rewards-of-sidewalk-labs-smart-city-on-torontos-waterfront.html

[5] www.theguardian.com/cities/2018/mar/01/smart-cities-data-privacy-eindhoven-utrecht

means that public-private partnerships may already be common in existing smart city projects.

Compounding this issue is that city planners, often coming from engineering or architectural backgrounds, may lack awareness of privacy issues as well as competence to address these issues on a technical level. This can make city planners susceptible to claims made by private corporations.

Finally, even when privacy protections are in place, surveillance in public spaces can still be problematic (Galič, 2019). For example, even though the surveillance deployed on Eindhoven's Stratumseind does not *identify* individuals, it is still configured to *reach* individuals and influence them to alter their behavior. This can have a negative effect on privacy because "privacy in public space focuses on facilitating the autonomous development of one's identity" Galič (2019), which includes privacy of association and freedom of speech. Public spaces therefore need to be accessible, not under exclusive control, allow for multiple use, tolerate some level of disorder, allow anonymous use, and allow for dissent. Any surveillance technology that allows profiling, sorting, and singling-out of people negatively affects these attributes of public space and thereby negatively affects social and political participation.

11.4.3 Challenges

These issues motivate why transparency for smart cities is an important research area. However, there are additional challenges over and above the challenges of studying transparency on the web or on mobile devices.

First, smart cities are bound to their physical locations in the world, and unlike IoT devices they cannot be set up in a lab environment. This also means that the services provided by smart cities may not be world-accessible and it may be necessary to be physically present in a city to study the properties of its services.

Second, the characteristics of smart cities have not been studied from a measurement point of view. As a result, the interaction points with smart city services and the boundaries of the black-boxes still have to be identified. Because of the diversity of cities and possible services, the interaction points and black-box boundaries may differ between cities and even between services.

Third, much of the data generated in a smart city may be inaccessible and not observable by researchers. Even though some data will be observable, for example, data generated in homes or offices from vantage points within these homes and offices, other data, like mobility data or data from surveillance of public spaces, may not be easily accessible. Research partnerships with cities and local councils may help alleviate this issue, however, developing these collaborations will take time, and data access is likely to be subject to stringent data protection rules.

These challenges present large potential barriers to research and may prevent many studies from taking place. Transparency research will have to devise new methods to overcome these barriers to ensure that smart cities and their public-private partnerships can be held accountable for their data use.

References

Acar, Abbas, Fereidooni, Hossein, Abera, Tigist, Sikder, Amit Kumar, Miettinen, Markus, Aksu, Hidayet, Conti, Mauro, Sadeghi, Ahmad-Reza, and Uluagac, Selcuk. 2020a. Peek-a-Boo: I See Your Smart Home Activities, Even Encrypted! In: *13th ACM Conference on Security and Privacy in Wireless and Mobile Networks*. WiSec '20. Linz: ACM.

Acar, Gunes, Englehardt, Steven, and Narayanan, Arvind. 2020b. No Boundaries: Data Exfiltration by Third Parties Embedded on Web Pages. *Proceedings on Privacy Enhancing Technologies*, **2020**(4), 220–238.

Acar, Gunes, Eubank, Christian, Englehardt, Steven, Juarez, Marc, Narayanan, Arvind, and Diaz, Claudia. 2014. The Web Never Forgets: Persistent Tracking Mechanisms in the Wild. Pages 674–689 of: *Proceedings of the 2014 ACM SIGSAC Conference on Computer and Communications Security*. CCS '14. Scottsdale, AZ: ACM.

Acar, Gunes, Juarez, Marc, Nikiforakis, Nick, Diaz, Claudia, Gürses, Seda, Piessens, Frank, and Preneel, Bart. 2013. FPDetective: Dusting the Web for Fingerprinters. Pages 1129–1140 of: *Proceedings of the 2013 ACM SIGSAC Conference on Computer & Communications Security*. CCS '13. Berlin: ACM.

Achara, Jagdish Prasad, Acs, Gergely, and Castelluccia, Claude. 2015. On the Unicity of Smartphone Applications. Pages 27–36 of: *Proceedings of the 14th ACM Workshop on Privacy in the Electronic Society*. WPES '15. Denver, CO: ACM.

Afroz, Sadia, Tschantz, Michael Carl, Sajid, Shaarif, Qazi, Shoaib Asif, Javed, Mobin, and Paxson, Vern. 2018. Exploring Server-Side Blocking of Regions. arXiv:1805.11606 [cs], May.

Agarwal, Lalit, Shrivastava, Nisheeth, Jaiswal, Sharad, and Panjwani, Saurabh. 2013. Do Not Embarrass: Re-Examining User Concerns for Online Tracking and Advertising. Pages 8:1–8:13 of: *Proceedings of the Ninth Symposium on Usable Privacy and Security*. SOUPS '13. Newcastle: ACM.

Agarwal, Pushkal, Joglekar, Sagar, Papadopoulos, Panagiotis, Sastry, Nishanth, and Kourtellis, Nicolas. 2020. Stop Tracking Me Bro! Differential Tracking of User Demographics on Hyper-Partisan Websites. Pages 1479–1490 of: *Proceedings of The Web Conference 2020*. WWW '20. Taipei: ACM.

Agarwal, Saharsh, Mani, Deepa, and Telang, Rahul. 2019 (June). *The Impact of Ride-Hailing Services on Congestion: Evidence from Indian Cities*. SSRN Scholarly Paper ID 3410623. Rochester, NY: Social Science Research Network.

Agarwal, Yuvraj, and Hall, Malcolm. 2013. ProtectMyPrivacy: Detecting and Mitigating Privacy Leaks on iOS Devices Using Crowdsourcing. Pages 97–110 of: *Proceedings of the 11th Annual International Conference on Mobile Systems, Applications, and Services*. MobiSys '13. Taipei: ACM.

Ahmad, Syed Suleman, Dar, Muhammad Daniyal, Zaffar, Muhammad Fareed, Vallina-Rodriguez, Narseo, and Nithyanand, Rishab. 2020. Apophanies or Epiphanies? How Crawlers Impact Our Understanding of the Web. Pages 271–280 of: *Proceedings of The Web Conference 2020*. WWW '20. Taipei: ACM.

Ali, Muhammad, Sapiezynski, Piotr, Bogen, Miranda, Korolova, Aleksandra, Mislove, Alan, and Rieke, Aaron. 2019a. Discrimination through Optimization: How Facebook's Ad Delivery Can Lead to Skewed Outcomes. arXiv:1904.02095 [cs], Sept.

Ali, Suzan, Osman, Tousif, Mannan, Mohammad, and Youssef, Amr. 2019b. On Privacy Risks of Public WiFi Captive Portals. Pages 80–98 of: Pérez-Solà, Cristina, Navarro-Arribas, Guillermo, Biryukov, Alex, and Garcia-Alfaro, Joaquin (eds.), *Data Privacy Management, Cryptocurrencies and Blockchain Technology*. Lecture Notes in Computer Science. Cham: Springer International Publishing.

Allix, Kevin, Bissyandé, Tegawendé F., Klein, Jacques, and Traon, Yves Le. 2016 (May). AndroZoo: Collecting Millions of Android Apps for the Research Community. Pages 468–471 of: *2016 IEEE/ACM 13th Working Conference on Mining Software Repositories* MSR.

Almeida, Mario, Bilal, Muhammad, Finamore, Alessandro, Leontiadis, Ilias, Grunenberger, Yan, Varvello, Matteo, and Blackburn, Jeremy. 2018. CHIMP: Crowdsourcing Human Inputs for Mobile Phones. Pages 45–54 of: *Proceedings of the 2018 World Wide Web Conference*. WWW '18. Lyon: International World Wide Web Conferences Steering Committee.

Alrizah, Mshabab, Zhu, Sencun, Xing, Xinyu, and Wang, Gang. 2019. Errors, Misunderstandings, and Attacks: Analyzing the Crowdsourcing Process of Ad-Blocking Systems. Pages 230–244 of: *Proceedings of the Internet Measurement Conference*. IMC '19. Amsterdam: ACM.

American Civil Liberties Union. 2019 (May). *Sandvig v Barr: Challenge to CFAA Prohibition on Uncovering Racial Discrimination Online*. www.aclu.org/cases/sandvig-v-barr-challenge-cfaa-prohibition-uncovering-racial-discrimination-online.

American Civil Liberties Union. 2020 (March). *Federal Court Rules 'Big Data' Discrimination Studies Do Not Violate Federal Anti-Hacking Law*. www.aclu.org/press-releases/federal-court-rules-big-data-discrimination-studies-do-not-violate-federal-anti.

Amnesty International. 2019. *Surveillance Giants: How the Business Model of Google and Facebook Threatens Human Rights*. Tech. rept. POL 30/1404/2019. London: Amnesty International.

Andow, Benjamin, Mahmud, Samin Yaseer, Wang, Wenyu, Whitaker, Justin, Enck, William, Reaves, Bradley, Singh, Kapil, and Xie, Tao. 2019 (Aug.). PolicyLint: Investigating Internal Privacy Policy Contradictions on Google Play. Pages 585–602 of: *28th USENIX Security Symposium*. USENIX Security 19. Santa Clara, CA: USENIX.

Andow, Benjamin, Mahmud, Samin Yaseer, Whitaker, Justin, Enck, William, Reaves, Bradley, Singh, Kapil, and Egelman, Serge. 2020. Actions Speak Louder than

Words: Entity-Sensitive Privacy Policy and Data Flow Analysis with PoliCheck. Pages 985–1002 of: *29th USENIX Security Symposium*. USENIX Security 20. USENIX.

Andreou, Athanasios, Venkatadri, Giridhari, Goga, Oana, Gummadi, Krishna P., Loiseau, Patrick, and Mislove, Alan. 2018. Investigating Ad Transparency Mechanisms in Social Media: A Case Study of Facebook's Explanations. In: *Proceedings of the 2018 Network and Distributed System Security Symposium*. San Diego, CA: Internet Society.

Andreou, Athanasios, Silva, Marcio, Benevenuto, Fabrício, Goga, Oana, Loiseau, Patrick, and Mislove, Alan. 2019 (Feb.). Measuring the Facebook Advertising Ecosystem. In: *NDSS 2019: Proceedings of the Network and Distributed System Security Symposium*. San Diego, CA: Internet Society.

Angwin, Julia. 2014. Privacy Tools: Opting Out from Data Brokers. *ProPublica*, Jan.

Angwin, Julia, and Parris, Terry Jr. 2016. Facebook Lets Advertisers Exclude Users by Race. *ProPublica*, Oct.

Angwin, Julia, Parris, Terry Jr., and Mattu, Surya. 2016a. Breaking the Black Box: What Facebook Knows About You. *ProPublica*, Sept.

Angwin, Julia, Mattu, Surya, and Parris, Terry Jr. 2016b. Facebook Doesn't Tell Users Everything It Really Knows.... *ProPublica*, Dec.

Angwin, Julia, Scheiber, Noam, and Tobin, Ariana. 2018. Facebook Job Ads Raise Concerns About Age Discrimination. *The New York Times*, Jan.

Aqeel, Waqar, Chandrasekaran, Balakrishnan, Feldmann, Anja, and Maggs, Bruce M. 2020. On Landing and Internal Web Pages: The Strange Case of Jekyll and Hyde in Web Performance Measurement. Pages 680–695 of: *Proceedings of the ACM Internet Measurement Conference*. IMC '20. Pittsburgh, PA: ACM.

Arshad, Sajjad, Kharraz, Amin, and Robertson, William. 2017. Include Me Out: In-Browser Detection of Malicious Third-Party Content Inclusions. Pages 441–459 of: Grossklags, Jens, and Preneel, Bart (eds.), *Financial Cryptography and Data Security*. Lecture Notes in Computer Science. Berlin, Heidelberg: Springer.

Arzt, Steven, Rasthofer, Siegfried, Fritz, Christian, Bodden, Eric, Bartel, Alexandre, Klein, Jacques, Le Traon, Yves, Octeau, Damien, and McDaniel, Patrick. 2014. FlowDroid: Precise Context, Flow, Field, Object-Sensitive and Lifecycle-Aware Taint Analysis for Android Apps. Pages 259–269 of: *Proceedings of the 35th ACM SIGPLAN Conference on Programming Language Design and Implementation*. PLDI '14. Edinburgh: ACM.

Ayenson, Mika D., Wambach, Dietrich James, Soltani, Ashkan, Good, Nathan, and Hoofnagle, Chris Jay. 2011 (July). *Flash Cookies and Privacy II: Now with HTML5 and ETag Respawning*. SSRN Scholarly Paper ID 1898390. Rochester, NY: Social Science Research Network.

Backstrom, Lars, and Kleinberg, Jon. 2014. Romantic Partnerships and the Dispersion of Social Ties: A Network Analysis of Relationship Status on Facebook. Pages 831–841 of: *Proceedings of the 17th ACM Conference on Computer Supported Cooperative Work & Social Computing*. CSCW '14. Baltimore, MD: ACM.

Bakshy, Eytan, Messing, Solomon, and Adamic, Lada A. 2015. Exposure to Ideologically Diverse News and Opinion on Facebook. *Science*, **348**(6239), 1130–1132.

Balebako, Rebecca, Leon, Pedro G., Shay, Richard, Ur, Blase, Wang, Yang, and Cranor, Lorrie Faith. 2012. Measuring the Effectiveness of Privacy Tools for Limiting

Behavioral Advertising. In: *In Web 2.0 Workshop on Security and Privacy*. San Francisco, CA: IEEE.

Ballatore, Andrea, Graham, Mark, and Sen, Shilad. 2017. Digital Hegemonies: The Localness of Search Engine Results. *Annals of the American Association of Geographers*, **107**(5), 1194–1215.

Bandy, Jack, and Diakopoulos, Nicholas. 2019. Auditing News Curation Systems: A Case Study Examining Algorithmic and Editorial Logic in Apple News. arXiv:1908.00456 [cs], Aug.

Barford, Paul, Canadi, Igor, Krushevskaja, Darja, Ma, Qiang, and Muthukrishnan, S. 2014. Adscape: Harvesting and Analyzing Online Display Ads. Pages 597–608 of: *Proceedings of the 23rd International Conference on World Wide Web*. WWW '14. Seoul: ACM.

Baron, Nancy. 2010. *Escape from the Ivory Tower: A Guide to Making Your Science Matter*. Washington, DC: Island Press.

Barth, Adam. 2011 (April). *HTTP State Management Mechanism*. Tech. rept. RFC 6265. Internet Engineering Task Force (IETF).

Bashir, Muhammad Ahmad, and Wilson, Christo. 2018. Diffusion of User Tracking Data in the Online Advertising Ecosystem. *Proceedings on Privacy Enhancing Technologies*, **2018**(4), 85–103.

Bashir, Muhammad Ahmad, Arshad, Sajjad, Wilson, Christo, and Robertson, William. 2016. Tracing Information Flows Between Ad Exchanges Using Retargeted Ads. Page 17 of: *25th USENIX Security Symposium*. Austin, TX: USENIX.

Bashir, Muhammad Ahmad, Arshad, Sajjad, Kirda, Engin, Robertson, William, and Wilson, Christo. 2018. How Tracking Companies Circumvented Ad Blockers Using WebSockets. Pages 471–477 of: *Proceedings of the Internet Measurement Conference 2018*. IMC '18. Boston, MA: ACM.

Bashir, Muhammad Ahmad, Arshad, Sajjad, Kirda, Engin, Robertson, William, and Wilson, Christo. 2019a. A Longitudinal Analysis of the Ads.Txt Standard. Pages 294–307 of: *Proceedings of the Internet Measurement Conference*. IMC '19. Amsterdam: ACM.

Bashir, Muhammad Ahmad, Farooq, Umar, Shahid, Maryam, Zaffar, Muhammad Fareed, and Wilson, Christo. 2019b. Quantity vs. Quality: Evaluating User Interest Profiles Using Ad Preference Managers. Page 15 of: *Proceedings of the 2019 Network and Distributed System Security Symposium*. San Diego, CA: Internet Society.

Bau, Jason, Mayer, Jonathan, Paskov, Hristo, and Mitchell, John C. 2013. A Promising Direction for Web Tracking Countermeasures. Page 5 of: *Web 2.0 Workshop on Security and Privacy*. W2SP.

Bertram, Theo, Bursztein, Elie, Caro, Stephanie, Chao, Hubert, Chin Feman, Rutledge, Fleischer, Peter, Gustafsson, Albin, Hemerly, Jess, Hibbert, Chris, Invernizzi, Luca, Kammourieh Donnelly, Lanah, Ketover, Jason, Laefer, Jay, Nicholas, Paul, Niu, Yuan, Obhi, Harjinder, Price, David, Strait, Andrew, Thomas, Kurt, and Verney, Al. 2019. Five Years of the Right to Be Forgotten. Pages 959–972 of: *Proceedings of the 2019 ACM SIGSAC Conference on Computer and Communications Security*. CCS '19. London: ACM.

Bertrand, Marianne, and Mullainathan, Sendhil. 2004. Are Emily and Greg More Employable Than Lakisha and Jamal? A Field Experiment on Labor Market Discrimination. *American Economic Review*, **94**(4), 991–1013.

Binns, Reuben, Zhao, Jun, Kleek, Max Van, and Shadbolt, Nigel. 2018a. Measuring Third-Party Tracker Power Across Web and Mobile. *ACM Trans. Internet Technol.*, **18**(4), 52:1–52:22.

Binns, Reuben, Lyngs, Ulrik, Van Kleek, Max, Zhao, Jun, Libert, Timothy, and Shadbolt, Nigel. 2018b. Third Party Tracking in the Mobile Ecosystem. Pages 23–31 of: *Proceedings of the 10th ACM Conference on Web Science*. WebSci '18. Amsterdam: ACM.

Bird, Sarah, Segall, Ilana, and Lopatka, Martin. 2020. Replication: Why We Still Can't Browse in Peace: On the Uniqueness and Reidentifiability of Web Browsing Histories. Pages 489–503 of: *Sixteenth Symposium on Usable Privacy and Security*. SOUPS 2020. USENIX.

Boda, Károly, Földes, Ádám Máté, Gulyás, Gábor György, and Imre, Sándor. 2012. User Tracking on the Web via Cross-Browser Fingerprinting. Pages 31–46 of: Hutchison, David, Kanade, Takeo, Kittler, Josef, Kleinberg, Jon M., Mattern, Friedemann, Mitchell, John C., Naor, Moni, Nierstrasz, Oscar, Pandu Rangan, C., Steffen, Bernhard, Sudan, Madhu, Terzopoulos, Demetri, Tygar, Doug, Vardi, Moshe Y., Weikum, Gerhard, and Laud, Peeter (eds.), *Nordic Conference on Secure IT Systems*. NordSec 2011. vol. LNCS 7161. Berlin, Heidelberg: Springer.

Bond, Robert M., Fariss, Christopher J., Jones, Jason J., Kramer, Adam D. I., Marlow, Cameron, Settle, Jaime E., and Fowler, James H. 2012. A 61-Million-Person Experiment in Social Influence and Political Mobilization. *Nature*, **489**(7415), 295–298.

Book, Theodore, and Wallach, Dan S. 2013. A Case of Collusion: A Study of the Interface Between Ad Libraries and Their Apps. Pages 79–86 of: *Proceedings of the Third ACM Workshop on Security and Privacy in Smartphones & Mobile Devices*. SPSM '13. Berlin: ACM.

Book, Theodore, Pridgen, Adam, and Wallach, Dan S. 2013 (May). Longitudinal Analysis of Android Ad Library Permissions. Page 9 of: *Mobile Security Technologies*. MoST.

Borgesius, Frederik J. Zuiderveen. 2016. Singling out People without Knowing Their Names – Behavioural Targeting, Pseudonymous Data, and the New Data Protection Regulation. *Computer Law & Security Review*, **32**(2), 256–271.

Borgolte, Kevin, and Feamster, Nick. 2020. Understanding the Performance Costs and Benefits of Privacy-Focused Browser Extensions. Pages 2275–2286 of: *Proceedings of The Web Conference 2020*. WWW '20. Taipei: ACM.

Bösch, Christoph, Erb, Benjamin, Kargl, Frank, Kopp, Henning, and Pfattheicher, Stefan. 2016. Tales from the Dark Side: Privacy Dark Strategies and Privacy Dark Patterns. *Proceedings on Privacy Enhancing Technologies*, **2016**(4), 237–254.

Brik, Vladimir, Banerjee, Suman, Gruteser, Marco, and Oh, Sangho. 2008. Wireless Device Identification with Radiometric Signatures. Pages 116–127 of: *Proceedings of the 14th ACM International Conference on Mobile Computing and Networking*. MobiCom '08. San Francisco, CA: ACM.

Brookman, Justin, Rouge, Phoebe, Alva, Aaron, and Yeung, Christina. 2017. Cross-Device Tracking: Measurement and Disclosures. *Proceedings on Privacy Enhancing Technologies*, **2017**(2), 133–148.

Bujlow, T., Carela-Español, V., Solé-Pareta, J., and Barlet-Ros, P. 2017. A Survey on Web Tracking: Mechanisms, Implications, and Defenses. *Proceedings of the IEEE*, **105**(8), 1476–1510.

Burklen, Susanne, Marron, Pedro Jose, Fritsch, Serena, and Rothermel, Kurt. 2005. User Centric Walk: An Integrated Approach for Modeling the Browsing Behavior of Users on the Web. Pages 149–159 of: *Proceedings of the 38th Annual Symposium on Simulation*. ANSS '05. Washington, DC: IEEE Computer Society.

Buttarelli, Giovanni. 2017. Privacy Matters: Updating Human Rights for the Digital Society. *Health and Technology*, **7**(4), 325–328.

Cabañas, José González, Cuevas, Ángel, and Cuevas, Rubén. 2018. Unveiling and Quantifying Facebook Exploitation of Sensitive Personal Data for Advertising Purposes. Pages 479–495 of: *27th USENIX Security Symposium*. USENIX Security 18. Baltimore, MD: USENIX Association.

Cahn, Aaron, Alfeld, Scott, Barford, Paul, and Muthukrishnan, S. 2016. An Empirical Study of Web Cookies. Pages 891–901 of: *Proceedings of the 25th International Conference on World Wide Web*. WWW '16. Montréal: International World Wide Web Conferences Steering Committee.

Calciati, Paolo, and Gorla, Alessandra. 2017. How Do Apps Evolve in Their Permission Requests?: A Preliminary Study. Pages 37–41 of: *Proceedings of the 14th International Conference on Mining Software Repositories*. MSR '17. Buenos Aires: IEEE Press.

Callejo, Patricia, Kelton, Conor, Vallina-Rodriguez, Narseo, Cuevas, Rubén, Gasser, Oliver, Kreibich, Christian, Wohlfart, Florian, and Cuevas, Ángel. 2017. Opportunities and Challenges of Ad-Based Measurements from the Edge of the Network. Pages 87–93 of: *Proceedings of the 16th ACM Workshop on Hot Topics in Networks*. HotNets-XVI. Palo Alto, CA: ACM.

Cao, Yinzhi, Li, Song, and Wijmans, Erik. 2017. (Cross-)Browser Fingerprinting via OS and Hardware Level Features. In: *Proceedings of the 2017 Network and Distributed System Security Symposium*. San Diego, CA: Internet Society.

Carbunar, Bogdan, and Potharaju, Rahul. 2015. A Longitudinal Study of the Google App Market. Pages 242–249 of: *Proceedings of the 2015 IEEE/ACM International Conference on Advances in Social Networks Analysis and Mining 2015*. ASONAM '15. Paris: ACM.

Carrascal, Juan Pablo, Riederer, Christopher, Erramilli, Vijay, Cherubini, Mauro, and de Oliveira, Rodrigo. 2013. Your Browsing Behavior for a Big Mac: Economics of Personal Information Online. Pages 189–200 of: *Proceedings of the 22Nd International Conference on World Wide Web*. WWW '13. Rio de Janeiro: ACM.

Carrascosa, Juan Miguel, Mikians, Jakub, Cuevas, Ruben, Erramilli, Vijay, and Laoutaris, Nikolaos. 2015. I Always Feel Like Somebody's Watching Me: Measuring Online Behavioural Advertising. Pages 13:1–13:13 of: *Proceedings of the 11th ACM Conference on Emerging Networking Experiments and Technologies*. CoNEXT '15. Berlin, Heidelberg: ACM.

Cavoukian, Ann. 2013. *Privacy by Design*. Tech. rept. Information and Privacy Commissioner of Ontario.

Celosia, Guillaume, and Cunche, Mathieu. 2020. Discontinued Privacy: Personal Data Leaks in Apple Bluetooth-Low-Energy Continuity Protocols. *Proceedings on Privacy Enhancing Technologies*, **2020**(1), 26–46.

Chen, G., Cox, J. H., Uluagac, A. S., and Copeland, J. A. 2016a. In-Depth Survey of Digital Advertising Technologies. *IEEE Communications Surveys Tutorials*, **18**(3), 2124–2148.

Chen, H., Leung, H., Han, B., and Su, J. 2017 (May). Automatic Privacy Leakage Detection for Massive Android Apps via a Novel Hybrid Approach. Pages 1–7 of: *Proceedings of the 2017 IEEE International Conference on Communications*. ICC. Paris: IEEE.

Chen, Le, Mislove, Alan, and Wilson, Christo. 2015. Peeking Beneath the Hood of Uber. Pages 495–508 of: *Proceedings of the 2015 Internet Measurement Conference*. IMC '15. Tokyo: ACM.

Chen, Le, Mislove, Alan, and Wilson, Christo. 2016b. An Empirical Analysis of Algorithmic Pricing on Amazon Marketplace. Pages 1339–1349 of: *Proceedings of the 25th International Conference on World Wide Web*. WWW '16. Montreal: International World Wide Web Conferences Steering Committee.

Chen, Le, Ma, Ruijun, Hannák, Anikó, and Wilson, Christo. 2018. Investigating the Impact of Gender on Rank in Resume Search Engines. Page 651 of: *Proceedings of the 2018 CHI Conference on Human Factors in Computing Systems*. Montreal: ACM.

Chen, Quan, and Kapravelos, Alexandros. 2018. Mystique: Uncovering Information Leakage from Browser Extensions. Pages 1687–1700 of: *Proceedings of the 2018 ACM SIGSAC Conference on Computer and Communications Security*. CCS '18. Toronto: ACM.

Chen, Terence, Chaabane, Abdelberi, Tournoux, Pierre Ugo, Kaafar, Mohamed-Ali, and Boreli, Roksana. 2013. How Much Is Too Much? Leveraging Ads Audience Estimation to Evaluate Public Profile Uniqueness. Pages 225–244 of: Cristofaro, Emiliano De, and Wright, Matthew (eds.), *Privacy Enhancing Technologies*. Lecture Notes in Computer Science, no. 7981. Berlin, Heidelberg: Springer.

Cheng, Long, Wilson, Christin, Liao, Song, Young, Jeffrey, Dong, Daniel, and Hu, Hongxin. 2020. Dangerous Skills Got Certified: Measuring the Trustworthiness of Skill Certification in Voice Personal Assistant Platforms. Pages 1699–1716 of: *Proceedings of the 2020 ACM SIGSAC Conference on Computer and Communications Security*. CCS '20. ACM.

Cheng, N., Wang, X. Oscar, Cheng, W., Mohapatra, P., and Seneviratne, A. 2013 (April). Characterizing Privacy Leakage of Public WiFi Networks for Users on Travel. Pages 2769–2777 of: *2013 Proceedings IEEE INFOCOM*.

Chittaranjan, Gokul, Blom, Jan, and Gatica-Perez, Daniel. 2013. Mining Large-Scale Smartphone Data for Personality Studies. *Personal Ubiquitous Comput.*, **17**(3), 433–450.

Christl, Wolfie. 2017. *Corporate Surveillance in Everyday Life*. Tech. rept. Cracked Labs, Vienna, Austria.

Christl, Wolfie, and Spiekermann, Sarah. 2016. *Networks of Control: A Report on Corporate Surveillance, Digital Tracking, Big Data & Privacy*. Vienna: Facultas.

Clark, Alexander, Fox, Chris, and Lappin, Shalom (eds.). 2013. *The Handbook of Computational Linguistics and Natural Language Processing*. 1st edition. Chichester: Wiley-Blackwell.

Clark, Sandy, Blaze, Matt, and Smith, Jonathan M. 2015. Smearing Fingerprints: Changing the Game of Web Tracking with Composite Privacy. Pages 178–182 of: Christianson, Bruce, Švenda, Petr, Matyáš, Vashek, Malcolm, James, Stajano, Frank, and Anderson, Jonathan (eds.), *Security Protocols XXIII*. Lecture Notes in Computer Science. Cham: Springer.

Clayton, Richard, and Mansfield, Tony. 2014 (June). A Study of Whois Privacy and Proxy Service Abuse. Page 19 of: *Proceedings (Online) of the 13th Workshop on Economics of Information Security*. State College, PA.

Clement, J. 2020 (Feb.). *Google: Ad Revenue 2001–2018*. www.statista.com/statistics/266249/advertising-revenue-of-google/.

Clifford, Scott, Jewell, Ryan M, and Waggoner, Philip D. 2015. Are Samples Drawn from Mechanical Turk Valid for Research on Political Ideology? *Research & Politics*, **2**(4), 1–9.

CNIL. 2019 (Jan.). *Deliberation of the Restricted Committee SAN-2019-001 of 21 January 2019 Pronouncing a Financial Sanction against GOOGLE LLC*. Tech. rept.

Cobb, Camille, Simko, Lucy, Kohno, Tadayoshi, and Hiniker, Alexis. 2020. A Privacy-Focused Systematic Analysis of Online Status Indicators. *Proceedings on Privacy Enhancing Technologies*, **2020**(3), 384–403.

Cockburn, Andy, Dragicevic, Pierre, Besançon, Lonni, and Gutwin, Carl. 2020. Threats of a Replication Crisis in Empirical Computer Science. *Communications of the ACM*, **63**(8), 70–79.

COMPASS Science Communication, Inc. 2017. *The Message Box Workbook*. Washington, DC: National Academies Press.

Conti, M., Cozza, V., Petrocchi, M., and Spognardi, A. 2015 (Nov.). TRAP: Using Targeted Ads to Unveil Google Personal Profiles. Pages 1–6 of: *2015 IEEE International Workshop on Information Forensics and Security*. WIFS.

Continella, Andrea, Fratantonio, Yanick, Lindorfer, Martina, Puccetti, Alessandro, Zand, Ali, Kruegel, Christopher, and Vigna, Giovanni. 2017. Obfuscation-Resilient Privacy Leak Detection for Mobile Apps Through Differential Analysis. In: *Proceedings of the 2017 Network and Distributed System Security Symposium*. San Diego, CA: Internet Society.

Cook, John, Nithyanand, Rishab, and Shafiq, Zubair. 2020. Inferring Tracker-Advertiser Relationships in the Online Advertising Ecosystem Using Header Bidding. *Proceedings on Privacy Enhancing Technologies*, **2020**(1), 65–82.

Cooper, Drew, Castiglione, Joe, Mislove, Alan, and Wilson, Christo. 2018. Profiling Transport Network Company Activity Using Big Data. *Transportation Research Record*, **2672**(42), 192–202.

Corner, Mark D., Levine, Brian N., Ismail, Omar, and Upreti, Angela. 2017. Advertising-Based Measurement: A Platform of 7 Billion Mobile Devices. Pages 435–447 of: *Proceedings of the 23rd Annual International Conference on Mobile Computing and Networking*. MobiCom '17. Snowbird, UT: ACM.

Couldry, Nick. 2016 (Sept.). *The Price of Connection: 'Surveillance Capitalism'*. http://theconversation.com/the-price-of-connection-surveillance-capitalism-64124.

Cozza, Vittoria, Hoang, Van Tien, Petrocchi, Marinella, and Spognardi, Angelo. 2016. Experimental Measures of News Personalization in Google News. Pages 93–104 of: Casteleyn, Sven, Dolog, Peter, and Pautasso, Cesare (eds.), *Current Trends in Web Engineering*. Lecture Notes in Computer Science. Cham: Springer.

Crump, Matthew J. C., McDonnell, John V., and Gureckis, Todd M. 2013. Evaluating Amazon's Mechanical Turk as a Tool for Experimental Behavioral Research. *PLOS ONE*, **8**(3), e57410.

Crussell, Jonathan, Stevens, Ryan, and Chen, Hao. 2014. MAdFraud: Investigating Ad Fraud in Android Applications. Pages 123–134 of: *Proceedings of the 12th Annual International Conference on Mobile Systems, Applications, and Services*. MobiSys '14. Bretton Woods, NH: ACM.

Dabrowski, A., Merzdovnik, G., Kommenda, N., and Weippl, E. 2016 (May). Browser History Stealing with Captive Wi-Fi Portals. Pages 234–240 of: *2016 IEEE Security and Privacy Workshops*. SPW. San Jose, CA: IEEE.

Dabrowski, Adrian, Merzdovnik, Georg, Ullrich, Johanna, Sendera, Gerald, and Weippl, Edgar. 2019. Measuring Cookies and Web Privacy in a Post-GDPR World. Pages 258–270 of: Choffnes, David, and Barcellos, Marinho (eds.), *Passive and Active Measurement*. Lecture Notes in Computer Science. Cham: Springer International Publishing.

Das, Anupam, Borisov, Nikita, and Caesar, Matthew. 2014. Do You Hear What I Hear?: Fingerprinting Smart Devices Through Embedded Acoustic Components. Pages 441–452 of: *Proceedings of the 2014 ACM SIGSAC Conference on Computer and Communications Security*. CCS '14. Scottsdale, AZ: ACM.

Das, Anupam, Borisov, Nikita, and Caesar, Matthew. 2016. Tracking Mobile Web Users Through Motion Sensors: Attacks and Defenses. In: *Proceedings 2016 Network and Distributed System Security Symposium*. San Diego, CA: Internet Society.

Das, Anupam, Borisov, Nikita, and Chou, Edward. 2018a. Every Move You Make: Exploring Practical Issues in Smartphone Motion Sensor Fingerprinting and Countermeasures. *Proceedings on Privacy Enhancing Technologies*, **2018**(1), 88–108.

Das, Anupam, Acar, Gunes, Borisov, Nikita, and Pradeep, Amogh. 2018b. The Web's Sixth Sense: A Study of Scripts Accessing Smartphone Sensors. Pages 1515–1532 of: *Proceedings of the 2018 ACM SIGSAC Conference on Computer and Communications Security*. Toronto: ACM.

Datta, Amit, Tschantz, Michael Carl, and Datta, Anupam. 2015. Automated Experiments on Ad Privacy Settings. *Proceedings on Privacy Enhancing Technologies*, **2015**(1), 92–112.

Datta, Amit, Lu, Jianan, and Tschantz, Michael Carl. 2019. Evaluating Anti-Fingerprinting Privacy Enhancing Technologies. Pages 351–362 of: *The World Wide Web Conference*. WWW '19. San Francisco, CA: ACM.

De Bock, KoenW, and Van den Poel, Dirk. 2010. Predicting Website Audience Demographics for Web Advertising Targeting Using Multi-Website Clickstream Data. *Fundamenta Informaticae*, **98**(1), 49–70.

De Cristofaro, Emiliano, Friedman, Arik, Jourjon, Guillaume, Kaafar, Mohamed Ali, and Shafiq, M. Zubair. 2014. Paying for Likes?: Understanding Facebook Like Fraud Using Honeypots. Pages 129–136 of: *Proceedings of the 2014 Conference on Internet Measurement Conference*. IMC '14. Vancouver: ACM.

De Domenico, Manlio, Lima, Antonio, and Musolesi, Mirco. 2013. Interdependence and Predictability of Human Mobility and Social Interactions. *Pervasive and Mobile Computing*, **9**(6), 798–807.

de Montjoye, Yves-Alexandre, Quoidbach, Jordi, Robic, Florent, and Pentland, Alex. 2013a. Predicting Personality Using Novel Mobile Phone-Based Metrics. Pages 48–55 of: Hutchison, David, Kanade, Takeo, Kittler, Josef, Kleinberg, Jon M., Mattern, Friedemann, Mitchell, John C., Naor, Moni, Nierstrasz, Oscar, Pandu Rangan, C., Steffen, Bernhard, Sudan, Madhu, Terzopoulos, Demetri, Tygar, Doug, Vardi, Moshe Y., Weikum, Gerhard, Greenberg, Ariel M., Kennedy, William G., and Bos, Nathan D. (eds.), *Social Computing, Behavioral-Cultural Modeling and Prediction*, vol. 7812. Berlin, Heidelberg: Springer.

de Montjoye, Yves-Alexandre, Hidalgo, César A., Verleysen, Michel, and Blondel, Vincent D. 2013b. Unique in the Crowd: The Privacy Bounds of Human Mobility. *Scientific Reports*, **3**(March), 1376.

de Montjoye, Yves-Alexandre, Radaelli, Laura, Singh, Vivek Kumar, and Pentland, Alex "Sandy". 2015. Unique in the Shopping Mall: On the Reidentifiability of Credit Card Metadata. *Science*, **347**(6221), 536–539.

Degeling, Martin, and Nierhoff, Jan. 2018. Tracking and Tricking a Profiler: Automated Measuring and Influencing of Bluekai's Interest Profiling. Pages 1–13 of: *Proceedings of the 2018 Workshop on Privacy in the Electronic Society*. WPES'18. Toronto: ACM.

Degeling, Martin, Utz, Christine, Lentzsch, Christopher, Hosseini, Henry, Schaub, Florian, and Holz, Thorsten. 2019 (Feb.). We Value Your Privacy ... Now Take Some Cookies: Measuring the GDPR's Impact on Web Privacy. In: *Network and Distributed Systems Security (NDSS) Symposium*. San Diego, CA: Internet Society.

Demetriou, Soteris, Merrill, Whitney, Yang, Wei, Zhang, Aston, and Gunter, Carl A. 2016. Free for All! Assessing User Data Exposure to Advertising Libraries on Android. In: *Proceedings 2016 Network and Distributed System Security Symposium*. San Diego, CA: Internet Society.

Derr, Erik, Bugiel, Sven, Fahl, Sascha, Acar, Yasemin, and Backes, Michael. 2017. Keep Me Updated: An Empirical Study of Third-Party Library Updatability on Android. Pages 2187–2200 of: *Proceedings of the 2017 ACM SIGSAC Conference on Computer and Communications Security*. CCS '17. Dallas, TX: ACM.

Deußer, Clemens, Passmann, Steffen, and Strufe, Thorsten. 2020. Browsing Unicity: On the Limits of Anonymizing Web Tracking Data. Pages 279–292 of: *2020 IEEE Symposium on Security and Privacy*. SP. San Francisco, CA: IEEE.

Dey, Sanorita, Roy, Nirupam, Xu, Wenyuan, Choudhury, Romit Roy, and Nelakuditi, Srihari. 2014. AccelPrint: Imperfections of Accelerometers Make Smartphones Trackable. In: *Proceedings of the 2014 Network and Distributed System Symposium*. San Diego, CA: Internet Society.

Diamantaris, Michalis, Marcantoni, Francesco, Ioannidis, Sotiris, and Polakis, Jason. 2020. The Seven Deadly Sins of the HTML5 WebAPI: A Large-Scale Study on the Risks of Mobile Sensor-Based Attacks. *ACM Transactions on Privacy and Security*, **23**(4), 19:1–19:31.

DiNitto, Diana, and Johnson, David H. 2015. *Social Welfare: Politics and Public Policy*. 8 edition. Boston, MA: Pearson.

Doctorow, Cory. 2020 (Aug.). *How to Destroy "Surveillance Capitalism."* https:// onezero.medium.com/how-to-destroy-surveillance-capitalism-8135e6744d59.

Dolin, Claire, Weinshel, Ben, Shan, Shawn, Hahn, Chang Min, Choi, Euirim, Mazurek, Michelle L., and Ur, Blase. 2018. Unpacking Perceptions of Data-Driven Inferences Underlying Online Targeting and Personalization. Pages 493:1–493:12 of: *Proceedings of the 2018 CHI Conference on Human Factors in Computing Systems*. CHI '18. Montreal: ACM.

Duan, Ruian, Bijlani, Ashish, Xu, Meng, Kim, Taesoo, and Lee, Wenke. 2017. Identifying Open-Source License Violation and 1-Day Security Risk at Large Scale. Pages 2169–2185 of: *Proceedings of the 2017 ACM SIGSAC Conference on Computer and Communications Security*. CCS '17. Dallas TX: ACM.

Dubois, Daniel J, Kolcun, Roman, Mandalari, Anna Maria, Paracha, Muhammad Talha, and Haddadi, Hamed. 2020. When Speakers Are All Ears: Characterizing Misactivations of IoT Smart Speakers. *Proceedings on Privacy Enhancing Technologies*, **2020**(4), 255–276.

Dwork, Cynthia, Hardt, Moritz, Pitassi, Toniann, Reingold, Omer, and Zemel, Richard. 2012. Fairness through Awareness. Pages 214–226 of: *Proceedings of the 3rd Innovations in Theoretical Computer Science Conference*. Cambridge, MA: ACM.

Eckersley, Peter. 2010. How Unique Is Your Web Browser? Pages 1–18 of: Atallah, Mikhail J., and Hopper, Nicholas J. (eds.), *Privacy Enhancing Technologies*. Lecture Notes in Computer Science, no. 6205. Berlin, Heidelberg: Springer.

Eckhoff, David, and Wagner, Isabel. 2018. Privacy in the Smart City – Applications, Technologies, Challenges and Solutions. *IEEE Communications Surveys & Tutorials*, **20**(1), 489–516.

Egele, Manuel, Kruegel, Christopher, Kirda, Engin, and Vigna, Giovanni. 2011 (Feb.). PiOS: Detecting Privacy Leaks in iOS Applications. Page 15 of: *NDSS Symposium*. San Diego, CA: Internet Society.

Enck, William, Gilbert, Peter, Han, Seungyeop, Tendulkar, Vasant, Chun, Byung-Gon, Cox, Landon P., Jung, Jaeyeon, McDaniel, Patrick, and Sheth, Anmol N. 2014. TaintDroid: An Information-Flow Tracking System for Realtime Privacy Monitoring on Smartphones. *ACM Trans. Comput. Syst.*, **32**(2), 5:1–5:29.

Englehardt, Steven, and Narayanan, Arvind. 2016. Online Tracking: A 1-Million-Site Measurement and Analysis. Pages 1388–1401 of: *Proceedings of the 2016 ACM SIGSAC Conference on Computer and Communications Security*. CCS '16. Vienna: ACM.

Englehardt, Steven, Reisman, Dillon, Eubank, Christian, Zimmerman, Peter, Mayer, Jonathan, Narayanan, Arvind, and Felten, Edward W. 2015. Cookies That Give You Away: The Surveillance Implications of Web Tracking. Pages 289–299 of: *Proceedings of the 24th International Conference on World Wide Web*. WWW '15. Florence: International World Wide Web Conferences Steering Committee.

Englehardt, Steven, Han, Jeffrey, and Narayanan, Arvind. 2018. I Never Signed up for This! Privacy Implications of Email Tracking. *Proceedings on Privacy Enhancing Technologies*, **2018**(1), 109–126.

Epp, Clayton, Lippold, Michael, and Mandryk, Regan L. 2011. Identifying Emotional States Using Keystroke Dynamics. Page 715 of: *Proceedings of the 2011 Annual Conference on Human Factors in Computing Systems*. CHI '11. Vancouver: ACM Press.

Epstein, Robert, and Robertson, Ronald E. 2015. The Search Engine Manipulation Effect (SEME) and Its Possible Impact on the Outcomes of Elections. *Proceedings of the National Academy of Sciences*, **112**(33), E4512–E4521.

Epstein, Robert, Robertson, Ronald E., Lazer, David, and Wilson, Christo. 2017. Suppressing the Search Engine Manipulation Effect (SEME). *Proc. ACM Hum.-Comput. Interact.*, **1**(CSCW), 42:1–42:22.

Ermakova, Tatiana, Fabian, Benjamin, Bender, Benedict, and Klimek, Kerstin. 2018. Web Tracking: - A Literature Review on the State of Research. *Hawaii International Conference on System Sciences 2018*. HICSS-51 (Jan.).

Eslami, Motahhare, Rickman, Aimee, Vaccaro, Kristen, Aleyasen, Amirhossein, Vuong, Andy, Karahalios, Karrie, Hamilton, Kevin, and Sandvig, Christian. 2015. "I Always Assumed That I Wasn't Really That Close to [Her]": Reasoning About Invisible Algorithms in News Feeds. Pages 153–162 of: *Proceedings of the 33rd Annual ACM Conference on Human Factors in Computing Systems*. CHI '15. Seoul: ACM.

Eslami, Motahhare, Vaccaro, Kristen, Karahalios, Karrie, and Hamilton, Kevin. 2017 (May). "Be Careful; Things Can Be Worse than They Appear": Understanding Biased Algorithms and Users' Behavior Around Them in Rating Platforms. In: *Eleventh International AAAI Conference on Web and Social Media*. Montreal: AAAI Press.

Eslami, Motahhare, Krishna Kumaran, Sneha R., Sandvig, Christian, and Karahalios, Karrie. 2018. Communicating Algorithmic Process in Online Behavioral Advertising. Pages 432:1–432:13 of: *Proceedings of the 2018 CHI Conference on Human Factors in Computing Systems*. CHI '18. Montreal: ACM.

European Data Protection Supervisor (EDPS). 2020 (July). *Outcome of Own-Initiative Investigation into EU Institutions' Use of Microsoft Products and Services*. Tech. rept. European Union, Luxembourg.

Falahrastegar, Marjan, Haddadi, Hamed, Uhlig, Steve, and Mortier, Richard. 2016. Tracking Personal Identifiers Across the Web. Pages 30–41 of: Karagiannis, Thomas, and Dimitropoulos, Xenofontas (eds.), *Passive and Active Measurement*. Lecture Notes in Computer Science. Cham: Springer.

Farooqi, Shehroze, Musa, Maaz, Shafiq, Zubair, and Zaffar, Fareed. 2020a. Canary-Trap: Detecting Data Misuse by Third-Party Apps on Online Social Networks. *Proceedings on Privacy Enhancing Technologies*, **2020**(4), 336–354.

Farooqi, Shehroze, Feal, Álvaro, Lauinger, Tobias, McCoy, Damon, Shafiq, Zubair, and Vallina-Rodriguez, Narseo. 2020b. Understanding Incentivized Mobile App Installs on Google Play Store. Pages 696–709 of: *Proceedings of the ACM Internet Measurement Conference*. IMC '20. Pittsburgh, PA: ACM.

Feal, Álvaro, Calciati, Paolo, Vallina-Rodriguez, Narseo, Troncoso, Carmela, and Gorla, Alessandra. 2020. Angel or Devil? A Privacy Study of Mobile Parental Control Apps. *Proceedings on Privacy Enhancing Technologies*, **2020**(2), 314–335.

Felt, Adrienne Porter, Barnes, Richard, King, April, Palmer, Chris, Bentzel, Chris, and Tabriz, Parisa. 2017 (Aug.). Measuring HTTPS Adoption on the Web. Pages 1323–1338 of: *26th USENIX Security Symposium*. USENIX Security 17. Vancouver: USENIX.

Felten, Edward W., and Schneider, Michael A. 2000. Timing Attacks on Web Privacy. Pages 25–32 of: *Proceedings of the 7th ACM Conference on Computer and Communications Security*. CCS '00. Athens: ACM.

Ferra, Fenia, Wagner, Isabel, Boiten, Eerke, Hadlington, Lee, Psychoula, Ismini, and Snape, Richard. 2020. Challenges in Assessing Privacy Impact: Tales from the Front Lines. *Security and Privacy*, **3**(2), e101.

Fielding, Roy, and Reschke, Julian. 2014 (June). *Hypertext Transfer Protocol (HTTP/1.1): Semantics and Content*. Tech. rept. RFC 7231. Internet Engineering Task Force (IETF).

Fifield, David, and Egelman, Serge. 2015. Fingerprinting Web Users Through Font Metrics. Pages 107–124 of: Böhme, Rainer, and Okamoto, Tatsuaki (eds.), *Financial Cryptography and Data Security*. Lecture Notes in Computer Science. Berlin, Heidelberg: Springer.

Foong, Eureka, Vincent, Nicholas, Hecht, Brent, and Gerber, Elizabeth M. 2018. Women (Still) Ask for Less: Gender Differences in Hourly Rate in an Online Labor Marketplace. *Proc. ACM Hum.-Comput. Interact.*, **2**(CSCW), 53:1–53:21.

Ford, Marcia, and Palmer, William. 2019. Alexa, Are You Listening to Me? An Analysis of Alexa Voice Service Network Traffic. *Personal and Ubiquitous Computing*, **23**(1), 67–79.

Fouad, Imane, Bielova, Nataliia, Legout, Arnaud, and Sarafijanovic-Djukic, Natasa. 2020. Missed by Filter Lists: Detecting Unknown Third-Party Trackers with Invisible Pixels. *Proceedings on Privacy Enhancing Technologies*, **2020**(2), 499–518.

Frik, Alisa, Haviland, Amelia, and Acquisti, Alessandro. 2020. The Impact of Ad-Blockers on Product Search and Purchase Behavior: A Lab Experiment. Pages 163–179 of: *29th USENIX Security Symposium*. USENIX Security 20. USENIX.

Fruchter, Nathaniel, Miao, Hsin, Stevenson, Scott, and Balebako, Rebecca. 2015. Variations in Tracking in Relation to Geographic Location. Page 8 of: *Proceedings of the 2015 Web 2.0 Workshop on Security and Privacy*. W2SP. San Jose, CA: IEEE.

Galán, A. Arrate, Cabañas, J. González, Cuevas, Á, Calderón, M., and Rumin, R. Cuevas. 2019. Large-Scale Analysis of User Exposure to Online Advertising on Facebook. *IEEE Access*, **7**, 11959–11971.

Galhotra, Sainyam, Brun, Yuriy, and Meliou, Alexandra. 2017. Fairness Testing: Testing Software for Discrimination. Pages 498–510 of: *Proceedings of the 2017 11th Joint Meeting on Foundations of Software Engineering*. ESEC/FSE 2017. Paderborn: ACM.

Galič, Maša. 2019. Surveillance, Privacy and Public Space in the Stratumseind Living Lab: The Smart City Debate, beyond Data. *Ars Aequi*, July, 570–579.

Gamba, Julien, Rashed, Mohammed, Razaghpanah, Abbas, Tapiador, Juan, and Vallina-Rodriguez, Narseo. 2020. An Analysis of Pre-Installed Android Software. Pages 197–213 of: *2020 IEEE Symposium on Security and Privacy*. SP. San Francisco, CA: IEEE.

Ge, Yanbo, Knittel, Christopher R, MacKenzie, Don, and Zoepf, Stephen. 2016 (Oct.). *Racial and Gender Discrimination in Transportation Network Companies*. Working Paper 22776. National Bureau of Economic Research.

Gervais, Arthur, Filios, Alexandros, Lenders, Vincent, and Capkun, Srdjan. 2017. Quantifying Web Adblocker Privacy. Pages 21–42 of: Foley, Simon N., Gollmann, Dieter, and Snekkenes, Einar (eds.), *Computer Security – ESORICS 2017*. Lecture Notes in Computer Science. Cham: Springer.

Gill, Phillipa, Erramilli, Vijay, Chaintreau, Augustin, Krishnamurthy, Balachander, Papagiannaki, Konstantina, and Rodriguez, Pablo. 2013. Follow the Money: Understanding Economics of Online Aggregation and Advertising. Pages 141–148 of: *Proceedings of the 2013 Conference on Internet Measurement Conference*. IMC '13. Barcelona: ACM.

Gjoka, Minas, Kurant, Maciej, Butts, Carter T., and Markopoulou, Athina. 2010 (March). Walking in Facebook: A Case Study of Unbiased Sampling of OSNs. Pages 1–9 of: *2010 Proceedings IEEE INFOCOM*.

Gómez-Boix, Alejandro, Laperdrix, Pierre, and Baudry, Benoit. 2018. Hiding in the Crowd: An Analysis of the Effectiveness of Browser Fingerprinting at Large Scale. Pages 309–318 of: *Proceedings of the 2018 World Wide Web Conference*. WWW '18. Lyon: International World Wide Web Conferences Steering Committee.

Gonzalez, Roberto, Soriente, Claudio, and Laoutaris, Nikolaos. 2016. User Profiling in the Time of HTTPS. Pages 373–379 of: *Proceedings of the 2016 Internet Measurement Conference*. IMC '16. Santa Monica, CA: ACM.

González Cabañas, José, Cuevas, Ángel, and Cuevas, Rubén. 2017. FDVT: Data Valuation Tool for Facebook Users. Pages 3799–3809 of: *Proceedings of the 2017 CHI Conference on Human Factors in Computing Systems*. CHI '17. Denver, CO: ACM.

Grace, Michael C., Zhou, Wu, Jiang, Xuxian, and Sadeghi, Ahmad-Reza. 2012. Unsafe Exposure Analysis of Mobile In-App Advertisements. Pages 101–112 of: *Proceedings of the Fifth ACM Conference on Security and Privacy in Wireless and Mobile Networks*. WISEC '12. Tucson, AZ: ACM.

Guha, Saikat, Cheng, Bin, and Francis, Paul. 2010. Challenges in Measuring Online Advertising Systems. Pages 81–87 of: *Proceedings of the 10th ACM SIGCOMM Conference on Internet Measurement*. IMC '10. Melbourne: ACM.

Gulyas, Gabor Gyorgy, Some, Doliere Francis, Bielova, Nataliia, and Castelluccia, Claude. 2018. To Extend or Not to Extend: On the Uniqueness of Browser Extensions and Web Logins. Pages 14–27 of: *Proceedings of the 2018 Workshop on Privacy in the Electronic Society*. WPES'18. Toronto: ACM.

Guo, Zhixiu, Lin, Zijin, Li, Pan, and Chen, Kai. 2020. SkillExplorer: Understanding the Behavior of Skills in Large Scale. Pages 2649–2666 of: *29th USENIX Security Symposium*. USENIX Security 20. USENIX.

Gutwirth, Serge, and Hildebrandt, Mireille. 2010. Some Caveats on Profiling. Pages 31–41 of: Gutwirth, Serge, Poullet, Yves, and De Hert, Paul (eds.), *Data Protection in a Profiled World*. Dordrecht: Springer Netherlands.

Habib, Hana, Zou, Yixin, Jannu, Aditi, Sridhar, Neha, Swoopes, Chelse, Acquisti, Alessandro, Cranor, Lorrie Faith, Sadeh, Norman, and Schaub, Florian. 2019 (Aug.). An Empirical Analysis of Data Deletion and Opt-Out Choices on 150 Websites. In: *Fifteenth Symposium on Usable Privacy and Security*. SOUPS 2019.

Han, Catherine, Reyes, Irwin, Feal, Álvaro, Reardon, Joel, Wijesekera, Primal, Elazari, Amit, Bamberger, Kenneth A, and Egelman, Serge. 2020. The Price Is (Not) Right:

Comparing Privacy in Free and Paid Apps. *Proceedings on Privacy Enhancing Technologies*, **2020**(3), 222–242.

Hannak, Aniko, Sapiezynski, Piotr, Molavi Kakhki, Arash, Krishnamurthy, Balachander, Lazer, David, Mislove, Alan, and Wilson, Christo. 2013. Measuring Personalization of Web Search. Pages 527–538 of: *Proceedings of the 22nd International Conference on World Wide Web*. WWW '13. Rio de Janeiro: ACM.

Hannak, Aniko, Soeller, Gary, Lazer, David, Mislove, Alan, and Wilson, Christo. 2014. Measuring Price Discrimination and Steering on E-Commerce Web Sites. Pages 305–318 of: *Proceedings of the 2014 Conference on Internet Measurement Conference*. IMC '14. Vancouver: ACM.

Hannák, Anikó, Wagner, Claudia, Garcia, David, Mislove, Alan, Strohmaier, Markus, and Wilson, Christo. 2017. Bias in Online Freelance Marketplaces: Evidence from TaskRabbit and Fiverr. Pages 1914–1933 of: *Proceedings of the 2017 ACM Conference on Computer Supported Cooperative Work and Social Computing*. CSCW '17. Portland, OR: ACM.

Hao, Shuai, Liu, Bin, Nath, Suman, Halfond, William G.J., and Govindan, Ramesh. 2014. PUMA: Programmable UI-Automation for Large-Scale Dynamic Analysis of Mobile Apps. Pages 204–217 of: *Proceedings of the 12th Annual International Conference on Mobile Systems, Applications, and Services*. MobiSys '14. Bretton Woods, NH: ACM.

Hara, Kotaro, Adams, Abigail, Milland, Kristy, Savage, Saiph, Callison-Burch, Chris, and Bigham, Jeffrey P. 2018. A Data-Driven Analysis of Workers' Earnings on Amazon Mechanical Turk. Pages 1–14 of: *Proceedings of the 2018 CHI Conference on Human Factors in Computing Systems*. Montreal: ACM.

Hargreaves, E., Agosti, C., Menasché, D., Neglia, G., Reiffers-Masson, A., and Altman, E. 2018 (Aug.). Biases in the Facebook News Feed: A Case Study on the Italian Elections. Pages 806–812 of: *2018 IEEE/ACM International Conference on Advances in Social Networks Analysis and Mining*. ASONAM.

Hargreaves, Eduardo, Agosti, Claudio, Menasché, Daniel, Neglia, Giovanni, Reiffers-Masson, Alexandre, and Altman, Eitan. 2019. Fairness in Online Social Network Timelines: Measurements, Models and Mechanism Design. *Performance Evaluation*, **129**(Feb.), 15–39.

Harkous, Hamza, Fawaz, Kassem, Lebret, Rémi, Schaub, Florian, Shin, Kang G., and Aberer, Karl. 2018. Polisis: Automated Analysis and Presentation of Privacy Policies Using Deep Learning. Pages 531–548 of: *27th USENIX Security Symposium*. USENIX Security 18. Baltimore, MD: USENIX.

He, Yongzhong, Yang, Xuejun, Hu, Binghui, and Wang, Wei. 2019. Dynamic Privacy Leakage Analysis of Android Third-Party Libraries. *Journal of Information Security and Applications*, **46**(June), 259–270.

Henze, Martin, Pennekamp, Jan, Hellmanns, David, Mühmer, Erik, Ziegeldorf, Jan Henrik, Drichel, Arthur, and Wehrle, Klaus. 2017. CloudAnalyzer: Uncovering the Cloud Usage of Mobile Apps. Pages 262–271 of: *Proceedings of the 14th EAI International Conference on Mobile and Ubiquitous Systems: Computing, Networking and Services*. MobiQuitous 2017. Melbourne: ACM.

Hils, Maximilian, Woods, Daniel W., and Böhme, Rainer. 2020. Measuring the Emergence of Consent Management on the Web. Pages 317–332 of: *Proceedings of the ACM Internet Measurement Conference*. IMC '20. Pittsburgh, PA: ACM.

Howe, Daniel C. 2015. Surveillance Countermeasures: Expressive Privacy via Obfuscation. *Datafied Research*, **4**(1), 88–98.

Howe, Daniel C, and Nissenbaum, Helen. 2017. Engineering Privacy and Protest: A Case Study of AdNauseam. Pages 57–64 of: *Proceedings of the 3rd International Workshop on Privacy Engineering*, vol. 1873. San Jose, CA: IEEE.

Hu, Desheng, Jiang, Shan, E. Robertson, Ronald, and Wilson, Christo. 2019a. Auditing the Partisanship of Google Search Snippets. Pages 693–704 of: *The World Wide Web Conference*. WWW '19. San Francisco, CA: ACM.

Hu, H., Peng, P., and Wang, G. 2019b (May). Characterizing Pixel Tracking through the Lens of Disposable Email Services. Pages 545–559 of: *2019 IEEE Symposium on Security and Privacy*. SP. San Francisco, CA: IEEE.

Hu, Xuehui Hu, de Tangil, Guillermo Suarez, and Sastry, Nishanth. 2020a. Multi-Country Study of Third Party Trackers from Real Browser Histories. Pages 70–86 of: *IEEE European Symposium on Security and Privacy*. Euro S&P. IEEE.

Hu, Yangyu, Wang, Haoyu, He, Ren, Li, Li, Tyson, Gareth, Castro, Ignacio, Guo, Yao, Wu, Lei, and Xu, Guoai. 2020b. Mobile App Squatting. Pages 1727–1738 of: *Proceedings of The Web Conference 2020*. WWW '20. Taipei: ACM.

Humbert, Mathias, Trubert, Benjamin, and Huguenin, Kévin. 2019. A Survey on Interdependent Privacy. *ACM Comput. Surv.*, **52**(6), 122:1–122:40.

Hunold, Matthias, Kesler, Reinhold, and Laitenberger, Ulrich. 2018. *Hotel Rankings of Online Travel Agents, Channel Pricing and Consumer Protection*. Working Paper 300. Düsseldorf Institute for Competition Economics (DICE) Discussion Paper.

Hupperich, Thomas, Tatang, Dennis, Wilkop, Nicolai, and Holz, Thorsten. 2018. An Empirical Study on Online Price Differentiation. Pages 76–83 of: *Proceedings of the Eighth ACM Conference on Data and Application Security and Privacy*. CODASPY '18. Tempe, AZ: ACM.

IAB Tech Lab. 2019 (March). *Ads.Txt Specification*. Tech. rept. 1.0.2.

IAB Technology Laboratory. 2018 (Nov.). *OpenRTB Specification v3.0*. https://github .com/InteractiveAdvertisingBureau/openrtb/blob/master/OpenRTB%20v3.0%20 FINAL.md.

Ikram, Muhammad, Onwuzurike, Lucky, Farooqi, Shehroze, Cristofaro, Emiliano De, Friedman, Arik, Jourjon, Guillaume, Kaafar, Mohammed Ali, and Shafiq, M. Zubair. 2017a. Measuring, Characterizing, and Detecting Facebook Like Farms. *ACM Trans. Priv. Secur.*, **20**(4), 13:1–13:28.

Ikram, Muhammad, Asghar, Hassan Jameel, Kaafar, Mohamed Ali, Mahanti, Anirban, and Krishnamurthy, Balachandar. 2017b. Towards Seamless Tracking-Free Web: Improved Detection of Trackers via One-Class Learning. *Proceedings on Privacy Enhancing Technologies*, **2017**(1), 79–99.

International Association of Privacy Professionals. 2016. *GDPR Complaint-Process Map*. https://iapp.org/resources/gdpr-tool/.

Invernizzi, L., Thomas, K., Kapravelos, A., Comanescu, O., Picod, J., and Bursztein, E. 2016 (May). Cloak of Visibility: Detecting When Machines Browse a Different Web. Pages 743–758 of: *2016 IEEE Symposium on Security and Privacy*. SP. San Jose, CA: IEEE.

Iordanou, Costas, Soriente, Claudio, Sirivianos, Michael, and Laoutaris, Nikolaos. 2017. Who Is Fiddling with Prices?: Building and Deploying a Watchdog Service for E-Commerce. Pages 376–389 of: *Proceedings of the Conference of the ACM*

Special Interest Group on Data Communication. SIGCOMM '17. Los Angeles, CA: ACM.

Iordanou, Costas, Smaragdakis, Georgios, Poese, Ingmar, and Laoutaris, Nikolaos. 2018. Tracing Cross Border Web Tracking. Pages 329–342 of: *Proceedings of the Internet Measurement Conference 2018.* IMC '18. Boston, MA: ACM.

Iqbal, Umar, Shafiq, Zubair, and Qian, Zhiyun. 2017. The Ad Wars: Retrospective Measurement and Analysis of Anti-Adblock Filter Lists. Pages 171–183 of: *Proceedings of the 2017 Internet Measurement Conference.* IMC '17. London: ACM.

Iqbal, Umar, Snyder, Peter, Zhu, Shitong, Livshits, Benjamin, Qian, Zhiyun, and Shafiq, Zubair. 2020. ADGRAPH: A Graph-Based Approach to Ad and Tracker Blocking. Pages 65–78 of: *IEEE Symposium on Security and Privacy.* SP. San Francisco, CA: IEEE.

Jiang, Shan, Chen, Le, Mislove, Alan, and Wilson, Christo. 2018. On Ridesharing Competition and Accessibility: Evidence from Uber, Lyft, and Taxi. Pages 863–872 of: *Proceedings of the 2018 World Wide Web Conference.* WWW '18. Lyon: International World Wide Web Conferences Steering Committee.

Jiang, Shan, Robertson, Ronald E., and Wilson, Christo. 2019. Bias Misperceived:The Role of Partisanship and Misinformation in YouTube Comment Moderation. *Proceedings of the International AAAI Conference on Web and Social Media,* **13**(July), 278–289.

Jin, Haojian, Liu, Minyi, Dodhia, Kevan, Li, Yuanchun, Srivastava, Gaurav, Fredrikson, Matthew, Agarwal, Yuvraj, and Hong, Jason I. 2018. Why Are They Collecting My Data?: Inferring the Purposes of Network Traffic in Mobile Apps. *Proc. ACM Interact. Mob. Wearable Ubiquitous Technol.,* **2**(4), 173:1–173:27.

Johnson, I., Henderson, J., Perry, C., Schöning, J., and Hecht, B. 2017. Beautiful... but at What Cost?: An Examination of Externalities in Geographic Vehicle Routing. *Proc. ACM Interact. Mob. Wearable Ubiquitous Technol.,* **1**(2), 15:1–15:21.

Jones, Jason J., Bond, Robert M., Bakshy, Eytan, Eckles, Dean, and Fowler, James H. 2017. Social Influence and Political Mobilization: Further Evidence from a Randomized Experiment in the 2012 U.S. Presidential Election. *PLOS ONE,* **12**(4), e0173851.

Kamkar, Samy. 2010 (Oct.). *Evercookie: - Virtually Irrevocable Persistent Cookies.* https://samy.pl/evercookie/.

Karami, Soroush, Ilia, Panagiotis, Solomos, Konstantinos, and Polakis, Jason. 2020. Carnus: Exploring the Privacy Threats of Browser Extension Fingerprinting. In: *Proceedings 2020 Network and Distributed System Security Symposium.* San Diego, CA: Internet Society.

Karegar, Farzaneh, Pettersson, John Sören, and Fischer-Hübner, Simone. 2020. The Dilemma of User Engagement in Privacy Notices: Effects of Interaction Modes and Habituation on User Attention. *ACM Transactions on Privacy and Security (TOPS),* **23**(1), 5:1–5:38.

Kawase, Ricardo, Papadakis, George, Herder, Eelco, and Nejdl, Wolfgang. 2011. Beyond the Usual Suspects: Context-Aware Revisitation Support. Pages 27–36 of: *Proceedings of the 22Nd ACM Conference on Hypertext and Hypermedia.* HT '11. Eindhoven: ACM.

Kenneally, Erin, and Dittrich, David. 2012 (Aug.). *The Menlo Report: Ethical Principles Guiding Information and Communication Technology Research.* Tech. rept. US Department of Homeland Security.

Khattak, Sheharbano, Fifield, David, Afroz, Sadia, Javed, Mobin, Sundaresan, Srikanth, Paxson, Vern, Murdoch, Steven J., and McCoy, Damon. 2016. Do You See What I See? Differential Treatment of Anonymous Users. In: *Proceedings 2016 Network and Distributed System Security Symposium.* San Diego, CA: Internet Society.

Klein, Amit, and Pinkas, Benny. 2019. DNS Cache-Based User Tracking. In: *Proceedings 2019 Network and Distributed System Security Symposium.* San Diego, CA: Internet Society.

Kliman-Silver, Chloe, Hannak, Aniko, Lazer, David, Wilson, Christo, and Mislove, Alan. 2015. Location, Location, Location: The Impact of Geolocation on Web Search Personalization. Pages 121–127 of: *Proceedings of the 2015 Internet Measurement Conference.* IMC '15. Tokyo: ACM.

Kohno, T., Broido, A., and Claffy, K. C. 2005. Remote Physical Device Fingerprinting. *IEEE Transactions on Dependable and Secure Computing,* 2(2), 93–108.

Kondracki, Brian, Aliyeva, Assel, Egele, Manuel, Polakis, Jason, and Nikiforakis, Nick. 2020. Meddling Middlemen: Empirical Analysis of the Risks of Data-Saving Mobile Browsers. Pages 1678–1692 of: *2020 IEEE Symposium on Security and Privacy.* SP. San Francisco, CA: IEEE.

Koop, Martin, Tews, Erik, and Katzenbeisser, Stefan. 2020. In-Depth Evaluation of Redirect Tracking and Link Usage. *Proceedings on Privacy Enhancing Technologies,* 2020(4), 394–413.

Kooti, Farshad, Grbovic, Mihajlo, Aiello, Luca Maria, Djuric, Nemanja, Radosavljevic, Vladan, and Lerman, Kristina. 2017. Analyzing Uber's Ride-Sharing Economy. Pages 574–582 of: *Proceedings of the 26th International Conference on World Wide Web Companion.* WWW '17 Companion. Perth: International World Wide Web Conferences Steering Committee.

Korolova, A. 2010 (Dec.). Privacy Violations Using Microtargeted Ads: A Case Study. Pages 474–482 of: *2010 IEEE International Conference on Data Mining Workshops.* Sydney: IEEE.

Kosinski, Michal, Stillwell, David, and Graepel, Thore. 2013. Private Traits and Attributes Are Predictable from Digital Records of Human Behavior. *Proceedings of the National Academy of Sciences,* 110(15), 5802–5805.

Kramer, Adam D. I., Guillory, Jamie E., and Hancock, Jeffrey T. 2014. Experimental Evidence of Massive-Scale Emotional Contagion through Social Networks. *Proceedings of the National Academy of Sciences,* 111(24), 8788–8790.

Kranch, Michael, and Bonneau, Joseph. 2015. Upgrading HTTPS in Mid-Air: An Empirical Study of Strict Transport Security and Key Pinning. In: *Proceedings 2015 Network and Distributed System Security Symposium.* San Diego, CA: Internet Society.

Krishnamurthy, Balachander, and Wills, Craig. 2009. Privacy Diffusion on the Web: A Longitudinal Perspective. Page 541 of: *Proceedings of the 18th International Conference on World Wide Web.* WWW '09. Madrid: ACM Press.

Krishnamurthy, Balachander, and Wills, Craig E. 2006. Generating a Privacy Footprint on the Internet. Pages 65–70 of: *Proceedings of the 6th ACM SIGCOMM Conference on Internet Measurement.* IMC '06. Rio de Janeiro: ACM.

Krishnamurthy, Balachander, Naryshkin, Konstantin, and Wills, Craig E. 2011. Privacy Leakage vs. Protection Measures: The Growing Disconnect. Page 10 of: *Web 2.0 Security and Privacy*. W2SP. Oakland, CA: IEEE.

Kristof, Victor, Grossglauser, Matthias, and Thiran, Patrick. 2020. War of Words: The Competitive Dynamics of Legislative Processes. Pages 2803–2809 of: *Proceedings of The Web Conference 2020*. WWW '20. Taipei: ACM.

Kulshrestha, J., Zafar, M.B., Noboa, L.E., Gummadi, K.P., and Ghosh, S. 2015. Characterizing Information Diets of Social Media Users. Pages 218–227 of: *Proceedings of the 9th International Conference on Web and Social Media*. ICWSM 2015. Oxford: AAAI Press.

Kulshrestha, Juhi, Eslami, Motahhare, Messias, Johnnatan, Zafar, Muhammad Bilal, Ghosh, Saptarshi, Gummadi, Krishna P., and Karahalios, Karrie. 2017. Quantifying Search Bias: Investigating Sources of Bias for Political Searches in Social Media. Pages 417–432 of: *Proceedings of the 2017 ACM Conference on Computer Supported Cooperative Work and Social Computing*. CSCW '17. Portland, OR: ACM.

Kumar, Vinayshekhar Bannihatti, Iyengar, Roger, Nisal, Namita, Feng, Yuanyuan, Habib, Hana, Story, Peter, Cherivirala, Sushain, Hagan, Margaret, Cranor, Lorrie, Wilson, Shomir, Schaub, Florian, and Sadeh, Norman. 2020. Finding a Choice in a Haystack: Automatic Extraction of Opt-Out Statements from Privacy Policy Text. Pages 1943–1954 of: *Proceedings of The Web Conference 2020*. WWW '20. Taipei: ACM.

Kurose, James, and Ross, Keith. 2016. *Computer Networking: A Top-Down Approach*. 7 edition. Boston, MA: Pearson.

Lambrecht, Anja, and Tucker, Catherine. 2019. Algorithmic Bias? An Empirical Study of Apparent Gender-Based Discrimination in the Display of STEM Career Ads. *Management Science*, **65**(7), 2966–2981.

Laperdrix, P., Rudametkin, W., and Baudry, B. 2016 (May). Beauty and the Beast: Diverting Modern Web Browsers to Build Unique Browser Fingerprints. Pages 878–894 of: *2016 IEEE Symposium on Security and Privacy*. SP. San Jose, CA: IEEE.

Le, Huyen, Maragh, Raven, Ekdale, Brian, High, Andrew, Havens, Timothy, and Shafiq, Zubair. 2019. Measuring Political Personalization of Google News Search. Pages 2957–2963 of: *The World Wide Web Conference*. WWW '19. San Francisco, CA: ACM.

Lécuyer, Mathias, Ducoffe, Guillaume, Lan, Francis, Papancea, Andrei, Petsios, Theofilos, Spahn, Riley, Chaintreau, Augustin, and Geambasu, Roxana. 2014. XRay: Enhancing the Web's Transparency with Differential Correlation. Pages 49–64 of: *23rd USENIX Security Symposium*. USENIX Security 14. San Diego, CA: USENIX.

Lecuyer, Mathias, Spahn, Riley, Spiliopolous, Yannis, Chaintreau, Augustin, Geambasu, Roxana, and Hsu, Daniel. 2015. Sunlight: Fine-Grained Targeting Detection at Scale with Statistical Confidence. Pages 554–566 of: *Proceedings of the 22nd ACM SIGSAC Conference on Computer and Communications Security*. CCS '15. Denver, CO: ACM.

Lerner, Ada, Simpson, Anna Kornfeld, Kohno, Tadayoshi, and Roesner, Franziska. 2016. Internet Jones and the Raiders of the Lost Trackers: An Archaeological

Study of Web Tracking from 1996 to 2016. In: *25th USENIX Security Symposium*. USENIX Security 16. Austin, TX: USENIX.

Leung, Christophe, Ren, Jingjing, Choffnes, David, and Wilson, Christo. 2016. Should You Use the App for That?: Comparing the Privacy Implications of App- and Web-Based Online Services. Pages 365–372 of: *Proceedings of the 2016 Internet Measurement Conference*. IMC '16. Santa Monica, CA: ACM.

Li, Ang, Wang, Alice, Nazari, Zahra, Chandar, Praveen, and Carterette, Benjamin. 2020. Do Podcasts and Music Compete with One Another? Understanding Users' Audio Streaming Habits. Pages 1920–1931 of: *Proceedings of The Web Conference 2020*. WWW '20. Taipei: ACM.

Li, M., Wang, W., Wang, P., Wang, S., Wu, D., Liu, J., Xue, R., and Huo, W. 2017a (May). LibD: Scalable and Precise Third-Party Library Detection in Android Markets. Pages 335–346 of: *2017 IEEE/ACM 39th International Conference on Software Engineering*. ICSE.

Li, Menghao, Wang, Pei, Wang, Wei, Wang, Shuai, Wu, Dinghao, Liu, Jian, Xue, Rui, Huo, Wei, and Zou, Wei. 2018. Large-Scale Third-Party Library Detection in Android Markets. *IEEE Transactions on Software Engineering*, 1–1.

Li, Song, and Cao, Yinzhi. 2020. Who Touched My Browser Fingerprint? A Large-Scale Measurement Study and Classification of Fingerprint Dynamics. Pages 370–385 of: *Proceedings of the ACM Internet Measurement Conference*. IMC '20. Pittsburgh, PA: ACM.

Li, Tai-Ching, Hang, Huy, Faloutsos, Michalis, and Efstathopoulos, Petros. 2015. TrackAdvisor: Taking Back Browsing Privacy from Third-Party Trackers. Pages 277–289 of: Mirkovic, Jelena, and Liu, Yong (eds.), *Passive and Active Measurement*. Lecture Notes in Computer Science. Cham: Springer.

Li, Yuanchun, Yang, Ziyue, Guo, Yao, and Chen, Xiangqun. 2017b. DroidBot: A Lightweight UI-Guided Test Input Generator for Android. Pages 23–26 of: *2017 IEEE/ACM 39th International Conference on Software Engineering Companion*. ICSE-C. Buenos Aires: IEEE.

Libert, T., Graves, L., and Nielsen, R. K. 2018. *Changes in Third-Party Content on European News Websites after GDPR*. Tech. rept. pubs:909043. Reuters Institute for the Study of Journalism.

Libert, Timothy. 2015. Exposing the Invisible Web: An Analysis of Third-Party HTTP Requests on 1 Million Websites. *International Journal of Communication*, **9**(0), 18.

Libert, Timothy. 2018. An Automated Approach to Auditing Disclosure of Third-Party Data Collection in Website Privacy Policies. Pages 207–216 of: *Proceedings of the 2018 World Wide Web Conference*. WWW '18. Lyon: International World Wide Web Conferences Steering Committee.

Library of Congress. 2020 (Sept.). *Recommended Formats Statement – Datasets – Resources (Preservation, Library of Congress)*. www.loc.gov/preservation/resources/rfs/data.html.

Linden, Thomas, Khandelwal, Rishabh, Harkous, Hamza, and Fawaz, Kassem. 2020. The Privacy Policy Landscape After the GDPR. *Proceedings on Privacy Enhancing Technologies*, **2020**(1), 47–64.

Liu, Bin, Sheth, Anmol, Weinsberg, Udi, Chandrashekar, Jaideep, and Govindan, Ramesh. 2013. AdReveal: Improving Transparency into Online Targeted

Advertising. Pages 12:1–12:7 of: *Proceedings of the Twelfth ACM Workshop on Hot Topics in Networks*. HotNets-XII. College Park, MD: ACM.

Liu, Tianming, Wang, Haoyu, Li, Li, Luo, Xiapu, Dong, Feng, Guo, Yao, Wang, Liu, Bissyandé, Tegawendé, and Klein, Jacques. 2020. MadDroid: Characterizing and Detecting Devious Ad Contents for Android Apps. Pages 1715–1726 of: *Proceedings of The Web Conference 2020*. WWW '20. Taipei: ACM.

Liu, X., Liu, J., Zhu, S., Wang, W., and Zhang, X. 2019. Privacy Risk Analysis and Mitigation of Analytics Libraries in the Android Ecosystem. *IEEE Transactions on Mobile Computing*, 1–1.

Liu, Xing, Zhu, Sencun, Wang, Wei, and Liu, Jiqiang. 2017. Alde: Privacy Risk Analysis of Analytics Libraries in the Android Ecosystem. Pages 655–672 of: Deng, Robert, Weng, Jian, Ren, Kui, and Yegneswaran, Vinod (eds.), *Security and Privacy in Communication Networks*. Lecture Notes of the Institute for Computer Sciences, Social Informatics and Telecommunications Engineering. Cham: Springer.

Liu, Yabing, Gummadi, Krishna P., Krishnamurthy, Balachander, and Mislove, Alan. 2011. Analyzing Facebook Privacy Settings: User Expectations vs. Reality. Pages 61–70 of: *Proceedings of the 2011 ACM SIGCOMM Conference on Internet Measurement Conference*. IMC '11. Berlin: ACM.

Lurie, Emma, and Mustafaraj, Eni. 2019. Opening Up the Black Box: Auditing Google's Top Stories Algorithm. *Proceedings of the 32nd International Florida Artificial Intelligence Research Society Conference*, **32**(May), 376–382. Sarasota, FL: AAAI Press.

Lyon, David. 2003. *Surveillance as Social Sorting: Privacy, Risk, and Digital Discrimination*. Psychology Press.

Ma, Ziang, Wang, Haoyu, Guo, Yao, and Chen, Xiangqun. 2016. LibRadar: Fast and Accurate Detection of Third-Party Libraries in Android Apps. Pages 653–656 of: *Proceedings of the 38th International Conference on Software Engineering Companion*. ICSE '16. Austin, TX: ACM.

Malloy, Matthew, McNamara, Mark, Cahn, Aaron, and Barford, Paul. 2016. Ad Blockers: Global Prevalence and Impact. Pages 119–125 of: *Proceedings of the 2016 Internet Measurement Conference*. IMC '16. Santa Monica, CA: ACM.

Marciel, M., Gonzalez, J., Kassa, Y. M., Gonzalez, R., and Ahmed, M. 2016 (Aug.). The Value of Online Users: Empirical Evaluation of the Price of Personalized Ads. Pages 694–700 of: *2016 11th International Conference on Availability, Reliability and Security*. ARES. Salzburg: IEEE.

Mashhadi, Afra, and Chapman, Clovis. 2018. Who Gets the Lion's Share in the Sharing Economy: A Case Study of Social Inequality in AirBnB. Pages 370–385 of: Staab, Steffen, Koltsova, Olessia, and Ignatov, Dmitry I. (eds.), *Social Informatics*. Lecture Notes in Computer Science. Cham: Springer.

Mathur, Arunesh, Acar, Gunes, Friedman, Michael J., Lucherini, Elena, Mayer, Jonathan, Chetty, Marshini, and Narayanan, Arvind. 2019. Dark Patterns at Scale: Findings from a Crawl of 11K Shopping Websites. *Proceedings of the ACM on Human-Computer Interaction*, 3(CSCW), 81:1–81:32.

Matic, Srdjan, Iordanou, Costas, Smaragdakis, Georgios, and Laoutaris, Nikolaos. 2020. Identifying Sensitive URLs at Web-Scale. Pages 619–633 of: *Proceedings of the ACM Internet Measurement Conference*. IMC '20. Pittsburgh, PA: ACM.

Matte, Celestin, Bielova, Nataliia, and Santos, Cristiana. 2020. Do Cookie Banners Respect My Choice? Pages 1612–1630 of: *2020 IEEE Symposium on Security and Privacy*. SP. San Francisco, CA: IEEE.

May, Anna, Wachs, Johannes, and Hannák, Anikó. 2019. Gender Differences in Participation and Reward on Stack Overflow. *Empirical Software Engineering*, **24**(4), 1997–2019.

Mayer, J.R., and Mitchell, J.C. 2012 (May). Third-Party Web Tracking: Policy and Technology. Pages 413–427 of: *2012 IEEE Symposium on Security and Privacy*. SP. San Francisco, CA: IEEE.

Mazel, Johan, Garnier, Richard, and Fukuda, Kensuke. 2019. A Comparison of Web Privacy Protection Techniques. *Computer Communications*, **144**(Aug.), 162–174.

Mazmudar, Miti, and Goldberg, Ian. 2020. Mitigator: Privacy Policy Compliance Using Trusted Hardware. *Proceedings on Privacy Enhancing Technologies*, **2020**(3), 204–221.

McDonald, Allison, Bernhard, Matthew, Valenta, Luke, VanderSloot, Benjamin, Scott, Will, Sullivan, Nick, Halderman, J. Alex, and Ensafi, Roya. 2018. 403 Forbidden: A Global View of CDN Geoblocking. Pages 218–230 of: *Proceedings of the Internet Measurement Conference 2018*. IMC '18. Boston, MA: ACM.

McGrath, Sean, and Theodorou, Andreas. 2020 (Sept.). *Exposing the Hidden Data Ecosystem Behind UK Charities*. https://proprivacy.com/privacy-news/exposing-the-hidden-data-ecosystem-of-the-uks-most-trusted-charities.

Mehrotra, Rishabh, Anderson, Ashton, Diaz, Fernando, Sharma, Amit, Wallach, Hanna, and Yilmaz, Emine. 2017. Auditing Search Engines for Differential Satisfaction Across Demographics. Pages 626–633 of: *Proceedings of the 26th International Conference on World Wide Web Companion*. WWW '17 Companion. Perth: International World Wide Web Conferences Steering Committee.

Melicher, William, Sharif, Mahmood, Tan, Joshua, Bauer, Lujo, Christodorescu, Mihai, and Leon, Pedro Giovanni. 2016. (Do Not) Track Me Sometimes: Users' Contextual Preferences for Web Tracking. *Proceedings on Privacy Enhancing Technologies*, **2016**(2), 135–154.

Merrill, Jeremy B., and Tobin, Ariana. 2019. Facebook Moves to Block Ad Transparency Tools —. . . . *ProPublica*, Jan.

Merzdovnik, G., Huber, M., Buhov, D., Nikiforakis, N., Neuner, S., Schmiedecker, M., and Weippl, E. 2017 (April). Block Me If You Can: A Large-Scale Study of Tracker-Blocking Tools. Pages 319–333 of: *2017 IEEE European Symposium on Security and Privacy*. EuroS P. Paris: IEEE.

Metwalley, Hassan, Traverso, Stefano, Mellia, Marco, Miskovic, Stanislav, and Baldi, Mario. 2015. The Online Tracking Horde: A View from Passive Measurements. Pages 111–125 of: Steiner, Moritz, Barlet-Ros, Pere, and Bonaventure, Olivier (eds.), *Traffic Monitoring and Analysis*. Lecture Notes in Computer Science. Cham: Springer.

Mhaidli, Abraham H., Zou, Yixin, and Schaub, Florian. 2019 (Aug.). "We Can't Live Without Them!" App Developers' Adoption of Ad Networks and Their Considerations of Consumer Risks. In: *Fifteenth Symposium on Usable Privacy and Security*. SOUPS 2019. Santa Clara, CA: USENIX.

Mikians, Jakub, Gyarmati, László, Erramilli, Vijay, and Laoutaris, Nikolaos. 2012. Detecting Price and Search Discrimination on the Internet. Pages 79–84 of: *Proceedings of the 11th ACM Workshop on Hot Topics in Networks.* HotNets-XI. Redmond, WA: ACM.

Mikians, Jakub, Gyarmati, László, Erramilli, Vijay, and Laoutaris, Nikolaos. 2013. Crowd-Assisted Search for Price Discrimination in e-Commerce: First Results. Pages 1–6 of: *Proceedings of the Ninth ACM Conference on Emerging Networking Experiments and Technologies.* CoNEXT '13. Santa Barbara, CA: ACM.

Miroglio, Ben, Zeber, David, Kaye, Jofish, and Weiss, Rebecca. 2018. The Effect of Ad Blocking on User Engagement with the Web. Pages 813–821 of: *Proceedings of the 2018 World Wide Web Conference.* WWW '18. Lyon: International World Wide Web Conferences Steering Committee.

Mishra, Vikas, Laperdrix, Pierre, Vastel, Antoine, Rudametkin, Walter, Rouvoy, Romain, and Lopatka, Martin. 2020. Don't Count Me Out: On the Relevance of IP Address in the Tracking Ecosystem. Pages 808–815 of: *Proceedings of The Web Conference 2020.* WWW '20. Taipei: ACM.

Moghaddam, Hooman Mohajeri, Acar, Gunes, Burgess, Ben, Mathur, Arunesh, Huang, Danny Yuxing, Feamster, Nick, Felten, Edward W, Mittal, Prateek, and Narayanan, Arvind. 2019. Watching You Watch: The Tracking Ecosystem of Over-the-Top TV Streaming Devices. Pages 131–147 of: *Proceedings of the 2019 ACM SIGSAC Conference on Computer and Communications Security.* London: ACM.

Montgomery, Douglas C. 2019. *Design and Analysis of Experiments.* 9 edition. Hoboken, NJ: John Wiley & Sons.

Mowery, Keaton, and Shacham, Hovav. 2012. Pixel Perfect: Fingerprinting Canvas in HTML5. Page 12 of: *Web 2.0 Workshop on Security and Privacy.* W2SP. San Francisco, CA: IEEE.

Mowery, Keaton, Bogenreif, Dillon, Yilek, Scott, and Shacham, Hovav. 2011. Fingerprinting Information in JavaScript Implementations. Page 11 of: *Web 2.0 Workshop on Security and Privacy.* W2SP. Oakland, CA: IEEE.

Mughees, Muhammad Haris, Qian, Zhiyun, and Shafiq, Zubair. 2017. Detecting Anti Ad-Blockers in the Wild. *Proceedings on Privacy Enhancing Technologies,* **2017**(3), 130–146.

Mulazzani, Martin, Reschl, Philipp, Huber, Markus, Leithner, Manuel, Schrittwieser, Sebastian, and Weippl, Edgar. 2013. Fast and Reliable Browser Identification with JavaScript Engine Fingerprinting. Page 10 of: *Web 2.0 Workshop on Security and Privacy.* W2SP. San Francisco, CA: IEEE.

Munson, Sean A., Lee, Stephanie Y., and Resnick, Paul. 2013 (June). Encouraging Reading of Diverse Political Viewpoints with a Browser Widget. In: *Seventh International AAAI Conference on Weblogs and Social Media.* Cambridge, MA: AAAI Press.

Murphy, Kevin P. 2012. *Machine Learning: A Probabilistic Perspective.* Illustrated edition. Cambridge, MA: The MIT Press.

Narayanan, Arvind, and Reisman, Dillon. 2017. The Princeton Web Transparency and Accountability Project. Pages 45–67 of: Cerquitelli, Tania, Quercia, Daniele, and Pasquale, Frank (eds.), *Transparent Data Mining for Big and Small Data,* vol. 32. Cham: Springer International Publishing.

Narayanan, Arvind, and Shmatikov, Vitaly. 2008. Robust De-Anonymization of Large Sparse Datasets. Pages 111–125 of: *IEEE Symposium on Security and Privacy, 2008.* Oakland, CA: IEEE.

Natatsuka, Atsuko, Iijima, Ryo, Watanabe, Takuya, Akiyama, Mitsuaki, Sakai, Tetsuya, and Mori, Tatsuya. 2019. Poster: A First Look at the Privacy Risks of Voice Assistant Apps. Pages 2633–2635 of: *Proceedings of the 2019 ACM SIGSAC Conference on Computer and Communications Security*. CCS '19. London: ACM.

Nath, Suman. 2015. MAdScope: Characterizing Mobile In-App Targeted Ads. Pages 59–73 of: *Proceedings of the 13th Annual International Conference on Mobile Systems, Applications, and Services*. MobiSys '15. Florence: ACM.

Nguyen, Duc Cuong, Derr, Erik, Backes, Michael, and Bugiel, Sven. 2019. Short Text, Large Effect: Measuring the Impact of User Reviews on Android App Security & Privacy. Page 15 of: *IEEE Symposium on Security and Privacy*. SP. San Francisco, CA: IEEE.

Niaki, Arian Akhavan, Cho, Shinyoung, Weinberg, Zachary, Hoang, Nguyen Phong, Razaghpanah, Abbas, Christin, Nicolas, and Gill, Phillipa. 2020. ICLab: A Global, Longitudinal Internet Censorship Measurement Platform. Pages 214–230 of: *2020 IEEE Symposium on Security and Privacy*. SP. San Francisco, CA: IEEE.

Nikiforakis, N., Kapravelos, A, Joosen, W., Kruegel, C., Piessens, F., and Vigna, G. 2013 (May). Cookieless Monster: Exploring the Ecosystem of Web-Based Device Fingerprinting. Pages 541–555 of: *IEEE Symposium on Security and Privacy*. SP. San Francisco, CA: IEEE.

Nikiforakis, Nick, Acker, Steven Van, Piessens, Frank, and Joosen, Wouter. 2012. Exploring the Ecosystem of Referrer-Anonymizing Services. Pages 259–278 of: Fischer-Hübner, Simone, and Wright, Matthew (eds.), *Privacy Enhancing Technologies*. Lecture Notes in Computer Science, no. 7384. Berlin, Heidelberg: Springer.

Nikiforakis, Nick, Joosen, Wouter, and Livshits, Benjamin. 2015. PriVaricator: Deceiving Fingerprinters with Little White Lies. Pages 820–830 of: *24th International Conference on World Wide Web (WWW)*. WWW '15. Florence: ACM.

Nissenbaum, Helen. 2004. Privacy as Contextual Integrity. *Wash. L. Rev.*, **79**, 119.

Nithyanand, Rishab, Khattak, Sheharbano, Javed, Mobin, Vallina-Rodriguez, Narseo, Falahrastegar, Marjan, Powles, Julia E., Cristofaro, Emiliano De, Haddadi, Hamed, and Murdoch, Steven J. 2016 (Aug.). Adblocking and Counter Blocking: A Slice of the Arms Race. In: *6th USENIX Workshop on Free and Open Communications on the Internet*. FOCI 16. Austin, TX: USENIX.

Ohm, Paul. 2009 (Aug.). *Broken Promises of Privacy: Responding to the Surprising Failure of Anonymization*. SSRN Scholarly Paper ID 1450006. Social Science Research Network, Rochester, NY.

Olejnik, Łukasz 2020 (Sept.). Shedding Light on Web Privacy Impact Assessment: A Case Study of the Ambient Light Sensor API. Pages 310–313 of: *2020 IEEE European Symposium on Security and Privacy Workshops*. EuroS PW. IEEE.

Olejnik, Łukasz, Tran, Minh-Dung, and Castelluccia, Claude. 2014. Selling off Privacy at Auction. In: *Proceedings 2014 Network and Distributed System Security Symposium*. San Diego, CA: Internet Society.

Olejnik, Łukasz, Acar, Gunes, Castelluccia, Claude, and Diaz, Claudia. 2016. The Leaking Battery. Pages 254–263 of: Garcia-Alfaro, Joaquin, Navarro-Arribas, Guillermo, Aldini, Alessandro, Martinelli, Fabio, and Suri, Neeraj (eds.), *Data Privacy Management, and Security Assurance*. Lecture Notes in Computer Science. Cham: Springer.

Oltramari, Alessandro, Piraviperumal, Dhivya, Schaub, Florian, Wilson, Shomir, Cherivirala, Sushain, Norton, Thomas B., Russell, N. Cameron, Story, Peter, Reidenberg, Joel, and Sadeh, Norman. 2018. PrivOnto: A Semantic Framework for the Analysis of Privacy Policies. *Semantic Web*, **9**(2), 185–203.

Overdorf, Rebekah, Juarez, Mark, Acar, Gunes, Greenstadt, Rachel, and Diaz, Claudia. 2017. How Unique Is Your .Onion?: An Analysis of the Fingerprintability of Tor Onion Services. Pages 2021–2036 of: *Proceedings of the 2017 ACM SIGSAC Conference on Computer and Communications Security*. CCS '17. Dallas, TX: ACM.

Pachilakis, Michalis, Papadopoulos, Panagiotis, Markatos, Evangelos P., and Kourtellis, Nicolas. 2019. No More Chasing Waterfalls: A Measurement Study of the Header Bidding Ad-Ecosystem. Pages 280–293 of: *Proceedings of the Internet Measurement Conference*. IMC '19. Amsterdam: ACM.

Pan, Elleen, Ren, Jingjing, Lindorfer, Martina, Wilson, Christo, and Choffnes, David. 2018. Panoptispy: Characterizing Audio and Video Exfiltration from Android Applications. *Proceedings on Privacy Enhancing Technologies*, **2018**(4), 33–50.

Papadopoulos, Panagiotis, Kourtellis, Nicolas, Rodriguez, Pablo Rodriguez, and Laoutaris, Nikolaos. 2017. If You Are Not Paying for It, You Are the Product: How Much Do Advertisers Pay to Reach You? Pages 142–156 of: *Proceedings of the 2017 Internet Measurement Conference*. IMC '17. London: ACM.

Papadopoulos, Panagiotis, Kourtellis, Nicolas, and Markatos, Evangelos. 2019. Cookie Synchronization: Everything You Always Wanted to Know But Were Afraid to Ask. Pages 1432–1442 of: *The World Wide Web Conference*. WWW '19. San Francisco, CA: ACM.

Papadopoulos, Panagiotis, Snyder, Peter, Athanasakis, Dimitrios, and Livshits, Benjamin. 2020. Keeping out the Masses: Understanding the Popularity and Implications of Internet Paywalls. Pages 1433–1444 of: *Proceedings of The Web Conference 2020*. WWW '20. Taipei: ACM.

Papaodyssefs, Fotios, Iordanou, Costas, Blackburn, Jeremy, Laoutaris, Nikolaos, and Papagiannaki, Konstantina. 2015. Web Identity Translator: Behavioral Advertising and Identity Privacy with WIT. Pages 3:1–3:7 of: *Proceedings of the 14th ACM Workshop on Hot Topics in Networks*. HotNets-XIV. Philadelphia, PA: ACM.

Parra-Arnau, Javier, Achara, Jagdish Prasad, and Castelluccia, Claude. 2017. MyAdChoices: Bringing Transparency and Control to Online Advertising. *ACM Trans. Web*, **11**(1), 7:1–7:47.

Pasquale, Frank. 2015. *The Black Box Society: The Secret Algorithms That Control Money and Information*. Cambridge, MA: Harvard University Press.

Peddinti, Sai Teja, and Saxena, Nitesh. 2010. On the Privacy of Web Search Based on Query Obfuscation: A Case Study of TrackMeNot. Pages 19–37 of: Atallah, Mikhail J., and Hopper, Nicholas J. (eds.), *Privacy Enhancing Technologies*. Lecture Notes in Computer Science. Berlin, Heidelberg: Springer.

Peddinti, Sai Teja, Bilogrevic, Igor, Taft, Nina, Pelikan, Martin, Erlingsson, Úlfar, Anthonysamy, Pauline, and Hogben, Giles. 2019. Reducing Permission Requests in Mobile Apps. Pages 259–266 of: *Proceedings of the Internet Measurement Conference*. IMC '19. Amsterdam: ACM.

Peer, Eyal, Brandimarte, Laura, Samat, Sonam, and Acquisti, Alessandro. 2017. Beyond the Turk: Alternative Platforms for Crowdsourcing Behavioral Research. *Journal of Experimental Social Psychology*, **70**(May), 153–163.

Perdisci, Roberto, Papastergiou, Thomas, Alrawi, Omar, and Antonakakis, Manos. 2020. IoTFinder: Efficient Large-Scale Identification of IoT Devices via Passive DNS Traffic Analysis. Pages 474–489 of: *IEEE European Symposium on Security and Privacy*. Euro S&P. IEEE.

Pham, Anh, Dacosta, Italo, Losiouk, Eleonora, Stephan, John, Huguenin, Kévin, and Hubaux, Jean-Pierre. 2019 (Aug.). HideMyApp: Hiding the Presence of Sensitive Apps on Android. Pages 711–728 of: *28th USENIX Security Symposium*. USENIX Security 19. Santa Clara, CA: USENIX.

Pitoura, Evaggelia, Tsaparas, Panayiotis, Flouris, Giorgos, Fundulaki, Irini, Papadakos, Panagiotis, Abiteboul, Serge, and Weikum, Gerhard. 2018. On Measuring Bias in Online Information. *SIGMOD Rec.*, **46**(4), 16–21.

Plane, Angelisa C., Redmiles, Elissa M., Mazurek, Michelle L., and Tschantz, Michael Carl. 2017. Exploring User Perceptions of Discrimination in Online Targeted Advertising. Pages 935–951 of: *26th USENIX Security Symposium*. USENIX Security 17. Vancouver: USENIX.

Pochat, Victor Le, van Goethem, Tom, and Joosen, Wouter. 2019. Rigging Research Results by Manipulating Top Websites Rankings. In: *26th Annual Network and Distributed System Security Symposium*. San Diego, CA: Internet Society.

Privacy International. 2019a (March). *Guess What? Facebook Still Tracks You on Android Apps (Even If You Don't Have a Facebook Account)*. http://privacyinternational.org/blog/2758/appdata-update.

Privacy International. 2019b (Sept.). *No Body's Business But Mine: How Menstruation Apps Are Sharing Your Data*. Tech. rept.

Pujol, Enric, Hohlfeld, Oliver, and Feldmann, Anja. 2015. Annoyed Users: Ads and Ad-Block Usage in the Wild. Pages 93–106 of: *Proceedings of the 2015 Internet Measurement Conference*. IMC '15. Tokyo: ACM.

Rabinowitz, Phil. 2020. *The Community Tool Box, Chapter 25: Changing Policies*. https://ctb.ku.edu/en/table-of-contents/implement/changing-policies/overview/main.

Rachovitsa, Adamantia. 2016. Engineering and Lawyering Privacy by Design: Understanding Online Privacy Both as a Technical and an International Human Rights Issue. *International Journal of Law and Information Technology*, **24**(4), 374–399.

Rafique, M. Zubair, Van Goethem, Tom, Joosen, Wouter, Huygens, Christophe, and Nikiforakis, Nick. 2016. It's Free for a Reason: Exploring the Ecosystem of Free Live Streaming Services. In: *Proceedings 2016 Network and Distributed System Security Symposium*. San Diego, CA: Internet Society.

Rama, Daniele, Mejova, Yelena, Tizzoni, Michele, Kalimeri, Kyriaki, and Weber, Ingmar. 2020. Facebook Ads as a Demographic Tool to Measure the Urban-Rural Divide. Pages 327–338 of: *Proceedings of The Web Conference 2020*. WWW '20. Taipei: ACM.

Ramesh, Reethika, Raman, Ram Sundara, Bernhard, Matthew, Ongkowijaya, Victor, Evdokimov, Leonid, Edmundson, Anne, Sprecher, Steven, Ikram, Muhammad, and Ensafi, Roya. 2020. Decentralized Control: A Case Study of Russia. In: *Proceedings 2020 Network and Distributed System Security Symposium*. San Diego, CA: Internet Society.

Rao, Ashwin, Kakhki, Arash Molavi, Razaghpanah, Abbas, Li, Anke, Choffnes, David, Legout, Arnaud, Mislove, Alan, and Gill, Phillipa. 2015. Meddle: Enabling

Transparency and Control for Mobile Internet Traffic. *Technology Science*, **2015103003**(Oct.).

Rashid, Fahmida Y. 2014 (April). *Surveillance Is the Business Model of the Internet: Bruce Schneier*. www.securityweek.com/surveillance-business-model-internet-bruce-schneier.

Rashidi, B., Fung, C., Nguyen, A., Vu, T., and Bertino, E. 2018. Android User Privacy Preserving Through Crowdsourcing. *IEEE Transactions on Information Forensics and Security*, **13**(3), 773–787.

Razaghpanah, Abbas, Nithyanand, Rishab, Vallina-Rodriguez, Narseo, Sundaresan, Srikanth, Allman, Mark, Kreibich, Christian, and Gill, Phillipa. 2018. Apps, Trackers, Privacy, and Regulators: A Global Study of the Mobile Tracking Ecosystem. In: *Proceedings of the 2018 Network and Distributed System Security Symposium*. San Diego, CA: Internet Society.

Reardon, Joel, Feal, Álvaro, Wijesekera, Primal, On, Amit Elazari Bar, Vallina-Rodriguez, Narseo, and Egelman, Serge. 2019 (Aug.). 50 Ways to Leak Your Data: An Exploration of Apps' Circumvention of the Android Permissions System. Pages 603–620 of: *28th USENIX Security Symposium*. USENIX Security 19. Santa Clara, CA: USENIX.

Reed, Mark S. 2018. *The Research Impact Handbook*. St Johns Well: Fast Track Impact.

Ren, Jingjing, Rao, Ashwin, Lindorfer, Martina, Legout, Arnaud, and Choffnes, David. 2016. ReCon: Revealing and Controlling PII Leaks in Mobile Network Traffic. Pages 361–374 of: *Proceedings of the 14th Annual International Conference on Mobile Systems, Applications, and Services*. MobiSys '16. Singapore: ACM.

Ren, Jingjing, Lindorfer, Martina, Dubois, Daniel J., Rao, Ashwin, Choffnes, David, and Vallina-Rodriguez, Narseo. 2018. Bug Fixes, Improvements, ... and Privacy Leaks - A Longitudinal Study of PII Leaks Across Android App Versions. In: *Proceedings of the 2018 Network and Distributed System Security Symposium*. San Diego, CA: Internet Society.

Ren, Jingjing, Dubois, Daniel J., Choffnes, David, Mandalari, Anna Maria, Kolcun, Roman, and Haddadi, Hamed. 2019. Information Exposure From Consumer IoT Devices: A Multidimensional, Network-Informed Measurement Approach. Pages 267–279 of: *Proceedings of the Internet Measurement Conference*. IMC '19. Amsterdam: ACM.

Reschke, Julian F., and Fielding, Roy T. 2014 (June). *Hypertext Transfer Protocol (HTTP/1.1): Message Syntax and Routing*. Tech. rept. RFC 7230. Internet Engineering Task Force (IETF).

Reyes, Irwin, Wijesekera, Primal, Reardon, Joel, On, Amit Elazari Bar, Razaghpanah, Abbas, Vallina-Rodriguez, Narseo, and Egelman, Serge. 2018. "Won't Somebody Think of the Children?" Examining COPPA Compliance at Scale. *Proceedings on Privacy Enhancing Technologies*, **2018**(3), 63–83.

Ribeiro, Filipe N., Henrique, Lucas, Benevenuto, Fabricio, Chakraborty, Abhijnan, Kulshrestha, Juhi, Babaei, Mahmoudreza, and Gummadi, Krishna P. 2018 (June). Media Bias Monitor: Quantifying Biases of Social Media News Outlets at Large-Scale. In: *Twelfth International AAAI Conference on Web and Social Media*. Palo Alto, CA: AAAI Press.

Ribeiro, Manoel Horta, Ottoni, Raphael, West, Robert, Almeida, Virgílio A. F., and Meira, Wagner. 2020. Auditing Radicalization Pathways on YouTube.

Pages 131–141 of: *Proceedings of the 2020 Conference on Fairness, Accountability, and Transparency*. FAT* '20. Barcelona: ACM.

Riederer, Christopher, Echickson, Daniel, Huang, Stephanie, and Chaintreau, Augustin. 2016. FindYou: A Personal Location Privacy Auditing Tool. Pages 243–246 of: *Proceedings of the 25th International Conference Companion on World Wide Web*. WWW '16 Companion. Montreal: International World Wide Web Conferences Steering Committee.

Robertson, Ronald E., Jiang, Shan, Joseph, Kenneth, Friedland, Lisa, Lazer, David, and Wilson, Christo. 2018a. Auditing Partisan Audience Bias Within Google Search. *Proc. ACM Hum.-Comput. Interact.*, **2**(CSCW), 148:1–148:22.

Robertson, Ronald E., Lazer, David, and Wilson, Christo. 2018b. Auditing the Personalization and Composition of Politically-Related Search Engine Results Pages. Pages 955–965 of: *Proceedings of the 2018 World Wide Web Conference*. WWW '18. Lyon: International World Wide Web Conferences Steering Committee.

Robertson, Ronald E., Jiang, Shan, Lazer, David, and Wilson, Christo. 2019. Auditing Autocomplete: Suggestion Networks and Recursive Algorithm Interrogation. Pages 235–244 of: *Proceedings of the 10th ACM Conference on Web Science*. WebSci '19. Boston, MA: ACM Press.

Roesner, Franziska, Kohno, Tadayoshi, and Wetherall, David. 2012. Detecting and Defending Against Third-Party Tracking on the Web. Pages 12–12 of: *Proceedings of the 9th USENIX Conference on Networked Systems Design and Implementation*. NSDI '12. San Jose, CA: USENIX Association.

Roth, Sebastian, Barron, Timothy, Calzavara, Stefano, Nikiforakis, Nick, and Stock, Ben. 2020. Complex Security Policy? A Longitudinal Analysis of Deployed Content Security Policies. In: *Proceedings 2020 Network and Distributed System Security Symposium*. San Diego, CA: Internet Society.

Samarasinghe, Nayanamana, and Mannan, Mohammad. 2019. Towards a Global Perspective on Web Tracking. *Computers & Security*, **87**(Nov.), 101569.

Sanchez-Monedero, Javier, Dencik, Lina, and Edwards, Lilian. 2019. What Does It Mean to Solve the Problem of Discrimination in Hiring? Social, Technical and Legal Perspectives from the UK on Automated Hiring Systems. arXiv:1910.06144 [cs], Sept.

Sandvig, Christian, Hamilton, Kevin, Karahalios, Karrie, and Langbort, Cedric. 2014 (May). Auditing Algorithms: Research Methods for Detecting Discrimination on Internet Platforms. Page 23 of: *Data and Discrimination: Converting Critical Concerns into Productive Inquiry*.

Sarker, Shaown, Jueckstock, Jordan, and Kapravelos, Alexandros. 2020. Hiding in Plain Site: Detecting JavaScript Obfuscation through Concealed Browser API Usage. Pages 648–661 of: *Proceedings of the ACM Internet Measurement Conference*. IMC '20. Pittsburgh, PA: ACM.

Scheiber, Noam. 2019. Facebook Accused of Allowing Bias Against Women in Job Ads. *The New York Times* (March).

Scheiber, Noam, and Isaac, Mike. 2019. Facebook Halts Ad Targeting Cited in Bias Complaints. *The New York Times* (March).

Schelter, Sebastian, and Kunegis, Jérôme. 2018. On the Ubiquity of Web Tracking: Insights from a Billion-Page Web Crawl. *The Journal of Web Science*, **4**(4), 53–66.

Schirck-Matthews, Angela, Hochmair, Hartwig, Strelnikova, Dariia, and Juhasz, Levente. 2019. Comparing the Characteristics of Bicycle Trips between Endomondo, Google Maps, and MapQuest. *Transportation Research Board Annual Meeting*. Washington, DC.

Schubert, Charlotte. 2018 (Jan.). *Do I Make Myself Clear? Media Training for Scientists*. www.sciencemag.org/features/2018/01/do-i-make-myself-clear-media-training-scientists.

Seneviratne, Suranga, Kolamunna, Harini, and Seneviratne, Aruna. 2015. A Measurement Study of Tracking in Paid Mobile Applications. Pages 7:1–7:6 of: *Proceedings of the 8th ACM Conference on Security & Privacy in Wireless and Mobile Networks*. WiSec '15. New York: ACM.

Shankland, Stephen, and Mihalcik, Carrie. 2019 (May). *Google Holds Firm on Chrome Changes That May Break Ad Blockers*. www.cnet.com/news/google-holds-firm-on-chrome-changes-that-may-break-ad-blockers/.

Shezan, Faysal Hossain, Hu, Hang, Wang, Jiamin, Wang, Gang, and Tian, Yuan. 2020. Read Between the Lines: An Empirical Measurement of Sensitive Applications of Voice Personal Assistant Systems. Pages 1006–1017 of: *Proceedings of The Web Conference 2020*. WWW '20. Taipei: ACM.

Shipp, Laura, and Blasco, Jorge. 2020. How Private Is Your Period?: A Systematic Analysis of Menstrual App Privacy Policies. *Proceedings on Privacy Enhancing Technologies*, **2020**(4), 491–510.

Shuba, Anastasia, and Markopoulou, Athina. 2020. NoMoATS: Towards Automatic Detection of Mobile Tracking. *Proceedings on Privacy Enhancing Technologies*, **2020**(2), 45–66.

Siby, Sandra, Juarez, Marc, Diaz, Claudia, Vallina-Rodriguez, Narseo, and Troncoso, Carmela. 2020. Encrypted DNS –> Privacy? A Traffic Analysis Perspective. In: *Proceedings of the 2020 Network and Distributed System Security Symposium*. San Diego, CA: Internet Society.

Silva, Márcio, Santos de Oliveira, Lucas, Andreou, Athanasios, Vaz de Melo, Pedro Olmo, Goga, Oana, and Benevenuto, Fabricio. 2020. Facebook Ads Monitor: An Independent Auditing System for Political Ads on Facebook. Pages 224–234 of: *Proceedings of The Web Conference 2020*. WWW '20. Taipei: ACM.

Sjösten, Alexander, Van Acker, Steven, and Sabelfeld, Andrei. 2017. Discovering Browser Extensions via Web Accessible Resources. Pages 329–336 of: *Proceedings of the Seventh ACM on Conference on Data and Application Security and Privacy*. CODASPY '17. Scottsdale, AZ: ACM.

Snowden, Edward. 2019. *Permanent Record*. 1st edition. New York: Metropolitan Books.

Soeller, Gary, Karahalios, Karrie, Sandvig, Christian, and Wilson, Christo. 2016. MapWatch: Detecting and Monitoring International Border Personalization on Online Maps. Pages 867–878 of: *Proceedings of the 25th International Conference on World Wide Web*. WWW '16. Montreal: International World Wide Web Conferences Steering Committee.

Solomos, Konstantinos, Ilia, Panagiotis, Ioannidis, Sotiris, and Kourtellis, Nicolas. 2019. Talon: An Automated Framework for Cross-Device Tracking Detection. In: *22nd International Symposium on Research in Attacks, Intrusions and Defenses*. RAID 2019. Beijing: USENIX.

Soltani, Ashkan, Canty, Shannon, Mayo, Quentin, Thomas, Lauren, and Hoofnagle, Chris Jay. 2009 (Aug.). *Flash Cookies and Privacy*. SSRN Scholarly Paper ID 1446862. Social Science Research Network, Rochester, NY.

Son, Sooel, Kim, Daehyeok, and Shmatikov, Vitaly. 2016. What Mobile Ads Know About Mobile Users. In: *Proceedings of the 2016 Network and Distributed System Security Symposium*. San Diego, CA: Internet Society.

Sørensen, Jannick Kirk, and Kosta, Sokol. 2019. Before and After GDPR: The Changes in Third Party Presence at Public and Private European Websites. Pages 1590–1600 of: *WWW '19 Companion Proceedings of the The Web Conference 2019*. San Francisco, CA: ACM Press.

Speicher, Till, Ali, Muhammad, Venkatadri, Giridhari, Ribeiro, Filipe Nunes, Arvanitakis, George, Benevenuto, Fabrício, Gummadi, Krishna P., Loiseau, Patrick, and Mislove, Alan. 2018 (Jan.). Potential for Discrimination in Online Targeted Advertising. Pages 5–19 of: *Conference on Fairness, Accountability and Transparency*. New York: ACM.

Srivastava, Animesh, Jain, Puneet, Demetriou, Soteris, Cox, Landon P., and Kim, Kyu-Han. 2017. CamForensics: Understanding Visual Privacy Leaks in the Wild. Pages 30:1–30:13 of: *Proceedings of the 15th ACM Conference on Embedded Network Sensor Systems*. SenSys '17. Delft: ACM.

Starov, O., and Nikiforakis, N. 2017a (May). XHOUND: Quantifying the Fingerprintability of Browser Extensions. Pages 941–956 of: *2017 IEEE Symposium on Security and Privacy*. SP. San Jose, CA: IEEE.

Starov, Oleksii, and Nikiforakis, Nick. 2017b. Extended Tracking Powers: Measuring the Privacy Diffusion Enabled by Browser Extensions. Pages 1481–1490 of: *Proceedings of the 26th International Conference on World Wide Web*. WWW '17. Perth, Australia: International World Wide Web Conferences Steering Committee.

Starov, Oleksii, Gill, Phillipa, and Nikiforakis, Nick. 2016. Are You Sure You Want to Contact Us? Quantifying the Leakage of PII via Website Contact Forms. *Proceedings on Privacy Enhancing Technologies*, **2016**(1), 20–33.

Starov, Oleksii, Zhou, Yuchen, Zhang, Xiao, Miramirkhani, Najmeh, and Nikiforakis, Nick. 2018. Betrayed by Your Dashboard: Discovering Malicious Campaigns via Web Analytics. Pages 227–236 of: *Proceedings of the 2018 World Wide Web Conference*. WWW '18. Lyon: International World Wide Web Conferences Steering Committee.

Starov, Oleksii, Laperdrix, Pierre, Kapravelos, Alexandros, and Nikiforakis, Nick. 2019 (May). Unnecessarily Identifiable: Quantifying the Fingerprintability of Browser Extensions Due to Bloat. Page 7 of: *Proceedings of the 2019 World Wide Web Conference*. WWW'19.

Stivala, Giada, and Pellegrino, Giancarlo. 2020. Deceptive Previews: A Study of the Link Preview Trustworthiness in Social Platforms. In: *Proceedings 2020 Network and Distributed System Security Symposium*. San Diego, CA: Internet Society.

Stock, Ben, Pellegrino, Giancarlo, Rossow, Christian, Johns, Martin, and Backes, Michael. 2016. Hey, You Have a Problem: On the Feasibility of Large-Scale Web Vulnerability Notification. Pages 1015–1032 of: *25th USENIX Security Symposium*. USENIX Security 16. Austin, TX: USENIX.

Storey, Grant, Reisman, Dillon, Mayer, Jonathan, and Narayanan, Arvind. 2017. The Future of Ad Blocking: An Analytical Framework and New Techniques. arXiv:1705.05568 [cs], May.

Stuart, Elizabeth A. 2010. Matching Methods for Causal Inference: A Review and a Look Forward. *Statistical Science*, **25**(1), 1–21.

Subramani, Karthika, Yuan, Xingzi, Setayeshfar, Omid, Vadrevu, Phani, Lee, Kyu Hyung, and Perdisci, Roberto. 2020. When Push Comes to Ads: Measuring the Rise of (Malicious) Push Advertising. Pages 724–737 of: *Proceedings of the ACM Internet Measurement Conference*. IMC '20. Pittsburgh, PA: ACM.

Sweeney, Latanya. 2013. Discrimination in Online Ad Delivery. *Commun. ACM*, **56**(5), 44–54.

Sy, Erik, Burkert, Christian, Federrath, Hannes, and Fischer, Mathias. 2018. Tracking Users Across the Web via TLS Session Resumption. Pages 289–299 of: *Proceedings of the 34th Annual Computer Security Applications Conference*. ACSAC '18. San Juan, PR: ACM.

Tannert, Benjamin, and Schöning, Johannes. 2018. Disabled, but at What Cost?: An Examination of Wheelchair Routing Algorithms. Pages 46:1–46:7 of: *Proceedings of the 20th International Conference on Human-Computer Interaction with Mobile Devices and Services*. MobileHCI '18. Barcelona: ACM.

Thebault-Spieker, Jacob, Terveen, Loren, and Hecht, Brent. 2017. Toward a Geographic Understanding of the Sharing Economy: Systemic Biases in UberX and TaskRabbit. *ACM Trans. Comput.-Hum. Interact.*, **24**(3), 21:1–21:40.

Toubiana, Vincent, Subramanian, Lakshminarayanan, and Nissenbaum, Helen. 2011. TrackMeNot: Enhancing the Privacy of Web Search. arXiv:1109.4677 [cs], Sept.

Tran, Chau, Champion, Kaylea, Forte, Andrea, Hill, Benjamin Mako, and Greenstadt, Rachel. 2020. Are Anonymity-Seekers Just like Everybody Else? An Analysis of Contributions to Wikipedia from Tor. Pages 974–990 of: *2020 IEEE Symposium on Security and Privacy*. SP. San Francisco, CA: IEEE.

Trevisan, Martino, Traverso, Stefano, Bassi, Eleonora, and Mellia, Marco. 2019. 4 Years of EU Cookie Law: Results and Lessons Learned. *Proceedings on Privacy Enhancing Technologies*, **2019**(2), 126–145.

Trickel, Erik, Starov, Oleksii, Kapravelos, Alexandros, Nikiforakis, Nick, and Doupé, Adam. 2019 (Aug.). Everyone Is Different: Client-Side Diversification for Defending Against Extension Fingerprinting. Pages 1679–1696 of: *28th USENIX Security Symposium*. USENIX Security 19. Santa Clara, CA: USENIX.

Trielli, Daniel, and Diakopoulos, Nicholas. 2019. Search As News Curator: The Role of Google in Shaping Attention to News Information. Pages 453:1–453:15 of: *Proceedings of the 2019 CHI Conference on Human Factors in Computing Systems*. CHI '19. Glasgow: ACM.

Tschantz, M. C., Datta, A., Datta, A., and Wing, J. M. 2015 (July). A Methodology for Information Flow Experiments. Pages 554–568 of: *2015 IEEE 28th Computer Security Foundations Symposium*. Verona: IEEE.

Tschantz, Michael Carl, Egelman, Serge, Choi, Jaeyoung, Weaver, Nicholas, and Friedland, Gerald. 2018a. The Accuracy of the Demographic Inferences Shown on Google's Ad Settings. Pages 33–41 of: *Proceedings of the 2018 Workshop on Privacy in the Electronic Society*. WPES'18. Toronto: ACM.

Tschantz, Michael Carl, Afroz, Sadia, Sajid, Shaarif, Qazi, Shoaib Asif, Javed, Mobin, and Paxson, Vern. 2018b. A Bestiary of Blocking: The Motivations and Modes behind Website Unavailability. In: *8th USENIX Workshop on Free and Open Communications on the Internet*. FOCI 18. Baltimore, MD: USENIX.

Ullah, I., Boreli, R., Kaafar, M. A., and Kanhere, S. S. 2014 (April). Characterising User Targeting for In-App Mobile Ads. Pages 547–552 of: *2014 IEEE Conference on Computer Communications Workshops*. INFOCOM WKSHPS. Toronto: IEEE.

Uluagac, A. S., Radhakrishnan, S. V., Corbett, C., Baca, A., and Beyah, R. 2013 (Oct.). A Passive Technique for Fingerprinting Wireless Devices with Wired-Side Observations. Pages 305–313 of: *2013 IEEE Conference on Communications and Network Security*. CNS. National Harbor, MD: IEEE.

United Nations. 1948 (Dec.). *Universal Declaration of Human Rights*. www.un.org/en/universal-declaration-human-rights/index.html.

Urban, Tobias, Tatang, Dennis, Holz, Thorsten, and Pohlmann, Norbert. 2018. Towards Understanding Privacy Implications of Adware and Potentially Unwanted Programs. Pages 449–469 of: Lopez, Javier, Zhou, Jianying, and Soriano, Miguel (eds.), *Computer Security*. Lecture Notes in Computer Science. Cham: Springer.

Urban, Tobias, Tatang, Dennis, Degeling, Martin, Holz, Thorsten, and Pohlmann, Norbert. 2019. A Study on Subject Data Access in Online Advertising After the GDPR. Pages 61–79 of: Pérez-Solà, Cristina, Navarro-Arribas, Guillermo, Biryukov, Alex, and Garcia-Alfaro, Joaquin (eds.), *Data Privacy Management, Cryptocurrencies and Blockchain Technology*. Lecture Notes in Computer Science. Cham: Springer International Publishing.

Urban, Tobias, Degeling, Martin, Holz, Thorsten, and Pohlmann, Norbert. 2020a. Beyond the Front Page:Measuring Third Party Dynamics in the Field. Pages 1275–1286 of: *Proceedings of the Web Conference 2020*. WWW '20. Taipei: ACM.

Urban, Tobias, Tatang, Dennis, Degeling, Martin, Holz, Thorsten, and Pohlmann, Norbert. 2020b. Measuring the Impact of the GDPR on Data Sharing in Ad Networks. Page 15 of: *15th ACM Asia Conference on Computer and Communications Security*. ASIA CCS '20. Taipei: ACM.

Utz, Christine, Degeling, Martin, Fahl, Sascha, Schaub, Florian, and Holz, Thorsten. 2019. (Un)Informed Consent: Studying GDPR Consent Notices in the Field. Pages 973–990 of: *Proceedings of the 2019 ACM SIGSAC Conference on Computer and Communications Security*. CCS '19. London: ACM.

Vaccaro, Kristen, Karahalios, Karrie, Sandvig, Christian, Hamilton, Kevin, and Langbort, Cedric. 2015. Agree or Cancel? Research and Terms of Service Compliance. In: *ACM CSCW Ethics Workshop: Ethics for Studying Sociotechnical Systems in a Big Data World*. Vancouver, ACM.

Vadrevu, Phani, and Perdisci, Roberto. 2019. What You See Is NOT What You Get: Discovering and Tracking Social Engineering Attack Campaigns. Pages 308–321 of: *Proceedings of the Internet Measurement Conference*. IMC '19. Amsterdam: ACM.

Vallina, Pelayo, Feal, Álvaro, Gamba, Julien, Vallina-Rodriguez, Narseo, and Anta, Antonio Fernández. 2019. Tales from the Porn: A Comprehensive Privacy Analysis of the Web Porn Ecosystem. Pages 245–258 of: *Proceedings of the Internet Measurement Conference*. IMC '19. Amsterdam: ACM.

Vallina, Pelayo, Le Pochat, Victor, Feal, Álvaro, Paraschiv, Marius, Gamba, Julien, Burke, Tim, Hohlfeld, Oliver, Tapiador, Juan, and Vallina-Rodriguez, Narseo. 2020. Mis-Shapes, Mistakes, Misfits: An Analysis of Domain Classification Services. Pages 598–618 of: *Proceedings of the ACM Internet Measurement Conference*. IMC '20. Pittsburgh, PA: ACM.

Vallina-Rodriguez, Narseo, Shah, Jay, Finamore, Alessandro, Grunenberger, Yan, Papagiannaki, Konstantina, Haddadi, Hamed, and Crowcroft, Jon. 2012. Breaking for Commercials: Characterizing Mobile Advertising. Pages 343–356 of: *Proceedings of the 2012 Internet Measurement Conference.* IMC '12. Boston, MA: ACM.

Vallina-Rodriguez, Narseo, Sundaresan, Srikanth, Razaghpanah, Abbas, Nithyanand, Rishab, Allman, Mark, Kreibich, Christian, and Gill, Phillipa. 2016. Tracking the Trackers: Towards Understanding the Mobile Advertising and Tracking Ecosystem. arXiv:1609.07190 [cs], Sept.

van Eijk, Rob, Asghari, Hadi, Winter, Philipp, and Narayanan, Arvind. 2019. The Impact of User Location on Cookie Notices (Inside and Outside of the European Union). In: *IEEE Security & Privacy Workshop on Technology and Consumer Protection.* ConPro '19. San Francisco, CA: IEEE.

Varmarken, Janus, Le, Hieu, Shuba, Anastasia, Markopoulou, Athina, and Shafiq, Zubair. 2020. The TV Is Smart and Full of Trackers: Measuring Smart TV Advertising and Tracking. *Proceedings on Privacy Enhancing Technologies,* **2020**(2), 129–154.

Vastel, A., Laperdrix, P., Rudametkin, W., and Rouvoy, R. 2018a (May). FP-STALKER: Tracking Browser Fingerprint Evolutions. Pages 728–741 of: *2018 IEEE Symposium on Security and Privacy.* SP. San Francisco, CA: IEEE.

Vastel, Antoine, Laperdrix, Pierre, Rudametkin, Walter, and Rouvoy, Romain. 2018b. Fp-Scanner: The Privacy Implications of Browser Fingerprint Inconsistencies. Pages 135–150 of: *27th USENIX Security Symposium.* USENIX Security 18. Baltimore, MD: USENIX.

Venkatadri, G., Andreou, A., Liu, Y., Mislove, A., Gummadi, K. P., Loiseau, P., and Goga, O. 2018 (May). Privacy Risks with Facebook's PII-Based Targeting: Auditing a Data Broker's Advertising Interface. Pages 89–107 of: *2018 IEEE Symposium on Security and Privacy.* SP. San Francisco, CA: IEEE.

Venkatadri, Giridhari, Lucherini, Elena, Sapiezynski, Piotr, and Mislove, Alan. 2019. Investigating Sources of PII Used in Facebook's Targeted Advertising. *Proceedings on Privacy Enhancing Technologies,* **2019**(1), 227–244.

Vieira, Carolina, Ribeiro, Filipe, Vaz de Melo, Pedro Olmo, Benevenuto, Fabricio, and Zagheni, Emilio. 2020. Using Facebook Data to Measure Cultural Distance between Countries: The Case of Brazilian Cuisine. Pages 3091–3097 of: *Proceedings of The Web Conference 2020.* WWW '20. Taipei: ACM.

Viennot, Nicolas, Garcia, Edward, and Nieh, Jason. 2014. A Measurement Study of Google Play. Pages 221–233 of: *The 2014 ACM International Conference on Measurement and Modeling of Computer Systems.* SIGMETRICS '14. Austin, TX: ACM.

Vincent, Nicholas, Johnson, Isaac, Sheehan, Patrick, and Hecht, Brent. 2019. Measuring the Importance of User-Generated Content to Search Engines. *Proceedings of the International AAAI Conference on Web and Social Media,* **13**(July), 505–516.

Vines, Paul, Roesner, Franziska, and Kohno, Tadayoshi. 2017. Exploring ADINT: Using Ad Targeting for Surveillance on a Budget – or – How Alice Can Buy Ads to Track Bob. Pages 153–164 of: *Proceedings of the 2017 on Workshop on Privacy in the Electronic Society.* WPES '17. Dallas, TX: ACM.

Vissers, Thomas, Nikiforakis, Nick, Bielova, Nataliia, and Joosen, Wouter. 2014 (July). Crying Wolf? On the Price Discrimination of Online Airline Tickets. In: *7th*

Workshop on Hot Topics in Privacy Enhancing Technologies. HotPETs 2014. Amsterdam.

Vissers, Thomas, Joosen, Wouter, and Nikiforakis, Nick. 2015. Parking Sensors: Analyzing and Detecting Parked Domains. In: *Proceedings 2015 Network and Distributed System Security Symposium.* San Diego, CA: Internet Society.

Wachter, Sandra. 2017 (Jan.). *Privacy: Primus Inter Pares – Privacy as a Precondition for Self-Development, Personal Fulfilment and the Free Enjoyment of Fundamental Human Rights.* SSRN Scholarly Paper ID 2903514. Social Science Research Network, Rochester, NY.

Wagner, Isabel, and Boiten, Eerke. 2018. Privacy Risk Assessment: From Art to Science, by Metrics. Pages 225–241 of: *13th International DPM Workshop on Data Privacy Management*, vol. LNCS 11025. Barcelona: Springer.

Wagner, James. 2018 (Oct.). *Trustworthy Chrome Extensions, by Default.*

Wan, Gerry, Izhikevich, Liz, Adrian, David, Yoshioka, Katsunari, Holz, Ralph, Rossow, Christian, and Durumeric, Zakir. 2020. On the Origin of Scanning: The Impact of Location on Internet-Wide Scans. Pages 662–679 of: *Proceedings of the ACM Internet Measurement Conference.* IMC '20. Pittsburgh, PA: ACM.

Wang, David Y., Der, Matthew, Karami, Mohammad, Saul, Lawrence, McCoy, Damon, Savage, Stefan, and Voelker, Geoffrey M. 2014a. Search + Seizure: The Effectiveness of Interventions on SEO Campaigns. Pages 359–372 of: *Proceedings of the 2014 Conference on Internet Measurement Conference.* IMC '14. Vancouver: ACM.

Wang, Haoyu, Liu, Zhe, Liang, Jingyue, Vallina-Rodriguez, Narseo, Guo, Yao, Li, Li, Tapiador, Juan, Cao, Jingcun, and Xu, Guoai. 2018. Beyond Google Play: A Large-Scale Comparative Study of Chinese Android App Markets. Pages 293–307 of: *Proceedings of the Internet Measurement Conference 2018.* Boston, MA: ACM.

Wang, W., Wang, X., Feng, D., Liu, J., Han, Z., and Zhang, X. 2014b. Exploring Permission-Induced Risk in Android Applications for Malicious Application Detection. *IEEE Transactions on Information Forensics and Security*, **9**(11), 1869–1882.

Wang, Yan, Chen, Yingying, Ye, Fan, Liu, Hongbo, and Yang, Jie. 2019. Implications of Smartphone User Privacy Leakage from the Advertiser's Perspective. *Pervasive and Mobile Computing*, **53**(Feb.), 13–32.

Webber, William, Moffat, Alistair, and Zobel, Justin. 2010. A Similarity Measure for Indefinite Rankings. *ACM Trans. Inf. Syst.*, **28**(4), 20:1–20:38.

Wei, Miranda, Stamos, Madison, Veys, Sophie, Reitinger, Nathan, Goodman, Justin, Herman, Margot, Filipczuk, Dorota, Weinshel, Ben, Mazurek, Michelle L., and Ur, Blase. 2020. What Twitter Knows: Characterizing Ad Targeting Practices, User Perceptions, and Ad Explanations Through Users' Own Twitter Data. Pages 145–162 of: *29th USENIX Security Symposium.* USENIX Security 20. USENIX.

Weinberg, Z., Chen, E. Y., Jayaraman, P. R., and Jackson, C. 2011 (May). I Still Know What You Visited Last Summer: Leaking Browsing History via User Interaction and Side Channel Attacks. Pages 147–161 of: *2011 IEEE Symposium on Security and Privacy.* SP. Oakland, CA: IEEE.

Weinshel, Ben, Wei, Miranda, Mondal, Mainack, Choi, Euirim, Shan, Shawn, Dolin, Claire, Mazurek, Michelle L., and Ur, Blase. 2019. Oh, the Places You've Been! User Reactions to Longitudinal Transparency About Third-Party Web Tracking and Inferencing. Pages 149–166 of: *Proceedings of the 2019 ACM SIGSAC Conference on Computer and Communications Security*. CCS '19. London: ACM.

Weissbacher, Michael, Mariconti, Enrico, Suarez-Tangil, Guillermo, Stringhini, Gianluca, Robertson, William, and Kirda, Engin. 2017. Ex-Ray: Detection of History-Leaking Browser Extensions. Pages 590–602 of: *Proceedings of the 33rd Annual Computer Security Applications Conference*. ACSAC 2017. Orlando, FL: ACM.

Whittaker, Zack. 2020. Oracle's BlueKai Tracks You across the Web. That Data Spilled Online. *TechCrunch*, June.

Wicker, Stephen B., and Ghosh, Dipayan. 2020. Reading in the Panopticon—: Your Kindle May Be Spying on You, but You Can't Be Sure. *Communications of the ACM*, **63**(5), 68–73.

Wills, Craig E., and Tatar, Can. 2012. Understanding What They Do with What They Know. Pages 13–18 of: *Proceedings of the 2012 ACM Workshop on Privacy in the Electronic Society*. WPES '12. Raleigh, NC: ACM.

Wu, Qianru, Liu, Qixu, Zhang, Yuqing, Liu, Peng, and Wen, Guanxing. 2016. A Machine Learning Approach for Detecting Third-Party Trackers on the Web. Pages 238–258 of: Askoxylakis, Ioannis, Ioannidis, Sotiris, Katsikas, Sokratis, and Meadows, Catherine (eds.), *Computer Security – ESORICS 2016*. Lecture Notes in Computer Science. Cham: Springer.

Wu, Shujiang, Li, Song, Cao, Yinzhi, and Wang, Ningfei. 2019 (Aug.). Rendered Private: Making GLSL Execution Uniform to Prevent WebGL-Based Browser Fingerprinting. Pages 1645–1660 of: *28th USENIX Security Symposium*. USENIX Security 19. Santa Clara, CA: USENIX.

Yang, Zhemin, Yang, Min, Zhang, Yuan, Gu, Guofei, Ning, Peng, and Wang, X. Sean. 2013. AppIntent: Analyzing Sensitive Data Transmission in Android for Privacy Leakage Detection. Pages 1043–1054 of: *Proceedings of the 2013 ACM SIGSAC Conference on Computer & Communications Security*. CCS '13. Berlin: ACM.

Yang, Zhiju, and Yue, Chuan. 2020. A Comparative Measurement Study of Web Tracking on Mobile and Desktop Environments. *Proceedings on Privacy Enhancing Technologies*, **2020**(2), 24–44.

You, W., Liang, B., Shi, W., Wang, P., and Zhang, X. 2018. TaintMan: An ART-Compatible Dynamic Taint Analysis Framework on Unmodified and Non-Rooted Android Devices. *IEEE Transactions on Dependable and Secure Computing*, 1–1.

Yu, Zhonghao, Macbeth, Sam, Modi, Konark, and Pujol, Josep M. 2016. Tracking the Trackers. Pages 121–132 of: *Proceedings of the 25th International Conference on World Wide Web*. WWW '16. Montreal: International World Wide Web Conferences Steering Committee.

Zarras, Apostolis, Kapravelos, Alexandros, Stringhini, Gianluca, Holz, Thorsten, Kruegel, Christopher, and Vigna, Giovanni. 2014. The Dark Alleys of Madison Avenue: Understanding Malicious Advertisements. Pages 373–380 of: *Proceedings of the 2014 Conference on Internet Measurement Conference*. IMC '14. Vancouver: ACM.

Zeber, David, Bird, Sarah, Oliveira, Camila, Rudametkin, Walter, Segall, Ilana, Wollsén, Fredrik, and Lopatka, Martin. 2020. The Representativeness of Automated Web Crawls as a Surrogate for Human Browsing. Pages 167–178 of: *Proceedings of The Web Conference 2020*. WWW '20. Taipei: ACM.

Zhang, Jiexin, Beresford, Alastair R, and Sheret, Ian. 2019a. SENSORID: Sensor Calibration Fingerprinting for Smartphones. Page 18 of: *Proceedings of the 40th IEEE Symposium on Security and Privacy*. SP. San Francisco, CA: IEEE.

Zhang, Mingxue, Meng, Wei, Lee, Sangho, Lee, Byoungyoung, and Xing, Xinyu. 2019b (Aug.). All Your Clicks Belong to Me: Investigating Click Interception on the Web. Pages 941–957 of: *28th USENIX Security Symposium*. USENIX Security 19. Santa Clara, CA: USENIX.

Zhao, Qingchuan, Zuo, Chaoshun, Pellegrino, Giancarlo, and Lin, Zhiqiang. 2019. Geo-Locating Drivers: A Study of Sensitive Data Leakage in Ride-Hailing Services. In: *Proceedings 2019 Network and Distributed System Security Symposium*. San Diego, CA: Internet Society.

Zhao, Shuai, Kalra, Achir, Borcea, Cristian, and Chen, Yi. 2020. To Be Tough or Soft: Measuring the Impact of Counter-Ad-Blocking Strategies on User Engagement. Pages 2690–2696 of: *Proceedings of The Web Conference 2020*. WWW '20. Taipei: ACM.

Zhu, Shitong, Hu, Xunchao, Qian, Zhiyun, Shafiq, Zubair, and Yin, Heng. 2018 (Feb.). Measuring and Disrupting Anti-Adblockers Using Differential Execution Analysis. In: *The Network and Distributed System Security Symposium*. NDSS.

Zimmeck, Sebastian, and Bellovin, Steven M. 2014. Privee: An Architecture for Automatically Analyzing Web Privacy Policies. Page 17 of: *23rd USENIX Security Symposium*. San Diego, CA: USENIX Association.

Zimmeck, Sebastian, Li, Jie S, Kim, Hyungtae, Bellovin, Steven M, and Jebara, Tony. 2017. A Privacy Analysis of Cross-Device Tracking. Page 19 of: *26th USENIX Security Symposium*. Vancouver: USENIX.

Zimmeck, Sebastian, Story, Peter, Smullen, Daniel, Ravichander, Abhilasha, Wang, Ziqi, Reidenberg, Joel, Russell, N. Cameron, and Sadeh, Norman. 2019. MAPS: Scaling Privacy Compliance Analysis to a Million Apps. *Proceedings on Privacy Enhancing Technologies*, **2019**(3), 66–86.

Žliobaitė, Indrė. 2017. Measuring Discrimination in Algorithmic Decision Making. *Data Mining and Knowledge Discovery*, **31**(4), 1060–1089.

Zuboff, Shoshana. 2019. *The Age of Surveillance Capitalism: The Fight for a Human Future at the New Frontier of Power*. 1st edition. New York: PublicAffairs.

Zuo, Chaoshun, Wen, Haohuang, Lin, Zhiqiang, and Zhang, Yinqian. 2019. Automatic Fingerprinting of Vulnerable BLE IoT Devices with Static UUIDs from Mobile Apps. Pages 1469–1483 of: *Proceedings of the 2019 ACM SIGSAC Conference on Computer and Communications Security*. CCS '19. London: ACM.

Index

DIFFUSION BONDING 2

Proceedings of the 2nd International Conference on Diffusion Bonding held at Cranfield Institute of Technology, UK, 28–29 March 1990.

PROGRAMME COMMITTEE

S. B. Dunkerton   The Welding Institute
R. M. Crispin   AEA Harwell Laboratory
R. Pearce   Consultmat
D. J. Stephenson   Cranfield Institute of Technology

DIFFUSION BONDING 2

Edited by

D. J. STEPHENSON

School of Industrial and Manufacturing Science,
Cranfield Institute of Technology, UK

ELSEVIER APPLIED SCIENCE
LONDON and NEW YORK

ELSEVIER SCIENCE PUBLISHERS LTD
Crown House, Linton Road, Barking, Essex IG11 8JU, England

Sole Distributor in the USA and Canada
ELSEVIER SCIENCE PUBLISHING CO., INC.
655 Avenue of the Americas, New York, NY 10010, USA

WITH 25 TABLES AND 213 ILLUSTRATIONS

British Library Cataloguing in Publication Data

Diffusion bonding 2.
1. Welding
I. Stephenson, D. J. (Derek John)
671.52

ISBN 1-85166-591-9

Library of Congress CIP data applied for

PREFACE

There is currently great interest in the process of diffusion bonding. The main thrust has been in the joining of advanced materials such as superplastic alloys, metal matrix composites and ceramics and, most importantly, to introduce the process into mass-production operations. Diffusion bonding has also led to reduced manufacturing costs and weight savings in conventional materials and developments in hot isostatic pressing have allowed greater design flexibility.

Since the first conference on Diffusion Bonding, held at Cranfield in 1987, considerable advances have been made and it was therefore considered appropriate to organise the Second International Conference on Diffusion Bonding which was held at Cranfield Institute of Technology on 28 and 29 March 1990. The meeting provided a forum for the presentation and discussion of recent developments in Diffusion Bonding and was divided into four main subject areas: steel bonding and quality control, diffusion bonding of aluminium alloys, bonding of high temperature materials and general applications. This structure is retained in the proceedings.

DAVID STEPHENSON

CONTENTS

Session 4: General Applications
(*Chair:* R. M. CRISPIN, *AEA Harwell Laboratory, UK*)

DIFFUSION BONDING – AN OVERVIEW

S B Dunkerton
The Welding Institute
Abington Hall
Abington
Cambridge   CB1 6AL
UK

ABSTRACT

Diffusion bonding is a microdeformation solid phase process finding application in niche areas. The mechanisms of bonding are generally understood, and data on modelling is available although limited to simple metal systems.

Application areas range from electronics and sensors to the aerospace and nuclear industries, and these applications are expected to continue and develop. An extension of these applications will result from developments in HIP bonding where the unit costs can be reduced for bulk production, and more complex geometries can be bonded.

Another driving force to extend the use of diffusion bonding, is the increasing development of new and advanced materials. Here, fusion processes are not generally applicable and diffusion bonding is one process offering potential for joints in materials such as metal matrix composites and ceramics.

This paper reviews the above applications and on-going developments for diffusion bonding.

INTRODUCTION

Of the modern joining techniques used in engineering today, solid phase processes probably have the longest history and a wide range of processes are now classified under the generic term of 'solid phase'. These processes vary dependent on the times, pressures and temperatures used and the methods of applying heat. At one extreme, cold pressure welding requires extensive deformation but no significant heating and is greatly restricted to the number of metals that can be joined (ie ductile fcc materials). Other processes include friction welding, magnetically impelled arc butt (MIAB) welding, explosive welding, leading to the other extreme of diffusion bonding. The latter process is characterised by its ability to join materials with minimal deformation and, in like materials, the absence of any identifiable bond line. It also has the attractive capability of joining a wide range of materials in both like and dissimilar combinations. These prime advantages are the key reasons for the process being used today in a wide range of industries extending from the electronics and nuclear field to engineering and aerospace components.

Diffusion bonding itself can be categorised into a number of variants, dependent on the form of pressurisation, the use of interlayers and the formation or not of a liquid phase. Each finds specific applications for the range of materials and geometries that need to be joined.

This paper will first review the process mechanism and range of diffusion bonding processes available, and will then provide a summary of where the process has found application to date and what developments are ongoing to move the process into new application areas.

PROCESS MECHANISM

In its simplest form, diffusion bonding involves holding pre-machined components under load at an elevated temperature whilst in a protective atmosphere. The loads used are usually below those which would cause macro-deformation of the parent material(s) and temperatures of 0.5-0.8Tm (where Tm = melting point in K) are employed. Times at temperature can extend to 60min and beyond but this depends upon the materials being bonded, the joint properties required and the remaining bonding parameters. Although the majority of bonding operations are performed in vacuum or an inert gas atmosphere, certain bonds have been produced in air[1].
An examination of the proposed sequence of stages in diffusion bonding (Fig. 1) emphasises the importance of the original surface finish. To form a bond it is necessary for the two metal surfaces to come into atomic contact and hence microasperities and surface contaminants must be removed from the bonding faces during bonding. Various models have been developed to provide an understanding of the mechanisms involved in forming a bond, with all being based on Cline's initial proposal[2] of a two stage mechanism. Firstly, the applied load causes plastic deformation of surface asperities reducing interfacial voids. Bond development then continues by diffusion controlled mechanisms including grain boundary diffusion and power law creep. A detailed review of existing models has been made by Wallach and Hill[3] which concludes that good agreement has been found between model and experiment for single phase metallic alloys. However, further work was identified particularly to include the effects of surface contaminants and to extend the modelling to other alloy systems and to the bonding of dissimilar materials.

PROCESS VARIANTS

Solid Phase Diffusion Bonding

Bonding in the solid phase is mainly carried out in vacuum or other protective atmosphere, with heat being applied by radiant, induction, direct or indirect resistance heating. Pressure can be applied uniaxially or isostatically. In the former case, a low pressure (3-10 MPa) is used to prevent macrodeformation of the parts (ie no more than a few percent). This form of the process therefore requires a good surface finish on the mating surfaces as the contribution to bonding provided by plastic yielding is restricted. Typically surface finishes of better than 0.4μm RA have been recommended[4] and in addition the surfaces should be as clean as practical to minimise surface contamination.

In hot isostatic pressing, much higher pressures are possible (100-200 MPa) and therefore surface finishes are not so critical, finishes of 0.8μm Ra and greater have been reported[5][6]. A further advantage of this process, is that the uniform gas pressurisation allows complex geometries to be bonded as against the generally simple butt joints possible with uniaxial pressurisation.

Where difficult materials need to be joined in the solid phase (and in particular metal to ceramic joints), it is possible to introduce single or multiple interlayers of other materials to aid the bonding process and to modify post-bond stress distributions.

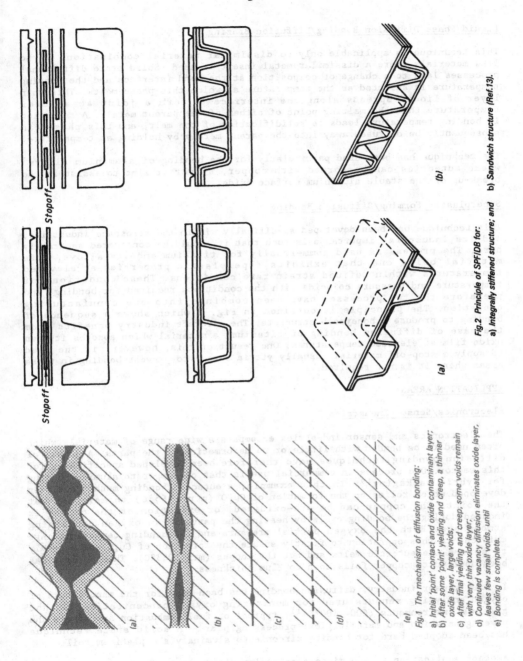

Fig.1 The mechanism of diffusion bonding:

a) Initial 'point' contact and oxide contaminant layer;
b) After some 'point' yielding and creep, a thinner oxide layer, large voids;
c) After final yielding and creep, some voids remain with very thin oxide layer;
d) Continued vacancy diffusion eliminates oxide layer, leaves few small voids, until
e) Bonding is complete.

Fig.2 Principle of SPF/DB for:
a) Integrally stiffened structure; and   b) Sandwich structure (Ref.13).

Liquid Phase Diffusion Bonding/Diffusion Brazing

This technique is applicable only to dissimilar material combinations or to like materials where a dissimilar metal insert is used. Solid state diffusional processes lead to a change of composition at the bond interface and the bonding temperature is selected as the temperature at which this phase melts. This thin layer of liquid spreads along the interface to form a joint at a lower temperature than the melting point of either of the parent metals. A reduction in bonding temperature leads to solidification of the melt, and this phase can subsequently be diffused away into the parent metals by holding at temperature.

The technique has been used particularly for the bonding of aluminium alloys[7] where eutectics can be formed with copper, silver or zinc to assist in the break-up of the stable aluminium surface oxide.

Superplastic Forming/Diffusion Bonding

This technique has been developed specifically within the aerospace industries, and its industrial importance is such that it should be considered separately here. The process is used commercially for titanium and its alloys, this material being one that exhibits superplastic properties at elevated temperatures within defined strain rate conditions. These conditions of temperature and pressure coincide with the conditions required for bonding, and therefore the two processes have been combined into one manufacturing operation. The principle is outlined in Fig. 2 which shows a sequence of bonding to produce a honeycomb structure. The aircraft industry benefits from the ease of diffusion bonding of titanium, a material which absorbs its own oxide film at elevated temperatures. One result of this, however, is the need to apply a stop-off material (usually yttria based) to prevent bonding in those areas where it is not required.

APPLICATION AREAS

Electronics/Sensor Industries

The electronics and sensor industries encompass a wide range of materials which often need to be bonded with little or no deformation of the parts. A number of diffusion bonding techniques have therefore been developed specifically for this sector. One process in commercial use is that of copper to alumina bonding for hybrid packaging[10]. In this example, a eutectic bonding method has been developed which relies on the formation of Cu_2O (m.p 1065°C) to melt and wet the joint. The copper can be pre-oxidised, or oxidation of the copper is induced during the bonding cycle by heating the parts in an oxygen containing atmosphere. Both the oxygen partial pressure and the bonding temperature are critical in this operation to firstly ensure the formation of Cu_2O and secondly to ensure the eutectic melts and not the copper (m.p 1083°C). This process has been applied to copper foils down to 25μm thickness.

In the sensor industry, diffusion bonding has been used for the manufacture of oxygen analysing sensors used for monitoring oxygen concentrations in hot gaseous environments (600-1400°C)[11], typical of fuel combustion systems in the power generation and metallurgical processing plant. A solid state technique has been adopted here for bonding zirconia to alumina via a platinum foil.

Another application in the micro-electronics field, is in the bonding of power device heat sinks[12]. Here, copper is required to be bonded to a berryllia package, and previously the parts would be brazed at temperatures of 800°C. However, the strains induced by the thermal cycling during brazing are sufficient to cause cracking of the ceramic. A low temperature bonding cycle was therefore required, and this was achieved by using interlayers between the

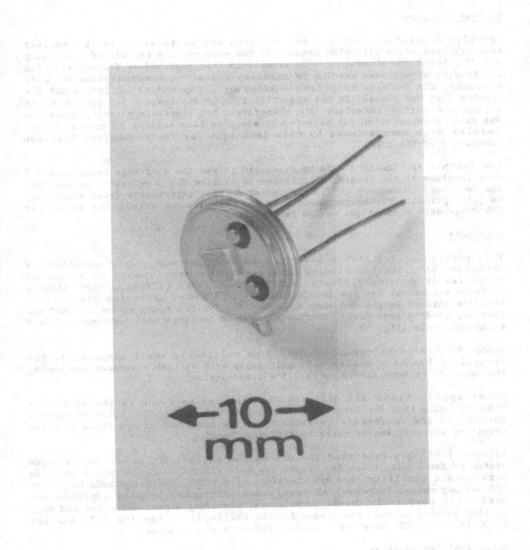

**Fig. 3   Small BeO chip diffusion bonded to header assembly – power device
heat sink.**

two materials of either gold or silver. A typical component produced in this way is shown in Fig. 3.

Nuclear Industry

Specific dissimilar material combinations are of interest to the nuclear industry, and often diffusion bonding is the only process capable of fulfilling all the joint requirements. One example is that reported by Yiasemides[5], for the bonding of depleted uranium to zircaloy-2 for the encapsulation of fuel elements. The modules comprised a zircaloy-2 cup and cover into which the uranium disc was placed. It was essential in this application for good bonding across the entire interface, and therefore a hot isostatic pressing operation was used. Encapsulation was affected by electron beam welding in vacuum. Target modules were manufactured by this technique for the Rutherford Appleton Laboratory of the SERC.

Two further applications — to be discussed in session 4 of this conference [6,7] have involved 1) the bonding of titanium to alumina for accelerator modules for the Daresbury Laboratory and 2) the use of ductile interlayers (pure aluminium) to join optically transparent materials and ceramics to metals for seals for UHV diagnostic windows and vacuum feedthroughs.

Aerospace

This particular industrial sector is one which has most widely exploited the technique of diffusion bonding because of the development of combined superplastic forming/diffusion bonding technology (SPF/DB). Many titanium airframe structures are now manufactured by this route, providing significant benefits through weight and cost savings[13][14]. Typical examples include hot air nozzles, landing gear doors, intricately shaped housings keel sections and heat exchanger ducts (Fig. 4).

Since the first development of SPF/DB on relatively small components, the technology has been scaled-up considerably with British Aerospace now having the capacity to bond sheets up to 2.5 x 1.8m section.

Other applications for diffusion bonding can be found in the aerospace industry, this time for aeroengine components. One application to be discussed further in the conference (session 4) is the novel use of pre-forms to allow repair of aircraft engine parts by diffusion bonding [15].

Fitzpatrick[16] has described the use of the process for manufacturing a new design of fan blade. These fan blades are made without clappers, which provide aerodynamic stability, and are therefore of a wider design and made hollow to off-set any weight increase. An 'activated' diffusion bonding approach was used, with copper and nickel interlayers, providing a cost effective and high quality joining method. Fan blades for the RB211-535 E4 (Boeing 757) and IAE V2500 (Airbus A320) have been manufactured with this process.

Other Application Areas

Diffusion bonding is being applied or developed for other industrial sectors, four others of which are worthy of mention for either their cheap manufacturing route or novelty.

Within the transport industries, materials and manufacturing processes have to be highly cost effective and it is therefore interesting to note that a diffusion bonding technique is being applied to the manufacture of disc-brakes, Fig. 5[17]. Here the disc pad material is a commercial mix of powders which is pre-placed on the metal disc and cold pressed. The discs are then stacked in a furnace and heated, during which time the brake pads are diffusion bonded to the disc.

Fig. 4   SPF/DB of titanium heat exchanger duct
          (Courtesy of British Aerospace plc).

Fig. 5   Disc brake - pad diffusion bonded to disc.

Diffusion bonding is being investigated as a route for valve manufacture, specifically in the hardfacing of small bore valves[18] where restricted access makes conventional hardfacing operations difficult. A hot isostatic pressing route is being adopted, with nickel and cobalt hardfacing alloys being bonded to steel. Work to date has shown that good quality metallurgical bonds are achieved, and the HIP approach enables angled interfaces to be bonded successfully, Fig. 6.

Also on valves, diffusion bonding is reported to be used for the hardfacing of exhaust valves in Japan[19]. In this application, hard wearing inserts of silicon carbide or silicon nitride are joined to Nimonic 80A, via compliant interlayers, typically of nickel and copper, Fig. 7.

A further application area lies in the field of heat exchangers, where miniaturisation is a major drive to increase efficiency and provide significant cost benefits. A new style of heat exchanger is now available commercially[20], and is known as the printed circuit heat exchanger. This comprises a series of flat metal plates chemically milled to provide fluid flow passages, which are diffusion bonded together to form blocks with precisely sized, shaped, routed and positioned passages. These are in turn welded to form the heat exchanger cores. Because no other materials are used in the bonding process, the exchangers can be used for a wide range of fluid types.

FUTURE DEVELOPMENTS

Clear indication of where diffusion bonding will move to in the 1990's is given in other papers in this conference. Considerable attention is being directed towards the bonding of superplastic aluminium alloys, as further weight and cost savings could be achieved within the aerospace industries if the SPF/DB technology could be transferred from titanium to aluminium. However, there are obvious difficulties related to the stable and tenacious oxide layer typical of all aluminium alloys. Work is therefore directed towards methods of overcoming this bonding problem, and also to the scaling-up of any new bonding techniques.

Another area where diffusion bonding will continue to receive much interest is in the bonding of ceramics to metals. A number of examples where the process is already being used for these dissimilar material combinations have already been stated. However, more demanding applications are expected particularly in engine parts, ranging from automotive to industrial and aeroengine components. Here, joints will be required that can tolerate much more severe operating conditions than previously covered. Both diffusion bonding and active metal brazing provide possible solutions to these joining difficulties, and an assessment of these bonding techniques has been made by Nicholas and Mortimer[21]. Work will also continue on the use of diffusion bonding for other advanced materials such as metal matrix composites and intermetallics, again with prime interest from the aerospace industries.

Away from aerospace applications, it is expected that HIP bonding will provide more cost effective manufacturing routes for mass-production parts, and here it is important for designers to be aware of the material combinations and designs that can be accommodated by this technique.

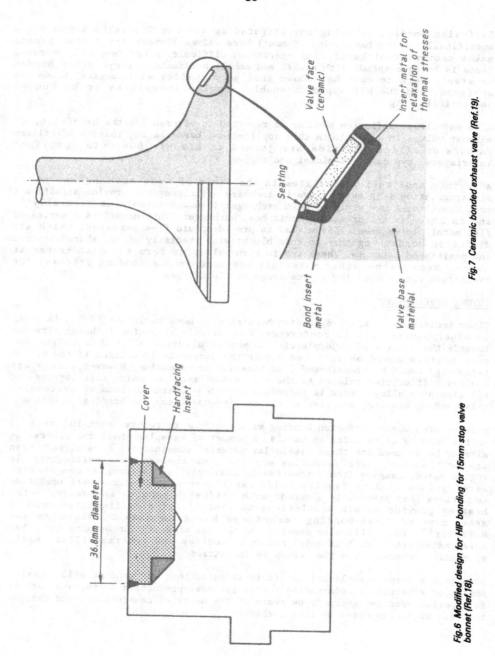

Fig. 7 Ceramic bonded exhaust valve (Ref.19).

Fig. 6 Modified design for HIP bonding for 15mm stop valve bonnet (Ref.18).

SUMMARY

A range of techniques are now available for diffusion bonding, offering scope for the joining of many new materials and configurations. This has led to increased attention being paid to the process, with new applications being developed on a regular basis. Although the greatest use of the process has been in the aerospace industry, there is increasing use in the electronics and automotive industry with the Japanese claiming success in the bonding of ceramics to metals for exhaust valves. Applications are also numerous in the USSR, with a report from 1981 stating that over 960 vacuum bonding machines are in operation in that country and are showing a good economic return[22].

There is therefore still considerable scope for the process and further efforts are expected to examine new techniques for the newer materials and to make the process more cost effective.

REFERENCES

1. Gubarev V V, Kazakov Yu V and Finkelstein M L, 'Diffusion Bonding in Air' Welding Production 1976 23 (7) pp 57–58.

2. Cline C L, Welding Journal 1966 45 pp 481–489.

3. Wallach E R and Hill A, 'Modelling of Diffusion bonding paper presented at Int. Conf on Diffusion Bonding Cranfield, England 7–8 July 1987.

4. Bartle P M, 'Diffusion Bonding: A Look to the Future', Welding Journal 1975 54 (11) pp 779–804.

5. Yiasemides G P, 'Diffusion Bonding using Hot Isostatic Pressing', Paper presented at Int. Conf. on Diffusion Bonding, Cranfield, England, 7–8 July 1987.

6. Private communication with Infutec Ltd.

7. Fulmer Research Institute Ltd, 'Diffusion Bonding of Aluminium Alloy Parts', UK Patent Spec. 1 485 051, 1974.

8. Joy T, 'The Application of Diffusion Bonding Technology to the Construction of an Electrostatic Particle Accelerator Tube', Paper presented at 2nd Int. Conf. on Diffusion Bonding, Cranfield, England 28–29 March 1990.

9. Milton J H and Govier R P, 'The Practical Application of Ductile Interlayer Diffusion Bonding', paper presented at 2nd Int. Conf. on Diffusion Bonding, Cranfield, England 28–29 March 1990.

10. Burgess J F etc, 'Direct Bonding of Metals to Ceramics for Electronic Applications', Book Advances in Joining Technology.

11. Bailey F P and Burbidge W E, 'Solid State Metal–Ceramic Reaction Bonding', Book Surfaces and Interfaces in Ceramic and Ceramic–Metal System Ed J Park/A Evans. Plenum Publishing Corporation 1981.

12. Stockham N R and Elliot S, 'Diffusion Bonding of Power Device Heat Sinks' Welding Institute Research Bulletin, May 1981 pp 128–131.

13. Hamilton C H and Stacher G, 'Recent Developments in Titanium Superplastic Forming/Diffusion Bonding', Paper presented at 28th National SAMPE Symposium April 12-14 1983.

14. Bottomley I and Ginty B, 'The Development of DB/SPF of Titanium for Military Applications' Paper presented at 2nd Int. Conf. on Diffusion Bonding, Cranfield, England, 28-29 March 1990.

15. Huchin J P and Barbot J P, 'Preform Diffusion Bonding in Aircraft Engine Repair', Paper presented at 2nd Int. Conf. on Diffusion Bonding, Cranfield, England 28-29 March 1999.

16. Fitzpatrick G A, 'Diffusion Bonding Titanium Structures for Aeroengine Components', Paper presented at Int. Conf. on Diffusion Bonding, Cranfield, England, 7-8 July 1987.

17. Private communication with T & N Technology.

18. McLeish J A, 'Small Bore Valve Hardfacing by Hot Isostatic Pressing' Paper presented at IMechE Conference (C373/012) 1989, pp 65-72.

19. Tech Alert article Professional Engineering July 1988, p65.

20. Johnston T, 'Miniaturised Heat Exchangers for Chemcial Processing', The Chemical Engineer, Dec 1986, pp 36-38.

21. Nicholas M G and Mortimer D A, 'Ceramic/Metal Joining for Structural Applications' Materials Science and Technology Vol 1, Sept 1985 pp 657-665.

22. Book: 'Diffusion Bonding of Materials' Ed. N F Kazakov, Pergeman Press ISBN 0-08-032550-5, 1985.

AMBIENT-TEMPERATURE CREEP FAILURE OF
SILVER-INTERLAYER DIFFUSION BONDS BETWEEN STEEL

G. A. Henshall [1], M. E. Kassner [2] and R. S. Rosen [1]

1 Chemistry and Materials Science Department
Lawrence Livermore National Laboratory
P. O. Box 808, Livermore, CA 94550 USA

2 Department of Mechanical Engineering
Oregon State University
Corvallis, OR 97331 USA

ABSTRACT

Silver-interlayer diffusion bonds have been fabricated using planar-magnetron sputtering. The bonds exhibit very high tensile strengths, despite the soft interlayer, because of the constraint provided by the base metal. However, these joints undergo delayed failure at relatively low tensile stresses at ambient temperatures, apparently by a ductile microvoid-coalescence mechanism at the bond interfaces. Two classes of delayed tensile failure were investigated. In the first case, the applied stress does not produce any plastic deformation in the base metal, and failure appears to be controlled by time-dependent plasticity within the silver interlayer as a result of the effective stress in the interlayer. The interlayer plasticity causes cavity nucleation and, eventually, interlinkage and failure. In the second case, time-dependent plasticity is observed in the base metals, and concomitant shear occurs within the softer silver under a high triaxial stress state. Here, the time-dependent plasticity of the base metal accelerates plasticity and failure in the interlayer. These models were substantiated by careful analyses of the stress and temperature-dependence of the rupture times, finite-element analysis of the stress state within the interlayer and microscopy of the interfaces loaded to various fractions of the expected rupture times. The findings reported here are applicable to bonds in which the interlayers are prepared by processes other than physical vapor-deposition.

1. INTRODUCTION

It has long been known that thin (e.g., 1 μm - 1 mm) interlayer bonds between higher strength base materials may have high ultimate tensile or rupture strengths despite the relatively low strength of the filler metal [1]. The high strength of the joint is due to the mechanical constraint provided by the stronger base metals which restricts transverse contraction of the interlayer. The constraint produces a triaxial state of stress and reduces the effective stress, thus reducing the tendency for the interlayer to plastically deform [1-8]. Plasticity of the base metal reduces the constraint and decreases the strength of the bond [8].

Recent work by the authors [9,10] has verified an earlier observation [11] of delayed or time-dependent tensile failure of solid-state interlayer bonds (of various composition) at ambient and elevated temperatures at stresses substantially less than the ultimate tensile strength, UTS. In those studies the bonds were prepared by the hot-hollow-cathode vapor-deposition process [9,10] and by interlayer foils [11]. The preliminary results [9,10] indicated that the ambient temperature creep of the base metals (e.g. to plastic strains of about 0.01 or less) relieves the constraint and the rupture life may be, correspondingly, degraded. That is, base-metal creep induces concomitant shear within the interlayer under a state of high triaxial stress which causes ductile failure within the interlayer. Therefore, the creep rate of the base metal controls the time-to-failure.

The purpose of this work was twofold. First, the validity of the "base-metal-accelerated" delayed-failure theory for bonds utilizing plastic base metals was checked. Creep-rupture tests were performed on diffusion-bonded specimens using silver interlayers deposited by planar-magnetron sputtering (PMS), a physical vapor-deposition process. The PMS process was preferred because of the superior quality and strength of the bond [12] and because this modern low-temperature joining process is increasingly utilized for joining ceramic and composite materials. Bonded specimens were loaded to various tensile stresses below the UTS and the creep rates of the base metals and the silver interlayer were measured. There should be some correspondence between these creep rates if a base-metal-control explanation of failure is viable. The role of plastic base metals in the fracture process was further investigated by conducting tensile-rupture tests of diffusion bonds made with stainless steel base metals of different yield strengths, and therefore different creep rates. The base-metal control theory predicts that lower base-metal creep rates, and lower corresponding creep rates within the interlayer, lead to longer times-to-rupture. The second purpose was to determine whether delayed failure occurs in interlayer bonds between elastic base metals, which do not creep over the range of applied stresses. This question is particularly relevant since many alloys, ceramics and composites fall within this category. Again, ambient and near-ambient temperature creep-rupture tests were performed at a variety of stresses below the UTS of the bond. Optical and electron microscopy, finite-element method (FEM) stress analysis and analyses of the temperature and stress sensitivity of the failure times were used to determine the failure mechanism.

2. EXPERIMENTAL PROCEDURES

Silver-interlayer diffusion bonds were fabricated using three kinds of base metals: maraging steel (0.002 plastic-strain offset yield stress, $\sigma_y.^{002}$, of about 1515 MPa), vacuum annealed Type 304 stainless steel ($\sigma_y.^{002} \simeq 220$ MPa), and cold-worked 304 stainless steel ($\sigma_y.^{002} \simeq 360$ MPa). The maraging steel deforms only elastically over the range of applied stress (less than 760 MPa). However, ambient-temperature creep is observed in the stainless steels at these stresses, even when significantly below the yield stresses. The base-metal blanks were machined into right circular cylinders, 15.3 mm in diameter and 38.8 mm in length. The surfaces of the ends to be coated of some maraging specimens were machined flat to 2 μm with a surface roughness of 0.1 μm arithmetic average. Other specimens were lapped (ground) flat using 1-μm diamond paste to 0.15 μm and to a surface roughness of 0.03 μm.

150-μm-thick silver-interlayer bonds were fabricated by PMS and hot isostatic pressing at 400 °C and 207 MPa, as described elsewhere [12]. The deposited silver layer (prior to bonding) has been confirmed by TEM to consist of columnar grains with an average diameter of about 0.25 μm. The column axes are essentially perpendicular to the base-metal surface and nearly coincident with the <111> crystallographic direction. The grains contain numerous growth twins, typically 10-15 nm in thickness. Recrystallization of most (50%-75%) of this structure occurs during the bonding step. A serrated, or wavy, high angle boundary generally remains, however, within the vicinity of the original silver surfaces. Typically, the recrystallized grains are greater than 1 mm long in the plane of the bond and encompass virtually the entire thickness of the original coating, i.e. 75 μm. The recrystallized grains contain numerous annealing twins. Figure 1 gives optical micrographs at two magnifications of silver-interlayer diffusion bonds prepared using the above process. Chemical (SIMS) analysis of the bonded interlayer did not reveal the presence of any significant quantity of impurities.

The mechanical behavior of the bonded interlayer was determined using torsion (low mechanical constraint) tests. The 0.1% offset effective (von Mises) yield stress was measured to be about 95 MPa whereas the 0.2% offset effective yield stress was found to be about 115 MPa, indicating both a high yield strength and hardening rate compared to annealed bulk-polycrystalline-silver [13]. The higher flow stresses can be rationalized, at least partially, by incomplete recrystallization and a refined substructure in the recrystallized grains.

Tensile creep-tests were performed at ambient temperature and at 72 °C using dead-weight type creep-rupture testing machines. Heating was accomplished by resistance furnaces that controlled the temperature within ±1 °C as measured by a thermocouple spot-welded to the specimen surface. Plastic strains were measured on unloaded samples by measuring specimen diameters using an optical comparator. Tests were performed in air of 30-40% relative-humidity, and the effects of any stress-corrosion cracking were not relevant [14,15].

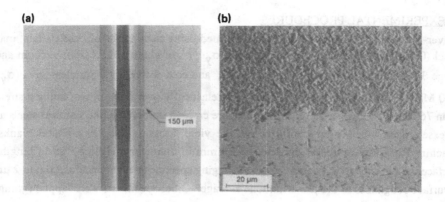

Fig. 1   (a) and (b) Optical micrographs of a silver-interlayer diffusion weld between stainless steel. The interlayers are 150 μm in thickness.

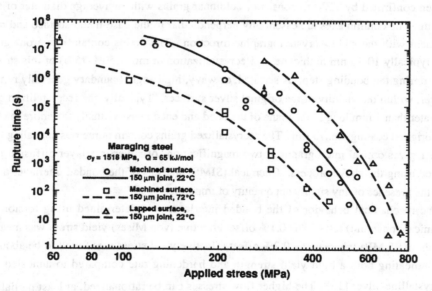

Fig. 2   The rupture-time versus applied stress for silver-aided diffusion bonds between maraging steel (elastic) base metals at ambient temperature and 72 °C.

3. RESULTS AND DISCUSSION

3.1 Elastic Base Metals

Delayed failure of the maraging-steel joints is clearly observed, as shown in Fig. 2. As the applied stress decreases, the time-to-rupture, t_r, increases. Further, delayed failure is observed at stresses less than 20% of the UTS (approx. 700 MPa). Tests were performed at ambient temperature (circles) and 72 °C (squares). Ambient temperature tests on maraging specimens for which the surfaces were lapped, rather than machined, prior to coating are indicated by triangles. At a given applied stress, lapped specimens fail at times approximately 50 times longer than those with machined base-metal surfaces. Ambient-temperature rupture-times are nearly 50 times longer than tests at 72 °C. Failure occurs at the center-plane of the interlayer or near the base-metal/interlayer interfaces after relatively small plastic strains. The fracture surfaces show strong evidence of ductile microvoid-coalescence at all stress levels [16,17].

Delayed failure of interlayer bonds between elastic base metals does not appear to be caused by environmentally-induced embrittlement [16]. Diffusive cavity-growth [18,19] does not appear tenable, since the equilibrium vacancy concentration and diffusivity of silver at ambient temperature are too low [20] to rationalize the short failure-times at higher stresses. Instead, we believe that delayed failure occurs by a rate-dependent mechanical process, such as creep of the silver interlayer resulting from the effective stress within the interlayer. The time-dependent plasticity can nucleate cavities that eventually lead to interlinkage and failure. Careful strain measurements indicate that the "macroscopic" plastic strain-to-failure in the silver interlayer is about 0.002 at higher stresses. The, albeit small, plastic strain could cause dislocation pile-ups at the three principal interfaces (as well as some other locations). A small number of dislocations in a pile-up could be sufficient to concentrate the stress at the interfaces and nucleate a small cavity or crack, particularly in the presence of large hydrostatic tensile stresses.

Cavity interlinkage, which probably leads to the catastrophic ductile delayed failure, may occur once a critical concentration (which would be a function of the applied load) of nuclei or cavities is attained at the interface(s). The concentration of interfacial cavities is apparently time-dependent. The nucleation, growth and/or interlinkage rate is expected to be a function of the creep rate of the silver at locations in the vicinity of the interface. Finite-element-method (FEM) stress analysis was performed on the 150-μm interlayer bonds [21] using the NIKE2D code [22,23]. These results are shown in Fig. 3, where the ambient-temperature "machined" data of Fig. 2 are plotted as a function of the effective (von Mises) stress at the center plane of the interlayer and the applied stress. The analysis revealed that the effective stress within the vicinity of the silver-silver (or other) interfaces is above the interlayer 0.01% offset yield stress (approx. 40 MPa) at all the applied loads for which delayed failure is observed. Therefore, nucleation of cavities associated with creep could occur at any of the applied stresses at which delayed failure is observed.

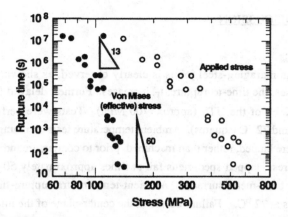

Fig. 3 The rupture time versus applied and effective stress within the interlayer for diffusion bonds between (machined) maraging steel at ambient temperature.

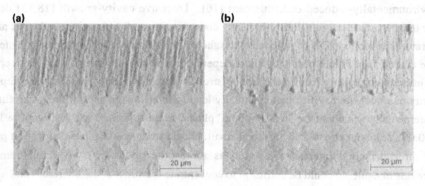

Fig. 4 Optical micrographs of the silver/silver interface in machined maraging steel specimens loaded to (a) 0%, and (b) 50% of the expected rupture time at a stress of 124 MPa .

The silver-plasticity explanation for delayed failure is consistent with the temperature dependence of t_r. The activation energy, Q, for creep of silver at ambient and near-ambient temperatures falls within the range of 50-71 kJ/mole for various substructures [13,24]. For the delayed failure of silver-interlayer diffusion bonds using maraging steel, Q is estimated from the data in Fig. 2 to be 65 kJ/mole [16], which falls within the range for silver plasticity.

To help verify the proposed theory to explain delayed-failure, the silver/silver and base-metal/silver interfaces were examined at various fractions of the creep-life. If delayed failure is the result of silver creep under high triaxial stresses that leads to void nucleation, growth and interlinkage, then cavities should be increasingly evident at or very near the interfaces with an increasing fraction of the expected rupture-time, $t_{r,ex}$. Therefore, specimens were loaded at different stresses for various fractions of $t_{r,ex}$, unloaded and examined for cavities. Using optical microscopy, small cavities at the three interfaces were frequently observed in specimens loaded to 10% or more of $t_{r,ex}$. The number of cavities present increased with increasing fraction of $t_{r,ex}$. Figure 4 presents optical micrographs of bonded specimens utilizing machined maraging steel that were (a) as-bonded (0% $t_{r,ex}$) and (b) loaded at 124 MPa for 50% of $t_{r,ex}$. Consistent with the proposed explanation for delayed failure, numerous cavities are evident in Fig. 4b at the silver/silver interface, as well as at grain boundaries in non-recrystallized regions.

Although the arguments given above support the silver-plasticity theory for delayed failure, some questions remain. For example, if creep is associated with the rate-controlling process for failure, then the stress sensitivity of t_r should be related to the stress exponent for plasticity of silver. In general, the stress exponent will be between the "constant-structure" stress exponent, N, and the "steady-state" stress exponent, n [13,16]. For silver deformed at ambient temperature N is about 200, whereas n is between 10 and 40 [13,24]. Torsion tests on the interlayer silver of this study showed that steady state is achieved after strains between 0.05 and 0.10. Therefore, for the silver relevant to this study, the apparent stress exponent should be about 200 as the plastic strain approaches zero [13], and between 10 and 40 for strains near 0.05 to 0.10 [24]. The stress exponent for failure of the silver-interlayer bonds between maraging steel is given by the slope of the t_r vs effective stress curve shown in Fig. 3. The slope varies from about 60 at high stresses to between 10 and 15 at low stresses. These values appear roughly consistent with the established steady-state stress exponent of silver but not with the constant-structure exponent. Therefore, consistency with the silver-plasticity theory is realized provided that the plastic strain accumulated to the onset of catastrophic ductile failure is near 0.05. As mentioned earlier, the measured "macroscopic" plastic strains over the interlayer thickness at the higher applied stress were only about 0.002 (perhaps even smaller at lower stresses), which is less than that which would appear to bring consistency. However, if the plastic deformation in the vicinity of the interfaces is higher than the macroscopic strain (e.g., a few percent, which we believe is possible), consistency is realized.

It is also difficult to explain the apparent cavity growth. Conventional and stereoscopic SEM, as well as thin foil TEM, have confirmed that the cavities like those observed in Fig. 4 have diameters roughly between 0.2 and 1 μm, with several small cavities frequently clustering to form the larger voids. If dislocation pile-ups are responsible for cavity nucleation, then the nuclei size would be on the order of a nm or so. An increase of 2 or 3 orders of magnitude in size cannot be readily rationalized by vacancy accumulation. Furthermore, this increase is not easily explained by "uniform" plastic deformation of the interlayer matrix. The cavity sizes could be rationalized by a sufficient strain level in the vicinity of the interfaces through the operation of a nuclei-interlinkage model [16]. An experimental investigation on this point is underway.

3.2. Plastic Base Metals

Figure 5 shows the stress-rupture behavior of 150-μm thick interlayer bonds that utilize two types of 304 stainless steel base metals: vacuum-annealed (squares) and cold-worked (triangles). The hollow symbols refer to ambient-temperature tests and the shaded symbols refer to 72 °C tests. All but two of the data refer to specimens that were machined prior to coating. The two lapped (triangles with dots) cold-worked specimens have longer rupture times, as was the case with the maraging specimens. Again, as the applied stress decreases, t_r substantially increases. The bend in the curve for specimens utilizing cold-worked stainless steel will be explained in Section 3.3. An important observation is that, for an applied stress that is common to both sets of stainless-steel data (e.g., 250 MPa), t_r for the cold-worked specimens is about a factor of 10^4 higher than for specimens that utilize the weaker (and less creep-resistant) annealed 304 stainless steel. The processing steps and geometry are identical for both kinds of specimens, so the dramatic difference of the rupture-times must be a consequence of the mechanical behavior of the __base__ metals. This confirms some sort of "base-metal acceleration" theory to rationalize the difference in the delayed-failure times.

Figure 6 shows the plastic strains in the base metal and the silver interlayer as a function of time for specimens utilizing annealed (a) and cold-worked (b) stainless steel. The base metal strains were measured near (within 50 μm) and away from (over 5 mm) the interlayer. In both cases, the plastic strain in the stainless steel increases with time[†]. The strain within the silver interlayer correspondingly increases. These results support the theory that creep in the base metal induces time-dependent plasticity in the silver interlayer. Recent FEM analyses [21] also show that base-metal creep produces concomitant shear within the soft silver interlayer under a state of high triaxial stress. The interlayer plasticity causes cavitation and failure just as in the

---

[†] The annealed 304 stainless steel base metal at the interface creeps less than in the gage section far from the interface. This behavior is caused by machining damage of the base-metal surface that is eventually coated with silver [17].

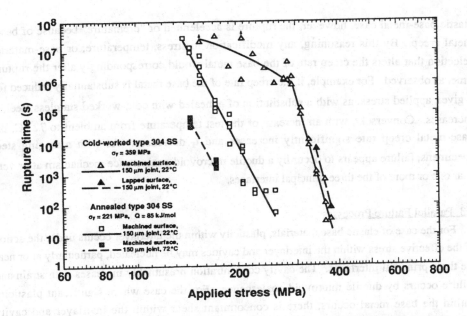

Fig. 5   The rupture time versus applied stress for silver-aided diffusion bonds between
         annealed and cold-worked stainless steel at ambient temperature and 72 °C. The base
         metals deform plastically at most of these applied stresses.

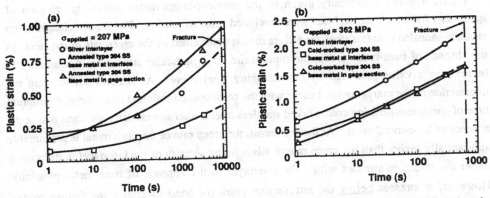

Fig. 6   The plastic strains in the silver interlayer and the base metal near (within 50 μm) and
         away (over 5 mm) from the interlayer versus time for bonded specimens using (a)
         annealed and (b) cold-worked stainless steel.

elastic base-metal case, however, the rupture is accelerated or "premature" because of base-metal creep. By this reasoning, any modification in stress, temperature, or base-material selection that alters the creep rate of the base metal would correspondingly alter the rupture time, as observed. For example, if the creep rate of the base metal is substantially reduced for a given applied stress, as with a substitution of annealed with cold-worked stainless steel, t_r increases. Conversely, with an increase of the test temperature from ambient to 72 °C, the base-metal creep rate significantly increases and t_r decreases. As with maraging steel specimens, failure appears to occur by a ductile microvoid-coalescence mechanism at or very near one or more of the three principal interfaces.

3.3 Parallel Failure Processes

For the case of elastic base materials, plasticity within the interlayer occurs under the action of the effective stress within the interlayer and cavities may be nucleated, particularly at or near the three principal interfaces. The cavity concentration presumably increases with strain and failure occurs by ductile microvoid coalescence. For the case where significant plasticity within the base metal occurs, there is concomitant shear within the interlayer and cavity nucleation can occur more rapidly at the same applied load. These two processes operate simultaneously and the faster process determines the rupture time. This last point may rationalize the "bend" in the t_r vs applied stress plot for bond-specimens that utilize cold-worked stainless steel.

Figure 7 gives a summary graph of the ambient-temperature stress-rupture data of specimens for which the surfaces were machined prior to coating. For the specimens using vacuum-annealed stainless steel, the failure time is determined by the creep rate of the steel. In the absence of base-metal creep, the rupture time at a particular stress would dramatically increase to a value predicted by the maraging steel curve. At stresses higher than the intersection of the maraging steel curve with the cold-worked stainless steel curve, the rupture time of specimens utilizing cold-worked stainless steel is also substantially less than that in the absence of base-metal creep. At these stresses, the creep rate of the base metal is presumably substantially higher than the creep rate of silver in the vicinity of the interface(s), deforming under the effective stresses within the interlayer in the absence of base-metal plasticity. However, at stresses below the intersection point (or bend location), the failure control changes. In this regime, the base-metal creep rate is relatively low and presumably less than that of the silver deforming under the effective stress within the interlayer. Consequently, below the crossover stress, the applied stress vs t_r trends of specimens using cold-worked stainless steel are quite similar to those using maraging steel and a bend appears in the curve.

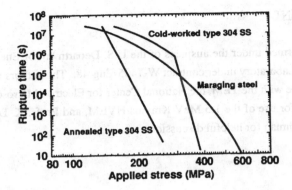

Fig. 7 Summary graph of the stress dependence of the rupture time for silver-interlayer bonds using annealed stainless, cold worked stainless, and maraging steel. All base metals were machined prior to coating.

4. CONCLUSIONS

Thin silver-interlayer diffusion bonds between maraging and type 304 stainless steel base metals were prepared using planar-magnetron sputtering. The maraging steel exhibits only elastic strain over the range of applied tensile stress, whereas the stainless steel exhibits plastic strain over most of the applied stress range. The following conclusions are based on experiments in which the bonded specimens were loaded in tension to various stresses below the ultimate tensile strength.

1. Delayed tensile-failure was observed for bonds between both elastic and plastic base metals. In the case of maraging steel (elastic) base metals, delayed failure occurred at stresses as low as 17% of the ultimate tensile strength of the bonds.

2. For bonds between maraging steel base metals, the time-to-failure is controlled by the creep rate of silver near the interfaces in the interlayer, which is determined by the effective stress within the interlayer.

3. Delayed failure may be accelerated by base-metal creep resulting from the effective stress in the base material. Plastic deformation of the base metal causes corresponding deformation in the interlayer, and cavities nucleate as with elastic base metals.

4. These findings are applicable to silver-interlayer bonds prepared by processes other than those utilizing physical vapor deposition (brazing, electroplating, solid foils etc.) and very possibly to other interlayer materials.

ACKNOWLEDGMENT

This work was performed under the auspices of the U.S. Department of Energy by Lawrence Livermore National Laboratory under contract W-7405-Eng-48. The authors wish to thank Mr. M. Wall for assistance with the TEM, the National Center for Electron Microscopy at Lawrence Berkely Laboratory for use of the 1.5 MeV Kraytos HVEM, and Profs. K. D. Challenger, W. D. Nix and J. C. Earthman for helpful discussions.

REFERENCES

1. E. Orowan, M.O.S. Armament Res. Dept. Rept., 1945, 16, 35.
2. N. Breds. and H. Schwartzbart, Welding J., 1956, 33, 610-s.
3. W. G. Moffatt and J. Wulff, Trans. AIME, 1957, 209, 442.
4. W. G. Moffatt and J. Wulff, J., Welding J., 1963, 42, 115-s.
5. N. Breds, Welding J., 1954, 33, 545-s.
6. R. Z. Shron and G. A. Bakshi, Welding Production, 1962, 9, 19.
7. H. J. Saxton, A. J. West, and C. R. Barrett, Metall. Trans., 1971, 2, 999.
8. A. J. West, H. J. Saxton, A. S. Tetelman and C. R. Barrett., Metall. Trans., 1971, 1, 1009.
9. R. S. Rosen, D. R. Walmsley and Z. A. Munir, Welding J., 1986, 65, 83-s.
10. J. W. Elmer, M. E. Kassner and R. S. Rosen, Welding J., 1988, 67, 157-s.
11. T. J. Moore and K. H. Holko, Welding J., 1970, 49, 395-s.
12. R. S. Rosen and M. E. Kassner, J. Vac. Sci. Tech. A, 1990 (in press).
13. M. E. Kassner, Metall. Trans., 1989, 20A, 2001-2010.
14. T. Takemoto and I. Okamoto, Welding. J., 63, 1984, 300.
15. A. T. Kuhn and R. M. Trimmer, Br. Corros. J., 1982, 17, 4.
16. M. E. Kassner, R. S. Rosen and G. A. Henshall, submitted to Metall. Trans., 1990.
17. R. S. Rosen, PhD dissertation, University of California, Davis, 1990.
18. A. C. F. Cocks and M. F. Ashby, Prog. Mater. Sci., 1982, 27, 189.
19. W. D. Nix, Mater. Sci. and Eng., 1988, A103, 103.
20. P. G. Shewmon, 'Diffusion in Solids', J. Williams, Jenks, OK, 1983.
21 G. A. Henshall, R. S. Rosen, M. E. Kassner and R. G. Whirley, submitted to Welding J., 1990.
22. J. O. Hallquist, Lawrence Livermore National Laboratory, Rept. UCRL-52678 Rev. 1, 1986 Livermore, CA.
23. G. L. Goudreau and J. O. Hallquist, J. Comp. Meths. Appl. Mechs. Eng., 1982, 30, 725.
24. R. W. Logan, R. Castro and A. K. Mukherjee, Scripta Metall., 1983, 17, 63.
25. H. J. Saxton, A. J. West, and C. R. Barrett, Metall. Trans., 1971, 2, 1019.

DIFFUSION BONDING BY HOT EXTRUSION OF INCOLOY 825 AND DUPLEX 2205
TO A LOW ALLOY STEEL

I. Gutiérrez and J.J. Urcola

CEIT(Centro de Estudios e Investigaciones Tecnicas de Guipúzcoa)
Paseo Manuel de Lardizábal, 15, SAN SEBASTIAN, Basque Country, Spain

J.M. Bilbao and L.M. Villar

TUBACEX S.A.

LLODIO, Alava, Basque Country, Spain.

AISI 4130 low alloy steel has been diffusion bonded to an Incoloy 825 and a Duplex 2205 stainless steel by an industrial hot extrusion process, the final product being a seamless clad tube with an internal lining of these corrosion resistant alloys. The microstructures of the as-extruded products have been analysed using optical metallography, SEM and STEM techniques. The interdiffusion of the different elements through the interface has been determined using EDS microanalysis both in SEM and STEM. For the combinations AISI 4130-Incoloy825 a region close to the original interface on the Incoloy side is observed, where a deformation substructure with subgrains, dislocations and an important amount of carbides $M_{23}C_6$ type are found. Different layers of austenite, martensite and ferrite-pearlite are observed on the steel side. In the case of the combinations AISI 4130-Duplex 2205 and close to the interface, a region with a low amount of ferrite with a big profussion of $M_{23}C_6$ carbides precipitated at the grain boundaries is observed, followed by regions with a higher amount of ferrite at grain boundaries to reach the original structure of the Duplex. The influence of several heat treatments consisting in quenching plus tempering in the region around the bonding have also been analysed.

INTRODUCTION

Surveys carried out by some oil companies have shown a clear trend at the near future for drilling wells at deeper depths. As well depth increases, the requirements of materials for tubing become more stringent. Due to the rise in temperature and pressure and because the tubings used have to sustain their own weight a high strength is required. An additional problem with deep oil and gas wells is the corrosion due to H_2S, HCl and CO_2.

Thus, the combination of these two factors: strength-corrosion resistance together with economical requirements have encouraged the development of bimetallic tubes, that is, a high strength low alloy steel with a thin metallurgically bonded, corrosion resistant clad alloy, produced in an economical way. These products could be also used in other applications like, pipe lines for oil transport, heat exchangers, in the chemical industry and cryogenic applications among others.

The present work describes the microstructures developed during diffusion bonding by hot industrial extrusion of inside linings of a Duplex 2205 stainless steel and an Incoloy 825 to an AISI 4130 low alloy steel

EXPERIMENTAL PROCEDURE

The bimetallic tubes were produced using 230mm AISI 4130 billets. These were perforated so that Duplex 2250 and Incoloy 825 bars could be alocated inside the holes and subsequently sealed following the procedure patented by TUBACEX S.A.(1). The assemblies were heated by low frequency induction heating to temperatures between 1170 and 1240ºC, pearced in a vertical 1200 Tn capacity hydraulic press. After reheating the pearced assemblies were extruded in a 3100 Tn capacity hydraulic press to 138 mm diameter tubes with a 10.5 mm total wall tickness. Finally they were hot rolled to 88.9 mm diameter tubes of 9.52 mm total wall thickness and air cooled. Metallographic specimen were cut from the tubes and prepared by conventional techniques to be observed optically and by SEM. Thin foils perforated at the interface for TEM observation were prepared using a combination of electropolishing and ion beam etching.

RESULTS AND DISCUSSION

AISI 4130-Incoloy 825. As-extruded.

Fig.1 shows an optical micrograph after an electrolitic etching using nital and exhibits a pearlite-bainite structure in the steel side.The decarburisation of the steel near to the bond is clearly apparent. It can be also observed an equiaxed structure exhibited by the Incoloy 825. Fig. 2 corresponds to a SEM micrograph of a specimen etched with nital.A ferrite zone- of around 20 μm size- located on the steel near the bond can be clearly appreciated, whereas the Incoloy shows some Ti-rich precipitates (black dots in the micrograph) in addition to some Cr-rich precipitates (dark grey in the micrograph). The size of this region with precipitates in the Incoloy is of around 15 μm. These regions with different microstructures on each of the materials are also clearly apparent in Fig. 1. The chemical analysis at and close to the interface - performed by EDS microanalysis- as a function of the distance from the interface is shown in Fig. 3. It clearly shows the interdiffusion of the different elements from the superalloy to the steel and the iron from the steel to the superalloy. The Cr seems to diffuse for longer distances than the rest of the elements and on the opposite the Ni shows the steeper variation of composition at the interface.

In Fig.4 can be observed the interface and the region close to it in the Incoloy side on the surface of a thin foil observed by SEM. The high amount of carbides close to the interface- within a distance around 10 μm from it- is clearly apparent. At longer distances the grain boundaries are decorated by the carbides. Analysis by EDS has shown they are rich in Cr and Mo, and presumably of $M_{23}C_6$ type.

Fig. 5 shows a region close to the interface analyzed by transmision electron microscopy. The line AA' represents the interface, which has an ondulated appearance at this magnification. The Incoloy presents a work hardened substructure of cells and dislocations, where an important amount of carbides $M_{23}C_6$ are also observed. The presence of these precipitates clearly indicates the easyness of carbon to diffuse from the steel to the Incoloy. On the steel side some arrangement in bands is apparent. The first of them, of less than 1 μm wide, is formed by austenite grains elongated in the direction parallel to the interface, with some dislocations, but completely free of carbides precipitated. This is a clear consequence of the difficulty of Cr to diffuse from the superalloy to the steel, in clear opposition with the facility of carbon to do it from the steel to the superalloy, as pointed

28

Fig.1. Optical micrograph of the as-extruded
AISI 4130-Incoloy 825 bond.

Fig.2. SEM micrograph of the as-extruded
AISI 4130-Incoloy 825 bond.

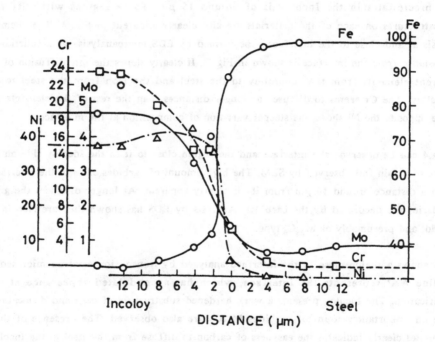

Fig.3. Concentration profiles of different elements
close to the AISI 4130-Incoloy 825 interface.

Fig.4. SEM micrograph of the interface and
the side region of the Incoloy 825.

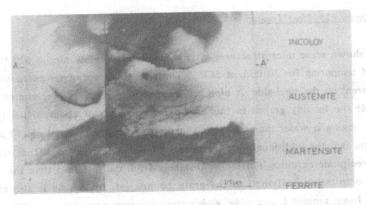

INCOLOY

A'

AUSTENITE

MARTENSITE

FERRITE

Fig.5. TEM micrograph of a region close to the interface(AA') of the AISI 4130-Incoloy 825
bond. On the steel side some arrangement in bands is indicated.

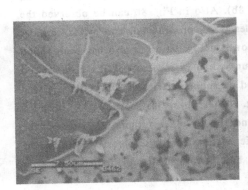

$M_{23}C_6$

Fig.6. SEM micrograph showing the austenite
band penetrating the steel grain boundaries in AISI 4130-Incoloy 825 bond.

Fig.7. TEM micrograph showing $M_{23}C_6$ carbides
precipitated in the Incoloy side, close to
the interface.

out above. Next to the austenite band a different one, with a thickness from 0.3 to several microns, is observed. It is formed by twinned plate martensite. The concentration of elements diffused from the superalloy in this region seems not to be enough to stabilize the austenite, but with some previsible amount of carbon they seem to provide the adecuated hardenability to obtain martensite by cooling. Finally the steel presents a structure formed by ferrite and pearlite, being the cementite scarce close to the interface. It is worth emphasizing that the band of austenite (rich in Cr and Ni) , pointed out before, penetrates occasionally the grain boundaries of the steel, as shown in Fig. 6. This could be a consequence of faster diffusion of Cr and Ni through the steel grain boundaries (pipe diffusion) as compared with bulk diffusion. On the other hand in the Incoloy side and close to the interface a proffuse precipitation of $M_{23}C_6$ carbides is found, as shown in Fig. 7.

AISI 4130-Incoloy 825. Heat Treated

In Fig. 8 are shown some microstructures after austenitizing for 30 min. at 920 ºC, water quenching and tempering for 30 min. at 513ºC. The typical aspect of tempered martensite is clearly apparent on the steel side. A high concentration of carbides precipitated are also observed inside the Incoloy grains. In this case over a distance of about 30 μm from the interface. This region is wider than that found in the as-extruded material of 10 μm. This clearly indicates that the additional heat treatments allows the carbon to diffuse for longer distances to precipitate carbides. For longer distances from the interface than the 30 μm the carbide precipitation is limited to the grain boundaries. In Fig. 8a is also clear the presence of a band, around 1 μm wide, which also penetrates some steel grain boundaries, as observed in the as-extruded material. The observation of the interface by transmission has shown that this band, as for the case of the as-extruded material consists of austenite, with some dislocations and carbide free (Fig. 8b). Also in Fig. 8b can be observed the Incoloy side consisting in dislocations and carbides $M_{23}C_6$ precipitated. This $M_{23}C_6$ carbides could be associated to grain boundaries, as shown in Fig. 9a , but also has been found precipitated inside the grains (in larger amounts than in the case of the as-extruded material), in these cases seem to be precipitated on subboundaries or dislocations, giving several geometrical forms, as shown in Fig. 9b. In these last cases it is found a crystallographic relationship cube to cube- found also by other authors (2)- between the precipitates and the matrix. This crystallographic relationship is also observed with one of the grains in the case of precipitation at grain boundaries. Small precipitates, with sizes

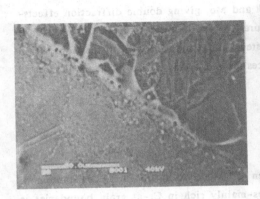

Fig.8. Microstructure of the AISI 4130-Incoloy 825
bond after a heat treatment of quenching
and tempering for 0.5 h. at 513°C.

a) SEM micrograph, and b) TEM micrograph
close to the interface.

Fig.9. TEM micrographs showing $M_{23}C_6$ carbides in the Incoloy 825, a) at grain boundaries,
and b) inside the grains.

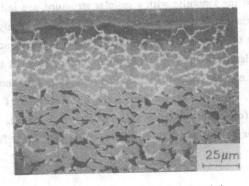

Fig.10. SEM micrograph of the as-extruded
AISI 4130-Duplex 2205 bond.

smaller than 0.1 µm of MC type, rich in Ti and Mo, giving double diffraction effects-reported also for some Ni alloys in the literature (3)- and in a paper of this Conference (4) for an Inconel 625, bonded to a low alloy steel, and associated with dislocations, grain boundaries or $M_{23}C_6$ carbides/matrix interfaces are also found in the Incoloy side close to the bonding.

AISI 4130-Duplex 2205. As-extruded.

Fig. 10 shows a SEM micrograph of a specimen etched electrolitically in a KOH solution. A large profussion of precipitation of carbides-mainly rich in Cr-at grain boundaries is observed in a region of around 50 to 70 µm close to the interface. This indicates a diffusion of carbon from the steel to the Duplex similar to that pointed out before for the Incoloy. The chemical analysis as a function of the distance from the interface is shown in Fig. 11. Again in this combination of materials the Ni is the element that diffuses for shorter distances.

In Fig. 12 is shown the evolution of the Duplex stainless steel microstructure -analyzed by STEM on a thin foil- and taking the interface as a reference. It is clearly apparent the presence of a band-called Zone 1-around 80 µm thick- where a high amount of carbides precipitated at grain boundaries can be observed. In this region the ferrite, normally associated to the austenite grain boundaries-see Zones 2 and 3 - is not observed. This region is followed by a second one-Zone 2- where the ferrite at the austenite grain boundaries appears and finally a Zone 3, where the right proportion of ferrite and austenite is observed. Analyzed the thin foil by transmision, it is apparent in Zone 1 the presence of carbides precipitated at austenite grain boundaries. The carbides have been analyzed by diffraction being $M_{23}C_6$ type. In the Zone 2, as shown in Fig. 13, the ferrite, presenting a subgrain structure, and the austenite with a cellular structure, are indicated. The two phases were identified from their diffraction patterns and the chemical analysis by EDS has shown a higher concentration of Cr and Mo in the ferrite and a higher concentration of Ni in the austenite. Some particles marked by P in the micrograph associated to the austenite-ferrite interface, which have not been identified, can be observed. Also some particles rich in Ti have been identified. Finally Fig. 14 shows the substructure of Zone 3 observed by Transmision of thin foils. An austenite grain (A), with a cellular structure, is clearly apparent in the center of the micrograph. The ferrite (F), identified by its diffraction

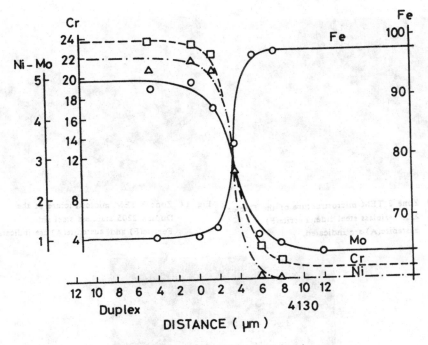

Fig.11. Concentration profiles of different elements
close to the AISI 4130-Duplex 2205 interface.

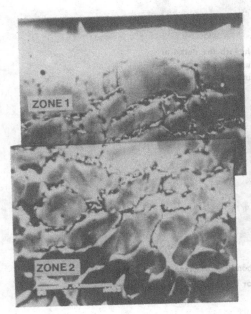

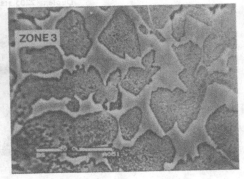

Fig.12. Sequence of microstructures from the bonding
interface in the Duplex 2205 stainless steel,
observed by STEM.

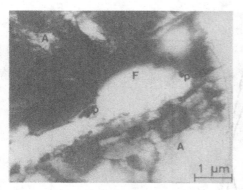

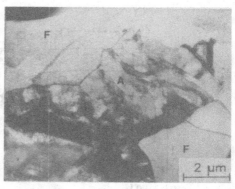

Fig.13. Zone 2 TEM microstructure of the Duplex 2205 stainless steel side. Ferrite(F) and austenite(A) are indicated.

Fig. 14. Zone 3 TEM microstructure of the Duplex 2205 stainless steel side. Ferrite(F) and austenite(A) are indicated.

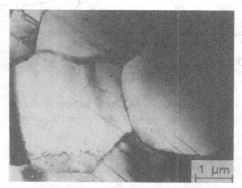

Fig. 15. TEM micrograph with the detail of ferrite substructure in Zone 3 of the Duplex 2205 stainless steel.

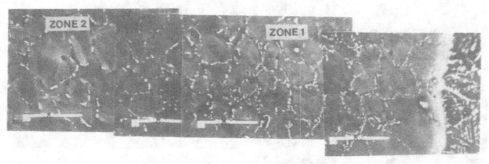

Fig. 16. Sequence of microstructures from the bonding interface in the Duplex 2205 stainless steel after quenching and tempering for 0.5 h. at 550ºC, observed by STEM.

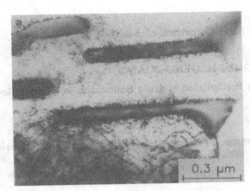 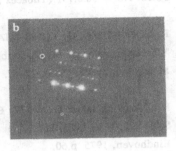

Fig.17. Detail of carbides precipitated in the Duplex 2205 stainless steel. a) TEM micrograph of $M_{23}C_6$ in lamellar form, b) Diffraction pattern showing the cube to cube
crystallographic relationship between carbide and austenite.

pattern, observed at more detail (Fig. 15) presents a subgrain structure with few dislocations
inside the subgrains.

AISI 4130-Duplex 2205. Heat treated

Fig. 16 shows the evolution of the microstructure with the distance from the bonding
interface in a tube quenched, after 30 min austenitizing at 950 °C, and tempered for 30
min. at 550ºC. The three zones reported above for the as-extruded material are clearly
apparent. Zone 1, 80 μm thick, without ferrite is very similar to that found in the as-
extruded material, but in Zone 2, with some amount of ferrite (dark in the micrograph), a
sensible amount of $M_{23}C_6$ carbides precipitated at the ferrite-austenite interface are
observed; these carbides, which were scarce in the as-extruded material, are consequence of
additional diffusion of carbon during the heat treatment. Zone 3, is basically the same to
that of as-extruded material, but with a higher proportion of ferrite. In several cases the
cube to cube crystallographic relationship, pointed out before, between the $M_{23}C_6$ and the
austenite has been found (See Fig. 17.b). This relation was also satisfied by carbides
precipitated in some kind of lamellar form as shown in Fig. 17a.

ACKNOWLEDGEMENTS

The authors want to thank the CICYT for the finantial support of the present work.

REFERENCES

1.- Patent No. # 50.8.733 (Tubacex S.A.) and Certificate of Addition 517.832.

2.- R. YONG-HUA, G. YONG-XIANG and H. GENG-XIANG.
"Characterization of $M_{23}C_6$ Carbides Precipitated at grain Boundaries in a Superalloy".
Metallography 22,(1989), 22-47.

3.- R.B. Scarling taken from J.W. Edington. Practical Electron Microscopy in Materials
Science 2. N.V. PHILIPS.
Eindhoven, 1975. p.60.

4.-B. López, I. Gutiérrez and J.J. Urcola, In this issue.

STUDY OF THE MICROSTRUCTURE OBTAINED AFTER DIFFUSION BONDING INCONEL 625
TO LOW ALLOY STEEL BY HOT UNIAXIAL PRESSING OR HIPPING

B. López, I. Gutiérrez and J.J. Urcola

CEIT
Centro de Estudios e Investigaciones Técnicas de Guipúzcoa
Paseo Manuel de Lardizábal, 15
Barrio de Ibaeta, San Sebastián, Spain

The microstructures obtained by diffusion bonding an Inconel 625 superalloy to an AISI 4130 low alloy steel, using two different bonding techniques: hot uniaxial pressing and hot isostatic pressing, have been studied using optical metallography, SEM and STEM techniques. The interdiffusion of the different elements through the interface and the chemical analysis of the different phases have been determined using EDS microanalysis both in SEM and STEM.

In specimens obtained by either diffusion bonding method, a profuse precipitation of $M_{23}C_6$ carbides, due to the diffusion of carbon from the steel, is clearly apparent. Due to the higher temperatures used during hipping as compared to hot pressing, a broader region of carbide precipitation is observed in the as-hipped specimens. For the hot pressed specimens the precipitation is prefferential in grain and twin boundaries. On the other hand, for as-hipped specimens, although precipitation is observed at grain and twin boundaries, it is also found inside grains along with a free precipitation zone around the grain boundaries. Additionally, large plate-like niobium carbides, were observed precipitated on grain and twin boundaries in the as-hipped specimens.

INTRODUCTION

It is difficult to find materials having appropriated corrosion resistance and mechanical properties to be used in particular applications where both properties are necessary. Some times the lack of such material can be solved with the use of coatings, but their limited thickness make them often not able for long term utilization. Diffusion bonding is one way of resolving the problem by bonding thick corrosion resistant layers to high strength substrates (i.e. high strength steels). This can be performed by several ways: co-extrussion, co-rolling, hot pressing and hipping among others. Co-extrussion to produce tubular products is a well stablished technique, (1,2) and high strength low alloy steel tubes with a corrosion resistant clad alloy metallurgically bonded to their insides and/or outsides have been produced with applications in pipe lines for oil and gas transport, heat exchangers, chemical industry among others. Although some combination of material have been tested (1,2), the research follows to find compatible materials to resolve some of the more demanding requirements.

The present work describes the microstructures developed during diffusion bonding by hot pressing and hipping of a Inconel 625 superalloy to an AISI 4130 low alloy steel

EXPERIMENTAL PROCEDURE

The starting materials were in form of 16 mm diameter bars. Discs 6.4 mm thick of AISI 4130 and 4.2 mm thick of Inconel 625 were cut from the bars. The discs were mechanically polished in emery paper and finished with 1 μm diamond paste. Finally they were carefully degreased before forming the assemblies for hot pressing or hipping.
Hot pressing of AISI 4130-Inconel 625-AISI 4130 discs assemblies, was carried out in an argon atmosphere in a servohydraulic 10 Tn machine fitted with a furnace reaching a maximum temperature of 1100 º C. Discs, assembled as for hot pressing, were introduced in mild steel cans, and vacuum sealed before hipping. In Table 1 are summarized the different tests carried out in the present work. Fig.1 shows two specimens tested by both techniques together with two cuts for metallography. Specimens were prepared by conventional techniques to be observed optically and by SEM. Thin foils perforated at the interface for TEM observation were prepared using a combination of electropolishing and ion beam etching.

RESULTS AND DISCUSSION

Figs. 1 a and b show how the Inconel 625 remains macroscopically nearly undeformed and the steel deforms plastically overflowing the Inconel during hot pressing at 1050 º. This is a consequence of the difference in hot strength of both materials being the Inconel stronger (~ 3 times) than the steel at this temperature (3).

Fig. 2 shows two optical micrographs of two bond regions between an AISI 4130 steel and an Inconel 625, after electrolitic etching using nital. In Fig. 2a, which corresponds to hot pressing at 1050ºC followed by slow cooling, the steel presents a ferrite-pearlite structure. On the other hand, Fig. 2b shows the bainitic structure of the steel side in a specimen tested by hipping at 1250ºC and fast cooled to room temperature. The decarburization of the steel close to the bond interface is clearly apparent in both figures. This region is small in the hot pressed specimen (150 μm), which correspond to a test carried out at low temperature (1050 °C) and large (400 μm) in the hipped specimen, tested at high temperature (1250 °C). The carbon diffused from the steel to the superalloy has allowed the precipitation of carbides. These are located at grain and twin boundaries in hot pressed specimens (Fig.2a) tested at low temperatures. At these low temperatures (1050ºC) pipe diffusion seems to be faster than lattice diffusion. On the other hand, at the high temperatures (1250 ºC) used for hipped specimens, both diffusion modes seem to be fast enough to produce a profuse precipitation of carbides both at the boundaries and inside the grains, as shown in Fig. 2b.

The chemical analyses at and close to the bond interface - performed by EDS microanalysis- as a function of the distance from the interface for specimens hot pressed at 900 and 1050ºC and for the hipped at 1175 and 1250ºC are shown in Figs. 3 and 4 respectively. It is clearly apparent the interdiffusion of the different elements from the superalloy to the steel and the iron from the steel to the superalloy. For each specimen, Cr seems to diffuse for longer distances than the rest of the elements and on the opposite Ni shows the steeper change of composition at the interface. On the other hand the increase of temperature from 900 to 1050ºC in hot pressing and from 1175 to 1250ºC in hipping gives longer interdiffusion distances. It is also apparent from the figures (compare Figs. 3 and 4) that hipping- with higher temperatures- allows longer diffusion distances.

Fig.5 represents the hardness variation in both sides close to the interface for a specimen hot pressed at 1050ºC (Fig. 5a) and for an hipped at 1250ºC (Fig. 5b). In both cases is clearly apparent the increase in hardness for the Inconel 625 in a region close to the interface. This hardening can be due in part to the precipitation of carbides in this region as has been pointed out above and/or to the dislocation substructure developed by work hardening in this region of the interface (see Figs.9 and 10). This also could explain the fact that the hardness in the hot pressed specimen is slightly higher. On the other hand, the difference in hardness in the steel side of both specimens agrees with the microstructural differences reported in Fig. 2. The ferrite-pearlite structure of Fig. 2a (hot pressed and slow cooled) presents a low hardness (specially in the ferrite grains) and the bainitic structure of Fig. 2b (hipped and fast cooled) presents a high hardness.

In Fig. 6 the interface and the region close to it in the Inconel side, analysed by SEM after electrolitic etching with nital, is shown. Fig. 6a corresponds to a hot pressing test performed at 1050ºC. The profuse precipitation of carbides at grain and twin boundaries is clearly apparent, indicating that carbon mainly diffuses by pipe diffusion, reaching regions within a distance of 150 μm from the interface. Figs. 6b and 6c correspond to specimens obtained by hipping at 1175 and 1250ºC respectively. Although the precipitation at grain and twin boundaries is very similar to that observed in the hot pressed specimen, in these cases a sensible amount of precipitates can be observed inside the grains. This precipitation due to lattice diffusion of carbon can be observed up to 40 μm from the interface after hipping at 1175ºC, reaching 60 μm for hipping at 1250ºC. In this case an appreciable grain growth has also taken place.

Carbide analysis by EDS in SEM has shown that they contain mainly Cr, Mo and Nb. Some of these carbides precipitate in form of real plates on the grain boundaries, as shown in Fig. 7 after a deep etching of the matrix.

The combination of EDS and diffraction in TEM has allowed the identification of several carbides. In Fig. 8a, obtained from a specimen hot pressed at 1050ºC, a carbide chain located at a grain boundary can be observed. In this grain boundary, placed at around 50 μm from the interface, carbides rich in Mo and rich in Nb are found alternatively. The carbides rich in Mo contain also sensible amounts of Ni, Cr and Fe and those rich in Nb contain also Ti. Diffraction pattern analysis has shown that the carbides rich in Mo are M_6C, with a fcc structure of parameter a= 1.185 nm, and those rich in Nb are of type MC with a F.C.C. structure of parameter a= 0.474 nm. Also some Nb_2C type carbides, assotiated to grain boundaries have been found in the specimen hipped at 1250ºC. In Fig. 8b, for a specimen hot pressed at 1050ºC, elongated carbides type MC, rich in Nb, are observed inside the Inconel grains. Carbides type $M_{23}C_6$, rich in Cr and Mo located at grain boundary can also be observed. This carbide follows a cube to cube crystallographic relationship with the Inconel F.C.C. lattice of one grain. This relationship, reported previously in the literature (4) has been also found in a work on diffusion bonding Incoloy 825 to a low alloy steel reported in this Conference (2).

Fig. 9 shows a region close to the bond interface of a specimen hot pressed at 1050ºC and analysed by TEM. The line AA' represents the interface, which has a wavy appearance at the present magnification. The Inconel presents a work hardened substructure with cells and dislocations. An important amount of big carbides of different types are also observed, together with a dispersion of finer (< 0.1 μm in size) MC carbides rich in Nb and Mo which produce a double diffraction effect, as can be observed in Fig. 10. This effect has been reported previously in the Incoloy bonded to a low alloy steel (2). These carbides, which have been identified in all specimens, although too big for precipitation hardening, can contribute to the hardening reported in Fig. 5 inhibiting the recovery and recrystallization of the work hardened region in the Inconel close to the interface.

Fig. 11 shows a region close to the bond interface of a specimen hipped at 1175ºC. The interface AA', with the present magnification, presents again an ondulated shape. In the Inconel side a substructure with few dislocations assotiated to grain boundaries and carbides can be observed. This substructure contrasts with the equivalent one corresponding to hot pressing (Fig. 9), where a heavily work hardened substructure was observed. This could be a clear consequence of the absence of shear strains in hipping compared with those imparted by hot pressing. The presence of this work hardened substructure close to the bond interface could explain the fact that the hardness in this region is higher in the hot pressed specimen than in the hipped one.

It is worth emphasizing that in all specimens analyzed, an austenite band of variable thickness, but around 4 μm parallel to the bond interface and in the steel side has been observed. This band, free of carbides, that has also been observed in a low alloy steel bonded to an Incoloy 825 (2) could be a consequence of the diffusion of Cr and Ni to the steel from the superalloy which stabilize the austenite in this side. The fact that it is nearly free of carbides seems to be a consequence of the fast carbon diffusion to the Inconel compared with Cr and Ni to precipitate there the carbides. Following this band and in the steel side structures typical of the steel are observed, being different for different cooling rates as pointed out before.

ACKNOWLEDGEMENTS

The Authors want to thank TUBACEX, S.A., for finantial support during the realization of this work.

REFERENCES

1) E.P. Lathan, D.B. Meadowcroft and L. Pinder, Mater. Sci. Technol., S, 1989, 813.

2) I. Gutiérrez, J.J. Urcola, J.M. Bilbao and L.M. Villar, in this issue.

3) B.López, Ph. D. Thesis work in course (San Sebastian).

4) R. Yong-Hua, G. Yong-Xiang and H. Geng-Xiang. Metallography 22, (1989), 22

Table 1 Experimental Details of the different Tests

Test Type	Temperature (º C)	Time	Pressure (MPa)
HOT PRESS	900	1 h. 30 min	73
	1050	1 hour	34
HIP	1175	1 hour	200
	1250	1 hour	200

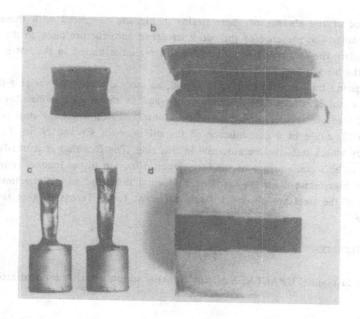

Fig. 1. Specimens tested by both techniques with cuts for metallography.
(a) (b) Hot Pressing (c) (d) Hipping.

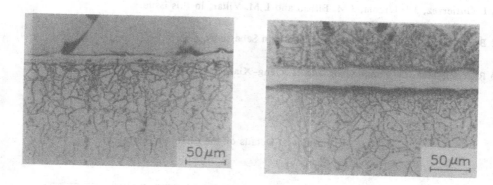

(a)   (b)

Fig. 2. Optical micrographs of the AISI4130 - Inconel 625 bond. a) Hot Pressed
Specimen b) Hipped Specimen.

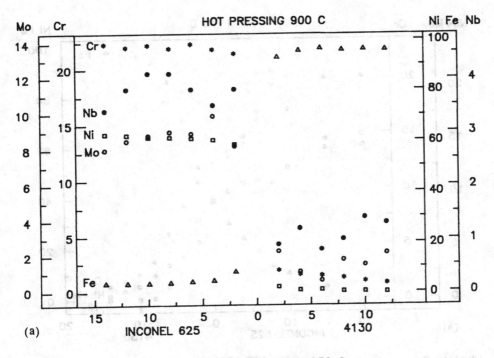

(a)

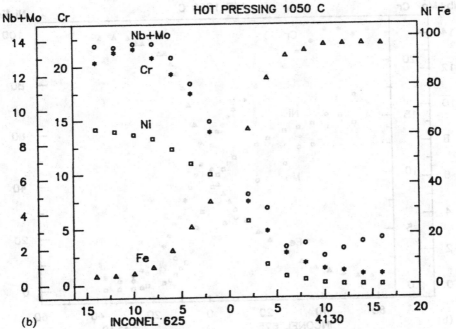

(b)

Fig. 3. Concentration profiles of different elements close to the bonding interface in specimens hot pressed at temperatures. a) 900°C b) 1050°C.

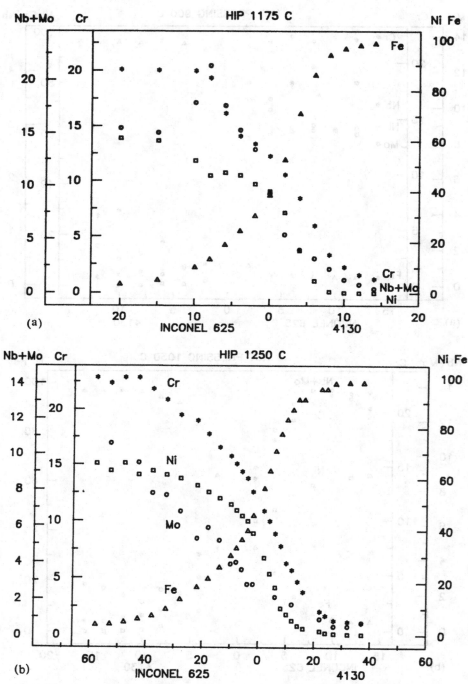

Fig. 4. Concentration profiles of different elements close to the bonding interface in specimens hipped at temperatures. a) 1175°C b) 1250°C.

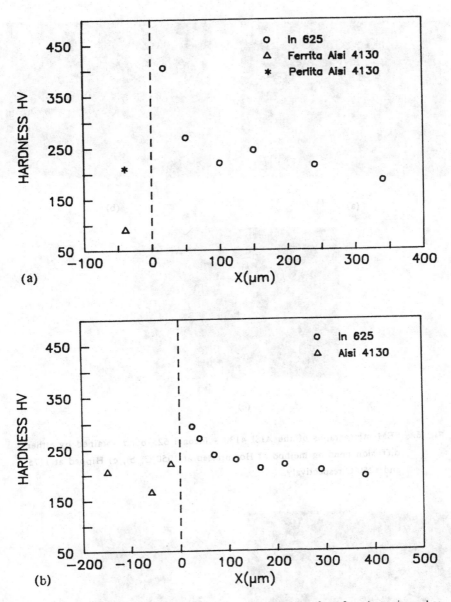

Fig. 5. Hardness variation in both sides close to the interface for a) specimen hot pressed at 1050°C b) specimen hipped at 1250°C.

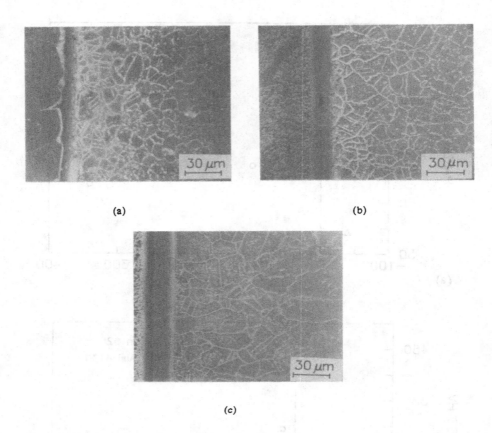

(a)

(b)

(c)

Fig. 6.   SEM micrographs of the AISI 4130 - Inconel 625 bond obtained by either diffusion bonding method a) Hot pressed at 1050°C, b), c) Hipped at 1175 and 1250°C respectivaly.

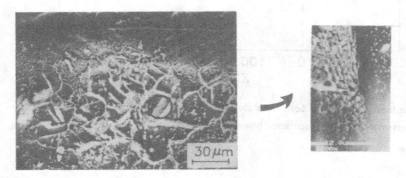

Fig. 7. SEM micrograph showing plate-like carbide precipitation on the grain boundaries.

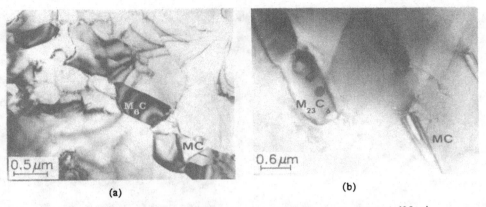

Fig. 8. TEM micrographs showing different types of carbides in the Inconel 625. a) at grain boundaries b) inside the grains.

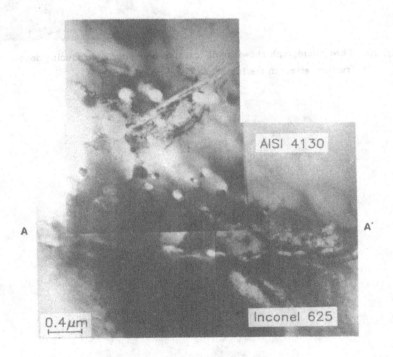

Fig. 9. TEM micrograph of a region close to the interface (AA') of the specimen hot pressed at 1050ºC.

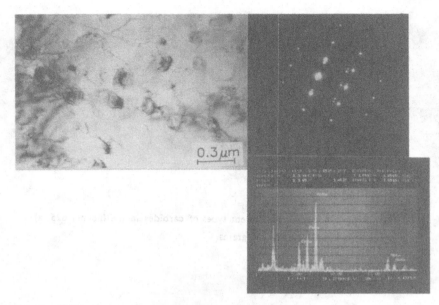

Fig. 10. TEM micrograph showing MC carbide precipitation producing double diffraction effect in the Inconel 625 close to the interface.

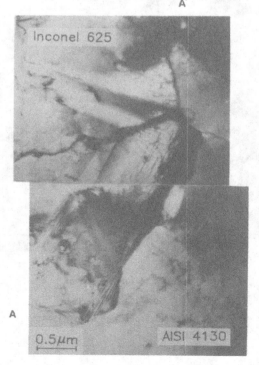

Fig. 11. TEM micrograph of a region close to the interface (AA') of a specimen
hipped at 1175°C.

HIP DIFFUSION BONDING OF AUSTENITIC TO FERRITIC STEELS

H V Atkinson*, M W Crabbe* and R Walker+

*School of Materials, University of Sheffield, Sir Robert Hadfield Building
Mappin Street, Sheffield, S1 3JD

+Infutec Ltd, Carlisle Close, Sheffield Road, Sheepbridge, Chesterfield,
Derbyshire, S41 9ED

Abstract

The HIP diffusion bonding of a strain hardening manganese steel to a low
alloy steel using a ductile Ni interlayer to relieve differential thermal
contraction stresses has been investigated.

Introduction

Hot Isostatic Pressing (HIPping) is a technique which has grown rapidly in
its commercial applications over the last decade. It has the potential to
diffusion bond dissimilar materials together in geometries which cannot be
achieved by other methods.

Strain hardening manganese steels, initially in the austenitic condition,
are notable for their toughness and wear resistance and are used in railway
points, drilling machines and rock-crushers. In such applications they
must often be attached to other less expensive steels such as low alloy
steels. This paper is a preliminary report on the HIP diffusion bonding of
such a manganese steel (Fe12.5%Mn 1.23%C) to a low alloy steel (Fe0.45%C
1.3%Cr 0.3%Mo 4.0%Ni).

The thermal expansivity of the manganese steel is significantly larger than
that of the low alloy steel (see Appendix 1). Differential thermal
contraction could therefore give rise to cracking during cooling from the
HIPping temperature. Nickel interlayers can be used to mitigate this
effect by providing a ductile intermediary with a thermal expansivity
coefficient larger than that of the low alloy steel and smaller than that
of the austenitic steel. However, too wide a nickel interlayer will be
deleterious, by its very ductility, to the mechanical properties of the
final product. This ductility might be offset to some extent by diffusion
into the nickel during the HIPping treatment, giving solid solution
hardening.

Previous work (Ref (1)) had shown that extensive cracking occurred with 25
μm and 100 μm Ni interlayer thicknesses, both at the bondline and within
the substrate metals, but not with 500 μm. One aim of the work reported
here was to further explore the regime between 100 μm and 500 μm interlayer
thickness. The central questions for investigation are:-

1) Have the components bonded, and to what extent?

2 Is there any cracking?

3) To what extent has interdiffusion occurred?

4)   What thickness of Ni interlayer is optimum for the joint?

Mechanical tests on the strength of the joints have not yet been carried out and therefore the answer to question 4) will be limited.

A significant feature of the previous work (Ref (1)) was the lines of what are either pores or particles lying parallel to the interface within the interlayer on both sides after diffusion bonding.   In some cases, the bondline cracks progressed via these features (see Fig 1). Cracks extended from the edges of the bond where the stresses due to differential thermal contraction are expected to be highest (Ref (2)) into the low alloy steel. In addition, there was extensive intergranular cracking within the manganese steel. (Fig 2).   The experimental procedure for the previous work was the same as that performed here except that the steel surfaces for bonding were ground prior to assembly for HIPping, in contrast with the polished surfaces used for this work.

Experimental Procedure

A can was assembled for HIPping as shown in Fig 3.   The Ni interlayers were made up from degreased Ni foil of 132 μm (99.5% purity with Fe the major impurity) and 30 μm thickness. The error on the former thickness is $\pm$ 1 μm and on the latter $\pm$ 2 μm.   Thus, the errors on the interlayer thicknesses are 660 $\pm$ 5 μm (5 x 132), 456 $\pm$ 7 μm (3 x 132 + 2 x 30), 324 $\pm$ 6 μm (2 x 132 + 2 x 30) and 132 $\pm$ 1 μm.   The austenitic steel (VEW K700) pieces were cut from bar 28.5 mm in diameter using a lubricated cutting wheel, ground to 1200 grit and polished on a 6 μm diamond wheel. The low alloy steel pieces, which came from bar $\sim$ 30 mm in diameter, were prepared in a similar way.   All components were thoroughly degreased in heated industrial methylated spirits prior to assembly in the encapsulating can which was made from mild steel tube with the end caps welded in place. The can was evacuated to 10^{-2} torr and then the evacuation tube sealed.

The can was heated at 20°C/min to 1120°C and HIPped at 15,000 psi for 3 hours.   The cooling rate was 10°C/min and the total cycle time $\sim$ 6 hours. During both the heating and cooling parts of the cycle, the temperature and pressure were applied and relieved in tandem. The HIPped can was sectioned using a lubricated slitting wheel and cut into pieces small enough to be mounted in conducting bakelite for polishing to 1 μm and conventional metallographic examination.   Specimens were etched for 15s in 2% nital for optical microscopy of the steels.   They were repolished to 1 μm prior to examination by Scanning Electron Microscopy (SEM).   Energy Dispersive X-Ray Analysis (EDX) was used to obtain profiles of elemental compositions across the diffusion bonded region.   The microstructure of the nickel interlayer was revealed by masking off the steels with nail varnish and etching with a mixture of dilute HCl (10cc), water (50cc) and meths (50 cc) saturated with 20 g $CuSO_4$.   If masking is not used the steel is excessively attacked by this etch.   Microhardnesses were obtained with a Leco 500 tester.

Results

1.   Optical Metallography

i)   Interlayer Thickness after HIPping

The measured interlayer widths were 165 μm, 336 μm, 452 μm and 656 μm ($\pm$5

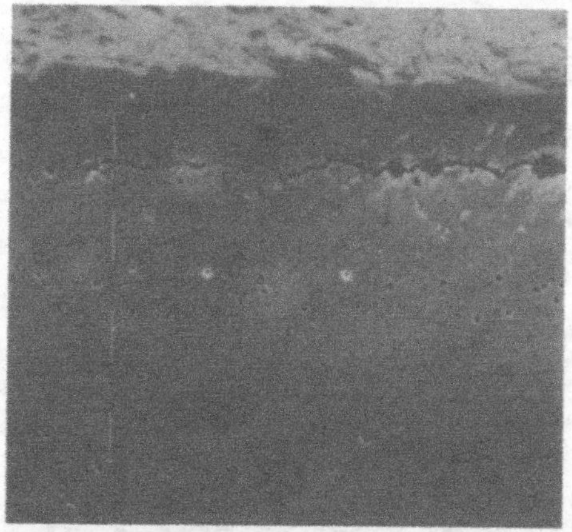

←Alloy steel

Fig 1   SEM micrograph of crack in the Ni interlayer progressing via pores. Interlayer thickness prior to HIPping was 25 μm. HIPping carried out at 1120°C, 15,000 psi for 3 hours.

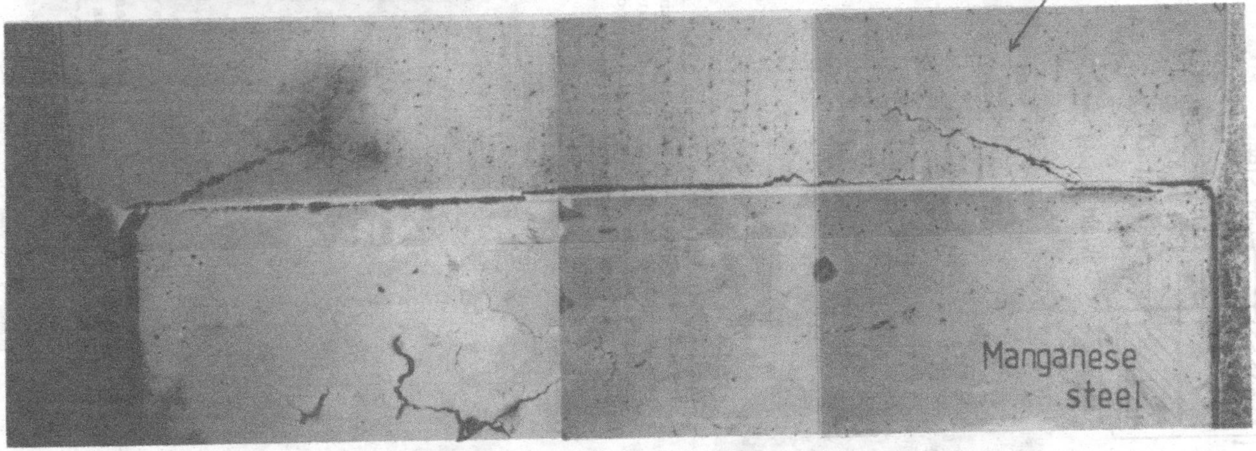

Alloy steel

←Manganese steel

Manganese steel

Fig 2   Optical micrograph of HIP diffusion bond between manganese steel and low alloy steel showing intergranular cracking within the bulk of the manganese steel, cracking within the 100 μm thickness Ni interlayer and cracks penetrating from the interface into the low alloy steel. Magnification ~ x8.

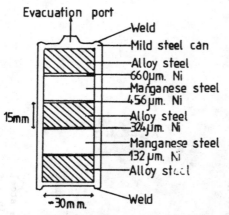

Evacuation port
Weld
Mild steel can
Alloy steel
660 μm. Ni
Manganese steel
456 μm. Ni
15mm
Alloy steel
324 μm. Ni
Manganese steel
132 μm. Ni
Alloy steel
~30mm.
Weld

Fig 3   Schematic diagram
of cross-section
through canned assembly
as-prepared for HIPping.

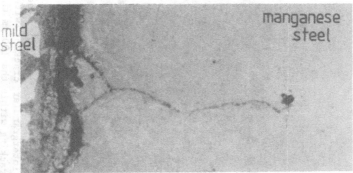

mild steel   manganese steel

Fig 4   Optical micrograph of "crack-like" feature penetrating from the interface between the mild steel can and the manganese steel into the manganese steel. These features appear to be networks of precipitates decorating grain boundaries rather than cracks as such. 132 μm interlayer thickness. Magnification ~x267.

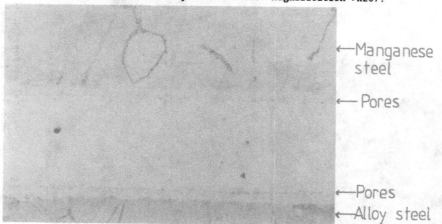

Manganese steel
Pores
Pores
Alloy steel

Fig 5   Lines of what are thought to be pores within the Ni, parallel to the steel/Ni interface on both sides of the interlayer. 132 μm interlayer thickness. Magnification ~x267.

μm in each case) in comparison with 132 μm, 324 μm, 456 μm and 660 μm respectively. Apart from the narrowest interlayer, it is within the bounds of error that the apparent interlayer widths after HIPping are the same as those before.

ii) Microstructure

After HIPping, all four interlayers appeared to have successfully bonded to the steels. No cracks were apparent within the bond region nor radiating from the bond region into the adjacent steels. There was no gross grain boundary cracking within the manganese steel. There were a few "crack-like" features penetrating from the mild steel can/manganese steel interface into the manganese steel (see Fig 4) but examination at high magnification suggested that these might be networks of precipitates decorating grain boundaries rather than cracks as such.

All the interlayers displayed systematic lines of dark round features parallel to the steel/Ni interfaces on both sides of the interlayers within the Ni (see Fig 5). These will be referred to as pores on the basis of SEM evidence (see below). For the 132 μm, 324 μm, 452 μm and 660 μm interlayer thicknesses respectively, they are situated 20, 15, 10 and 15 ± 2 μm from the apparent interface after HIPping. They vary in size and spacing. It is within the bounds of error that the pores lie at the original interfaces between the Ni and the adjacent steels prior to HIPping. However, it should be noted, given the comment in Section 1.i) above, that the errors are such that the interlayer thickness after HIPping could be the same as before, and that the lines of pores do consistently lie within the interlayer as it appears after HIPping.

The low alloy steel is in the martensitic condition after HIPping. The manganese steel is in the austenitic condition with carbide precipitated around the grain boundaries and present in an acicular morphology within the grains. Within a region ∼ 1 mm wide adjacent to the interface with the mild steel can the carbides disappear (Fig 6). In the mild steel can itself there is an increased volume fraction of pearlite adjacent to the same interface. Conversely the mild steel is denuded of pearlite adjacent to the low alloy steel. After the etch to reveal the microstructure of the interlayer itself, very fine networks of precipitates were revealed around some of the Ni grain boundaries.

2) Microhardness

The microhardness of the manganese steel is typically 200-230 Vickers, of the low alloy steel typically 730-760 Vickers and of the Ni interlayer typically 130-180 Vickers. The microhardness values across the interlayers are relatively uniform.

3) Scanning Electron Microscopy (SEM)

SEM examination of the dark, round features within the interlayers lying systematically parallel to the diffusion bonded interfaces suggested that these features are pores rather than particles (see Fig 7). (The dark line and adjacent marks running across the SEM micrograph in Fig 7(a) indicate where EDX analyses have been carried out).

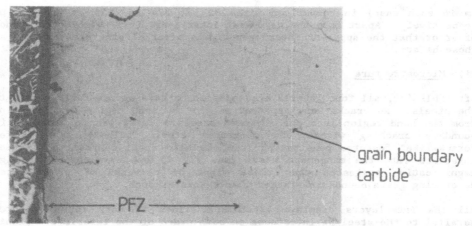

Fig 6   Optical micrograph showing precipitate free zone ~ 1mm wide in
         the manganese steel adjacent to the mild steel can.   132 μm
         interlayer thickness. Magnification ~ x67.

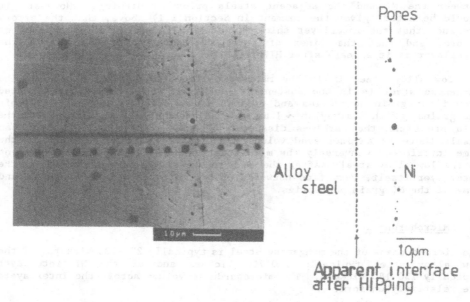

Fig 7   (a) Scanning Electron Micrograph of interface between low alloy
         steel and 324 μm Ni interlayer showing line of pores lying within
         the Ni parallel to the interface.

         (b) Tracing of the same field of view to clarify the size and
         distribution of pores.

4)   Energy Dispersive X-Ray Analysis (EDX)

The diffusion profiles for the major elements (Fe, Mn, Ni) were obtained for the 132 μm and 324 μm interlayers. The measurements were made at 4 μm and 6 μm intervals respectively. The results are summarised in Figs 8 and 9. Carbon, the other element of particular interest, cannot be detected with the EDX system. The results are reproducible to within ± 0.1 w/o. The compositions in the bulk agree well with the quoted alloy compositions for manganese steel and low alloy steel.

The composition in the centre of the 132 μm interlayer (∼165 μm in width after HIPping) is 0.5 wt% Si, 1.16 wt% Mn, 0.8 wt% Fe, balance Ni. The composition in the centre of the 324 μm interlayer (∼336 μm in width after HIPping) is 0.30 wt% Mn, 0.25 wt% Fe, balance Ni.

In both Figs 8 and 9, the Mn profile shows a distinct plateau   55-60 μm wide spanning from the apparent edge of the interlayer after HIPping into the interlayer on the manganese steel side. The plateaus are virtually identical in profile for the 132 μm and 324 μm interlayers. The onset of the rise in Mn from the plateau to the bulk value in the manganese steel coincides with the apparent edge of the interlayer after HIPping. The fall from the plateau value towards the middle of the Ni interlayer follows the fall in the Fe profile in both cases.

Discussion

1)   Integrity of Bond

In contrast with the previous work, there is no apparent cracking either in the bond region or elsewhere, even with the narrowest (132 μm) interlayer. The only difference in experimental procedure in comparison with the previous work was the surface preparation of the steels (ie ground surfaces previously, polished here). It is difficult to envisage surface roughness alone having a pronounced effect on the generation of cracks. This suggests the critical interlayer thickness, above which cracking does not occur, is between 100 μm and 132 μm. Mechanical testing would help to identify whether the 132 μm interlayer bond has a low fracture toughness due to high residual stresses. In addition, although the manganese steel has not cracked intergranularly, grain growth has occurred to a significant extent during HIPping, such that, with the presence of the grain boundary carbides, the manganese steel will be in a brittle condition. Heat treatment after HIPping will be required to alleviate this.

2)   Origin of Systematic Lines of Pores

The systematic lines of pores within the Ni interlayer parallel to the interface could act as preferential crack propagation paths in service. It is therefore important to identify their origin. There are two major possible explanations.

i)   Surface contamination (oxide or carbonaceous) or adsorbed gas on the surfaces of the materials to be bonded has produced the spherical pores. If this were the cause of the porosity, the pores would be expected to occur along the line of the original interface. The errors are such that it is not possible to identify unequivocally whether the pores do lie along the

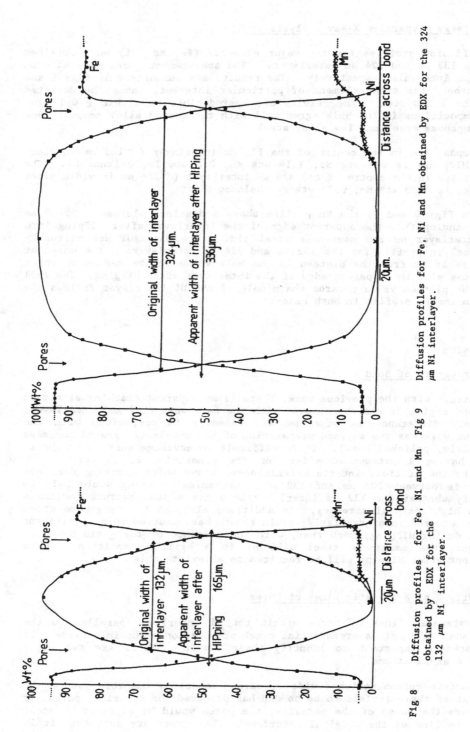

Fig 8   Diffusion profiles for Fe, Ni and Mn obtained by EDX for the 132 μm Ni interlayer.

Fig 9   Diffusion profiles for Fe, Ni and Mn obtained by EDX for the 324 μm Ni interlayer.

The compositions for the bulk in the specifications for the alloys are indicated by dotted lines.

original interface. The suggestion could be further investigated by reproducing the can assembly described here with the single change of variable to diffusion pump evacuation of the can. The pores might arise from particle drop-out during polishing for metallographic examination, but some particle retention would be expected and no particles could be found in the SEM.

ii) The pores are Kirkendall porosity formed as the result of the vacancy current that accompanies the unequal mass flow in a diffusion couple, with the Ni diffusing out of the interlayer faster than the Fe (and Mn) are diffusing in. The fact that the Matano interface (used in the calculation of interdiffusion coefficients) for the 132 μm interlayer coincides with the original position of the bond, as expected if no Kirkendall porosity occurs, undermines this hypothesis.

In either eventuality, it is noteworthy that the pores have either survived HIPping, where the very aim is the removal of porosity, or have been generated during the cool down period after HIPping despite the decrease in pressure and temperature in tandem. The differential thermal contraction stresses will tend to cause tension within the Ni adjacent to the manganese steel. This might counteract the isostatic pressure during cool down.

3)   Diffusion Profiles

The most important features of the diffusion profiles are as follows:-

i)   Significant interdiffusion has occurred. For example, in Fig 8, comparing the original width of the Ni interlayer with the Ni profile the Ni has diffused about 20 μm into the adjacent steels. Similarly the Fe has just penetrated to the middle of the 132 μm interlayer with a composition there of 0.8 w/o in comparison with the maximum Fe impurity concentration in the Ni of 0.5 w/o. Solid solution hardening does not have a significant effect on the hardness of the interlayer though, as the microhardness profiles across the interlayers are fairly flat. This suggests that if the ductile interlayer did prove a source of weakness in the system under mechanical testing, the Ni interlayer must be replaced with a harder material, although one which will still act as a stress reliever during cooling. In addition, as interdiffusion occurs, at a particular plane in the bond an Fe 36% Ni alloy will be created. This is the composition of Invar which has a thermal expansivity of 0 K^{-1}. Such a layer would be expected to cause stresses rather than relieve them.

ii)   The profiles for Fe and Ni are smooth but that for Mn shows a plateau. This is difficult to explain, particularly as there are no second phase particles apparent in the microstructures which could account for such observations. If there were a limit on the solid solubility of Mn in Fe/Ni alloys such that as the Ni diffused into the steel the Mn was rejected ahead of the diffusion front such a plateau might occur behind the diffusion front. However, it is unlikely that such a limit occurs in the phase diagram. Another possible explanation is that the pores act as a diffusion barrier so that two separate diffusion couples develop. It is not clear then why the Ni and Fe profiles are smooth while that for the Mn shows a plateau. The plateau could also be associated with the nature of the dependence of manganese diffusivity on the %Ni in Fe.

4) Diffusion Between the Bonded Steels and the Mild Steel Can

The optical metallography suggests there is significant diffusion of carbon from the manganese steel into the mild steel can, and from the mild steel can into the alloy steel. This finding has practical implications since in the regions of denudation or enrichment the properties of the steels will be changed. The affected layers might have to be machined off prior to HIPping or different encapsulation geometries/materials investigated.

Summary

The HIP diffusion bonding of a low alloy steel to a strain hardening manganese steel using a ductile Ni interlayer to relieve differential thermal contraction stresses has been investigated. No cracking was observed even with the thinnest interlayer (132 μm) but mechanical tests are required to further investigate the mechanical integrity. The origin of systematic lines of pores within the interlayer has not been unequivocally identified. Significant interdiffusion between the Ni and the steels, and between the mild steel can and the steels has occurred. The plateau in the Mn profile between the interlayer and the manganese steel is difficult to explain.

Acknowledgements

We would like to thank HIP Ltd for the provision of HIPping facilities and Dr J A Whiteman for assistance with SEM. In addition, we are grateful to Prof H Jones, Dr C W Haworth, Dr B A Rickinson, Dr A Hartley and Mr S G Moseley for helpful discussions.

References

1. H V Atkinson and S Mohammed. Unpublished.

2. K Suganuma and T Okamoto, "Interlayer Bonding Methods for Ceram-ic/Metal Systems with Thermal Expansion Mismatches", p 71-88 in 'Fundamentals of Diffusion Bonding'. Edited by Y Ishida, Publ Elsevier 1987. Proc 1st Seiken Int Symp on "Interface Structure, Properties and Diffusion Bonding", Tokyo, Japan, 2-4 Dec 1985.

3. R E Reed-Hill, "Physical Metallurgy Principles", Publ Van Nostrand Reinhold 1964, p 272-277.

APPENDIX

Thermal Expansivity Data (10^{-6} K^{-1}) between 20°C and x°C

The data is taken from the VEW information sheets for the K600 low alloy steel and K700 austenitic steel.

	x°C					
	100	200	300	400	500	600
Low Alloy Steel	11.0	12.5	13.0	13.5	14.0	14.5
Austenitic Steel	18.2	19.4	20.8	21.7	20.8	19.8

CONTROL OF DIFFUSION BONDING QUALITY

D. Kotelnikov,
Tcherkassy's Branch of the Kiev Politechnical Institute
Tcherkassy USSR

ABSTRACT

This paper presents an empirical model to predict the diffusion bonding parameters required to produce high quality joints. A four stage approach is used to define the optimum manufacturing parameters for a given combination of materials. As an example, the case for a cylindrical magnetoconductor is discussed.

INTRODUCTION

A cylindrical magnetoconductor made out of ferromagnetic and diamagnetic materials 310 + X18H9T and 310 + σp.XO,8 (Fig. 1) is the main part of an electric valve. Usual methods for joining, such as brazing or welding by fusion, are unacceptable due to low strength, porosity, cracks and wide scatter of magnetic and traction parameters. Moreover a 100-hour heat treatment is necessary for the welded magnetoconductors. A further consideration is the waste of materials during the manufacturing process which can be higher than the mass of a magnetoconductor.

The analysis of the different ways of manufacturing magnetoconductors shows that precision diffusion bonding (DB) in vacuum is the most advantaged method. The major problem arises from the complicated interaction between process parameters and DB quality. Special investigations are required to optimise the process. This paper presents an analytical method which makes it possible to select the optimal modes for DB of metals and alloys. It consists of four stages.

MODEL DEVELOPMENT

The first stage is an analysis of DB quality (Table 1). It is established that a width of a joint is a criterion of DB quality. The correlation between the width of a joint (b) and the zone of diffusion mass transfer (x) was found. Their dimensions vary in the range of 1 - 25 and 15 - 200 micrometers respectively.

The second stage requires a prediction of the optimal DB parameters which can guarantee DB quality. The average diffusion coefficients determined by an X-ray spectral investigation of diffusion joints at a DB pressure of 10MPa are shown in Table 2.

The following assumptions were taken for this case:

- DB quality is achieved if the transition structures or common grains appear in a contact zone between connected surfaces as a result of diffusion and recrystallisation processes [1-6].

- DB is sufficient at a width of a joint of 2 - 10 micrometers which corresponds to the width of 10 - 40 micrometers of a diffusion zone;

- minimum DB temperature (1183K) corresponds to $\alpha \rightarrow \gamma$ transition of iron when a large-grained structure and a minimal coercitivity for the alloy are reached;

- the diffusion and recrystallisation are accompanied by the unrestrictive mutual dissolving of Fe, Ni, Cr and restrictive (compound formation) - Fe and Ti [16,17] during DB alloy310 + X18H10T;

- the restrictive solution and the eutectoid mixture are formed during DB;

- DB time is defined by the dependence:

$$t = \frac{\tilde{X}^2}{D} = \frac{20^2.10^{-8}}{2.10^{-9}} = 2000s,$$

where $\tilde{X}$ - the average width of diffusion for the temperature 1323K at the pressure - 10MPa, vacuum - 0.04Pa and $R_a \approx 6$ micrometers.

Proceeding from the above mentioned assumptions the starting parameters are changed for DB of $\sigma p.X0.8 + 310$: P = 10MPA, T = 1323K, t = 2000s. The time for DB of 310 + X18H10T may be lowered due to an increase of the temperature, for instance, at a temperature of 1323K t can be reduced to about 1000s. The predicted parameters can give a strength of a diffusion joint equal to or greater than the strength of the lower strength metal.

The third stage is an experimental examination of the DB process. DB parameters were changed as follows:

for 310+X18H9T $\Delta P = \pm 3MPa$, $\Delta T = \pm 50K$, $\Delta t = \pm 300s$;

for 310+$\sigma p.X0.8$ $\Delta P = \pm 4MPa$, $\Delta T = \pm 50K$, $\Delta t = \pm 600s$.

The following dependencies were determined empirically,

for alloy310+X18H10T

$$\sigma_B = +341.1+20.7X_1+25.3X_2+13X_3+6.1X_1X_2-1.4X_1X_3+3.8X_2X_3-1.1X_1X_2X_3$$

$\alpha_H = +124+23X_1+19X_2+11X_3-4X_1X_2-6.0X_1X_3+4X_2X_3-3.0X_1X_2X_3$

$\varepsilon = 1.97+0.78X_1+0.7X_2+0.52X_3+0.1X_1X_2+0.02X_1X_3-0.02X2X_3-0.45X_1X_2X_3$

for alloy а10+σp.X0.8

$\sigma_B = 245.7+41.8X_1+15X_2+15.1X_3-8.3X_1X_2-3X_1X_3+6.8X_2X_3-4.7X_1X_2X_3$

$\alpha_H = 102+36X_1+19X_2+11X_3+3X_1X_2+10X_1X_3-7X_2X_3-6X_1X_2X_3$

$\varepsilon = 1.9+0.77X_1+0.7X_2+0.54X_3+0.080X_1X_2+0.08X_1X_2+0.02X_1X_2-0.02X_2X_3-$
$-0.43X_1X_2X_3$

The variables X_1, X_2, X_3 are temperature, applied pressure and time of DB respectively, σ_B - the maximum strength, α_H - the impact elasticity, ε - the relative deformation of bonded parts during DB which is defined by technical demands.

The influence of DB parameters and width of joint on strength is shown on Figure 2. The joint strength equal to a base metal strength may be reached at the width of joint b = 3 - 4 micrometers. However, the strength is sensitive to temperature and time of DB and therefore to guarantee the strength of the DB joint a width of joint of b = 5 - 8 micrometers is required.

The fourth stage is a change of optimal process mode:

for   310+X18H9T - T=1373±10K, P=15±1MPa, t=900±30s;

for   310+σp.X0.8 - T=1273±10K, P=10±1MPa, t=1800±30s.

These modes guarantee the following DB quality:

for   310+X18H10T - σ_{B_1}>370MPa, α_{H1}>156 KJ/m^2 , ε_1< 3%;

for   310+σp.X0.8 - σ_{B_2}> 280MPa, α_{H2} > 150 KJ/m^2 ε_2 < 3.1%.

The DB quality after the change of parameters from the optimum values may be determined from Figure 2 as follows:-

$$b_1 = 2.64.10^5 \exp\left[\frac{-3.2.10^5}{2RT}\right]\sqrt{t}, \text{ [µm]};$$

$$\sigma_{B1} = 20.4.10^5 \, \exp\left[\frac{-1.6.10^5}{RT}\right]\sqrt{t} + 330 \quad [MPa];$$

$$\alpha_{H1} = 0.167T + 9.67P - 222, \, [KJ/m^2]$$

$$b_2 = 1.08.10^5. \, \exp\left[\frac{-2.84.10^5}{2RT}\right]\sqrt{t}, \, [\mu m];$$

$$\sigma_{B2} = 1.43.10^5. \, \exp\left[\frac{1.42.10^5}{RT}\right]\sqrt{t} + 160, \, [MPa].$$

The required control of temperature during heating -up and then isothermal exposure (2) for DB may be determined on the basis of a mathematical model for the thermocycle $T=(t,B,I,U,R)$, derived by a method of a group arguments calculation [20]. : For heating-up, $T = f\{Z_1[y_1(t,I);y_2(U;R)];$ $Z_2.\{y_3(B;R);y_4(I;R)]\}=0.033-2.17+2.85Z_2+19.5Z_1-20Z_1Z_2\pm7K;$

where $z_1 = 0.02+0.973z_1+0.254z_2;$ $Z_2=-0.25+0.754z_3+0.524z_4;$
$y_1 = 6.54+141t+19.0I,03t.I;y_2=0.13+0.02U+0.25R;$
$y_3 = 0.58-0.24B-0.222R-0.25B.R.;y_4=9.26-68.9I+843R+121I^2+23.4I.R.;$

For isothermal exposure, $T=1.16+3.2.10^{-4}I+2.41.10^{-5}U\pm5K;$

where t - time of DB [min], I - current of a glow discharge [A], U - voltage between electrodes [100V], B - vacuum [cm Hg]; R - anode resistance [100 ohm].

The DB process allows the bonding and heat treatment processes of 310 to be combined to obtain a minimum coercitivity. It is described by the following dependencies:

H_c^{1273}=79.6 (1.12+1.10^{-4}·t), A/m

H_c^{1373}=79.6 (1.1.10^{-4}.t), A/m, when the cooling velocity on $\alpha \rightarrow \gamma$ transition should be 0.011 - 0.028°C/s to guarantee value of H_c>0.65A/m.

CONCLUSIONS

Subsequent testing of DB joints for the two alloys show their leakproofness, vacuum density and a fatigue strength of 110 and 50 MPa for 1.10^6 cycles (Figure 3), which guarantees DB quality. Not a single defective DB joint was received during 10 years of working in this mode.

REFERENCES

1. Larikov L. N., Riabov V. R., Falchenko V. M. Diffusion processes in a solid state on welding. - Moscow: Machinostronic, 1975.-192p.

2. Kasakov N. F., Shishnova A. P., Lado L. V. Using of a metallographic analysis for a clearing of a mechanical properties of a welded joints - In a book: Diffusion bonding in vacuum. Moscow : MTIMP, 1971, pp32-55.

3. Kotelnikov D. I. Investigations of technology and an equipment of a diffusion welding: Dissertation, Kiev, KPI, 1968 - 150pp

4. Kapralov B. P., Sigachev A. P. Investigation of a diffusion welding in vacuum of a molybdenum with iron. - In book: IY Conf. "Diffusion welding of metals, alloys and nonmetallic materials", May, 1966, MTIMP, 1968, pp94-106.

5. Venzovskii I. V., Hondishev A. F. Diffusion bonding heterogeneous materials in electronic: Ibid.

6. Malevskii U. B., Markashova L. I., Nesmich V. S. Role of the recrystallisation at welding in solid state. - In book: Diffusion bonding in vacuum. Moscow: MTIMP, 1971, pp87-98.

7. Kazakov N. F., Mizzoev K. M., Malimova M. N. Microstructure investigations of hard alloys joined with steel. - Ibid, p185-194

8. Shepetina G. A., Charouhina K. E. Investigation of diffusion welding in vacuum of steel 18XMBA with hard alloy. - Ibid, pp125-130.

9. Investigation of diffusion welding of EVP. G. V. Konushkov, N. F. Kazakov, V. I. Erekin, N. I. Fedorov. - Ibid, pp140-148.

10. Application of diffusion welding for bonding alloys with steel G. A. Schepetina, A. V. Kitaev, V. A. Gorshkov, A. V. Mamontova. - Ibid, pp239-245.

11. Technological parameter influence on transfer mass at diffusion welding of nickel/U. . Malerskii, L. I. Markashova, D. D. Pereverzev, V. S. Nesnich. In book YII Conference on diffusion welding in vacuum. Moscow, MTIMP, 1973, pp42-47.

12. Investigation of diffusion bonding of Cu and Pt./E.A. Iour, A. N. Kvasha, V. V. Nichowshkin, V. E. Prihodiko. - Ibid, pp48-51.

13. Velikonoia M., Limpel I. First steps in diffusion welding in Yugoslavia. - Ibid, pp166-175.

14. Diffusion welding at titanium./E.S. Karakozov, L. M. Orlova, V. V. Peshkov, V. I. Grigorievski. - Moscow, Metallurgica, 1977-p.277

15. Diatlov V. I., Kotelnikov D. I. Investigation of banding of armo-Fe with steel. - In book: V conference. Moscow, MTIMP, 1980, pp198-203.

16. Metallochemical properties of periodical system elements/ II. Kornilov, N. M. Matveev, L. I. Priashina, R. S. Poliakova. - Moscow, Nauka, 1966, p351.

17. Hansen M., Anderko U. Structures of binary alloys, Moscow, Metallurgia, 1962, Vol.I, 863 p. Vol.II, 625p.

18. Zait V. Diffusion in metals. - Moscow, Inostr. Liter. 1958, 384p.

19. Novikov V. U., Kazahov N. F. Optimisation of diffusion welding modes of steels   10 and X18H10T by factor plan experiments. In book: Protective covering in machine building. Krasnoyarsk: Polytechnical Institute, 1973, pp131-140.

20. Ivahnenko A. H. Enristic systems of auto-organisation in technical cybernetics. Kiev, Technika, 1972.

TABLE 1

Materials	σ_B, MPa	δ, %	a_H, J/cm²	X, μm	B, μm	Nature of diffusion	Literature Source
Steel 15+Ni	400	9	65	15-30(M,X)	6...8	availability of joint	2
12X18HAT+Fe	400..410	-	-	60...75(X)	6...8	-//-	3
Mo+IX13	460	-	-	40...80(MX)	-	transition zone	4
W+Ni	-	-	-	35(X)	10	-//- joint	5
12X18HgT+12X18HgT	-	-	-	50..70(M)	5.10	common grains in bonding zone	3
Steel145+12X1HAT	380..540	-	87...175	60..70(M,X)	6...8	-//- joint	3
XH77-T1-0+XH77T1-0	740-760	42.56	-	-	-	-//- common grain	6
BK8+Ni+T15H6+Ni	200..210	-	-	15..20(M)	1..5	-//- transition zone	7
18X2H4BA+BK20	-	-	-	80..200	5..7	-//-	8
Cu+Cu	210	-	-	-	2	-//-	9
Cu+carbon steel	140	-	-	-	2	-//-	9
Cu+X18HAT	180	-	-	-	2	-//-	9
BKX+36HXT1-0	600..800	-	-	40..500(M,X)	8.10	-//-	10
Ni+Ni	-	-	-	30..40(M,X)	5.10	-//-	11
Cu+Pt	150	-	-	-	10	-//-	12
brass+Al	-	-	-	40(X)	5	-//-	13
Cu+Al	-	-	-	20(X)	-	-//-	13
Fe+Ni	-	-	50..60	20..25(X)	-	-//-	1
12X2H4A	-	-	-	20..25(X)	-	-//-	1
Ti-alloys	-	-	-	-	8..25	small grain zone	14

Width of transfer mass zone was defined by metallographic (M) or X-ray (X) methods

TABLE 2

Diffusant	T,K	D cm^2/s	D$_o$ cm^2/s	Q$_o$ J/mole	Literature Source
Fe	1203..1395	-	$1.04 \cdot 10^{-3}$	200640	18
	1243..639	-	5.8	310156	18
Cr	1473	$(1.7..81.) \cdot 10^{-9}$	-	56430	18
	1423	$6.8 \cdot 10^{-10}$	-	-	15
	1623	$(2.2..5.3) \cdot 10^{-8}$	-	-	18
Cu	-	-	3	254980	18
Ni	1473	$9.3 \cdot 10^{-11}$	-	-	18
Cr	1473	$4.5 \cdot 10^{-9}$	-	-	15
Ni	1473	$2 \cdot 10^{-9}$	-	-	15
Fe	1473	$2 \cdot 10^{-9}$	-	-	15
Fe	1333..1.533	$(0.8..9.0) \cdot 10^{-9}$	-	-	1

- Fe is base metal for all case, Q - average diffusion factor, D$_o$ - constant,

Q$_o$ - activation energy.

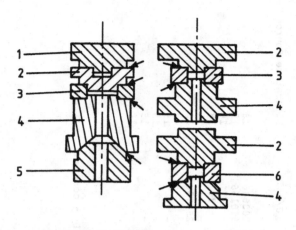

FIGURE 1.   MAGNETOCONDUCTORS MANUFACTURED FROM PARTS: 1,3,5 –
FROM STEEL X18110T, 2,4 – FROM STEEL 10,6 – FROM BRONZE
δp,X0,8; INDICATORS SHOW THE DIFFUSION BONDING.

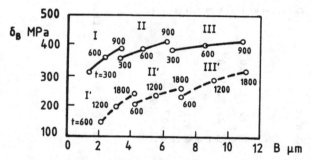

FIGURE 2.   DEPENDENCE STRENGTH OF BONDINGS Э10+X18H10T (SOLID LINE,
P=15 MPa) and Э10+δpX0, 8 (DOTTED LINE, P=10 MPa) ON WIDTH
WELD JOINT "b", DEFINED BY TEMPERATURES: I–I=1273, II–T=1373,
III–T=1473 k, I'–T=1223 k, II'–T=1273 k, III'–T=1373 k.

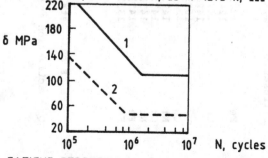

FIGURE 3.   FATIGUE STRENGTH TEST RESULTS BONDING Э10+X18H10T (1)
and Э10+δp,X 0,8 (2).

Development of Diffusion Bonding Techniques
for Al-Li base Alloy AA8090

R.A.Ricks, G.J.Mahon, N.C.Parson, T.Heinrich* and P.-J.Winkler*

Alcan International Ltd., Southam Road, Banbury, Oxon. OX16 7SP

*M.B.B. Central Laboratories, Ottobrunn, D 8000, Muenchen, 80. F.R.G.

ABSTRACT

AA8090 superplastic sheet is now commercially available allowing the intrinsic low density of the alloy to be combined with the complexity of shape possible from superplastic forming routes. In order to take full advantage of this technology and produce lightweight expanded structures, a selective bonding technique is required which produces a joint with adequate room temperature strength and capable of withstanding the stresses associated with the superplastic forming operation. Such technology is established in the production of titanium alloy components but has been hampered in aluminium alloys due to the stability of the oxide layer always present on surfaces exposed to the atmosphere.

A variety of bonding techniques have been investigated including diffusion bonding, thin foil interlayers, and roll clad zinc interlayer (transient liquid phase bonding) routes. Detailed metallographic data demonstrating bond line integrity is reported along with room temperature shear strengths and peel strengths measured at superplastic forming temperatures. It will be shown that diffusion bonding and solid state bonding with interlayers invariably produces oxide debris at the bond line which limits the strength of the bond. Successful bonds can be produced using transient liquid phase bonding, satisfying high and low temperature strength requirements, providing the correct combinations of boning technique and process parameters are used.

Introduction

For many years scientists have sought to emulate in aluminium alloys the diffusion bonding achievements of Ti and Ti base alloys without the natural oxide instability and oxygen solubility inherent in these alloys to assist bond formation. The highly stable and tenacious oxide formed on the surface of all aluminium alloys effectively prevents true diffusion bonding taking place unless stringent surface modifications are made (eg. 1,2) and these are usually only possible in conditions of high vacuum (3) which may not be easily achievable in a production environment and would certainly add to the cost of the bonding technology. Nevertheless many claims to achieve diffusion bonding exist in the patent literature (eg. 4,5), many quoting impressive shear strength data, invariably acquired at ambient temperature, although at least one publication reports difficulty in achieving consistenty high properties from the bond (6). Clearly if diffusion bonding, or any related bonding technique, is eventually to be used in any structural application, including in combination with superplastic forming, reliable, consistent bonds must be developed which could provide useful bond strengths at both ambient and, for superplastic forming applications, elevated temperatures. Such bond strengths need not require parent metal strength, provided consistency is ensured and the component can survive the fabrication process and provide acceptable service properties. Indeed in view of the relatively large bond areas often employed for more practical reasons, the design strength of any bond may well be considerably less than that of the parent metal.

One consideration of diffusion bonding, which is often overlooked, is the low level of bond deformation achieved during bond formation, allowing net shaped components to be produced without the need for expensive post bonding machining operations. Low joint deformation can be achieved in true diffusion bonding, but many reported bonding experiments often use excessive pressure to achieve adequate bond strengths (presumably due to metal/metal contact after oxide rupture) and the final component shape may differ significantly from the starting shapes of the individual sheets. Furthermore, for superplastic forming after bonding in aluminium alloys, there exists a constraint on the time at elevated temperature (ie. during bonding) since the microstructure is inherently unstable and excessive recovery and recrystallisation must be avoided to ensure adequate formability without cavitation and premature failure.

With these constraints in mind the following programme of work was initiated between Alcan International Ltd. (Banbury) and M.B.B. Central Laboratories (Ottobrunn) to develop practical bonding processes in superplastic Al-Li alloy AA8090 (Al-2.4%Li-1.2%Cu-0.6%Mg-0.14%Zr). Both solid state and transient liquid phase bonding routes have been studied and the advantages and disadvantages of each route discussed. Bond strength requirements will be considered and the successful combination of bonding with subsequent superplastic forming will be discussed.

Experimental

Initial bonding experiments were conducted in a custom built bonding rig at M.B.B., allowing bonding to be carried out under vacuum (10^{-4} bar) or inert gas using R.F. induction heating of specimen and platens. Various experimental conditions were evaluated, including specimen faying surface preparation, and these data are reported in the following sections. Transient liquid phase bonding has been achieved by roll bonding surface layers of high purity Zn base alloys to the surface of the 8090 alloy to provide a low melting point material with reasonable solubility in aluminium (7). In all cases a bond time of 60mins was employed since previous studies in house had shown this to be the practical limit of thermal exposure before unacceptable loss of superplastic performance in the 8090. Figure 1 shows the experimentally determined pressure limitation as a function of temperature to ensure less than 5% thickness deformation during bonding, and this curve was employed to define maximum pressure at any temperature of bonding. A sample size of 50x50mm was chosen, comprising two pieces of 2mm thick sheet bonded together. After appropriate surface treatment all specimens were ultrasonically degreased in trichlorethylene and dried immediately prior to bonding. After bonding four specimens 10mm wide were machined to provide shear-lap test pieces (figure 2) or, T-peel test pieces (figure 3) depending on test mode chosen. For the latter the bottom sheet was bent through 90° along a central line and inserted in a slot cut in the bottom platen, thus allowing only half the area to be bonded. This method was prefered to stop-off agents since less bond damage occured during subsequent specimen handling. For some solid state bonding experiments thin foil interlayers were employed produced by laboratory rolling appropriate starting material to a thickness of 100μm. This interlayer material was invariably used in the fully soft condition and chemically cleaned (NaOH, HNO_3) and degreased prior to insertion between the faying surfaces. Bonds were tested using standard mechanical testing procedures for shear lap specimens (and see next section) and examined by optical and transmission electron microscopy (T.E.M.). Specimen preparation for the latter consisted of machining 3mm discs of material containing the bond line along a diameter followed by either jet-electropolishing or ion-beam machining to perforation.

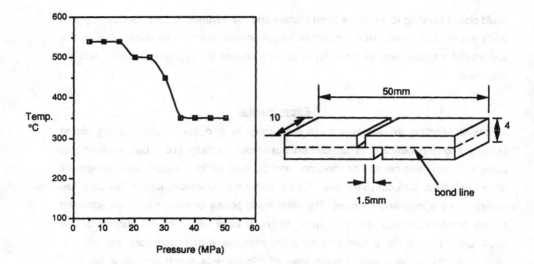

Figure 1
Experimental pressure limitation as a function of
temperature to achieve <5% deformation

Figure 2
Geometry of shear lap specimen used in this
investigation

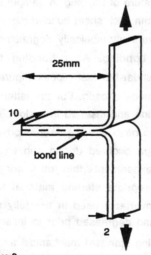

Figure 3
Geometry of hot T-peel specimen used in this
investigation

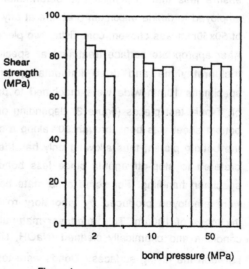

Figure 4
Effect of bonding pressure on room temperature
bond shear strength

Results and Discussion

a) Solid state bonding experiments

Initial experiments were conducted to assess the effect of pressure on bond strength at constant temperature (500°C). For these experiments a standard specimen surface treatment was employed consisting of abrasion using a "Scotchbrite" alumina filled nylon pad. This was found to give an easily reproducable surface finish which, after degreasing, was found by surface analysis to be free from major contaminants. Figure 4 shows the effect of pressure on room temperature bond shear strength and indicates that little benefit is to be gained with excessive pressure even if 50MPa is used and excessive deformation (~20%) is tolerated in this alloy. Typical bond shear strengths lie in the range 70-85MPa which is approximately 30% of the parent metal shear strength in this condition. The effect of bonding temperature on room temperature bond shear strength is shown in figure 5. Higher bond strengths may be achieved at 540°C compared with 500°C albeit with increased scatter in the data. Under these conditions of pressure (10MPa) bond deformation was still limited to 5% (figure 1).

The effect of faying surface treatment was assessed by considering the R_A value (mean surface roughness) of a number of surface treatments including shot peening (shot blasting was avoided due to the tendency to embed the angular particles in the soft alloy surface). Figure 6 shows the mean surface roughness of the surfaces developed by the various techniques and figure 7 shows the resultant room temperature bond shear strengths at two bonding temperatures. Although there is considerable scatter the data do suggest that higher bond strengths may be achieved with rougher surfaces, although the surface produced with a rotary steel brush could develop severe surface tearing if excessive pressure were used. It is possible under these conditions of bonding that the enhanced strength with roughness is due to to deformation of touching surface asperities causing metal/metal contact after oxide rupture. With touching asperities the overall bond deformation will cease once the contact area increases such that the local material flow stress is reached. With larger asperities (rougher surface) although the bond area should remain the same, each contact point will undergo higher deformation possibly leading to higher bond strength. This mechanism of bonding would not be expected to be sensitive to atmosphere, provided undue oxidation were avoided since atmospheric contact of the developing metal/metal regions would not occur. Bonds made in both argon and vacuum showed little difference in strength which lends supportive evidence to this bonding mechanism.

Metallographic examination of the bonds created under conditions described above revealed a readily identifiable bond line decorated with coarse precipitates (figure 8) formed during the relatively slow cool down to ambient temperature. Many

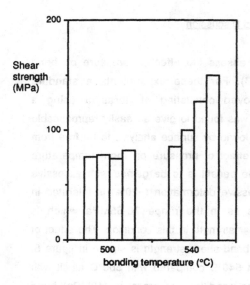

Figure 5
Effect of bonding temperature on room temperature
bond shear strength

Figure 6
Mean surface roughness value (RA) for 8090
with differing surface treatments

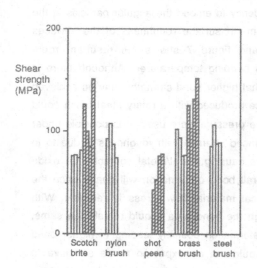

Figure 7
Effect of faying surface preparation on room
temperature bond shear strength

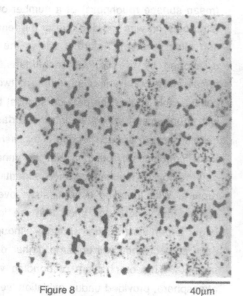

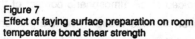

Figure 8
Optical micrograph showing bond line in 8090

regions of the bond appeared featureless and this was confirmed by T.E.M. of foils prepared containing the bond line, as shown in figure 9a. Along any particular bond line the density of fine precipitates or oxide dispersoids varied from zero (ie. a clean bond seen as a high angle grain boundary)(figure 9a) to a heavily decorated bond were mechanical oxide disruption had not taken place. Close examination of the oxide containing regions of the bond line (figure 9b) revealed that the morphology of the dispersoids consisted of discrete, spherical particles, inconsistent with simple mechanical disruption which would leave films of insoluble oxide after exposure to modest temperatures used in bonding this alloy. One explanation for this oxide morphology is that, concommitant with the mechanical disruption of the oxide film, chemical attack had also taken place. The elements Mg and Li, present in the 8090 are known to form more stable oxides and compounds than Al_2O_3, which is the kinetically prefered oxide on 8090 formed at room temperature (8), and could thus assist disruption of the faying surface oxide during bonding. This hypothesis was tested by the fabrication of a series of alloys containing all the alloying elements in 8090 except either Mg, or Li, or both. This work has been reported previously (9) but for completeness the essential findings will be reported here. If both Li and Mg were omitted from the alloy extremely poor bonds were developed under similar bonding conditions, having practically zero strength at room temperature (figure 10). T.E.M. examination of the bond line revealed a different oxide morphology to that shown in figure 9b for the 8090 alloy, in the alloy containing no Mg or Li regions of continuous oxide were readily observed (figure 11) indicating that chemical oxide disruption had not taken place during bonding in this alloy. Addition of either Mg or Li to this alloy (Al-1.2%Cu-0.14%Zr) improved the achievable bond strengths (figure 10), although attainment of 8090 strength levels was not possible. T.E.M. examination of these alloys revealed chemical oxide film disruption in these alloys (9), although to a lesser extent than seen in the 8090 alloy.

The bond strength data and results of metallographic examination have revealed that the likely mechanisms of bonding in 8090 are as follows;

a) mechanical deformation of faying surface asperities creating metal/metal
   bonding at such sites after oxide rupture. These sites are recognisable in
   the final microstructure by the featureless grain boundaries which form.

b) bonding is assisted at sites where mechanical oxide rupture does not occur
   by chemical disruption of the faying surface oxide. This generates a spherical
   reaction product (probably Li/Mg aluminate) and in doing so improves
   the final bond strength.

The need for both mechanisms to operate to develop useful bond strengths is supported by published bond strength data for pure aluminium samples (mechanism

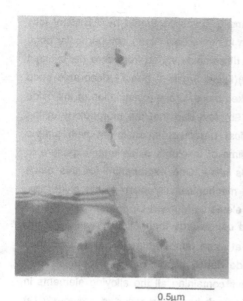

0.5μm

Figure 9a
T.E.M. image showing clean bond line formed in
8090

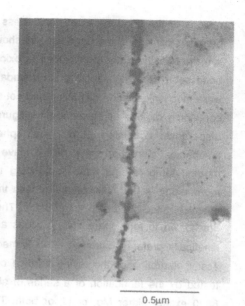

0.5μm

Figure 9b
T.E.M. image showing dispersoid decorated
bond line in 8090

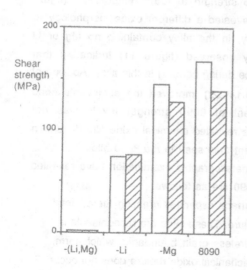

Shear
strength
(MPa)

200

100

0

-(Li,Mg)   -Li   -Mg   8090

Figure 10
Effect of alloy content on room temperature bond
shear strength

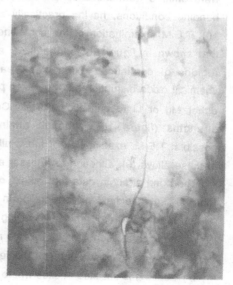

0.5μm

Figure 11
T.E.M. image showing continuous oxide film at bond
line in alloy lacking Mg and Li

b) above will not operate)(10) where poor strengths were developed with only mechanical oxide disruption.

At this stage in the investigation the hot peel strength of the bonds was determined as discussed in the previous section. Hot T-peel tests were carried out in a modified superplastic tensile testing machine operating at a strain rate of 1×10^{-3} s^{-1} at 520°C, if necessary with a superimposed hydrostatic back pressure of argon of up to ~4MPa. The results from this method of testing revealed that at typical superplastic forming temperatures for this alloy, very low peel strengths (figure 12) in the range 1-1.5 N/mm were recorded. A simple calculation reveals that with such a peel strength at superplastic forming temperature the limitation of force on the bond line to avoid debonding would require (for 2mm thick sheet) a superplastic material having a flow stress of less than ~0.5MPa. Clearly such a low flow stress is not achievable at any practical strain rate (11) and typical flow stress values for 8090 in the strain rate range of maximum strain rate sensitivity are of the order 2-4MPa which implies bond peel strengths ~5x higher than developed by the solid state bonding experiments described above.

In view of the observed increase in room temperature bond shear strength of the solid state bonds as Li and Mg were added to the alloy, one possible route for increasing the effectiveness of the chemical bond formation would be to use a thin interlayer of a soft, chemically active alloy foil between the faying surfaces. Under conditions of pressure and temperature the deformable interlayer should accommodate the surface asperities of the 8090 and allow chemical attack of the alumina on the faying surfaces. Two inherent problems may exist with this approach:

a) two bond lines will be created thus increasing the chance of failure due to poor bonding

b) the mechanical deformation of the 8090 asperities will be reduced due to soft, deforming interlayer thus reducing this contribution to bond strength.

Three thin foil interlayer alloys were chosen for investigation, together with a pure Al foil for control, as follows

Al-0.5%Ga

Al-1.3%Li

Al-4.5%Mg   (all wt%)

all of which are known to attack alumina on aluminium. Alloy compositions were chosen as the maximum alloy addition which still enabled 100μm foil to be rolled. Using these soft, deformable interlayer foils a series of experiments was conducted to assess the shear and hot T-peel strengths of bonds made at 500°C and 540°C under similar pressure and time conditions as discussed previously. Room temperature shear strength data are shown in figure 13, from which it may be seen that the alloy

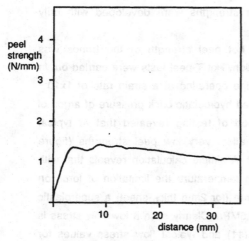

Figure 12
Peel strength of solid state bonds in 8090 at 520°C

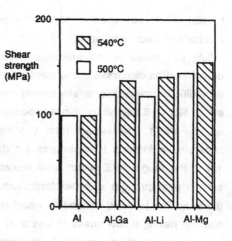

Figure 13
Room temperature shear strengths of bonds made with deformable interlayers

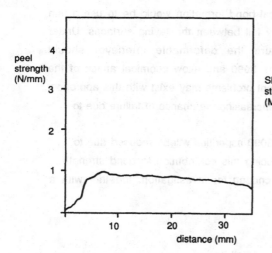

Figure 14
Peel strengths of bonds made with thin foil interlayers at 520°C

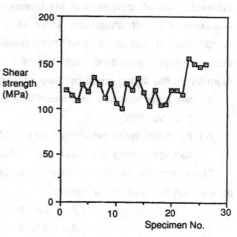

Figure 15
Room temperature shear strengths of transient liquid phase bonds made with roll clad Zn alloy interlayer.

foils give greater strength than the pure Al foil, supporting the view that chemical oxide disruption takes place, and of the choices of interlayer material the Al-Mg foil appears to produce the highest shear strength values, now in excess of 150MPa (~70% of the parent metal shear strength). However, hot T-peel strength data (figure 14) shows that the strength of the bonds under these conditions is significantly weaker than those bonds made with no interlayer. These data highlight an important detail of bond strength assessment. Under lap-shear conditions the entire bond area is simultaneously stressed and the additional chemical oxide disruption may well develop enhanced bond strengths, as seen in the interlayer bonds. Under T-peel testing conditions the bond area is sequentially tested in tension and clearly the areas of chemical oxide disruption do not significantly contribute to bond strength compared with the mechanical oxide rupture at contact asperities. For the purposes of this investigation neither solid state bonding technique produced bond strengths sufficient to allow subsequent superplastic forming and alternative bonding technology was considered.

b) Transient liquid phase bonding

Several surface coatings are being investigated in this joint programme but this manuscript will only consider the use of high purity Zn-Cu alloys roll bonded to the surface of 8090. These alloys melt at ~420°C thus at 540°C there is ample superheat to ensure liquation and promote diffusion. All transient liquid bonding relies on diffusion to remove excess solute and allow isothermal solidification and thus the total amount of solute for removal is critical. Roll bonding technology can only produce Zn-Cu alloy layers ~30µm thick before severe surface cracking develops, probably enhanced by Li and other solute diffusion into the Zn layer, thus large amounts of Zn/Cu need to be removed by diffusion. Nevertheless respectable bond shear strengths may be developed after 60mins at 540°C with little deformation of the bond (12) and with good reproducibility as shown in figure 15. Optical metallography of these bonds reveals that excess Zn remains at grain boundary sites in the microstructure (figure 16) allowing rapid bond strength attainment albeit with some loss in overall properties, as reflected in the lower recorded shear strength values. The real advantages in this form of bonding are best seen under hot T-peel testing conditions (figure 17) which show that peel strengths at 520°C in excess of 5N/mm may be achieved. With peel strengths of this nature it is conceivable that subsequent superplastic forming may be attempted with success , as demonstrated in previous publications (12). Further development of these bonding technologies has allowed transient liquid phase bonding of 8090 in times as short as 15mins thus ensuring good retention of superplastic properties, and this technology is now being assessed for the production of two sheet (and eventually three sheet) superplastically formed structures (figure 18)

Figure 16
100µm
Optical micrograph showing bond generated in
8090 clad with Zn alloy

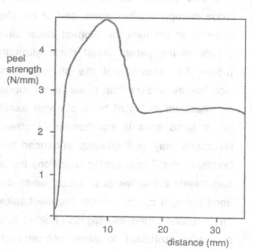

peel
strength
(N/mm)

distance (mm)

Figure 17
Peel strength of Zn clad 8090 bond at 520°C

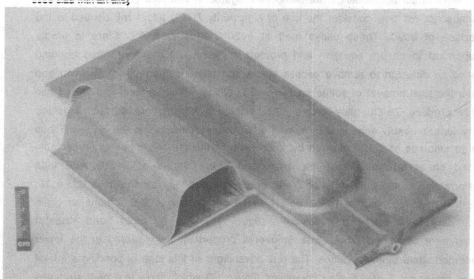

Figure 18
Two sheet bonded and superplastically formed component employing transient liquid phase bonding of 8090
alloy

Summary and Conclusions

From the data reported above it is clear that bond strengths developed in aluminium alloys will fall short of parent metal strength if bonding conditions similar to those used in this investigation are used, which are seen to be practical and viable in production environments. The solid state bonding experiments show that the method of strength assessment is important in comparing relative bonding technology suitability. For the purposes of this study the somewhat lower room temperature shear strengths achieved with transient liquid phase bonding were acceptable given the higher hot peel strengths achieved by this route. It should be recommended that shear strength data are not used as a standard assessment of bond strength and reliability owing to the possibility of recording very high shear strength values from bonds which may have almost no tensile peel strength. Finally the real value of diffusion or transient liquid phase bonding lies in the achievement of many desirable bond features, including low deformation, rapid bond strength formation if subsequent superplastic deformation is desired and adequate bond strength to survive service conditions. The results of this investigation to date indicate that transient liquid phase bonding is best suited to achieving this combination of features.

Acknowledgements

The authors wish to thank Alcan International for permission to publish this manuscript. The T.E.M. data was acquired as part of an Alcan funded Ph.D. study by Mr E.R. Maddrell at the University of Cambridge under the supervision of Dr.E.R. Wallach.

References

1.   D.V.Dunford and P.G.Partridge
     J. Mat. Sci. **22**, (1987), 1790

2.   P.G.Partridge and D.V.Dunford
     J. Mat. Sci. **22**, (1987), 1597

3.   D.Hauser, P.A.Kammer and J.H.Dedrick.
     Weld. Res. Sup. Jan. 1967. p11ff.

4.   European patent appl. No 0 350 220

5.   U.S. Patent No 4,732,312

6.   J.Pilling and N.Ridley
     Mat. Sci. Tech. **3**, 1987, 353.

7.   U.K. Patent Appl. No 2,134,833

8.   C.F.Knights, V.J.Moore, J.C.Riviere and L.S.Welch
        A.E.R.E. Harwell report No. G4060

9.   E.R.Madrell, R.A.Ricks and E.R.Wallach
        Proc. 5th Int. Conf. Al-Li alloys, Williamsburg, VA. (1989)
        Eds. T.H.Sanders and E.A.Starke, p.451

10.   T.Enjo, K.Ikeuchi and K.Furukawa
        J. Jap. Inst. Light Met. July 1985, p.388

11.   R.A.Ricks and N.C.Parson
        Proc. 5th Int. Conf. Al-Li alloys, Williamsburg, VA, (1989)
        Eds. T.H.Sanders and E.A.Starke, p.169

11.   R.A.Ricks, P.-J.Winkler, H.Stoklossa and R.Grimes
        ibid. p.441

DIFFUSION BONDING OF SUPERPLASTIC ALUMINIUM ALLOYS USING A TRANSIENT LIQUID PHASE INTERLAYER (ZINC)

D.W. Livesey and N. Ridley

Materials Science Centre

University of Manchester/UMIST

Grosvenor Street, MANCHESTER, M1 7HS.

Abstract

The effects of a vapour deposited zinc interlayer on the strength of diffusion bonds produced in three Al-based alloys: 7475, 8090 and Supral 220, has been investigated. The bonding pressure was applied mechanically and the bond strengths were evaluated using a constrained lap shear compression test. The integrity of the bond was also examined using optical and scanning electron microscopy. For 7475 alloy, maximum shear strengths of up to ~ 270 MNm^{-2} (T621 condition) were obtained, while the corresponding strengths for 8090 and Supral 220 were up to 210 MNm^{-2} (T6 condition), and 100 MNm^{-2}, respectively. Although an appreciable variability of shear strength was noted for bonds formed between chemically cleaned and zinc coated surfaces, the application of ion-beam etching prior to coating led to a significant improvement in bond strength and/or to a reduction in bond strength variability.

1. Introduction

There is considerable interest in extending the diffusion bonding (DB) and superplastic forming (SPF) technology which has been developed for titanium alloys to other superplastic materials. However, in the case of aluminium alloys the problems associated with the tenacious surface oxide have made it difficult to obtain reproducible high quality bonds.

Previous procedures used to produce diffusion bonds in Al alloys have been reviewed recently by Pilling[1] and by Partridge [2]. The methods have included the bonding of chemically cleaned surfaces using static compression [3, 4] or gas pressure [5]; the use of Al and Al alloy interlayers [6, 7]; the deposition of protective coatings on, or implantation in, argon sputter cleaned surfaces [2, 8-10]; the application by vapour deposition, or roll cladding, of transient liquid interlayers to the surfaces to be bonded [4, 11].

In the present work the surfaces of the SP aluminium alloys to be bonded have either been chemically cleaned, or chemically cleaned and then ion-beam etched, prior to the vapour deposition of zinc coatings. The surfaces have then been bonded in air by static compression.

2. Experimental

2.1 Materials and Surface preparation

The three superplastic aluminium alloys to be bonded were Al - 7475 (nominal wt % composition: Al - 5.5 Zn - 2.3 Mg - 1.5 Cu - 0.2 Cr, Al-8090 (Al - 2.5 Li - 1.2 Cu - 0.6 Mg - 0.12 Zr) and Supral 220 (Al-6 Cu-0.4Zr-0.2 Mg - 0.25 Si - 0.1 Ge). The 7475 alloy was manufactured by Alcoa, and the 8090 and Supral 220 alloys were produced by British Alcan. The materials were received in the form of sheet of approximately 3mm thickness.

Rectangular blanks measuring 22mm x 88mm were machined from the sheets. One surface of each blank was polished to a P1200 grit finish, with the final grinding stage giving fine scratches lying parallel to the length of the specimen. Talysurf measurements gave a surface roughness, or R_A value, of 0.08 μm. Specimens were ultrasonically cleaned and given a chemical treatment involving pickling in hot 10% Na OH solution followed by immersion in 30% nitric acid. Surfaces were then coated with zinc to a depth of 1.5- 12 μm by vapour deposition in an Edwards coating unit. The zinc was heated in a molybdenum crucible located beneath the specimen, and gave an even layer of predictable thickness. To examine the effect of argon-ion cleaning, the specimen was made cathodic and a potential of 5000 V was used to produce a glow discharge for 10-30 minutes prior to vapour deposition.

2.2 Bonding procedure

The 7475 and 8090 specimens were diffusion bonded at 515°C, and the Supral 220 at 460°C, by static compression, in air, between stainless steel plattens. A pre-load of approximately 10% of the full bonding load was maintained while the specimen was heated to test temperature. Bonding pressures and times varied from 2 MPa - 5 MPa and 2½ hours - 10 hours, respectively.

2.3 Testing of bonds

Lap shear tests were performed in a constraining jig and involved the application of a compressive force to produce a shear stress on the overlapped region. Specimen buckling was avoided by this method and an

overlap of 1.33 t used, where t is sheet thickness. Shear strengths quoted
are the maximum load the sample is able to support, divided by the bonded
area tested. The bonded specimen was machined into 2 test pieces each
having a bond area of ~ 60 mm^2. The Al-7475 was given a standard T621 heat
treatment, the Al-8090 a standard T6 heat treatment while the Supral 220
was not heat treated, before testing. The rate of loading of the lap shear
test pieces was 0.5 mm min^{-1}. Typical stress-displacement curves are shown
in Fig. 1 for bonds of various shear strengths and for the parent metals.
It can be seen that the stronger bonds display a small but significant
degree of plasticity prior to failure for all three alloys, and that the
stress-displacement curves have the same shape as is shown by the parent
metals. The overlap used did not led to peeling of the test piece, as has
been discussed by Partridge (2). The bond integrity was also examined by
optical and scanning electron microscopy on sections through the bond
region. In some cases composition profiles were obtained for different
zinc coating thicknesses by electron probe microanalysis (SEM) through the
bond region.

3. Results

3.1 Al-7475

Specimens were bonded after chemical cleaning and zinc coating, or after
ion-beam cleaning and zinc coating. The maximum thickness of zinc which
was investigated was 12 μm. Bonding was carried out at 515°C, which is the
optimum temperature for SPF. The lap shear strength of the parent metal
after heat treatment (T621) was 307 MNm^{-2}.

Bond shear strengths for selected test conditions are given in Table 1. It
was noted that for nearly all test conditions the bond strength increased

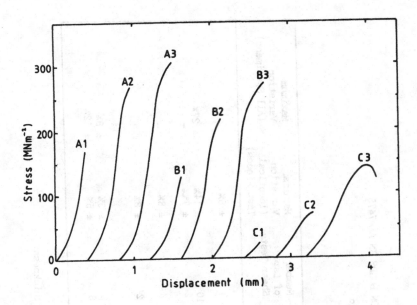

Fig. 1: Lap shear, stress-displacement curves for 7475(A) and 8090(B) both bonded at 515°C; 3 MPa; 3 μm Zn, and Supral 220(C) bonded at 460°C; 5 MPa; 3 μm Zn. A1, B1 and C1, chemically cleaned. A_2, B_2 and C_2, ion beam etched for 10 minutes. A3, B3 and C3, parent metal.

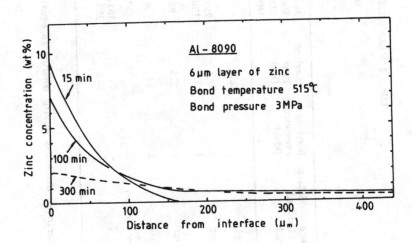

Fig 2.: Zinc concentration profiles for various bonding times. 8090.

TABLE I : LAP SHEAR STRENGTHS OF DIFFUSION BONDS IN AL-7475

BONDING TEMPERATURE 515°

* Surface Condition (after chemical cleaning)	Bonding Pressure (MPa)	Bonding Time (Hours)	Average Shear Strength (MNm^{-2})	Maximum Shear Strength (MNm^{-2})	Number of Lap Shear Tests	Maximum Variation (Identical Test Pieces)	Maximum Variation (All Specimens)
1.5 μm zinc	3	2.5	131.6	139.4	2	± 6%	-
3 μm zinc	3	2.5	228.6	259.5	10	± 14%	± 27%
	4	2.5	196.5	209.5	2	± 7%	-
6 μm zinc	3	2.5	85.7	92.9	2	± 8%	-
12 μm zinc	3	10	136.3	146.7	2	± 8%	
Ion-beam cleaned 10 mins. + 3 μm zinc	2	2.5	151.4	155.4	6	± 3%	± 8%
	3	2.5	259.4	273.4	8	± 5%	± 12%

* The interlayer thickness during bonding is equal to twice the coating thickness.

with increase of bonding pressure from 2 to 3 MPa. Bonding at the latter pressure led to compressive strains of 5-10%. A further increase in pressure gave unacceptably high levels of specimen distortion with little change in bond shear strength. An increase in the bonding time from 2½ to 10 hours did not increase shear strength except for chemically cleaned specimens coated with the thickest layers of zinc (12 μm).

The chemically cleaned and coated specimens showed a maximum variation of ± 14% for the bond strengths of test pieces from the same bonded specimen, for optimum bonding conditions (Table 1). However, overall scatter for a series of specimens bonded under the same conditions was higher at ± 27%. Ion beam cleaning for ~ 10 minutes followed by deposition of 3 μm of zinc resulted in a slight improvement in shear strengths up to ~ 270 MNm^{-2}. In addition, the scatter between test pieces from the same specimen was reduced to ± 5%, under optimum bonding conditions, and scatter from all tests to ± 12%. Increasing the time of ion beam etching did not result in further improvement.

3.2 Al-8090

The lap shear strength of the base material was measured at 272 MNm^{-2}. Tests were performed at a temperature of 515°C which is near that for optimum superplastic deformation in this alloy. At 2 MPa pressure very low bond strengths were observed while above 3 MPa specimens were highly distorted. Coating with 3 μm of zinc after chemical cleaning gave a maximum of bond strength of ~ 185 MNm^{-2}. Increasing the zinc layer beyond 3 μm had an adverse effect on bond strength. Bond shear strengths are listed in Table 2.

TABLE 2 : LAP SHEAR STRENGTHS OF DIFFUSION BONDS IN AL-8090

BONDING TEMPERATURE 515°C

Surface Condition (after chemical cleaning)	Bonding Pressure (MPa)	Bonding Time (Hours)	Average Shear Strength (MNm^{-2})	Maximum Shear Strength (MNm^{-2})	Number of Lap Shear Tests	Maximum Variation (Identical Test Pieces)	Maximum Variation (All Specimens)
3 μm zinc	2	2.5	19.3	38.2	6	± 27%	± 100%
	3	2.5	164.3	185.6	8	± 18%	± 23%
6 μm zinc	2	2.5	54.7	63.2	2	± 16%	–
	3	2.5	164.8	169.5	2	± 3%	–
Ion-beam cleaned 10 mins + 3 μm zinc	2	2.5	10.4	33.2	6	± 7%	± 219%
	3	2.5	189.3	216.1	8	± 5%	± 14%

Ion beam cleaning before coating increased the maximum shear strengths to values of ~ 220 MNm^{-2} and reduced scatter (Table 2). This effect was observed after only 10 minutes exposure to argon ions. Scatter was reduced for maximum variation between identical test pieces (from ± 18% to ± 5%) and maximum variation between all test pieces (from ± 23% to ± 14%) for bonding under optimum condition. Ion-beam cleaning for 30 minutes produced no further improvement in bond strengths or scatter of data.

3.3 Supral 220.

Diffusion bonding was not as successful as with 7475 or 8090 alloys. Maximum bond strengths of up to 100 MNm⁻ were achieved but reproducibility was poor, (Table 3). The lap shear strength of the base material was measured at 140 MNm^{-2}. Specimens were bonded in the chemically cleaned/zinc layer condition. The thickness of the layer was varied from 3 to 6 μm.

At a bonding pressure of 3 MPa bond strengths were low. For a pressure of 5 MPa higher bond strengths were achieved and a zinc layer thickness of 6 μm gave the highest average and maximum shear strengths, 77 MPa and 102 MPa, respectively. Ion beam cleaning for 30 minutes, followed by deposition of 3 μm of zinc, did not result in an increase in the average or maximum shear strengths, but there was an improvement in reproducibility.

4. **Discussion**

4.1 Bonding of 7475 and 8090 alloys.

The present results show that the use of zinc as a transient liquid interlayer can result in the production, under static loading conditions, of high strength diffusion bonds in the superplastic sheet alloys 7475 and

TABLE 3 : LAP SHEAR STRENGTHS OF DIFFUSION BONDS IN SUPRAL 220
BONDING TEMPERATURE 460°C

Surface Condition (after chemical cleaning)	Bonding Pressure (MPa)	Bonding Time (Hours)	Average Shear Strength (MNm⁻²)	Maximum Shear Strength (MNm⁻²)	Number of Lap Shear Tests	Maximum Variation (Identical Test Pieces)	Maximum Variation (All Specimens)
3 μm zinc	3	2.5	32.0	40.1	6	± 12%	± 25%
	5	2.5	54.0	59.7	6	± 11%	± 30%
6 μm zinc	3	2.5	15.5	23.2	2	± 50%	–
	5	2.5	77.5	101.9	2	± 32%	–
Ion-beam cleaned for 10 mins + 3 μm zinc	3	2.5	31.8	36.0	6	± 6%	± 23%
	5	2.5	66.9	71.3	6	±5%	± 6%

8090. In previous work on the bonding of 7475 after chemical cleaning, but without the use of interlayers, it was observed that although high bond shear strengths could be obtained (> 100 MNm^{-2}), there was frequently a wide variability in strength. The reasons for this were not identified but might have been due to variations in oxide distribution on the bonding interfaces.

A further factor which contributed to bond strength variability was the observation that good bonds often failed prematurely in tension and in peel, despite the use of constrained lap-shear testing (with tensile loading). In the present work a constrained lap-shear test with compressive loading appears to have overcome the previous testing problems.

For the 7475 alloy it can be seen from Table 1 that the optimum conditions for bonding at 515°C, were for a 3 μm deposit of zinc (6 μm for the 2 surfaces in contact), with an imposed pressure of 3 MPa for a time of 2½ hours. For chemically cleaned surfaces these conditions gave an average shear stress of 228 MNm^{-2} with a maximum of 260 MNm^{-2} being recorded. The maximum variation between 2 lap shear test pieces taken from the same specimen was ± 14%, with ± 27% for all tests (10 in all). After ion beam cleaning for 10 minutes the respective shear strengths were 260 MNm^{-2} and 273 MNm^{-2}. The scatter between duplicate measurements was reduced to ± 5%, and between several test specimens to ± 12%.

For the 8090 alloy (Table 2) the optimum conditions for bonding at 515°C were identical to those for 7475 alloy. For chemically cleaned surfaces these conditions gave an average shear stress of 164 MNm^{-2} with a maximum of 185 MNm^{-2}. The maximum variation between duplicate test pieces was ±

18%, and for all tests, ± 23%. Ion beam cleaning for 10 minutes gave improved shear strengths of 189 MNm^{-2} and 216 MNm^{-2} respectively, with markedly reduced scatter.

Despite the high values obtained in the present work for both 7475 and 8090, the bond strengths are still below those of the base metal. However, the work has identified a method of surface preparation, thickness of zinc coating, and conditions of pressure and time to give the highest bond strength and consistency. The beneficial effects of ion beam cleaning are probably due to the removal of loosely bonded surface contaminants rather than complete oxide removal, immediately prior to the deposition of the zinc interlayer.

The present strengths for 7475 have exceeded most of the values reported in the literature to date e.g. Byun and Yavari [7] obtained shear strengths of ~ 170 MNm^{-2}, when Al interlayers were used, while Dunford, Gilmore, and Partridge [10] have reported 180 MNm^{-2} for 7010 clad sheet, sputter-coated with 1 μm of silver.

An alternative method to the production of interlayers by vapour deposition or ion implantation, would be to roll clad the alloy using a thin foil of zinc. Recent work by Ricks et al [11] on roll clad 8090 involved the production of relatively thick surface layers of zinc, ~ 50 μm (total thickness ~ 100 μm). Specimens bonded at a pressure of 5 MPa for 1 hour at ~ 520°C gave an average shear bond strength of ~ 120 MNm^{-2}, with values lying between 100 - 160 MNm^{-2}, which is significantly less than that obtained for 8090 in the present work.

The most remarkable results to date are those reported recently by Kennedy of up to 320 MNm^{-2} (parent metal strength) for 7475 without interlayers (5). After surface preparation by an undisclosed procedure, specimens were bonded using a low gas pressure of ~ 0.7 MPa (100 psi) for 4 hours at 516°C. Specimen strengths (T6 condition) were measured by tensile loaded lap-shear testing. Unlike static loading bonding procedures, gas pressure will always give a uniform pressure over the bonding surfaces, and it is not clear whether it is this, or the surface preparation, which is the dominant factor leading to high bond strength.

4.2 Diffusion bonding of Supral 220.

Diffusion bonding of Supral 220 using zinc interlayers with, or without, ion-beam etching did not prove to be as successful as for 7475 and 8090 alloys. The maximum average bond shear strength was only about 50% of the parent metal strength. This may be partially due, at least, to the relatively low bonding temperature of 460°C, which is the optimum superplastic forming temperature for the alloy. The use of a higher bonding temperature is likely to lead to grain growth, and to a reduction of the significant contribution that grain boundaries make to the bonding process (3), despite the increased diffusivity. However, the bonding behaviour at higher temperatures, using a zinc interlayer, remains to be examined.

4.3 Mechanism of bonding; diffusion of zinc.

Diffusion bonding of aluminium alloys without interlayers probably takes place by a 2-stage process: (i) Asperities make contact and undergo plastic collapse and creep as the surfaces are brought together. The surfaces become more intermeshed until full contact is made. Metal/metal bonding is unlikely due to the thin but tenacious surface layer of Al_2O_3. (ii) The oxide film is ruptured as the specimen spreads laterally. Eventually, all interfacial voids are filled by diffusion and creep processes. It is believed that the effect of a layer of zinc, which is molten at bonding temperatures of > 400°C, is to penetrate the layer of Al_2O_3 and form a low melting point liquid region. The applied pressure will displace some of this liquid, and lead to a more efficient break-up of the oxide layer. Subsequent diffusion of zinc into the adjacent sheet material results in solidification of the liquid region.

The extent of Zn diffusion has been studied in 8090 alloy using a SEM with analyser facilities. The results in Fig. 2 show that for a zinc layer of 3 μm thickness (total width 6 μm) a bonding pressure of 3 MPa reduces the zinc concentration in the interface to ~ 5 wt % after 2½ hours, and to ~ 2.5 wt % at 30 μm from the interface. After 10 hours the concentration is reduced to 1-2 % at the bond line. Parallel studies carried out using pure aluminium specimens have shown that the rate of zinc diffusion is greatly enhanced by increasing the bonding temperature to 600°C, although this would not be practical for the superplastic alloys.

4.4 Metallographic observations

Metallographic examination by optical and scanning electron microscopy of sections through bonds having a range of lap shear strengths has enabled the bond line to be identified, although evidence of interfacial discontinuities decreased with increasing bond strength. Fig. 3a shows a clearly defined bond line for a lower strength bond in 7475, while the high strength bond in Fig. 3a shows a fully recrystallised bond line. Examination of the fracture surfaces of lap shear test specimens indicated

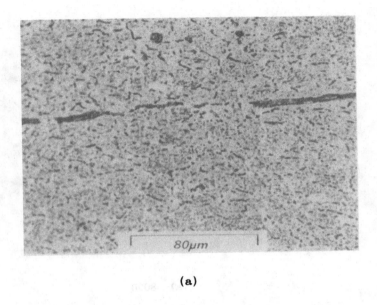

(a)

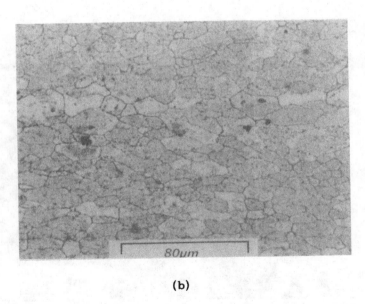

(b)

Fig. 3: Bond lines in 7475 (a) Shear strength, (chemically cleaned) 120 MNm^{-2}.

(b) Shear strength, 273 MNm^{-2} (ion beam cleaned).

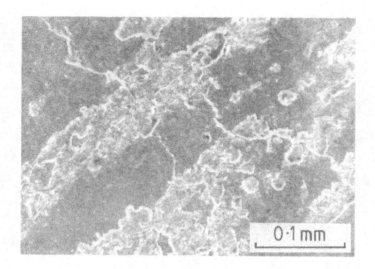

(a)   8090

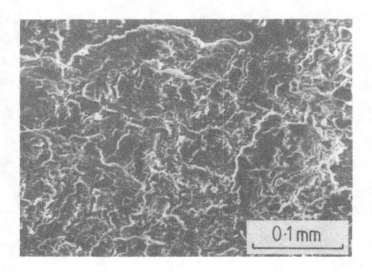

(b)   7475

Fig. 4:   (a) Poor bond; chemically cleaned; 2 MPa; 2½ hours.
          (b) Good bond; ion beam cleaned; 3 MPa, 2½ hours.

that the morphologies were of 2 main types (Fig. 4). For fractures associated with low bond strength, regions of the original planar ground surface were visible with interspersed areas of ductile tearing. For fractures, resulting from high bond strengths, virtually all the fracture surface consisted of ductile tearing with features characteristic of both shear and tensile failure.

5. Summary

Transient liquid phase diffusion bonds have been produced by static compression of superplastic aluminium alloys 7475 and 8090, having a vapour deposited interlayer of zinc. Bonds were evaluated using constrained lap shear compression testing and metallography. While appreciable variations of shear strength were noted for bonds formed from chemically cleaned and zinc coated surfaces, the use of ion-beam etching prior to coating gave a significant improvement in bond strength and/or bond strength variability. For 7475 (T621 condition) and 8090 (T6 condition) maximum shear strengths of ~ 270 MNm^{-2} and > 200 MNm^{-2} were obtained, compared with parent metal strengths of 307 and 272 MNm^{-2}, respectively. Optimum bonding conditions involved a pressure of 3 MPa, a bonding time of 2½ hours, and a bonding temperature of 515°C with a 3 μm coating of zinc (6 μm for two surfaces in contact). In all specimens it was possible to metallographically detect the bond line.

Similar studies on Supral 220 at 460°C led to less satisfactory results. The maximum shear strength recorded was ~100 MNm^{-2} compared with a parent metal strength (non-heat treated) of ~140 MNm^{-2}. Ion beam cleaning reduced scatter but did not improve strength levels.

6. Acknowledgements

The present investigation was financially supported by an SERC/MOD Grant. The authors are grateful to Dr. P.G. Partridge, of RAE, for helpful discussions of the work.

7. References

1. J. Pilling, in Superplasticity and Superplastic Forming, (ed. C.H.Hamilton and N.E. Paton), TMS, Warrendale, PA, USA (1988), 475-489.

2. P.G. Partridge, in Superplasticity, AGARD-LS-168, Agard, Neuilly-sur-Seine, France (1989), 5.1-5.19.

3. J.Pilling and N. Ridley, J. Mater. Sci. Technol., 3 (1987), 353-359.

4. N. Ridley, J. Pilling, A. Tekin and Z.X. Guo, in Diffusion Bonding (ed. R. Pearce), SIS, Cranfield, UK, (1987), 129-142.

5. J. Kennedy, in Ref. 1, pp. 523-527.

6. T.D. Byun and R.B. Vastava, Proc. of Symposium on Welding, Bonding and Fastening, (ed. J.D. Buckley and B.A. Stein), NASA Langley Research Centre, Hampton, VA, USA (1984), 231-245.

7. T.D. Byun and P. Yavari, in Superplasticity in Aerospace, Aluminium, (ed. R. Pearce and L. Kelly), SIS, Cranfield, UK, (1985), 285-295.

8. J. Harvey, P.G. Partridge and A.M. Lurshay, Mater. Sci. Eng., 79 (1986) 191.

9. J. Harvey, P.G. Partridge and C.L. Snooke, J. Mater. Sci. 20 (1985) 1009-1014.

10. D.V. Dunford, C.G. Gilmore and P.G. Partridge, in Ref. 4, pp. 143-157.

11. R.A. Ricks, P.J. Winkler, H. Stoklossa and R. Grimes, in Al-Li 5, (ed. T.H. Sanders and E.A. Starke), MCPE, Birmingham, UK, (1989) 441-449.

INFLUENCE OF SURFACE PREPARATION ON THE DIFFUSION WELDING OF HIGH STRENGTH ALUMINIUM ALLOYS

by
H.M.Tensi and M. Wittmann
Technische Universität München, FRG,
Institut für Werkstoff- und Verarbeitungswissenschaften

ABSTRACT

Diffusion Bonded joints have been produced between sheets of the high strength aircraft and aerospace Aluminium alloys AA 7475 and Al-Li 8090/2091. For these materials the combination of Diffusion Bonding and Superplastic Forming would lead to considerable design flexibility and cost reductions. So an enormous increase of their application potential for aircraft structural components would result from the development of DB/SPF-technologies (1).

This paper reports some effects of different surface preparation methods on the bond quality which were investigated in connection with a modified bonding process. The preparation methods included grinding, brushing and "RF ion etching" (sputter cleaning) with a subsequent sputter deposition of Cu, Ag or Au. Grinding was accomplished in air and also in argon atmosphere in order to minimize the immediate formation of the natural oxide layer. From the argon chamber the ground specimens were then directly shifted into the bonding chamber without beeing exposed to air.

Surface and depth profile analyses were carried out by means of Glow-Discharge-Source (GDS) Plasma-Emission-Spectroscopy in order to verify the surface characteristics of the sheets to be bonded.

The DB-joints were produced in a Diffusion Bonding Hot-Press which admits a defined application of the weld pressure during the heating phase and also rapid cooling after the bonding process. This process was especially developed for the Diffusion Bonding of high strength Aluminium sheets.

Shear tests at room temperature exhibited that excellent strengths up to 410 MPa are possible. Besides the shear strength also the peel strength was measured at room temperature and at SPF temperature (516°C). The results were correlated with joint characteristics found by metallographic methods and observations by Scanning-Electron-Microscope (SEM).

INTRODUCTION

The quality of diffusion bonded joints is highly dependent on the geometric and the physical state of mating surfaces (2). For the Diffusion Bonding of Aluminium alloys the main problem is the tenacious oxide layer which forms again in oxidizing atmosphere immediately after its removal. The Aluminium oxide is very compact and stable and therefore prevents pure metal to metal contacts and diffusional processes which are necessary for the joint formation. The thickness of the natural oxide film which forms in a normal atmosphere is about 10 nm. Thus a successful production of DB-joints of Aluminium alloys requires surface preparation methods which either avoid the formation of an oxide layer or which cause a fragmentation of the oxide during the welding process itself (3). The disruption of oxide layers necessarily requires a certain degree of bulk deformation for surface extension and extrusion of material through gaps in the fractured surface layer.

EXPERIMENTAL PROCEDURE

Materials and preparation methods

Sheets of the high strength Aluminium alloy AA 7475 and the Al-Li-based alloys 2091 and 8090 were the materials to be bonded. Table 1 shows the nominal weight composition of the tested alloys.

Table 1: Nominal weight composition of examined Al-alloys

alloy sheet	composition in wt %					
	Zn	Cu	Mg	Li	Zr	Cr
7475/2mm (Alcoa)	5.2-6.2	1.2-1.9	1.9-2.6	/	/	0.18-0.25
2091/1.7mm (Pechiney)	/	1.8-2.5	1.1-1.9	1.7-2.3	0.04-0.16	/
8090/1.7mm (Alcan)	/	1.0-1.4	0.5-0.9	2.3-2.6	0.08-0.16	/

Blanks of 25 x 100 mm with the 100 mm length parallel to the sheet rolling direction were diffusion bonded in the self made vaccum hot press described later. Prior to bonding the surfaces of the specimens were prepared by different methods.

The examined surface treatments were:

1. Grinding in air   and cleaning with ethanol,
2. Grinding under a protective argon atmosphere,
3. Chemical cleaning followed by brushing,
4. Mechanical cleaning by grinding followed by "RF ion etching" and a subsequent sputter coating with Copper, Silver or Gold.

The sheets were diffusion bonded immediatly after finishing the surface preparation by grinding or scratch brushing. The sputter coated specimens which were prepared in groups of about 30 pieces had to be stored up in a vaccum container during the time between sputter coating and Diffusion Bonding.

Surface analyses

Surface analyses were accomplished in order to classify the physical state of the surfaces to be bonded or to find explanations for differences in the bond quality due to different preparation methods. For this purpose GDS-Plasma-Emission-Spectroscopy was available for depth profile analyses.

The results from the surface analyses revealed some interesting characteristics concerning the different surface states:
The depth profile of a Copper coated Al-Li 2091 sheet (Figure 1) shows that the oxide layer on the Al surface was removed completely by "RF ion etching" before the Copper atoms were deposited on the clean surface. On the Copper surface itself nevertheless an oxide layer has formed as well as on the pure Aluminium. The thickness of the oxide layer could not be determined exactly because the etching rates are only known approximately. Its size may be in the range of 10 nm. On the Copper surface also C and H were detected probably due to cleaning the Cu-surface with ethanol before the analysis was started.

The Silver coated specimens did not show any oxide film on the surface. Surprisingly in the interface between the sputter layer and the Aluminium surface a considerable amount of oxygen was

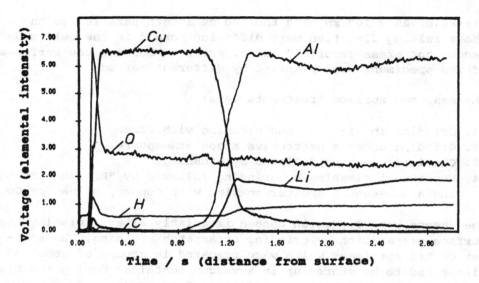

Figure 1. Elemental depth profile of Cu-coated Al-Li 2091 using
GDS-Plasma-Emission-Spectroscopy; surface ground

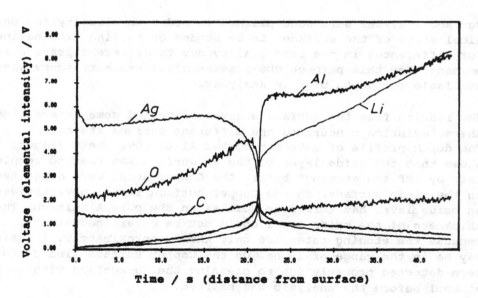

Figure 2. Elemental depth profile of Ag-coated Al-Li 8090 using
GDS-Plasma-Emission-Spectroscopy; surface brushed

detected. The concentration profile (see Fig. 2) indicates, that up-hill diffusion of Oxygen through the Ag-layer must have occured. The result is the formation of Al_2O_3 and LiO near the interface. This configuration appears detrimental for the production of a good bond, which was confirmed by mechanical tests.

Welding process and testing of joints

The welding experiments were carried out in a DB-Hot-Press with a vaccum chamber which had been developed especially for the diffusion bonding of high strength Aluminium sheets. The bonding process is characterized by the application of the weld pressure from the beginning of the heating phase and a defined temperature control in the cooling phase. This pilot plant even provides the option of quenching the specimens from bonding temperature. It has proved that low cooling rates, above all in Al-Li alloys, result in an extensive precipitation of intermetallic phases. Such phases cause reduced bond strengths due to their brittle behaviour. The welding temperature was 500 – 510°C.

The bond quality was investigated by overlap shear tests at room temperature and peel tests at room-temperature and SPF temperature (516°C). Additionally metallographic and fractographic methods were employed for a further characterization of the joints and of their fracture behaviour.

RESULTS FROM MECHANICAL TESTS

Influence of surface preparation on the shear strength

The effect of surface coating on the bond shear strength was measured and compared with the results from uncoated specimens. The range of clad layer thickness was 300 – 3000 Å for Cu, 1000 – 3400 Å for Ag and 1000 Å for Au. The uncoated specimens were ground with SiC emery papers of different grade in order to investigate the influence of the surface roughness on the bond quality.
Also the effect of a post bondig artifical ageing was investigated. This did not need an extra solution treatment because the bonds were quenched in cold water.

The shear strength data of AA 7475 are plotted in Figure 3. They indicate that the best results were obtained in the uncoated and

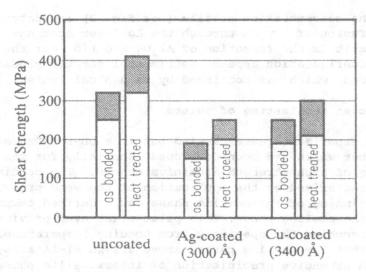

Figure 3. Shear strengths of diffusion bonded AA 7475 sheets at room temperature for different surface finishes

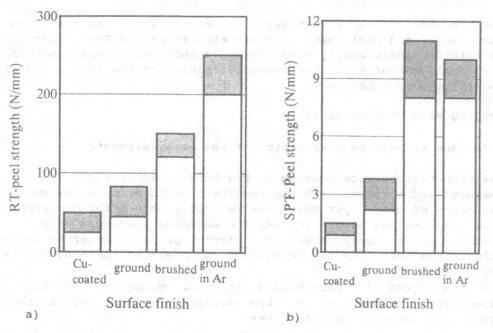

Figure 4. Effect of surface finish on the peel strength of AA7475 sheets: a) at room temperature b) SPF-temperature

artifically aged condition. The shear strength values are in the range between 320 and 410 MPa. Surprisingly the shear strengths of Cu- and Ag- coated bonds were lower. Au-coated specimens showed even worse quality. Many Au-coated specimens failed during the preparation before they could be tested. Obviously artifical ageing increases the shear strength independant from the surface treatment. The influence of the interlayer thickness seems to be negligible. DB-joints between Al-Li 8090/2091 sheets exhibited lower bond strengths compared with AA 7475 bonds. A strong influence of the surface roughness of uncoated specimens could be demonstrated for the Al-Li alloys: increasing surface roughness results in increasing shear strengths.

Influence of surface preparation on the peel strength

Peel tests were accomplished at room temperature and under SPF-conditions (516°C). The influences of the preparation methods, grinding, scratch brushing and sputter coating were investigated. The results are presented in Figure 4a and b. They exhibit considerable differences in the bond strengths for both test conditions.

At room temperature Cu coated bonds had very low peel strengths of 25 - 50 N/mm. The peel strengths of ground specimens (grade 1000) were in the range of 45 - 83 N/mm. For brushed surfaces RT peel strengths 120-150 N/mm were achieved. The best results however were obtained with surfaces prepared by grinding in Argon atmosphere. Their peel strengths were in the range of 200 - 250 N/mm were measured. At SPF temperature nearly the same tendency was found. The peel strengths of sputter coated bonds (1 - 1,5 N/mm) were totally inacceptable. Medium values of 2,5 - 3,8 N/mm were measured for ground surfaces. Excellent peel strengths could be produced when the surfaces were scratch brushed or ground under Argon. Values of 8 - 11/8-10 N/mm were obtained using these preparation methods. This makes the subsequent SPF of diffusion bonded sheets without any mechanical support of the DB-zone feasible.

Some of the brushed joints could not be completely peel tested under SPF conditions because after a certain degree of peeling the sheets deformed superplasticly and finally failed in the base material.

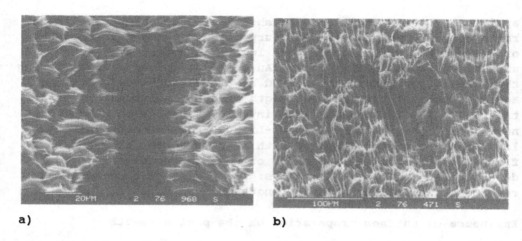

a)   b)

Figure 5. SEM-micrographs a) peel split of a AA 7475 DB-joint
          after hot peel test under SPF conditions b) "SPF-fai-
          lure" of parent metal

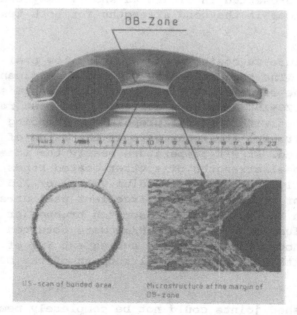

Figure 6. DB/SPF-principle part (torus) of AA 7475 sheets with
          ultrasonic c-scan of the bond and microstructure in the
          aperture zone (4)

SEM observations of the hot peeled surfaces and especially of the peel split revealed an extremely ductile fracture behaviour (see Fig. 5a). When the bonded sheets are seperated whiskers form similar to parts which were glued with a viscous adhesive. The base material failure exhibits equal characteristics (Fig 5b). Under SPF conditions the grains seem to be embedded in a doughy paste which results in low flow stresses and extreme deformability.

The possibility to produce DB/SPF parts without any support of the DB joint during the SPF deformation was examined by the production of a demostration part. The torus shown in Figure 6 was made of two AA 7475 discs which were diffusion bonded in the center ($\emptyset$ = 35 mm) and conventionally welded at the outer circumference. The torus then was formed at SPF temperature by gas pressure injection through a small pipe.

DISCUSSION AND PROSPECTS

The experimental results from the present research confirm the hypotheses of oxide fragmentation by plastic deformation of the surface region which enhances the joint formation through metal to metal contacts. Increasing local deformation due to a higher surface roughness leads to higher bond strengths. Uncoated brushed surfaces and surfaces ground in Argon lead to maximum bond qualities.

Sputtered interlayers seem unfavourable for the diffusion bonding of Aluminium alloys although the sputter materials themselves are considered easy to be bonded. The moderately stable oxides which are formed on Silver and Copper surfaces are considered advantageous for the Diffusion Bonding. Copper is additionally known for its ability to assimilate surface contaminants in the base metal.

The reason for the poor weldability of Ag-coated Aluminium sheets may however be found in the depth profile plotted in Figure 3. Probably the deposited Silver layer was not dense enough to prevent the migration of oxygen through Silver towards the Aluminium margin. There an interfacial oxide layer could form which is responsible for the low bond strengths. Probably the same effect causes the poor bonding of Au-coated sheets.

Besides the above described positive properties of Copper the fact that it forms thick soft oxides is detrimental to diffusion bonding because they tend to smear along the weld interface. Only small areas are therefore available for welding in this case.

In summary the results exhibit that diffusion bonded joints can be produced in a quality which is required for the combined use with Superplastic Forming. Uncoated sheets bonded immediately after the surface finish exhibit promising bond strengths. If the transfer of the encouraging results from the laboratory status to the production level is possible the manufacture of diffusion bonded and superplasticly formed Al-components can be expected.

REFERENCES

1. Winkler, P.J., Diffusion Bonding and Superplastic Forming, two complementary manufacturing techniques. Proceedings of Int. Conf. on Superplasticity and Superplastic Forming, Blaine, USA, Aug. 1988
2. Jellison, J.L., The role of surface contaminants in the solid-state welding of materials. Treatise on clean surface technology, volume 1, Plenum Press, New York, London, 1988, 205-234
3. Kazakov, N.F., Diffusion Bonding of materials. Pergamon Press, Frankfurt, 1981
4. Tensi, H.M., Wittmann, M., Friedrich, H.E., Schmidt,J.J., Diffusion bonding of high strength aircraft and aerospace aluminium alloys. Light weight alloys for aerospace applications, Proceedings of a TMS-symposium, Las Vegas, USA, 1989

The authors whish to thank SPECTRUMA-Instruments, Kirchheim, FRG for the generous support.

DIFFUSION BONDING OF THIN ALUMINIUM FOILS

Y. BIENVENU and J.L. KOUTNY

Ecole des Mines de Paris
Centre des Matériaux P.M. Fourt
BP 87, 91003 Evry, Cedex, France

ABSTRACT

Diffusion bonding of thin aluminium (Al-3 Mg) foils with thicknesses down to 8 μm was possible at relatively low temperatures (400°C) when a thin silver coating was applied prior to hot uniaxial pressing. The most critical point was the control of the deformation of the foils. Diffusion related phenomena were studied by metallography and the soundness of the assemblies was evaluated by "peeling" tests.

1. Introduction

In order to manufacture a small component for a detector, it is necessary to sandwich a very thin foil (8 μm) of Al-3 Mg between two thicker (> 50 μm) templates of the same material (Fig. 1). This is a preliminary report on the difficulties encountered and on some solutions attempted.

Aluminium-magnesium alloys are primarily solid solution strengthened and strain hardened. They are not heat treatable. Cold working may increase the mechanical properties (tensile strength up to 350 MPa), they offer excellent corrosion resistance. The material is often used in foils for the manufacture of parts of microphones, loudspeakers and of radiation windows.

The requirements for the assembly are :

- the 8 μm foil should remain flat after the joining process and retain its strength and elastic modulus,
- the overall thickness of the assembly must be precise and reproducible (± 3 μm for example). The surface roughness of the templates should also be limited after joining. This precludes large deformations of the foils and templates.

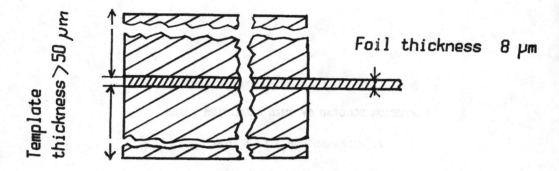

Figure 1 : Schematic drawing of the assembly of Al-3Mg sheets to foil.

Aluminium alloys are difficult to weld and additionally thin geometry of the parts for the present application increases these problems. Adhesive bonding is feasible but it results in rupture strengths of the order of 50 MPa (in tension) and the final thickness of the assembly (brazing or welding) is also too imprecise for the required geometry. Diffusion joining is thus the only process considered for that application.

Diffusion brazing with a transitory liquid phase created by the adjunct of a zinc interlayer, or of a coating, is one solution, since eutectic brazing can operate at 380°C in this system. However the application considered for the component precludes formation of zinc vapour and brazing processes would dissolve the thin foil. Solid state diffusion bonding is the solution at this stage and we will consider the possibility to apply it with and without interlayers.

2. Materials and bonding technology

The Al-3% Mg alloys are produced by Billiton B.V. (N.L.) as cold rolled products : sheet for the templates (thickness > 50 μm) and foil (8 μm). The composition includes 0.1% Mn which improves stress corrosion resistance and hardens the material. It was impossible to derive any valuable metallographic information from the foil (8 μm) which showed an extremely small grain size. In the template some silicon was detected in the smaller aluminium-magnesium precipitates (3-5 μm), and also some iron in tiny (< 3 μm) aluminium-silicon-manganese-iron precipitates. Annealing at temperatures above 150°C causes the iron and manganese containing precipitates to coarsen while the aluminium-magnesium precipitates tend to dissolve (in agreement with the phase diagram, Fig. 2). One hour annealing treatments at 400°C reduce the rupture strength from 300 MPa to 220 MPa and the conventional elastic limit from 280 MPa to 120 MPa, but the elongation at rupture increases markedky. These results were obtained from tensile specimens punched out in a 100 μm thick sheet (2), no test could be carried out on the 8 μm foil.

The surface roughness was less than one micrometer, elongated lines result from cold rolling.

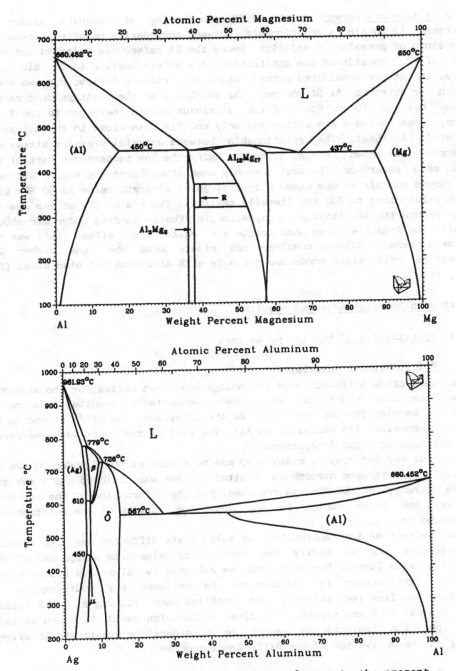

Figure 2 : Phase diagram informations relevant to the present
application of diffusion bonding : a) Al-Ag system
b) Al-Mg system (no data on the Al corner of the
ternary (15)).

A <u>literature survey</u> on the diffusion bonding of aluminium alloys was undertaken to obtain a relationship between compressive uniaxial stress and temperature of pressing. A majority, among the 13 references selected out of a total of 22, considered the application of a silver coating to the aluminium alloys, the others considered copper, magnesium, zinc or indium, but two chose silicon or eutectic Al-Si powders. The thickness of the coatings used ranged between 0.1 and 10 μm. Most of the aluminium alloys belonged to the 7 xxx series, some to the 6 xxx series and only one (14) was close to the alloys of the study (Al-5Mg). The relationship between uniaxial pressing stress and temperature is shown in Fig. 3. We are using the low temperature part of the graph as a reference. The most commonly used atmospheres are argon, nitrogen and vacuum and air in one case. A typical joint strength value is 50 MPa with a high value close to 200 MPa (tensile testing). The aim of the silver coating is to reduce the sensitivity to oxydation, diffusion bonding under air should actually be feasible when both parts are coated with silver (this was not the case here). Silver coatings are widely used when one wisker low temperature solid state bonds and not only with aluminium but also steel (17) (2-14, 16)

3. Diffusion bonding tests and results

3.1. Optimization of bonding parameters

3.1.1. Without interlayer

A very crude diffusion bond technology was first tested for the assembly of two templates under air which not unexpectedly resulted in an oxide diffusion barrier forming on parts of the interface. The oxide proved to be rich in magnesium (in addition to Al). The rest of the tests were performed under nitrogen or argon (+ hydrogen).

Without any interlayer, using a 30 min hold time at 500°C under 20 MPa of stress, in a nitrogen atmosphere limited success was achieved and a maximum tensile strength of 60 MPa was recorded, but the deformation of the assembly (5%) was too large, which is not suprising in view of the relationship illustrated in Fig. 3.

The effect of ion implantation on solid state diffusion was also tested. The objective was to modify the surface of aluminium alloys and of the inevitable oxide layers. For this study we selected two aluminium alloys which differed significantly in composition, to evidence any modification on diffusion profiles (we selected zinc profiles when joining a 7 xxx series alloy against a 2 xxx series). No clear conclusion could be drawn at this stage, but ion implantation cannot be considered a substitute to silver coating in the activation of the diffusional process.

3.1.2. With an interlayer

The current bonding technology for the present application relies on a thin (0.1-2 μm) **silver coating** (sputtering) of the templates and not of the

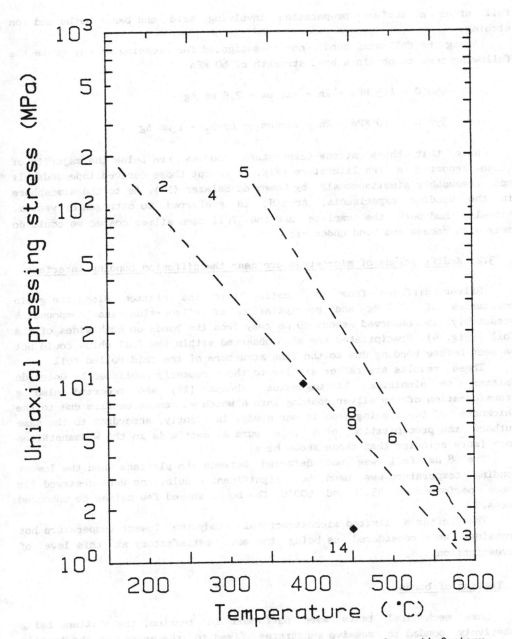

Figure 3 : Relationship between stress and temperature for satisfactory
diffusion bonding - with interlayers - numbers refer to
papers in the list of references - only No. 14 considers
Al-Mg alloys.
♦ selection of bonding conditions in the present study on
Al-3Mg + silver coating.

foil after a surface preparation involving acid and basic baths and ion etching.

Among the following conditions investigated for pressing we may quote the following ones to obtain a bond strength of 60 MPa :

450°C - 1.5 MPa - 2h - vacuum - 2.5 μm Ag

or   390°C - 10 MPa - 2h - vacuum or Ar-H$_2$ - 1 μm Ag

Note that these stress-temperature couples are below the majority of those reported in the literature (Fig. 3) except those derived independantly and presumably simultaneously by Gomez de Salazar (14). As to the atmosphere in the bonding experiments, Ar-5 H$_2$ is preferred to nitrogen or vacuum. Actually had both the template and the foil been silver coated we could do away with vacuum and bond under air.

3.2. Modifications of microstructure near the diffusion bonding interface

Silver diffuses from the coating into the platten along the grain boundaries of Al-3 Mg and precipitation of silver-aluminium compounds δ presumably was observed about 20 μm away from the bonds on both sides of the foil (Fig. 4). Precipitates are also observed within the foil which could not be seen before bonding due to the fine structure of the cold rolled foil.

These results are rather similar to those recently published by Gomez de Salazar on aluminium 5% magnesium sheets (14) who reported also a transformation of the silver coating into δ which we cannot confirm due to the thickness of the coating used in our study. Incidently, according to the same authors the precipitation of δ in a pure Al matrix is in the Widmanstätten form (more acicular than those shown here).

The 8 μm foil was not deformed between the plattens when the lowest bonding temperature was used, but significant ondulations were observed for bonds performed at 450°C and 500°C. The bonds showed few oxides or unbonded areas.

Thus after a limited microstructural study the lowest temperature hot pressings were considered as being the most satisfactory at this level of investigation.

4. Testing of bonds

Some mechanical tests were performed in tension, the plattens being adhesively bonded to massive substrates fixed to the grips of the tensile testing machine. The adhesive bonding can carry 50 MPa. Bonds between Al-3 Mg foils and platten were declared satisfactory when the rupture initiated within the adhesive. Most bonds passed that test.

Also a very crude peel test was tried using a sharp steel blade to separate the materials. Most bonds could not be damaged.

5. Planeity of the assembly

Difficulties were met when the 8 μm foil was bonded to the templates as part of the foil is free of the template in the component. This section of the foil usually has some waviness after diffusion bonding and ways are sought to retighten it again. One of the means is to perform different heat treatments to the foil and the templates prior to bonding to, create differential changes in dimensions. Other ways are currently preferred to reach this effect but the mechanisms remain to be elucidated and it is too early in the development of the technique to give a report on that crucial aspect of component manufacturing.

Acknowledgements

The authors are indebted to Drs. M. Jeandin and J.C. Le Flour, to Mr. J.D. Bartout, Mr. D. Pachoutinsky and to Miss V. Codazzi for their contributions to the experimental work and for simulating discussions on an unusual bonding case. They also wish to thank Dr. Pivin (University Paris-Sud/Orsay) for performing ion implantations.

References

1. T.B. Massalski, J. Murray, L.H. Bennett, H. Baker, Binary Alloys phase diagrams, A.S.M., Metals Parks, Oh, USA, (1986).
2. J. Harvey, P.G. Partridge and A.M. Lurshay, Materials Science and Engineering, 79, (1986) pp 191-199.
3. A.E. Dray and E.R. Wallach, Diffusion Bonding of Al alloys, Diffusion Bonding Int. Conf. Cranfield, 1987, R. Pearce ed, pp 125-129.
4. D.V. Dunford, C.G. Gilmore and P.G. Partridge, Effect of the silver coating thickness on the shear strength of diffusion bonded clad Al-Zn-Mg (7010) alloy, ibid, pp 143-159.
5. P.G. Partridge, J. Harvey et al, Patent GB 211 769 1A 28-3-83.
6. O. Ohashi and T. Hashimoto, Atmospheric diffusion welding of silver ion plated materials, J. Jap. Weld. Soc. (1980), 9, pp 647-651.
7. Mel Schwartz, Metals Joining Manual, Mc Graw Hill, (1979) also Diffusion Welding Proc. Conf., Las Vegas, Nev. USA, AWS ed, Miami, USA (1980).
8. P.G. Partridge and D.V. Dunford, On the testing of diffusion bonded overlap joints between Al-Zn-Mg (7010) sheet, J. Mat. Sci. Letters, 22 (5), (1987), pp 1597-1608.
9. P.G. Partridge and D.V. Dunford, The peel strength of diffusion bonded joints, J. Mat. Sci. Lett., 22) (1987), pp 1597-1608.
10. Diffusion welding of 390 Aluminium alloy hydraulic valve bodies, Proc. Conf. 11th Int. Die Casting Congress (Proc. Conf.), Cleveland, Ohio, (1981), paper G.T 81-083, p 6.
11. J.L. Jellison and F.J. Zanner, "Solid State Welding" in Metals Handbook, vol 8, A.S.M., Metals Park, Ohio, pp 672-690.

12. P.G. Partridge, J. Harvey and D.V. Dunford, Diffusion Bonding of aluminium alloys in the solid state, Proc. Conf. AGARD, Nato, CP 398, (1986) pp. 8.1-8.23

13. Guinn E. Metzger, Diffusion Brazing of aluminium alloys, US AFML report (1970).

14. J.M. Gomez de Salazar, P. Hierro, A.J. Criado and A. Ureña, Prakt. Met. 255, (1988), pp 532-543.

15. G. Petzow and G. Effenberg, Ternary Alloys, vol. 1 (silver based ternary systems) VCH, Weinheim, F.R.G., ((1988).

16. G.A. Henshall, M.E. Kassner and R.S. Rosen, Ambient Temperature creep failure of Ag-aided diffusion bonds between steels, This conference.

LASER SURFACE MODIFICATION OF 8090 ALLOY
WITH SILICON FOR DIFFUSION BONDING

by

J.N. Kamalu [+] and **D.S. McDarmaid** [++]

+ Manufacturing Engineering Department, University of Dundee.

++ Material and Structures Dept., Royal Aerospace Establishment,
Farnborough, Hants.

Summary

Surface modification of 1.6 mm thick 8090 (Al-Li-Cu-Mg-Zr) sheet with silicon has been investigated using laser processing technology. An alloy which melts at about 550 $^{\circ}$C has been produced and the laser parameters for production of shallow porosity-free tracks of this alloy in the sheet surface, with no distortion of the sheet, have been determined. Bonding trials at 560 $^{\circ}$C have successfully joined two sheets together although on sectioning, evidence of solidification cracking was observed at the bond interface.

INTRODUCTION

The development of low density Al-Li alloys has generated much interest in the aerospace industry, none more so than that for the Al-Li-Cu-Mg-Zr (8090) alloy which can also be superplastically formed. Further significant cost and weight savings could be achieved if multi-sheet components could be produced, as with titanium alloys, by a combination of superplastic forming and diffusion bonding.

The aim of this investigation was to produce shallow tracks of a modified surface alloy using laser processing which could melt just above the superplastic forming temperature (530 ^{o}C) to breakdown the oxide surface and produce localised regions of bonding on cooling to the forming temperature. Thus, multi-layered sheet assemblies could be selectively bonded, cooled and formed in one operation without removal from the press. This processing route would enable accurate control of the bonding pattern and eliminate problems of location and movement of thin interface foils and of capillary flow of the liquid phase at the bond interface as the liquid phase would be retained in a predetermined 'groove' pattern.

EXPERIMENTAL PROCEDURES

Silicon powder was introduced into the surface of 1.6 mm thick 8090 sheet by the pre-placing method and by a powder feed system using a laser. The laser was a 2 Kw CO_2 axial flow system built by Control Laser. The silicon powder was sieved (Table 1) to remove the fraction greater than 125 um and heated to remove moisture and any volatile substances. The 8090 sheet surface was degreased and dried prior to processing.

For the pre-placing method, the powder was mixed with a sodium silicate binder, lightly painted onto the sheet surface, and dried at 200 ^{o}C prior to laser processing. The use of the binder enabled the molten surface to be shielded with an argon atmosphere during the laser processing.

The powder feed system used argon as the powder carrier and allowed the silicon to be injected into the laser-generated melt pool. The argon gas also acted as a protective atmosphere.

PROCESS REQUIREMENTS

The laser processing was required to be such that (i) no distortion of the substrate occurred; (ii) the surface alloyed region (Figure 1) should be at least 1 mm wide and 0.3 mm deep; and (iii) there should be no porosity.

RESULTS AND DISCUSSION

1. Techniques

(a) Pre-placed method

The presence of the powder layer increased the beam absorption and the laser power had to be reduced to 1.1 Kw to prevent substrate distortion. Reduction of the specific energy input by increasing the speed or the beam diameter adversely affected the process control and could not be used. This method, however, gave poor reproducibility of the melt tracks as it was difficult to ensure uniform thickness of the pre-placed layer and unacceptable levels of porosity were obtained (figure 2), probably from the presence of the binder although some may have been a consequence of entrapped argon from the gas shield.

(b) Continuously-fed powder

Reproducible melt tracks were obtained with low or zero porosity and the laser power did not have to be significantly reduced. The melt zone characteristics for different beam diameters and laser speed were, therefore, investigated in more detail. Increasing the laser beam diameter from 2 mm to 7 mm increased the melt width and reduced the melt depth (figure 3). No alloying was observed when the beam diameter was increased to 8 mm. The effect of laser speed is shown in figure 4. For speeds slower than 20 mm/s, substrate distortion occurred. With increased speed, both the depth and width of the melt reduced. Although a range of processing parameters could be used to meet the melt zone requirements, a laser beam diameter of 5 mm and a laser speed of 40 mm/s were selected to produce tracks for the bonding experiments.

2. **Characterisation of the alloyed region**

The silicon content of the melt region varied from 100% at the top of the clad bead to 0% at the melt zone/substrate interface, and the primary silicon particles were angular (figure 5). Electron microprobe analysis of the matrix material below the melt interface (figure 1) confirmed that alloying had occurred (figure 6) and differential scanning calorimetry of the alloyed material revealed the formation of a phase which melted at about 550 ^{o}C (figure 7). X-ray diffraction analysis, however, failed to identify this phase and further studies are in progress.

3. **Bonding**

The laser-treated surfaces were ground to a 240 silicon carbide finish and degreased prior to bonding. The specimens for bonding were held for 15 minutes at 560 ^{o}C in a still air furnace. The specimens were then cooled to 530 ^{o}C and held for 1 hour to simulate the superplastic forming cycle prior to air cooling.

Although bonding occurred, microsections through the bonded region revealed the presence of a discontinuous interface in the same plane as the sheet surface, Figure 8. The discontinuous interface, however, was not planar and, in some instances, extended through the second phase particles. These particles were globular and had a more homogeneous distribution than the angular primary silicon particles that were present before bonding. Cracked particles were not observed within the alloy region. The composition of the particles was not determined completely although they contained aluminium and silicon. The silicon content of the alloy matrix was also increased to about 14 wt % and the marked silicon gradient prior to bonding was removed, cf figures 6 and 9. The above observations indicate that the alloyed region had melted during the bonding cycle and that the discontinuous interface was a consequence of solidification cracking rather than incomplete bonding. It is possible that the solidification cracking could be eliminated or sealed if the hydrostatic back pressure imposed to prevent internal cavitation during the superplastic forming process was applied prior to the cooling stage.

ACKNOWLEDGEMENTS

The authors would like to thank Professor W.M.Steen of Liverpool University and Professor D.R.F.West of Imperial College, London, for their support and colleagues at Imperial College where the work was done.

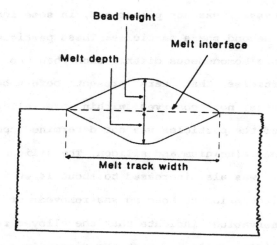

Figure 1 : Schematic diagram of laser clad track.

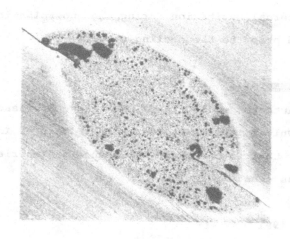

Figure 2 : Typical micrograph of bond produced using pre-placed powder (X 40).

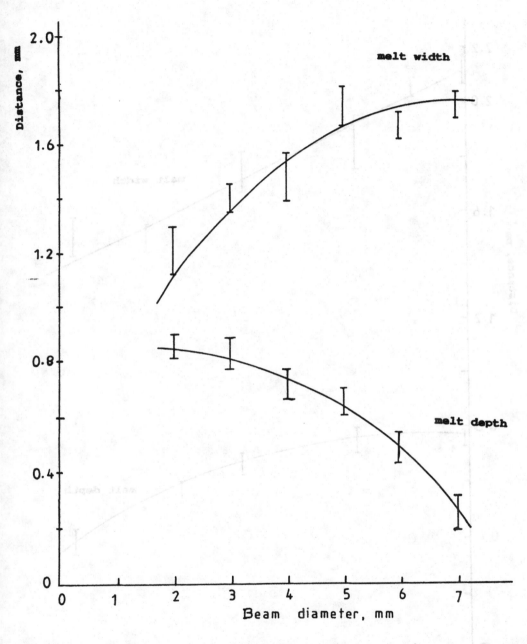

Figure 3 : Variation of melt width and melt depth with beam diameter. (Laser power = 1.85 Kw, cladding speed = 40 mm/s).

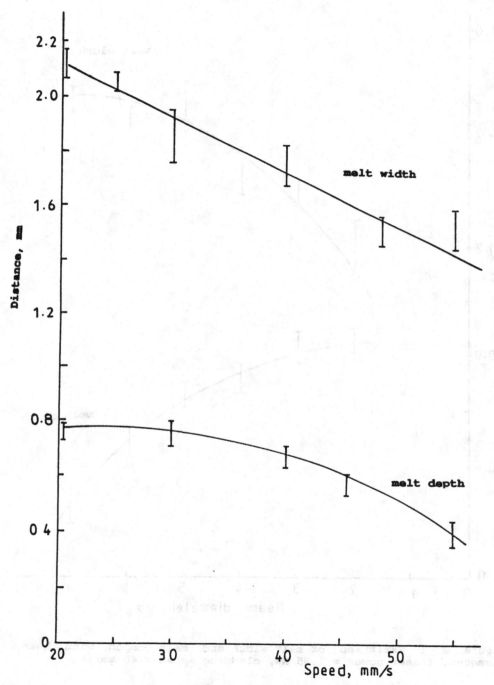

Figure 4 : Effect of cladding speed on melt depth and melt width.
(Laser power = 1.85 Kw; beam diameter = 5 mm).

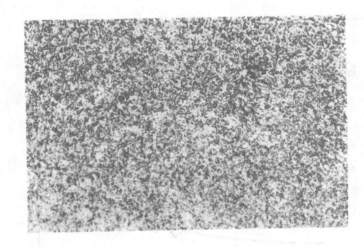

Figure 5 : Optical micrograph showing angular primary silicon particles within the melt zone prior to bonding (X 340).

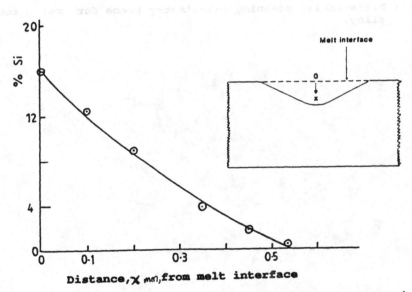

Figure 6 : Silicon distribution within the melt zone matrix alloy.

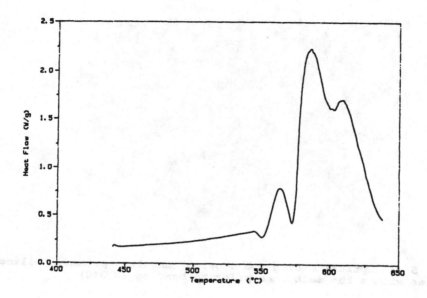

Figure 7 : Differential scanning calorimetry trace for melt zone alloy.

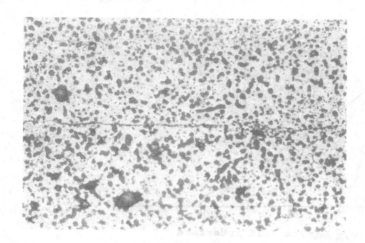

Figure 8 : Typical joint interface region with alloyed melt zone (X 340).

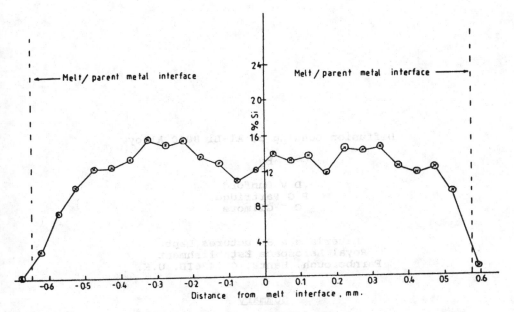

Figure 9 : Silicon distribution within bond region.

Table 1 : Sieve analysis of silicon powder

Size band (um)		wt %
Lower limit	Upper limit	
125	–	58.04
90	125	17.40
75	90	7.21
63	75	4.14
53	63	3.52
45	53	6.78
38	45	2.57
32	38	0.73
–	32	0.21

Diffusion Bonding of Al-Li 8090 Alloy

by

D V Dunford
P G Partridge
C J Gilmore

Materials & Structures Dept
Royal Aerospace Establishment
Farnborough, Hants. GU14 6TD. U.K.

<u>Summary</u>

Shear strengths (τ) of solid state and liquid phase diffusion bonds have been determined for Al-Li 8090 aluminium alloy sheet at various overlap lengths (L). These results have been compared to measured base metal strengths using the same test piece and testing technique. When L < 3 mm a plateau region was obtained where τ was independent of L; in this plateau region τ=191 ± 8 MPa (solid state) and 190 MPa (liquid phase). Strengths were independent of test piece type or of thickness of sheet or interlayer. Similar strength behaviour was obtained for the base metal with strengths in the plateau region of 203 ± 4 MPa. The slightly lower bond strength is caused by the planar bond interface (solid state) or the coarse grained interfacial region (liquid phase). Joint strengths were however greater than those previously reported for 8090 alloy and about a factor 7 greater than those for adhesive bonded joints.

1. Introduction

Superplastic forming (SPF) has become an established manufacturing process for titanium and aluminium alloy sheet components [1] and when combined with diffusion bonding (SPF/DB) substantial cost and weight savings can be achieved in titanium aerospace structures compared with conventional riveted titanium structures [2]. Diffusion bonding (DB) is more difficult for aluminium alloys because of their stable surface oxide film [3-5]. Some bond strength data have shown unacceptably large scatter and low minimum strength values [6] whilst other data [7,8] indicate bond shear strengths equal to that of the base metal. The major causes of scatter in measured bond shear strength values for thin sheet are incomplete surface contact, prior bond interface contamination or peel stresses generated in the overlap shear test piece [5,9]. Interlayers have been used in both the solid and liquid states to improve surface contact and to reduce the effect of surface films [10 - 13].

The new generation of aluminium alloys with lithium additions have low density, high specific strengths [14] and can exhibit superplastic behaviour [15], which makes them particularly attractive for SPF/DB processing. However lithium containing alloys oxidise more readily than lithium free alloys [16] and are reported to be more difficult to diffusion bond [17,18]. Published strength data for diffusion bonded Al-Li alloy joints are summarised in Table 1 [4,18-20]. Strengths greater than 100 MPa were obtained for solid state bonds, with or without the use of an interlayer and for liquid phase bonds with a Zn interlayer, but again there was significant scatter in the strength values. To obtain a more precise measure of the shear strength of DB 8090 Al-Li alloy, the effect of overlap length has been determined for bonds made in both the solid and liquid states; similar tests were carried out on the base metal for comparison. The results obtained are described in this paper.

2. Experimental Technique

8090 Al-Li alloy sheet with a composition (wt%) of Al-2.5%Li-1.3%Cu-0.8%Mg-0.12%Zr-0.1%Fe-0.05%Si was used in thicknesses of 2.5 - 4 mm. The sheets were in either the unrecrystallised or partially recrystallised condition. Surfaces to be bonded were mechanically polished to a 1 μm diamond or 1200 SiC grit finish then washed and ultrasonically cleaned in acetone. For liquid phase bonding a physical vapour deposition (PVD) process was used to deposit the Cu interlayer. The surface oxide film was first removed by argon ion bombardment and the surface was then ion plated with a known thickness of copper as described in ref 3. For thicker interlayers an 8μm thick foil was inserted between the coated surfaces.

Diffusion bonding was carried out in a hot press at a temperature and pressure to give a final overall through thickness deformation of 6 - 12%. Bonded sheets were heat treated to the STA condition before testing. This consisted of a solution heat treatment of 20 mins at 530°C, water quenched followed by an ageing cycle of 5 hours at 185°C then air cooled. Two single overlap shear test pieces were used, Type 1 and Type 2 in Fig.1a and 1b respectively. A 5 mm wide section was cut from the edge of the bonded sheets to determine the microstructure before and after heat treatment. Surface slots were cut to the depth of the bond line after heat treatment in type 2 bonded sheets to produce test pieces with overlap lengths (L) of 1.9 - 15.1 mm. Bond shear tests were carried out in a jig described elsewhere [22].

Tensile properties of the base metal were determined after re-heat treatment to the STA condition or after a bond thermal cycle (TC) followed by STA. The shear strength of the base metal sheet was obtained by making a type 2 test piece from 4 mm thick sheet using 2 mm deep slots (0.5 t) to give overlap lengths in the range 2-5.3 mm. Shear tests were carried out on sheet in the TC + STA condition.

Fracture surfaces were studied using a Jeol T220 scanning electron microscope (SEM). Specimens for examination by transmission electron microscopy (TEM) were dimpled at the bond interface prior to subsequent thinning to perforation using standard electro-polishing techniques. Secondary electron imaging of the foil surface was used to locate and confirm the presence of the bond interface before thorough evaluation in the transmission mode.

3. Results

3.1 Microstructure of DB joints

A section through a DB joint in unrecrystallised 3 mm thick sheet is shown in Fig.2. The bond line (A-A) is indistinguishable from the surrounding planar grain boundaries associated with pancake like grains in the base alloy at B. TEM micrographs prepared from a DB joint in partially recrystallised 4 mm thick sheet are shown in Fig 3. There was no evidence of porosity or continuous oxide films at the bond interface at A-A in fig 3a, although some fragmented oxide particles could be seen. Misorientations of about 10° obtained across this interface indicated that the bond interface was actually a conventional large angle boundary. The uniformity of the $\delta'(Al_3 Li)$ precipitates up to and on both sides of this boundary shows no significant Li depletion occurred prior to bonding. This grain boundary nevertheless appears very resistant to migration since an impinging grain boundary at C only formed an equilibrium 120° configuration at the triple point near the bond interface, Fig 3b. A solid state DB joint in an 8090 based 20 wt.% SiC particulate reinforced MMC is shown in figure 4. In spite of the presence of the particles good bond strengths can be obtained. Introducing a copper layer and bonding above the Al-Cu eutectic temperature produced the bond interface microstructure shown in Fig.5. In the as bonded condition residual needles of the $CuAl_2$ phase are present at A in Fig.5a, but these disappear after heat treatment to the STA condition leaving a coarse grained region at the bond line at B in Fig.5b. There is no evidence of a planar bond interface, which is consistent with melting having occurred.

3.2 Strength of DB joints and base alloy

All bonded joints failed, after post bonding heat treatment to the STA condition, at the bond interface. Results of shear strength (τ) versus overlap length (L) for solid state bonds are shown in Fig 6. A plateau in the τ v L curve was obtained for L < 3 mm. For L > 3 mm τ decreased with increase in L. This agrees with previous results [9] which show a change from almost pure shear in the plateau region to mixed shear and tension (peel) with increasing L. The liquid phase diffusion bonded joints showed a similar trend and comparable strength levels. The shear strength for similar overlap lengths in the plateau region was 191 ± 8 MPa for solid state bonds and about 190 MPa for the liquid phase bonds with no significant effect on the shear strength of test piece type or of thickness of sheet or interlayer.

The τ v L curve obtained for the base metal in the TC + STA condition was similar to that for the DB joint but the plateau occurred at 203 ± 4 MPA (Fig 6). The mean plateau value for the base metal was 12 MPa greater than for the DB joint. Tensile strengths for the base metal in the STA and TC + STA conditions were 428 MPa and 398 MPa respectively.

3.3 Fractography

Shear fractures for a solid state bonded joint and a base metal test piece manufactured from 4 mm partially recrystallised sheet with similar overlap lengths in the plateau region (L~2 mm) and similar shear strength are shown in Fig 7. The surfaces showed evidence of flat intergranular fracture regions (at A) with diameters approximately equal to those of the grains in the base metal. There was little evidence of ductile shear fracture. The base metal and liquid phase bond fractures were rougher than the solid state DB fractures; this is attributed to the marked planarity of the grain boundaries at the solid state bond line (Fig 2).

Increased overlap length (L>3 mm) changes the bond fracture mode from intergranular to a mixture of inter- and trans-granular fracture in both the solid state and liquid phase bonds. In the former, surface pits caused by pullout were observed on the bond fracture as discussed in more detail elsewhere [22]. Fractographs of liquid phase DB joints are shown in figure 8. The large grained bond region produced a coarse intergranular fracture surface (Fig 8a) and larger pullout pits about 5 grains deep (Fig 8b).

4. Discussion

DB shear strengths measured in the plateau region of 191 ± 8 MPa (solid state) and 190 MPa (liquid phase) compare favourably with base metal strengths measured for similar overlap length and thermal condition. These bond shear strengths are greater than any previously reported for Al- Li alloys bonded in either the solid or liquid states (Table 1) and about a factor 7 greater than adhesive bonded Al-Li alloy joints [23]. The results for solid state bonded joints indicate that the presence of lithium in aluminium alloys makes DB easier and not more difficult as has been reported elsewhere [17]. This improved bondability is probably caused by the high diffusivity of Li and Mg in the aluminium lattice and the greater tendency for Li and Mg rich oxide films at the bond interface to ball up and become discontinuous [19].

Present results confirm previous tests that indicated valid shear strength values may only be obtained using short overlap lengths (L < 3 mm)in a plateau region apparent on a r v L curve[9]. The reduced sensitivity to overlap length and the presence of fracture surfaces exhibiting only one fracture mode may be a consequence of the uniform stress system operating at these short overlap lengths [24,25] . The reduction in strength with increased overlap length can be attributed to an increased peel component in the fracture process.

In this paper DB joint strengths have been compared with those for the base metal given the same thermal cycle and tested under the same conditions. Base metal shear strengths are often calculated from base metal tensile data assuming a shear/longitudinal tensile strength ratio of 0.6 which has been reported for many aluminium alloys [26]. Using measured longitudinal strength for the 8090 base metal in the TC + STA condition of 398 MPa the predicted shear strength would be;

$$r = 0.6\sigma_L = 239 \text{ MPa} \qquad (1)$$

This value is greater than even the maximum measured base metal value of 209 MPa. However the fracture plane (L-T) in the shear test is characteristic of that obtained in the short transverse (ST) direction and this suggests that the tensile strength in this direction should be substituted for σ_L . σ_{ST} cannot be obtained for thin sheet, but for Al-Li alloy (8090 or 2090) plate in the STA condition [27,28] the ratio of σ_{ST}/σ_L is 0.88. Substituting this into equation 1 gives $r = 210$ MPa which is in good agreement with measured base metal strengths.

There is clear evidence from the TEM work that the bond
interface becomes a conventional grain boundary with no defects
(Fig 3).
The strengths of DB joints in the plateau region were only 94% of
the measured base metal strength. This is attributed to the ease of
fracture along the planar boundary in the solid state bond. Planar
bond interfaces have also been obtained for solid state DB joints
in clad 7010 and 7475 alloys [3,8,29], although in the case of
7475 base metal strengths were reported. These interfaces may be
caused either by the pinning of grain boundaries by oxide particles
(or intermetallics) [4,29], or the inherent resistance to grain
boundary migration in the base metal. Planar interfaces are not
observed if a liquid phase is used [20] and the lower observed
strength in this case is attributed to the increase in grain size
in the bond region caused by melting and resolidification.

Conclusions

1. Diffusion bonded joints have been produced in 8090 Al-Li alloy
   in the solid or liquid phase states with shear strengths of 191
   + 8 MPa and 190 MPa respectively.

2. The solid state bond interface was a conventional large angle
   grain boundary with no evidence of porosity or oxide films. The
   planarity of the bond interface led to slightly lower shear
   strength compared with the base metal.

3. Liquid phase bonding produced a coarse grained interfacial
   region with no evidence of a planar bond interface.

4. The reduction in strength with increased overlap length is
   caused by a change in the stress state from pure shear to mixed
   shear and peel.

Acknowledgments

The authors wish to thank A J Shakesheff and D S McDarmaid for
many helpful discussions and M Sheppard for help with experimental
work.

References

1. H E Friedrich   Superplasiticity and Superplastic Forming,
   R Furlan   TMS, 1988 p649
   M Kullick

2 D Stephen   Designing with Titanium, Inst. of Metals
                   1986 p108

3 P G Partridge   AGARD conference on Advanced Joining of
   J Harvey   Aerospace Metallic Materials, No.398
   D V Dunford   Sept 1985 p8-1

4 D V Dunford   Proc. Intern. Conf. on Superplasticity in
   P G Partridge   Aerospace - Aluminium, Cranfield, SIS,
                   July 1985 p257

5 P G Partridge   AGARD Lecture Series on Superplasticity
                   No.164, Sept 1989 p5-1

6 J Pilling   Mater. Sci. Eng, 3, 353, 1987
   N Ridley

7 T Byun   Welding Bonding and Fastening, NASA Pub.2387
   P Yavari   1984 p23

8 J Kennedy   Superplasticity and Superplastic Forming,
                     TMS, 1988 p523

9 P G Partridge   J Mater. Sci. 22 1597 1987
   D V Dunford

10 M M Schwartz   Metals Joining Manual, 1979

11 C L Cline   Welding J. Suppl. 45, p481s, 1966.

12 J T Niemann   Welding Res. Suppl. p285s, 1978.
   G W Wille

13 R A Morley   Welding J. 59, p29, 1980.
   J Caruso

14 C J Peel   Metals and Materials, August p449 1987
   B Evans
   D S McDarmaid

15 D S McDarmaid   Al-Li IV Conference, Paris 1987, p c3-257
   A J Shakesheff

16 P G Partridge   Int. Met. Rev, Inst. Met, 1990 in the press

17 J Pilling   Superplasticity and Superplastic Forming,
                     TMS 1988 p475

18 M R Edwards   Al-Li V Conference, Williamsburg 1989 p431
   E Klinklin
   V E Stoneham

19 E R Maddrell   ibid p451
   R A Ricks
   E R Wallach

20 R A Ricks   ibid p441
   P J Winkler
   H Stoklossa
   R Grimes

21 J Harvey   J. Mater. Sci., 20, 1009, 1985
   P G Partridge
   C L Snooke

22 D V Dunford   J. Mater. Sci., 1990 in the press
   P G Partridge

23 D J Arrowsmith   Al-Li III , Inst. Metals, 1986 p584
   A W Clifford
   D A Moth
   D J Davies

24 A J Kinloch   J. Mater. Sci. 17 617 1982

25 L J Hart-Smith   Delamination and Debonding of Materials, ASTM, STP 876 1985 p238

26   Source Book on Selection and Fabrication of Aluminium Alloys, ASM 1978 p1

27 D Dew-Hughes   Mater. Sci. and Tech. 4 106 1988
E Creed
W S Miller

28 K T V Rao   Met. Trans. 19A 549 1988
W Yu
R O Ritchie

29 D V Dunford   Proc. Intern. Conf. on Diffusion Bonding, Cranfield, U.K, 1987 p143
C J Gilmore
P G Partridge

TABLE 1

SHEAR STRENGTHS OF DIFFUSION BONDED 8090 Al-Li ALLOY

Bonding technique	Sheet thickness(t) and surface finish	Overlap length (ℓ)	Environment	Bonding conditions	Post bond heat treatment	Shear stress τ	Reference
Hot platen, clad sheet Ag coated. Solid state.	t = 1.8mm 1μm diamond polish	3.6mm (2t)	air/ argon	280-300°C 100-130 MPa 45 mins 10% deformation	16h 530°C, WQ (SHT) + 5h 185°C (STA)	104 MPa (SHT) 98 MPa (STA)	4
Hot platen, clad sheet with or without Ag coating. Solid state.	t = 3.5mm 1200 SiC grit ground surface or 1μm diamond polish	6mm (~2t)	air/ argon	538 ± 5°C 50 MPa (max) 0.5-5.8h above 500°C	24h 530°C	34-110 MPa (1200 grit,No Ag) 50-56 MPa (1μm diamond,No Ag) 0-60 MPa (1μm diamond, Ag)	18
Induction heating. Solid state.	t ~ 3mm 180 SiC grit ground surface	~3mm (1t)	vacuum <10^{-2} Pa	525°C 2.5 MPa 40 mins 10%(max)deformation		125-175 MPa	19
Hot platen. Zn-1% Cu clad layer. Liquid phase.		1.5mm	air or air/ argon	500-540°C ~5 MPa 1 hour		100-160 MPa	20

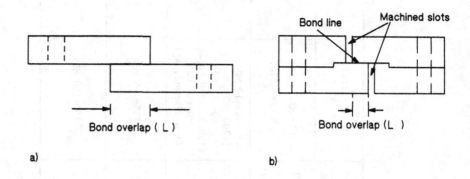

a)   b)

Figure 1   Single overlap shear test pieces;
                (a) Type 1, (b) Type 2.

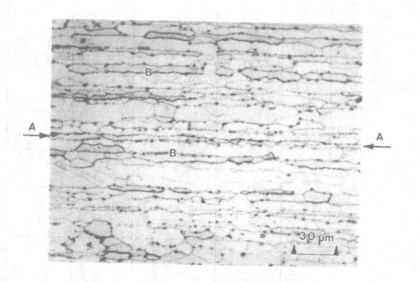

Figure 2   Section through a solid state DB joint
                in unrecrystallised 2.5 mm thick sheet.
                Bond interface at A-A.

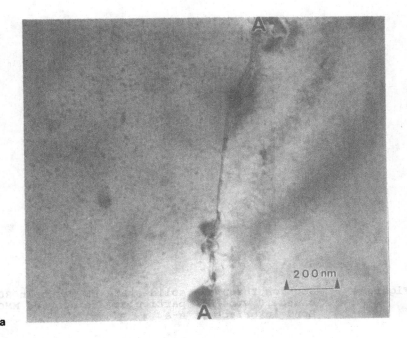

a

b

Figure 3   Transmission electron micrographs of a solid
            state diffusion bond.
            Bond interface at A-A.

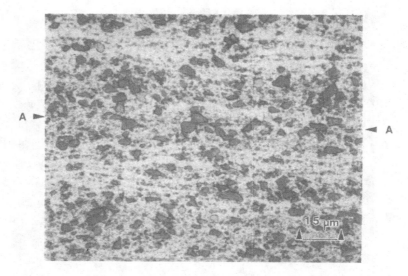

Figure 4   Section through a solid state DB joint in 8090
based 20 wt.% SiC particulate reinforced MMC.
Bond interface at A-A.

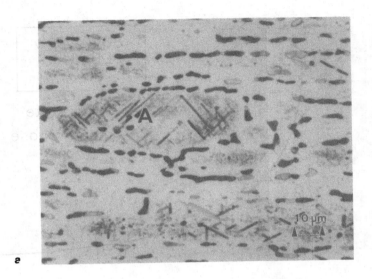

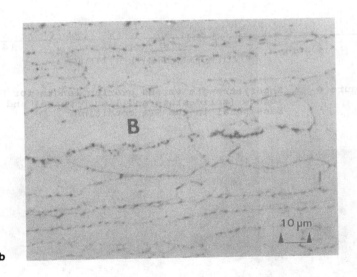

Figure 5   Section through a liquid phase DB joint;
a) as bonded, b) STA.

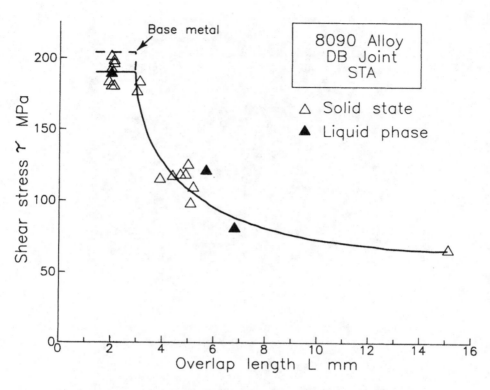

Figure 6   Shear strength versus overlap length for DB joints (solid state and liquid phase) and 8090 base metal in the STA condition.

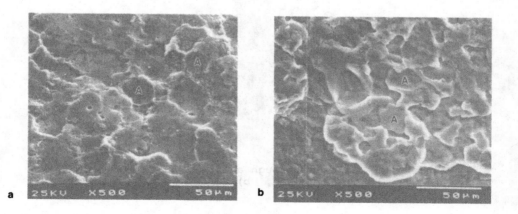

Figure 7   SEM fracture surfaces of a sheared joint in; a)   DB (solid state), b) base metal.

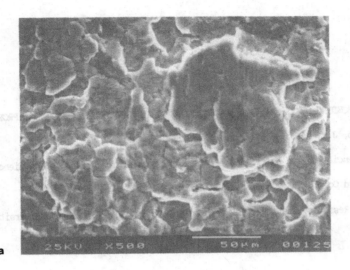

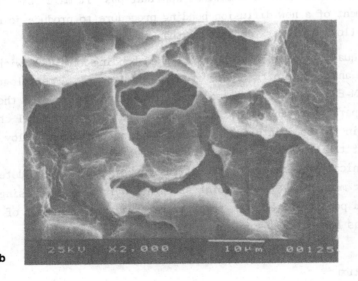

Figure 8   SEM fracture surfaces of a sheared liquid
               phase DB joint.

DIFFUSION BONDING OF Ti-6Al-4V ALLOY: METALLURGICAL ASPECTS AND MECHANICAL PROPERTIES

F.A. Calvo, J.M. Gómez de Salazar, A. Ureña, J.G. Carrión*

Dept. Ciencia de los Materiales e Ingeniería Metalúrgica. Facultad de Ciencias Químicas. Universidad Complutense de Madrid. SPAIN.

*Dept. de Residuos, Instituto de Tecnología Nuclear, CIEMAT. Ciudad Universitaria, Madrid. SPAIN.

Abstract

This paper presents the results obtained on the diffusion bonding of Ti-6 Al-4 V alloy for aeronautical applications. It main objetive is the development of a new diffusion bonding procedure to produce joints in ti tanium alloys at lower temperature than the current methods.

High quality joints have been produced bonding at 850 ºC with pressures of 4 MPa and times in the range from 90 and 120 min. A metallographic study by SEM-EDS has been performed to determinated the role of the diffusion bonding parameters and their influence on the microstructural changes occured in the bond interface. Grain growth of the parent alloy and the increase of the bonded area with time has been also measured.

Mechanical properties of the diffusion joints have been determined using different mechanical tests. Joint strenghts were meassured using tensile, shear and peel test, at room temperature. Fracture behaviour of the tested joints has been also described.

I. Introduction

The study of diffusion bonding of Ti-6Al-4V alloy has been developed as a result of the experience obtained from the investigation on superplastic forming of this and other titanium alloys for their application in the fabrication of aircraft structures. Ti-6Al-4V alloy (1) and most of Ti alloys formed as sheets (2-3) can be subjected to a combined

145

process of diffusion bonding (DB) with superplastic forming (SPF) to produce complex components in one operation with substantial cost and weight savings. Authors that have studied this process have proposed different experimental conditions for SPF/DB of Ti–6Al–4V (4–9), but they restricted diffusion bonding temperature in a very narrow range (920 – 930 °C) where the SPF condition of the material is the best (3) provided the optimum volumetric equilibrium between the microstructural phases that compound the alloy (10).

However, the requirement that both bonding and forming must be carried out at high temperatures is one of the limitations that exhibits the aplication of SPF/DB to Ti alloys. For these reasons, there is a considerable interest on the extension of SPF/DB technology in Ti alloys to lower temperatures.

The present paper describes the results of an experimental work in which the main objective was to develope a solid state bonding process available for Ti alloys using bonding temperatures of 850 °C which aproximately corresponds with the 50% of the titanium alloys melting point.

Diffusion bonds obtained in this research were studied by metallographic techniques to determine the microstructural changes showed by the alloy after the thermomechanical treatment involved in the diffusion bonding process. Both formation of new phases and grain growth of the parent alloy were investigated. The quality of the bonds was estimated with different mechanical proofs (tensile, lap shear and peel strength tests) using different bonding conditions. Fractography of tested bonds made possible to determine the relation between the bonded area and the mechanical properties.

II. Experimental technique

2.1. Materials and Preparation

The parent materials used in this investigation were received in the form of 1.0 and 2.5 mm thick sheets, and in 28 mm thick plate, both in the annealed condition. The chemical compositions are given in Table 1.

Metallographic studies and mechanical tests were carried out on the bonded joints. Different types of specimens were designed and prepared for each kind of test. For

TABLE I.- Chemical composition of parents materials.

Elements Materials	CHEMICAL COMPOSITION (%)							
	Al	V	Fe	O	C	N	H	Ti
SHEETS	6.20	4.30	0.08	-	0.05	0.009	0.005	Bal.
PLATE	6.15	4.40	0.09	-	0.05	0.010	0.005	Bal.

Fig.1.: Parent alloy microstructure

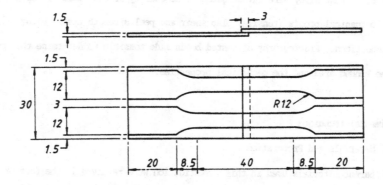

Fig.2.: Dimensions of tensile specimens for diffusion bonded cylinders

microstructural studies, pairs of rectangular specimens of 20 x 15 mm were cut from the 1 mm thick sheet and bonded at different conditions. The microstructure of the as-received material was characterized in one of these specimens using different metallographic techniques. This microstructure is shown in Fig. 1. It is principally α-phase, that form the alloy matrix and present β aggregates on grain boundaries of α matrix. Inside α grain can be observed a very fine precipitate. It was identified as α₂ phase.

For the shear test, pairs of rectangular specimens of 50 x 30 mm were cut from the 1 mm thick sheet and bonded as Fig. 2 shows. The overlap length was 3 mm, and after bonding they were machined two shear test pieces from each bonded specimen. Overlap area of these test pieces was 6 x 3 mm.

Peel test piece blanks of 100 x 17 mm made from 2.5 mm thick sheet, were bonded at one end, with a bonding length of 17 mm as shows Fig. 3. They were bending into a suitable shape for peel testing.

Butt joints between cylindrical specimens of 10 mm diameter and 20 mm length mede from the plate material, were obtained. The tensile strength of these joints was measured using cylindrical tensile test pieces (ASTM A370). They were machined from bonded specimens with the bond interface positionned of the middle of the gauge length. Dimensions of these specimens were represented in Fig. 4.

For cylindrical specimens the areas to be bonded were prepared following two different methods. Part of them were machined (turned) to 1.5 μm average roughness and the other were ground with 600 grade emery paper to 0.1 μm. The flat specimens (sheet) were prepared only in the second way. Just before bonding, all specimens were cleaned with acetone in an ultrasonic bath.

2.2. Bonding procedure.

Diffusion joints were made using two different bonding machines. One used induction heating and applied the load by a mechanical screw feed system. The other one applied the pressure by a lever system and used external resistance heating. Both equipments had high vacuum systems and all diffusion bonds were produced in a vacuum range of 10^{-3}–10^{-4} torr.

Diffusion bonding tests for all types of specimens were made at 850 °C. Pressures of

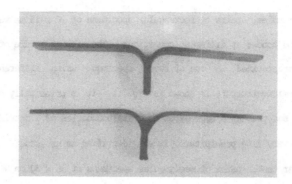

Fig.3.: Peel test pieces

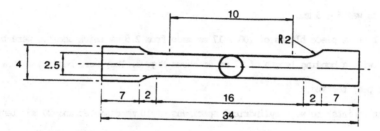

Fig.4.: Dimensions of shear specimens for diffusion bonded sheets

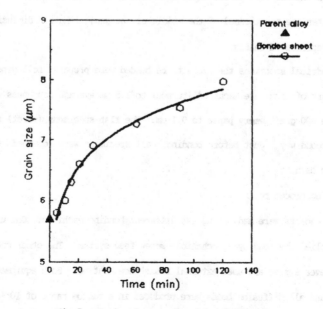

Fig.5.: Grain size growth with bonding time

2 and 4 MPa and bonding times between 30 and 120 minutes were studied with the above surface conditions.

The thermal bonding cycles that the Ti–6Al–4V alloy experimented for the different tested specimens were similar. The heating speed was 0.4 °C/s and after the set bonding time, the specimens were cooled in the vacuum chamber with low cooling rates in the range of 0.07–0.1 °C/s.

III. Results and discusions.

3.1. Microstructure.

Metallographic study of transverse sections of the diffusion bonds was carried out using light and scanning electron microscopy. In the as–bonded condition the biphasic structure of the parent alloy is preserved, although the α–phase grain grew. Although grain growth was observed during bonding (Fig. 5); for tested bonding times, the grain size was always kept in the range required to develop superplastic properties. This grain growth is attached with the transformation of β phase into acicular α during the cooling after bonding procedure.

The precipitates observed inside the α–grain in the as–received material, appeared also after bonding cycle. However, increasing bonding time did favour the homogeneitation of the alloy elements in the metallic matrix and the dissolution of those agregates. After 120 minutes of bonding, precipitates could not be observed (Fig. 6a and b).

EDS microanalysis proved that the intercristaline precipitate is a Ti–Al compound (Fig. 7), probably the ordered solid solution TiAl₃ (α₂ phase). This α₂ phase produced an strengthening of the α–matrix, and a desencrease of the parent alloy ductility (11).

All the bonded specimens shown superficial enrichment in α–phase (Fig. 8), because the high solubility that oxygen presents in α–Ti. The high hardness of α–phase turned the alloy excessive britle and it makes difficult the following machined process. For the elimination of this α–phase layer is necessary to apply a chemical milling to the bonded pieces (12).

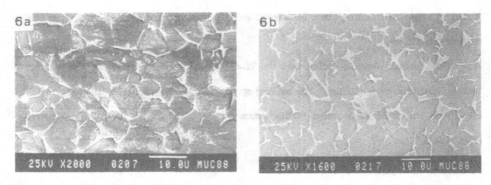

Fig.6.: Diffusion bonds in Ti–6Al–4V sheet at 850 °C and 4 MPa. Bonding time: a) 60 min., b) 120 min.

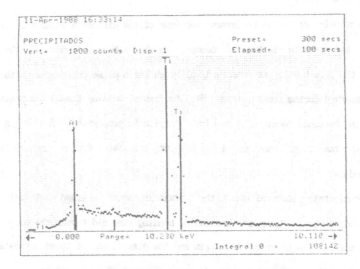

Fig.7.: EDS microanalysis of Ti₃Al precipitates

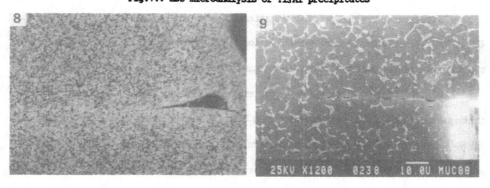

Fig.8.: Superficial enrichment in α phase
Fig.9.: Edge effect in diffusion bonded Ti–6Al–4V sheet

Diffusion bonds presented a very high microstructural quality for all bonding times tested. The original bond interface desappeared and no voids were observed for bonding condition used. Complete recristallitation was observed trough bond interface. However, most of the bonded specimens showed a lack of union at their edges. This effect due to the microscopical gradient of pressure that there is in this part of the bond interface. This fact explains the presence of a very high proportion of cavities at the edges of some specimens which number and size desencrease towards the center of the specimens (Fig. 9). The evolution of the interfacial voids comfirmed the theoretical model proposed by Guo and Ridley (13) based on the shrinkage of lenticular voids (Fig. 10a and b) by diffusion and creep mechanisms.

3.2. Tensile tests.

The results of tensile tests on cylindrical bonded pieces showed high strength bonds could be obtained for Ti-6Al-4V joints when bonding temperatures of 850 °C were used. Maximum tensile strength of 960 MPa (approximately 90 % of the parent alloy tensile strength) was reached for bonding conditions of 850 °C, 4 MPa and 90 min, using ground surfaces (0.1 μm). Increasing the bonding pressure from 2 to 4 MPa had little effect on the tensile strength, but the increase of bonding time from 90 to 120 minutes produced a light softening of the bonded alloy. It was related with the dissolution of α_2 precipitates and the grain growth of α-matrix observed for longer bonding times. Thes results are graphically shown in Fig. 11a and b.

It is interesting to note the effect on the mechanical properties of the sourface roughness of bonded areas. Although tensile strength of turned specimens is only ligthly lower than the value obtained for grounded specimens (Fig 11a); a high dependence between the elongation and the surface finish was observed (Fig 11b). While joints with roughness surface of 0.1 μm failed trough the parent alloy with a great elongation, similar to the as-received material one (≈ 15 %); joints bonded with higher roughness failed though the bond interface with hardly necking. The load-elongation curve exhibited by a high quality bond during a tensile test is compared with the curve obtained for a high roughness bonded specimen in Fig. 12. In the firt one a significant plastic deformation has occurred in the

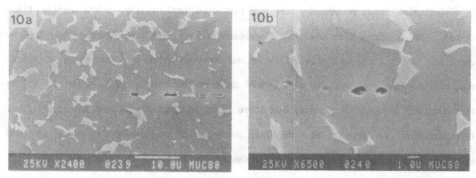

Fig.10.: a) Interracial voids close to the specimen edge; b) Detail of lenticular voids

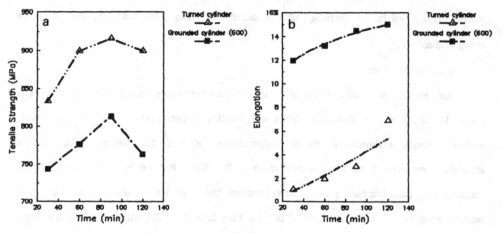

Fig.11.: Effect of the bonding time and surface roughness on the mechanical tensile properties of diffusion bonded Ti-6Al-4V cylinder: a) Tensile strength; b) Elongation

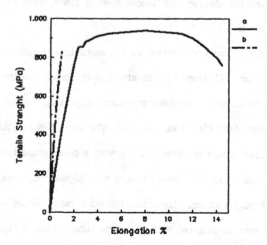

Fig.12.: Tensile strength versus elongation curves: a) groud specimens; b) turned specimens

bond region prior to tensile fracture. This plasticity was absent in poor bons and these interfaces were subsequently found to have unbonded areas. The fractographic study of both kind of tested joints showed this fact (Fig. 13a and b). This study made also possible to determinate the evolution of the bonded area proportion and its dependence with the bonding conditions (Fig. 14).

3.3. Lap shear tests

The results of lap-shear tests on diffusion bonds of Ti-6Al-4V were strongly dependent on test piece configuration. The distorsion generated in the specimen during bonding when small backing blocks of 3 x 30 mm were used to apply pressure in preliminary bonding trials, introduced important errors in the shear strength evaluation. These problems were avoided by using two restraining clamps during bonding.

The average results of shear tests of all restrained diffusion joints, bonded at different times, are showed in Fig. 15. The shear strength values of these bonds are in the range of 628-816 MPa. Although a certain increase of shear strength was produced with increasing bonding times, all measured values were lower than the tensile strength of the parent alloy in the as-received condition. The maximum failure strength obtained for the longest bonding time used (120 minutes) reached only the 76% of that value.

However, all diffusion bonds tested failed by tensile through the parent material close to the overlap area. The failure was always initiated at the edge of the overlap, so that initial crack growth started in the bond interface and when the crack tip hit the high integrity bond, the failure progressed through the parent material. This phenomenon is less pronounced in joints bonded for longer times. Thus, it explains the strength increase observed with bonding time.

In spite of failure occurred at parent alloy, the failure stress was taken to be that supported by the bond when this phenomenon is produced. The true shear strengths of diffusion bonds tested would be higher than these values.

3.4. Peel tests

The true peel strength of diffusion bonded joint is very difficult to evaluate because of the strong dependence between this value and other design parameters, such as

154

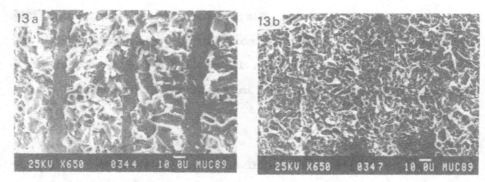

Fig.13.: Fracture surfaces of difusion bonded cylinders: a) high strength bond; b) low strength bond with unbonded areas

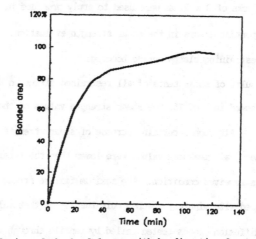

Fig.14.: Evolution of the bonded area with bonding time for turned specimens

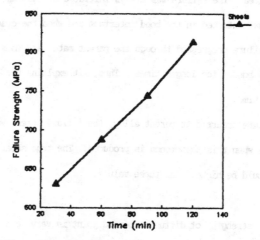

Fig.15.: Effect of bonding time on shear strength of overlap bonds

the test piece configuration and testing technique. However, it was interesting to get some information of peel stress behavior of Ti-6Al-4V diffusion bonds. Peel strengths obtained were in the range of 90-200 N/mm.

Specimens with low peel strength (<100 N/mm) presented a broken load vs. deformation curve for peel test (Fig. 16a). This is because the peel crack appeared to grow in a series of jump that induces a drop in the peel stress. Fractographic SEM studies of the joints shows this crack propagation: areas with plastic deformation alternate with large zones of low quality joint, where the crack growth rate was very high (Fig. 17a).

Joints with high peel strength (≈200 N/mm) showed peel test curves where the load remained almost constant during crack growth (Fig. 16b). Failure surfaces of these specimens show large plastic areas, developed during the slow crack growth period (Fig. 17b). These joints were obtained for bonding times longer than 60 minutes.

IV. Conclusions

High quality diffusion bonded joints can be produced for Ti-6Al-4V alloy using bonding temperatures of 850 °C, which is lower than that of the superplastic forming process.

The best mechanical properties were obtained using bonding pressures of 4 MPa and times in the range of 90-120 minutes. For these conditions, the grain size of the parent alloy was kept in the range required for superplastic forming.

The maximum tensile strength obtained was 90% of the tensile strength of the parent alloy in the as-received condition. Shear strength up to 76% of that value were also obtained.

In spite of the peel strength depended on a combination of factors, results suggest that high peel strength can be obtained at 850 °C.

References

(1) J. Pilling, D.W. Livesey, J.B. Hawkyard, N. Ridley. Metals Science, 18 (3), 1984.

(2) C. Hammond. Superplastic Forming of Structural Alloys. Proc. Conf.. AIME, 1982.

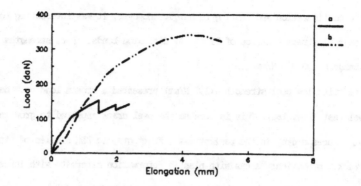

Fig.16.: Load-elongation curve for peel test in bonded specimens. Bonding conditions:
a) T_b= 850 °C; P_b= 4 MPa; t_b= 120 min
b) T_b= 850 °C; P_b= 2 MPa; t_b= 30 min

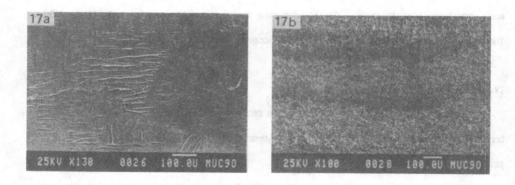

Fig.17.: Fracture surfaces of diffusion bonded joint in peel test

(3) C. H. Hamilton. Superplastic Forming. Proc. Conf.. AMS, 1984.

(4) S. Bownall. Metalworking Production, 129 (2), 1985.

(5) B. Kellock. Machinery and Production Engineering. 143 (3), 1985.

(6) M. Ohsumi, M. Shimizu, A. Takakashi, T. Tsuzuku. Mitsubishi Heavy Industries Ltd.

   Technical Review, Feb. 1984.

(7) A. Arieli, R.B. Vastava. Superplastic Forming. Proc. Conf.. AMS, 1984.

(8) R. Sawle. Superplastic Forming of Structural Alloys. Proc. Conf.. AIME, 1982.

(9) L. Ascani. Innovation in Materials and their Applications. Proc. Conf. ASM, Chicago Oct.

   1977, 19-36.

(10) O.D. Sherby and O.A. Ruano. Superplastic Forming of Structural Alloys. Proc. Conf..

   AIME, 1982.

(11) ASM Committee on Titanium and Titanium Alloys. Metals Handbook vol.3, pp. 763-774.

    (9th ed.)

(12) W.T. Harris. "Chemical Milling". Clarendon Press, 1976.

(13) Z.X. Guo and N. Ridley. Materials Science and Technology, 3 (11), 1987. 945-953.

Resistance Diffusion Bonding of a Titanium Aluminide

A. Cox,* W. A. Baeslack III,** S. Zorko*** and C. English***

*Edison Welding Institute
Columbus, Ohio 43212

**Department of Welding Engineering
The Ohio State University
Columbus, Ohio 43210

***GE Aircraft
Cincinnati, Ohio 45215

ABSTRACT

Diffusion bonds and fusion welds have been produced between sheets of Ti-6wt%Al-4wt%V and Ti-14.8wt%Al-21.3wt%Nb titanium aluminide using the capacitor-discharge resistance spot welding process. Diffusion bonds in Ti-6wt%Al-4wt%V were characterized by beta grain growth across the bond line and the presence of occasional interface defects. Despite fracture through the bond region, optimum tensile-shear strengths for the diffusion bonds were comparable to those of fusion spot welds which failed by "nugget pullout". High quality, defect-free diffusion bonds were also produced in a Ti-14.8wt%Al-21.3wt%Nb alpha-two titanium aluminide. The bond region was characterized by the growth of equiaxed beta grains across the bond line and an absence of interface defects. Fusion welds in the titanium aluminide exhibited a coarse, columnar beta grain structure. High cooling rates experienced in both the diffusion bonds and fusion welds in the titanium aluminide promoted the retention of beta phase down to room temperature throughout a large proportion of the bond and weld zones. Tensile-shear fracture of the titanium-aluminide welds initiated near the weld outer periphery and propagated principally through the unaffected base metal. The average fracture strength of the diffusion bonds produced at high axial force was markedly superior to that of bonds produced at low axial force and fusion welds. This difference was attributed to a more severe notch geometry at the outer periphery of the latter weld types.

INTRODUCTION

Requirements for high performance gas-turbine engines and airframe structures in the 1990's will demand the development of advanced aerospace materials which can provide mechanical property combinations superior to those exhibited by current alloys. Alpha-two titanium aluminides, which are based on the ordered Ti_3Al intermetallic (DO_{19} superlattice), offer the potential for significantly improved elevated-temperature properties versus conventional near-alpha titanium alloys. Although the inherent brittleness of the binary compound has precluded its utilization in engineering applications, ternary and quaternary alloying element additions to the basic Ti_3Al chemistry have resulted in alpha-two titanium aluminides (more precisely, alpha-two + beta alloys) with improved ductility and toughness.

Since titanium aluminides are being developed principally for structural applications, joinability will be an important factor in ultimately determining their utility. Initial weldability studies on a first-generation alpha-two titanium aluminide, Ti-14.8wt%Al-21.3wt%Nb, found that moderate cooling rates associated with conventional gas tungsten-arc welding result in the formation of a fine, acicular alpha-two microstructure which exhibits low ductility and susceptibility to solid-state cracking. More recent Nd:YAG laser welding studies (2) on this alloy showed that extremely high cooling rates promote the formation of an ordered-beta microstructure (B2 superlattice) which exhibits a ductility nearly equivalent to that of the unaffected base metal and good resistance to cracking. Although high energy density welding processes, such as laser and electron beam welding, may be suitable for the joining of monolithic titanium aluminides, such fusion welding techniques may not be feasible for fiber-reinforced alpha-two titanium aluminides due to severe fiber degradation. Consequently, the effective joining of these materials will require the application of solid-state welding processes, such as diffusion bonding. Capacitor-discharge resistance spot welding (CD-RSW) offers a strong potential for producing diffusion bonds between thin sheets of both monolithic and fiber-reinforced titanium aluminides. The extremely rapid weld thermal cycle associated with this process is desirable in that it would minimize thermal effects on reinforcing fibers. In addition, the process promotes an extremely high cooling rate which can potentially provide a more ductile, crack-resistant ordered-beta weld microstructure. In the present study, solid-state resistance diffusion bonds and conventional fusion spot welds were produced in both Ti-14.8wt%Al-21.3wt%Nb (hereafter designated as Ti-15-21 and in conventional Ti-6wt%Al-4wt%V (hereafter designated as Ti-6-4) for comparative purposes using the CD-RSW process. The influence of welding parameters on the weld type (ie. solid-state versus fusion), microstructure, mechanical properties and fracture characteristics were determined for each alloy and comparatively evaluated.

EXPERIMENTAL PROCEDURE

Ti-15-21 and Ti-6-4 sheets 1.70 and 0.762 mm in thickness, respectively, were provided in the alpha+beta rolled and mill-annealed condition. Chemical compositions of each alloy are provided in Table 1. Microstructures of both alloys exhibited equiaxed alpha (Ti-6-4) or alpha-two (Ti-15-21) grains with small islands of beta phase located principally at alpha or alpha-two grain boundary triple points. Coupons for spot welding were sectioned to a nominal size of 20 mm in width x 50 mm in length, with the length oriented transverse to the sheet rolling direction. Prior to welding, coupons were pickled in a solution of 5 ml HF + 40 ml HNO_3 + 55 ml H_2O, rinsed with distilled water, methanol and dried. Preliminary welding trials were performed in order to determine an optimum range of welding voltages and forces which provided satisfactory interface contact while minimizing surface

deformation. Final iteration welds for mechanical property analysis were subsequently produced over a range of voltages from 150 to 180 volts for Ti-6-4 and 230 and 280 volts for the Ti-15-21 in order to produce both solid-state and fusion welds. Table 2 summarizes the welding forces and voltages evaluated for each of the materials, and the corresponding peak welding currents and cycle times.

Subsequent to welding, representative coupons were sectioned transversely at the weld centerline, mounted in epoxy, polished down to 0.05 micron alumina and etched with Kroll's reagent for examination using light microscopy. In addition, transmission-electron microscopy (TEM) samples were sectioned from the center of selected Ti-15-21 diffusion bonds, jet electropolished and examined using a JEM 2000FX electron microscope. Mechanical property analysis included Knoop microhardness testing (500 gm load) and tensile shear testing. Tensile-shear test specimens were clamped 12 mm on each end and tensile tested at an extension rate of 0.134 mm/s. Fracture stresses provided in Table 2 were calculated based on actual metallographic measurements of the weld diameter, including both the fusion and solid-state bonded interface regions in fusion welds. Each fractured tensile-shear specimen was cross-sectioned, mounted in epoxy and metallographically prepared for identification of the fracture path.

RESULTS AND DISCUSSION

Macroscopic Examination

CD-RSW welds evaluated in this study were produced at relatively low energy inputs as compared to conventional resistance spot welds in titanium. Consequently, defects associated with excessive heat input, such as excess deformation of the sheet surfaces and/or the expulsion of molten metal from the fusion zone were not observed. The use of low energy inputs also promoted the formation of smaller bonded or fused interface regions versus optimum fusion spot welds. However, except for the diffusion bonds produced in Ti-15-21, bond and weld diameters met minimum requirements as set forth in Mil-Spec. MIL-W-6858D (3). (Note that this specification officially applies only to fusion spot welds).

Microstructure Analysis

Figure 1A shows the cross-section through a solid-state bond produced between Ti-6-4 sheets using the CD-RSW process (160 Volts, 7.12 kN electrode force). At the outer periphery of the bond, the microstructure appeared similar to the equiaxed alpha + beta microstructure exhibited by the unaffected base metal (Fig. 1B). Examination of this region at increased magnification (Fig. 1C), however, indicated that it had actually experienced temperatures above the beta transus (that temperature where the low-temperature HCP alpha phase transforms completely to the high-temperature BCC beta phase on heating) during the weld thermal cycle. The thermal excursion of this region to peak temperatures only marginally above the beta transus for an extremely short duration allowed only minimal beta grain growth and negligible homogenization of V and Al which was originally partitioned to the beta and alpha phases, respectively. On subsequent rapid cooling, Al-rich, V-depleted beta phase regions which were originally alpha grains transformed to fine, acicular alpha-prime (HCP) martensite (Fig. 1C), while V-enriched beta regions were likely retained as beta phase. Evidence of a nearly continuous bond line in this region indicated incomplete bonding and only limited beta grain growth across the interface. Nearer to the center of the bond region, peak temperatures were appreciably higher, which promoted extensive beta grain growth across the interface and homogenization of alloying elements in the high-temperature beta phase (Fig. 1D). As in the outer periphery, extremely rapid cooling rates promoted solid-state transformation of this region to alpha-prime martensite. Examination of this interface region at increased magnification (Fig. 1E) showed the occasional presence of voids along the bond line.

An increase in voltage to 180 volts promoted appreciable melting at the Ti-6-4 sheet interfaces and the formation of a fusion zone (Fig. 2A). Outside of the fusion zone, a region of solid-state bonding existed in which the microstructure varied from the equiaxed-alpha appearing microstructure at the weld outer periphery, to a compositionally homogenous, coarsened beta grain/alpha-prime martensite microstructure adjacent to the fusion line (Figs. 2B and C). In general, the solid-state bond in this region of the fusion weld appeared superior to that observed in the solid-state weld, with negligible bond line defects. The weld fusion zone solidified by the epitaxial nucleation of columnar beta grains directly upon equiaxed beta grains at the fusion boundary. These columnar grains grew in a direction parallel to the maximum temperature gradient at the solid-liquid interface (ie., parallel to the electrode axis), ultimately impinging at the weld centerline to create an irregular beta grain boundary, as shown in Fig. 2D. As expected, rapid cooling rates experienced in the fusion zone promoted beta decomposition to alpha-prime martensite.

Figure 3A shows the cross-section through a diffusion bond produced between Ti-15-21 sheets using a voltage of 230 Volts and an electrode force of 8.9 kN. As indicated, except at the outer periphery, complete bonding was achieved across the weld interface. Examination of the bond outer periphery at increased magnification showed that nearly the entire bond line had experienced peak temperatures above the beta transus, but that as in the outer periphery of the Ti-6-4 bonds, insufficient time was available for homogenization of alloying elements and beta grain growth (Fig. 3B). At the center of the bond, homogenization was more extensive, as indicated by the more "diffuse" appearance of the original alpha grain morphologies (Fig. 3C). Noticible beta grain growth was also observed across the bond interface in this region. Light microscopy analysis suggested that the microstructure consisted of alpha-two (possibly martensitic as in the Ti-6-4 welds) and retained beta. However, analysis using TEM and selected-area diffraction indicated this region to consist primarily of retained-beta phase. Except at the outer periphery, bonding appeared complete across the interface with no evidence of voids or other lack of bonding defects.

The diffusion bonds produced at an identical voltage (230 Volts) but lower axial force (7.12 kN) experienced a higher heat input into the bond region (Fig. 4A). This higher energy input was attributed to a greater interface resistance (due to the lower force) promoting greater I^2R heating at the interface. Near the outer periphery (Fig. 4B), the microstructure appeared similar to that observed in the high force bond, but with a greater extent of alloying element homogenization. Nearer to and at the axial bond centerline (Figs. 4C and D), evidence of appreciable beta grain growth across the interface and possible incipient melting at beta grain boundaries (heavily etched) were evident. Note that the heavily-etched grain boundaries which liquated at peak temperatures differed from the room temperature beta grain structure due to grain boundary migration on cooling. Although not examined with TEM, it is believed that regions near the center of the bond, where appreciable homogenization of alloying elements occurred, were retained as beta phase on cooling to room temperature. Except at the outermost periphery, the bond line exhibited an absence of defects.

Figure 5A shows a cross-section through the fusion weld produced in Ti-15-21 sheet using 280 Volts and an electrode force of 7.12 kN. As in Ti-6-4, the weld exhibited both a fusion zone and a surrounding region of solid-state bonding. At the weld outer periphery, a thermal excursion only slightly above the beta transus minimized beta grain growth and homogenization of base metal microstructure compositional variations (Fig. 5B). Nearer to the fusion line, greater compositional homogenization and appreciable beta grain boundary migration and grain growth were observed (Fig. 5C). As in the Ti-6-4 fusion weld, coarse, columnar beta grains solidified epitaxially from coarsened beta grains in the near HAZ. The cellular-dendritic solidification substructure exhibited by these grains (Fig. 5B) is quite apparent in the room temperature microstructure, and attributed to the segregation of Nb during weld solidification and the slow diffusivity and minimal homogenization of this element during weld cooling. Based on previous laser welding studies (2), it is suggested that the FZ structure contained entirely retained, ordered beta phase. As shown in Figure 5A, this weld was characterized by the limited extrusion of "flash" from the interface region at the outer periphery of the weld.

Mechanical Properties

Knoop microhardness values at the center of diffusion bonds and fusion zones in Ti-6Al-4V are shown in Table II, and ranged from about 375 in the diffusion bonds to 385 in the fusion welds. These values, which were higher than that of the base metal, were consistent with the presence of alpha-prime martensite in these locations. Hardnesses at the center of diffusion bonds in Ti-15-21 varied from about KHN 375-385 in the high force bonds to KHN 350-360 in the low force bonds. Fusion zone hardnesses in welds produced at both force levels were somewhat higher ranging from KHN 385-390. These hardnesses were appreciably greater than that of the alpha-two + beta base metal microstructure (DPH 220) and also marginally greater than that of ordered, retained-beta microstructures in water quenched (1) and Nd:YAG laser welds (2).

Tensile-shear strengths and stresses are shown in Table 2. The average tensile-shear strength of Ti-6-4 diffusion bonds produced at 160 Volts was 5.64 kN, which was quite similar to average strengths of 5.47 and 5.69 kN for the fusion welds produced at 170 and 180 Volts, respectively. These values meet minimum requirements as set forth by MIL-Spec. MIL-W-6858D for fusion welds in titanium sheet of this thickness (3). The average tensile shear stress of 313.5 MPa for the optimum diffusion bonds was superior to that of the fusion welds and quite comparable to that of conventional fusion spot welds in Ti-6Al-4V sheet (4). Tensile-shear strengths of diffusion bonds produced at low force and the fusion welds in Ti-15-21 titanium aluminide were appreciably lower than joints in Ti-6-4, despite exhibiting larger bond/weld diameters. In contrast, the diffusion bond produced at high force exhibited high strength (6.41 kN) and fracture stress (354.7 MPa) levels superior to the Ti-6-4 bonds and welds. As for all alloy/parameter combinations evaluated, tensile-shear strength levels of the three specimens tested at this optimum condition were quite consistent with values of 388, 357 and 320 MPa.

Fracture Analysis

Failure of resistance diffusion bonds in the Ti-6-4 sheet occurred macroscopically by shear fracture through the bond region. Analysis of the fracture path by metallographic cross-sectioning of the failed specimens revealed fracture along the bond interface only at the outer weld periphery, possibly promoted by the presence of occasional defects at the interface. Fracture through the central weld region was principally remote from the bond line. Failure of fusion welds in Ti-6-4 sheet occurred by fracture around the outer periphery of the weld fusion zone, commonly known as "nugget pullout." It is of interest to note that despite the different modes of fracture between the solid-state and fusion welds, fracture strengths and stresses were quite similar.

Fracture along the bond interface was observed only for a single resistance diffusion bond in Ti-15Al-21Nb produced at the lower axial force (Fig. 6A). As shown in Fig. 6B, fracture initiated at a notch between the extruded "flash" at the weld outer periphery and the base sheet. Crack propagation occurred along the bond line at the weld outer periphery, but remote from the bond line near the center of the bond region. All other tensile-shear specimens fractured through the unaffected base metal in the manner shown in Figure 7A. As shown in Figure 4A for a diffusion bond produced at low force and Fig. 7B for a fusion weld, fracture initiated at the notch between the extruded flash and the sheet surface, propagating through the unaffected base metal to the surface. In contrast, fracture of the solid-state weld produced at high force appeared to initiate on the sheet surface away from the weld outer periphery (Fig. 7C). Note that the extrusion of metal from the weld region and the associated notch formation did not occur in these welds due to the lower net energy input and reduced interface deformation (despite the higher force level). The greater fracture strengths of the high pressure diffusion bonds versus the low pressure diffusion bonds and fusion welds appeared to be associated primarily with this difference in fracture initiation behavior. The present study has demonstrated the strong potential of the CD/RSW process for producing high quality diffusion bonds in Ti-6-4 and Ti-15-21 titanium aluminide sheet materials. It has also shown that joint properties in the low-ductility titanium aluminide are highly dependent on the notch geometry at the weld outer periphery, and that parametric studies optimizing weld mechanical properties must consider this effect. Such notch effects will certainly become of even greater significance when considering the axial fatigue behavior of diffusion bonds in this material.

CONCLUSIONS

1. High-integrity diffusion bonds were produced in Ti-6Al-4V sheet using the CD-RSW welding process. Diffusion bond tensile-shear strengths met minimum requirements for fusion spot welds as set forth in Mil. Spec. MIL-W-6858D, despite shear fracture through the bond region versus nugget pullout in the fusion welds.

2. Defect-free resistance diffusion bonds were also produced in Ti-15Al-21Nb titanium aluminide sheet. Tensile-shear strengths and stresses of diffusion welds produced with high electrode force were appreciably greater than diffusion bonds produced at low force and fusion welds.

3. Reduced tensile properties of fusion welds in Ti-15Al-21Nb were attributed to fracture initiation at a notch created in the outer weld periphery by the slight extrusion of metal from the weld interface. Despite initiation at this notch, crack propagation occurred nearly exclusively through the base metal. The absence of this notch in the diffusion bonds produced at high force promoted fracture initiation remote from the outer periphery and correspondingly higher tensile-shear strengths.

REFERENCES

1. Baeslack, W. A. III and Mascorella, T., "Weldability of a Titanium Aluminide," Welding Journal 68, 1989, p. 483s-498s.

2. Baeslack W. A. III, Cieslak, M. J. and Headley, T. J., "Structure, Properties and Fracture of Pulsed Nd:YAG Laser Welded Ti-14.8 wt%Al-21.3wt%Nb Titanium Aluminide," Scripta Metallurgica 22, 1988, p. 1155-1160.

3. Military Specification: MIL-W-6858D, "Welding, Resistance: Spot and Seam," 1978.

4. Jarboe, D. M., "Resistance Spot Welding of Ti-6Al-4V Alloy," Bendix Technical Report BDX-613-2447, 1980.

ACKNOWLEDGEMENTS

The authors express appreciation to Dr. Jerry Gould of the Edison Welding Institute for his technical contributions. The authors are also indebted to EWI for the use of their resistance welding and mechanical testing facilities. Work performed at OSU was supported by GE Aircraft, Cincinnati, Ohio.

Table 1. Chemical Compositions of Ti-6-4 and Ti-15-21 Base Metals (wt%)

Element	Ti-6Al-4V	Ti-15Al-21Nb
Al	6.6	14.80
V	4.3	-
Nb	-	21.30
Fe	0.14	0.065
O	0.1	0.058
N	0.01	0.007
H	0.0083	-
Ti	bal.	bal.

Table 2. Welding Parameter[a] and Mechanical Properties[b] for Capacitor Discharge Resistance Spot Welds Produced in Ti-6-4 and Ti-15-21 Titanium Aluminide

Specimen Type[c]	Voltage V	Current amps	Time ms	Force kN(psi)	Weld Type[d]	Central Interface Hardness
Ti-6-4	150	5,300	12.8	7.12(1,600)	SS	375
Ti-6-4	160	5,800	15.5	7.12(1,600)	SS	375
Ti-6-4	170	6,235	14.7	7.12(1,600)	FW	380
Ti-6-4	180	6,735	16.5	7.12(1,600)	FW	385
Ti-15-21	230	6,735	10.3	7.12(1,600)	SS	350-360
Ti-15-21	230	6,835	11.5	8.90(2,000)	SS	375-385
Ti-15-21	280	8,500	11.4	7.12(1,600)	FW	385-390
Ti-15-21	280	8,535	11.6	8.90(2,000)	FW	380-390

Weld Diameter mm (in.)	Tensile-Shear Strength kN (lbs.)	Tensile-Shear Stress MPa (ksi)	Fracture Mode[d]
4.50(0.177)	4.71(1,060)	303.8(44.1)	BLS
4.63(0.182)	5.64(1,268)	313.5(45.5)	BLS
4.80(0.189)	5.47(1,230)	302.5(43.9)	NP
5.08(0.200)	5.69(1,280)	275.6(40.0)	NP
4.80(0.189)	4.17(938)	228.1(33.1)	BLS/OP
4.80(0.189)	6.41(1,442)	354.7(51.5)	OP
5.59(0.220)	3.54(797)	144.4(21.0)	OP
5.59(0.220)	4.10(923)	167.4(24.3)	OP

[a]RWMA Class 2 copper electrodes, 6.35 mm diameter, flat surfaces
[b]Average of 2-3 specimens per condition
[c]SS-Solid State Weld, FW-Fusion Weld
[e]BLS-Bond Line Shear, NP-Nugget Pullout, OP-Outer Periphery

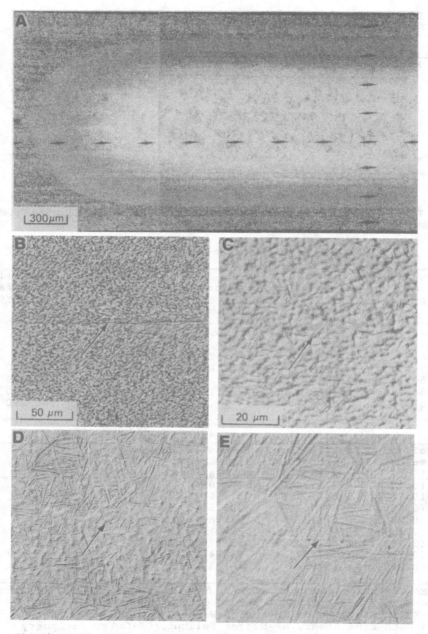

Figure 1. Light Micrographs of Diffusion Bond Produced Between Ti-6-4 Sheets Using CD-RSW Process (160 Volts, 7.12 kN Electrode Force): (A) Cross-Section Through Bond Region, Vertical Hardness Traverse Indicates Axial Bond Center-line; (B,C) Bond Region at Outer Periphery; (D,E) Bond Region at Axial Centerline. Arrows in (B-E) Indicate Bond Line.

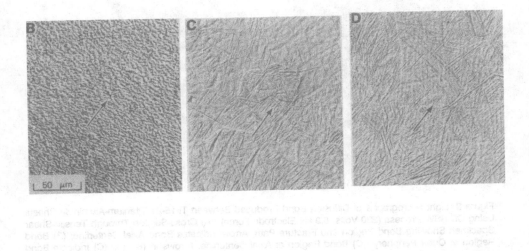

Figure 2. Light Micrographs of Fusion Weld Produced Between Ti-6-4 Sheets using CD-RSW Process (180 Volts, 7.12 kN Electrode Force): (A) Cross-Section Through Weld Zone, Vertical Hardness Traverse Indicates Axial Weld Centerline; (B) Bond Region at Outer Periphery of Solid-State Bonded Region; (C) Bond Region at Inner Periphery of Solid-State Bonded Region; (D) Axial Centerline of Fusion Zone. Arrows in (B) and (C) Indicate Bond Line, Arrow in (D) Indicates Beta Grain Boundary Along Horizontal Weld Centerline.

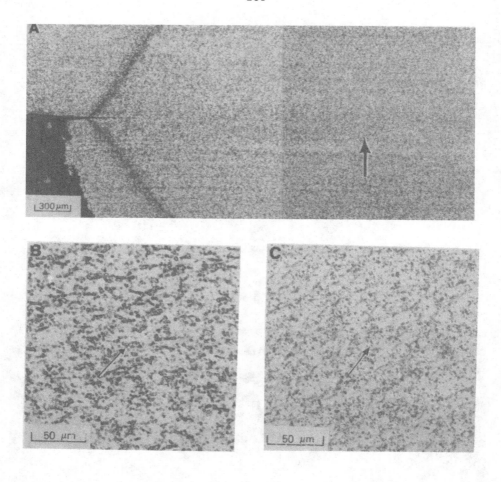

Figure 3. Light Micrographs of Diffusion Bond Produced Between Ti-15-21 Titanium-Aluminide Sheets Using CD-RSW Process (230 Volts, 8.9 kN Electrode Force): (A) Cross-Section Through Tensile-Shear Specimen Showing Bond Region and Fracture Path, Arrow Indicates Bond Axial Centerline; (B) Bond Region at Outer Periphery; (C) Bond Region at Axial Centerline. Arrows in (B) and (C) Indicate Bond Line.

Figure 4. Light Micrographs of Diffusion Bond Produced Between Ti-15-21 Titanium-Aluminide Sheets Using CD-RSW Process (230 Volts, 7.12 kN Electrode Force): (A) Cross-Section Through Tensile-Shear Specimen Showing Bond Region and Fracture Path, Arrow Indicates Bond Axial Centerline; (B) Bond Region at Outer Periphery; (C) Bond Region Between Outer Periphery and Axial Centerline, (D) Bond Region at Axial Centerline. Arrows in (B-D) Indicate Bond Line.

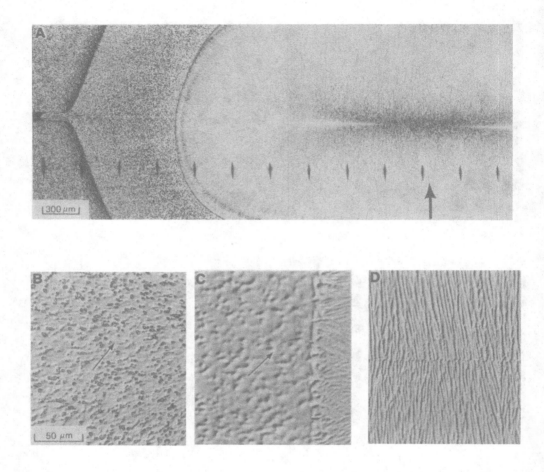

Figure 5. Light Micrographs of Fusion Weld Produced Between Ti-15-21 Titanium-Aluminide Sheets Using CD-RSW Process (280 Volts, 7.12 kN Electrode Force): (A) Cross-Section Through Weld Region, Arrow Indicates Weld Axial Centerline; (B) Bond Region at Outer Periphery of Solid-State Bonded Region; (C) Bond Region at Boundary Between Solid-State Bonded Region and Weld Fusion Zone; (D) Axial Centerline of Weld Fusion Zone. Arrows in (B) and (C) Indicate Bond Line.

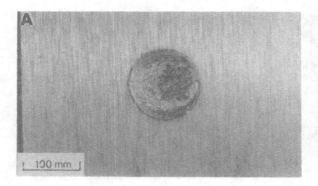

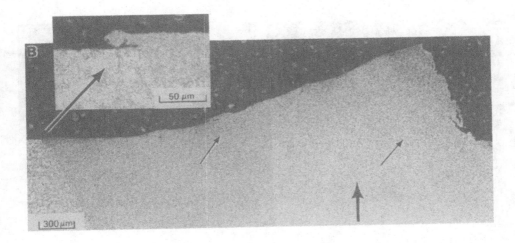

Figure 6. Light Micrographs Showing Fractured Tensile-Shear Specimen Produced Between Ti-15-21 Titanium-Aluminide Sheets Using CD-RSW Process (230 Volts, 7.12 kN Electrode Force): (A) As-Fractured Specimen; (B) Cross-Section Across Crack Path With Inset Showing Outer Edge of Bond. Large Arrow Indicates Bond Axial Centerline, Small Arrows Indicate Bond Line.

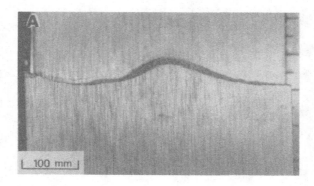

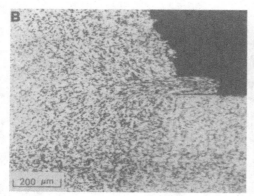

Figure 7. Light Micrographs of Fractured Tensile-Shear Specimens Produced Between Ti-15-21 Titanium-Aluminide Sheets Using CD-RSW Process: (A) Typical As-Fractured Specimen; (B) Cross-Section Across Fracture Path for Weld Produced at 280 Volts, 7.12 kN Electrode Force; (C) Cross-Section Across Fracture Path for Bond Produced at 230 Volts, 8.90 kN Electrode Force. Arrow in (C) Indicates Bond Line.

30 SECONDS SOLID STATE BONDING OF METALS

Thierry DEVERS, Martine HOURCADE.

Laboratoire de Metallurgie du Conservatoire National des Arts et Métiers
2, Rue Conté 75003 PARIS
tel: (1) 40.27.25.86 (FAX 42.71.93.29)

Solid state diffusion bonding as enables to join dissimilar metals, which are difficult by the conventional methods of fusion welding.

Requiring only rather low temperatures, this technic avoids in particular the indesirable structural transformations, but requires bonding duration ranging from some dozens of minutes to several hours according to the caracteristics of the specimens [1], [2], [3].

The possible industrialisation of this technique, makes it necessary to reduce the bonding time considerably and, consequently to find new manufacturing routes .

This target requires first a faster heating process such as induction heating and secondly a rather high pressure (max 300 MPa) to be applied at room temperature, in order to overcome the handicap of the short diffusion time, which reduces possibilities for pore resorption. Morover, during the entire heating process, the pressure is modulated so that it always stays just below the flow stress of the weakest metal.

This dynamic loading process must crush, as much as possible, the asperities of the surface, so that a clean contact between the surfaces be quickly achieved without too high deformation ot the specimens.

To check the potentialities of this new technology of dynamic diffusion bonding (DDB) and to compare to the classical technique, we experimented feasibility tests on titanium/tantalum and zircaloy/tantalum butt joints previously studied at the Laboratoire de Métallurgie (CNAM).

Our purpose was to minimize the bonding duration for an optimal quality of butt joints.

THE DYNAMIC DIFFUSION BONDING EQUIPMENT (fig 1)

The equipment built in our laboratory includes a vacuum chamber heated by high frequency induction and a dynamic unidirectional loading system.

a) Induction heating is performed by the solenoid located around the specimens, outside the glass chamber. A thermocouple directly bonded to the specimens or an optical pyrometer measures the sample temperature.

The specimens are isolated from the bars by refractory discs ($Si_3 N_4$).

172

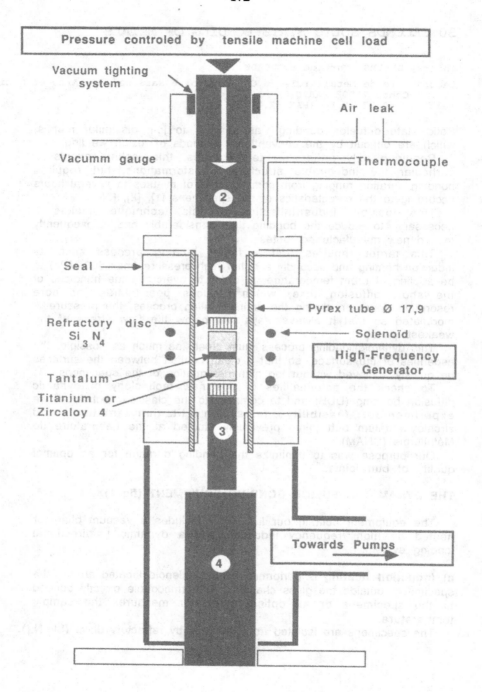

Pressure controled by tensile machine cell load

Vacuum tighting system

Air leak

Vacumm gauge

Thermocouple

2

Seal

1

Pyrex tube Ø 17,9

Refractory disc
Si$_3$N$_4$

Solenoïd

High-Frequency Generator

Tantalum

Titanium or Zircaloy 4

3

Towards Pumps

4

FIGURE 1

b) The pressing system includes:

- an INSTRON tensile-compression machine equiped with a 0-10.000 daN load cell.
- pressing bars. The dynamic application of the pressure is ensured by the upper bars. The lower bars are static. The dimensions of the bars 1 and 3 determine the maximum pressure at 300 MPa.

c) The vacuum achieved may reach 10^{-5} torr vacuum at the level of the specimens.

THE MATERIALS AND SPECIMENS USED

Table 1 shows the chemical composition of the materials used (T50, Zy4 and Ta)

	H2	O2	Fe	C	Cr	Ti	Sn	Zr
T50	>.006*	.21*	.04*	.015*	-	reste	-	-
Zy4	3 **	.127*	.21*	70*	.11*	-	1.4*	reste
Ta	Nuclear purity (≤50 ppm)							

* in weight %;   ** in ppm

Table 1. Chemical composition of materials

The tensile properties of the 3 metals at room temperature are given in table 2 (measures on test pieces similar to the ones used to test our butt joints (fig 3)).

	$Re_{0,2}$(MPa)	Rm(MPa)	A%
T50	430	529	39
Zy4	380	550	19
Ta	232	260	52

Table 2. Tensile properties

A tantalum plate (2mm thick), is sandwiched (fig1) between the two cylinders (8 mm diameter and 10mm heigh). Before bonding, the faying surfaces are given a final fine grinding to Ra ≤ 0,14 µm (paper P 1200), and then are degreased, chimicaly pickled (table 3), washed and dried.

	Pickling bath composition	Conditions
T 50 ou Zy4	78% H2O, 20% HNO3 2% HF	1mn at 20°C
Ta	45% H2O, 45% HNO3 10% HF	1mn at 20°C

Table 3. Chemical pickling conditions

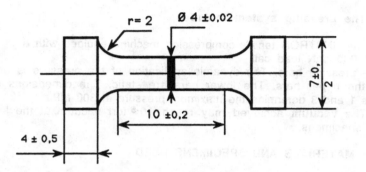

Figure 2 :TENSILE TEST SPECIMEN

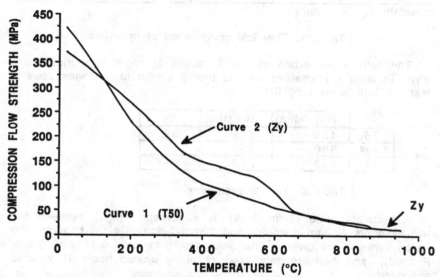

FIGURE 3: EFFECT OF TEMPERATURE ON FLOW STRENGTH OF T50 AND ZY4

EXAMINATION AND TESTING OF JOINTS

Metallographic examination

Polished sections of bonds are observed by scanning electron microscopy (SEM) by means of a back scattering electron detector (BSE).

Mechanical testing

After bonding tensile test specimens are machined (dimensions shown in figure 2). Considering the configuration of our joints, this type of test is really severe; the difference of mechanical caracteristics of the two metals generates, throughout the interface, a triaxiality of the stresses and, consequently, an additional shear stress at the level of the bond line.

RESULTS AND DISCUSSION

1) Determination of Ti and Ta flow strength

During the heating process, the pressure on the specimens must close follow the flow strength of the weakest metal; for this purpose, one must determine the curves of the Ti or Zy yield compression strength as fonction of temperature.

The curve 1 in figure 3 shows a smooth decrease of flow strength of titanium between 20 to 875°C. The curve 2, concerning Zy4, shows a plateau between 300 and 550°C. The steep inflexion linked to the hardening of metal could be due to an interaction between oxygen and the dislocations (S.I Hong and al)[4].

2) Butt joint between Ti and Ta

Our previous studies on the joining of titanium and tantalum by static diffusion bonding have demonstrated (on test pieces similar to the ones used in the present study) that it is possible to obtain a fracture away from the bond line within tantalum. The bonding conditions were: one hour at 885°C; preload at 20°C: 50 MPa; pressure of 5 MPa during bonding temperature level.

These results being taken into account, and in order to remain below the transformation point $\alpha \rightarrow \alpha + \beta$ (885°C for our alloy), we decided to operate at 865°C. We had then to optimize the pressure and the duration of the isothermal level.

Effect of preload

Series of bonding tests enabled to ascertain the positive effect of the preload, a reduction of the residual micropores after the mechanical polishing, and also an improvement of the mechanical properties of bonded joints.

At 20°C the preload was set at 300 MPa or 200 MPa [1], then the load was gradually lowered during the heating so as to reach 16 MPa during the isothermal level.

bonding time (s)	0	120	300
Preload 200MPa	Rm=55 MPa	Rm=206 MPa	Rm=330 MPa*
Preload 300MPa	Rm=232 MPa	Rm=350 MPa*	Rm=334 MPa*

* Rupture in the Ta

Table 4. Effect of preload on butt-joint tensile properties

Table 4 shows that, at a preload of 200 MPa, the rupture in tantalum is obtained for bonding time of 300 s compared to 120 s only at 300MPa. In addition, for durations from 0 to 120 s, the tensile strengths of the joints for a 200 MPa preload are far inferior to those obtained at 300 MPa.

The micrographic examination of the 120 s bonding sample (at 200 MPa) shows several isolated remaining pores (≥ 5 μm) which explains the low mechanical strength of this joint.

Effect of bonding time

The purpose of these experiments was to ascertain, the minimal bonding duration resulting in a tensile fracture within tantalum.

Considering the previous results, these bonds were carried out under a 300 MPa preload. Figure 4 shows that:
- the maximum tensile strength (Rm≥ 330 MPa) is reached with a minimal bonding time of 12 s.
- the fracture occurs in tantalum away from the bond line with an isothermal level lasting 30 s at minimum.

Polished sections of the joint of the 30 s test piece shows (photo 1) that the diffusion zone (2,5 μm), consists of (according to the binary phase diagram):
- a wide two-phase layer α + β, shaped during the cooling, characterised by "needle" structure of Widmanstätten type.
- on the titanium side, a dark single phase layer which is α solid solution of titanium.
- on the tantalum side, a thin clear layer of β tantalum.

---

[1]The preload of 200 MPa was lowered on after 200°C

177

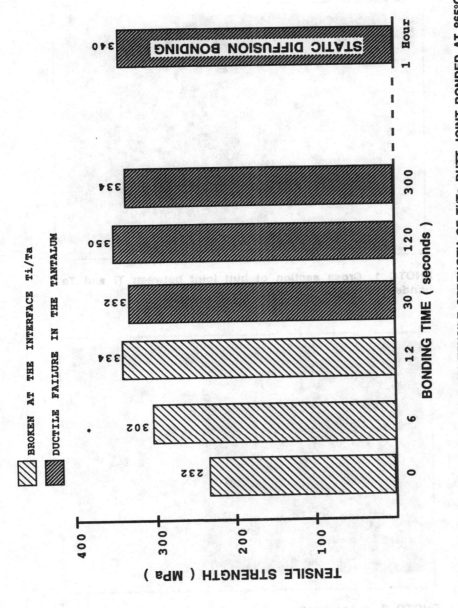

FIGURE 4. EFFECT OF BONDING TIME ON TENSILE STRENGTH OF Ti/Ta BUTT JOINT BONDED AT 865°C

PHOTO 1. Cross section of butt joint between Ti and Ta bonded at 885°C /30 seconds

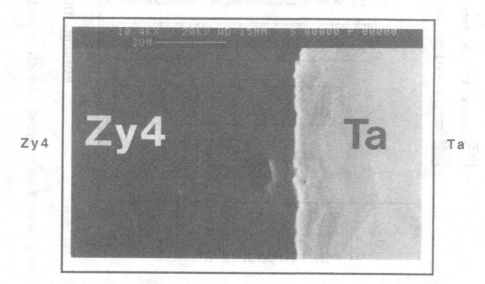

PHOTO 2. Cross section of butt joint between Zy4 and Ta bonded at 950°C /30 seconds

Some residual little pores (≤ 0,1μm) remain at the initial interface without any consequence on the quality of joints for a bonding time equal or superior to 30 s.

Conlusions

- This DDB process, with a 300 MPa preload, permits a great reduction of the bonding time, compared to the conventional diffusion bonding technic: from one hour to 30 seconds in the same temperature range (865 and 885°C).
- The diffusion zone is then very thin (2,5 μm for 30 s).
- The preload intensity is a determining factor for the resorption of the residual pores, both in number and dimensions.

3) Butt joint between Zy4 and Ta

Our previous studies on diffusion bonding between zirconium and tantalum [2], had shown that a minimum 4 hours duration (at 950°C) was necessary to obtain a strong jonction, with a fracture of the joint in the tantalum.

We tried to ascertain the reduction of bonding time that could be gained thanks to the DDB.

Taking into account the results on the butt joint between Ti and Ta, the preload chosen for these tests is 300 MPa and the pressure during the bonding is of 13 MPa. We selected the same bonding temperature than in our prievious studies, namely 950°C.

The results (figure 5) show that the fracture occurs in tantalum after 30s of bonding. The micrographic examination of this welded joint boundary shows (photo 2) that the diffusion zone (≈ 3 μm) is made up of:
- on the zircaloy side, the two-phase α + β layer (Widmanstätten structure).
- on the tantalum side, a thin layer of solid solution (β tantalum).
- a very few small residual pores,at the limit of these two areas. Because of the short time, the pores remain at the initial interface, the diffusion front having already by-passed these little defects.

The conclusions that can be drawn from these results are the following:
- the DDB enables to greatly reduce the bonding duration compared to the former process: 30 seconds instead of 4 hours of bonding (950°C)
- the thikness of the diffusion zone is greatly reduced and the residual pores are, despite a very short diffusion time, located away from the bond line. The restriction on the thickness of the diffusion zone formulated by M. Veyrac and al[2], seems not to be strictly respected in our case. The location of the pores in the diffusion zone probably explains the differences observed in the behaviour of our two joints.

CONCLUSIONS

This study proves that DDB, benefiting from the classical diffusion bonding and of a duration below the minute (at leust for these joints), could become cost effective compared with the conventional processes of

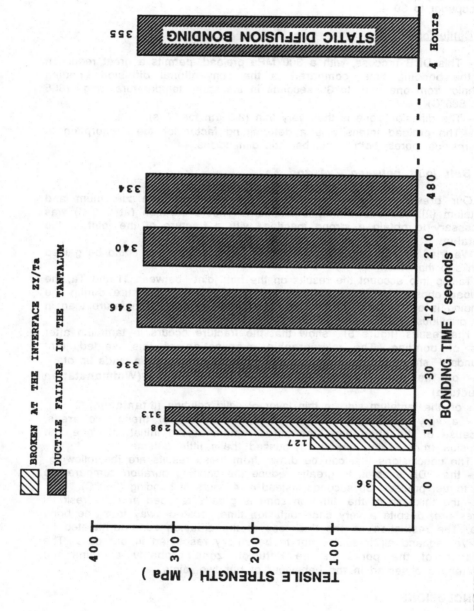

FIGURE 5. EFFECT OF BONDING TIME ON TENSILE STRENGTH OF ZY4/Ta BUTT JOINT BONDED AT 950°C

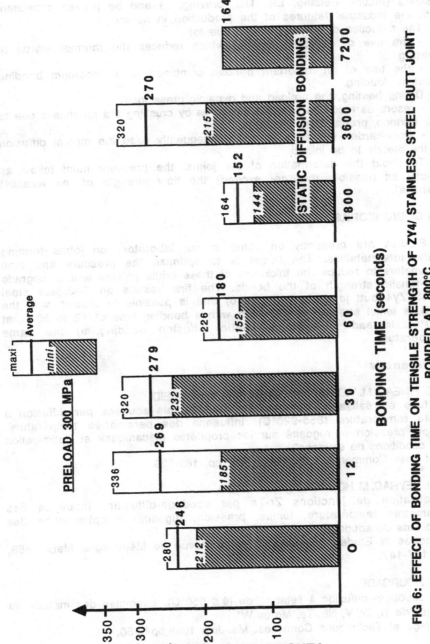

FIG 6: EFFECT OF BONDING TIME ON TENSILE STRENGTH OF ZY4/ STAINLESS STEEL BUTT JOINT BONDED AT 800°C

welding (friction welding, EB, TIG, brazing, .,) and be proven consistent with the industrial features of the production in series.

The reduction of bonding time is due to:

- the use of induction heating which reduces the thermal inertia of heating
- the use of an important preload combined to an optimum bonding pressure loading.

During heating, the preload and dynamic pressing:

- resorb as much as possible the pores by crushing the roughness due to the surface preparation treatment,
- work-harden the surfaces and consequently ease the mutual diffusion of the metals to be joined.

To avoid the deformation of the joints, the pressure must follow as strictly as possible (but not exceed) the flow strength of the weakest material.

ON GOING WORKS

Studies are presently on going in our laboratory on joints forming brittle intermetallics. The target is to optimize the pressure and time parameters to reduce the thickness of these brittle phases and to upgrade the tensile strength of the bonds. The first results on Stainless steel (316L)/Zy4 butt joint show (figure 6) that is possible to obtaint, with the DDB, a tensil strenght of 270 MPa with a bonding time of 12 to 30 s, at 800°C, instead 1 hours in static diffusion bonding at the same temperature.

References

[1] S. PINEAU, M. VEYRAC, M. HOURCADE, B. HOCHEID
" Etude et réalisation de jonctions titane-tantale soudées par diffusion à haute température (855-920°C): influence des paramètres température, temps, pression et rugosité sur les propriétés mécaniques et optimisation des conditions de soudage".
J. of Less Common Metals, 109, 1985, pp. 169-196.

[2] M. VEYRAC, M. HOURCADE, B. HOCHEID
"Réalisation de jonctions Zr-Ta par soudage-diffusion. Influence des paramètres température, temps, pression, rugosité et optimisation des conditions de soudage".
Mémoires et Etudes Scientifiques de la Revue de Métallurgie, Mars 1988, pp. 137-147.

[3] M. HOURCADE.
" Le soudage- diffusion à l'état solide ($\theta \leq$ 950°C). Exemples des métaux ou alliages de Ti, Zr, V, Nb, Ta, Mo ou W".
Soudage et Techniques Connexes, Mai-Juin 1989,pp48-56.

[4] S.I HONG et al.
"Elongation minimum of Zircaloy 4".
Journal of Nuclear Material n° 67, 1977, pp 254.

THE DIFFUSION BONDING OF ENGINEERING CERAMICS TO NICKEL BASED SUPERALLOYS BY HOT ISOSTATIC PRESSING (HIPPING)

S.G. Moseley, J. Blackford, H. Jones and G.W. Greenwood.
School of Materials, Sir Robert Hadfield Building, Mappin Street,
Sheffield, South Yorkshire, S1 3JD.

R.A. Walker.
Infutec Limited, Carlisle Close, Sheffield Road, Sheepbridge,
Chesterfield, Derbyshire, S41 9ED.

This present work is investigating the HIP diffusion bonding of NITRASIL Si_3N_4 and REFEL SiC ceramics to the nickel-based superalloys INCOLOY 909 and INCONEL 718.

Bonding, both with and without the use of interlayers, is being studied with the aim to produce strong, reliable joints that can withstand the stringent conditions they are likely to meet in service.

Two bond geometries are currently under scrutiny. The first, without the use of interlayers, is a cylindrical design with the ceramic component inserted into a pre-drilled hole in the metal, for subsequent testing in shear. The axial compressive loading technique ("indentation test") similar to that used for push-out testing of fibre-reinforced composites is being utilised. This geometry enables detailed analysis to be performed on the residual radial clamping stress at the interface on cooling, the interfacial frictional shear stress, Poisson's effect, and the true bond shear strength.

The second is a tensile geometry where the effects of differing interlayer materials, multiple interlayers and interlayer thicknesses are being examined.

Various post-HIP heat treatments, in vacuum and air, are being utilised to fully comprehend the kinetic and thermodynamic aspects of the interfacial phenomena in all the systems studied. Subsequent testing of the heat-treated specimens then enables a correlation to be made between bond strength and microstructural properties.

All this information, when combined, gives a full analysis of bond strength as a function of all variables, including bond design, HIP parameters, post-HIP treatments and interlayer materials.

INTRODUCTION

Since the first diffusion bonding conference at Cranfield in July 1987, extensive research has been undertaken on ceramic to metal diffusion bonding. Much emphasis has been placed on design of the joint to compensate for the effect of differences in the coefficient of thermal expansion between the materials, a factor contributing to the limited strength achieved in many diffusion bonded systems. There has been a movement away from planar interface geometries towards more complex three-dimensional bond configurations, as can be seen in Figure 1. The use of interlayers has also increased, with a number of types now being successfully utilised, as illustrated in Fig. 2. The trend towards producing larger bonded areas (Fig. 3) is most promising, and results primarily from the use of the two aforementioned techniques. The commercial utilisation of ceramic to metal diffusion bonded joints is increasing, as users and manufacturers become more aware of the requirements for achieving a satisfactory bond (Fig. 4).

The present paper details fundamental investigations into the diffusion bonding of Refel SiSiC to Incoloy 909 and Inconel 718 nickel-based superalloys, involving experimental investigation of interfacial layer characteristics in these systems over a range of temperatures, and detailing how the generated microstructure at the interface affects bond strength.

EXPERIMENTAL PROCEDURE

As noted above, alloys used in this study were Incoloy 909 and Inconel 718, the compositions of which are given in Table 1. The Refel SiSiC material is α-SiC with approximately 10% free silicon at the SiC grain boundaries. A bonding geometry has been chosen whereby a squat cylinder of ceramic (aspect ratio 1:1) is inserted into a pre-drilled hole in the alloy bar prior to HIPping, with less than $50\,\mu m$ of free space between alloy and ceramic at the outset. Several such specimens are then encapsulated in mild steel, separated from one another by inert boron nitride discs (to prevent metal-to-metal diffusion bonding during HIPping), and evacuated down to a steady hold at 10^{-4} torr prior to sealing for HIPping. The ceramic bars were 6.5mm in diameter, and the alloy bars were 25.4mm in diameter. Figure 5 illustrates the capsule and specimen geometry. Bonding is carried out under recognised commercial HIPping conditions for the chosen alloys, (1160°/3 hours/103 MPa) during which the alloys plastically deform onto the surface of the ceramic, giving intimate contact and allowing diffusion to occur across the interface and form the diffusion bond. Specimens were then removed from the mild steel capsule by sectioning through the BN discs, and subjected to post-HIP heat treatments at various temperatures between 750 and 1150°C for up to 480 hours. Measurements of the extent of reaction after these treatments allowed detailed investigation of reaction zone growth behaviour. Reaction rate constants and apparent activation energies could then be determined. Phase identification was by fully quantitative analysis using the LINK analysis system on a CAMSCAN scanning electron microscope. In conjunction with this characterisation of interface behaviour, evaluation of interfacial bond strength was performed using a "push-out" testing procedure (Fig. 6). The contribution to absolute strength of bond shear strength, interfacial friction and residual clamping stress was then calculated by means of the analysis of Hsueh et al [1-4].

RESULTS AND DISCUSSION

1) IN718 - SiSiC

Figure 7 shows the interfacial microstructure generated during HIP diffusion bonding of IN718 to SiSiC at 1160°C and 103 MPa for 3 hours. The reaction on the ceramic side of the couple gives a complex mixture of (primarily) nickel silicides with some iron and chromium silicides also present, and large quantities of carbon as graphite flakes. Within the alloy is formed a continuous layer of an M_6C-type carbide, rich in Cr, Ni, Si, Fe, Mo and Ti. Other (unidentified) phases are also present in the complex two layer reaction zone, but in far lesser proportions. Reaction zone growth plots were constructed following post-HIP heat treatments in air over a range of temperatures (Fig. 8). There is a marked increase in the rate of growth at 1050°C and above, evident from the change in slope of the lines and the measured reaction rate constants (Table 2). The constructed Arrhenius plot clearly shows this increase in reaction rate (Fig. 9). The majority of the measured reaction zone growth at $\geq$ 1050°C is of the silicide-rich zone adjacent to the ceramic. Between 900 and 1000°C both zones grow at approximately equal rates, and at 900°C the silicide-rich zone is consumed by the growing carbide zone. The main reaction products remain the same after all heat treatments, though as mentioned above, their proportions do change depending on temperature.

This reaction behaviour for IN718-SiSiC has been found to be very similar to that for previously reported systems of a similar type [5-11]. The major diffusing species across the ceramic-metal interface are nickel diffusing inwards from the alloy to the ceramic, and silicon and carbon diffusing outwards from the ceramic into the alloy, in an interchange reaction. In this study, iron and chromium from the alloy are also observed to diffuse into the ceramic, though in lesser proportions than the nickel. These metallic elements initially diffuse along the free silicon grain boundaries of the SiC, and react to form silicides. The low melting points of the nickel silicides formed (see below) allow the zone to become at least partially liquid at the bonding temperature. It is known that an Ni-Si liquid of $\geq$60 atomic % Ni can dissolve SiC [10] and it is assumed that this is the reaction that consumes the ceramic until the silicon content of the liquid increases to such a point that it no longer occurs. The carbon is liberated as graphite at this stage of the reaction, though some is carried out of this region by convection through the liquid, to enter the alloy and form the observed carbide zone within the alloy. Many reaction products are observed in the silicide-rich region within the ceramic, primarily NiSi, Ni_3Si_2 and $NiSi_2$, with some (unidentified) iron and chromium silicides, and the graphite. The melting range of this region has been observed to be between 1010 and 1030°C, from DTA. This is higher than that expected from mixed nickel silicide eutectics ($NiSi$-$NiSi_2$: 966°C, $NiSi$-Ni_3Si_2: 964°C) probably due to the iron and chromium silicides. The change in the slope of the Arrhenius plot (Fig. 9) is due to this melting phenomena, as the reaction changes from solid-state diffusion controlled to liquid phase mass transport controlled. Fig. 10 is a specimen subjected to a 1200°C post-HIP heat treatment, showing Ni-Si dendrites. The carbide formed is similar in type to the η'-Cr_3Ni_2SiC observed in the previous studies, though in this case Fe, Mo and Ti replace some of the Cr in the structure. Close to this carbide zone in the alloy, the Si modifies the alloy structure slightly, and more γ' phase is observed than would normally be expected in the IN718.

Comparison of the Arrhenius plot for this IN718-SiSiC system to the other similar (though less complex) systems to which reference was made earlier [5-11], shows that it has the greatest temperature stability, in spite of the reactivity of the ceramic resulting from its free silicon. This is not unexpected, however, on the basis of previous suggestions that the more complex the alloy the greater is its stability in contact with SiC [7]. So, even though IN718 has more silicide and carbide formers, the number of phases formed increases, and the overall driving force for the reaction is reduced. The continuous carbide layer also acts as a barrier to nickel source strength.

The calculated apparent activation energies are 167 kJmol^{-1} below the silicide melting temperature, and 683 kJmol^{-1} above this point. The lower value is in good agreement with previously reported values of 184 kJmol^{-1} for NiCrAl-SiC [7] and 227 Jmol for an Ni-based superalloy - SiC [7].

Mechanical testing on as-HIPped specimens yielded interfacial shear strengths of 120 to 141 MPa, and further tests are currently in progress for heat treated specimens. Future work will incorporate hot testing.

2) IN909 - SiSiC

Fig. 11 shows the interfacial microstructure generated during HIP diffusion bonding of IN909 to SiSiC at 1160°C and 103 MPa for 3 hours. A complex reaction zone is observed, this time consisting of three distinct regions. As with the IN718-SiSiC system, formed adjacent to the ceramic is a region consisting primarily of a mixture of nickel silicides with some iron and (in this case) cobalt silicides. The carbide zone adjacent to this silicide zone consists mainly of $M_{23}C_6$ -type carbide, rich in Fe, Ni, Ci and Si, and as with the silicide zone, forms at a location within the prior ceramic. The outermost reaction layer, formed within the alloy itself, consists of a number of carbide phases. Predominant after HIPping is an M_6C-type carbide rich in Ni, Nb, Fe, Co, Si and Ti, and the silicon can readily enter this structure and enhance its growth during the bonding operation. Also observed is an $M_{23}C_6$-type carbide, with a predominantly cellular morphology after HIPping. Reaction zone growth plots were constructed following post-HIP heat treatments in air over a range of temperatures (Fig. 12). There is again observed a marked increase in the rate of growth of the overall reaction zone at 1050°C and above, evident from the change in slope of the lines and the measured reaction rate constants (Table 2). The constructed Arrhenius plot clearly shows this increase in reaction rate (Fig. 9). The main effect observed during these heat treatments is the change in morphology of the carbide phases in the outermost reaction zone, adjacent to the alloy. Higher temperature heat treatments enhance the growth of the cellular $M_{23}C_6$ carbide and changes the morphology of the M_6C carbide from blocky to Widmanstatten, and it must be noted that both these high temperature structures are detrimental to the mechanical properties of the bond. Heat treatments at lower temperatures favour the blocky carbide phase. There is also a change in the relative proportions of each reaction layer within the overall zone after the various heat treatments. Lower temperatures give the main growth outwards in the outermost reaction zone, while higher temperatures cause the silicide zone to grow inwards at the expense of the middle reaction layer, though this layer in turn consumes the outermost layer. Figs. 13 and 14 show this behaviour.

The mechanisms of forming these reaction zones are virtually identical to those mentioned previously for the IN718-SiSiC system. Again, the silicide-rich layer is at least partially liquid at the HIP bonding temperature, and once more the liberated carbon precipitates as graphite flakes, with some carbon moving outwards along with silicon, to form the two distinct carbide rich layers observed. DTA identified the onset of melting at around 1030°C for the mixed silicides, and the enhanced rate of reaction growth above this temperature is due to convective mass transfer through this partially molten layer. In this system however, the carbides formed are not continuous through the reaction layers, and it is assumed that because of this they do not act as a barrier to further inward diffusing species and so do not limit further reaction, resulting in the large reaction zone widths observed.

Of all systems compared in the Arrhenius plot (Fig. 9), IN909-SiSiC has the least temperature stability, and compared to the IN718-SiSiC system below 1000°C, for a given reaction rate constant, the IN909-SiSiC system must be 300°C lower in temperature. The calculated apparent activation energies are 160 kJmol^{-1} below 1000°C and 730 kJmol^{-1} above 1050°C, indicating similar reaction mechanisms to the other highlighted systems.

Mechanical testing on as-HIPped specimens yielded interfacial shear strengths of 98 to 115 MPa, and further tests are currently in progress for heat treated specimens. Preliminary tests show that as-HIPped specimens and those subjected to heat treatments below 950°C fail at a location close to the original interface between ceramic and metal, but those specimens subjected to higher temperature heat treatments fail between the outermost region and the alloy, since the structure of the alloy is also affected detrimentally by the higher temperature.

CONCLUSIONS

(1)   Despite the free silicon present in the ceramic, the interface with Inconel 718 has greater temperature stability than other similar ceramic-metal systems (ie. lower reaction rates at any given temperature, provided that temperature is below the melting range of the mixed silicides in the reaction zone).

(2)   The mechanisms of the reaction appear to be similar to those of other systems, but the complexity of the alloy proves advantageous in limiting severe reaction and in slowing down the rate of reaction.

(3)   Room temperature bond strengths are promising though the effect of time at elevated temperature on this strength has yet to be determined, and further work on bond strength at high temperature is necessary.

(4)   It is recommended that a joint of IN718-SiSiC should not be used above 900°C to avoid the formation of liquid at the interface which could have disastrous effects on the properties of the joints.

(5)   From the studies of the Incoloy 909-SiSiC system, it is concluded that it is not only the extent of the reaction zone which affects bond integrity, but also the types of reaction product formed, together with their proportions and morphologies which also play a significant role.

(6)   The high reactivity of this system suggests it is necessary to use a metallic interlayer between the ceramic and alloy to act as a diffusion barrier, particularly to prevent the inward diffusion of nickel to the ceramic. Work is currently in progress using cobalt foils to achieve this.

(7)   Optimisation of HIPping parameters is also currently in progress, and detailed mechanical testing programs are to be undertaken.

ACKNOWLEDGEMENTS

This work has been undertaken under the auspices of a SERC/CASE Award with HIP Ltd, Chesterfield and we are grateful to HIP Ltd for permission to publish this work.

REFERENCES

[1]   C.H. HSUEH, J.Mat.Sci. Lett. 8 (1989) 739-742.

[2]   C.H.HSUEH, J.Mat.Sci 25 (1990) 818-828.

[3]   C.H.HSUEH, "Fibre Pullout Verses Push-Down for Fibre-Reinforced Composites with frictional interfaces", J.Mat.Sci., in press.

[4]   C.H. HSUEH, M.K. FERBER, and P.F. BECHER, "Stress-displacement relation of fibre for fibre-reinforced ceramic composites during (indentation) loading and unloading", J.Mat.Res., in press.

[5]   R.L. MEHAN and D.W. McKEE, J.Mat.Sci. 11 1976) 1009-1018.

[6]   R.L. MEHAN and R.B. BOLAN, J.Mat.Sci. 14 (1979) 2471-2481.

[7]   M.R. JACKSON, R.L. MEHAN, A.M. DAVIS and E.L. HALL, Metall.Trans.A., 14A (1983) 355-364.

[8]   E.L. HALL, Y.M. KOUH, M.R. JACKSON and R.L. MEHAN, Metall.Trans.A., 14A (1983) 781-790.

[9]   E.L. HALL, R.L. MEHAN and M.R. JACKSON, Metall.Trans.A, 14A (1983) 1549-1560.

[10]   J.R. McDERMID, M.D. PUGH and R.A.L. DREW, Metall.Trans.A., 20A (1989) 1803-1810.

[11]   T.G. NIEH, J.J. STEPHENS, J. WADSWORTH and C.T.LIU, Proc.Conf., "Interfaces in polymer, ceramic and metal matrix composites", June 13-17, 1988, Ohio, USA.

[12]   T.TANAKA, H. MORIMOTO and H. HOMMA, Proc.Conf., "Hot Isostatic Pressing", Antwerp, 25-28 April 1988.

[13]   E. BUTLER, M.H. LEWIS, A. HEY and R.V. SHARPLES, "Ceramic Joining in Japan", a DTI Report, June 1986.

[14]   T. WHALEN, Proc. 1st European Symposium on Engineering Ceramics, 25-26 February 1985, London, pp 177-184.

Alloy	C	Mn	Si	Cr	Ni	Mo	Al	Ti	Nb+Ta	Co	B	Fe	Nb
IN718	0.05	0.10	0.18	18.25	53.00	3.05	0.50	1.00	5.25	0.25	0.004	18.60	
IN909	0.01		0.40		38.00		0.03	1.50		13.00		42.00	4.70

TABLE 1 : Compositions of alloys (weight percent)

System	750°C	800°C	850°C	900°C	950°C	1000°C	1050°C	1100°C	1150°C
IN909 -SiSiC	-9.98		-8.93		-8.66		-7.73		-5.72
IN718 -SiSiC		-11.73	-11.48	-11.13	-10.84	-10.24	-9.37	-8.58	-7.33

TABLE 2 : Reaction rate constants (log k) as a function of temperature (units of k, cm^2 s^{-1})

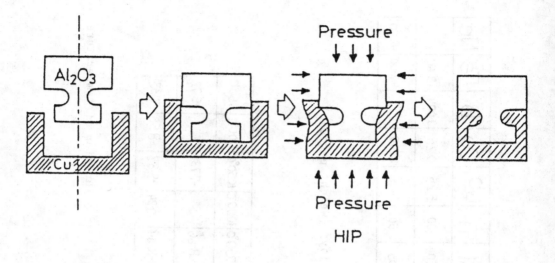

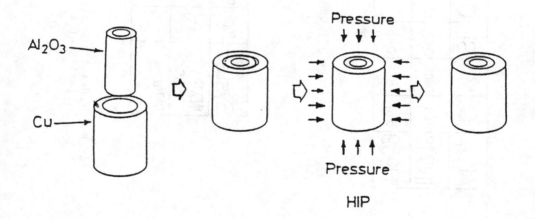

FIG.1: Complex ceramic-metal bond configurations made possible by the use of HIPping. (12)

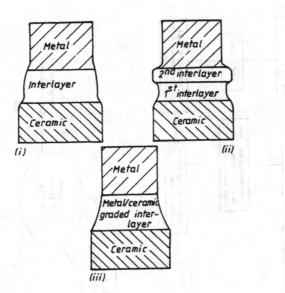

FIG.2: Interlayer configurations used in ceramic-metal joining. (13)

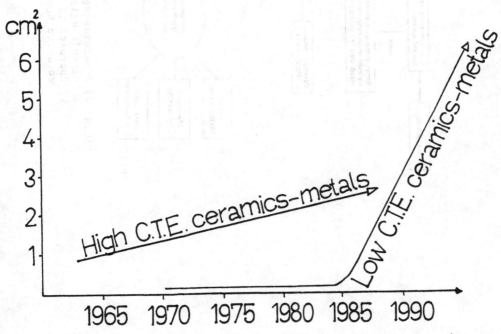

FIG.3: Trends in the size of ceramic-metal bonded areas in recent years.

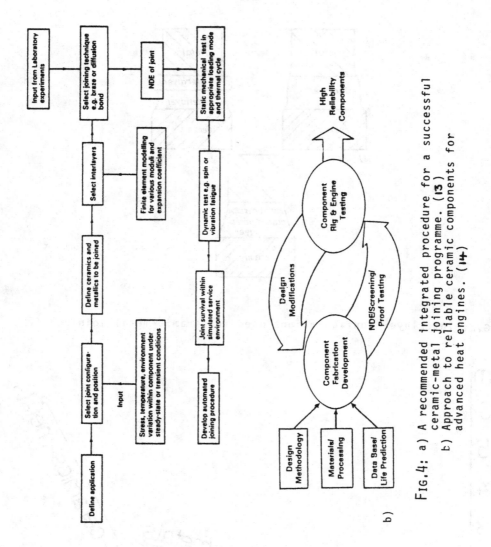

FIG. 4: a) A recommended integrated procedure for a successful ceramic-metal joining programme. (13)
b) Approach to reliable ceramic components for advanced heat engines. (14)

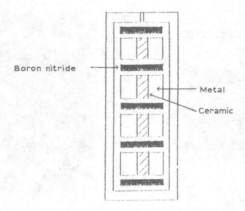

FIG.5: Schematic illustration of capsule and specimen geometry.

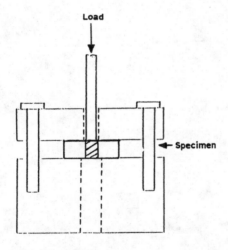

FIG.6: Schematic illustration of shear testing rig geometry.

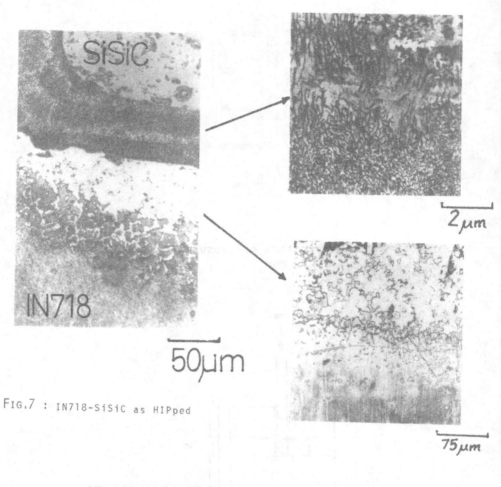

FIG.7 : IN718-SiSiC as HIPped

FIG.10 : IN718-SiSiC after 24 hours at 1200°C

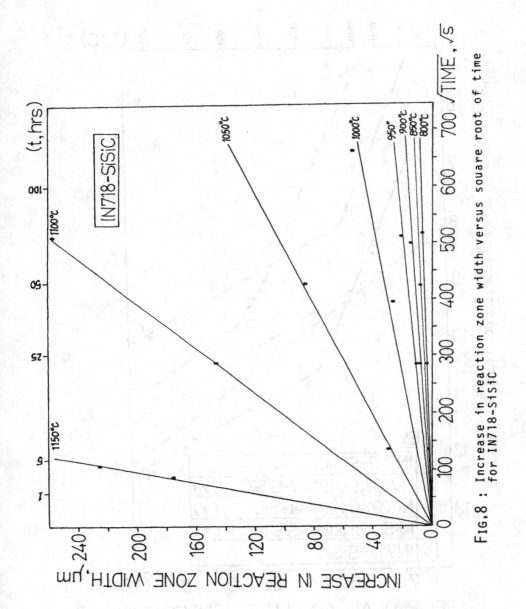

FIG. 8 : Increase in reaction zone width versus square root of time
for IN718-SiSiC

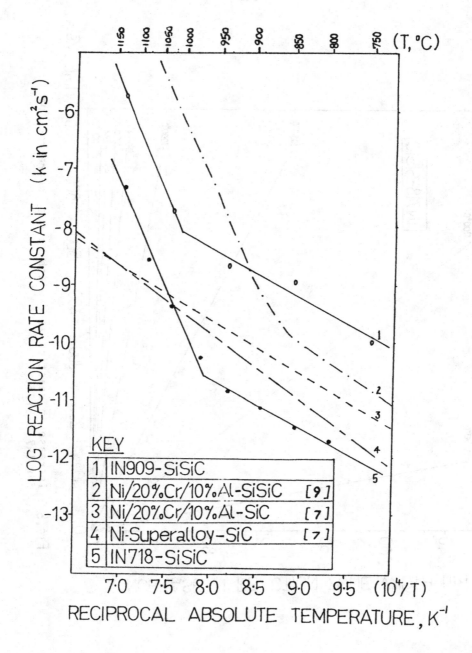

FIG.9 : Arrhenius Plot of reaction rate constant versus reciprocal absolute temperature

IN909

SiSiC

1mm

→←original interface

FIG.11 : IN909-SiSiC as HIPped

100μm

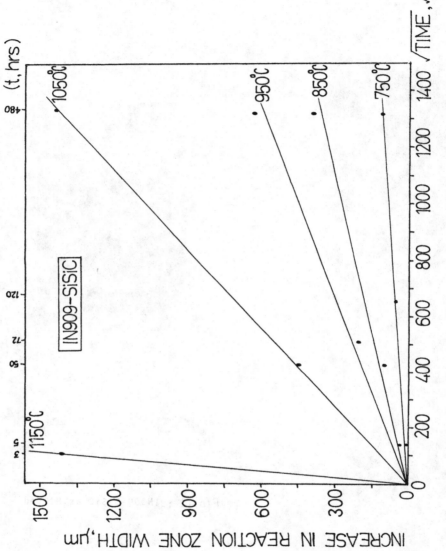

Fig.12 : Increase in reaction zone width versus square root of time
for IN909-SiSiC

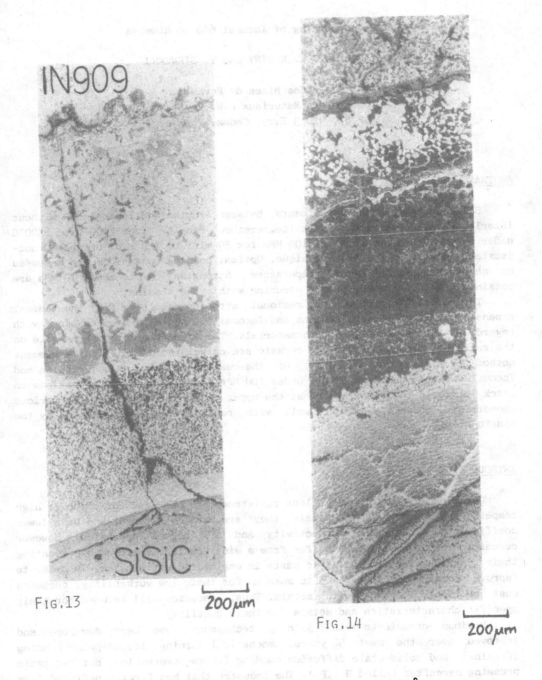

FIG.13 : IN909-SiSiC after 5 hours at 850°C

FIG.14 : IN909-SiSiC after 480 hours at 1050°C

Diffusion bonding of Inconel 600 to Alumina

C. COLIN, J.L. KOUTNY and Y. BIENVENU

Ecole des Mines de Paris,
Centre des Matériaux P.M. Fourt,
BP 87, 91003 Evry, Cedex, France

ABSTRACT

Solid-state bonding experiments, between Alumina and Inconel 600 without interlayers, are carried out at temperatures ranging from 1100°C to 1300°C under Argon at a pressure of 100 MPa for 30 min. to 120 min. using the hot-isostatic pressing (H.I.P.) technique. Optimal bonding conditions are assessed by shear testing at room temperature. Strengths up to about 70 MPa are obtained with fracture primarily occuring within the Alumina.

The critical problem of residual stresses resulting from the thermal expansion mismatch between Alumina and Inconel 600 has also been examined with regard to the thickness of both materials. The effects of components size on the residual stresses within the ceramic are calculated using a finite element method (F.E.M.). On the basis of the results of calculation, Alumina and Inconel 600 are bonded at 1300°C under 100 MPa for 60 min. The observations on crack close to the interface or at the upper ceramic surface, for the various geometries, correlate rather well with residual stresses computed by the elasto-plastic model.

INTRODUCTION

Ceramics exhibit an excellent resistance to wear and corrosion at high temperatures. Compared to metals they are usually stronger and have lower coefficients of thermal conductivity and of thermal expansion. However ceramics remain brittle and suffer from a wide scatter in strength preventing their introduction as monolithic parts in engineering structures. In order to improve their reliability and to make up for their low workability, ceramics must be tighly combined with metals. Thus, ceramics will be used for their specific characteristics and metals for their ductility.

Various ceramic-to-metal joining techniques have been developed and improved over the past 50 years, mechanical joining, liquid-phase bonding (brazing) and solid-state diffusion bonding (thermocompression, hot isostatic pressing hereafter called H.I.P.). The industry that has first benefitted from these techniques is Electronics with hermetic sealings. However, recent advances in energy conversion systems (Aerospace and the motor-car industry) have broadened the field of applications of metal/ceramic bonding. These new applications require much higher operating temperatures, stronger bonds and the ability to withstand corrosive, radiation and vibrational conditions. Solid-state diffusion bonding seems to be most promising technique because it offers the possibility to produce an interfacial structure stable even at elevated temperatures.

In general, two problems should be solved in order to join ceramics to metals without defects. The first one arises from the difference in the structure between ceramics and metals -ceramics are ionic or covalent whereas in metals the electrons are delocalized-. Secondly, the large thermal expansion mismatch creates stress concentration after cooling from the bonding temperature and may induce cracks in the ceramic. The former problem has been solved either by a mechanical anchoring of the metal on the ceramic body (solid-state bonding without interlayer [1]) or by metallizing of ceramics with a reactive element (brazing [2]). The latter problem has been overcome either by embedding ceramics into metals [1] because ceramics are prone to cracking in tension but resist compression, or by inserting an appropriate interlayer between parent materials. Several kinds of interlayers have been examined. A soft metal such as Al [3-7] and Cu [8-10] relieves the residual stresses through elastic, plastic and creep deformation but it is not sufficient since these metals cannot resist the effects elevated temperature and thermal cycling or thermal shock. Therefore laminated interlayers have been proposed, for example, Al/Invar [11], Ni/W [12,13], Mo/W [14], Fe/W [15], Cu/W [12] and Ti/Mo [16]. A hard metal with a low thermal expansion coefficient is inserted to constrain the shrinkage deformation of the soft metal and parent metal. According to the thickness of the insert metal layers, the ceramic may crack at the edges or longitudinally at the core or may not crack at all if the shrinkage deformation of the soft metal and ceramic is well balanced [17]. Lastly, as dissimilar materials could not be bonded by the conventional diffusion method previously cited or even by H.I.P. as a result of insufficient reaction at the interface, a composite interlayer i.e. a mixture of the materials to be bonded themselves, makes then bonding possible [18] because a mechanical interlocking force adds to the weak chemical bonding. In addition this new method looks effective for the relief of the residual stresses, due to its thermal expansion coefficient , which is intermediate between those of the dissimilar materials. A further advantage is that the addition of a third element is not required. These various methods, however still remain problematic to join large components. Indeed, the residual stresses become more critical as bonding areas are increased [19,20] and may exceed the fracture stress of the ceramic.

If we consider the two main solid-state diffusion bonding technologies , H.I.P. offers several advantages over uniaxial hot pressing (so-called thermocompression). In the first place, the isostatic nature of the pressure allows to apply a uniform pressure over all the joint irrespective of its geometrical complexity (three-dimensional interfaces). The high pressure (about 100-200 MPa) easily ensures the contact between the two bodies through surface deformation of either parent metal or interlayer, if any. In other respects, the H.I.P. process allows the increase of the pressure regardless of the yield point of the metal at elevated temperatures. In addition, it can prevent the formation of pores linked to limited deformation of the metal for a short period and/or to a gas phase such as O_2 or N_2 produced by solid-state interfacial reaction. Secondly the only deformation which occurs is that which is required to bring the surfaces into intimate contact and therefore H.I.P. offers the possibility to fabricate near-net-shapes. This is unlike uniaxial pressing where the applied stresses are unbalanced and therefore some macroscopic plastic flow and distorsion can occur leading to unbonded areas much more numerous than with isostatic pressing. In addition to all these features H.I.P. can be performed at lower temperature making it easier to control the formation of a reaction layer. Three bonding parameters should usually be adjusted : bonding temperature, bonding pressure and bonding time. In the case of bonding between ceramic and metal without interlayer by H.I.P., the bonding temperature is above 0.5 times the melting point of the metal, the bonding pressure is conventionally fixed between 100 and 200 MPa, and the bonding time is determined by the degree of reactivity between the materials.

The advantages offered by H.I.P. bonding over uniaxial hot pressing have to be weighed against the processing cost involved with canning and the cost of the development work necessary to optimize the H.I.P. technology. The purpose of the present study is to investigate the potential of the H.I.P. technique. The research programme is supported by the EEC DG XII (Euram 0039) and the three partners are focussing on several aspects (see annex). The junctions of interest are In 600-alumina.

The work at the Ecole des Mines de Paris will now be presented at greater length, the objectives being the study of the effect of parameters like H.I.P. temperature, bonding time at maximum temperature on the soudness of the In 600/alumina assembly and on the room temperature shear strength. The effect of component geometries, primarily the thickness of ceramic and metal, on residual stresses will experimentally be studied. These experimental results will be validated with finite element analysis, allowing for both elastic and plastic behaviour of the workpieces. At the end of this study, one should be in a position to propose a strong joint with a geometry leading reasonable residual stresses.

EXPERIMENTAL PROCEDURE

Materials

The alumina used in this work is manufactured by C.I.C.E. (St Gobain) with the trade name TS15. This material is claimed by the manufacture to be at least 97.7% pure with 1.38% SiO_2 and to have a density of 3.75 g/cm^3. The 22 mm diameter disc samples are supplied as-ground with thickness ranging from 1 to 40 mm.

The metal is In 600 a nickel base superalloy which is widely used in nuclear engineering (heat exchanger). Its chemical composition (in weight %)

is listed in Table I. It is supplied by TECHPHY (IMPHY S.A.) in the form of 30 mm diameter hot rolled rods. These latters are ground to 22 mm diameter and are cut into discs of appropriate thickness. One face of these discs is polished to optical flatness.

According to literature, the surface roughness seems to have some influence on the mechanical properties of a joint. Some say that a rough surface prevents complete contact at the interface under limited pressure [21] and that the deep scratches on the surface of the ceramic are usually subjected to severe residual stresses [22, 23], and others say that a rough bond face may have an anchoring effect that promotes joining by mechanical interlocking [24]. It is very difficult to say which effect dominates. All materials are thoroughly cleaned by ultrasonic agitation in trichloroethane before being bonded. Indeed to achieve an excellent interdiffusion, the bonding surfaces must be free of any contaminants. Typical properties of the ceramic and of the alloy shown in Table II demonstrate the difference between properties like the elastic modulii and the coefficients of thermal expansion.

Bonding procedure

Ceramics and metals are sprayed with a stop-off product except for the faying surfaces in order to facilitate the removal of the container. Several metal + ceramic pairs are stacked in a 316L stainlees steel container as shown in figure 1, separated by inert bodies (discs 2 mm thick and 22 mm diameter). The container is evacuated to about 10^{-5} torr and hermetically sealed. Indeed, it is important to ensure that no gas is trapped at the interface which could either react to form compounds inhibiting interdiffusion or form gas pockets. Up to four containers are placed into the hot zone and the high pressure cell of the H.I.P. facility (National Forge H.I.P. 2000 unit). Ar gas is used as pressure transmitting medium. The samples are pressed under about 30 MPa at room temperature. Then the pressure and the temperature are simultaneously raised to 100 MPa and 1100-1300°C, respectively. The heating rate is about 10°C/min. After reaching the desired bonding temperature, a dwell-time ranging from 30 to 120 min is achieved. Lastly, the pressure and temperature are slowly lowered (0.35 MPa/min and 6°C/min, respectively). A slow cooling rate is adopted in this work to minimize stresses developing at the interface as a result of the large thermal expansion mismatch between dissimilar materials. The diagrams shown in figure 2 are for standard operating conditions, mainly : 1300°C, 60 min and 100 MPa. The containers are then stripped off and the samples are cleaned by polishing the outer surface because a misalignment of the two materials may occur during bonding.

Evaluation of strength

Strength is one of the critical properties for structural applications. There is an ASTM standard (designation F19-64 [25]) for measuring the tensile strength of brazed joints between metallized ceramics, but it requires complex-shape specimens and more convenient tests are needed. Actually tensile, bend and shear tests are three of the most popular methods among which the simpler is the shear test. However, the stress at the interface is not simple shear since to the applied shear stress the distribution of residual stresses superimposes which is not uniform along the interface.

The strength of the bonded specimens is assessed by shear tests conducted at room temperature at a cross-head speed of 0.05 mm/min using a ZWICK 1474 tensile tester. The conception of the shear test facility, shown in figure 3, minimizes the bending moment originating from distance between loading points by using two ball-bearings. The type of joint tested is illustrated in figure 4. In order to obtain the scatter in strength, two or three specimens bonded in the same conditions are tested. The scatter is the result of the distribution of internal flaws induced by residual stresses. Indeed during the joining and cooling treatment, unbonded areas may result and networks of cracks can be formed reducing the strength of ceramic/metal joints. To take into account these defects one may consider the statistics of strength data by using Weibull theory which is based on the weakest link in the chain [22, 26]. After the shear test, a macroscopic examination allows to derive information on the fracture mechanism.

RESULTS AND DISCUSSION

Strength as a function of H.I.P. temperature and time

The influence of individual bonding parameters on the room temperature shear strengths of the joints are shown in figures 5 and 6. The fracture path is affected differently, by variations in these parameters. It can be located either at the interface due to primarily a lack of reactivity or within the ceramic.

Figure 5 indicates that there is a threshold bonding temperature (1100°C equal to ~ 0.8 T_m, where T_m is the melting point of parent metal) below which no measurable bonding is produced and above which the strength increases with bonding temperature, reaching about 65 MPa. When bonded at 1100°C and 1200°C the joints failed systematically at the interface and those bonded at 1300°C failed within the ceramic. It was also noticed that the joints bonded at the two lowest temperatures were not reproductible. Most of them fractured either when removing from the container, or after holding in air for about a twenty days prior to testing. On the other hand, the surviving samples exhibited a reasonable strength at 1200°C (about 25 MPa) if they were rapidly tested after bonding. It was observed however that the extent of reaction in the form a darkened area was much less at 1100°C than 1200°C. The formation of a strong bonds at 1300°C probably involves a chemical interaction. It can be ascribed to the formation of the mullite or of the spinel phase $NiAl_2O_4$ already identified by other researchers [27-29]. Therefore in a attempt to better understand the process of the reaction, experiments were conducted in the same bonding conditions with pure alumina and lower strengths were then achieved irrespective of the selected bonding conditions. For example at 1300°C the pure alumina displayed a strength of 25 MPa compared to 65 MPa (with silica added). In both cases the samples fractured within the alumina.

In contrast to this major effect of temperature, the bonding time had a less marked influence on the bond strength as shown in figure 6. The use of longer times slightly weakened the samples bonded at 1300°C. It was noticed that strength values were less scattered than those obtained by changing temperature. All samples fractured within the alumina. This result indicated that a large amount of residual stresses had developed in the joint. The fracture mechanism is the following : the crack initiates at the interface, deviates within the alumina and continues to produce the final fracture.

Residual thermal stress analysis

As anticipated a large stress concentration may be introduced in the joint during the cooling to room temperature, as a result of thermal expansion mismatch between the dissimilar materials. In some cases unfortunately these thermal stresses are large enough because a degradation of strength by cracking of the ceramic or even failure of the joint. For the simple geometries, analytical solutions are available [30-32]. But an important drawback of the analytical calculations is that they yield only very approximate results, since the temperature dependance of the materials properties and the metal plasticity are not taken into account.

A more general approach is to solve the problem numerically using finite element calculations. This allows to extend the computation to any kind of complex-shaped components and to include plastic and creep effects in addition to elastic effects. Usually it is very difficult to obtain accurate data on the plasticity and the creep behaviour of metals at elevated temperatures. Furthermore, such computations require great efforts and long CPU time. It is why a great number of elastic calculations have been carried out by several researchers [19, 20, 33, 34]. They studied the influence of joint geometry on the maximum stress level. Elastic calculations lead to an overestimation of the residual stresses, although qualitatively the results are often acceptable. It may be expected that more accurate results will be obtained by carrying out elastic-plastic calculations [7].

The purpose of the present work is to assess the distribution, nature and level of the residual stresses in the alumina as the thickness of the dissimilar materials varies, in order to minimize these stresses for practical applications. To validate this stress modelling, experiments have been carried out with alumina discs bonded to In 600 at 1300°C for 60 min under 100 MPa. After bonding, the cracking of the joints was revealed using a penetrating dye. The cracking of the alumina near the interface or on the upper surface was compared with residual stresses computed by the elastoplastic model. For reference, elastic calculations have also been performed. The grid with its boundary conditions are illustrated in figure 7. An isoparametric 8-node elements with 4 integration points are used. The physical and mechanical properties of the parent metal, as a function of temperature, have been determined or compiled from available literature (figure 8), those of the ceramic have been taken as being constant (table II). The F.E.M. calculations are based on the following assumptions :

1. The joint is cooled in 50°C steps from 1300°C to 50°C (and in a final step of 30°C down to room temperature),
2. The initial residual stress of the joint is 0 MPa at 1300°C,
3. The temperature of the joint is uniform at each calculation step, although the thermal conductivities and heat capacities are very different for the two materials,
4. The Von Mises flow rule is assumed to be valid.

Tensile stresses in alumina have been mainly considered, because it is the most important factor influencing the reliability of the joint. Depending on the geometry of the assemblies, these stresses may lead to two type of alumina cracking. One is located at the free lateral surface in the vicinity of the interface and the other at the upper surface.

But these two modes of cracking are not generated by the same stresses. In the former case, it is the maximum principal stress ($\sigma_{p\ max}$) at the interface that governs the degradation of the ceramic, while in the latter case it is the maximum radial stress ($\sigma_{rr\ max}$) and/or circumferential stress ($\sigma_{\theta\theta\ max}$) that predominates. Figures 9 and 10 show the maximum principal stress generated in alumina as a function of the the alumina and of the In 600 thicknesses, respectively. The values obtained from the thermo-elastic stress analysis are compared to those obtained from a thermo-elasto-plastic stress analysis to show that plastic deformation of In 600 allows an important stress relieving within the ceramic. This plastic deformation was contiguous to the interface and could reach from 1.7 to 4.3% according to considered geometry. Note that the elastic or plastic curve reaches a plateau beyond a thickness of 10 mm for the alumina bonded to 44 mm thick In 600 (figure 9). Below about 5 mm in thickness, $\sigma_{p\ max}$ decreases below the fracture stress of alumina (plastic curve). It is apparent that the thinner alumina discs makes the joint more stable. But the end user cannot tolerate too thin a ceramic which could be substituted by plasma sprayed coatings. Compared with the conventional coating process, the present bonding method has the advantage of producing a dense ceramic layer with high bonding strength and a surface hardness equivalent to that of the bulk ceramic. On the basis of the above calculations, a series of In 600 (44 mm thick) bonds was undertaken for alumina thicknesses ranging from 2 to 40 mm. Figure 11 indicates that cracking appears from a critical thickness of 8 mm close to the interface. When the ceramic thickness reachs 40 mm, the specimen fractured without any applied stress, a convex fracture surface was observed in such a joint. This failure path is characteristic of the presence of great residual stresses in the joint but also indicates a relatively good interfacial strength. Otherwise interfa-

interfacial peeling will occur. Thus numerical modelling of residual stresses in the ceramic seems to satisfactorily interpret the tendency to cracking near the interface. The residual stresses as function of the thickness of the In 600 exhibit a maximum located at about 4 mm, then a plateau is reached at beyond 16 mm (figure 10). This maximum is much less marked in plastic than elastic, but the trend is similar.

The plots of σ_{rr}, $\sigma_{\theta\theta}$ in figures 12 and 13 may be used to predict whether the cracking, if any, should occur radially ($\sigma_{\theta\theta} > \sigma_{rr}$) or in the form of rings ($\sigma_{rr} > \sigma_{\theta\theta}$) on the upper surface of the ceramic. From observations made on some 42 assemblies - 7 values of t_c and 6 of t_m - (figure 14), the thicker (8 and 16 mm) ceramics did not crack on the upper surface but were inclined to crack close to the interface and for the thinner ceramics (2, 3 and 4 mm), the surface cracks showed a mixed mode (radial and circumferential) at the centre for 1, 2 and 4 mm thick metals and radial near the rim of the upper surface ($\sigma_{\theta\theta}$ is the main component of the stress tensor and remains high enough to cause damage). However thinner ceramics did not crack close to the interface. The predictions of the model both for the cracking at the interface and at the free ceramic surface were found to be in a good agreement with these observations.

CONCLUSION

Solid-state diffusion bonding by H.I.P. was found to be a promising route for Alumina/In 600 junctions without interlayers. Optimal conditions for bonding have been worked out, high temperatures are more effective than low temperatures and this may be attributed to a greater chemical reactivity between the dissimilar materials. The maximum shear strength (70 MPa) is reached for relatively short bonding times (30 min) at 1300°C under 100 MPa.

Also , the critical problem of residual stresses resulting from the thermal expansion mismatch has been examined. Although numerous approximations were used, the numerical elastoplastic model used to compute the residual thermal stresses in ceramic, developed upon cooling, is able to interpret satisfactory the tendency to cracking both at the free lateral surface of the ceramic in the vicinity of the interface ($\sigma_{p\ max}$) and at the upper surface of the ceramic ($\sigma_{rr\ max}$ and/or $\sigma_{\theta\theta\ max}$). It was also observed that the initiated cracks at the upper surface did not propagate through the whole thickness of the ceramic but stopped close to the interface by a branching phenomenon. There is an optimum ratio of ceramic to metal thickness for minima residual stresses. Usually, the use of the thinner ceramic enhances bond integrity. When the plastic deformation of In 600 is allowed the level of computed residual stresses in the Alumina become acceptable. A more accurate computation would need a better knowledge of the temperature dependance of the material properties. It would also be necessary to take into account the residual stress redistribution in the ceramic during its cracking by releasing the nodes at a crack. In addition, to improve the accuracy of the finite element analysis, the presence of reaction products at Al_2O_3/In 600 interface may be considered because it is susceptible to greatly reduce the shear stresses along the interface. The computed maximum tensile stresses (debased $\sigma_{P\ max}$), occuring at the free ceramic surface in the vicinity of the interface, are usually singular in nature and are influenced by the local mesh width. It was noticed that $\sigma_{P\ max}$ tends to increase with decreasing mesh width. Thus a small grid is prefered to a coarse grid. Therefore when one conducts a finite element stress analysis of the bonded dissimilar materials as a function of geometric factors (respective thicknesses), it is necessary to pay careful attention to keep the mesh width constant. Finally, for a better description of the system studied, the strength of the interface should be taken into account on the basis of the local criterion.

ACKNOWLEDGEMENTS

The financial support of the E.E.C. DG XII is gratefully acknowledged (Euram program 0039). The authors wish to thank C.I.C.E. (St GOBAIN) for kindly supplying the alumina (TS15) and for its marked interest in our results. They wish to thank their partners (UCL and CEA) for stimulating discussions.

REFERENCES

1.   T. Tanaka, H. Morimoto and H. Homma, "Joining of alumina to copper by H.I.P.", Proceedings of International Conference on Hot Isostatic Pressing of Materials : Applications and Developments, Addendum Ed., 3.37-3.40, ANTWERP 25th-27th April 1988.

2.   R.E. Loehman and A.P. Tomsia, "Joining of Ceramics", The American Ceramic Society Bulletin, vol. 67, n°2, 375-380, 1988.

3.   K. Suganuma, T. Okamoto, M. Koizumi and M. Shimada, "Joining of silicon nitride to silicon nitride and to Invar alloy using an aluminium inter-layer", Journal of Materials Science, vol. 22, n°4, 1359-1364, 1987.

4.   J.T. Klomp, "Bonding of metals to ceramics and glasses", The American Ceramic Society Bulletin, vol. 51, n°9, 683-688, 1972.

5.   M.G. Nicholas and R.M. Crispin, "The fabrication of steel-alumina joints by diffusion bonding", Proceedings of the British Ceramic Society, Engineering with ceramics, R.M. Davidge Ed., n°32, 33-40, March 1982.

6.   M.G. Nicholas and R.M. Crispin, "Diffusion bonding stainless steel to alumina using aluminium interlayers", Journal of Materials Science, vol. 17, n°11, 3347-3360, 1982.

7.   C. Colin, D. Broussaud, F. Grivon and A. Wicker, "Solid-state bonding of partially stabilized zirconia to metals", Proceedings of the third international symposium on Ceramic Materials and Components for Engines, V.J. Tennery Ed., 492-502, Las Vegas, USA, 27-30 November 1988.

8. R.M. Crispin and M.G. Nicholas, "Ceramic-metal diffusion bonding using interlayers of copper and silver", Fortschrittsber Deutsche Keramische Gesellschaft, Vol. 1, n°2, 212-222, 1985.

9. T. Yamada, H. Sekiguchi, H. Okamoto, S. Azuma, A. Kitamura and K. Fukaya, "Diffusion bonding SiC or Si_3N_4 to Nimonic 80A", High Temperature Technology, vol. 5, n°4, 193-200, November 1987.

10. W.E. Borbidge, R.V. Allen and P.T. Whelan, "A review of the reaction bonding technique for joining ceramics to metals", Journal de Physique, Colloque C1, Supplément au n°2, Tome 47, C1-131-C1-137, February 1986.

11. K. Suganuma, T. Okamoto, M. Koizumi and M. Shimada, "Method for preventing thermal expansion mismatch effect in ceramic-metal joining", Journal of Materials Science Letters, Vol. 4, n°5, 648-650, 1985.

12. T. Yamada, H. Sekiguchi, M. Okamoto, S. Azuma, A. Kitamura and K. Fukaya, "Diffusion bonding SiC or Si_3N_4 to Nimonic 80A, "High Temperature Technology, Vol. 5, n°4, 193-200, November 1987.

13. T. Yamada, H. Sekiguchi, H. Okamoto, S. Azuma and A. Kitamura", Diffusion bonding SiC or Si_3N_4 to metal", Proceedings of the Second International Symposium on Ceramic Materials and Components for Engines, W. Bunk and H. Hausner Eds., 441-448, Lübeck-Travemünde FRG, April 14-17, 1986.

14. K. Suganuma, M. Takagi, Y. Miyamoto, M. Koizumi, T. Okamoto and H. Nakata, "Joining of Silicon Nitride to Molybdenum under High Pressure", Nippon-Seramikkusu-Kyokai-Gakujutsu-Rombunshi, Vol. 96, n°11, 1051-1056, 1988.

15. K. Suganuma, T. Okamoto, Y. Miyamoto, M. Shimada and M. Koizumi, "Joining Si_3N_4 to type 405 steel with soft metal interlayers", Materials Science and Technology, Vol. 2, n°11, 1156-1161, November 1986.

16. F. Hatakeyama, K. Suganuma and T. Okamoto, "Solid-state bonding of alumina to austenitic stainless steel", Journal of Materials Science, Vol. 21, n°7, 2455-2461, 1986.

17. T. Tanaka, H. Morimoto and H. Homma, "Joining of Ceramics to Metals", Nippon Steel Technical Report, n°37, 31-38, April 1988.

18. K. Suganuma, T. Okamoto, M. Shimada and M. Koizumi, "New method for solid-state bonding between ceramics and metals", Communications of the American Society, Vol. 66, n°7, C-117-C-118, 1983.

19. K. Suganuma, T. Okamoto, M. Koizumi and M. Shimada, "Effect of thickness on direct bonding of silicon nitride to steel", Communications of the American Ceramic Society, Vol. 68, n°12, C-334-C-335, December 1985.

20. K. Suganuma and T. Okamoto, "Interlayer bonding methods for ceramic/metal systems with thermal expansion mismatches", Fundamentals of diffusion bonding, Proceedings of the First Seiken International Symposium on Interface Structure, Properties and Diffusion Bonding, Y. Ishida Ed., Elsevier, Amsterdam - Oxford - New York - Tokyo, 71-88, Tokyo, Japan, 2-4 December 1985.

21. M. Nakamura, K. Kubo, S. Kanzaki and H. Tabata, "Joining of silicon nitride ceramics by hot pressing", Journal of Materials Science, Vol. 22, n°4, 1259-1264, 1987.

22. K. Suganuma, T. Okamoto, M. Koizumi and M. Shimada, "Effects of surface damage on strength of Silicon Nitride bonded with Aluminum", Advanced Ceramic Materials, Vol. 1, n°4, 356-360, 1986.

23. R.L. Mullen, R.C. Hendricks and G. Mc Donald, "Interface roughness effect on stresses in ceramic coatings", Ceramic Engineering and Science Proceedings, Vol. 8, n°7-8, 559-571, 1987.

24. C. Beraud, M. Courbiere, C. Esnouf, D. Juve and D. Treheux", Study of copper-alumina bonding", Journal of Materials Science, Vol. 24, n°12, 4545-4554, 1989.

25. "Standard Method for tension and vacuum testing metalized ceramic seals", ASTM F19-64.

26. K. Suganuma, T. Okamoto, M. Koizumi and M. Shimada, "Acoustic emission from ceramic/metal joints on cooling", The American Ceramic Society Bulletin, Vol. 65, n°7, 1060-1064, 1986.

27. F.P. Bailey and W.E. Borbidge, "Solid-state metal-ceramic reaction bonding", Surfaces and interfaces in ceramic and ceramic-metal systems, J.A. Pask and A.G. Evans Eds, Materials Science Research, Vol. 14, Plenum Press, New York, 525-533, 1981.

28. C.A. Calow, P.D. Bayer and I.T. Porter, "The solid-state bonding of nickel, chromium and nichrome sheets to α-Al$_2$O$_3$", Journal of Materials Science, Vol. 6, n°2, 150-155, 1971.

29. J.A. Wasynczuk and M. Rühle, "Microstructural characterization of Ni/Al$_2$O$_3$ diffusion bonds", J.A. Pask and A.G. Evans Eds., Materials Science Research, Vol. 21, Plenum press, New-York and London, 1986.

30. A.G. Evans, M. Rühle and M. Turwitt, "On the mechanics of failure in ceramic/metal bonded systems", Journal de Physique, Colloque C4, Suppl. n°4, Tome 46, C4-613-C4-626, April 1985.

31. C.H. Hsueh and A.G. Evans, "Residual stresses in metal/ceramic bonded strips", Journal of the American Ceramic Society, Vol. 68, n°5, 241-248, 1985.

32. M. Wittmer, C.R. Boer, P. Gudmundson and J. Carlsson, "Mechanical properties of liquid-phase-bonded copper-ceramic substrates", Journal of the American Ceramic Society, Vol. 65, n°3, 149-153, 1982.

33. K. Suganuma, T. Okamoto, M. Koizumi and M. Shimada, "Effect of inter-layers in ceramic-metal joints with thermal expansion mismatches", Communications of the American Ceramic Society, Vol. 67, n°12, C-256-C-257, 1984.

34. H.P. Kirchner, J.C. Conway, J.R. and A.E. Segall, "Effect of joint thickness and residual stresses on the properties of ceramic ahesives joints : I, Finite element analysis of stresses in joints", Journal of the American Ceramic Society, Vol. 70, n°2, 104-109, 1987.

APPENDIX : Brief overview of the work carried out by Euram partners.

   - combination of bonding and of a final densification of both the metal and the ceramic : in charge of CEA. Initial densification is done by CIPing (and "fixing" for the ceramics). Interlayers (graded powder layers IN 600-alumina) have to be used to accomodate the differences in the kinetics of densification,
   - mechanical interlocking of In 600 powder compacts on a dense alumina part machined with a groove. Satisfactory results were then obtained,
   - comparison with uniaxial hot pressing (Université Catholique de Louvain La Neuve). This technique is convenient to directly produce test samples for tensile and toughness measurements tests. U.C.L. bonded dense alumina and In 600 compacts with and without copper inserts. With the copper, it is recommended to operate the uniaxial hot pressing under a limited partial oxygen pressure. Tensile strengths in excess of 50 MPa have been obtained for a cylindrical test sample geometry. K_{IC} values have been obtained from bonding tests on square section samples with a notch machined in the ceramic near the interlayer, the value of about 4-5 MPa$\sqrt{m}$ is close to that of the ceramic alone up to 500°C. Direct bonding (under a good vacuum) may lead to similar toughness values but up to higher temperatures (800°C). All partners are involved in the microstructural studies and studies of metal/ceramic reactions.

TABLE I : Chemical composition of In 600.

Elements	Ni	Cr	Fe	Mn	Si	Ti	Al	C	Cu	Co	P	S
(weight %)	73.1	16.25	~ 7	0.83	0.27	0.25	0.16	0.027	0.02	0.02	0.011	0.0008

TABLE II : Properties of materials at room temperature.

Properties / Materials	Density	Melting point °C	Coeff. of Thermal Expansion $10^{-6}C^{-1}$	Poisson's ratio	Elastic modulus GPa	Thermal conductivity $W.m^{-1}.K^{-1}$	Yield Strength MPa	Strength MPa
Al_2O_3 (TS15)	3.75	-	7.8	-	330	30	-	330** 220**
In 600	8.45	1371-1427	12.1	0.29	214	14.8	283	662*

** bending strength   * tensile strength

213

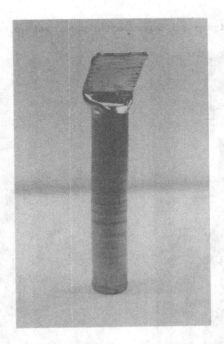

Figure 1 : Deformation of container after bonding (1300°C, 60 min, 100 MPa).

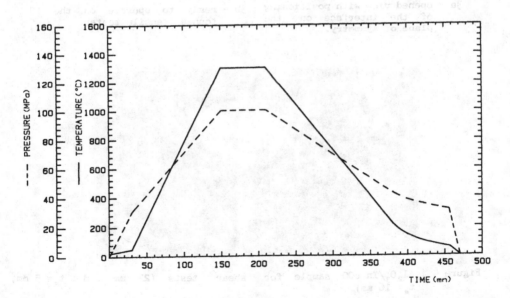

Figure 2 : Standard H.I.P. cycle (pressure-temperature versus time) for 1300°C - 60 min - 100 MPa.

Figure 3 : Experimental shear set-up.

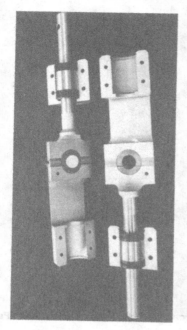 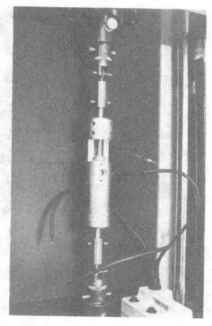

3a - opened view with positioning of the interface on the plane of symmetry.

3b - ready to operate on the 10 tonnes tensile tester.

Figure 4 : Al_2O_3/In 600 sample for shear tests (22 mm o.d ; t_c = 5 mm, t_m = 16 mm).

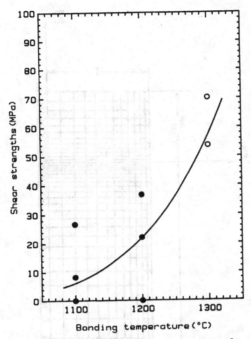

Figure 5 : Shear strengths of samples bonded for 60 min under 100 MPa at various temperatures. Filled symbols refer to samples that failed at alumina/In 600 interfaces.

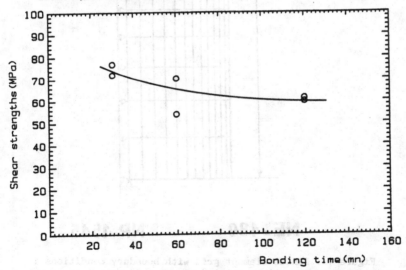

Figure 6 : Shear strengths of samples bonded for various times under 100 MPa at 1300°C.

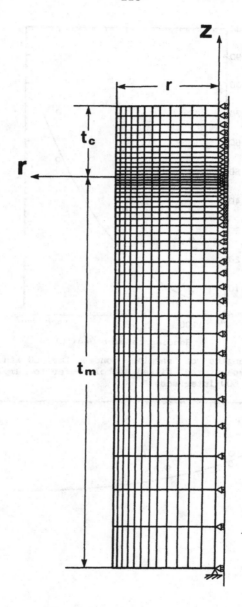

NE=480   **NP=1545**

Figure 7 : Finite element grid with boundary conditions :
(r = 11 mm ; t_c= 8 mm ; t_m= 44 mm)

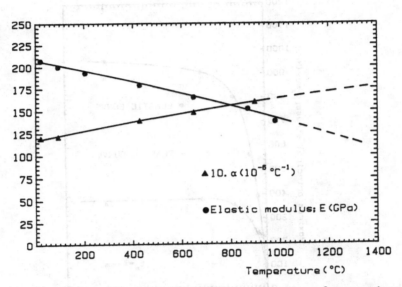

Figure 8a : Physical properties of In 600 as a function of temperature :
Variation of the elastic modulus :
$E(T) = -7.97.10^{-6}T^2 - 59.41.10^{-3} T + 206.55$
where E is in GPa and T in °C.
Variation of the coefficient of thermal expansion :
$\alpha(T) = -0.84.10^{-12}T^2 + 5.58.10^{-9}T + 11.65.10^{-6}$
where α is in 10^{-6} °C^{-1} and T in °C.

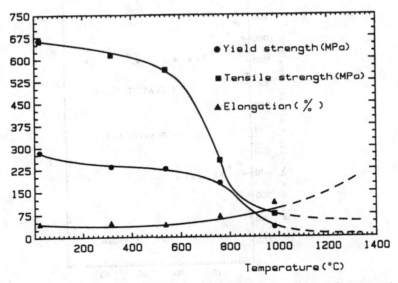

Figure 8b : Mechanical properties of In 600 as a function of temperature.

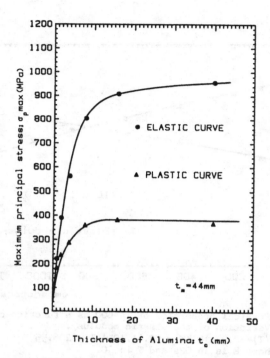

Figure 9 : **Maximum principal stress at the free lateral surface close to the interface as a function of the thickness of alumina** (r = 11 mm ; t_m = 44 mm).

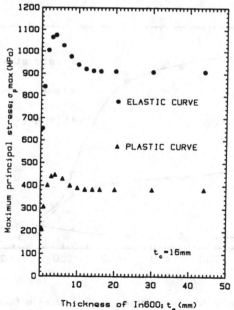

Figure 10 : **Maximum principal stress at the free lateral surface close to the interface as a function of the thickness of In 600** (r = 11 mm ; t_c = 16 mm).

219

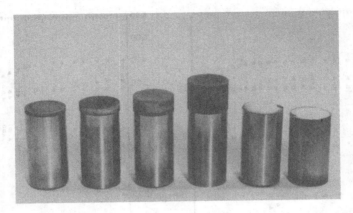

Figure 11 : Al$_2$O$_3$/In 600 bonds with increasing ceramic thickness from left to right t$_c$= 2, 4, 8, 16 and 40 mm. The In 600 thickness is constant (44 mm).

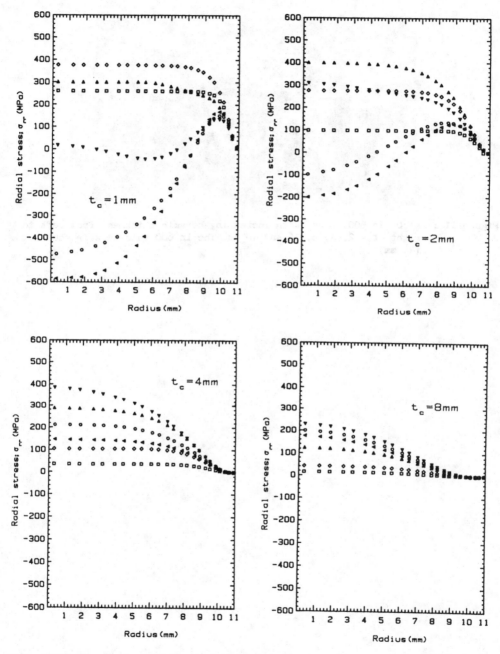

Figure 12 : Computed radial stress distribution as a function of radius for various thicknesses of metal.

(□ t_m = 0.5 mm ; ◇ t_m = 1 mm ; △ t_m = 2 mm ; ▽ t_m = 4 mm ; ○ t_m = 8 mm ; ◁ t_m = 16 mm).

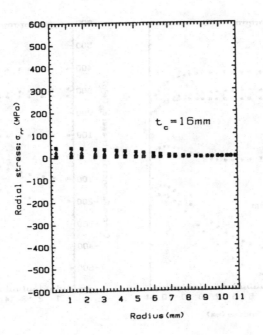

Figure 12 : Computed radial stress distribution as a function of radius for various thicknesses of metal.
(□ t_m= 0.5 mm ; ◇ t_m= 1 mm ; △ t_m= 2 mm ; ▽ t_m= 4 mm ; ○ t_m= 8 mm ; ◁ t_m= 16 mm).

222

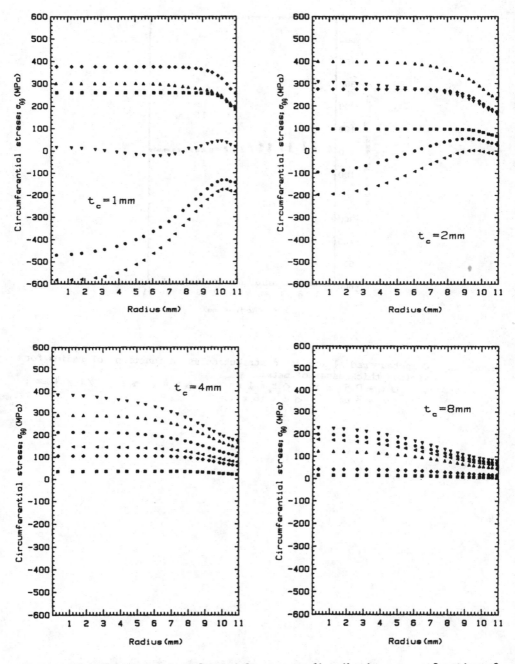

Figure 13 : Computed circumferential stress distribution as a function of radius for various thicknesses of metal.
(■ t_a = 0.5 mm ;   ◆ t_a = 1 mm ;   ▲ t_a = 2 mm ;   ▼ t_a = 4 mm ;
● t_a = 8 mm ;   ◀ t_a = 16 mm).

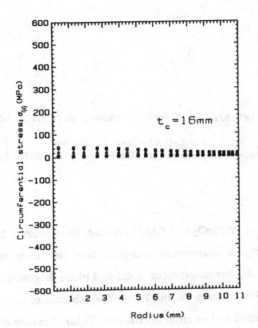

Figure 13 : Computed circumferential stress distribution as a function of
radius for various thicknesses of metal.
(■ t_m = 0.5 mm ; ◆ t_m = 1 mm ; ▲ t_m = 2 mm ; ▼ t_m = 4 mm ;
● t_m = 8 mm ; ◀ t_m = 16 mm).

Figure 14 : Full set of Al_2O_3/In 600 junctions with seven ceramic thicknesses
(1, 2, 3, 4, 5, 8 and 16 mm) and six metal thicknesses (0.5, 1, 2,
4, 8 and 16 mm).

INTERFACES IN METAL/CERAMIC DIFFUSION BONDS

C-D Qin and B. Derby

Department of Materials, University of Oxford, OX1 3PH

Abstract

Diffusion bonds of Pd/ZrO$_2$ and Pd/Al$_2$O$_3$ made in vacuum at 1100°C 10 MPa have been studied. Their strengths measured by four-point bend tests show strong bonding occurred in the Pd/ZrO$_2$ bands. Investigation of published phase diagrams suggested this to be due to an eutectic reaction between Pd and ZrO$_2$. The existence of such a reaction was further characterised by optical and electron microscopy (TEM). Possible eutectic temperatures were found at 707 and 890° by differential thermal analysis (DTA).

TEM results of Pd/Al$_2$O$_3$ found no reaction layer between these two materials. This possibly explains the low strengths of these diffusion bonds.

Introduction

Better understanding of the interface in diffusion bonding could develop new interlayer alloys for joining materials. A number of metal/ceramic diffusion bonded systems have been studied in the past for the presence of interface reactions. The presence or absence of interface reactions is of considerable importance in understanding the evolution of strength during the diffusion bonding process and enabling a prediction of conditions leading to optimum joint properties. There have been a number of investigations of interfaces between zirconia and other materials, in particular between NiO and Zirconia [1], Pt and zirconia [2], Pd and zirconia [3][4][5] and Pt, Ni, Zr and zirconia [3]. In the present work the interface defects and the eutectic reaction products between Pd and zirconia have been studied by optical microscopy and transmission electron microscopy (TEM). The eutectic reaction observed explains their strong bonding, as eutectic reaction forming liquid phases will enhance the wetting capability between these two materials, and the reaction layer may also provide strong chemical bonding. Such a reaction is further confirmed by differential thermal analysis (DTA) of the Pd and zirconia mixed powders. Two probable reaction temperatures are found to be about 707°C and 890°C. Similar efforts have also been tried in Pd/alumina diffusion bonded interfaces, however, no reaction in this system has been found.

TEM results of Pd/alumina interfaces show that there is no reaction layer between these two materials. This explains why such a bonding is generally very weak.

Experimental

Yttria stabilized TZP zirconia and alumina bars of dimensions 11x11x14 mm were cleaned and one face polished to a 3 micron surface finish. Two blocks were assembled around a thin metal foil to provide a sandwich for bonding at 10MPa in vacuum for various bonding times. TEM specimens were produced from metal/ceramic multilayers fabricated under identical conditions to those used for bonding. The multilayers were cut into 0.2 mm thick slices which were dimpled and ion beam milled to perforation. A Philips CM12 microscope operated at 120kV was used to examine the interfaces. DTA analysis was made for well mixed Pd/zirconia (Pd/alumina) powders (1mole/1mole) compressed under identical conditions to those used for bonding, pure Pd and zirconia powders respectively, thus any signal from the mixing will be revealed comparing these three DTA data.

Results

Optical Microscopy

To investigate the initial stage of eutectic reaction 1 minute bonding time was used. Fig.1 shows strips of Pd melted inside a grain, which has been suggested to be the eutectic nuclei in the eutectic composition after Zr and/or O diffused into the stripes. The well defined geometry should define the low order crystollography orientations. The real interface composes two interfaces after the eutectic reaction, i.e., interface of ceramic/eutectic layer and eutectic layer/Pd. Fig.2a is an over view of the Pd surfaces. It shows the fracture passage changes from eutectic layer/Pd (bright region) to ceramic/eutectic layer (dark region) during fracture of the metal/ceramic interface from left hand side to right hand side. Note also the eutectic patterns inside each grain in the bright region. Fig.2b shows islands of dark regions which is the interface of the ceramic/eutectic. This basically shows that the bonding between ceramic to the eutectic products is stronger than that the eutectic products to the metal.

In contrast to the short time bonding, long time (2 hours) bonding causes the eutectic products growing to large crystals (~2 micron). This is shown in fig. 3a and 3b respectively. Fig.3c shows the ceramic part is well reacted to fit the eutectic grains, thus the fracture passage is zig-zaged to increase the fracture energy and resistance.

Differential thermal analysis

Fig.4 is a diagram of the DTA data for Pd, Pd/zirconia and zirconia. Two extra peaks were found for Pd/zirconia at 707 and 890°C. Peak at 1195°C was observed at both zirconia and Pd/zirconia. However the peak presented in pure Pd at about 815°C was absent in Pd/zirconia.

Electron microscopy

In fig.5a TEM of the interface region of Pd/alumina is shown. There is no apparent reaction in this interface region. In fig.5b Pd/zirconia interface shows a clearly defined interfacial reaction product zone of variable thickness but of 0.5 micron in average. Some very small particles are visible in this region between Pd and zirconia.

Discussion

Much thinner reaction layers at metal/ceramic interfaces were reported during in situ heating experiments on MgO particles supported by a Pd grid [6]. In that case the driving force for any reaction was believed to be the solution energy of Mg in Pd. Such redox reactions at metal/ceramic interfaces where the solution energy rather than the oxidation energy is dominant have been postulated in the past [7].

There are many intermediate intermetallic compounds possible between Pd and Zr (fig.6)[8]. The compound Pd/Zr_2 is of particular interest because of its steep eutectic valley with pure Zr which leads to a liquid phase below $1100^{\circ}C$. The driving force for this reaction will be the solution energies of Zr and O in Pd. It is proposed that the interfacial reaction and interdiffusion occurs until the composition of the interlayer is such as to promote melting. The liquid phase then wets the interface to create a completed bond. Results from DTA suggests that the real eutectic reaction temperature for system of Pd/zirconia is about 707 or $890^{\circ}C$, which is lower than the eutectic reaction temperatures for Pd/Zr. This may be because of the presence of oxygen. The actual bonding at $1100^{\circ}C$ has actually endured these two phase change temperatures. It is noted the eutectic products consist of various small particles, hence the actual reaction is very complicated.

The Pd and Al system also shows possible intermediate intermetallic compounds (fig.6) but no reaction has yet been found. This difference is possible an effect of different solution energies for Al and O in Pd.

The absorb peak in DTA of pure Pd at about $815^{\circ}C$ is coincident with the temperature for PdO to decompose [9]. As the Pd is only protected by argon gas flow in DTA, oxidation is probable for pure Pd while for Pd/zirconia the reaction between the components is dominant. Oxidation of Pd before about $815^{\circ}C$ is a continuous process thus no peaks are detected. The peak at $1195^{\circ}C$ for zirconia is the phase change from monoclinic zirconia to tetragonal zirconia [10].

Conclusions

(1) Eutectic reaction between palladium and zirconia explains the high strength of the bonding at $1100^{\circ}C$. The reason for the low bonding strength of Pd/alumina is suggested to be the absent of similar eutectic reaction.

(2) DTA can be used to detect any possible reaction and to tell eutectic reaction temperatures between metal/ceramic diffusion bonding.

Acknowledgements

We are most grateful for the funding from SERC and Johnson Matthey for supply of the Pd foil. We also appreciate Deliang Zhang for the initiation and help in DTA analysis and Dr B. Cantor for providing the DTA analysis apparatus.

References

1) V.P. Dravid, P. Vinayak, C.E. Lyman, M.R. Notis, and A. Revcolevschi, Ultramicroscopy 29 60, (1987).
2) M. Pharaoh and G.J. Tatlock, Inst. Phys. Conf. Series 93, 2 413, (1988).
3) B. Derby, in 'Diffusion Bonding', Ed. R. Pearce, 195, Cranfield U.K. (1986).
4) N. James and B. Derby, 3rd Inter. Conf. on Joining Metals, Ceramics and Glass, Ed. W. Kraft, 73, DGM (1988).
5) C-D Qin and B. Derby, in 'Properties of Joints', BABS Autumn Conf., 14-15 Nov. (1989).
6) D.F. Lynch, A.F. Moodie and C.E. Warble, J. Mater. Sci. Lett. 15 1069, (1980).
7) J.T. Klomp, in "Ceramic Microstructures '86: Role of Interfaces", eds. J.A. Pask and A.G. Evans, Mater. Sci. Res. 21 307, Plenium (1987).
8) Binary Alloy Phase Diagrams, eds. T.B. Massalski, J.L. Murrar, L.H. Bennett, H. Baker and L. Kacprzak, ASM, (1986).
9) Rare Metals Handbook, ed. C.A. Hampel, Reinhold Pub. Corp., New York, (1954).
10) Advances in Ceramics, eds. F. Yan and A.H. Heuer, 3 241, (1981).

Fig. 1 Optical microscopy of the eutectic nuclei on the Pd foil.
Interfacial of Pd/zirconia was made at $1100^{o}C$ 10MPa 1 minute. The well
defined geometry reflects the crystallography orientations. It shows
that Pd foil melts locally in the beginning of the eutectic reaction.

Fig. 2 An overview of the broken interface made at $1100^{o}C$ 10MPa 1
minute. (a) shows the breaking passage (from left to right hand side)
changes from eutectic layer/Pd (bright area) to zirconia/eutectic
interface (dark area). Note also the strip-like eutectic reaction
products in the bright area. (b) islands of grains (dark area) are
formed from fracture along zirconia/eutectic interface. Majority of
the fracture is along the eutectic/Pd interface.

Fig. 3 Optical microscopy of the Pd/zirconia interface. (a) the zirconia/eutectic layer interface at initial stage of bonding at 1100°C 10MPa 1 minute. Note the fine structure of the interface. (b) in contrast to (a) the well grown interfacial eutectic reaction products are seen as shiny small grains about 2 micron in sizes after 2 hours bonding. (c) the morphology on the zirconia side after 2 hours bonding. It shows zirconia and Pd are well contacted via the eutectic reaction products shown in (b).

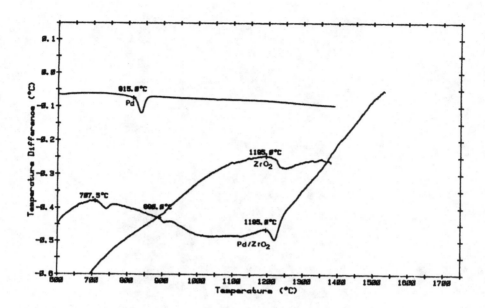

Fig. 4 Diagram of DTA results for Pd, Pd/zirconia and zirconia. The peaks correspond to the phase transformation temperatures of the analysed materials. The peak for Pd is 815°C, Pd/zirconia 707, 890 and 1195°C and zirconia 1195°C.

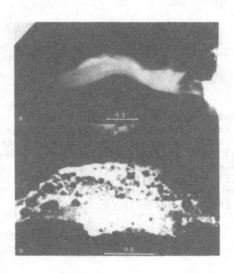

Fig.5 (a) TEM of Pd/alumina interface (marked AA). No apparent reaction is observed; the interface is very sharp. (b) TEM of Pd/zirconia interface. A reaction zone, which is about 0.5 micron and consists of various sizes of small particles, is observed between these two materials.

Assessed Al-Pd Phase Diagram

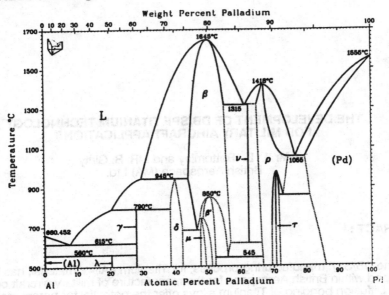

Pd-Zr Phase Diagram

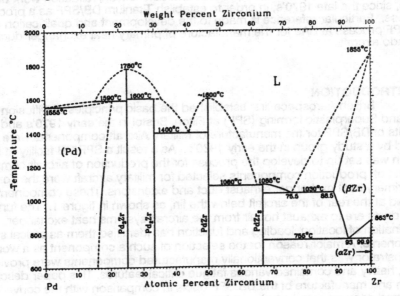

Fig. 6 Phase diagrams of Al-Pd and Pd-Zr [8].

* All the units in the micrographs are in micron.

THE DEVELOPMENT OF DB/SPF TITANIUM TECHNOLOGY FOR MILITARY AIRCRAFT APPLICATIONS

by
Mr. I. E. Bottomley and MR. B. Ginty
British Aerospace (MA) Ltd.

ABSTRACT :

The DB/SPF manufacturing process, for Titanium 6Al/4V material, has been developed within British Aerospace for the manufacture of military aircraft components. Diffusion bonding of Titanium alloys offer the potential for parent metal joint strengths, and when combined with SPF complex aircraft components offering significant cost and wieght savings can be manufactured. This paper describes the manufacturing development and process characterisation/validation work undertaken, since the late 1970's, in order to establish Titanium DB/SPF as a production process. Particular reference is made to the development and qualification of the DB/SPF process at BAe for the manufacture of primary heat exchanger ducts on the Tornado aircraft.

1.0 INTRODUCTION

British Aerospace first established the basic principles of Diffusion Bonding (DB) and Superplastic forming (SPF) at Filton, Bristol in the early 1970's and the benefits of DB/SPF for the manufacture of Military Aircraft components were highlighted by a study group in the early 1980's. As a result a SPF/DB facility at BAe, Warton was set up to develop the process for the production of aircraft components. The first off production components selected for military aircraft were the Tornado IDS primary heat exchanger exhaust duct and extensions. These components are situated at the rear of the aircraft below the fin, as shown in figure 1. The function of these ducts are to exhaust hot air from the aircraft systems heat exchanger. The combination of location, loading and function has identified them as critical structural components. A major reason for the selection of such a component as a working demonstrator was that conventionally manufactured components were proving costly, heavy and contained various fatigue critical features. This paper describes the design and manufacture of the DB/SPF ducts in comparison with the conventional fabricated components, including BAe's approach to the airworthiness qualification. In parallel and supporting the development and manufacture of the production ducts a general DB/SPF development programme was conducted, this is also described briefly.

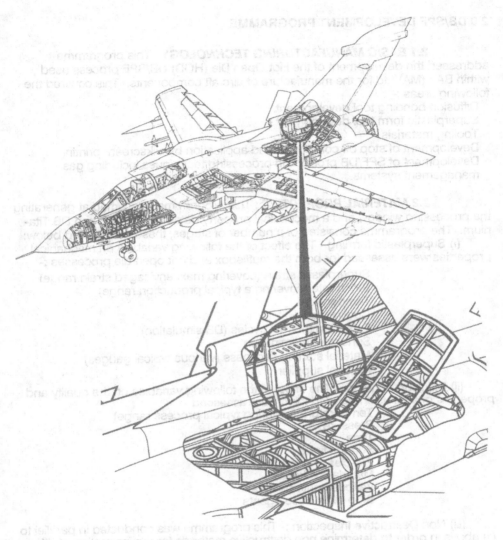

Figure 1: Tornado SPF/DB Heat Exchanger Exhaust Duct

2.0 DB/SPF DEVELOPMENT PROGRAMME

2.1 BASIC MANUFACTURING TECHNOLOGY : This programme addressed the development of the Hot Open Die (HOD) DB/SPF process used within BAe (MA) Ltd for the manufacture of aircraft components. This covered the following areas :-
Diffusion bonding tool development.
Superplastic form tool development.
Tooling materials.
Development of stop off compound and application by silkscreen printing.
Development of SPF/DB production processing techniques including gas management systems.

2.2 MATERIAL PROPERTIES : This programme was aimed at generating the processing window and a mechanical property database for SPF and DB Titanium. The programme consisted of a number of stages, these are detailed below:
(i) Superplastic forming - The effect of the following variables on mechanical properties were assessed for both the mufflebox and hot open die processes :-
Superplastic strain (covering max. envisaged strain range)
Strain rate (covering a typical production range)
Temperature
Cooling rate
Extended thermal cycles (DB simulation)
Surface contamination
Material starting thickness (various typical gauges)
Material supplier
(ii) Diffusion bonding :- The effect of the following variables on the quality and properties of a diffusion bonded joint, were assessed -
Temperature (covering typical process range)
Pressure
Time
Surface finish
Pre-cleaning treatment
Material thickness
Various contaminants
Stop off/release agents

(iii) Non Destructive Inspection :- This programme was conducted in parallel to (ii) above in order to determine non destructive methods for the inspection of diffusion bonded joints and to define detectable defect standards.

2.3 STRUCTURAL ELEMENTS TEST PROGRAMME : This programme consisted of the manufacture of a number of DB/SPF test elements with a variety of internal core configurations. These elements were then tested to demonstrate and verify their structural integrity under static and fatigue loading. Other programme objectives were to ;
manufacture different core configurations;
identify problem areas;
prove pressure/time profiles;
confirm thinning predictions;
establish contamination levels;
optimise NDE procedures.
generate design data, i.e. skin/core ratios, bond widths, core angles etc.

2.4 DEMONSTRATOR TEST PROGRAMME : This covered the manufacture of military aircraft demonstrator components to simulate typical design and manufacturing activities in order to address production problems associated with manufacture of aircraft structures. These demonstrator programmes also include full scale tests to verify design assumptions and confirm structural behaviour. Subsequent to the initial heat exchanger duct programmes further developments have continued such that a complete foreplane structure has now been manufactured and tested sucessfully.

3.0 TORNADO HEAT EXCHANGER DUCT PROGRAMME

3.1 DESIGN
3.1.1 Conventional - The original heat exchanger exhaust duct assembly was designed as four fabricated and welded sub assemblies, as shown in figure 2. These can be considered as forward and aft (extension) ducts. The aft ducts form a socket into which the forward ducts locate therefore a fit tolerance needs to be maintained (a maximum allowable gap of 0.2mm). The working environment of these components dictated the material for manufacture as Titanium alloy and Titanium 2.5% Copper alloy was used.

3.1.2 DB/SPF - In designing the DB/SPF components interchangability with the conventionally formed components had to be maintained whilst at the same time providing savings in the manufacturing process and significant improvements in service performance. As a result of preliminary trade studies, manufacturing development trials and the requirement to maintain the same internal vane configuration the design evolved as a four sheet accordion core structure, as shown in figure 3. This design meant that the parts count for the forward ducts was reduced from 18 to 4 and from 14 to 4 for the aft (extensions). To facilitate manufacture by the DB/SPF process the material was changed to the Titanium 6Al/4V alloy.

3.2 MANUFACTURE :
3.2.1 Conventional - The manufacturing methods used for both the forward ducts and extensions are essentially the same and are described as follows;

Considering first of all the manufacture of the splitter vanes, of which five would be required for each sub assembly, these would be manufactured so :-
    Profile blank by ;
    Hot rubber pre-form at 350°C
    Creep form/hot size at 650°C
The half pressings are also manufactured using a similar process. Assembly would then continue by TIG welding together of the two half pressings. The material being Titanium any welding must then be carried out under an inert atmosphere, usually in a welding chamber. 100% radiographic examination of the welded joints was then carried out because of the classification of the part. The splitter vanes are then positioned in a jig and resistance spot welded in placed. This process is repeated for each sub assembly.

As can be seen from the description above the process was both lengthy in terms of manufacturing time and required a large number of tools per sub-assembly, hence the potential for cost reductions by the change to DB/SPF manufacture was substantial.

3.2.2 DB/SPF - Using the Hot Open Die DB/SPF process developed at BAe (see paragraph 2.1) the duct sub-assemblies are manufactured in pairs, not individually as for the conventionally manufactured components. This manufacturing route reduced the number of tools for the manufacture of a complete aircraft set from 54 to 22, see table 1. A detailed explanation of the manufacturing process and

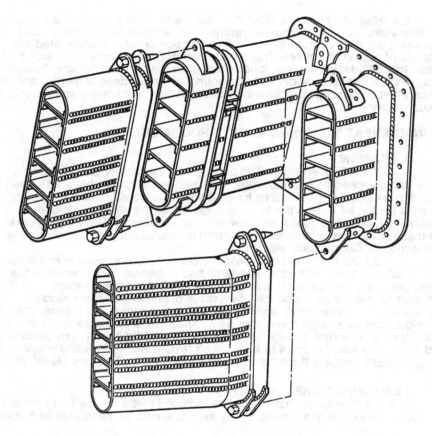

Figure 2: Heat Exchanger Duct Assembly Conventional Multi-Piece Welded Design

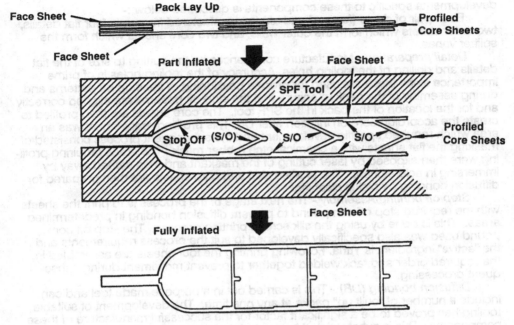

Face Sheet

Pack Lay Up

Profiled Core Sheets

Face Sheet

Part Inflated

Face Sheet

SPF Tool

Stop Off (S/O)   S/O   S/O

Profiled Core Sheets

Face Sheet

Fully Inflated

Figure 3: Schematic of Accordian Core Concept

	Conventional		DB/SPF	
	Parts Count	Tools No.	Parts Count	Tools No.
Fwd Duct Port	9	13	} 4	} 11
Fwd Duct S/board	9	13		
Aft Duct Port	12	14	} 4	} 11
Aft Duct S/board	12	14		
Totals	42	54	8	22

Table 1: Comparison of Parts/Tool Count, Conventional vs DB/SPF

developments specific to these components is described below :-

Each pair of ducts (forward and aft) is manufactured from only four flat details, two outer sheets which form the outer walls, and two core sheets which form the splitter vanes.

Detail preparation - Manufacture commences by the cutting to size of the flat details and drilling of the tooling holes. Accuracy of the tooling holes is of prime importance since these are used for precise positioning of the stop off patterns and during assembly of the pack to ensure that the stop off patterns are aligned correctly and for the location of the pack in the SPF tool. The core sheets are then profiled to create the accordion core on inflation after DB. This profiling requirement was an area which required specific development and the subsequent process consisted of masking the flat sheets with a chemical etch rubber mask. The areas requiring profiling were then exposed by laser cutting of the maskant and then etched away by immersing in acid etchant. The profiled skin and core sheets are then prepared for diffusion bonding by pickle cleaning.

Stop off printing/Assembly - The next stage of the process is to print the sheets with the required stop off compound to prevent diffusion bonding in predetermined areas. This is done by using the silk screen printing process. The stop off compound used was also specifically developed to suit the process requirements and the "active" ingredient is Yttria. Following printing the four sheets are assembled in the required order and tack welded together to prevent movement during subsequent processing.

Diffusion bonding (DB) - This is carried out in a purpose made tool and can include a number of "built up" packs at any one time. The development of suitable tooling has proved to be a significant factor for the successful manufacture of these components. This is substantiated by the fact that as tooling has developed the incidence of rejection due to no bonds has reduced to less than 1%. Diffusion bonding is carried at temperature (above 900°C) using gas pressure, for about 90 minutes. One of the advantages of carrying out DB as a separate operation prior to SPF is that, in order to generate confidence in the process, the bonded packs can be subjected to NDE inspection by ultrasonic "C" scan.

Superplastic forming (SPF) - Is then carried out using the Hot Open Die process at a temperature of 925°C. This requires form tooling that is manufactured from heat resisting steel and BAe use a 22-4-9 alloy steel. Expansion of the pack is achieved by the introduction of argon gas between the sheets, the pressure of the gas follows a predetermined profile which has been calculated to form the material at the optimum strain rate for SPF of $1.5 \times 10^{-4} \text{sec}^{-1}$. At the end of the SPF cycle the component is removed from the press and allowed to cool in air, the parts are then subjected to the chemical milling process to remove the oxygen contaminated surface layer.

For the final processing, i.e. attachment of bracketry etc., the components are treated as conventional sub-assemblies.

3.3 QUALIFICATION

3.3.1 Process verification - The DB/SPF process, in general, relies heavily on process control for maintaining component quality and integrity, therefore strict control documentation and procedures had to be introduced to satisfy the quality assurance requirements. The requirements start with the raw materials that are to be used and cover every aspect of the processing route. The manufacturing process can be broken down into a number of stages in order appreciate the process verification requirements, these are shown schematically in figure 4 and briefly discussed below ;

1. DIFFUSION BONDING - From the results of the basic technology programme a manufacturing window for the diffusion bonding process was determined,

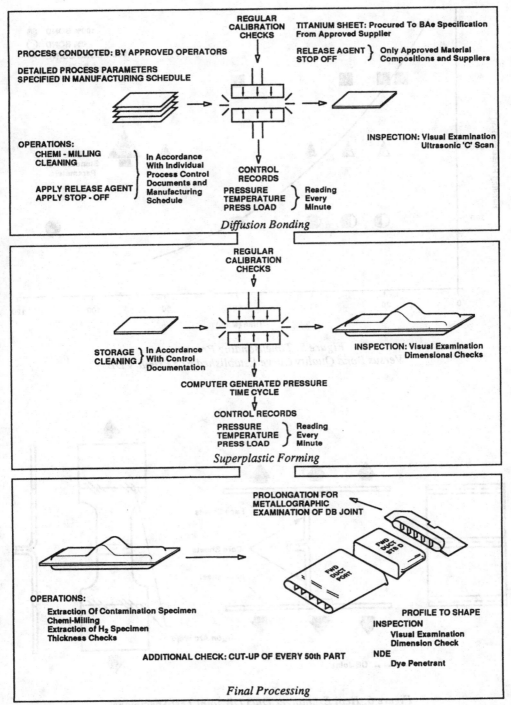

Figure 4: Heat Exchange Duct Process Control Requirement

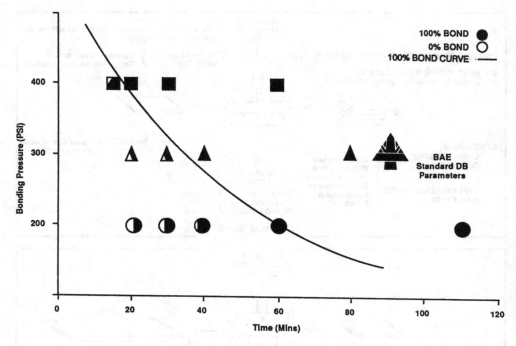

Figure 5: Time/Bonding Pressure
Versus Bond Quality Curve Established For Primary DB

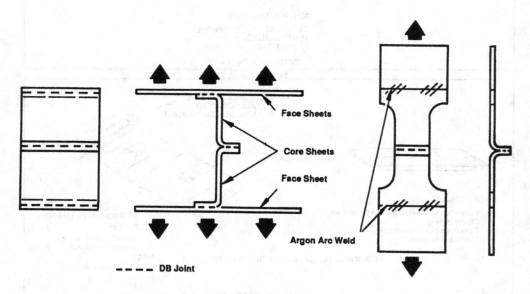

Figure 6: Heat Exchanger Duct DB Joint Test Specimens

see figure 5. Manufacturing parameters were then selected to achieve **overkill** and therefore compensating for any variations in processing parameters, within the allowable tolerances.

2. SUPERPLASTIC FORMING - After non destructive examination and visual inspection the DB pack is submitted for SPF. As with the DB process strict process control and monitoring is required to verify this operation.

3. FINAL PROCESSING - After the final SPF operation final process checks are carried out to verify the quality of the resultant DB/SPF component.

3.3.2 Component verification - In order to confirm the material and joint properties of the DB/SPF parts the components were subjected to the following test work ;

(i) Cut up testing - An important part of the airworthiness clearance was the demonstration of reproducibility, confirmation of DB joint strengths and overall quality of these components. This was carried out by full detailed cut up testing of a number of development and the first five off production components. The tests carried out on ducts consisted of detailed dimensional inspection, Hydrogen content determination (before and after chemical milling), contamination depth determination (before and after chemical milling by selective masking), mechanical testing (fatigue and static) on joints, SPF material and test specimen fractographic examination. The heat exchanger duct joint test specimens are shown in figure 6. Each 50th component was also subjected to full cut up testing in order to monitor component reproducibility and quality. The conclusions of the testing were :
Under strict process control and optimised processing parameters :-
1. The Hydrogen contents are below specification maximum
   after processing.
2. The depth of surface contamination can be assessed representatively by
   extraction of "off part" samples to facilitate controlled removal.
3. Diffusion bond lap shear strength is that of the parent material.
4. Diffusion bonded joints do not peel under static or fatigue loading.
5. The fatigue strength of a diffusion bonded joint is dictated by the local
   notch geometry produced.

(ii) Continuous assessment - As part of the quality assurance requirements until sufficient confidence in the process could be established lap shear joint test prolongation specimens and metallographic specimens were removed from excess material of each duct to provide joint quality and contamination depth details to verify component quality.

4.0 CONCLUSIONS :
The DB/SPF manufacturing process for the Tornado heat exchanger ducts has shown significant cost and manufacturing time savings, the exhaustive development and airworthiness testing has led to extremley high confidence in the process. The heat exchanger ducts have now been in service for approximately 5 years and as such supports the high confidence level in the process. As a result DB/SPF is now an approved manufacturing process at BAe (MA) Ltd and major structural components, foreplanes and outboard flaperons, are now designed for the European Fighter Aircraft (EFA) to be manufactured using the process.

THE APPLICATION OF SPF/DB TO DISSIMILAR METAL JOINTS

by

P G Partridge
T S Baker *

Materials and Structures Dept.
Royal Aerospace Department
Farnborough
Hants

ABSTRACT

High strength dissimilar metal joints have been made between Ti-6Al-4V titanium alloy and S526 stainless steel by pre-machining grooves in the steel surface and superplastically forming (SPF) the titanium-alloy into the grooves and diffusion bonding (DB). These monlithic joints with a corrugated bond interface failed in the steel at a load 2-7 times greater than the load for equivalent joints with planar interfaces. The strength and fracture behaviour of these joints is described.

1. Introduction

There is increasing interest in making joints between dissimilar materials e.g. Ti/Al alloys, Ti/steel, metal/metal matrix composite, in order to exploit the individual properties of these advanced materials, but mechanical joints can present problems. With MMC's it may be difficult to machine to close tolerances and to avoid stress concentrations and with all materials the joints may be susceptable to crevice corrosion or fretting fatigue. Ideally a monolithic joint is required.Such a joint can be produced by diffusion bonding [1,2]. However to avoid the formation of brittle intermetallics at the bond interface it is usually necessary to introduce coatings or foils as diffusion barriers [1,3,4].

A bond interface in a dissimilar metal overlap shear test piece is shown schematically at A-A in Fig.1. The shear plane and bond interface plane are common and the joint shear strength is invariably limited by the strength of the weakest interlayer or intermetallic phase at the bond interface [5]. For this reason the shear strength of a dissimilar metal joint seldom exceeds 60% of the weakest of the two metals being joined and is often very much less than this value. The effect of this low interface strength is accentuated by the planarity of the bond interface which allows cracks once nucleated to propagate rapidly with little energy dissipation [6-9].

It may be possible to manufacture a corrugated bond interface between dissimilar metals and this non-planar interface may lead to a dramatic increase in the strength of the joint. Examples of the interface contours that can be produced when a superplastic alloy

* Now at the Atomic Research Establishment, Aldermaston, Berks.

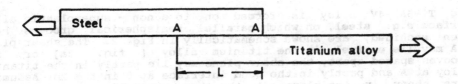

Common shear plane and bond interface A-A

L = Overlap length

Fig 1 Dissimilar metal joint with planar bond interface

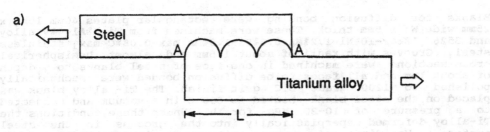

a)

Shear plane in titanium at A-A

b)

Shear plane in titanium at A
and bond interface at B

Fig 2 Corrugated bond interface produced by hemispherical grooves in
a steel surface

e.g Ti-6Al-4V alloy is formed on to a non - superplastic alloy surface e.g. steel, on which parallel hemispherical grooves have been machined, are shown schematically in Figs 2. The shear plane A-A may lie entirely in the titanium alloy [fig. 2a] or, for grooves spaced apart, the shear plane may lie partly in the titanium alloy at A and partly in the bond interface at B in fig.2b. Assuming pure shear in the plane A-A ,the shear strength of the joint will depend either on the shear strength of the Ti-alloy alone [Fig2a] or partly on the shear strength of the Ti-alloy and partly on the shear strength of the bond interface [Fig.2b].

The effect of a simple corrugated diffusion bond interface on the shear and fracture behaviour of Ti-6Al-4V/stainless steel joints has been studied. The results obtained and their significance for the design of high strength dissimilar metal joints are discussed in this paper.

2. Experimental technique.

Blanks for diffusion bonding were rectangular plates 40mm long x 25mm wide[W] x 5mm thick. These were machined from Ti-6%Al-4%V alloy and S526 [18%Cr-10%Ni-1.2%Mn-0.6%Si-1.0%Mn max-0.08%C max] stainless steel. Grooves with radii of about 1.5mm and almost hemispherical cross-sections were machined in one face of steel blanks to a depth of about 1mm and all faces to be diffusion bonded were mechanically polished to 1200 grade SiC grit finish. The Ti- alloy blank was placed on the steel blank, heated to 850 C in a vacuum and subjected to a pressure of 10-20 MPa for 1h. Under these conditions the Ti-alloy deformed superplastically into the grooves in the steel surface. Vanadium and copper foils were inserted between some blanks to produce Ti-alloy /V/Cu/steel diffusion bonded joints; such joints have been shown to have high shear strength [3,4].

In the present programme single overlap shear test pieces were machined from the bonded blanks with with the overlap length L in the range 4.2-12.6 mm as shown in Figs.1 and 2b. In the shear test the tensile axis was aligned in and parallel to the mid-plane of the test piece by the use of spacers at the pin-holes. For grooved test pieces flat plates were lightly clamped across the overlap length to delay the onset of bending and peel. The cross-head speed was about 7mm/min

3. Results

3.1. Manufacture of Ti-6Al-4V/stainless steel joints by SPF/DB.

Hemispherical grooves in a steel surface are shown in a section through a diffusion bonded joint in Fig.3; the grooves at A were completely filled after a deformation of ~14% under a pressure of 15MPa . The macroscopic grain flow in the Ti-alloy near the grooves resembles that for a forged product and this macrostructure is likely to increase the resistance to shear in the Ti- alloy compared with the same shape machined from bar or extruded sections.

Another possibility is the introduction of non-metallic fibres or particulates during the DB stage to form a metal matrix composite and to provide local strengthening near the bond interface. Matrix coated SiC fibres are ideal for this purpose. An example of continuous SiC fibres which have been coated with a Ti-6Al-4V alloy matrix [10] and embedded in Ti-alloy during forming into a groove in a steel surface is shown at A in fig.4.

245

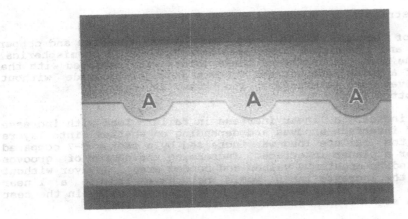

fig 3 Hemi-spherical grooves in steel surface completely filled by superplastically formed Ti-alloy at A, pressure 15MPa .

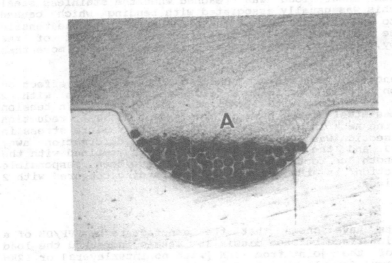

fig 4 Section through Ti-6Al-4V alloy coated 100um diameter SiC-fibres diffusion bonded in Ti-alloy in a groove in the steel surface.

3.2 Shear strength of joints.

A series of bonded joints were made with vanadium and copper interlayers and corrugated interfaces with 1,2 or 3 hemispherical grooves. The shear strengths of these joints were compared with the strengths of a joint made without grooves and joints made without either grooves or interlayers. The shear strength data are plotted in fig.5.

The plots indicate a linear increase in failure load with increase in number of interface grooves and depending on whether interlayers were used the failure load was increased by a factor 2-7 compared with that for a planar interface. Increasing the number of grooves inevitably led to greater L values and bonded area. However without the grooves the increase in L would not have led to a linear increase in load, since peel would have occurred early in the test and led to a significant reduction in the failure load.

3.3 Failure mode of joints

The maximum shear load was reached when the stainless steel deformed and this was usually associated with bending which caused the alloys to peel apart. Although in the soft state the tensile strength of the stainless steel is only about 40% of that of the Ti-6Al-4V alloy, cold work can increase this percentage to more than 80%.

The presence of interlayers appeared to have little effect on the deformation behaviour or failure load of test pieces with 2 grooves. The test piece with 3 grooves [fig.6] failed in tension in the stainless steel at the base of groove 3 at A. The reduction of area in the neck in groove 3 was 30% and the failure stress in the net cross section was 1060MPa.There was little deformation away from groove 3 and the larger overlap length combined with the increased strength due to the interlayers may have been responsible for the reduction in the extent of the bending compared with 2 grooved test piece.

4. Discussion

The results have shown that the manufacture by SPF/DB of a corrugated DB interface between dissimilar metals increased the load for failure of the joint from ~3KN [with no interlayers] or 12KN [with interlayers] for planar interfaces to ~21KN for the test piece with interlayers and 3 grooves. The increase in load with increase in the number of grooves may reflect the greater resistance to crack growth and to peel along the bond interface in this type of joint The problem of peel clearly only arises in the type of stressing experienced in the overlap test piece. In components the design would ensure that the DB joint was subjected to shear stresses only.

A corrugated DB interface might be manufactured between two closely matched machined parts but the machining costs could be prohibitive. The combination of part machining one metal to a low tolerance and superplastic forming the second metal offers lower costs as well as better grain flow characteristics at the interface.

Of particular significance in the present tests is the ability of the monolithic diffusion bonded corrugated joint to transfer the shear load to the base metal and away from the weaker bond interface

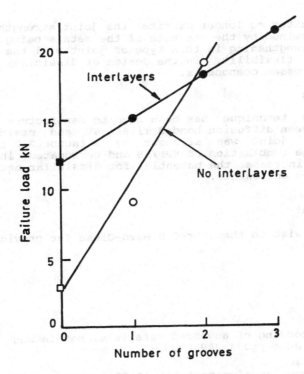

fig 5   Failure load v number of grooves for Ti-alloy/stainless
         steel overlap shear test pieces.

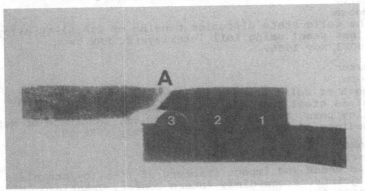

fig 6   3 groove test piece after tensile failure in stainless
         steel, side view .

so that the latter no longer dictates the joint strength, which may now be determined by the strength of the metals being joined. The mechanical strengthening in this type of joint will therefore allow much greater flexibility in the design of dissimilar metal joints for highly stressed components.

5. Conclusions

An SPF/DB technique has been used to manufacture a corrugated interface between diffusion bonded Ti-6Al-4V and stainless steel. This type of joint was stronger by a factor 2-7 than a planar interface. The combination of SPF/DB and corrugated interfaces is expected to increase the potential for dissimilar metal joints in highly stressed components.

Acknowledgement

The authors wish to thank Dr C M Ward-Close for providing fig.8.

REFERENCES

1 P G Partridge
   C M W-Close
   Diffusion bonding of advanced materials. Metals and
   Materials June pp334-339 1989

2 P G Partridge
   Diffusion bonding of materials. AGARD Lecture series
   No.168 on Superplasticity pp 5.1-5.29 Oct 1989

3 T S Baker
   P S Moore
   On the solid state diffusion bonding of Ti-6Al-4V alloy to
   stainless steel using foil interlayers. RAE Tech
   Rep 86073 Nov 1986.

4 T S Baker
   P S Moore
   Strength of solid state diffusion bonded joints between
   stainless steel 304L and IMI318 and between IMI550
   Ti-alloy bars. Designing with Titanium, Institute of Metals
   Proceedings of Bristol Conference, July 1986 p87

5 T S Baker
   P G Partridge
   Tensile shear and impact fracture of Ti-alloy/stainless
   steel joints. Proceedings Intern Confer, Cranfield July
   1987 p103-104.

6 J R Williams
   Welding technology in the aircraft industry. American
   Welding Society p55 1981

7 P G Partridge
   D V Dunford
   On the testing of diffusion bonded overlap joints between
   clad Al-Zn-Mg alloy sheet. RAE TR 86033 June 1986. J Mater.
   Sc. 22 1597-1608 1987

8   D V Dunford
    P G Partridge
    Peel strengths of diffusion bonded joints between clad
    Al-alloy sheet. J Mater. Sc. 22 1790-1798 1987

9   D V Dunford
    P G Partridge
    Strength and fracture behaviour of diffusion bonded joints
    in Al-Li (8090) alloy   Part 1 Shear strength. RAE TR 89052
    Sept 1989

10 C M W-Close
    P G Partridge
    A fibre coating process for advanced metal matrix
    composites   RAE TR 89033 July 1989

HIP-diffusion bonding of ODS-materials by use of plasma sprayed encapsulation

by

K.H. Hammelmann H.P. Buchkremer, and D. Stöver
Institut für Angewandte Werkstofforschung
Forschungszentrum GmbH Jülich/Germany

ABSTRACT

Diffusion bonding is a possible joining for ODS-materials. The Hot - Isostatic - Pressure (HIP) bonding technique for the three different ODS-materials MA6000, MA754, MA956 and the alloy Incoloy800H by use of mild steel- capsules as well as by application of the plasma spray encapsulation technique was studied.

In the first stage of experiments the optimum HIP-parameters have been determined, while in the second stage the method of Low-Pressure-Plasma-Spray (LPPS) encapsulation has been investigated. Some variation of surface roughness were conducted as well. The quality of the bonds has been checked by tensile strength measurements and metallography.

1. Introduction

Diffusion-welding of ODS-alloys by means of the HIP-bonding-technique offers several well known advantages not offered by other joining processes /1,2,3/. Because of the evident differences in their temperature dependent strength the investigated ODS-materials require the knowledge of exact bonding conditions. So in the first stage of experiments the proper HIP-conditions have to be determined.

The HIP-parameters (hold time, temperature and pressure) have been varied in a certain range taking care of the limited number of available specimens.

Two cylindrical rods of 8 mm in diameter x 30 mm in length were put into a mild steel capsule. The capsule was electron beam welded under vacuum conditions and then HIP'ed. In order to determine the optimum HIP-parameters 42 pairs have been investigated (s. Table 1).

Twelve specimens No. 47 - 49 were LPPS encapsulated. This method of encapsulation promises more simplicity and in some cases savings compared to the usual encapsulation technique. Therefore, in the second stage of experimental runs all the specimens (Table 3) have been LPPS encapsuled. To determine the influence of roughness in terms of bond strength was a further aim of this series of experiments.

2. Specimen Preparation

The processing route with the single steps of fabrication of LPPS encapsulated specimens are shown in Fig. 1.
The two cylindrical rods were mounted in the LPPS vacuum chamber. Then the chamber was evacuated to $(3 - 5) \cdot 10^{-2}$ mbar and the sample surface was sputtered to remove oxides and adsorbed impurities. After that plasma spraying was carried out at an Argon pressure of about 50 mbar. A coating with about 40 mm width and $500 - 800$ μm in thickness was sprayed on both cylinders resulting in one specimen consisting of two gastight bonded cylinders. After cooling down and He-leak testing the prefixed samples were diffusion bonded by a subsequent HIP step.

The coating materials used consisted of the Steel 100 Cr6 as well as the superalloy UDIMET 700. Both metal powders had a grain size distribution < 45 μm and were sprayed with a Leybold AG LPPS facility (Plasma gun: Electroplasma 03 CA) applying the in table 2 listed parameters.

After HIP'ing the joined rods were machined to a tensile/creep test specimen. Under equal HIP conditions two identical specimens of each material combination (Table 1) were fabricated in order to carry out tensile tests at RT as well as at 800°C, whereby the tensile strength, yield strength and elongation could be determined.

3. Mechanical testing results

Table 1 shows the results of the tensile tests. In the first part of table 1 (No. 1 - 24) the HIP-conditions are different, in order to obtain the proper welding parameters for the following tests in the second part (table 1 No. 25 - 49).

During machining 24 specimens of 95 failed. The most part of these specimens were HIP'ed at a low pressure of 40 MPa. As a consequence a HIP pressure of 40 MPa turned out to be unsufficient. A higher pressure is required for the materials (MA754, MA6000) with resulting high strength at elavated temperatures. The obtained bonding strength vs. HIP-pressure is shown in Fig. 2 - 4. As can be seen from Fig. 3 and 4 the bonding strength increases with HIP-pressure for MA754 and MA6000. Within the shown limits no dependence on HIP-pressure is visible in Fig. 2 for MA956.

No difference in bonding strength has been detected between the two applied HIP-temperatures (1050°C and 1150°C). For further experiments the lower temperature was used avoiding recristallisation effects which occur at the elevated temperatures. The hold time should be kept as low as possible because of grain growth effects and other microstructural changes /1/. Some specimens failed after a time of 0.5 h; a hold time t = 2.0 - 2.5 h seemed to be suitable for further experiments.

In Fig. 5 the Ni and Fe diffusional profiles (elemental line scans of EDX) for 3 specimens of the material combination M754/Incoloy 800H are shown. The bond strength of the 3 specimens are equal in a range of ± 10 % (Table 1). The fracture of the specimens 29w + 30k occured in the bond zone, of 29k in the base material of Incoloy 800H. This curves show a significant interdiffusion of Ni and Fe in the respective joining partner.

An other example is displayed in Fig. 6 giving the Fe and Ni profiles for the material combination MA956/Incoloy800H. Two curves of the specimens 14w and 37w show a good interdiffusion. In these cases the fracture occured in the base material of MA956, whereas specimen 36k shows a steep gradient in concentration thus indicating poor diffusion in the bonding zone. Here the fracture occured in the bond zone at a tensile strength of ~ 50 % reference value of base material of MA956. The experimental conditions for the specimens 36k, 14 w and 37w were identical, so further investigations will be necessary.

The following parameters could cause unsufficient bonding strength:

a) **Untightness** of the capsule leading to ineffective HIP-pressure
b) **Precipitation** of elements and recristallisation in the bonding zone
c) **Too large roughness** of the bonding surfaces

ad a) The leaktests of the specimen has been elaborately performed, however, for the LPPS-specimens further developments are necessary to improve the leaktest procedure.

ad b) With means of Scanning-Electron-Microscop (SEM) some precipitation and recristallisation effects have been measured. Fig. 10a and 10b show metallographic SEM-pictures of the specimen 29k. The fracture occured in the base material, the bonding zone is visible in the middle of the pictures. An agglomeration of Ti and Al particles (light points probably TiO_2 and Al_2O_3) in the bonding zone is visible. This has been obtained for many specimens, but no reduction in strength has been observed for this specimens. Some optical microscop (OM) and SEM investigations were made, a change in grain structure has'nt been observed.

ad c) The roughness influence of the bonding surface as function of the strength has been examined. The roughness Ra (DIN 4762) is defined:

$$Ra = \frac{1}{X_m} \int_0^{X_m} |Y| \cdot dx$$

x, y = system of coordinates

Table 3 summarized the results of the roughness and tensile tests.

The LPPS encapsulated specimens were HIP'ed for 2.5 h hold-time, at 200 MPa pressure and 1050°C temperature.
Fig. 7 - 9 show the tensile strength as function of the roughness Ra. No roughness influence is visible for the pairs Incoloy 800H/MA754, Inc. 800H/MA956, Inc. 800H/MA6000 and MA956/MA956. That's not admissible for the pairs MA754/MA754 and MA6000/MA6000. The roughness has been flattened by the HIP-pressure for the weaker material Incoloy800H and MA956. The material flow strength at the HIP-temperature is essentially lower (R_{max}~60MPa) as the applied HIP-pressure (P_{HIP}=200MPa). The material strength for MA754 and MA6000 on the other hand applied lies above the HIP-pressure. A HIP-pressure of 400 MPa - not applied here but possible with the HIP-II facility - will be sufficient to flatten the harder MA754 and MA6000. Generally, one can state that the influence of the bond surface roughness is unimportant if sufficiently high HIP-pressures are applied. Optical microscopic investigations of the bond surface confirmed this.

The investigation of the LPPS encapsulated series showed, that 10 specimens (of 38) failed during machining (table 3). The failure rate up to now is higher as for the tube encapsulating. As stated above the leaktest must be improved, because HIP-pressure is at least partly ineffective, if the encapsulation is untight. But the experiments confirmend that the LPPS encapsulation is a simple and practicable method for HIP-diffusion bonding.

4. Conclusions

The correct choice of HIP-parameters is essential for HIP-diffusion bonding of ODS-materials. To avoid uncontrolled recristallisation, for all the investigated materials (MA754, MA956, MA6000 and Inc.800H) the upper value of temperature should be limited to 1050°C. The minimum HIP-pressure which is necessary depends on the material used. For MA956 and Incoloy800H we recommend a HIP-pressure range of 150 - 200 MPa, for MA754 = 250 - 350 MPa and MA6000 = 380 - 400 MPa. Using these parameters the welding-time of 2.0 - 2.5 h is sufficient with respect to undesired grain growth and formation of brittle phases. The influence of the bond surface roughness is negligible if a correct choice of the HIP-pressure is performed. Furthermore, the experiments have qualified the method of LPPS-encapsulation, however, in order to reduce the failure rate the applied leaktest method must be improved.

5. References

/1/ C. Verport, M. Wazmy
    HIP-diffusion bonding of ODS MA6000
    3rd Int. Conference London, 1986.

/2/ D. Stöver, H.P. Buchkremer
    HIP-diffusion bonding of ODS-material
    2nd Int. HIP-Conf. Gaithersburg, 1989.

/3/ Z. Wisenholz, J. Mironi
    Diffusion bonding of stainless steel 304L
    Haifa, Israel, 1986.

Table 1

HIP-Parameter and Results of Tensile testing for HIP-bonded ODS-Alloys

No.	Materialcombinat.	Specimen-quantity	HIP-parameter time/pres./temp	Tens. strength		Yield strength		Elongation	
				RT	800°C	RT	800°C	RT	800°C
-	-	-	h /MPa /°C	MPa	MPa	MPa	MPa	%	%
1	MA754/MA754	2	2.0/ 40/1050			no results			
2	"	2	2.0/ 40/1150	521	n.r.	459	n.r.	-	-
3	"	2	2.0/360/1050	806	202	496	~100	-	1.94
4	"	2	2.0/360/1150	839	186	481	~100	-	2.96
5	"	2	0.5/ 40/1150			no results			
6	"	2	8.0/ 40/1150			"			
7	MA956/MA956	2	2.0/ 40/1050			no results			
8	"	2	2.0/ 40/1150	893	39	720	-	10.90	57.40
9	"	2	2.0/360/1050	715	53	700	-	0.43	32.0
10	"	2	2.0/360/1150	725	49	700	47	2.58	69.84
11	"	2	0.5/ 40/1150			no results			
12	"	2	8.0/ 40/1150			"			
13	MA956/Incol.	1	2.0/ 40/1050			no results			
14	"	1	2.0/ 40/1150	-	61	-	59		
15	"	1	2.0/360/1050	-	61	-	59		
16	"	1	2.0/360/1150	-	58	-	59	n.r.	
17	"	1	0.5/ 40/1150			no results			
18	"	1	8.0/ 40/1150	-	59	-	57		
19	MA6000/MA6000	2	2.0/ 40/1050			no results			
20	"	2	2.0/ 40/1150			"			
21	"	2	2.0/360/1050	1151	n.r.	1117	n.r.	1.34	1.35
22	"	2	2.0/360/1150	n.r.	530	n.r.		n.r.	2.15
23	"	2	0.5/ 40/1150			no results			
24	"	2	8.0/ 40/1150			"			
25	MA754/MA754	2	2.5/120/1150	729	132	475	106	9.08	0.86
26	"	2	"	583	n.r.	478	n.r.	3.38	
27	"	2	"	n.r.	124	n.r.	-		1.29
28	Ma754/MA754	2	"	627	220	487		5.6	2.8
29	MA754/Incoloy	2	"	518	147	186			
30	MA754/Incoloy	2	"	472	171	174			
31	MA956/MA956	2	"	739	51	702	45	1.45	26.80
32	"	2	"	236	52	174	45	1.83	31.99
33	"	2	"	881	47	710	42	3.33	127.20
34	"	1	"	794	-	690			
35	MA956/MA956	2	"	831	190	800	~90	0.8	11.8
36	MA956/Incoloy	1	"	292	-	227			
37	MA956/Incoloy	2	"	233	56	229	55		
38	MA956/Incoloy	2	2.5/120/1150	n.r.	136	n.r.	~90		
39	MA6000/MA6000	2	2.5/200/1150	1071	315	1058	-	0.59	0.59
40	"	2	"	915	275	910	-	0.48	6.88
41	"	1	"	1127		1036	-	2.10	
42	"	2	"	1123	n.r.	1098	-	0.10	
43	"	2	"	1040	258	1040		0.38	
44	MA6000/MA6000	2	"	891	40	726	-	8.6	143.0
45	MA6000/Incoloy	2	"	468	127	320	98		
46	MA6000/Incoloy	2	2.5/200/1150	282	36	227	34		
47	MA956/MA956(LPPS)	4	2.5/120/1150	663	67	663	-	1.94	19.4
48	MA956/MA956(LPPS)	4	2.5/120/1150	732	55,52	692	-	65.5	57.1
49	MA956/MA956(LPPS)	4	2.5/120/1050	204	52	204	-	1.18	59.6

Table 2
LPPS encapsulation parameter

Plasma features	LPPS run No.1	LPPS Run No.2
material	100 Cr6	Udimet 700
chamber pressure	55 mbar	55 mbar
sputter current	150 A	150 A
plasma "	1395 A	1420 A
power (elektr.)	51 kw	60 kw
carrier gas	7 slpm	7 slpm
powder feed rate	¯ 90 g/min	¯ 94 g/min

Table 3
Mechanical test results of HIP bonded ODS alloys by different surface roughness
HIP-conditions: p = 200 MPa, t = 2.5 h, T = 1050°C

Nr.	Materialcombinat.	Number	Roughness Ra measured value	Tensile strength RT	800°C	Yield strength RT	800°C	Elongation RT	800°C
-	-	piece	µm(max)	MPa	MPa	MPa	MPa	%	%
1	MA754/Incoloy 800H	2	0.42	550	134	226	≈100	27.32	2.46
2	"	2	4.50	547[1]	160	207	≈100	57.30	2.79
3	"	2	25.50	532[1]	36	228	36	46.50	0.82
4	"	2	2.50	384	126	290	≈100	4.10	0.44
5	"	2	0.45+25.5	442	191	430	≈100	12.80	5.69
6	MA754/MA754	2	0.45	554	51	474	51	1.23	0.03
7	"	2	21.5	468	131	443	131	0.82	0.41
8	MA956/Incoloy 800H	2	0.42	n.r.	201[1]	n.r.	≈120	n.r.	48.60
9	"	2	4.2	438	121	223	≈120	10.90	2.90
10	"	2	24.1	n.r.	184[1]	o.E.	≈120	n.r.	67.90
11	"	2	3.5	n.r.	132	n.r.	¯120	n.r.	14.65
12	"	2	0.40+26.1	208	193	191	≈120	0.55	14.00
13	MA956/MA956	2	0.4	n.r.	164[1]	n.r.	≈120	n.r.	37.71
14	"	2	20.52	132	142[1]	v.B.	≈120	0.11	38.80
15	MA6000/Incoloy 800H	2	0.6	454,449	n.r.	216,252	n.r.	7.7,17.4 n.r.	
16	"	2	23.5	n.r.	221,122	o.E.	≈100	n.r. 9.6,1.6	
17	"	2	4.1	238	156	228	≈100	0.26	1.86
18	MA6000/MA6000	2	0.4	1167	96	1152	v.B.	0.60	0.97
19	"	2	21.1	582	104	v.B.	"	0.27	0.52

Index 1: Fracture in bulk material
Index 2: n.r. no results (Fracture by machining)

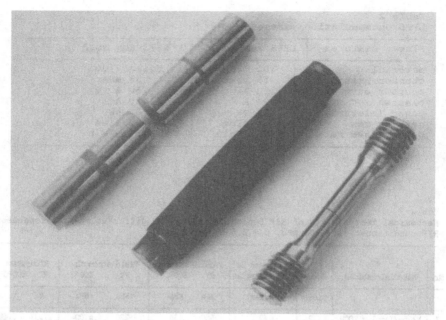

Fig. 1a Steps of fabrication for LPPS tensile/creep specimen

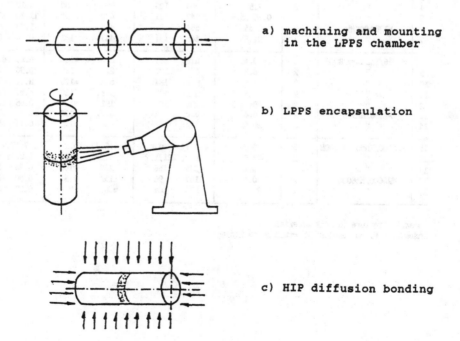

a) machining and mounting
   in the LPPS chamber

b) LPPS encapsulation

c) HIP diffusion bonding

**Fig. 1b Schematic of the plasma sprayed encapsulation and
HIP diffusion bonding**

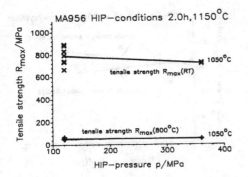

Fig.2 Tensile strength versus HIP pressure (MA956)

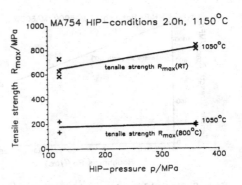

Fig.3 Tensile strength versus HIP pressure (MA754)

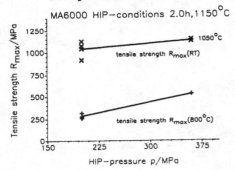

Fig.4 Tensile strength versus HIP pressure (MA6000)

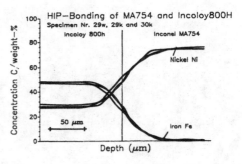

Fig.5 Diffusion profile of Nickel and Iron

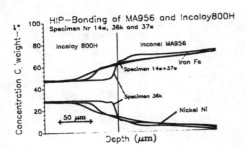

Fig.6 Diffusion profile of Ni and Fe (MA956)

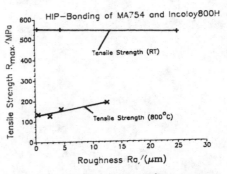

Fig.7 Tensile strength versus roughness (MA754/Inc 800)

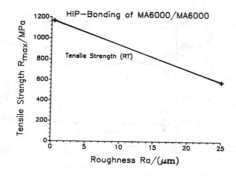

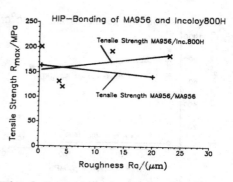

Fig.8 Tensile strength versus roughness (MA6000/MA6000)

Fig.9 Tensile strength versus roughness (MA956/Inc800)

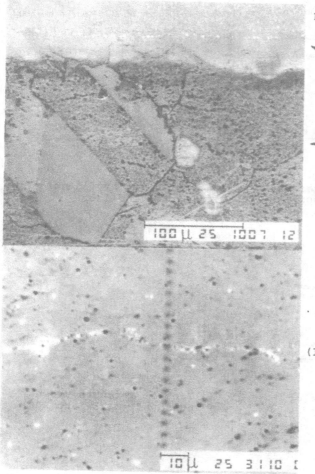

Fig. 10a Bonding zone of specimen 29k (line scan EDX)

MA754

Incoloy 800H

Fig. 10b Bonding zone of specimen 29k (light points AL and Ti)

COMPONENT ASSEMBLY USING HIP DIFFUSION BONDING

R M Walker . D J Roberts . and B A Rickinson

INFUTEC Limited, Chesterfield

This paper reviews the application of process conditions developed in HIP equipment to generate sound metal-to-metal diffusion bonds. A number of examples are chosen to illustrate the capabilities of the process: modular valve assembly from stock components; valve cladding by sheet material; ultrasonic test block manufacture, and a multi-alloy part assembled from a variety of starting materials. The capabilities for solid stage diffusion bonding over large areas by HIP with a resulting narrow and controlled diffusion are evident from the examples chosen.

1. Diffusion Bonding - The Process Options

The process of diffusion bonding is by no means new but has been considered for over 25 years as somewhat theoretical and having only limited practical use. During the past five years, as a direct consequence of the requirements of the aerospace industry, much interest and considerable resources have been diverted to process development. Probably the most publicised area of investigation has been concerned with the manufacture, on a fully commercial basis, of superplastically formed/diffusion bonded panel structures in titanium and its alloys to create light weight components of high specific stiffness. This increase in interest has created, not unexpectedly, a wide range of potential applications for the process, sometimes in areas where joining of particular combinations of materials was thought impossible.

In simple terms diffusion bonding is defined as the process of joining two components by atomic movement, where the relative numbers of atoms crossing the interface in both directions is controlled by the activation energies of diffusion for the various atomic species. To a large extent the overall interface reaction rate is controlled by the temperature at which the bonding operation is carried out and the time of exposure at elevated temperature.

It is important to reflect that diffusion bonding occurs in the solid state. It therefore follows that such a joining technique offers many advantages over conventional fusion processes in that there is no heat affected zone and no cast structure. Under ideal conditions the strength of the bond produced should be at least the same as the weaker of the materials being joined.

Diffusion bonding can be practiced in two principle forms. Using the uniaxial diffusion bonding approach, the materials to be joined are held together under a modest uniaxial load, typically around 10 MPa. The temperature - pressure combination is such as to allow bonding without plastic yielding. This process has been used successfully for some years although it is somewhat limited by the geometry and size of the materials to be joined.

The second category, that of diffusion bonding using Hot Isostatic Pressing is limited only by the size of HIP vessel and the particular combination of materials. Hot Isostatic Pressing or HIPping has been used for more than 25 years to remove discreet internal porosity from a range of engineering materials with the overall aim of increasing quality and part performance.

The HIPping process (Fig. 1) involves subjecting components to simultaneous elevated temperature and pressure for a period of time. Isostatic gas pressure is developed by means of a high purity gas, usually argon. By contrast this process relies on the yield strength of the material at the elevated temperature, typically 2/3 Tm, being lower than that of the surrounding gas pressure. If this criteria is fulfilled then discreet or non surface breaking voids within the body of the component will shrink in size by plastic flow induced by the net external stress. At an advanced stage of densification internal surfaces of the pore are squeezed together to allow diffusion across the prior pore surfaces. A diffusion bond is thus formed and the defect is completely removed from the material.

If we consider the analogous situation where surface asperities touch, then provided the gaps between the mating surfaces are sealed from the external HIPping atmosphere the HIPping process will treat the interfacial voidage as a series of discrete pores. In this way solid phase joining of materials with complex geometry can be effectively controlled.

Figure 1 - Modern Hot Isostatic presses have the
capability to process diffusion bonded
structures up to 1.15 m in diameter and
2.2 m in height. Temperature control
may be varied between 300 - 1410°C and
gas pressures up to 103 MPa (15,000 psi).

(Photograph - Courtesy of H.I.P. Limited, Chesterfield)

2. Diffusion Bonding for Valve Manufacture

2.1 Modular Valve Construction

The production of specialised body castings and to some extent forgings, has long been a problem for valve manufacturers. This stems mainly from the high cost of patterns and tools which often need to be amortised within a short production run. From a supply standpoint the production lead time on new designs of valve bodies where patterns and the manufacturing methodology do not exist, can be measured in months rather than weeks. Clearly, in both cases this situation may be unacceptable to the end user. If a typical valve body is analysed, its various features may be broken down into functional modules. Figure 2 illustrates a titanium valve body that has been manufactured from a collection of bar stock components of very simple geometry by HIP diffusion bonding. Individual segments are seal welded together to allow each interface pocket to be evacuated. Thereafter the product was HIP processed at 920°C for 3 hours at 15,000 psi to develop a high integrity monolithic structure. The advantages of this type of "modular construction" are very considerable, and some specific points are listed below:

1) Ability to reduce manufacturing times - bar material - ex-stock.

2) Overall flexibility to custom-design one-off parts.

3) Wide application of technique to all forms of material supply (cast and wrought stock and powder).

4) Improved cost effectiveness for small batch quantities.

5) Improved mechanical properties and integrity by comparison to through penetration welds or cast parts.

6) No patterns required.

2.2 Valve Surfacing

Although Figure 2 illustrates a technique involving the bonding of similar materials it has already been demonstrated that the flanges or internal bore/seat structures can be modified to suit use, ie, to provide increased resistance to corrosion and erosion caused by contaminated oil or sour gas. The common high strength steels tend to be rather poor in their susceptibility to stress corrosion cracking and therefore it is popular practice to weld deposit corrosion resistant materials

265

Figure 2 – A cross branched valve body in titanium
alloy produced by HIP diffusion bonding
of bar stock sections. Diameter of top
flange – 130 mm

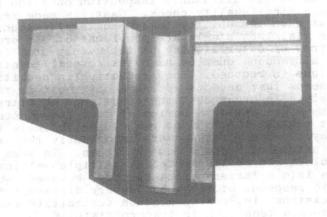

Figure 3 – Half section of an alloy steel bonnet
component clad on all internal surfaces
with IN625 bar tube and consolidated powder.

within the internal cavities. Welding access is a
potential problem for such finishing.

Using the same principle of modular construction by HIP
a well-head component has been produced that uses a high
strength alloy steel blank with a corrosion resistant
material bonded to all the wetted surfaces, (Fig. 3).
Such corrosion resistant materials can be used in the
form of cut lengths of tube and discs of sheet material,
or as powder. By means of encapsulation and subsequent
evacuation procedures the assembly may be prepared for
HIPping to effect diffusion bonds between the high
strength steel and IN625, C263 etc. Ancillary
encapsulating materials are usually removed after HIP
processing to expose the clad surfaces. The advantages
of this method of construction are as follows.

1) Potential cost saving on construction when
   compared to machining from solid bar or forged
   blanks of the desired high value material.

2) No macro dilution effects from the application of
   the corrosion resistant material at the interface
   unlike a fusion welded deposit.

3) Improved quality control when compared to a
   manual or semi automatic welding process.

4) Freedom from internal defects.

3. Implanting of Defects for Test Block Applications

The inspection of large castings weighing upwards of 3 tonnes
is often made extremely difficult by the combination of
material analysis and casting geometry. For such parts it is
common practise to use ultrasonic inspection on a 100 per
cent basis as a final quality check. Castings made from
materials that have the ability to attenuate ultrasound such
as austenitic stainless steels are problematic. In order
that these types of materials may be fully inspected the
frequency of ultrasound must be such that overall sensitivity
of the technique is reduced. This reduction in sensitivity
effectively means that defects are more difficult to find and
size accurately. In order that the competence of ultrasonics
operators can be evaluated, a series of test components are
required that contain the type of real defects likely to be
encountered by the inspectors. More importantly the exact
position and nature of defects must be known. In some cases
such a test block can be fabricated by multiple welding of
small defects into a larger parent casting, however, where
the ultrasonic response of the weld is very different from
that of the casting, ie. coarse grained austenititc stainless
steels then such a technique is inappropriate.

In such cases an implant block of equivalent grain structure
to the casting and containing the known defects is positioned
within a machined pocket on the casting and seal welded into

place. The seal weld forms a gastight envelope between the
parent casting and the implant block which is subsequently
evacuated and sealed. The whole assembly is then HIPped and
in turn a diffusion bond between the implant block and parent
casting is formed. After removal of the light seal weld and
suitable disguise of the defect (if this is surface breaking)
the assembly is checked for the integrity of the bond
interfaces. It has been shown that the bond interface
between the implant block and the parent casting is
transparent to ultrasound using the common probe frequencies
used for inspection in the UK and USA.

For some applications, as for example in the manufacture of
simple training blocks, planar defects may be implanted in
predetermined positions. Ultrasonic reflectors for example
mica sheets may be positioned at the bottom of flat bottomed
holes which are later filled by plugs of similar substrate
material. The diffusion bonding of the assembly provides an
outwardly perfect component whose internal structure is
flawed in precise locations. Such a technique is clearly
ideal for classroom demonstrations, or for calibration in the
field. The effect of the thermal cycle during HIP processing
has been shown to have no measurable effect on ultrasonic
response before and after processing.

4.   A Multi-alloy Modular Approach

In a logical extension of the HIP bonding technology it is
clearly evident that the following opportunities are
available by the process.

1)   Solid to solid diffusion bonding.

2)   Solid to powder diffusion bonding.

3)   Diffusion bonding of similar materials.

4)   Diffusion bonding of dissimilar materials, (with and
without alloy interlayers.

Purely as a technology demonstrator the "flywheel" type
component, see Fig. 4 has been manufactured. This component
effectively shows the ease by which dissimilar materials can
be joined together in a single HIP processing operation. In
this example the ends of the shaft have been clad to enhance
corrosion and perhaps rolling fatigue properties by the
application of a nickel base alloy consolidated from a powder
alloy. The large collar has been machined from a disc of
alloy steel and subsequently diffusion bonded to the shaft of
similar composition thereby demonstrating the ability to
substantially reduce both material and machining costs. Bars
of a Monel alloy have been diffusion bonded into the collar
at regular intervals to form part of a revolution counting
device. Finally, to provide corrosion protection within the
cooling water channel on the shaft axis, an austenitic
stainless steel tube has been diffusion bonded to the
ferritic mild steel body. It should be restated that all

a)

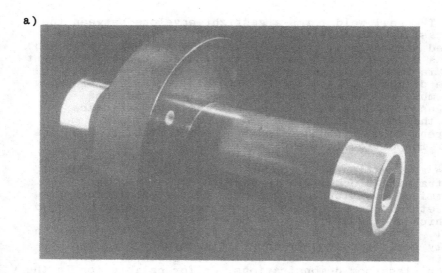

b)

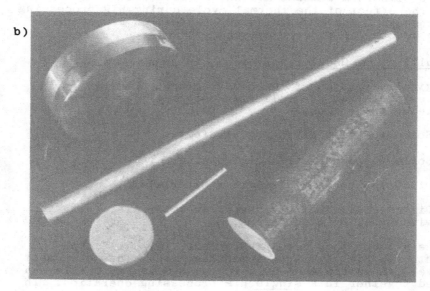

Figure 4 – The fully finished multi alloy flywheel
shown in a) should be contrasted to the
stock material depicted in b) utilised for
HIP bonding construction.

    i)   Alloy steel bar for shaft and collar.
   ii)   Stainless steel tube for central liner.
 iii)   Monel bar for rev. counter insertions.
  iv)   Nickel based alloy powder used to
        prepare bearing surfaces.

such high integrity interface bonding effects were developed within one thermal treatment.

5. Conclusion

The practical implications for HIP diffusion bonding are only now being fully realised. This situation has been substantially influenced by the increasing size of HIP equipment leading to consequent improvements in process economics. Engineering designs whose material selection has been compromised by traditional manufacturing methods can now be re-assessed to utilise expensive materials cost effectively. HIP diffusion bonding has developed a niché which is set for expansion.

Diffusion Bonded Windows for Diagnostics of Fusion Plasmas
H J Milton, A A Newton, H H H Watson
AEA Fusion, UKAEA/Euratom Fusion Association,
Culham Laboratory, Abingdon, Oxon OX14 3DB, UK

1. Introduction

At Culham the technique of diffusion bonding has been developed for joining
optically transparent materials to metal housings to make windows for fusion plasma
experiments. These windows are used for optical access to the plasma chamber
both for viewing the natural emissions of the plasma in the ultra violet to the
infra-red wavelength range and for the use of probing laser beams. The windows
have the advantage of ultra high vacuum capability with prolonged high
temperature service and are used on machines such as JET (Joint European Torus
located at Culham) and other large plasma machines around the world.

The diffusion bonding technique in this case joins quite dissimilar materials, one of
which is brittle. The usual method of matching expansion coefficients of materials
is not always possible and we have used interlayers of ductile metals. In addition
to joining the usual window materials we have developed this process to produce
ceramic to metal joints for insulating vacuum feed-throughs using alumina and
machinable glass ceramics.

In this paper we describe the requirements for windows for fusion experiments,
the methods of production with special emphasis on the diffusion bonding and we
list the sizes and performance achieved. Circular windows up to $\varphi = 130$ mm
diameter have been supplied and are in routine use.

Application to Fusion Plasma Machines

A variety of optical techniques are used to study and measure the properties of
plasma produced within fusion plasma machines such as JET. Optical access to the

metal containment vessel is required through high-specification windows of crystalline quartz, synthetic sapphire and fused silica. Commercially produced windows are not available which combine adequate optical performance, prolonged high temperature capability and suitability for use in high transient magnetic fields at up to several tesla.

The specification for windows is:-

1. Ultra High Vacuum (UHV) quality with a guaranteed leak rate of less than 10^{-9} millibar litre per second.

2. All materials to be non-magnetic.

3. Fully bakeable on a repetitive basis to at least 400 and preferably 500°C with a life at high temperature greater than 3000 hours.

4. High transparency throughout the ultra-violet to far infra-red wavelength and millimetre microwave ranges.

5. Various geometries for many mounting configurations.

6. To be fitted to the plasma vessel by remote control TIG welding.

The initial requirement was for windows of crystalline quartz for transmitting laser light at 3.5 and 200 μm wavelengths for interferometers to measure the plasma electron density. This material has anisotropic expansion characteristics and suffers a phase change at 573°C accompanied by expansion anomalies and a high risk of shattering. Together, these properties preclude the use of conventional window sealing geometries, and also the use of conventional sealing processes which either rely on the high temperature metallisation of the joint interface, or on brazing at high temperatures with active-metal containing alloys. The UHV requirements (bakeability and low vapour pressure) also preclude the use of activated low temperature solders used in some commercial windows, the use of silver chloride as a cement, or of any known organic adhesives.

The technique of using an expansion-matched glass frit as a high temperature cement (as suggested by Mozeleski[1] at Princeton) was further developed at Culham. However, windows could not be made to meet the JET bake-out requirements and the bonding layer was prohibitively brittle. Instead, we overcame all the foregoing problems by developing ductile interlayer diffusion bonding techniques.

2 Problems in Sealing to Quartz

2.1 Thermal Expansion Behaviour

Crystalline quartz has similar mechanical properties to most common glasses, being brittle and having relatively low tensile strength. Hence when sealed into a metal housing to make a window it is important to ensure that the tensile components of thermal stresses in the quartz due to differential expansion between quartz and metal are kept to appropriately low values. Such stresses can develop both during initial cooling from the sealing temperature and subsequent thermal cycling in service. The magnitude of these stresses depends on the thermal expansion characteristics of the quartz, of the metal to which it is sealed and of the sealing material, the elastic moduli of these materials and the sealing geometry. It also depends on the yield strengths/creep strengths of the metal and sealing material over the temperature range from ambient to the solidus of the bonding material or, if fusion is not involved, the temperature of bonding.

The structure and optical behaviour of crystalline quartz is anisotropic. This requires diagnostic windows for JET to be "Z-cut" ie to be orientated so that the plane of the windows is perpendicular to the crystalline optical Z axis. The anisotropy of structure likewise results in anisotropic thermal expansion. The thermal expansion behaviour is also dramatically affected by a phase-change from

Expansion of crystalline quartz and 304 stainless steel
against temperature.
Fig.1

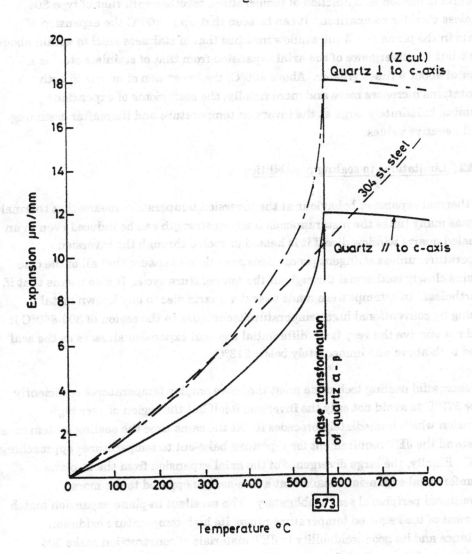

α quartz to β quartz at the "inversion" temperature of 573°C. These expansion characteristics are summarised in Figure 1, where the fractional thermal expansion of quartz is plotted as a function of temperature, together with that of type 304 stainless steel for comparison. It can be seen that up to 400°C the expansion of quartz in the plane of a Z cut window matches that of stainless steel to within about 0.02% but the divergence of the axial expansion from that of stainless steel is a factor of about 9 times greater. Above 400°C, the expansion of quartz in both orientations increases more and more rapidly, the coefficients of expansion becoming indefinitely large at the inversion temperature and thereafter assuming small negative values.

2.2 Limitations to sealing possibilities

The thermal expansion behaviour at the inversion temperature means that thermal stresses many times the instantaneous fracture strength can be induced even in an unsealed quartz window disc if it is heated or cooled through the inversion temperature, unless stringent precautions are taken to ensure that all of the disc remains closely isothermal throughout the temperature cycle. It also means that if, nevertheless, an attempt were made to seal a quartz disc to any known metal housing by conventional high temperature techniques in the region of 800-850°C it could not survive the very large differential thermal expansion stresses as the seal cooled both above and immediately below 573°C.

Any successful sealing technique must therefore employ temperatures sufficiently below 573°C to avoid not only the inversion itself but the region of very high expansion which immediately precedes it. At the same time the sealing system must withstand the JET requirement for repetitive bake-out to temperatures approaching 500°C. Finally, the large divergence of the axial expansion from the in-plane circumferential expansion means that a face-seal as opposed to the more conventional peripheral seal is obligatory. The excellent in-plane expansion match over most of the required temperature range, its high temperature oxidation resistance and its good weldability to JET materials of construction make 304 stainless steel the preferred non-magnetic material for such a face-seal. However, no low vapour pressure brazing alloy for making the joint between stainless steel and quartz was commercially available. It would have needed to have an active-metal content and a solidus above 500°C, yet a liquidus safely below the inversion temperature. Development of such an alloy did not appear to be easy. Even had such an alloy been available, problems in limiting its uncontrolled spread over the optical aperture seemed likely. By contrast, some relevant previous experience in the Group made solid-state diffusion bonding, using ductile aluminium interlayers, seem an extremely viable method of sealing which would solve all of the foregoing problems. This turned out to be the case.

3 Development of Diffusion Bonding for Crystal Quartz Windows

3.1 Relevant Previous Experience

The Special Techniques Group at Culham first made vacuum-tight aluminium interlayer diffusion bonds to stainless steel in 1965, when developing ultra high vacuum sealing flanges. These used 1mm diameter aluminium wire gaskets flattened between the sealing surfaces of the flanges. After service at temperatures up to 400°C such seals only remained vacuum tight providing none of the clamping bolts had yielded. Reliability of the vacuum seal was greatly improved for joints where easy demountability was not required, by baking the assembled flanges on the evacuated system at 500°C for several hours. This produced a diffusion bond at the interfaces strong enough to allow the bolts to be removed for subsequent service, and to require the use of heavy jacking screws for flange separation.

In 1972, several years prior to the requirement for quartz windows, our attention had been drawn to early work by Nicholas and Crispin at Harwell on the production of expansion-matched solid state diffusion bonds between alumina ceramics and titanium using aluminium foil interlayers and bonded in vacuum or argon. Bonding pressures of 50-100 MPa were used in the temperature range of 500-600°C.

We had made limited use of the technique at this time to make a miniature multiple-stacked alumina-titanium insulator and a large high voltage alumina insulator for a 60 kV EB welder. The latter was made by diffusion bonding the flat

ends of a thick-walled alumina tube directly to aluminium end-caps. These had 60°
knife-edges machined on their sealing faces, the tips of which were flattened by
the bonding pressure. Despite the very high expansion mismatch at the bonding
temperature of ~1%, test pieces showed that this type of assembly was extremely
robust. This confirmed our design hypothesis that the residual stresses in the
alumina would be limited to safe values by a combination of factors. The most
important are the low hot yield strength of aluminium and its high creep rate
during the initial stages of slow cooling in vacuum from the bonding temperature of
580°C down to about 200°C. Additional factors which are important during the final
stages of cooling are the high mechanical compliance of the reduced cross-section
near the tips of knife-edges, and the low elastic modulus of aluminium.

3.2 Further Development Work

Our early experience in making UHV seals had demonstrated that an aluminium
interlayer diffusion seal to stainless steel would require a bonding temperature of
at least 500°C. It remained to be shown whether aluminium would bond to quartz,
and if so, at what temperature. (Success seemed likely because of the possibility
of the exchange of valency electrons at the interface of the joint). The question
was answered in an economical fashion by making a test-joint between a solid (and
therefore non-compliant) cylinder of stainless steel and a readily available thick
disc of fused silica. Silica is chemically identical to crystalline quartz, has a
similar tensile strength, but an extremely low rate of thermal expansion. The test
exploited the consequent self-stressing of such an assembly (due to differential
contraction) as it cooled from a trial bonding temperature of 500°C. The silica
shattered extensively, but no trace of interfacial failure could be detected in any of
the fragments, thus demonstrating that a diffusion bond to quartz should also be
developed at this temperature which would be greater than its fracture strength.
A final consideration was whether residual stresses in a quartz window disc bonded
to stainless steel at this temperature would be sufficiently low for such an assembly
to be viable.

Reference to Figure 1 shows that the expansion of quartz in the plane of a window on cooling from 500 to 400°C diverges from that of stainless steel by about 2 μm/mm. If such a thermal strain were developed entirely in the quartz in a non-compliant bonding situation, the corresponding maximum shear stresses would be prohibitively large. However, this potential thermal strain is only about a fifth of that inherent in the aluminium to alumina EB insulator, where the stress relief mechanisms discussed above were effective in enabling a fully viable assembly to be manufactured*. It was therefore decided to manufacture an 85mm diameter prototype aluminium-bonded quartz to stainless steel window, using a ferrule consisting of a flanged deep-drawn cylinder of type 304 stainless steel, with a wall-thickness chosen to give maximum compliance consistent with mechanical strength. The diffusion bond was to be made over the width of the face of the flange by flattening a small diameter centrally-placed aluminium wire, in conformity with our previous experience.

A specially modified vacuum furnace was used to optimise bonding conditions for this prototype window, and for subsequent production. This was equipped with an external hydraulic ram arranged to maintain axial forces of up to 60 kN through a vacuum seal. The arrangement is shown schematically in Fig. 2. Typical vacuum conditions during bonding were a total pressure of a few times 10^{-6} mbar and a partial pressure of oxygen of less than 1×10^{-8} mbar. Cylindrical stainless steel tensile pieces were used, 25 mm in diameter (see Figure 3). These were hollow so that the UHV vacuum-tightness of the bonds could be checked.

---

* In later work Nicholas and Crispin[2] carried out relevant studies of residual stresses in the case of an expansion-mismatched alumina-aluminium-stainless steel system with non-compliant geometry. They showed how the measured bond strength of such joints could be improved significantly by an optimised stress-relieving heat treatment. (The restricted, high temperature, range in which the expansion mismatch occurs in our own work, and slow cooling in vacuum makes additional heat treatment unnecessary).

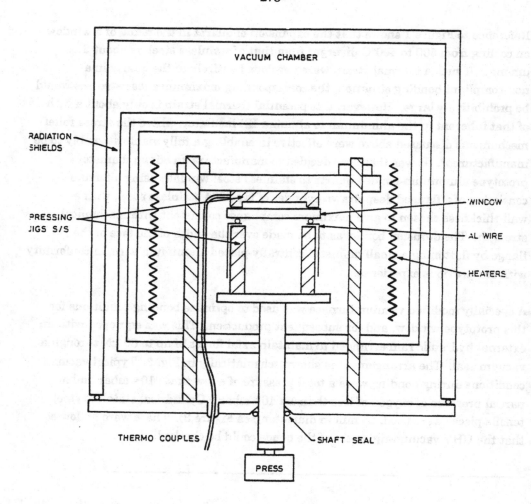

VACUUM FURNACE WITH HYDRAULIC PRESS

Fig.2

Key: Clockwise from Top Right

Stainless Steel - Stainless Steel (unbaked)

Stainless Steel - Quartz-Stainless Steel (unbaked)

Inconel-Inconel (after baking)

Fig 3 TENSILE/VACUUM TEST PIECES

All stainless steel to stainless steel bonds between pairs of these test-pieces were vacuum-tight to < 1 x 10^{-9} mbar L/s, and had tensile strengths in the range 95-106 MPa, close to the UTS of the aluminium. Stainless steel to quartz bond-strengths were similarly tested by bonding quartz discs between pairs of the stainless-steel test-pieces. The strength of these bonds was limited by the tensile strength of the quartz, with failure strengths typically in the range 60-65 MPa. All bonds were again leak-tight to < 1 x 10^{-9} mbar L/s prior to tensile testing and no bond failures at the interfaces occurred.

The 85mm diameter prototype window was immediately leak tight and extremely resistant to both thermal and mechanical abuse. The experience gained from manufacturing tensile test pieces and the prototype led to a number of adaptations of the basic design and the manufacture of several hundred windows with diameters of up to 130 mm. Four examples are shown in Fig. 4. More recently, strip windows with straight sides and semicircular ends, up to 107 mm long by 22 mm wide have been made.

4. BONDING TO OTHER MATERIALS

Requirements for good transmission in the near ultraviolet, the near infra red and millimetre microwave wavelengths demanded the sealing of sapphire and fused silica windows to suitable metals. Further development work was therefore carried out to exploit the diffusion bonding process developed for crystal quartz for this purpose. The different expansion characteristics of some of the materials considered are shown in Figure 6 and their optical properties in Fig. 5.

a) Synthetic Sapphire

From the point of view of expansion matching and non magnetic properties, titanium, tantalum and molybdenum appeared to be the most suitable ferrule materials for bonding to sapphire. However, none of these materials could be directly TIG welded into the stainless steel or Inconel 600 port tubes as required for JET. One of the lowest expansion, non-magnetic, weld-compatible materials which also meets JET's UHV criteria is Inconel 625, and despite its relatively large

Key: Clockwise from Top Right:

36 mm aperture Sapphire-Inconel-Stainless Steel Diagnostic window (for direct insertion into hot plasma)
14 mm diameter Alumina-Titanium Insulator Stack
15 mm aperture Crystalline Quartz-Stainless Steel Window Sub-assembly
13 mm bore Alumina-Titanium-Stainless Steel Miniconflat UHV Isolator
36 mm aperture Sapphire-Inconel Window Sub-assembly
62 mm aperture Crystalline Quartz-Stainless Steel Diagnostic Window
Central: 110 mm aperture Sapphire-Inconel Window Sub-assembly

Fig 4 ALUMINIUM DIFFUSION-BONDED COMPONENTS

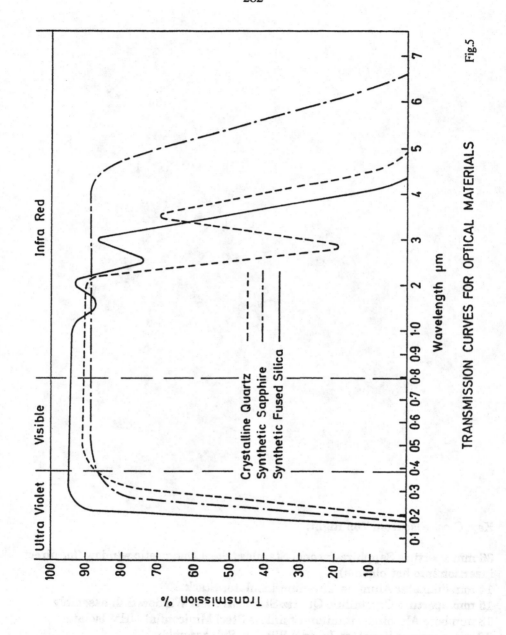

TRANSMISSION CURVES FOR OPTICAL MATERIALS

Fig.5

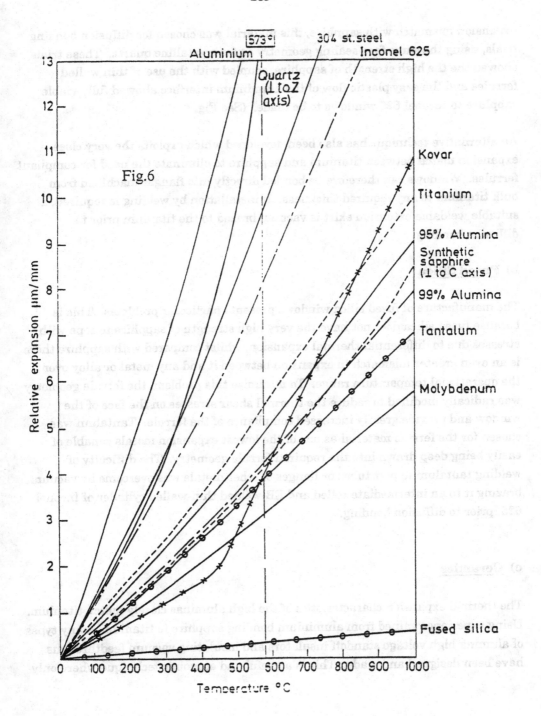

Fig.6

expansion mismatch with sapphire, this material was chosen for diffusion bonding trials, using the same face-sealing geometry as for crystalline quartz. These trials showed the the high strength of sapphire, coupled with the use of thin walled ferrules and the easy plastic flow of the aluminium interface allowed fully viable sapphire to Inconel 625 windows to be made. (See Fig. 4)

An alternative technique has also been developed which exploits the very close expansion match between titanium and sapphire to eliminate the need for compliant ferrules. Windows can therefore be bonded directly into flanges machined from bulk titanium to any required thickness. If installation by welding is required, a suitable weldable extension skirt is vacuum brazed to the titanium prior to diffusion bonding.

b) Fused Silica

The manufacture of fused silica windows presents particular problems. This is because fused silica does not have the very high strength of sapphire to cope with stresses due to differential thermal expansion, whilst compared with sapphire there is an even greater mismatch in expansion between it and any metal or alloy over the operational temperature range. To minimise this problem, the ferrule geometry was radically modified to reduce the thermal shear stresses on the face of the window and provide greatly increased compliance of the ferrule. Tantalum was chosen for the ferrule material as one of the lowest expansion metals capable of easily being deep drawn into the required ferrule geometry. The difficulty of welding tantalum to port tubes or flanges of other metals was overcome by vacuum brazing it to an intermediate rolled and EB-welded thin-walled cylinder of Inconel 625, prior to diffusion bonding.

c) Ceramics

The thermal expansion characteristics of the high aluminas closely match titanium. Using experience gained from aluminium bonding sapphire to titanium, many types of alumina high voltage standoff insulators and insulating vacuum feedthroughs have been designed and made. This is a useful and economic technique where only a few of any type are required. Aluminium diffusion-bonded alumina-titanium insulators are much more rugged than those produced by high temperature brazing because of lower residual stresses. Measured tensile strengths are typically two to three times greater. We have exploited this with great success in situations where mechanical failure of conventional stand off insulators due to uneven load-sharing has occurred in service. Substitution of diffusion-bonded direct replacements has solved many such problems. The process has also been successfully applied to bonding machinable glass ceramic (Macor) to stainless steel. Prototype or small batches of urgently required insulators can be made very quickly and economically as the Macor parts can be machined in-house and can often be bonded to standard type 304 stainless steel vacuum connectors. Here, the fracture toughness of the Macor due to its micaceous structure, as well as the easy plastic flow characteristics of the aluminium interface, makes this combination of materials a practical proposition, despite the expansion mismatch. Some examples of these fabrications are shown in Figs. 4, 7 and 8.

5. PERFORMANCE OF ALUMINIUM BONDED ASSEMBLIES

5.1 Thermal Endurance

Aluminium bonded windows were developed against a JET specification for repeated thermal cycling from room temperature to a temperature to be chosen in the range 400 to 500°C depending on the life-times achieved. Test windows were evacuated on a UHV system fitted with a partial pressure analyser to detect any leakage and cycled in air to a series of different peak temperatures in the range of interest. The thermal cycle ramp rate was 100°C per hour and the soak period at maximum temperature during each cycle was 10 hours. No catastrophic failures were observed at any stage of an extensive life-testing programme.

For quartz and sapphire windows, the eventual end of life is signalled by a small leak at the aluminium to metal-ferrule interface. Once initiated, the leak slowly but steadily increases. This behaviour is associated with the growth of brittle intermetallic phases at the interface. Above a thickness of the order of 2 µm, this layer starts to fail by shearing at each successive thermal cycle.

Key: Clockwise from Top Right:

62 mm aperture Crystalline Quartz-Stainless Steel Diagnostic Window
Alumina-Titanium High Voltage stand-off insulator
Alumina-Titanium Stainless Steel Mini Conflat UHV Isolator
Macor-Stainless Steel KF 40 High Vacuum Isolator

Fig 7 ALUMINIUM DIFFUSION-BONDED COMPONENTS

Top:

Alumina-Titanium-Stainless Steel UHV Conflat DN200CF

Bottom:

Alumina-Titanium-Stainless Steel Conflat DN16CF

Fig 8 SIZE RANGE OF UHV CERAMIC ISOLATORS

For crystalline quartz windows sealed to type 304 stainless steel, baked at 500°C (the temperature at which the diffusion bonds were formed), continuing diffusion causes rapid growth of the intermetallic layer. Leakage starts to occur after 8 thermal cycles and an 80 hour total soak time. However, the diffusion rate depends exponentially on temperature and at a maximum operating temperature of 400°C, no incipient leakage occurs after more than 300 thermal cycles and cumulative soak times at 400°C of more than 3,000 hours. For sapphire to Inconel 625, the formation of the intermetallic layer is approximately five times slower and we have demonstrated lifetimes greater than 3,000 hours at 470°C, incurring more than 300 thermal cycles.

The fused silica to tantalum system is less well understood, but we have measured lifetimes greater than 3,000 hours at 450°C, again incurring more than 300 thermal cycles. At 500°C, the oxidation rate of unprotected tantalum in air becomes prohibitively high. No failures during thermal testing of any of the types of window have been in the aluminium to window bond-interface.

All of our windows are designed to be mounted so that atmospheric pressure keeps the bond in compression. This ensures that accidental mechanical damage which may crack an evacuated window is unlikely to cause failure by catastrophic implosion. It also means that any possible failure mechanism caused by the otherwise desirable low hot yield strength and high creep rate of aluminium can be disregarded. Nevertheless, it was of interest to carry out long term hydraulic pressure tests in the reverse direction. These demonstrated that all types of window will withstand a reverse pressure of at least 2 bar. (Higher pressures were not investigated for fear of cracking very expensive window discs).

5.2 Corrosion Performance

The chemistry of aluminium is amphoteric and it is a highly electropositive metal. Hence its contact with most other metals in an aqueous environment constitutes a corrosion cell. This causes slow electrochemical attack of a diffusion bond even in demineralised water, and rapid attack in aqueous acidic or alkaline solutions. We have exploited the latter phenomenon throughout our development programme, routinely employing hot dilute alkaline solutions to separate test joints in a few hours for salvaging the components for re-use. We also discovered that the rate of attack in demineralised water during a long-term pressure test on a quartz window was such that approximately 25% of the outer periphery of the 3 mm wide bond area was corroded in 72 hours. However, corrosion stopped completely when the window was dried out. This window and several others, stored for more than seven years in a normal industrial laboratory atmosphere remain fully viable UHV components. Hence neither brief contact with water in the liquid phase, nor prolonged exposure to normal humidities is a problem (providing that condensation does not occur). Cleaning in any of the organic solvents used for UHV components is completely safe, as is brief immersion in some non-ionic aqueous detergent solutions followed by ultrasonically demineralised water rinses and oven drying.

Some sixty quartz windows supplied to the Plasma Physics Laboratory at Princeton, USA have been in use for the last 5 years and occasionally cleaned as above and proved fully reliable throughout this period. However, operating experience on JET subsequent to the development of aluminium bonded diagnostic windows revealed the need for cleaning the torus with aqueous solutions with the windows in situ. The torus is a large chamber ~80 m³. Personnel can enter for internal operations, fixing limiters, diagnostics etc, and maintenance. Consequently debris is deposited on the internal surfaces of the vessel. This contamination is removed by high pressure washing with a very dilute alkali solution followed by rinsing with demineralised water. Chemical and electrochemical corrosion of the diffusion bonded joints occurred when residual washing water remained in contact with the aluminium for many hours before removal by baking (which produced a saturated steamy atmosphere) prior to pumping.

Trials of joints immersed in JET water-wash residues with pH values close to 7, show electrochemical corrosion proceeding to the point where severe erosion of the interlayer occurred in 24 hrs. In the absence of a more chemically resistant bonding technique, protection of the joints during pressure washing is achieved by blanking-off the window ports with close-fitting caps to prevent ingress of moisture.

6. DEVELOPMENT OF GOLD DIFFUSION BONDING

Although most UHV systems are unlikely to be contaminated with aqueous solutions, JET's later requirements highlighted the need for a more chemically resistant diffusion bonded joint, still retaining the desirable properties of the aluminium interlayer bond, and extended high temperature operation at the full bakeout temperature of 500°C.

We therefore developed diffusion bonding using gold interlayers. Gold is not attacked by dilute acid and alkali solutions and it does not oxidise. The rate of diffusion of gold into ferrule materials is much slower than that of aluminium and it does not form brittle phases with the constituents of most ferrule materials, (as required for prolonged bakeout at temperatures well above 450°C). A final reason for using gold is its low yield strength, providing a compliant bed for the fragile window discs.

Development work was performed on the expansion matched stainless steel to crystalline quartz system. Unlike aluminium, gold does not bond directly to quartz so a low temperature priming process was developed for the quartz surfaces. During bonding an annealed gold wire is compressed between the primed quartz and the stainless steel ferrule having a suitably prepared surface to enhance bonding at 500°C.

Initial testing was carried out on a total of 10 windows of 30mm diameter and tensile test pieces similar to those used for aluminium interlayer bonding. During testing to destruction, the tensile test pieces invariably failed by plucking a complete ring of quartz from the disc, the interfaces remaining intact.

During life testing, 10 windows of 30 and 85 mm diameter and a similar number of tensile test pieces have been successfully cycled up to 320 times to a temperature of 520°C from a base temperature of 350°C for total times at temperature in excess of 4500 hours.

This work is continuing in parallel with trials to develop gold bonding to synthetic sapphire, fused silica, alumina and diamond.

7. <u>CONCLUSIONS</u>

Diffusion bonding has been developed for making transparent windows for fusion experiments capable of ultra high vacuum performance and high temperature cycling. The use of aluminium interlayers in the form of wire gives strong, ductile, and reliably vacuum tight joints between a wide range of similar amd dissimilar materials. The ductility of the joints is adequate to keep the stresses developed by repetitive differential thermal expansion and contraction to safe values between materials with differences in temperature coefficients of expansion of up to 6ppm.

The technique has been proved to be ideal for bonding brittle 'glasslike' materials to metal housings for the production of rugged, leak tight assemblies capable of repetitive thermal cycling to temperatures in excess of 400C with lifetimes at temperature of a minimum of 3000 hrs.

A newly developed diffusion bonding technique using a gold interlayer shows no evidence of deterioration in aqueous solutions and offers the advantage of higer bakeout temperatures for extended periods.

8. <u>ACKNOWLEDGEMENTS</u>

Many important contributions to the work described in this paper were made by the late Rodney Govier.

We are grateful to Mr P Millward of the Joint European Undertaking for his encouragement and for his support of the development work required to enable the JET diagnostic window specifications to be met.

Table 1 Characteristics of aluminium diffusion bonded windows

Window Material	Clear Diameter	Maximum usual Operating Temperature*
Crystalline Quartz	16-120 mm	400°C
Fused Silica	30-90	450°C
Synthetic Sapphire	12-110	470°C

* At least 300 thermal cycles to the quoted temperatures are permissible, with cumulative soak times of at least 3,000 hours. Windows are usually tested and can operate at higher temperatures for shorter periods.

References (1) M Mozeleski, Princeton University, unpublished internal memorandum 'Crystalline Quartz Windows'.

(2) M G Nicholas and R M Crispin AERE Harwell Report No. R10331 September 1981 'Diffusion Bonding Stainless Steel to alumina using aluminium interlayers'.

LOW TEMPERATURE DIFFUSION BONDING OF HIGH CARAT GOLD USING IN SITU GOLD-CADMIUM ALLOYS

D.Decroupet and G.Demortier

Laboratoire d'Analyses par Réactions Nucléaires (L.A.R.N.),

Institute for Studies in Interfaces Sciences (I.S.I.S.),

Facultés Universitaires Notre-Dame de la Paix,

22, rue Muzet, B-5000 Namur (Belgium)

ABSTRACT

Gold-cadmium alloys are highly suitable for the solid state bonding of gold because their low melting temperatures lead to an enhanced mobility as compared to that in pure gold. Local gold-cadmium alloys are realized in pure gold and 18 carats gold foils. The cadmium diffusion into gold is performed from the thermal decomposition of cadmium sulphide in air at temperatures ranging from 650°C to 850°C. The quantitative analysis (three-dimensional concentration maps) of those alloys is achieved using proton induced X-ray emission (PIXE). From the distributions of Cd in depth we obtain the diffusion coefficients of cadmium into pure gold and 18 carats gold-copper-silver alloys.

Gold substrates locally prepared by this procedure are used as the first component for the diffusion bonding on another pure gold part. Optical and electron microscopies of solders show that the joint region appears as a simple juxtaposition of the two initial gold parts. Electron microscopy of a section through the contact region reveals that the interface almost disappears. The concentration of cadmium in the joint is often below the detection limit for the electron microprobe, but the high sensitivity of the PIXE microprobe is sufficient to determine the composition of the soldered region even with a Cd concentration below 0.1%. The redistribution of cadmium on about 30 microns on both sides of the joint is observed. This diffusion bonding process can be used in jewelry craft.

INTRODUCTION

Due to their low melting temperatures, gold-cadmium alloys are convenient materials for the diffusion bonding of high carat gold. Cadmium additions to gold alloys are therefore often used in the preparation of gold brazing alloys. The low melting temperature ensures an enhanced mobility leading to high diffusion rates, at temperatures far below the melting point and consequently to the possibility of solid state bonding processes [1].

Au-Cd alloys are prepared in selected narrow regions of pure gold and 18 carats (750°/oo Au, 125°/oo Ag, 125°/oo Cu) gold foils rolled to a thickness of 50 microns. The cadmium diffusion into these foils is performed from the thermal decomposition of cadmium sulphide in air [2,3,4], at temperatures ranging from 650°C to 850°C and for diffusion periods up to 20 minutes [5]. Analytical results obtained by nuclear reactions as well as secondary ion mass spectroscopy (SIMS) demonstrate that intermetallic alloys are produced despite the presence of sulphur, carbon and oxygen during the diffusion process [6,7]. Mössbauer spectroscopy shows that the diffusion of cadmium from CdS into gold leads to solid solutions, in agreement with the Au-Cd phase diagram in the gold-rich region [8,9].

ANALYSIS OF THE ALLOY COMPOSITION

The three-dimensional composition of the gold-cadmium and gold-silver-copper-cadmium alloys is determined using the proton induced X-ray emission technique (PIXE) [10,11]. This method is an ideal tool because the characteristic X-ray energies of the various elements are well separated (Cu Kα = 8.0 keV, Au Lβ = 11.5 keV, Au Lγ = 13.4 keV, Ag Kα = 22.0 keV, Cd Kα = 23.0 keV). These X-rays are detected by an energy dispersive Si(Li) detector, whose entrance window is shielded with a zinc filter (35 microns) in order to selectively reduce the dominant gold LX-rays [12].

The most widely used electron microprobe analysis cannot be applied because the silver and cadmium K X-rays are not produced by 20 keV electrons and the interference of the respective L-X rays hinders the quantitative study of the alloys with a solid state detector [13]. The elemental composition determined by scanning the incident beam on the surface of the alloys indicates their homogeneity [16]. Local variations of the elemental concentrations are detected with a PIXE microprobe using a focalised proton beam with a resolution of 5 microns [14,15,16]. The sample displacement by 2.5 microns steps allows a detailed scanning of the sample surface [18]. A scan on a plane cut through the diffusion region allows the investigation of the depth distribution of cadmium in the gold foils (figure 1).

DETERMINATION OF THE COEFFICIENTS OF DIFFUSION

The cadmium depth profiles presented in figure 1 show typical diffusion curves as long as the cadmium does not migrate across the gold foil. These diffusion curves allow us to calculate the diffusion coefficient for cadmium in pure gold and 18 carats gold (figure 2). The diffusion coefficient for cadmium in gold is about one order of magnitude higher than the self diffusion coefficient of gold [19,20].

This higher mobility of the cadmium atoms as compared to that of the gold atoms can be explained by the valence effect which has a considerable influence when the vacancy mechanism is dominant [21,22]. The interaction of an atom of solute carrying a charge Z_1e with a vacancy is more favourable than the interaction of a solvent atom of charge Z_2e with this vacancy when $Z_1 > Z_2$, because the vacancy acts as a charge - Z_2e. In the case of gold-cadmium alloys, $Z_2 = 1$ for gold and $Z_1 = 2$ for the cadmium atoms which therefore are rapidly diffusing in gold.

The calculation of the diffusion coefficient for cadmium in pure gold from the analytical results at various times and temperatures gives an activation energy of $1,4 \ 10^5$ J/mole. This value, as compared to the $1,75 \ 10^5$ J/mole for the self diffusion of gold [23], confirms the favourable diffusion of cadmium in gold. As our results concern only a small temperature range (which cannot

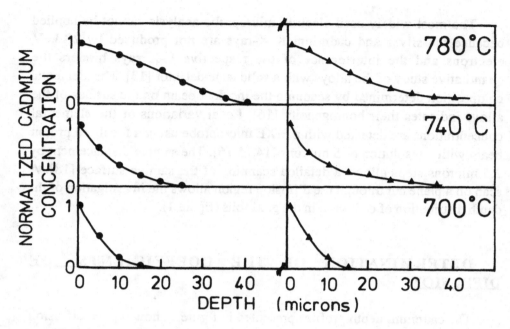

<u>Figure 1</u> :   Cadmium depth profiles at various temperatures after a diffusion period of 10 minutes. The beam diameter used for the PIXE microprobe analyses was 5 µm. <u>Left part</u> : cadmium diffusion in pure gold. <u>Right part</u> : cadmium diffusion in 18 carats gold-silver-copper alloy.

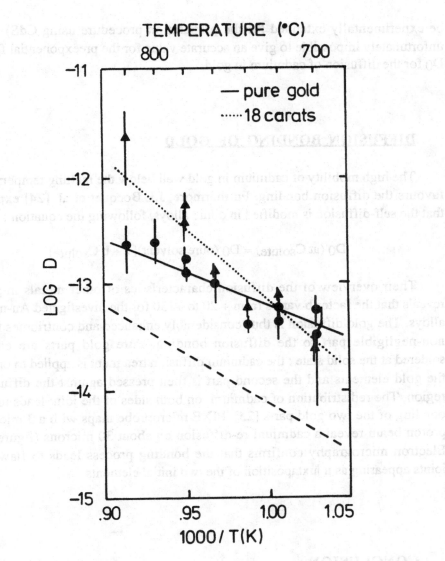

<u>Figure 2</u> :   Diffusion coefficients (in m²/s) for the diffusion of cadmium
from CdS into pure gold (●) and 18 carats gold alloys (▲).
The broken line shows the self-diffusion coefficient for pure
gold.

be experimentally extended for the preparation procedure using CdS), it is unfortunately impossible to give an accurate value for the preexponential factor D_0 for the diffusion of cadmium in gold.

DIFFUSION BONDING OF GOLD

The high mobility of cadmium in gold well below the melting temperature favours the diffusion bonding. Furthermore, J.L.Bocquet et al. [24] explain that the self-diffusion is modified in dilute alloys, following the equation :

$$D_0 \text{ (at } C_{solute}) = D_0 \text{ (pure solvent)}[1 + b \, C_{solute}]$$

Their overview of the diffusion characteristics of other metals in gold reveals that the factor b varies from + 20 to +130 for the investigated Au-metal alloys. The gold diffusion is thus considerably enhanced and contributes for a non-negligible part to the diffusion bonding. Pure gold parts are easily soldered at the solid state : the cadmium diffusion treatment is applied to one of the gold elements and the second part is then pressed against the diffusion region. The redistribution of cadmium on both sides of the joint leads to the bonding of the two gold parts [25]. PIXE microprobe maps with a 3 microns proton beam reveal a cadmium re-diffusion on about 30 microns (figure 3). Electron micrography confirms that the bonding process leads to flawless joints appearing as a juxtaposition of the two initial elements.

CONCLUSION

Gold-cadmium alloys realized by cadmium diffusion from cadmium sulphide into pure gold are highly suitable for the diffusion bonding of gold. The significant lowering of the melting temperature after the introduction of cadmium into gold leads to high diffusion coefficients allowing the necessary migration for the solid state bonding. The redistribution of the elements in the

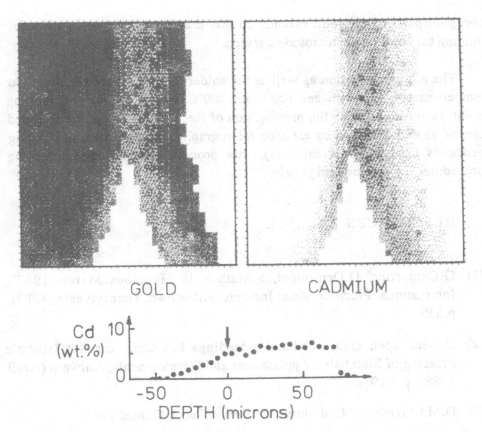

Figure 3 : Concentration maps of gold (90 to 100 weight %) and cadmium (0 to 10 weight %) through the region of the joint realized at 750°C between a pure gold sphere and a pre-treated foil. Each step is 10 microns.

The lower part of the figure shows the cadmium profile across the joint, and indicates the rediffusion of cadmium on about 30 microns into the gold sphere (each step is 5 microns, the beam diameter about 3 microns). The position of the joint is pointed out by the arrow.

two gold parts of the joint extends on less than 50 microns on each side, limiting the contact to a microscopic region.

The alloy preparation as well as the soldering process are performed at temperatures ranging between 700°C and 800°C, well below the gold melting point, favouring thereby the preservation of the initial shape of the soldered pieces, as demonstrated by electron micrography. As the diffusion bonding proceeds fastly (a few minutes), this process can improve soldering procedures, i.e. for modern jewelry.

REFERENCES

[1] G.Demortier, D.Decroupet, S.Mathot, in "Precious Metals 1987", International Precious Metal Institute, Allentown, Pennsylvania (1987), p.335

[2] D.Decroupet, G.Demortier, Proceedings Int. Conf. on Hot Isostatic Pressing of Materials : Applications and Developments, Antwerp (April 1988), p.3.19

[3] D.M.Chizhikov, "Cadmium", Pergamon Press, Oxford 1966

[4] Jin, Li, Xi, Jian, Chen, Applied Surf.Sci. 32 (1988), 218

[5] D.Decroupet, S.Mathot, G.Demortier, J.Mat.Sci.Lett. 8 (1989), 849

[6] D.Decroupet, G.Demortier, "PIXE microprobe studies of gold-cadmium alloys processed by local diffusion", Nucl.Instr. and Methods B49 (1990) 501

[7] D.Decroupet, Ph.D Thesis, to be published (1990)

[8] D.Decroupet, G.Demortier, LARN report N°891 (1989)

[9] H.Okamoto, T.B.Massalski, "Phase diagrams of binary gold alloys", ASM International (1987)

[10] G.Demortier, in Microbeam Analysis, eds. A.D.Romig Jr. and J.I.Goldstein, San Francisco Press (1984), p.249

[11]   S.A.E.Johansson, J.L.Campbell, "PIXE, a novel technique for elemental analysis", J.Wiley and Sons (1988).

[12]   G.Demortier, in "Precious Metals 1987", International Precious Metal Institute, Allentown, Pennsylvania (1987), p.55

[13]   G.Demortier, Y.Houbion, Oxford J.Archaeology, 6(1) (1987), 109

[14]   G.J.F.Legge, Nucl.Instr. and Methods B3 (1984), 561

[15]   G.J.F.Legge, Nucl.Instr. and Methods, B40/41 (1989), 675

[16]   F.Watt, G.W.Grime, "Principles and applications of high energy ion microbeams", Adam Hilger, Bristol (1987)

[17]   R.D.Vis, "The proton microprobe : applications in the biomedical field", CRC Press (1985)

[18]   M.Piette, G.Demortier, F.Bodart in "Microbeam Analysis", eds. A.D.Romig Jr. and W.F.Chambers, San Francisco Press (1986), 333

[19]   D.Duhl, K.I.Mirano, M.Cohen, Acta Metall. 11 (1963), 1

[20]   H.M.Gilder, D.Lazarus, J.Phys.Chem. Solids, 26 (1965), 2081

[21]   N.F.Kazakov, "Diffusion bonding of materials", Mir Publishers, Moscow (1985)

[22]   J.Philibert, "Diffusion et transport de matières dans les solides", Editions de Physique, Les Ulis (1985)

[23]   C.J.Smithells, "Metals reference book", Butterworths, London (1976)

[24]   J.L.Bocquet, G.Brébec, Y.Limoge, Chapt.8 of "Physical Metallurgy", R.W.Cahn and P.Haasen eds., Elsevier Science Publishers (1983).

[25]   G.Demortier, D.Decroupet, S.Mathot, "Performances of PIXE and nuclear microprobes for the study of gold soldering processes". (Nucl.Microprobe Technology and Applications Conference, Melbourne, Australia, feb.1990)

A New Aspect of Eutectic Bonding for Gold Soldering.

S. MATHOT* and G. DEMORTIER

Laboratoire d'Analyses par Réactions Nucléaires (LARN)
Facultés Universitaires Notre-Dame de la Paix,
22, rue Muzet, B-5000 Namur (Belgium)

Abstract.

The mechanism of diffusion of silicon in polycrystalline gold has been studied by PIXE, high energy deuteron microprobe ,optical and electron microscopies. A silicon film deposited on gold annealed at a temperature slightly higher than the Au-Si eutectic temperature (363°C) diffuses by precipitation of a gold-silicon eutectic alloy in the grain boundaries of the substrate.

In regard to this mechanism of diffusion, we propose a diffusion bonding procedure based on the re-diffusion, at 400°C, of this alloy from the grain boundaries of one of the two bonded gold pieces. The microstructure of the region of the joint after it was torn off is interpreted as the result of a re-diffusion of the eutectic gold-silicon alloy at the interface.

*IRSIA fellowship

1. Introduction.

Eutectic solders are commonly used in electronic industry. The Au-Si eutectic alloy (Tf = 363°C) is widely used for silicon chip bonding on a metal lead frame or on a metallized region deposited on an insulating substrate (die bonding). When this Au-Si eutectic solder is applied as a joining alloy, the silicon chip can be bonded at a temperature just above 363°C on its lead frame previously coated with a gold film [1,2,3].

In practice, a gold film is deposited on the back side of the silicon chip and alloyed at (or above) the Au-Si eutectic temperature to form a gold-silicon eutectic alloyed layer on the silicon surface. One advantage of this process is that no joining alloy must be inserted between the chip and the lead frame, but the procedure induces a further penetration of gold in silicon leading to indesirable electrical behaviors [3,4].

The aim of this work is to present an alternative bonding procedure in which the Au-Si eutectic alloy is formed by diffusion in the coated lead frame and not on the back side of the silicon crystal itself. The time of heating of the electronic device and therefore the diffusion of gold in the silicon crystal would then be less important. We present an application of this procedure of eutectic bonding to the soldering of pure gold pieces.

By metallograpic observations and elemental analysis by prompt nuclear techniques (high energy proton and deuteron microprobes) we have studied the mechanism of diffusion of silicon in gold. The mechanism of bonding is interpreted from the microstructure of the joint between two bonded pieces of gold.

2. Bonding procedure preparation.

The specimens are thin pure gold foils (99.99 %) partly masked for the silicon deposition in order to appreciate the diffusion of silicon from the film along the surface.

Silicon films of thicknesses ranging from 0.1 to 1 µm are evaporated onto thin foils of pure gold. These polycrystalline gold foils are obtained by rolling at room temperature.The silicon depositions are performed at a pressure of 1×10^{-6} Torr using an electron gun. While depositing the silicon, the gold foils are maintained at 400°C.during 15 to 60 minutes in order to allow silicon diffusion. The foils are then cooled down to room temperature and the silicon film is removed by chemical etching.

Pieces of pure gold (foils or granules) may be soldered on these foils prepared by silicon diffusion. For this purpose, the pure gold piece is put on the region where the silicon has been introduced by diffusion and the two pieces are simply reheated at a temperature of 400°C. After a few minutes, the two pieces are bonded, giving a perfectly invisible joint [Figure 1].

3. Analytical procedure.

The metallographic structure of the foils after the silicon diffusion has been observed by optical and electron microscopies. The surface of the gold foils at the limit of the masked region exhibits structural modifications of the surface only for samples prepared at a temperature above the gold-silicon eutectic temperature (363°C). At a lower

Figure 1 :   Pure gold granule (1 mm in diameter) bonded on a 15 μm
gold sheet in which silicon has diffused at 400 °C. The
bonding of the granule is obtained by the re-diffusion of
silicon at 400 °C.

temperature, one observes a poor adherence of the silicon film to the gold substrate.

Figure 2 shows electron micrographs of the surface of a gold foil after silicon diffusion at 400°C during 1 h. Figure 2 (a) represents the limit of the zone masked during the silicon deposition. The top part of this micrograph concerns the silicon film. In the lower part, we observe an important modification along the gold grain boundaries. The microstructure of these grain boundaries in the masked zone suggests that a eutectic gold-silicon alloy has been formed during the silicon diffusion [Figure 2 (b)].

In order to complete the metallographic observations, the PIXE (Proton Induced X-ray Emission) microprobe was used to determine the composition of the gold-silicon alloy formed.

A beam of 2.5 MeV proton is focused (5 µm in diameter) on the polycrystalline gold foil to scan narrow regions situated at the limit of the deposited silicon film or at the back side of the foil. With this spatial resolution (of the same order of magnitude than the surface broadening of the grain boundaries), the PIXE microprobe results give the absolute silicon concentration in the grain boundaries and into the grains [5].

A typical silicon map obtained on the back side of a polycrystalline gold foil (14 µm thick) after silicon diffusion during 1 h at 400°C is giving in figure 3. These maps are obtained by collecting the emitted K X-rays of silicon and M X-rays of gold with an energy-dispersive solid state detector. The absolute silicon concentration in different regions is obtained by a comparison with a bulk eutectic gold-silicon alloy.

Figure 3(a) shows that silicon has migrated through the foil along paths corresponding to the gold grain boundaries. An other representation of these silicon concentrations, given in the 3-dimensional plot (X, Y and concentration) in figure 3(b), indicates that the silicon

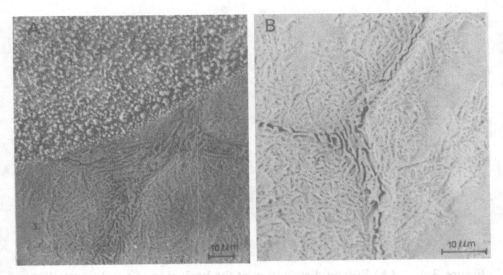

Figure 2 :   (A) SEM micrograph of the gold surface after silicon diffusion at 400 °C for 1 hour. The gold foil was masked during the silicon deposition (lower part). The micrograph indicates that the silicon diffuses from the silicon film (1) and forms a Au-Si a eutectic alloy in the grain boundaries (2) with ramifications at the surface of the grains (3).

(B) SEM micrograph of the structure of the grain boundaries at a few hundred microns from the limit of the silicon film.

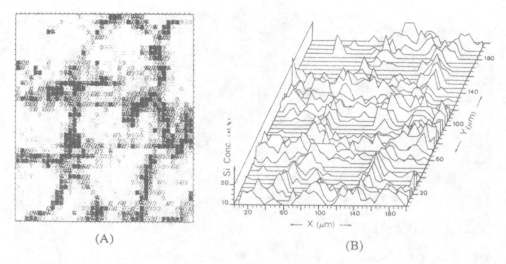

(A)

(B)

Figure 3 : (A) Silicon distribution at the back side of a polycrystalline gold foil (14 μm thick) after silicon diffusion at 400 °C for 1 hour (PIXE results). The precipitation of silicon is obvious only along the gold grain boundaries.

(B) 3-dimensional plot (X, Y and concentration) of figure (A). The concentration of silicon in the grain boundaries is close to the composition of the eutectic Au-Si alloy (19 at.% of silicon).

concentration is quite constant in the grain boundaries and close to the composition of the eutectic Au-Si alloy (19 at. % of Si). The silicon concentration decreases rapidly when the beam is scanned from the grain boundaries into the grains.

PIXE results concern depths of less than two microns behind the scanned surface. In order to measure the silicon concentration into deeper layers, we have used the spectroscopy of protons induced by the exoenergetic $^{28}Si(d,p)^{29}Si$ nuclear reaction. A beam of 2.75 MeV deuterons is focused (5 μm in diameter) on the surface of the gold foil. Silicon concentrations in various depths are obtained by counting the emitted protons [6]. The energy of these emitted protons is a smooth function of the depth at which they are produced. By scanning the beam on a narrow region on the surface of the gold foil, the proton spectroscopy allow us to obtain a set of maps which represent the silicon contents at different depths up to 16 μm under the surface.

Figure 4 shows a set of 7 maps obtained on a region (65 x 60 μm) of the front side (the side on which the silicon film is deposited) of a gold foil (16 μm thick) after silicon diffusion at 400°C during 1 h. The gold foil is made of small grains deformed by the rolling procedure with a thickness often equal to that of the foil. It can be seen that silicon is present in the full depth of the foil but only along well-defined paths corresponding to the gold grain boundaries.

4. Interpretation of the mechanism of bonding.

The results of PIXE and metallographic observations show that a eutectic gold-silicon alloy is formed preferably along the gold grain boundaries during silicon diffusion in gold at a temperature just above the eutectic. The process may be explained from the gold-silicon phase

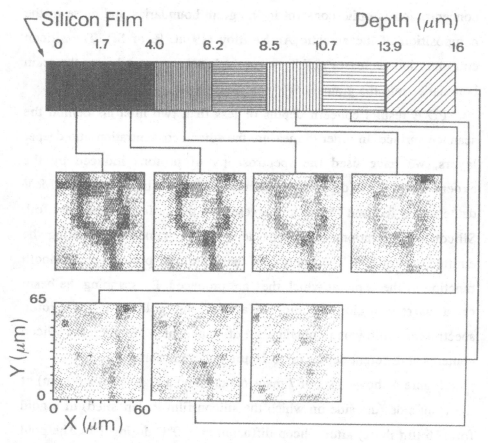

Figure 4 : Set of seven distribution maps (65 x 60 μm²) of silicon showing the relative concentrations at different depths below the surface of a gold foil (16 μm thick) after silicon diffusion for 1 hour (results obtained by nuclear reactions induced by a deuteron microprobe).

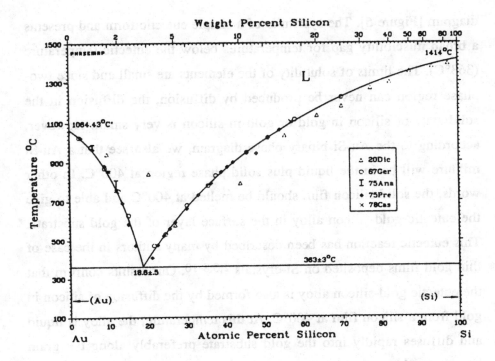

<u>Figure 5</u> :   Gold-silicon phase diagram [7].

diagram [Figure 5]. The system is of a simple eutectic form and presents a broad miscibility gap for temperatures below the eutectic temperature (363°C). The limits of solubility of the elements are small and since two-phase region can never be produced by diffusion, the diffusion in the solid state of silicon in gold or gold in silicon is very small. However, according to the Au-Si binary phase diagram, we also see that a Au-Si mixture will be in the liquid plus solid phase region at 400°C. In other words, the solid silicon film should be melted at 400°C and able to give the eutectic gold-silicon alloy in the surface layer of the gold substrate. This eutectic reaction has been described by many authors in the case of thin gold films deposited on Si-crystals [2,3,8-10]. Our results confirm that the eutectic gold-silicon alloy is also formed by the diffusion of silicon in gold from a silicon film at 400°C. At this temperature, the alloy is liquid and diffuses rapidly into the gold substrate preferably along the grain boundaries due to its high free energy.

This mechanism of diffusion explains the proposed diffusion bonding procedure. In a first step, the eutectic gold-silicon alloy is formed in the grain boundaries of a gold piece by the diffusion of silicon at 400°C. After that, the excess of silicon is chemically removed and an other piece of pure gold is put on the selected region. The two pieces maintained in contact are annealed during a few minutes at 400°C. At this temperature, the gold-silicon eutectic alloy present in the surface and in the grain boundaries of one of the two pieces is melted and may rapidly diffuse at the interface, allowing the closure within interatomic distances necessary to join the two pieces by establishing interatomic bonds. A permanent joint is formed as the melted Au-Si eutectic alloy is cooled.

We have examined the bond microstructure after failures in the interface of gold foils (12 μm thick) bonded by silicon diffusion at 400°C. The bonded specimens were epoxied to a tensile test fixture. The experiment has shown that the epoxy bond was not strong enough to force failures to occur in all the bond surface. Fragments of the second gold foil (foil without preparation by silicon diffusion) remain on the first after failures [Figure 6(a)].

Figures 6(b), 6(c) and 6(d) show electron micrographs of the elongated side of one of these fragments. One sees that the bond was made on the pure gold foil only along the grain boundaries of the first foil prepared by silicon diffusion. Small parts of the eutectic gold-silicon alloy formed in the grain boundaries of the first foil have been torn off and are present on the second foil (upper part of the picture). These small fragments show the outlines of the grains of the first foil on the surface of the second.

The fact that the bond is only realized opposite to the grain boundary can be due to the chemical etching of the first foil before the bonding. The chemical etching is necessary in order to remove the excess of silicon after silicon deposition and diffusion. But the treatment also dissolves part of silicon of the eutectic gold-silicon alloy formed at the surface of the foil. So, this surface alloy is poorer in silicon and is not suitable to be melted at 400°C. Consequently the eutectic gold-silicon alloy formed only in depth is melted and may diffuse to form the bond. This diffusion bonding procedure could be improved by an annealing of the diffused foils after etching and before the final bonding in order to form the eutectic alloy at the surface again.

In addition to the fact that the bond is made at a low temperature, one advantage of this bonding procedure is that one piece can be prepared at selected regions before the joining procedure.

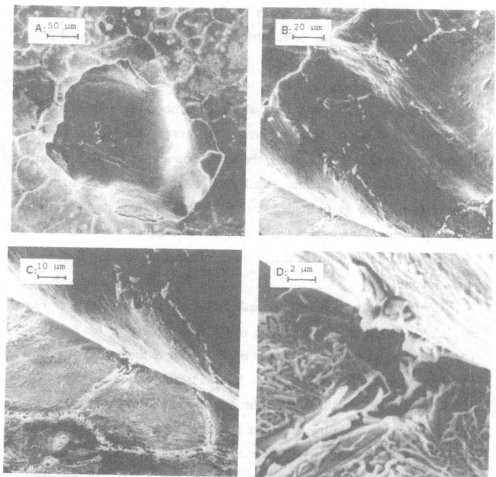

Figure 6 : SEM micrograph (A) of the joint between two gold foils
(12 μm thick) bonded by silicon diffusion at 400 °C. A
portion of the second foil (pure gold) remains bonded to
the one in which silicon has been introduced by diffusion.
SEM micrographs (B, C and D) at various magnifications
of the structure of the joint between the two foils confirm
that the bond is made only along the grain boundaries of
the first foil where gold-silicon eutectic alloy is present.

5. Conclusions.

A diffusion bonding procedure based on the re-diffusion of a eutectic gold-silicon alloy (initially produced by diffusion in one of the two pieces to be bonded) is proposed.

An elemental analysis of silicon in gold by PIXE and deuteron microprobes and metallographic observations show that the mechanism of diffusion of silicon in gold at 400°C goes through the formation of the eutectic gold-silicon alloy preferably along the gold grain boundaries. This eutectic alloy is liquid at the temperature of diffusion and then rapidly diffuses.

The soldering of gold pieces is also made at 400°C. The principle of the soldering is the melting of the gold-silicon alloy (formed by the diffusion in one piece) and the re-diffusion of this alloy at the interface with the other piece. This mechanism is confirmed by observations of the bond microstructure after a forced mechanical failure.

References

[1] B. G. STREETMAN, Solid State Electronic Devices, Prentice / Hall Int., N. Y., (1980)

[2] H. KATO, Jpn. J. Appl. Phys., 28 (6) (1989) 123

[3] F. G. YOST, J. Elect. Mat., 3 (2)(1974) 353

[4] A. TRAN et al., Metal. Trans. A, 18 (1987) 701

[5] S. MATHOT , G. DEMORTIER, Nucl. Instr. & Meth. B49 (1990) 505

[6] S. MATHOT, G. DEMORTIER, Nucl. Instr. & Meth. B50 (1990) 52

[7] H. OKAMOTO, T.B. MASSALSKI, Bul. alloys Phase Diag., 4 (2) (1983) 190

[8] P.H. CHANG, G.BERMAN and C.C. SHEN, Journal of Applied Physics, 63 (5) (1988) 1473

[9] A.HIRAKI, Japanese Journal of Applied Physics, 22 (4) (1983) 549

[10] A.K.GREEN and E.BAUER, Journal of Applied Physics, 47 (4) (1976) 1284